Competitiveness, Organizational Management, and Governance in Family Firms

Cesar Camisón
University of Valenica, Spain

Tomás González
University of Valencia, Spain

A volume in the Advances in Business Strategy and Competitive Advantage (ABSCA) Book Series

IGI Global
DISSEMINATOR OF KNOWLEDGE

Published in the United States of America by
IGI Global
Business Science Reference (an imprint of IGI Global)
701 E. Chocolate Avenue
Hershey PA, USA 17033
Tel: 717-533-8845
Fax: 717-533-8661
E-mail: cust@igi-global.com
Web site: http://www.igi-global.com

Library of Congress Cataloging-in-Publication Data

Names: Camison, Cesar, 1958- editor. | González Cruz, Tomás, editor.
Title: Competitiveness, organizational management, and governance in family firms / Cesar Camison and Tomás González, editors.
Description: Hershey, PA : Business Science Reference, [2020] | Includes bibliographical references and index. | Summary: “”This book examines the separation of ownership and management, on the one hand, and the institutional development of family governance instruments, on the other, to help uncover the asymmetric effects of these two choices”--Provided by publisher”-- Provided by publisher.
Identifiers: LCCN 2019032930 (print) | LCCN 2019032931 (ebook) | ISBN 9781799816553 (hardcover) | ISBN 9781799816584 (paperback) | ISBN 9781799816560 (ebook)
Subjects: LCSH: Family-owned business enterprises--Management.
Classification: LCC HD62.25 .C655 2020 (print) | LCC HD62.25 (ebook) | DDC 658--dc23
LC record available at https://lccn.loc.gov/2019032930
LC ebook record available at https://lccn.loc.gov/2019032931

This book is published in the IGI Global book series Advances in Business Strategy and Competitive Advantage (ABSCA) (ISSN: 2327-3429; eISSN: 2327-3437)

British Cataloguing in Publication Data
A Cataloguing in Publication record for this book is available from the British Library.

Advances in Business Strategy and Competitive Advantage (ABSCA) Book Series

Patricia Ordóñez de Pablos
Universidad de Oviedo, Spain

ISSN:2327-3429
EISSN:2327-3437

Mission

Business entities are constantly seeking new ways through which to gain advantage over their competitors and strengthen their position within the business environment. With competition at an all-time high due to technological advancements allowing for competition on a global scale, firms continue to seek new ways through which to improve and strengthen their business processes, procedures, and profitability.

The **Advances in Business Strategy and Competitive Advantage (ABSCA) Book Series** is a timely series responding to the high demand for state-of-the-art research on how business strategies are created, implemented and re-designed to meet the demands of globalized competitive markets. With a focus on local and global challenges, business opportunities and the needs of society, the **ABSCA** encourages scientific discourse on doing business and managing information technologies for the creation of sustainable competitive advantage.

Coverage

- Strategic Management
- Balanced Scorecard
- Value Chain
- Joint Ventures
- Tacit Knowledge
- Cost Leadership Strategy
- Business Models
- Foreign Investment Decision Process
- Entrepreneurship & Innovation
- Adaptive Enterprise

IGI Global is currently accepting manuscripts for publication within this series. To submit a proposal for a volume in this series, please contact our Acquisition Editors at Acquisitions@igi-global.com or visit: http://www.igi-global.com/publish/.

The Advances in Business Strategy and Competitive Advantage (ABSCA) Book Series (ISSN 2327-3429) is published by IGI Global, 701 E. Chocolate Avenue, Hershey, PA 17033-1240, USA, www.igi-global.com. This series is composed of titles available for purchase individually; each title is edited to be contextually exclusive from any other title within the series. For pricing and ordering information please visit http://www.igi-global.com/book-series/advances-business-strategy-competitive-advantage/73672. Postmaster: Send all address changes to above address.

Titles in this Series

For a list of additional titles in this series, please visit: https://www.igi-global.com/book-series/advances-business-strategy-competitive-advantage/73672

Advanced MIS and Digital Transformation for Increased Creativity and Innovation in Business
Gülay Ekren (Sinop University, Turkey) Alptekin Erkollar (ETCOP, Austria) and Birgit Oberer (ETCOP, Austria)
Business Science Reference • © 2020 • 251pp • H/C (ISBN: 9781522595502) • US $225.00

Improving Business Performance Through Innovation in the Digital Economy
Ionica Oncioiu (Titu Maiorescu University, Romania)
Business Science Reference • © 2020 • 272pp • H/C (ISBN: 9781799810056) • US $225.00

Ethical Consumerism and Comparative Studies Across Different Cultures Emerging Research and Opportunities
Ebtihaj Ahmed Al-A'ali (University of Bahrain, Bahrain) and Meryem Masmoudi (University of Bahrain, Bahrain)
Business Science Reference • © 2020 • 248pp • H/C (ISBN: 9781799802723) • US $155.00

Handbook of Research on Managerial Practices and Disruptive Innovation in Asia
Patricia Ordoñez de Pablos (University of Oviedo, Spain) Xi Zhang (Tianjin University, China) and Kwok Tai Chui (The Open University of Hong Kong, Hong Kong)
Business Science Reference • © 2020 • 451pp • H/C (ISBN: 9781799803577) • US $235.00

Entrepreneurial Innovation and Economic Development in Dubai and Comparisons to Its Sister Cities
Heather C. Webb (Dubai Men's College, UAE) and Hussain A. Al Numairy (Dubai Men's College, UAE)
Business Science Reference • © 2020 • 364pp • H/C (ISBN: 9781522593775) • US $210.00

Theoretical and Applied Mathematics in International Business
Bryan Christiansen (Global Research Society, USA) and Fatima Shuwaikh (Université Paris Saclay, France)
Business Science Reference • © 2020 • 358pp • H/C (ISBN: 9781522584582) • US $225.00

Strategic Marketing for Social Enterprises in Developing Nations
Nigel Chiweshe (University of KwaZulu-Natal, South Africa) and Debbie Ellis (University of KwaZulu-Natal, South Africa)
Business Science Reference • © 2019 • 373pp • H/C (ISBN: 9781522578598) • US $195.00

Handbook of Research on Entrepreneurship, Innovation, and Internationalization
Nuno Miguel Teixeira (Polytechnic Institute of Setúbal, Portugal) Teresa Gomes da Costa (Polytechnic Institute of Setúbal, Portugal) and Inês Margarida Lisboa (Instituto Politécnico de Leiria, Portugal)
Business Science Reference • © 2019 • 761pp • H/C (ISBN: 9781522584797) • US $395.00

IGI Global
DISSEMINATOR OF KNOWLEDGE

701 East Chocolate Avenue, Hershey, PA 17033, USA
Tel: 717-533-8845 x100 • Fax: 717-533-8661
E-Mail: cust@igi-global.com • www.igi-global.com

Table of Contents

Detailed Table of Contents

This chapter develops an additive model of the microeconomic sources of family firm (FF) competitiveness. Its main contribution is the proposal of a new explanatory framework with a perspective incorporating both ex post competitiveness and its determinants in a chain of multi-level causality. Based on fully-specified theory, the framework is designed to explain the complementarity of the effects of the firm's country, industry, district, strategy, and distinctive competences, focusing where appropriate on the case of the FF. The theoretical model also sheds light on the forces that influence the accumulation of sustainable competitive advantages. To that end, this chapter incorporates a particular focus on how the ownership and control structure affects the accumulation of intangible assets that give rise to the so-called family effect.

Family businesses are described as organizations owned by one or more members of the same family. Most of the business organizations in the world consists of family firms. However, although they constitute a larger share in almost all of the economies, in their first 5 years of operation, 90% of the family businesses disappear. Of the remaining 10%, 67% die or change ownership after first generation. Only 12% survive under current ownership past the third generation. Therefore, in order to maintain the continuity of the business, family businesses have to achieve competitive advantage. One way to achieve competitive advantage is through becoming market oriented. In this connection, the purpose of this chapter is to identify the role of market orientation and the four basic organizational capabilities (entrepreneurial ability, management ability, global ability, and building partnerships ability) on gaining competitive advantage by systematically reviewing relevant concepts, thereby contributing to the existing literature.

Section 4
Family Firm Financial Behavior

Section 5
Family Firm Survival and Resilience

Preface

Interest in the Family Enterprise (FE) as an object of study is indisputable. The rapid formation of new EFs has contributed significantly to economic dynamism during the early stages of industrial modernization in developed countries (Jones & Rose, 1993; Nenadic, 1993, 1994; Payne, 1984), and even in the precommercial stage. Between the 16th and 18th centuries, when the institutional framework that guaranteed contracts was nonexistent, the uncertainty in commercial relations between traders and craftsmen was mitigated by the development of codes of conduct that favored greater social cohesion; logically, family relations in business strengthened this cohesion and thus contributed to favoring exchange (Valdaliso & López-García, 2000). The uncertainty derived from an incipient legal framework. Further the risk associated with trade thus contributed to the fact that the dominant mercantile form was based on family organizations which were characterized by a total overlap between management and the family, as well as between the social capital and the patrimony of the owners (Colli, 2003). The industrial revolution changed technology and production processes, the structure of markets and the company's own internal organization. This revolution, together with the establishment of a legal framework that regulated commercial relations more effectively, contributed to the fragmentation of the shareholding structure and a growing dissociation between ownership and control of companies (Berle & Means, 1932). However, it did not destroy the family-enterprise relationship, so that the family continued to play a transcendental role in business during and after the industrial revolution (Valdalizo & López-García, 2000).

It is therefore not surprising that many of the world's oldest companies are family owned[1], including the following: Château de Goulaine, which has been based in France since the year 1000 and whose business is winemaking; Barone Ricasoli, an Italian company which was founded in 1141 and, since then, has been dedicated to wine production; Barovier & Toso, Italian manufacturer of the famous Murano glass that was born in 1295 (with 28 generations on its shoulders); John Brooke & Sons, which was founded in 1541 in the United Kingdom (for its 15th generation), in the textile business. Spain has three references in the list; all of them are dedicated to the production of wines of different types: Codorniu (1551), Osborne y Compañía (1772), and Torres (1800), to which González Byass (1835) should be added as a symbol of the Spanish wine sector, which, by the middle of the 19th century, represented 2% of exports. The list of longest-lived EFs points to the predominance of countries such as Japan and the Mediterranean (Italy, with eight family businesses among the 25 oldest in the world, France, and Spain, followed at a great distance by Germany, Great Britain, and Holland), which can be explained by the rooting of the family as the nucleus of social organization.

Today, the FE continues to play the same role in the economic transition of developing countries, as is the case in East Asia (Claessens, Djankov, & Lang, 2000; Lam, Mok, Cheung, & Yam, 1994; Mok, Lam, & Cheung, 1992). In emerging economies, the private business sector is also fraught with family-controlled organizations, such as the Korean *chaebol*, the *sagas* that control Indian economy (including the Marwari, Parsee, Bajaj, Mittal, Ambani, and Tata), or the powerful and diversified Japanese corporations (*zaibatsu*) between the end of the 19th century and 1945. The international expansion of the Mittal steel group and Tata Motors (which has grown with impressive purchases, such as the Anglo-Dutch steel group Corus, and emblematic brands of the British Empire, such as Jaguar and Land Rover) is a clear sign of its competitive strength.

However, the active presence of FEs is not a history of the past nor of the early stages of the industrialization process. As Bhattacharya and Ravikumar (2001) revealed in the theoretical modelling of its evolution, the Family Firm (FF) continues to be an organizational form with great weight in developed economies with advanced capital markets, after successfully overcoming the vicissitudes of successive industrial and technological revolutions. The FF is the core on which the business fabric orbits in all capitalist economies for its contribution to job and wealth creation (Astrachan & Shanker, 2003; Eddy, 1996; Heck & Stafford, 2001; Klein, 2000; Martikainen, Nikkinen, & Vähämaa, 2009; McConaughy, Matthews, & Fialko, 2001; Miller, Le Breton-Miller, Lester, & Cannella, 2007; Morck, Wolfenzon, &Yeung, 2005; Morck & Yeung, 2003, 2004; Shanker & Astrachan, 1996; Upton & Petty, 2000), perhaps with the exception of countries with strong legal protection of minority shareholders (La Porta, López-de-Silanes, & Shleifer, 1999).

Some of the known estimates allow to more accurately calibrate the economic contribution of FE in the modern economy. At the European level, studies estimate their share to be between 75% and 99% of the business fabric, generating 65% of gross domestic product (GDP) and continental employment (Jones & Rose, 1993). Thus, Colli (2003) figures its presence between 75% and 95% in Italy, between 70% and 80% in Spain, and around 75% in the United Kingdom. For the United States, the first calculations of the 1980s placed its weight on total supply at 95% (Dyer, 1986; Ward, 1987) and up to 98% (Davis, 1983), absorbing almost half of the GDP. In the following decade, Shanker and Astrachan (1996), depending on the definition adopted, estimated their number between 4.1 and 20.3 million organizations, which would contribute between 12% and 48% of the GDP, 15% to 59% of the employed population, and 19% to 78% of new jobs. Also, Sharma, Chrisman, and Chua (1996) put their weight above 80%, and 50% of employment and GDP. Instead, Gersick, Davis, Hampton, and Lansberg (1997) evaluated their presence between 65% and 80% of GDP.

In Spain, the most solvent specialized studies began with Gallo's work (Gallo, 1995; Gallo & García-Pont, 1989), which assesses the relative importance of EFs in Spain in 71% of all companies and in 62% of the working population. Subsequently, Merino and Salas (1993) and Galve and Salas (2003) evaluated the presence of EF in the Spanish manufacturing population of 10 or more employees, based on the data provided by the Business Strategy Survey, and for the period 1991-1998. Their numbers put the participation of family businesses in this group at 40.9% in 1991 and 33.0% in 1998, this being a trend towards constant weight loss in all company size strata and in all manufacturing industry subsectors. The Instituto de la Empresa Familiar (2015) estimated its number at approximately 2.8 million, equivalent to 85% of the productive fabric, representing 70% of private employment and GDP, and contributing 59% of national exports (Table 1). Other approximations speak of the fact that EFs in Spain account for 65-80% of total companies, employ 65%-75% of the active population, and represent between 50%-70% of the GDP and 59% of exports (Amat, 1998; Consejo General de Cámaras de Comercio, 2008; Gallo, Cappuyns & Estapé, 1995; Reyes & Sacristán, 2003).

Table 1. Summary of data on the contribution of family businesses to the business fabric and economy in Spain, the European Union, and the United States

Number of family businesses in Spain	2.8 million
Proportion of family businesses over total businesses in Spain	85%
Proportion contributed to GDP and private employment in Spain	70%
Percentage of market capitalization in Spain	30%
Percentage over total listed companies in Spain	50%
Distribution of the Generational Cycle in Spanish EFs	
Fourth or more	1%
Third	3%
Second	25%
First	65%
Number of employees contributed in Spain	10.13 million
Contribution to Spanish exports	59%
Number of family businesses in the European Union (EU)	17 million
Proportion of family businesses to the total number of businesses in the EU	60%
Proportion of family businesses over 100 largest businesses in the EU	25%
Number of employees contributed in the EU	100 million
Proportion of family businesses to total businesses in the USA	80%
Proportion of employment provided by family businesses in the USA	50%

Source: Instituto de la Empresa Familiar (2015)

The above-mentioned data prove the special importance of the EF among small and medium enterprises (SMEs). The international success of EFs in the textile, garment, and haute couture sectors, which are located in northern Italy, is a benchmark for the competitive potential of family-controlled SMEs (Galve & Salas, 2003). Donckels and Fröhlich's (1991) study of eight European Union countries concluded that 60% of SMEs were family-owned. Smaller EFs have also been the basis of Chinese export dynamism over the last 40 years (Galve & Salas, 2003). In the case of Spain, for 1998 data, Galve and Salas's (2003) study indicates that the relative importance of FE decreases continuously as organizational size increases: While the number of FE only represents 6.1% of companies with more than 500 employees, in companies with fewer than 20 employees the percentage rises to slightly more than half, the latter being the only segment in which they are in the majority. The comparison of this scenario with that of 1991 highlights that the trend is the same, although the proportion of EFs in all segments was higher (ranging from 10.1% of large firms to 62.4% of smaller ones), and they also continued to be the majority in the segment of companies with personnel up to 50 employees.

Camisón's (1997) research on the evolution of Spanish industrial SMEs in the decade 1984-1994 revealed that EFs had continued to be the majority in this productive fabric, although their weight had decreased. This is evident observing the number of companies with family capital (which fell from 60.3% to 55.6%) and those in which the main partners are natural persons who are linked to family capital (falling from 58.2% to 52.1%). In both cases, EFs had decreased in favor of EnF, but above all of companies with foreign capital. In the line Galve and Salas (2003) pointed out, the decade 1984-

1994 contemplated a significant decrease in the average presence of family capital in the total capital of Spanish industrial SMEs, which decreased from 86.4% to 60.2%. However, this decrease in family ownership has not essentially damaged their degree of majority control of the property. The study also provided clear evidence of the high weight of first-generation family SMEs, which remained at 59.4% (with a reduction of 5.7%) at the end of the period, and of the growth of second-generation family SMEs (which reached 34%, with a gain of 4.2%). Instead, third-generation or higher family SMEs barely accounted for 6.6% (growing of 1.5%).

Although most FEs are microenterprises, the number of these organizations with meaningful volumes of activity is significant, to the extent that many of the world's largest corporations (most of them are listed on the stock exchange) are family-owned enterprises. Many of them even occupy leadership positions in the businesses in which they operate, including illustrious names such as BMW, Michelin, Mars, and C&A. The EF in Spain also brings together a selected team of the most successful national companies within the domestic market (e.g., the Corte Inglés or Mercadona—the subject of a case study by Harvard University) and in international markets (e.g., Porcelanosa, Zara or Puig). Morck et al. (2005) highlighted the prevalence of large EF corporations with a concentration of corporate control in the hands of a few families and, consequently, the rarity of shareholder dispersion. In Europe, most listed companies remain under family control (Faccio & Lang, 2002; Franks & Mayer, 2001; La Porta et al., 1999). Thus, Faccio and Lang's (2002) study among listed companies in 13 European countries (including Spain) showed that 44% were family-controlled, and that the percentage of social control of a few families was very high: 15 French, German, and Italian families controlled 33.8%, 25%, and 21.9% of the market value of family businesses in their respective countries (the percentage in Spain is 13.5%). Sticking to the largest companies in each country, they found that of the 20 largest companies, three, six, and four were family-owned in Germany, France, and Italy, respectively. A singular reference is Sweden, where half of its 20 most important multinational companies belonged to an industrial group controlled for generations by the Wallenberg family. The predominance of EF among large corporations is equally documented in countries such as the United States, with dispersed shareholding structures as a model of managerial capitalism (Anderson & Reeb, 2003; Bhattacharya & Ravikumar, 2001; Gadhoum, Lang, & Young, 2005). More than one-third of the companies which are listed on the index of the largest Standard & Poor´s 500 companies remain under the control of the founder or his/her descendants, who own about 18% of their property (Business Week, 2003). A similar percentage of the companies that appear in the *Fortune* 500 ranking are controlled by families (Gersick et al., 1997). Its weight is equally relevant among listed companies worldwide (Burkart, Panunzi, & Shleifer, 2003). This evidence contradicts the image of the established moderate corporation since Berle and Means's (1932) research, in which ownership is fragmented among minority investors, and control is concentrated in the hands of professional managers.

These empirical evidences lead to profile the problem of EF's competitiveness as a relevant issue of interest. The importance of the FF in the creation of wealth, the generation of employment, and the well-being of a significant part of the population justifies the value of research on revealing its origins, nature, strengths, and weaknesses, so that it is possible to design strategies that strengthen its competitiveness and future development.

Competitiveness has probably one of the most commonly used terms in recent decades. In any case, if the concept is on the rise, it is not due to a passing fad, but responds to deep concerns about the change in the reference environment of economic and social agents. Entrepreneurship is currently taking place in an open and highly competitive environment, against a backdrop of economic processes as relevant as the globalization of markets, the internationalization of economies, the emergence of new international competitors, the transformation of demand or the rise in the importance of intangibles. Changes in the environment make traditional comparative and competitive advantages obsolete. Besides, they force companies to continually question the essence of market competition and renew themselves to ensure their profitability, growth, and survival. At this point, it is necessary to stress that all companies, both those with an international presence and those not including many local FF, are exposed to competition from foreign markets. All markets are susceptible to being modified by the conditions the globalized market determines. Technology, access to customers, the way of doing business, even the local market, shape globalization and, in turn, are exposed to the conditions international markets impose.

Thus, wondering about the determinants of the company's competitiveness is wondering about how the organization is adapting to the international competition in which it is immersed, about its learning of the habits and customs an open economy requires. The company's survival is at stake in its ability to face this challenge with management and future perspectives that are different from traditional management systems. "Being competitive" is vital for the creation of wealth and the growth of companies, sectors, economies operating within a system of competition (i.e., in competitive environments) where protective barriers are diluted and the degree of competition subsequently increases.

In addition, the debate on competitiveness is a capital topic, because it evokes a question of caliber: The theoretical model that the observer adopts and that is intimately related to the discipline or current of thought from which he/she approaches the analysis. The theoretical controversy over the above-mentioned basic problems is rooted in the very divergences deriving from the basic discipline protecting the researcher, with several competing approaches advocating different explanatory frameworks. The issue lies at the crossroads between disparate fields, such as industrial economics, finance, strategic management, neoeconomic institutionalism, international economics, organizational theory, and marketing. In particular, enterprise competitiveness, the origins of value creation, and persistent differences in performance between firms are at the core of the basic issues of industrial economics and strategy (Porter, 1991; Rumelt, Schendel, & Teece, 1991). It is therefore not strange that competitiveness and competitive advantage have attracted the interest of multiple special issues of prestigious journals since the 1990s. Examples are *The Academy of Management Executive* (1998, vol. 12, nº 4; 1999, vol. 13, nº 1; 2002, vol. ; 2004, vol. 18, no. 4), with focus also on value creation (2007, vol. 32, no. 1), and the *Strategic Management Journal* (2003, vol. 24, no. 10), with focus on competitive heterogeneity.

The state of the art recognizes that performance levels differ significantly, with some companies exhibiting abnormally high results and others below average (Kessides, 1990; Rumelt, 1991), and that such abnormal results have been sustained over time (Jacobson, 1988). The reflection on the weight of endogenous and exogenous factors that determine the company's competitive capacity is therefore a fundamental task.

Paradoxically, despite the existing consensus on the importance of understanding the origin and sustainability of competitive advantages and sustained abnormal results (economic rents), the consolidation of a theoretical framework which is capable of explaining competitiveness at the enterprise level and the empirical contrasting weight of the different effects predicted by the literature are still irregular and insufficient. The debate on the determining factors of competitiveness and the multiplicity of interests that coexist around it make it a complex and glassy issue. The essential reasons for this lack of definition arise from: 1) The lack of concreteness of the unit of reference (i.e., nation vs. industry vs company); 2) the disagreement on the point where to fix the concept (causes vs. consequences, or in other terms, ex-ante and ex-post competitiveness); 3) the amplitude of macroeconomic, environmental, sectorial, and internal factors of the companies that converge on it; 4) already on a second plane, questions referring to the temporal and geographical scenario.

Although business and entrepreneur are the star players, business competitiveness is conditioned, to some extent, by the environment in which they develop their activities. Therefore, the debate on the importance of the national environment in business competitiveness persists. National competitiveness is a highly controversial issue. Economists such as Krugman (1994), for whom it is a misleading and dangerous word, and supporters of the theory of international strategic competition (Kogut, 1985, 1991, 1993; Nelson & Rosenberg, 1993; Porter, 1990, 1992; Porter, Takeuchi, & Sakakibara, 2000) attribute to the national competitive base a decisive role in the international competitiveness of the country's companies.

On the other hand, not all microeconomic factors are equally relevant to competitive effects, and a resounding frivolity persists in the allocation of the adjective to factors, reflecting the limited managerial understanding of the concept. Specifically, the "family effect" remains a research challenge for researchers who are interested in the organizational form of FF and in the effects of family ownership on variability of firm performance and competitiveness. The recognition of the existence of a "family effect" that emanates from the mechanisms of government and the quality of its management has been advancing (Dyer, 2006). In addition, works such as Hoopes and Miller's (2006) study argue that concentration of ownership and family involvement influence control costs, investment choices, and capacity development, concluding that the firm's government has relevant effects on the portfolio of resources and capabilities, and therefore on its competitiveness.

However, the relationship between an organizational form of FF and performance remains anchored in contradictory predictions and empirical outcomes (e.g., Barontini & Caprio, 2006; Daily & Dollinger, 1992; Demsetz & Villalonga, 2001; Nordqvist & Melin, 2002; Westhead, Cowling, & Storey, 1997). The reason for this state of affairs lies in certain problems that hindered the consolidation of a body of consistent knowledge until the 1990s (Casson, 1999)[2]. The first of these is the very definition of the object of study (e.g., Astrachan, Klein, & Smyrnios, 2002; Galve & Salas, 2003). The bias that imprints on research the variability in the criteria for measuring the family character of a company has slowed down the generalization and extrapolable value of empirical results (Wortman, 1994). The second of the obstacles is of an informative nature. It alludes to the difficulties in collecting data on the collective formed by the FF among the public secondary sources, and which gives more value to primary research (e.g., the one from which the editors yield results) . Nevertheless, information problems also stem from the complexity and obscurity of family-enterprise ties (scientific progress is impossible without their revelation) and from the belief that the emotional charge in the organization questions the scientific nature of its research. The timeliness of the object of study itself has also been criticized with arguments relating to conflicts for separating the two areas that intermingle, namely the family and the company. One line points to the redundancy of investigating the FF with previous work on the general company or on family relations (Lansberg, Perrow, & Rogolsky, 1988). Another position insists on the complexity of simultaneously studying two different objects (i.e., the family and the company). Indeed, academic specialization tends to restrict one of them by slowing down the prognosis of the relations between the family and the company, despite the fact that the overlap of the two fields makes it inevitable (Lansberg, 1983). A current of opinion even understands that the boom of this model actually occurs when family owners are losing the majority control of capital, and thus control of its management. In other words, interest in the FF would be born precisely when it begins to cease to be so. This argument has a strong ideological content, which is not explicitly stated, but underlies tacitly in the belief that the efficiency and rationality that should govern mercantile relations force to circumvent the dynamics of the owner family in the organizational behavior.

The complexity of the FF as an object of study is particularly visible in the issue of competitiveness. As a business, the FF should be subject to the same regularities as any other business organization. However, as a family-owned business, some of these regularities may manifest anomalies that do not fit the general pattern.

Despite all these problems, the FF has been attracting increasing interest from scientific communities based in economics and business administration. A number of noteworthy events have contributed decisively to this, multiplying the awareness of the FF. One of these basic changes was the creation in the United States of the Family Business Institute and its launch of initiatives such as the *Family Business Review*, which has provided an open window for a better knowledge of its reality through theoretical and applied research. A similar movement has awakened in Spain the foundation of the Family Business Institute, which hosts a good number of the largest national business groups, and the constitution of the network of FF chairs in a significant number of universities.

The consolidation of the FF as an object of academic study is reflected in the gradual appearance of journals which are devoted to its research. Along with the pioneering *Family Business Review*, new publications, such as the *Journal of Family Business Strategy*, can be reviewed. In addition, other magazines in the field of management have received monographic issues on the family business. A unique emphasis is the case of *Entrepreneurship Theory & Practice,* which has dedicated special issues to EF every year since 2003.

This broadening of the theoretical and empirical knowledge of the FF comes from different fields of knowledge. Neubauer and Lank (1998) point to four traditions: The study of the figure of the entrepreneur and the entrepreneurial spirit; research on the creation of enterprises and SMEs; the prognosis of entrepreneur-led enterprises; literature focusing on the FF issue itself. These authors visualize these four sources as circles with a rather scarce common area, because researchers are predisposed to stay within the borders of one of them and are unlikely to interact with other researchers with different interests. However, more fruitful than this disciplinary vision may be the one that cares about the company's theories applied to increasing knowledge about the FF. This wealth of origins of FF interests has been further accentuated when strategy specialists have placed their vision on this gender of organizations (Chrisman, Chua, & Sharma, 2005; Chrisman, Steier, & Chua, 2008; Sharma, Chrisman & Chua, 1997).

In conclusion, the "family effect" remains a challenge for researchers who are interested in both the FF's organizational form and in the effects of familiar ownership on the firm's strategy, structure, and performance. Governance mechanisms, management quality, ownership concentration, and family involvement, all have relevant effects in terms of influencing monitoring costs, investment decisions, the development of the portfolio of resources and capabilities, and FF competitiveness. Nevertheless, to date, few studies have opened the black box of the "family effect."

CHAPTER DESCRIPTIONS

This book is organized in 15 chapters, which are grouped into seven sections. Each section focuses on a fundamental issue that calls for further clarification.

Section 1: The Reconciliation Between the Demographic and the Essential Approach Through the Competence-Based View

This section presents three chapters that propose a promising vein of research to throw light into the *black box* that mediates the relationship between the "family effect" and family-firm performance. These chapters propose an undelaying logic that tries to build causal relations between family involvement and family-firm demographic proxies, organizational capabilities, organizational behavior, and orientations, and finally, performance.

Chapter 1: *A Theoretical Framework for the Analysis of the Relationship Between Family Firms and Competitiveness.* César Camisón. This theoretical contribution shows a promising vein of research by properly tying family-firm demographic features, governance and management structures, and their impact on resources and on the endowment of capabilities, which therefore explain family-firm behavior and performance.

Chapter 2: *The Role of Market Orientation and Organizational Capabilities of Family Businesses on Competitive Advantage.* Özgür Atılgan. This theoretical contribution shows, from a competence-based view, which combination of capabilities, namely managerial, entrepreneurial, partnership, and dynamic, lead to superior market orientation. This chapter shows an interesting direction to new research in the family-business field, which is linking demographic proxies to the endowment of capabilities and capabilities to organization-behavioral outputs, such as market orientation.

Chapter 3: *A Configurational Approach to Analyze Family Governance and Family-Firm Outcome Preferences.* Antonio Carlos Cuenca and Tomás F. González-Cruz. The chapter explores a sample of family-firms looking for a taxonomy made from the degree of development of the family government system. The chapter reports four groups and shows that a family-business with developed family government systems tends to give greater relevance to nonfinancial outcomes, to the detriment of the purely operational and financial outcomes.

Section 2: Family Firm and Competitiveness

In a turbulent age, when sustained competitive advantage is a mirage or, even worse, a trap, remaining competitive is not an outdated research issue. This section presents chapters analysing the way family-firms can remain competitive.

Chapter 4: *Family Firm Competitiveness and Organizational Ambidexterity.* Montserrat Boronat-Navarro and Alexandra García Joerger. This chapter reviews the state of the art of the published research analysing the relationship between family-business and organizational ambidexterity. The chapter identifies potential and specific family-firm antecedents that promote and enable organizational ambidexterity. It calls for additional qualitative research to gain better understanding of how family-ownership promotes or blocks such organizational capability.

Chapter 5: *The Accumulation of Distinctive Competences in Family Firms.* César Camisón and Alba Puig-Denia. This chapter analyses a sample of 1,019 Spanish family-firms that belong to the tourism industry. From a capabilities-based view, the authors' survey shows that managerial competences become the most important barrier to the accumulation of distinctive competences. In line with previous research, the family-firm capability to develop and retain competent managers is the key to competitiveness. Then, the family influence is a double edge sword, depending on its impact on firm government and management and its consequences on managerial capabilities.

Section 3: Family Firm Strategic Behavior

Since Le Breton-Miller and Miller's (2008) call to gain better understanding of family firm strategic behaviour, different papers have analyzed this issue through key strategy dimensions (e.g., competitive strategy, internationalization, cooperation, M&A, and innovation). This section presents three examples of this vein of research.

Chapter 6: *Which Competitive Strategy Fits Better to Different Family-Business Profiles? A Configurational Approach.* Tomás F. González-Cruz and Norat Roig-Tierno. This chapter analyzes which combination of family-firm features, as well as environmental turbulence, together with the strategic choice –in terms of competitive strategy–, are present when performance is present. Results show that family businesses that follow a differentiation strategy in turbulent environments, as well as those that follow a low-cost strategy in nonturbulent environments, achieve better performance. In both cases, a family CEO and the presence of a board of directors contribute as complementary conditions.

Chapter 7: *Factors Determining the Internationalization of Spanish Family Small and Medium Enterprises.* Marta Fernández-Olmos. This chapter analyses, from a resource-based approach, a panel data from 702 industrial small and medium family-businesses. This chapter enlarges the vein of research analysing family-business internationalization, and contributes by considering family-business heterogeneity and separating the decision to internationalize from the enacted internationalization degree. Results show how both managerial capabilities and product innovation are critical to internationalization. As firm size and age, knowledge and relations the family or the firm managers provide have a positive impact on small and medium family-business internationalization.

Chapter 8: *Technological Innovation in Family Firms.* Mario Ossorio. This chapter reviews recent and relevant contributions to the issue it tackles. It shows that fear to loose ownership control and family-first logics have become barrier to innovation. Also, previous performance, dominant coalition's aspirations, industry growth, and, over all, an independent board, and competent managers are moderating factors. In any case, this chapter ends calling for additional research based on quantitative methodologies which are able to produce generalizable results.

Section 4: Family Firm Financial Behavior

It is naïve, partial, and even counterproductive separating strategic from financial behavior, especially for the case of family firms, where the firm supposes a relevant portion of financial questions about the financial behavior and capital structure of family firms.

Chapter 9: *Leverage and Family Firms: A Multi-Theoretical Approach.* Sergio Camisón-Haba, José Antonio Clemente, Beatriz Forés, and Melanie Grueso-Gala. This chapter combines different theoretical frameworks (e.g., Pecking-order theory, trade-off theory, socioemotional wealth theory, and the theory of preferences) to analyze which logic drives family-firm financial behaviour in terms of leverage. Results show the family business's preference towards debt as a way of maintaining the stock control and preserving socioemotional wealth.

Chapter 10: *Ownership and Operating Performance of Spanish Family IPO Firms.* Fuencisla Martínez Lobato, C. José García Martín, and José Emilio Farinós Viñas. This chapter shows that although family firms are oriented to retain control in the hands of family owners, when they make the decision to go public, they are governed by the same criteria as nonfamily firms, and they experience the same changes in their ownership structure and operating performance.

Section 5: Family Firm Survival and Resilience

This section addresses an old and relevant issue, which needs new research. The family firm has a long orientation in its objectives and the purpose of survival in the next generations. Therefore, succession, generational change, and the strategic vision for progressing towards a model of long-lived organization are very relevant topics for the family firm.

Chapter 11: *Keys to the Survival of the Family Firm: Long-Lived Family Firms.* César Camisón and José Antonio Moreno. This chapter follows the competence-based view and shows that, while functional capabilities have direct and significant impact on short-term economic performance, dynamic capabilities explain long-term performance.

Chapter 12: *The Role of Family Ownership in Survival and Bouncing Back: Good and Bad News?* María Iborra, Vicente Safón, and Consuelo Dolz. This chapter presents a suggestive piece of research that analyzes a relevant and long forgotten topic, as is the effect of family ownership on SME resilience. This chapter draws on the socioemotional wealth theory and on organizational resilience literature to examine how family firms behave when facing a threatening and stressful external event (e.g., the most recent world financial and economic crisis). Data analysis on a sample of 3,133 firms shows the dual and complementary nature of family-firm financial and nonfinancial goals. The chapter states that family-owned SMEs show higher survival rates than their nonfamily counterparts, and they present similar rates of recovery.

Section 6: Family Firm Performance

Family-firm performance is an open issue and object of open calls for new research in top journals. There is a need to develop more comprehensive outcome models that reflect family intentions and preferences. This section includes two chapters with contributions about sustainability and innovation as relevant aspects of this dimension.

Chapter 13: *The Quadruple Sustainability: Economic, Social, Environmental, and Family.* Beatriz Forés, José Antonio Clemente Almendros, and José María Fernández Yáñez. This chapter addresses the issue of firm outputs in its different dimensions and shows that family businesses report high economic, social, and environmental performance. The chapter provides explanations from the socioemotional wealth theory.

Chapter 14: *Understanding Family Firm Profitability Heterogeneity: Differences Within Family Managed Firms and the Interaction Effect of Innovative Effort.* Maria J. Martinez-Romero, Rubén Martínez-Alonso, Alfonso A. Rojo-Ramírez, and Julio Diéguez-Soto. This chapter contends that "innovative effort" is a proper construct to understand the way by which family involvement introduces heterogeneity between family businesses. A panel data containing 3, 164 observations shows that those family firms with an increase in the number of family members who are involved in the firm present higher profitability, and that the innovative effort reinforces the positive relationship between family involvement and firm profitability.

Section 7: Analysing the Family Firm from the Family Side

The last section addresses one of the most disregarded and promising issues in family-business research, which is analyzing the family firm from the family side. This implies differentiating the levels of analysis which exist in every family firm and its relationships.

Chapter 15: *Investigating Inner Dynamics in Family Firms: A Multilevel Analysis.* Filippo Ferrari. This chapter is an original and provocative piece of qualitative research, consisting of multiple case analyses that focus on the relationships between different levels at the family firm, namely firm (organization), family (group), and family members (individuals). The chapter shows how dysfunctional relationships destroy value creation. This kind of investigation is a necessary and promising vein of research in order to better understand family-firm dynamics and outputs.

AIMS OF THE BOOK

In this book, the editors' approach, while facing prevailing issues to the academic community, makes a clear distinction between the separation of ownership and management, on the one hand, and the institutional development of family governance instruments, on the other. This helps to uncover the asymmetric effects of these two choices. It also allows to examine which of the two strategies that are employed in FFs to reinforce managerial capital (i.e., contracting external managerial professionals vs. succession planning for family leadership) has a greater positive impact on the "family effect," thus helping to achieve better managerial capabilities.

The specific objectives of this book are:

1. Proposing a typology of FFs in order to analyse the differences in this population in terms of strategy, resources, capabilities, and governance and management structures.
2. Modeling the effects of the strategy, capabilities, ownership, and governance and management structures, along with other variables which are exogenous to the organization, based on the results of the different types of FF.
3. Identifing the differences in the processes of accumulation and protection of resources and capabilities among different types of FF, as well as the determinants of the development of dynamic and managerial capabilities in each one.
4. For the different types of FF, analyzing the effect of corporate governance design, and the way in which the family organizes itself in relation to the business, on the development of managerial, innovative, and entrepreneurial capabilities, and subsequently FF performance. Similarly, analysing the extent to which this relationship is moderated by the complexity of the family, family involvement, managerial discretion, and managerial succession planning by the family.
5. Exploring models of fit between the different dimensions of FF design (i.e., strategy, endowment of capabilities, and governance structure) that lead to better performance.

Other specific objectives of the book include:

1. Evaluating the relative importance of the factors—both internal and external to the organization—that influence the results of the different types of FF, highlighting their differences and providing reasons for these differences.
2. Analyzing the different profiles of the various types of FF in terms of allocation of resources and capabilities, theoretically explaining the causes of these differences, and empirically validating their determinants.
3. Analyzing whether the resources and capabilities of the FF are valuable not simply because they meet VRIO requirements, but due to their value in relation to the strategy and the level of development of other assets.
4. Analyzing which governance structures—in relation to both the firm and the family—best enhance the development of managerial, innovative, and entrepreneurial capabilities, and result in superior performance of the different types of FF.
5. Similarly, analyzing the extent to which this relationship is moderated by the complexity of the family and the business, and by family involvement in governance, management, and work.
6. Evaluating the need for fit and the costs of misfit and overfit.
7. Making a clear distinction between the separation of ownership and management, on the one hand, and the institutional development of family governance instruments, on the other. This will help us to uncover the asymmetric effects of these two choices on the development of capabilities, on performance and on the progress made by the FF towards one of the identified models.
8. Investigate which of the two strategies to strengthen managerial capital in the FF (external recruitment of a managerial professionals versus succession planning for a change in family leadership) has a more positive impact on the "family effect," thus helping to achieve better managerial capabilities and sustained improvements in performance.

The collection of high-level papers by specialists in these topics can have a notable impact on the state of the art in the field of family business, given that the knowledge currently existing in these five aspects is still incipient. The achievement of this reference work role in the topics studied will also benefit from the fact that it also outlines promising paths for future research on how to manage, survive, and grow family firms.

As usual in IGI Global's collection *Edited References*, the editors looked for chapters that included concise discussions of the latest models and concepts about the defined topics. Indeed, the contributions offer descriptions detailing the latest innovative and trending content in specific areas.

This book is also informative reading for anyone interested in the field of family firms from a strategic perspective, whether scholars, consultants, professionals or practitioners (e.g., managers and family entrepreneurs).

The book has the potential to appeal to managers and owners of family firms seeking a more in-depth understanding of the keys to success and survival of the organizations they lead. Likewise, it can provide interesting supporting material for graduate and undergraduates courses and masters to specialize in family firms.

In addition, the book can attract researchers in the field, given its aim to position itself at the knowledge frontier. It can thus represent a valuable resource for doctoral programmes and relevant research.

REFERENCES

Amat, J. M. (1998). *La continuidad de la empresa familiar*. Barcelona: Ediciones Gestión 2000.

Anderson, R. C., & Reeb, D. M. (2003). Founding-family ownership and firm performance: Evidence from the S&P 500. *The Journal of Finance*, *58*(3), 1301–1328. doi:10.1111/1540-6261.00567

Astrachan, J. H., Klein, S. B., & Smyrnios, K. X. (2002). The F-PEC scale of family influence: A proposal for solving the family business definition problem. *Family Business Review*, *15*(1), 45–58. doi:10.1111/j.1741-6248.2002.00045.x

Astrachan, J. H., & Shanker, M. C. (2003). Family businesses´ contribution to the U.S. economy: A closer look. *Family Business Review*, *16*(3), 211–219. doi:10.1177/08944865030160030601

Barontini, R., & Caprio, L. (2006). The effect of family control on firm value and performance: Evidence from continental Europe. *European Financial Management*, *12*(5), 689–723. doi:10.1111/j.1468-036X.2006.00273.x

Berle, A., & Means, G. (1932). *The modern corporation and private property*. New York: MacMillan.

Bhattacharya, U., & Ravikumar, B. (2001). Capital markets and the evolution of family business. *The Journal of Business*, *74*(2), 187–220. doi:10.1086/209670

Burkart, M., Panunzi, F., & Shleifer, A. (2003). Family business. *The Journal of Finance*, *58*(5), 2167–2210. doi:10.1111/1540-6261.00601

Camisón, C. (1997). *La competitividad de la PYME industrial española: estrategia y competencias distintivas*. Madrid: Civitas.

Casson, M. (1999). The economics of the family firm. *The Scandinavian Economic History Review*, *47*(1), 10–23. doi:10.1080/03585522.1999.10419802

Chrisman, J. J., Chua, J. H., & Sharma, P. (2005). Trends and directions in the development of a strategic management theory of the family firm. *Entrepreneurship Theory and Practice*, *29*(5), 555–575. doi:10.1111/j.1540-6520.2005.00098.x

Chrisman, J. J., Steier, L. P., & Chua, J. H. (2008). Toward a theoretical basis for understanding the dynamics of strategic performance in family firms. *Entrepreneurship Theory and Practice*, *32*(6), 935–947. doi:10.1111/j.1540-6520.2008.00264.x

Claessens, S., Djankov, S., & Lang, L. H. P. (2000). The separation of ownership and control in East Asian corporations. *Journal of Financial Economics*, *58*(1-2), 81–112. doi:10.1016/S0304-405X(00)00067-2

Colli, A. (2003). *The history of family business 1850-2000*. Cambridge, UK: Cambridge University Press.

Consejo General de Cámaras de Comercio. (2008). *Pyme familiar: Puente al futuro*. Madrid: Consejo General de Cámaras de Comercio.

Daily, C. M., & Dollinger, M.-J. (1992). An empirical examination of ownership structure in family and professionally-managed firms. *Family Business Review*, *5*(2), 117–136. doi:10.1111/j.1741-6248.1992.00117.x

Davis, P. (1983). Realizing the potential of the family business. *Organizational Dynamics*, *12*(1), 47–56. doi:10.1016/0090-2616(83)90026-8

Demsetz, H., & Villalonga, B. (2001). Ownership structure and corporate performance. *Journal of Corporate Finance*, *7*(3), 209–233. doi:10.1016/S0929-1199(01)00020-7

Donckels, R., & Fröhlich, E. (1991). Are family business really different: European experiences from Stratos. *Family Business Review*, *4*(2), 149–160. doi:10.1111/j.1741-6248.1991.00149.x

Dyer, W. G. (1986). *Cultural changes in family firms*. San Francisco: Jossey-Bass.

Dyer, W. G. (2006). Examining the "family effect" on firm performance. *Family Business Review*, *19*(4), 253–273. doi:10.1111/j.1741-6248.2006.00074.x

Eddy, P. (1996). Lessons, legends and legacies: Serving the family business. *Journal of Financial Planning*, *9*(6), 76–79.

Faccio, M., & Lang, L. (2002). The ultimate ownership of Western European corporations. *Journal of Financial Economics*, *65*(2), 365–395. doi:10.1016/S0304-405X(02)00146-0

Franks, J., & Mayer, C. (2001). Ownership and control of German corporations. *Review of Financial Studies*, *14*(4), 943–977. doi:10.1093/rfs/14.4.943

Gadhoum, Y., Lang, L. H. P., & Young, L. (2005). Who controls US? *European Financial Management*, *11*(3), 339–363. doi:10.1111/j.1354-7798.2005.00287.x

Gallo, M. A. (1995). *La empresa familiar. Textos y casos*. Barcelona: Editorial Praxis.

Gallo, M. A., Cappunys, K., & Estapé, M. J. (1995). Family business in Spain: Tracks followed and outcomes reached by those among the largest thousand. *Family Business Review*, *8*(4), 245–254. doi:10.1111/j.1741-6248.1995.00245.x

Gallo, M. A., & García-Pont, C. (1989). La empresa familiar en la economía española. *Papeles de Economía Española*, *39-40*, 67–85.

Galve, C., & Salas, V. (2003). *La empresa familiar en España. Fundamentos económicos y resultados*. Bilbao: Fundación BBVA.

Gersick, K. E., Davis, J. A., Hampton, M., & Lansberg, I. (1997). *Generation to generation—Life cycles of the family business*. Boston: Harvard Business School Press.

Heck, R. K. Z., & Stafford, K. (2001). The vital institution of family business: Economic benefits hidden in plain sight. In G. K. McCann & N. Upton (Eds.), *Destroying myths and creating value in family business* (pp. 9–17). Deland, FL: Stetson University Press.

Hoopes, D. G., & Miller, D. (2006). Owner preferences, competitive heterogeneity, and strategic capabilities. *Family Business Review*, *19*(2), 89–101. doi:10.1111/j.1741-6248.2006.00064.x

Instituto de la Empresa Familiar. (2015). *La empresa familiar en España*. Barcelona: Instituto de la Empresa Familiar.

Jacobson, R. (1988). The persistence of abnormal returns. *Strategic Management Journal*, *9*(5), 415–430. doi:10.1002mj.4250090503

Jones, C., & Rose, M. B. (1993). Family capitalism. *Business History*, *35*(4), 1–16. doi:10.1080/00076799300000126

Kessides, I. N. (1990). Internal versus external market conditions and firm profitability: An exploratory model. *Economic Journal (London)*, *100*(September), 773–792. doi:10.2307/2233658

Klein, S. (2000). Family business in Germany: Significance and structure. *Family Business Review*, *13*(3), 157–181. doi:10.1111/j.1741-6248.2000.00157.x

Kogut, B. (1985). Designing global strategies: Comparative and competitive value-added chains. *Sloan Management Review*, 15–27.

Kogut, B. (1991). Country capabilities and the permeability of borders. *Strategic Management Journal*, *12*(S1), 33–47. doi:10.1002mj.4250120905

Kogut, B. (Ed.). (1993). *Country competitiveness. Technology and the organizing of work*. New York: Oxford University Press.

Krugman, P. (1994). Competitiveness: A dangerous obsession. *Foreign Affairs*, *73*(2), 28–44. doi:10.2307/20045917

La Porta, R. L., López-de-Silanes, F., & Shleifer, A. (1999). Corporate ownership around the world. *The Journal of Finance*, *54*(2), 471–517. doi:10.1111/0022-1082.00115

Lam, K., Mok, H. M. K., Cheung, I., & Yam, H. C. S. (1994). Family groupings on performance of portfolio selection in the Hong Kong stock market. *Journal of Banking & Finance*, *18*(4), 725–742. doi:10.1016/0378-4266(94)00017-4

Lansberg, I. (1983). Managing human resources in family firms: The problem of institutional overlap. *Organizational Dynamics*, *12*(1), 39–46. doi:10.1016/0090-2616(83)90025-6

Lansberg, L., Perrow, E., & Rogolsky, S. (1988). Family business as an emerging field. *Family Business Review*, *4*(2), 1–8. doi:10.1111/j.1741-6248.1988.00001.x

Martikainen, M., Nikkinen, J., & Vähämaa, S. (2009). Production functions and productivity of family firms: Evidence from the S&P 500. *The Quarterly Review of Economics and Finance*, *49*(2), 295–307. doi:10.1016/j.qref.2007.11.001

McConaughy, D., Matthews, C. H., & Fialko, A. S. (2001). Founding family controlled firms: Performance, risk, and value. *Journal of Small Business Management*, *39*(1), 31–49. doi:10.1111/0447-2778.00004

Merino, F., & Salas, V. (1993). *Estrategia y resultados de la empresa familiar*. Barcelona: Universidad Autónoma de Barcelona, Documento de Investigación 9307.

Miller, D., Le Breton-Miller, I., Lester, R. H., & Cannella, A. A. Jr. (2007). Are family firms really superior performers? *Journal of Corporate Finance*, *13*(5), 829–858. doi:10.1016/j.jcorpfin.2007.03.004

Mok, H. M. K., Lam, K., & Cheung, I. (1992). Family control and return covariations in Hong Kong's common stocks. *Journal of Business Finance & Accounting*, *19*(2), 277–293. doi:10.1111/j.1468-5957.1992.tb00625.x

Morck, R., Wolfenzon, D., & Yeung, B. (2005). Corporate governance, economic entrenchment, and growth. *Journal of Economic Literature*, *43*(3), 655–720. doi:10.1257/002205105774431252

Morck, R., & Yeung, B. (2003). Agency problems in large family business groups. *Entrepreneurship Theory and Practice*, *27*(4).

Morck, R., & Yeung, B. (2004). Family control and the rent-seeking society. *Entrepreneurship Theory and Practice*, *28*(4), 391–409. doi:10.1111/j.1540-6520.2004.00053.x

Nelson, R. R., & Rosenberg, N. (1993). Technical innovations and national systems. In R. R. Nelson (Ed.), *National innovation systems* (pp. 3–21). New York: Oxford University Press.

Nenadic, S. (1993). The small family firm in Victorian Britain. *Business History*, *35*(4), 86–114. doi:10.1080/00076799300000130

Nenadic, S. (1994). The family and the small firm in late nineteenth-century Britain. In M. Muller (Ed.), *The structure and strategy of small and medium enterprise*. Berlin: Spriger.

Neubauer, F., & Lank, A. G. (1998). *The family business: Its governance for sustainability*. Routledge.

Nordqvist, M., & Melin, L. (2002). The dynamics of family firms: An institutional perspective on corporate governance and strategic change. In D. Fletcher (Ed.), *Understanding the small family business*. London: Routledge.

Payne, P. L. (1984). Family business in Britain: A historical and analytical survey. In A. Okochi & S. Yasvoka (Eds.), *Family business in the era of industrial growth: Its ownership and management* (pp. 171–206). Tokyo: University of Tokyo Press.

Porter, M. E. (1990). The competitive advantage of nations. *Harvard Business Review*, *68*(2), 73–93.

Porter, M. E. (1991). Towards a dynamic theory of strategy. *Strategic Management Journal*, *12*(S2), 95–117. doi:10.1002mj.4250121008

Porter, M. E. (1992). *Capital choices: Changing the way America invests in industry*. Washington, DC: The Council of Competitiveness.

Porter, M. E., Takeuchi, H., & Sakakibara, M. (2000). *Can Japan compete?* London: Macmillan Press.

Reyes, L., & Sacristán, M. (2003). Análisis de las diferencias de comportamiento de las empresas familiares cotizadas. *Revista Europea de Dirección y Economía de la Empresa*, *12*(2), 57–70.

Rumelt, R. P. (1991). How much does industry matter? *Strategic Management Journal*, *12*(3), 167–185. doi:10.1002mj.4250120302

Rumelt, R. P., Schendel, D., & Teece, D. (1991). Strategic management and economics. *Strategic Management Journal*, *12*(S2), 5–29. doi:10.1002mj.4250121003

Shanker, M. C., & Astrachan, J. H. (1996). Myths and realities: Family businesses´ contribution to the U.S. economy. A framework for assessing family business statistics. *Family Business Review*, *9*(2), 107–123. doi:10.1111/j.1741-6248.1996.00107.x

Sharma, P., Chrisman, J. J., & Chua, J. H. (1996). *A review and annotated bibliography of family business studies*. Boston: Kluwer. doi:10.1007/978-1-4419-8768-6

Sharma, P., Chrisman, J. J., & Chua, J. H. (1997). Strategic management of the family business: Past research and future challenges. *Family Business Review*, *10*(1), 1–35. doi:10.1111/j.1741-6248.1997.00001.x

Upton, N., & Petty, W. (2000). Venture capital investment and U.S. family business. *Venture Capital*, *2*(1), 27–39. doi:10.1080/136910600295792

Valdaliso, J. M., & López-García, S. (2000). *Historia económica de la empresa*. Barcelona: Crítica.

Ward, J. L. (1987). *Keeping the family business healthy: How to plan for continuing growth, profitability, and family leadership*. San Francisco: Jossey-Bass.

Westhead, P., Cowling, M., & Storey, D. J. (1997). *The management and performance of unquoted family companies in the United Kingdom. Centre for Small and medium Sized Enterprises*. Warwick Business School.

Wortman, M. S. (1994). Theoretical foundations for family-owned businesses: A conceptual and research based paradigm. *Family Business Review*, *7*(1), 3–27. doi:10.1111/j.1741-6248.1994.00003.x

ENDNOTES

1 William T. O´Hara and Peter Mandel, directors of the Bryant College´s Institute for Family Enterprise and editors of *Family Business Magazine*, have compiled a list of the world's 100 oldest family businesses from a variety of sources, including Tercentenarians, a British organization that hosts family businesses which are over 300 years old, and Les Henokiens, a similar institution in France that encompasses bicentennial family businesses. The ranking is available at www.cojoweb.com/ref-companies-worlds-oldest.html and www.familybusinessmagazine.com.

2 Narrative reviews of the state of EF research can be found in the following papers: Debicki, Matherne, Kellermans, & Chrisman, 2009; Poutziouris, Smyrnios, & Klein, 2006; Basco, 2006; Chrisman, Chua, & Sharma, 2005; Sharma, Chrisman, & Chua, 1996, 1997.

Section 1

The Reconciliation Between the Demographic and the Essential Approach Through the Competence-Based View

Chapter 1
A Theoretical Framework for the Analysis of the Relationship Between Family Firms and Competitiveness

César Camisón
University of Valencia, Spain

ABSTRACT

This chapter develops an additive model of the microeconomic sources of family firm (FF) competitiveness. Its main contribution is the proposal of a new explanatory framework with a perspective incorporating both ex post competitiveness and its determinants in a chain of multi-level causality. Based on fully-specified theory, the framework is designed to explain the complementarity of the effects of the firm's country, industry, district, strategy, and distinctive competences, focusing where appropriate on the case of the FF. The theoretical model also sheds light on the forces that influence the accumulation of sustainable competitive advantages. To that end, this chapter incorporates a particular focus on how the ownership and control structure affects the accumulation of intangible assets that give rise to the so-called family effect.

INTRODUCTION

The ***ownership and control structure*** is one of the basic characteristics that influence the strategic and operational decision-making of any organization; as such, it has important implications for corporate governance and economic performance (Vives, ed., 2000; Shleifer & Vishny, 1997; Short, 1994; Jensen, 1986). The comparative efficiency of different ownership and control structures (organizational forms) is an issue that has captured the interest of researchers in the field of agency theory (Thomsen & Pedersen, 2000; Li & Simerly, 1998; Gedajlovic & Shapiro, 1998; Shleifer & Vishny, 1997; Short, 1994; Oswald & Jahera, 1991; Jensen, 1986; Fama & Jensen, 1985; Williamson, 1985; Jensen & Meckling, 1976) for the past 80 years, ever since the seminal work of Berle & Means (1932).[1] On the basis of this theory,

DOI: 10.4018/978-1-7998-1655-3.ch001

the focus of interest has turned first to how the organizational form can protect or weaken the position and power base of senior management, as well as the analysis of the agency problem and the efficiency of the ownership concentration of various organizational forms (Fama & Jensen, 1985). Subsequently, the emphasis has turned to the role of the ownership structure—and particularly the type of owner—in organizational behaviour (Judge, 2012). This line of research recognizes the heterogeneity of the owner group and emphasizes that the identity of the owners is key to how they exercise their power and how this is reflected in the organization's strategy, structure, processes and outcomes (Thomsen & Pedersen, 2000; Nickel, Nicolitsas & Dryden, 1997; Hansmann, 1996, 1988; Short, 1994; Gedajlovic, 1993; Mc-Connell & Servaes, 1990; Cubbin & Leech, 1983; Levin & Levin, 1982). Managerial discretion, the structure and dynamics of management systems, and the planning of relationships between management and owners can change substantially depending on the type of owners, their shareholder complexity and their degree of involvement in the management of the company. The literature has focused on the implications of the ownership interest and/or corporate governance of institutional investors, large shareholders (blockholders), and minority shareholder advocacy organizations. Only in a second phase has the focus of agency theory turned to the ***family identity of capital owners*** (Kellerman, Eddleston, Barnett & Pearson, 2008; Naldi et al., 2007).

Studies such as that by Hoopes & Miller (2006) argue that ownership concentration and family involvement influence control costs, investment choices and capacity development, concluding that the firm's governance has relevant effects on its portfolio of resources and capabilities and hence on its competitiveness. Related research has further explored which model of ownership and corporate governance is most effective for coordinating, protecting and monetizing the firm's intangible assets (Capasso, 2004; Holland, 2001; Salas, 1993a,b, 1992a,b). This line of thinking connects contract theory to the resources- and capabilities-based view (RCBV) (Teece, Pisano & Shuen, 1997; Leonard-Barton, 1992). It has been acknowledged that the strategic value of intangible assets should not obscure the fact that some of their intrinsic features may hinder or prevent their successful accumulation. Dynamic analysis of the flow of new resources and capabilities thus puts the focus on the actions the firm should take in order to neutralize the negative effects inherent in those characteristics of intangible assets. The intended design of the ownership and control structure and the internal organization play a central role.

The convergence between the dynamic aspects within the RCBV—with its offshoot centred on *familiness*—and institutional theory has lately given rise to the idea that the firm's strategy, structure and business results can be affected by the family identity of the owners of the firm's capital, as well as by the existence of managerial discretion (Kellerman, Eddleston, Barnett & Pearson, 2008; Naldi, Nordqvist, Sjöberg & Wiklund, 2007; Brunninge, Nordqvist & Wiklund, 2007; Hoopes & Miller, 2006; Holland, 2001; Morck & Yeung, 2004b; Capasso, 2004). The family firm (hereafter FF) has thus been studied as a distinct organizational form characterized by certain specific features (e.g., Salvato, Chirico, Melin & Seidl, 2019; Gallo, 1995; Donnelley, 1964; Calder, 1961), including a particular ownership and governance structure. Of course, the FF is a company and therefore subject to the same sources of competitive advantage and problems as any other such economic agent. Of particular interest, then, are the motivations that are exclusively the domain of FFs. Family-controlled capital and the fact that the positions of owner, owner-employee and owner-manager are often held by family members can affect the competitiveness of family organizations. Dyers (2006) indicates that there is a ***family effect*** which influences performance through governance mechanisms and managerial quality (e.g., Barontini & Caprio, 2006; Westhead, Cowling & Storey, 1997) as well as through specific strategies (Westhead, 1997; Harris, Martínez & Ward, 1994).

However, Carney (2005) highlights the need for greater clarity in the reasoning behind how FF ownership, governance and control structures materialize and how they shape the development of resources and capabilities. The "family effect" remains a challenge for researchers interested in the organizational form of FF and in the effects of family ownership on the behaviour, strategy, structure, and performance of the firm. A growing body of work[2] is opening the black box of the "family effect". This chapter focuses on three of the ***problems that revolve around the family effect and that need to be further developed***: the competitiveness of the FF as compared to the NFF (non-family firm); the strengths and weaknesses that distinguish each organizational form; and the distinct sources of competitive advantages and disadvantages associated with family ownership.

This research thus aims to provide elements that can contribute to the formulation of an FF theory capable of uncovering the heterogeneity and root causes of FF competitiveness. To that end, this chapter puts forward an explanatory model of *ex post* business competitiveness that addresses the set of internal and external organizational mechanisms underpinning the generation and sustainability of competitive advantages (*ex ante* competitiveness) and the achievement of economic profitability. The model is first applied to the dimensions characteristic of any company, and subsequently to the unique framework of the FF. This approach, already introduced in a previous study (Camisón & Monfort, 2011), seeks to expand the explanatory frontiers of FF competitive dynamics by introducing a set of internal firm-specific variables as drivers.

This contribution to a better understanding of FFs through the theoretical framework of strategic management follows the pioneering work of Ward (1988) and Sharma, Chrisman & Chua (1997). In order to address the questions on ex post FF competitiveness, as Chrisman, Chua & Sharma (2005) point out in their review of the literature, and Chrisman, Steier & Chua (2008) reaffirm in their introduction to the fifth special issue on the topic published by *Entrepreneurship Theory & Practice* between 2003 and 2009, the challenge is to extend the theoretical horizons of FF research from a strategic management perspective. Particularly notable examples focused on these questions are the new firm theories developed since the 1980s within the strategic management approach, in which the drivers of competitive advantages are a central issue (Barney, 1986b, 1991; Porter, 1991; Rumelt, Schendel & Teece, 1991). Research into FF competitiveness can then be approached through the line of study that offers an understanding of the relative importance of the different environmental and organizational factors determining the variability in firm behaviour and results (Galve & Salas, 2003: 21).

The results of the research into the relative impact of such factors on performance (Hawawini, Subramanian & Verdin, 2003; McGahan, 1999; Mauri & Michaels, 1998; McGahan & Porter, 1998, 1997; Rumelt, 1991; Schmalensee, 1985) indicate that the main source of variability is the firm effect, i.e., the idiosyncratic features of each firm. Moreover, the multifaceted reality of the world of FFs, which encompasses a wide range of different organizations, presents certain problems; indeed, to speak generically of the FF— even if it is simply to make a distinction between FFs and NFFs, is too limited a perspective. Therefore, in order to open the black box of FF competitiveness, it is necessary to reveal the heterogeneity of this population. This will help identify the specific attributes of FFs that enable them to survive and achieve economic profitability. The exploration of FF diversity can be approached from several different angles. This chapter focuses on the three most theoretically relevant elements: (1) the variety of the portfolio of resources and capabilities; (2) the features of ownership, governance and management structures; (3) the establishment of an FF typology that can be used to consistently classify organizations of this type. Strategic management research has addressed these facets primarily through the prism of RCBV, agency theory, and the approach based on organizational forms. Most related studies are based on one of these approaches. However, it can be argued that in order to advance the knowledge of this subject, a multi-theoretical approach is required; one which combines the three theoretical perspectives outlined above.

After this introduction, the rest of this chapter is structured into five sections. The first section sets out a systematic overview the concept of FF and its distinctive characteristics. The concept of competitiveness is then introduced and an approach to measuring it is proposed, distinguishing between ex ante and ex competitiveness. The following section identifies the various external factors and the firm-specific internal issues when it comes to competing and achieving a competitive advantage. Sources of competitive advantage may arise from the general environment, the competitive environment of the industry, the territorial environment, strategic similarity and the internal heterogeneity of the firm's portfolio of resources and capabilities. The "family effect" has also been incorporated into the wide-ranging yet classical analysis of aspects affecting competitiveness. However, this is still a cross-sectional approach to the issue of competitiveness, as although it may be able to explain the variability of competitive positions and financial performance in a certain place and time, it does not provide the basis for explaining the reasons behind such asymmetries. A more in-depth exploration of the microeconomic bases of competitiveness also requires a longitudinal perspective, in order to examine how a firm's advantages over its competition are created. To do so requires a focus on the influence of ownership and control structures on the generation and sustainability of competitive advantage, with a particular emphasis on the implications of the FF profile in this regard.

CONCEPTUALIZATION AND STRUCTURAL COMPLEXITY OF THE FAMILY FIRM

One of the problems commonly faced by the authors who contributed to early FF research was the lack of a universally agreed definition of what was meant by this term, both in the legal sphere and in the scientific community.

This lack of an accepted definition of the FF caused considerable problems to legislators who, from the late 1990s on, were involved in drafting legislation that could meet the needs of these entities in terms of their treatment under the tax code. For example, Gallego (2012) points out that despite growing awareness of the importance of FFs in Spanish law, this type of firm has not traditionally been defined or regulated under private law. This situation was first addressed through the tax regulations: despite the general lack of a definition, tax regulations sought to define the FF strictly for fiscal purposes, in order to apply specific taxes, without the definition specified in this area bringing the matter to a close or entirely delimiting the concept of what should be understood as an FF.

At the same time, issues relating to the academic conceptualization of FF complicated the task of making comparisons between studies (Litz, 1995; Astrachan, Klein & Smyrnios, 2002) or developing the scientific analysis of this subject (Basco, 2006); without a consensus as to the definition of an FF, it is difficult to formulate an underlying theory on which to base the analysis. Furthermore, just as in any other scientific field, it was first necessary to pin down the concept of the object of study (the FF in this case) in order to develop a solid theoretical framework. Consequently, a significant proportion of the existing literature related to the FF is focused on defining it and distinguishing it from other types of company (Pérez et al., 2007).

The authors involved in developing the legislation were in agreement that an FF could be identified on the basis of the relationship between the concepts of business and family, but apart from this general observation, they differed on how to define it. Roca Junyent (2005), one of the architects of the legislation in this area, pointed out that the multiple existing definitions of the concept of the FF proposed by different authors rested on a variety of different elements. These include the generations of the family involved in the firm; the percentage of the family's ownership interest in the firm's capital; the owning family performing executive functions or similar; the intention to maintain the family ownership interest in the firm; and the descendants of the founder having control over the management and/or the governance of the firm.

Despite the problem of the FF definition, there was an undeniably pressing need to move forward on the legislation governing FF. Thus, in 2000 the Grupo Parlamentario Popular presented a motion before the Senate, calling for the Government to submit a draft Legal Statute on the Family Business to Parliament in the shortest time possible. This motion was ultimately amended and adopted, in the sense of providing the Senate Treasury Committee with a Report on the Analysis of the Family Business. Lacking a definition of this type of firm, the motion considered that in order for a company to be deemed an FF, it must feature a series of elements, detailed as follow (exact wording included in the footnotes):

1. It must be a company, regardless of its legal form. It can be a civil or commercial company, or even a sole proprietorship intending future continuity.
2. Ownership must be held by a family group. There is no requirement in Spanish commercial or civil law stipulating a minimum percentage that should be in the hands of a family group, nor is it defined what is meant by "family" for this purpose.[3] As such, it can be understood that it is sufficient to hold a percentage of the ownership or capital that grants control of the company[4], and to interpret the concept of family in a broad sense. What is more, even if the company belongs to a single owner but the intention is to pass the company on in the future to the owner's children or spouse, this company can be deemed a family firm
3. The family governs the company. This idea does not necessarily imply that the family or any of the members of the family directly manage the company, although that would be a typical situation, especially in the first generations. Rather, the day-to-day direct management of the firm can be handled by professionals, while the strategic governance and control remains in the hands of family members.
4. There must be a desire for the firm to endure beyond the life or the active life of the founder and the current owners. Going beyond strictly legal implications, the idea of continuity is the key to characterizing and giving meaning to the concept of family business. The continuity of the firm relates to family members' will and desire to keep the firm within the family group, as a legacy to pass on to future generations.

Since FF status offers advantages under certain Spanish tax laws a series of requirements are stipulated that need to be met in order to be classified as such; hence, the practical importance of the FF definition, although this does not curtail a broader concept of what constitutes an FF. These requirements include but are not limited to the following: the company should be run for commercial purposes; it should constitute the livelihood of one or some of the family members; and a substantial part of the running of the company should be done by members of the family unit (Gallego, 2012).

It follows that all the elements that researchers have identified as setting FF apart from NFF should be salient features of the FF definition (Chrisman, Shua & Sharma, 2005). Classifying a company as an FF or an NFF is based on both objective elements (capital, family participation) and subjective elements (recognition as a family business or the intentions of the dominant group) (Basco, 2006).

However, there is a common factor in any conceptualization, relating to the existence of a profound connection between the business and the family. In the words of Ayala & Navarrete (2004), this connection is "the conviction that the company and the family are two distinct social institutions with specific objectives, the convergence of which gives rise to a new system: the family business". This nexus engenders a structure of governance, ownership and control that differs from that of the NFF, and that delineates the characteristics of the FF. As Chua et al. (1999) suggest, it is the pattern of ownership, governance, management and succession that makes FFs unique.

The literature has provided many different approaches to and definitions of the concept of the FF. Following a thorough review of the literature, Sharma et al. (1996) reported 34 different definitions. Thus, the concept of FF has been widely discussed in the literature but without achieving a generally-accepted definition that precisely defines the characteristics to be taken into account when denoting a company as an FF.

Table 1 shows a summary prepared by Barroso, Sandino & Bañegil (2012), which sets out the extensive exploration of FFs over the period from 1975 to 2006. The definitions can be categorized into two main groups: single-criterion definitions, or those based on a single relevant factor; and multicriteria definitions, or those based on more than one relevant criterion. Single-criterion definitions are comparatively few and tend to be based on ownership factors (Barnes & Hershon, 1976; Lansberg, Perrow & Rogolsky, 1988; Donckels & Fröhlich, 1991) or management/control factors (Barry, 1975; Handler, 1989; Neubauer & Lank 2003). Multicriteria definitions, which are more common, jointly account for ownership and management/control factors, along with elements such as the desire for continuity, the family's influence on the business, and the desire to leave a legacy, among others.

This summary clearly shows that two criteria have traditionally been predominant when it comes to providing a definition of the FF: ownership and management. On the basis of the contributions made by the various authors reviewed, it can be argued that, on the one hand, there is a certain consensus on the role of ownership: namely, that the family must own a sufficient proportion of the share capital to have effective control of the company. On the other hand, there has been more intense debate on the role of management, with a range of positions adopted. Thus, for example, Daily & Dollinger (1993) state that for a company to be defined as an FF, it must be managed by the family (which excludes companies that are family-owned but managed by agents from outside the family), while other authors such as Graves & Thomas (2006) hold that it is enough for one family member to be part of the management team.

A number of other elements have been taken into account, which underline the complexity involved in developing a comprehensive, rigorous definition of the FF. These include the number of generations of the owning family; the family's degree of influence over the firm; the family's commitment to the business; whether the activity remains the same or the firm changes and even diversifies its activities; and the desire for continuity, to mention just some of the most relevant. After reviewing 258 FF definitions, Hernández, Sarkar & López (2017) were able to identify the eight concepts that form the conceptual framework of this type of organization (Figure 1), which they have shown can be useful for classification purposes.

Table 1. The concept of the family firm and its evolution over the period 1975-2006

<table>
<tr><th></th><th>Dimensions</th><th>Authors</th><th>Definition</th></tr>
<tr><td rowspan="2">Single-criterion definitions</td><td>Ownership</td><td>Barnes & Hershon (1976: 106)
Lansberg, Perrow & Rogolsky (1988: 2)
Donckels & Fröhlich (1991:152)</td><td>"If controlling ownership is vested in the hands of an individual or of the members of a single family"
"A business in which members of a family have legal control over ownership"
"If family members holds at least 60% of the equity"</td></tr>
<tr><td>Management / control</td><td>Barry (1975: 42)
Handler (1989: 262)
Neubauer & Lank (2003: 37)</td><td>"An enterprise that, in practice, is controlled by the members of a single family"
"An organization whose major operating decisions and plans for leadership succession are influenced by family members serving in management or on the board"
A proprietorship, partnership, corporation or any form of business association where the voting control is in the hands of a given family.</td></tr>
<tr><td rowspan="4">Multicriteria definitions</td><td>Ownership and management</td><td>Davis (1983: 47)
Gallo & Sveen (1991: 181-182)
Graves & Thomas (2006)
Welsch (1993: 40)</td><td>"An organization in which policy and direction are subject to the significant influence of one or more family units. This influence is exercised through ownership and sometimes through the participation of family members in management"
"A business where a single family owns the majority of stock and has total control. Family members also form part of the management and make the most important decisions concerning the business"
"One that is majority family-owned and has at least one family member in the management team"
"One in which ownership is concentrated, and owners or relatives of owners are involved in the management process."</td></tr>
<tr><td>Desire for continuity and family influence</td><td>Fahed-Sreih & Djoundourian (2006: 227)</td><td>"Any company that is controlled or influenced by a single family with the intention of staying in it."</td></tr>
<tr><td>Desire for continuity and management</td><td>Chua, Chrisman & Sharma (1999: 25)</td><td>"A business governed and/or managed with the intention to shape and pursue the vision of the business held by a dominant coalition controlled by members of the same family or a small number of families in a manner that is potentially sustainable across generations of the family or families."</td></tr>
<tr><td>Management, ownership and Desire for continuity</td><td>Claver, Rienda & Pertusa (2004: 231)</td><td>"Any organization where majority ownership and management is in the hands of a family and there is a desire for continuity in future generations, instilling a sense of identity in its members through the family culture"</td></tr>
</table>

Source: Barroso et al. (2012).

By around 2007, it was becoming increasingly evident that there was a need to find a more operational, functional definition limited to identifying observable and measurable characteristics that differentiate the FF from other businesses. In response to this need, in April 2008, an official definition of the FF was approved by the two main institutions representing this type of entity at the international level: the European Group of Family Enterprises (GEEF) and the board of the Family Business Network (FBN).

Figure 1. Structure of the definition of the family firm concept.
Source: Hernández, Sarkar & López (2017: 8).

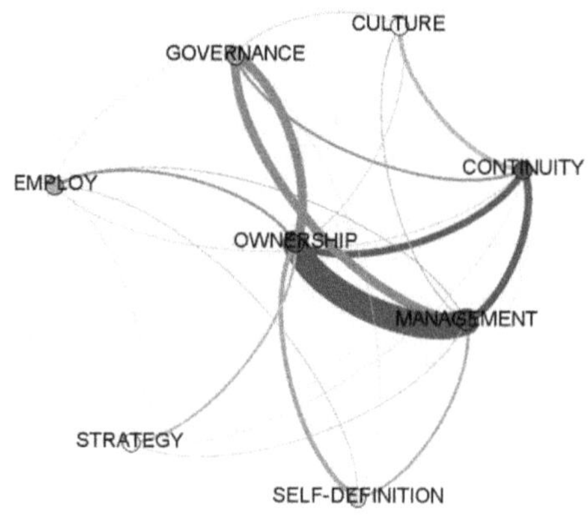

According to this definition, a company, whatever its size, is a family business if:

1. "The majority of the voting rights are in the possession of the person(s) from the family who established the firm, or in the possession of the natural person(s) who has/have acquired the share capital of the firm, or in the possession of their spouses, parents, child, or children's direct heirs.
2. The majority of decision-making rights are indirect or direct.
3. At least one representative of the family or kin is formally involved in the management or governance of the firm.
4. Listed companies meet the definition of family enterprise if the person who established or acquired the firm (share capital) or their families or descendants possess 25 per cent of the decision-making rights mandated by their share capital.[5]"

Given that the use of different definitions in FF research has led to significantly different results and conclusions, it becomes evident how important it is to have an agreed definition, such as the one presented above. By way of example, Barroso, Sandino & Bañegil (2012) mention Westhead & Cowling's 1998 study of UK firms. These authors attempted to classify a set of companies as either FF or NFF using several alternative definitions, which had been constructed by combining four key elements under more or less strict criteria. These elements were recognition of the family nature of the business (family perception), ownership, management, and intergenerational succession.

The definitions that the authors constructed by combining these four elements were progressively more restrictive, and the results of the study changed depending on which definition was used. Logically, this is to be expected as the sample became smaller as more restrictions were put on becoming part of the FF group. Thus, under the least restrictive definition, the authors found that FFs comprised 78.5% of the total set under study, whereas when using the more restrictive definition they comprised only 15%. The implication to be drawn from examples such as this one is that the FF definition is critical to determining the relative proportion of firms that are FFs and their contribution to the economy.

In order to perform an *ex post* and *ex ante* competitiveness analysis, this study uses the broad definition proposed by Shanker & Astrachan (1996), according to which an FF is a company in which the founder or his/her descendants have majority ownership and control of strategic decisions. This concept requires that a given family own part of the share capital and, additionally, a majority of the voting capital, so that family members have sufficient power to decide the strategy of the organization. As such, FFs are generally characterized as having a high concentration of capital in the hands of owners that share a family connection. The family group's reluctance to lose control of the firm prove an obstacle both to an open capital increase and to attracting external financing. Although this broad concept of the FF does not require the direct participation of the family in the implementation of company strategy and management, there is typically a low degree of managerial discretion in such situations due to the position of owner and manager being held by the same person, a member of the nuclear family. Therefore, the FF organizational model differs from both the managerial business model and the prevailing organizational form in Germany and Japan, which is characterized by the greater relevance of external financing and the active presence of bank creditors in corporate governance.

Each FF has its own particular structure, but there are certain patterns that are common to all. As can be seen in Figure 2, the FF is also a more intricate form of business organization than the NFF, due to the complex system resulting from the addition of a third dimension—the family—to the two dimensions common to every firm: ownership and business. The complexity of the FF was originally represented by Tagiuri & Davis (1982), who proposed the classic three-circle model. This model was later further developed by Gersick, Davis, Hampton & Lansberg (1997), who analysed the interactions that arise between these elements. If the "business" component is separated out from the staff employed as managers or employees and the board of directors, the resulting environment is even more complex, with four dimensions. This representation clearly depicts the increased number of positions as a result of distinguishing between these four axes. The typical NFF of a certain size (obviously excluding micro-enterprises and possibly also a fair number of small enterprises) is characterized by the existence of seven distinct groups of members of the organization, who differ from one another in terms of their roles in the organization. The CEO, who normally performs the role in position 7, is responsible for managing all seven sets of roles in such a way that they complement each other and pursue the firm's mission and objectives. The FF model adds just one more dimension: the family. Nevertheless, as a result of that addition, the number of roles that the CEO (who normally occupies position 15) must manage has more than doubled.

In a first step, each circle can be considered separately, without accounting for the intersections. Thus, the *family* circle includes all members within the family. With regard to the circle of *managers/employees*, it comprises all persons working in the company who receive a salary for the work they do. Thirdly, the *ownership* circle includes the holders of the shares of the company, that is, all those who have a series of rights and duties relating to the company. Finally, the board of directors brings together owners and their representatives, as well as potential outside experts. If these circles were observed independently, there would be no overlap in the roles of the members in each circle.

However, the model shows how the different areas found in the FF overlap. While defining the duties of management, control and responsibility in any company is challenging, it is an even trickier problem in the specific case of the FF; it is not clearly defined who is responsible for each of these actions in FFs, with informal structures and overlapping roles emerging (Donnelley, 1964; Burack & Calero, 1981; Hayes, 1981; Kets de Vries, 1993b, 1996; Harvey & Evans, 1994; Ibrahim & Ellis, 1994; Tagiuri & Davis, 1992; Ginebra, 1997).

This proliferation of roles can go some way to explaining the negative dynamics that are often associated with these types of organizations. They not only make the tasks of governance and management significantly more complex, but also lead to a rise in latent conflicts between the actors who perform

Figure 2. The typical family firm model

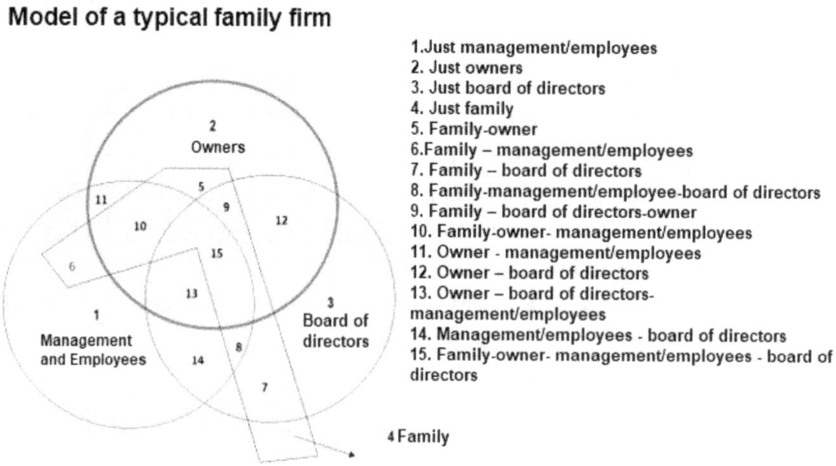

Figure 3. The typical non-family firm model

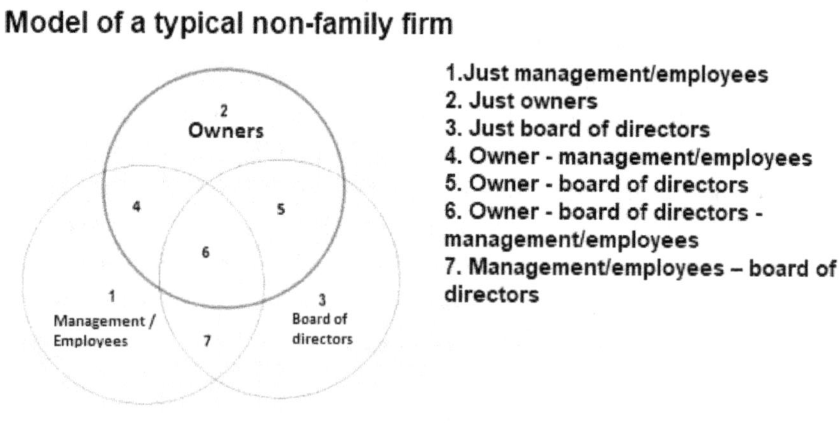

the different roles, above and beyond those stemming from the classic agency relationship. The institutional overlap between family and business can lead to problems that manifest themselves in normative contradictions; what is expected of individuals from a family perspective often conflicts with what is expected of them according to business principles (Galve, 2002). For example, a family member who is not an employee or owner could be in favour of giving opportunities to other family members, while an employee who is not a family member may think that family members should only be given opportunities if they are genuinely better than other candidates. Conversely, a family owner who also holds a managerial position will try to encourage the recruitment of family employees. Thus, the relationships that can arise and the roles to be performed in an FF are multiple and sometimes diffuse, which causes conflict of interests between different members of the company structure.

When the FF is founded, the owner at that time also tends to be the person with overall responsibility for the firm. Thus, both these roles are concentrated in the same person, who directs, controls and takes responsibility for the business. In such cases, the variety of systems and areas of intersection become more complex in later phases of the firm's development, and even more so with the incorporation of new generations into the company. As such, it becomes necessary to develop appropriate governance bodies and mechanisms to ensure that possible conflicts that may emerge from the dynamics of these relationships do not threaten the survival of the company.

THE COMPARATIVE COMPETITIVENESS OF THE FAMILY FIRM

An Unresolved Problem

The central role of FFs in modern developed economies and the theoretical work aimed at justifying the effectiveness of this organizational model in facing up to the challenges of the globalized economy and knowledge base, come into direct conflict with the claims of prestigious economic historians such as Landes (1951), Chandler (1990) and Lazonick (1991); they argue that the raison d'être of the FF is limited to the early stages of the industrialization process. Further, they claim that the FF constitutes a conservative and even disadvantageous institution for the current state of economic development.

However, this prediction contradicts the active presence of FFs in developed economies with advanced capital markets (Bhattacharya & Ravikumar, 2001), with strong empirical evidence of such firms' persistence. Reports of FF success stories in all sectors of the economy is interpreted by one line of research as a sign of the competitive strength FFs have managed to acquire by exploiting their specific features (Stinnett & De Frain, 1985; Alcorn, 1982).

The competitiveness of FFs as compared to NFFs remains an unresolved question due to contradictory empirical results and the variety of indicators and performance dimensions used in the analyses.

Ex Ante and Ex Post Competitiveness

The analysis of competitiveness must be based on a clear definition of the concept. This term can be understood as indicating the ability of a company, through the efficient management of a certain combination of available resources (internal and external to the organization) and the development of specific strategies, to configure a product offering that is attractive to a significant share of the market. Furthermore, it refers to the ability of the company, in competition with other companies in open markets, to develop a competitive advantage that is sustainable over time and to achieve a favourable competitive position from which to maintain and increase its market share while achieving superior financial results and satisfactory revenue growth without having to resort to abnormally low remuneration of the factors of production" (Camisón, 1997: 80-81).[6]

Following a review of the literature, four main dimensions of the firm's ex post competitiveness can be identified: financial performance, market performance, survival, and competitive position (Figure 3)

Producing goods and services that are successful in international markets but do not generate profits lacks economic logic. Therefore, the second competitiveness criterion is the achievement of outstanding results that are superior to those of the competition over a prolonged period of time (thus excluding results that are temporarily abnormally high). Economists refer to ***normal profit***, defined as that which enables the long-term survival of the company, and that equals the real or opportunity cost of the resources used to generate that income (which is determined by the minimum income demanded by investors). In a normal competitive market, normal profit tends to be the industry average. On the other hand, the term

Figure 4. Ex ante and ex post competitiveness

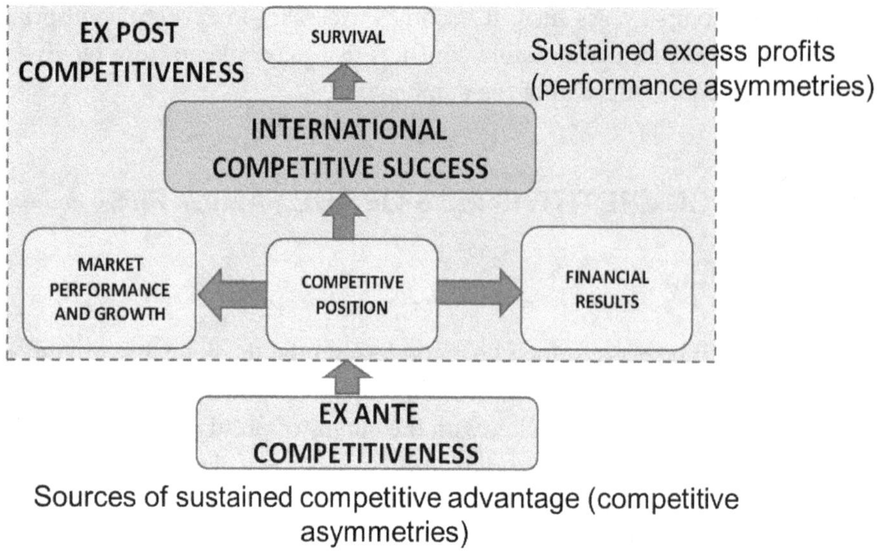

economic profit refers to the excess profits obtained by a firm, above the normal profit, and which do not immediately induce a competitive response or more competition (Grant, 1991a: 134; Alchian, 1991). Competitiveness must therefore yield economic profits that can be maintained over time; in other words, that cannot be easily eliminated by the mechanisms of market competition.

The first approach to a firm's ability to compete is based on the consequences of market competition, which are reflected in the firm's ***financial results.*** Viewed from this angle, the improvement in a firm's competitiveness can be measured through the evolution of certain indicators of its performance and financial situation, such as profitability of capital, productivity, financial solvency or cost efficiency (Camisón & Cruz, 2008). Although these competitiveness indicators are widely used, they do not enable an understanding of the factors that lead to these results—the ultimate sources of entrepreneurial competitiveness—which would enable the firm to take action to improve them. Financial performance measures are "contaminated" by numerous elements, some of which may be unrelated to gains in competitiveness (for example, the cyclical evolution of the economy) while others actually reflect gains in competitiveness arising from institutional and industrial structures, from the general environment, and from the effectiveness and efficiency of the behaviour of the agents whose decisions influence the configuration of the institutions, processes, and organizations. The second problem with these indicators is that past profitability can only serve as a measure of future competitiveness if it is appropriately employed. The balance sheet and the profit and loss statement cannot reveal the weaknesses and ailments affecting the company's competitive health. The firm can be in good financial health internally, while demonstrating competitive cost efficiency and a capacity to generate income at the level of the existing competition, and yet still lack future prospects for competitiveness. The markets, products and distinctive competences of the firm play a decisive role.

The firm's competitiveness can also be reflected in its ***market performance***, which can be captured by observing its revenue growth, as well as the firm's impact on the markets. The ***growth of the firm*** can be measured by its sales growth (in absolute or relative terms) and its gain of market share. ***Sales growth*** is a robust indicator of a firm's competitiveness as it reflects the firm's ability to develop a product offering that is attractive to a significant share of the market, using a stock of resources and capabilities that endow the firm (as well as the product range) with a differential element to make it stand out from the competition. In turn, the ***market share*** that a firm achieves reveals consumers' interest in its quality-price offer, and how this translates into attracting new customers to its products. Financial theory and much of the strategic literature have emphasized that there must be a trade-off between the gain of market share and the profitability of capital, under the hypothesis that the former is a strong predictor of cash flow generation and thus the two will be related.

A third criterion for measuring competitiveness is ***survival***. Survival is an innate goal of any system (Luhmann, 1996). This is all the more true in the case of the FF, whose determination to endure over time is patently reflected in the desire to transfer ownership (and often control) to future generations. Survival is therefore a powerful and useful indicator for assessing the success of an FF. However, no firm can achieve long-term survival in the market without a sustainable competitive advantage that protects it from competition and enables it to adapt to the changing environment. Nor can firms survive without achieving an economic performance that yields an appropriate return on capital investment and financing for new investments, as well as meeting a performance threshold that would be the minimum acceptable to the dominant coalition (Gimeno & Folta, 1997).

It has been widely argued in the related literature that FF survival is tied to economic performance and to the satisfaction of family members (Sharma et al., 2001; Morris et al., 1997; Handler, 1989). The ***satisfaction*** of the owning family primarily depends on the firm's financial outcomes, effective manage-

Table 2. Family firm outcome model

		Family Firm Systems	
	Outcomes	**Firm(s) Outcomes**	**Family Outcomes**
Financial	Outcomes that reflect the fulfillment of financial goals	Block Ia: Firm-specific financial outcomes Financial outcomes associated with key firm outcomes that include financial outcomes and product market outcomes. Examples include: • Profitability • Growth • Liquidity	Block IIa: Family-specific financial outcomes Financial outcomes important to the family regardless of involvement with the firm's ownership or operations. Examples include: • Family Control • Family income and portfolio value • Family market returns • Firm patient and survivability capital determined by family • Family wealth • Family credit • Family assets (e.g., real estate, stock in firms other than the family firm) • Philanthropic value (i.e., tax deductions)
Non-financial internal	Non-financial outcomes that reflect the fulfillment of goals that are associated and linked to those within the boundaries of the family or firm	Block Ib: Firm-specific non-financial internal outcomes Non-financial outcomes associated with effective and efficient internal operations, falling within the boundaries of the firm. Examples include: • Objective measures such as product quality & process efficiency • Subjective measures such as job satisfaction, organizational commitment, & stewardship climate	Block IIb: Family-specific non-financial internal outcomes Non-financial outcomes associated with effective and efficient family processes. Examples include: • General family well-being • Emotional well-being • Family happiness • Family cohesion (emotional & cognitive) • Psychological meaning & identity • Autonomy • Belonging • Transgenerational sustainability intentions • Satisfaction with fulfillment of familial obligations.
Non-financial external	Non-financial outcomes that reflect the fulfillment of goals that are associated and linked to thoughts and perceptions of those beyond the boundaries of the family or firm.	Block Ic: Firm-specific non-financial external outcomes Non-financial outcomes associated with the perceptions of those beyond the boundaries of the firm(s) regardless of family's involvement with firm(s). Examples include: • Customer loyalty • Customer satisfaction • Firm reputation • Firm image • Social responsibility	Block IIc: Family-specific non-financial external outcomes Non-financial outcomes associated with the perceptions of those beyond the boundaries of the family regardless of the family's involvement with firm(s). Examples include: • Community embeddedness • Family image & prestige • Family legacy
		Several firm-centric goals & few family-centric goals ←	→ **Few firm-centric goals & several family-centric goals**

Source: Holt, Pearson, Carr & Barnett (2017: 187).

ment of the succession process that resolves concerns about the firm's survival, and the attainment of other non-financial goals and values typical of the FF. The latter includes securing employment for family members, ensuring the economic security of forthcoming generations and their predecessors, family harmony, social prestige, family reputation, the sense of begetting and belonging to a worthy project, contributing to community well-being, or a sense of social justice (Rosenblatt et al., 1985; McKiernan & Morris, 1994; Tagiuri & Davis, 1992). Holt, Pearson, Carr & Barnett (2017) conducted a review of the literature and presented a broad overview (see Table 2) of the goals observed in FFs and the variety of indicators they use to measure the success or failure of the business.

Although these four elements are correlated, they do not occupy the same plane. The competitive position is the main determinant of the quality and sustainability of the company's economic profits. The firm's competitive position is the primary manifestation of its ex post competitiveness, since it is the first aspect in which the effects of the firm's competitive advantages materialize. In turn, this provides the basis for maintaining and increasing its market share while achieving superior financial results and satisfactory revenue growth (Camisón, 1997: 80-81).

Against this background, some studies have reported a positive and direct family effect on the creation and development of the firm (Astrachan, Zahra & Sharma, 2003) and its performance (Anderson & Reeb, 2003; McConaughy, Matthews & Fialko, 2001; Miller & Le Breton-Miller, 2006), whereas others report a non-significant relationship (Galve & Salas, 2003). The relationship between the organizational form of an FF and its performance is the subject of contradictory predictions and empirical outcomes (e.g., Barontini & Caprio, 2006; Demsetz & Villalonga, 2001; Nordqvist & Melin, 2002). The differences between the financial performance of the FF and NFF depend on the indicator and the business cycle (Camisón, Forés & Puig-Denia, 2016).

Empirical evidence on FF survival compared to NFF survival is also controversial. Neubauer & Lank (1998: 44) refer to some studies on the longevity of FF in several countries, which seem to suggest that the FF model involves particularly serious problems that can shorten the average life expectancy of such firms. According to these authors, the fragility of the FF is reflected in the fact that between two-thirds and three-quarters go bankrupt or are sold by the founding family during the first generation; moreover, only between 5% and 15% of FFs reach the third generation of the founding group. A particularly upsetting example of this is Kongo Gumi, a Japanese company dedicated to the construction of temples, which was founded in the year 578. The company managed to survive through 58 generations, by applying an essential principle: the presidential chair should be passed on to the best prepared son and not necessarily to the first-born, as dictated by Japanese culture. However, the secularization of Japanese society undermined its traditional business and although the firm attempted a diversification strategy, the bursting of the housing bubble in Japan in the 1990s led the firm further into indebtedness until it eventually went bankrupt in 2006.

The predominance of first-generation FFs, and the sharp drop in the number of these firms that manage to prosper beyond the second generation, have been taken to support the prediction of a high mortality rate and serious problems with generational and managerial change. The empirical reference typically cited is that of Ward (1987): in his study of FFs in the United States and Europe, the author estimates that only 33% of them were passed on from the first to the second generation, with a 50% survival rate over subsequent generations; therefore, the percentage of FFs surviving past the second and third generation is 16% and 8%, respectively. The research by Craig & Moores (2006) points to an equally troubling mortality rate: at the end of the first generation, between two-thirds and three-quarters of FFs go bankrupt or the family lose control. Moreover, only around 15% endure into the third generation as a family firm in line with the idea of its founder. Focusing on Spanish FFs, Amat (1998: 60) estimates the probability of surviving through the first generational change at 10-15%, 30-35% in the second, and a 50% chance of surviving the third generation. Galve & Salas (2003: 82) also conclude that FFs find it harder to survive, as indicated by the fact that only 24.2% of companies over 25 years of age are FFs (compared to 75.8% of NFFs), and this percentage has even declined slightly since 1991. However, these data can also be interpreted in a different way: focusing exclusively on FFs, we see that 25.7% are between 16 and 25 years old and 26.5% are over 25 (both percentages having grown significantly since 1991), that is, 52.2% have reached or surpassed the threshold of the first generational change (almost 5 percentage points higher than in 1991). This survival rate is not markedly lower than that of the NFF. In the case of the NFF, 15.7% are aged 16-25 years and 40.8% are 25 or over, giving a total of 56.5%. Moreover, in the period under study, this rate decreased by 6 percentage points.

Other studies provide evidence that also casts doubt on the greater longevity of the NFF. Thus, the study by Camisón (2001a) on Valencian industrial firms points out that the average age of the FF is higher than that of the NFF (a significant difference of 29 years compared to 21 years, respectively). Research by the same author on Spanish industrial SMEs (Camisón, 1997) also reports a longer average life of FFs, although the difference narrowed in the decade under study: in 1984, the average FF age was 23.6 years and average NFF age was 16.1 years, while a decade later the corresponding ages were 24.9 and 20.1 years, respectively. Given that the average duration of a generation is 25-30 years, and that most of Spain's production industries emerged from the 1960s on (86.9% and 79.1%, respectively), the relative share of the first and second generation of FFs could be better explained by their youth rather than their lack of competitiveness. However, the data reported by Galve & Salas (2003) and Camisón (1997) point to a decreasing share of FFs in recently-established companies, which may reveal a preference by entrepreneurs for other organizational models and funding sources, independent of family control.

In addition to assessing ex post competitiveness—referring to the various indicators that measure the results achieved by the company at a certain point in time—it is necessary to understand ex ante competitiveness—referring to the drivers of business success (Camisón, 1997: 81; Salas, 1993: 109). This difference corresponds to the traditional distinction between means and ends; or in other words, between determinants/predictors (means) and results (ends). Meeting consumers' needs and creating value (or capturing income) is only feasible when the firm enjoys sustainable competitive advantages. A firm is competitive when it achieves better results than its rivals (in terms of profitability, growth, market share and survival) thanks to certain competitive advantages that allow it to sell more and/or higher-priced products, yielding higher profits, and which are difficult for competitors to imitate. There are therefore two dimensions to the concept of competitiveness: ***ex ante and ex post competitiveness*** (Figure 3). [7]

Determinants of Ex Post Competitiveness

The proposed summary explanatory model of FFs' international competitiveness focuses on the chain of ex ante competitiveness and the subsequent indicators of ex post competitiveness, which can ultimately provide an explanation for the firm's international competitive success.

Firm performance provides a measure of its ability to compete, captured through observation of the financial and commercial effects produced by competing and surviving in the market, as well as other non-financial outcomes. Strategic research attempts to explain the firm's competitive potential before it starts to compete, and the differences in performance between firms in the same industry based on multiple elements both internal and external to the organization. Theory indicates that the firm's resources and capabilities and the attractiveness of the environment (a priori potential) and its results (consequences) should be strongly correlated, with the former being the cause of the latter.

In an initial classification, it can be stated that the competitiveness of the company and its ongoing achievement of economic profits is basically dependent on two types of factors or sources: (1) external factors of competitiveness, which determine the degree to which the organizational environment influences business competitiveness; (2) internal sources of competitive advantages stemming from the heterogeneity of the internal context of each organization. Figure 4 summarizes this conceptual framework and the theoretical relationships that can be expected between the different levels of competitiveness. More conventionally, the strategic management literature (Camisón, 1996a; Canals, 1995, 1991; Salas, 1993b; Cuervo, 1993b; Nelson, 1991; Porter, 1991, 1990 a,b; Whipp, Rosenfeld & Pettigrew, 1989; Rumelt, 1984) has classified the different drivers of competitive advantage into three groups: country advantages (international differences), industry advantages (cross-industry differences) and firm advantages (cross-company differences).

In line with neoclassical economic theory, the country effect reflects the comparative advantages enjoyed by firms in a particular country due to that country's specific resources and capabilities; that is, its factor endowment. The firm effect, which is underpinned by different theoretical approaches (the main one being the RCBV), captures the firm's unique attributes that endow it with competitive advantages or disadvantages compared to its competitors in the business, and which therefore influence the variation in strategies and performance between organizations of the same industry. The industry effect, supported by the tenets of industrial economics, refers to the common features of an industry (which affect all competitors equally) as the main determinant of intra-industry performance and persistent differences in the performance of companies competing in different activities.

Figure 5. Ex ante competitiveness as the source of ex post competitiveness, and its determinants.

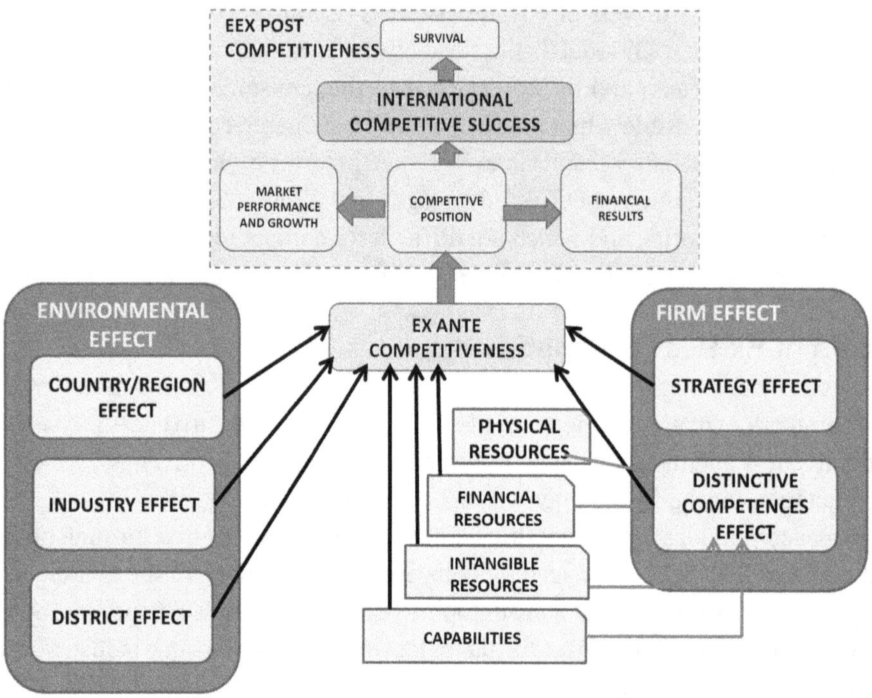

Other studies have contributed to the analysis of the strategic heterogeneity of companies, including the firm effect capturing the influence of the diversification of the portfolio of activities (McGahan, 1999; McGahan & Porter, 1999, 1997; Schmalensee, 1985). There is also an intermediate level of analysis between industry and firm level—the strategic group—used to analyse the effect of competitive similarity between companies within the same industry (González & Ventura, 2002; Khanna & Rivkin, 2001). A year effect has also been included to account for the temporary effects generated by cyclical variations in the economy, and captured by an industry-year interaction term (McGahan & Porter, 1999, 1997; Roquebert, Phillips & Westfall, 1996; Rumelt, 1991). Lastly, the competitiveness analysis must take into account the influence of the territorial framework. It is important not to approach the notion of territory from a reductionist perspective, viewing it in purely spatial terms relating to its uniform, static aspects; nor should it be reduced to the spatial framing of the markets. Rather, it is more useful to interpret it as a district in the Marshallian sense of the term. The firm's location in a territory with a given wealth of shared resources stemming from external economies and the social and relational atmosphere embedded in the environment, highlights the fact that the firm's behaviour may be significantly influenced by the district effect (Camisón, 2004; Porter, 1990; Brusco, 1982; Becattini, 1979).

The empirical research into the relative effect on performance of the different kinds of competitive advantages has largely contributed evidence (albeit with certain contradictory results) of the predominant importance of the firm effect in explaining intra-industry differences in performance (Bamiatzi et al., 2016; Bamiatzi & Hall, 2009; Roquebert et al., 1996). There is empirical evidence of higher profit differentials between companies belonging to the same industry than between companies in different industries (Mauri & Michaels, 1998; Rumelt, 1991; Hansen & Wernerfelt, 1989; Cool & Schendel, 1987) and of greater profitability asymmetry between companies in the same strategic group than between said groups (McNamara, Deephouse & Luce, 2003; Cool & Schendel, 1987, 1988).

In summary, the predominance of the firm effect points to persistent heterogeneous scenarios, the roots of which lie in initially asymmetric endowments of resources and capabilities. These assets are rare, lasting, of limited transferability, and imperfectly imitable due to barriers to duplication (Rumelt, 1991, 1984; Barney, 1991; Grant, 1991a; Dierickx & Cool, 1989; Lippman & Rumelt, 1982); imperfectly substitutable for strategically equivalent assets (Collis & Montgomery, 1995; Collis, 1994; Amit & Schoemaker 1993; Peteraf, 1993; Barney, 1991, 1986b; Dierickx & Cool, 1989); and their rents are appropriable by the firm. The RCBV postulates that sustainable advantages over the competition lie in the wealth of a firm's strategic assets at a given moment in time (Barney, Wright & Ketchen, 2001; Barney, 1986b, 1991; Peteraf, 1993; Rumelt, 1991; Grant, 1991a; Wernerfelt, 1984) and the firm's dynamic capability to protect, renew and expand those assets (Easterby-Smith, Lyles & Peteraf, 2009; Eisenhardt & Martin, 2000; Helfat & Peteraf, 2003; Teece, 2007; Teece & Pisano, 1998; Teece, Pisano & Shuen, 1997; Zollo & Winter, 2002; Leonard-Barton, 1992; Nelson & Winter, 1982).

In particular, the RCBV has emphasized the role of ***intangible assets***, in both the strategic analysis and the strategy implementation phase (Itami & Roehl, 1987). The value of intangible assets as a source of economic profits and sustainable competitive advantages can be explained by the fact that they are forms of knowledge with different degrees of specificity, codifiability and complexity. These features make them more readily eligible as strategic assets. The literature has thus studied the role of intangible assets as a source of success. In this regard, key intangible assets include the history and culture of the company (Hall, 1992, 1993; Fiol, 1991; Itami & Roehl, 1987; Barney, 1986a), managerial talent (Barney & Tyler, 1990; Hambrick & Finkelstein, 1987), interpersonal relationships between managers (Barney, 1986a), reputation (Hall, 1992, 1993; Itami & Roehl, 1987; Klein & Lefler, 1987; 1981; Klein, Crawford

& Alchian, 1978), a clear vision of the future for an organization based on a charismatic leader (Zucker, 1987), the unique organizational architecture (Nelson & Winter, 1982), the differentiated skills and knowledge of its human resources (Barney & Wright, 1998; Lado & Wilson, 1994; Hall, 1992, 1993), and information on its clients (Itami & Roehl, 1987).

Resources and Capabilities in the Context of the FF: The Concept of Familiness

The literature has extensively studied the relative importance of these factors in explaining performance variability in all types of companies, but to date there are no published papers that have proposed and empirically tested the causes of ex ante FF competitiveness.

Given the unique characteristics of FFs, the specific features that differentiate them from NFFs will inevitably be a strong determinant of their competitive behaviour, continuity and, ultimately, success or failure. The literature includes many studies examining the strengths and weaknesses of FFs from non-academic perspectives. Some are based on the authors' own professional experience (as managers or consultants); and while others may even focus on particular case studies, they are generally lacking the rigorous protocols that demonstrate the reliability of the data collection and analysis—a *sine qua non* for accepting the results as valid. For its part, academic research has presented detailed analyses of the effects of FFs' differential characteristics on their results and value creation (e.g., McConaughy et al., 2001; Chrisman et al., 2005; Villalonga & Amit, 2006; Andres, 2008; Nieto et al., 2009), from two main theoretical perspectives: agency theory and the RCBV (Basco, 2006; Chrisman et al., 2003, 2005; Astrachan, 2010).

The most fruitful line of research aimed at explaining the competitive advantages and disadvantages of the FF is based on the concept of ***familiness*** (Pearson, Carr & Shaw, 2008; Habbershon, 2006; Habbershon, Williams & MacMillan, 2003; Habbershon & Williams, 1999). This term denotes the unique set of resources and capabilities that an FF possesses because of the interaction of different systems: the family as a whole, the individual family members, and the business. In other words, familiness refers to the resources and capabilities stemming from the involvement of the owning family; as such, it can be key to the analysis of the relationship between FF advantages and outcomes. However, the mere existence of specific resources or capabilities in a given company, due to its FF status, does not necessarily imply an advantage. In this sense, the influence of these assets can be positive (distinctive familiness) or negative (constrictive familiness). By this point, the issue has become immersed in a wealth of empirical results that are hard to systematize, and it has not yet been possible to sort the FF-specific factors that produce competitive advantages and disadvantages.

The FF-specific features yield a number of advantages and disadvantages that can affect various aspects of the business and determine the direction the organization will follow. Table 3 summarizes the most important ones. It should be noted that some of the characteristics typically found in FFs appear in both columns, suggesting that, depending on the point of view or the subject under study, they may be either beneficial or harmful. For example, while selecting employees and managers on the basis of family ties or kinship can lead to greater commitment and loyalty on their part, and benefits stemming from shared values, nepotistic practices can also pose serious disadvantages when it comes to achieving business success. Recruiting family members without due concern for their ability to perform certain tasks will prove an obstacle to building a sustainable competitive advantage, especially in the case of managers. Furthermore, while family involvement may lead to better knowledge of the business, this will tend to be more informal in nature. As such, it becomes hard for the firm to follow a strategic vision, with more

Table 3. Advantages and disadvantages of the family firm

ADVANTAGES	DISADVANTAGES
Family-employee incentives linked to family wealth/well-being Pollak (1985)	***Entrenchment*** Morck et al. (1988); Gallo & Vilaseca (1998); Gómez-Mejía et al. (2001); Schulze et al. (2001, 2003)
More knowledge and experience of the business Leach, (1993); Kets de Vries (1993b, 1996); Ibrahim & Ellis (1994); Gallo (1995); Ginebra (1997); Poutziouris (2001)	***Informal structures and overlapping roles*** Donnelley (1964); Burack & Calero (1981); Hayes (1981); Kets de Vries (1993b, 1996); Harvey & Evans (1994); Ibrahim & Ellis (1994); Tagiuri & Davis (1992); Ginebra (1997)
Commitment, dedication and family pride Calder (1961); Donnelley (1964); Horton (1986); Kets de Vries (1993b, 1996); Leach (1993); Ibrahim & Ellis (1994); Gallo (1995, 2002); Poza (1995); Cauffman (1996); Taiguri & Davis (1992); Ginebra (1997); Poutziouris (2001).	***Unprofessional management and human resources*** Westhead (1997); Fiegener et al. (1996); Gallo & Melé (1998); Jorissen et al. (2001); Matlay (2002); Fernández & Nieto (2005)
Greater monitoring capacity (Pollak, 1985)	***Spillover of family conflicts into the business*** Horton (1986); Gilbert (1989); Levinson (1971); Kets de Vries (1993b, 1996); Leach (1993); Harvey & Evans (1994); Ibrahim & Ellis (1994); Tagiuri & Davis (1992); Galve (2002)
Altruism Becker (1981); Fama & Jensen (1983); Pollak (1985); Simon (1993); Eshel et al. (1998); Eaton et al. (2002); Carney (2005)	***Altruism*** Gómez-Mejia et al. (2001); Schulze et al. (2001, 2003)
Loyalty, trust, communication and concern for employees Donnelley (1964); Davis (1983); Pollak (1985); Ward (1988); Leach (1993); Ibrahim & Ellis (1994); Gallo (1995, 2002); Tagiuri & Davis (1992); James (1999); Ibrahim et al. (2001); Poutziouris (2001)	***Nepotism*** Calder (1961); Burack & Calero (1981); Kepner (1983); Kets de Vries (1993b, 1996); Ibrahim & Ellis (1994); Gallo (1995); Cauffman (1996); Tagiuri & Davis (1992); Ginebra (1997); Poutziouris (2001).
Convictions, values and shared vision Donnelley (1964); Ibrahim & Ellis (1994); Taiuri & Davis (1996); Denison et al. (2004)	***Autocratic and paternalistic management style*** Calder (1961); Burack & Calero (1981); Kets de Vries (1993b, 1996); Leach (1993); Ibrahim & Ellis (1994); Gallo (1995); Cauffman (1996); Ginebra (1997); Poutziouris (2001)
Flexibility and speed in decision-making Davis (1983); Hall (1988); Kets de Vries (1993b, 1996); Leach (1993); Gallo (1995); Goffee & Scase (1985); Poza (1995); Cauffman (1996); Tagiuri & Davis (1992); Ginebra (1997); Poza et al. (1997); Donckels & Lambrecht (1999).	***Debt*** Burack & Calero (1981); Ginebra (1997); Poutziouris (2001)
Financial and operational autonomy Donnelley (1964); Kets de Vries (1993b, 1996); Poza (1995); Cauffman (1996); Ginebra (1997); Donckels & Lambrecht (1999); Poutziouris (2001).	***Problems with financing and acquisition of key resources and capabilities*** Donnelley (1964); Miller & Rice (1988); Kets de Vries (1993b, 1996); Friedman & Friedman (1994); Gallo (1995); Cauffman (1996); Ginebra (1997) & Donckels & Lambrecht (1999); James (1999); Carney (2005)
Long-term vision and commitment Donnelley (1964); Danco (1975) Davis (1983); Leach (1993); Kets de Vries (1993b, 1996); Ibrahim & Ellis (1994); Gallo (1995); Ginebra (1997); Poutziouris (2001).	***Problems of succession and coercion of descendants*** Gilbert (1989); Ginebra (1997). Calder (1961); Burack & Calero (1981); Leach (1993); Kets de Vries (1993b, 1996); Ibrahim & Ellis (1994); Gallo (1995)

Source: Own elaboration based on Fuentes et al. (2008), Galve (2002) & Chrisman et al. (2005)

informal business structures and overlapping roles emerging. In turn, these factors hinder management's effective leadership of the organization, as the role of each member of the company is not well defined.

Within the company's stock of strategic assets, coordination capabilities are vital for functional and dynamic capabilities to be activated and deployed in an integrated manner. Of all these coordination capabilities, managerial capabilities are fundamental: they enable the coordination of functional capabilities and make it possible to explore new combinations of resources and capabilities. They thus help create a mission that guides the formulation and implementation of strategy, on the basis of which the rest of the organizational competences can be developed (Camisón, 2005; Barney, 1986b; Collis, 1994; Lado, Boyd & Wright, 1992). The value of managerial capabilities in generating economic profits lies in the wealth of tacit and specific knowledge contained therein, which is specific to a certain historical and organizational context (Barney, 1991; Hambrick, ed., 1988; Hambrick et al., 1996). Moreover, they are socially constructed through complex interactions between key stakeholders and through experiential learning. All these features constitute powerful isolating mechanisms that make imitation difficult, and represent a source of sustainable competitive advantage (Castanias & Helfat, 1991; Hamel, 2007).

Although having a long-term vision and commitment is identified as an advantage, this aspect is closely tied to FF continuity through other members of the family in order to preserve the family wealth and control of the business, which are considered personal goals of the family. Viewed from this angle, it can be seen as more an issue of keeping family members in the company; specifically, it becomes a problem of succession. Succession is one of the most extensively analysed aspects in the field of family business; it is considered one of the key challenges for the vast majority of FFs (Benavides et al., 2011) and in some cases is even seen as a threat to such organizations (Cabrera & García, 2000). Succession involves the search for suitable candidates to manage and/or take on responsibility for the company. The search is usually centred on the family itself, to maintain the family nature of the firm. Nevertheless, suitable candidates cannot always be found within the family; moreover, some family members may be coerced into leading the family business, a fact that will negatively influence the development of an entrepreneurial and leadership orientation. These factors undermine the possibility of developing efficient managerial capabilities. Furthermore, reluctance to recruit external professionals is a reflection of conservative behaviour that can create aversion to change, which in turn hinders the development of managerial capabilities.

Aspects related to altruism have both positive and negative implications for the firm. Altruism is a powerful force in family life and, by extension, within the FF (Schulze et al., 2003). It compels parents to take care of their children, encourages family members to be considerate to one another, fosters the family's commitment to the firm, and generates more communication within the FF, thereby reducing information asymmetries between family agents and increasing the use of informal agreements (Daily & Dollinger, 1992; Simon, 1993; Eshel, 1998). However, altruism entails certain practical difficulties in applying specific sanctions, leading to moral hazard problems. For instance, it is hard for family agents to take actions that may harm the well-being of other family members, even if their behaviour or level of productivity are not appropriate (Galve, 2002). Thus, parents behaving altruistically can lead to spoilt, selfish behaviour on the part of their children (Buchanan, 1975), without repercussions for the children. This reasoning can be extended to the sphere of FF. On the other hand, altruism and managerial entrenchment, combined with the intention and desire to maintain family control, can negatively influence FF performance, cancelling out the value of its capabilities and hindering or delaying the development of new capabilities (Gómez-Mejía et al., 2001; Schulze et al., 2001, 2003). In this regard, altruistic behaviour within the FF may lead to the recruitment and continued employment of staff and

Table 4. Family firm advantages that can become obstacles to the development of managerial capabilities and firm success

ADVANTAGES		DISADVANTAGES	SOME OBSTACLES TO THE DEVELOPMENT OF MANAGERIAL CAPABILITIES.
Family-employee incentives linked to family wealth/well-being		*Entrenchment*	Problems supporting change. Problems developing strategic and entrepreneurial orientation. Low level of professionalization
More knowledge and experience of the business		*Informal structures and overlapping roles*	Leadership problems.
Commitment, dedication and family pride		*Unprofessional management and human resources*	Problems of professionalization and knowledge of management methods. Orientation that is more personal than professional. Lack of a strategic vision
Greater monitoring capacity		*Spillover of family conflicts into the business*	Problems in accepting diverse opinions. Problems in decision-making.
Altruism		*Altruism*	Problems of professionalization and knowledge of management methods. Orientation that is more personal than professional.
Loyalty, trust, communication and concern for employees		*Nepotism*	Problems of professionalization and knowledge of management methods. Orientation that is more personal than professional.
Convictions, values and shared vision		*Autocratic and paternalistic management style*	Problems in decision-making, in fostering a spirit of dialogue and in effective leadership.
Flexibility and speed in decision-making		*Debt*	Problems of effective leadership and acceptance of diverse opinions. Limited strategic vision of the business
Financial and operational autonomy		*Problems with financing and acquisition of key resources and capabilities*	Inward-looking rather than entrepreneurial orientation, and limited strategic vision of the business.
Long-term vision and commitment		*Problems of succession and coercion of descendants*	Not very capable successors. Little expertise in management methods and principles. Negative effects on leadership and entrepreneurial capacity.

Source: own elaboration

managers who are poorly qualified to carry out a certain activity. In such cases, these staffing decisions are based more on considerations related to family and kinship than on candidates' qualifications or suitability for the post. This has an adverse effect on the firm's managerial capabilities and thus the rest of its capabilities. Table 4 shows, in broad terms, how certain features identified as advantageous could become disadvantages hindering the proper development of managerial capabilities.

The literature has also provided contradictory evidence, with some studies identifying FFs as especially entrepreneurial, innovative, dynamic and proactive (Nordqvist et al., 2009) and reports of positive effects of the involvement of new family generations on the entrepreneurial behaviour of the FF (Kellermanns, Eddleston, Barnett & Pearson, 2008). These strategic assets have given rise to a school of thought which postulates that FFs can achieve a sustainable competitive advantage (Sirmon & Hitt, 2003; Habbershon & Williams, 1999). Conversely, other studies associate family involvement with adverse risk-taking behaviour (Naldi, Nordqvist, Sjöberg & Wiklund, 2007) and with certain characteristics that are incompatible with an entrepreneurial orientation, such as an unwillingness to implement strategic changes (Brunninge, Nordqvist & Wiklund, 2007), greater conservatism, low innovation and high risk aversion (Ward, 1986; Zahra, 2005, Naldi et. al, 2007). Agency theory has proved no less controversial (Miller & Le-Breton, 2006; Anderson & Reeb, 2003; Schulze, Lubatkin & Dino, 2003; Schulze, Lubatkin, Dino & Buchholtz, 2001, 2002).

CORPORATE AND FAMILY GOVERNANCE STRUCTURES AS DETERMINANTS OF DIFFERENCES IN RESOURCES AND CAPABILITIES OF FAMILY AND NON-FAMILY FIRMS

The strategic value of intangible assets should not obscure the fact that there are major barriers to their development (Camisón, 1997: 345-346). These obstacles include the extended period of time required to accumulate them, which causes diseconomies in terms of how long they take to begin to produce positive income flows (Jensen, 1986; Dierickx & Cool, 1989; Salas, 199; Vives, ed., 2000); their nature as a public good, which can cause certain externalities and appropriability problems due to free-rider behaviour; and asset specificity and complementarity, which can complicate transactions involving these assets and diminish their collateral value to third parties, given the uncertainty about their residual value.

The ownership and governance structures are key to understanding the organizational and financial design decisions that the company must make in order to coordinate, protect and monetize the accumulated intangible assets, while neutralizing the negative effects inherent to these assets (Figure 5). According to Salas (1992) and Osterman (1994), the ideal organizational design in order to compete on the basis of intangibles requires structures that promote the setting of long-term objectives and the adoption of a commitment-oriented management system.

The issues related to ownership, control, the owner's orientation, the dilution of ownership and the governance mechanisms that regulate the effect of separating ownership and control have attracted growing interest in the FF literature. Agency theory is based on the analysis of the conflicts of interest that arise in situations where ownership and control are separate. It starts from the idea proposed by Adam Smith (1796) that the manager who does not own the business is hardly likely to act as diligently as the owner. This idea was further developed by Berle & Means (1932), who suggested that in cases where there is a conflict of interest, the manager of the company will seek to further his own interests to the detriment of the objectives of the owner of the company. For their part, Jensen & Meckling (1976) laid

Figure 6. The causality chain of competitiveness: the role of intangible assets and the ownership and governance structure.

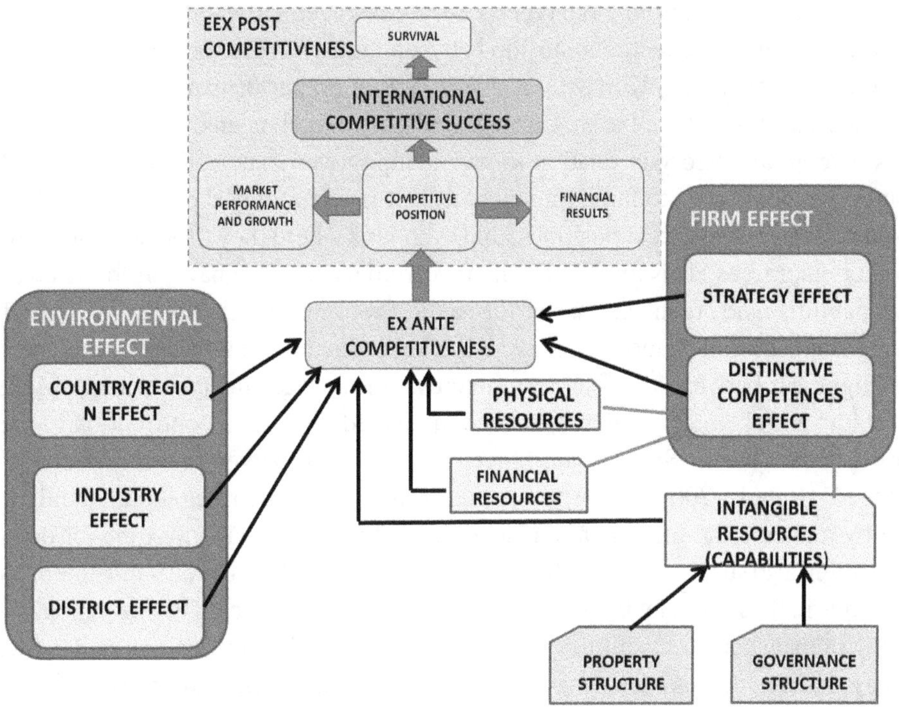

the foundations for modern agency theory by focusing on the problems that emerge due to the separation of ownership and control. Conceptually, agency theory can be directly applied to the context of the FF (Astrachan, 2010), taking into consideration that the objectives set by the firm also include non-economic benefits (Chrisman et al., 2003).

Carney (2005) suggests that the FF governance structure places constraints on managerial capabilities, hindering the acquisition of resources and capabilities and thus generating competitive disadvantages. Specifically, the fact that FFs often restrict decision-making roles to an insider group—usually family members—with access to privileged information (Chandler, 1990; Demsetz & Lehn, 1985), inhibits their ability to accumulate intangible capabilities and develop the routines and organizational systems required to coordinate various functions and a large number of people (Kogut & Zander, 1992).

The literature maintains that the nature of these capabilities as a public good can lead to certain externalities and problems of appropriability due to free-rider behaviour, arising when skilled professionals leave the organization, taking this knowledge with them. On the other hand, the setting of long-term goals is fostered in FFs, due to the closer alignment between ownership and management. This minimizes the adverse effects of the departure of specialized managerial knowledge (Camisón, 1997). However, family involvement can also generate problems relating to the lack of separation between ownership and management, as well as issues concerning the leadership and succession required to ensure the professionalism and competence of the management team and the board of directors (Miller, Minichilli & Corbetta, 2013, Minichilli, Corbetta & MacMillan, 2010). The literature has reported evidence that family involvement in FF governance and management has both positive and negative effects on the firm's endowment of certain managerial capabilities, such as entrepreneurial orientation (Zahra, 2005, Zahra, Hayton & Salvato, 2004, Zahra, Neubaum & Huse, 2000) or innovation (Lichtenthaler & Muethel, 2012), albeit without clearly defining the type of family involvement in question. It should not come as a surprise, therefore, that the direct relationship between family involvement and performance has been found to be non-significant (e.g., Kim & Gao, 2013), or that FF performance has been shown to decline with generational transitions (van Essen, Carney, Gedajlovic & Heugens, 2015).

The focus on contract theory in relation to ownership, governance and management structures has led to less attention being paid to family involvement. It is commonly the case in FFs that core family members hold middle-management positions, and even jobs where they have no control over or responsibility for other employees. This form of family involvement can also have profound consequences for managerial capabilities and organizational performance. Preliminary analysis suggests that the leadership of the management team can be more effective when subordinates are also family members. This is due to the close alignment between the long-term interests of both groups (as owners). Moreover, family workers constitute a highly-committed workforce motivated to make a contribution to the growth and continuity of the firm (Davis, Schoorman, Mayer & Tan, 2000). Given their economic and emotional interests in the FF (Bubolz, 2001), these non-managerial family employees should facilitate the work of management by reducing the time spent on supervision and thus freeing up time for other managerial tasks. But one might also suspect that conflicts can arise more readily between family members occupying different positions in the hierarchy if there are power struggles and or conflicting visions of FF strategy. A deterioration in managerial capabilities could also stem from the problems associated with attracting external managerial talent; candidates may be wary of obstacles to their authority and decision-making capacity as a result of having employees who are theoretically subordinate but who also belong to the owning family. When the family has a strong presence in the firm, managers end up being constrained by the family dynamics (Gómez-Mejía, Núñez & Gutiérrez, 2001). In addition, family involvement can be associated with adverse risk-taking behaviour (Naldi et al., 2007) and with higher governance costs due to altruism (Jensen, 1994)—in this case familial altruism (Schulze et al., 2007; Dyer, 2006; Lubatkin, Schulze, Ling & Dino, 2005; Schulze et al., 2003, 2002, 2001; Gómez-Mejía et al., 2001). Relatively little academic research has focused on these issues and their impact on firm results; moreover, findings to date have not been conclusive. Despite the strategic value of managerial capabilities and the potential problems affecting their accumulation, an understanding of the factors that influence their development remains incomplete. The literature has emphasized the effect of individual socio-demographic differences (e.g., Ford & Gioia, 2000) and the learning process that underpins the acquisition of the skills required for managerial tasks, whether the investment in human capital is private or organizational (e.g., Ortín, 1998, special issue Academy of Management Learning & Education, September 2015). However, there has been little focus on examining the influence of the ownership and control structure on the acquisition and development of certain resources and capabilities—in particular, managerial capabilities.

Despite the abundant literature on the combinations of corporate governance and family which promote the acquisition and development of capabilities, very few published papers have adopted a contingency perspective or considered the possibility of different solutions which comply with the principle of equifinality (e.g., De Massis, Chirico, Kotlar & Naldi, 2014, Braun & Sharma, 2007; Corbetta & Salvato, 2004). The special issue on governance published by the *Academy of Management Journal* in December 2014 is a good example of this. This aspect presents another problem to be investigated.

THE HETEROGENEITY OF FAMILY FIRMS

Another broad line of research has sought to explain the variation in business outcomes based on the similarity/differentiation of the firm's competitive position within its industry. To that end, an intermediate level of analysis between industry and firm level has been introduced, giving rise to the so-called "strategy effect". This effect reflects the intra-industry performance differential attributable to the adoption of a certain competitive position by a group of competitors, which is superior to alternative options and which is stable over time. The main theoretical underpinnings of this effect are the concepts of strategic similarity, the strategic group and competitive positioning.

Following Deephouse (1999), strategic similarity can be defined as the distance between a firm's strategic position and its competitors' strategic positions. Strategic similarity refers to homogeneity between organizations employing the same strategic option, and heterogeneity between different groups of competitors occupying different positions within an industry.

According to Porter's *theory of competitive advantage*, a firm's competitive success can be explained not only by the industry effect outlined above, but also by a second factor, the positioning effect, which recognizes the specificity of each company as reflected in the relative position that the company has secured in its market. Therefore, Porter defines the role of strategy in generating and maintaining a differentiated competitive position that allows a firm to generate higher profits than competitors. Porter (1980, 1985) also observed the internal heterogeneity of each sector, disaggregating the industry into strategic groups with differentiated competitive positions. Barriers to mobility, based on the costs of change and barriers to imitation (McGee & Thomas, 1986), could lead to differences in performance between the different strategic groups (Porter, 1979; Caves & Porter, 1977) and help ensure that the competitive advantages and economic profits achieved by the successful groups are sustainable over time.

González & Ventura (2002) and Khanna & Rivkin (2001) have empirically shown the relative importance of the strategic group effect as a determinant of profitability, together with industry and firm effects. However, studies such as that of McNamara, Deephouse & Luce (2003), which add to the classic work of Cool & Schendel (1988, 1987), again conclude that within-group differences in performance are larger than between-group differences. Thus, the strategy effect is likely to be unique to each company. The heterogeneity of firms within each strategic group, due to their portfolio of resources and capabilities and the way in which they combine them to formulate and implement their strategy, is sufficient to generate notable asymmetries that set their market positions and their results apart from those of other firms.

Therefore, one way of advancing the state of the research is to take the analysis down to the level of the different types of FF. No previous studies have analysed what type of FF and what type of FF governance achieves the best results in relation to the strategy adopted. Indeed, there is only one such paper (Basco, 2014), which analyses FF performance according to the competitive strategy adopted. Therefore, defining the different types of FF and the variation in their results constitutes a promising line of research. Similarly, although the literature is filled with empirical studies that have proposed a myriad of generic classifications for companies (e.g., Conant, Mokwa & Varadarajan, 1990; Snow & Hrebiniak, 1980; Porter, 1980; Miles & Snow, 1978), there is limited configurational research within the field of the FF (e.g., Cannella, Jones, & Withers, 2015; Casillas, Moreno, & Barbero, 2010). Frankly, the few studies that have been published—with the possible exceptions of Yu, Lumpkin, Sorenson & Brigham (2012) and Hernández-Linares, Sarkar & López-Fernández (2017)—leave room for improvement in that they use only a small number of variables to identify groups of firms and overlook some key attributes of FFs, such as the governance structures and values of the firm and family. This gap in the research prompted the 2019 publication of the special issue on "Typologies and taxonomies of family business" in *Family Business Review* (volume 32, number 2). Progress has been made in research into FF heterogeneity and how this variability is linked to relevant measures of organizational performance, through various studies that apply a configurational approach to capture asymmetries (Neubaum, Kammerlander & Brigham, 2019; Sánchez.Ruiz, Daspit, Holt & Rutherford, 2019; Kosmidou & Ahuja, 2019; Stanley, Hernández-Linares, López-Fernández & Kellermanns, 2019; Rau, Schneider-Siebke & Günther, 2019).

FUTURE RESEARCH DIRECTIONS

The "family effect" remains a challenge for researchers interested in both the FF's organizational form and in the effects of family ownership on the firm's strategy, structure and performance. Governance mechanisms, managerial quality, ownership concentration, and family involvement all have relevant effects in terms of influencing monitoring costs, investment decisions, the development of the portfolio of resources and capabilities, and FF competitiveness. Nevertheless, few studies to date have opened the black box of the "family effect ".

The authors draw attention to the factors underlying the generation and protection of managerial capabilities, with a particular focus on corporate governance design and management structure, analysing the moderating effect exerted on this relationship by family complexity, the development of instruments for family-business conciliation, and family involvement in three areas (governance, management and work), as well as the extent to which these mechanisms are standard in the different FF types. Other interesting topics for study include the effect of the configuration of firm and family governance structures on organizational performance, and the contingency effect of fitting corporate governance to family involvement and complexity.

CONCLUSION

This chapter focuses on four of the fundamental issues requiring further clarification: (1) determinants of the variation in competitiveness among FFs; (2) the different FF types and the variation in their performance; (3) the endowment of resources and capabilities that distinguishes the excellent FF and the differences between the various FF types in this regard; and (4) the factors underlying the configuration of firm and family governance structures. The review of the literature has revealed the sources of competitive advantages and drivers of economic profits in the field of FFs. The family effect is particularly strong when it comes to the portfolio of resources and capabilities The heterogeneity of FFs also calls for FF typologies and taxonomies which classify FFs according to their key defining elements. In order to provide a comprehensive conceptualization of the FF which appropriately accounts for its components, the authors have also reviewed the related literature, pointing to the potential of each as competitive advantages and disadvantages.

ACKNOWLEDGMENT

This study has been funded by the Ministry of Science, Innovation and Universities and the Agencia Estatal de Investigación (the Spanish State Research Agency), with co-financing from the European Regional Development Fund (ERDF). [Reference ECO2016-26796-P]

REFERENCES

Alchian, A. A. (1991). Rent. In J. Eatwell, M. Milgate, & P. Newman (Eds.), *The world of economics* (pp. 591–597). Nueva York, NY: W.W. Norton. doi:10.1007/978-1-349-21315-3_79

Alcorn, P. B. (1982). *Success and survival in the family-owned business*. Nueva York, NY: McGraw-Hill.

Amat, J.M. (1998). *La continuidad de la empresa familiar.* Barcelona, España: Ediciones Gestión 2000.

Anderson, R., & Reeb, D. (2003). Founding-family ownership and firm performance: Evidence from the S&P 500. *The Journal of Finance*, *58*(3), 1301–1328. doi:10.1111/1540-6261.00567

Andres, C. (2008). Large shareholders and firm performance – An empirical examination of founding-family ownership. *Journal of Corporate Finance*, *14*(4), 431–445. doi:10.1016/j.jcorpfin.2008.05.003

Astrachan, J. H. (2010). Strategy in family business: Toward a multidimensional research agenda. *Journal of Family Business Strategy*, *1*(1), 6–14. doi:10.1016/j.jfbs.2010.02.001

Astrachan, J. H., Klein, S. B., & Smyrnios, K. X. (2002). The F-PEC scale of family influence: A proposal for solving the family business definition problem. *Family Business Review*, *15*(1), 45–58. doi:10.1111/j.1741-6248.2002.00045.x

Astrachan, J. H., Zahra, S. A., & Sharma, P. (2003). *Family-sponsored ventures*. Kansas City, MO: Kauffman Fondation.

Ayala, J. C., & Navarrete, E. (2004). Efectos, tamaño y sector sobre la rentabilidad, endeudamiento y coste de la deuda de las empresas familiares riojanas. *Cuadernos de Gestión*, *4*(1), 35–53.

Bamiatzi, V., Bozos, K., Cavusgil, S. T., & Hult, G. T. M. (2016). Revisiting the firm, industry and country effects on profitability under recessionary and expansion periods: A multi-level analysis. *Strategic Management Journal*, *22*(1), 1–26.

Bamiatzi, V., & Hall, G. (2009). Firm versus sector effects on profitability and growth: The importance of size and interaction. *International Journal of the Economics of Business*, *16*(2), 205–220. doi:10.1080/13571510902917517

Barnes, L. B., & Hershon, S. A. (1976). Trasfering power in the family business. *Harvard Business Review*, 105–114.

Barney, J. B. (1986). Organizational culture: Can it be a source of sustained competitive advantage? *Academy of Management Review*, *11*(3), 656–665. doi:10.5465/amr.1986.4306261

Barney, J. B. (1986). Strategic factor markets: Expectations, luck and business strategy. *Management Science*, *32*(10), 1231–1241. doi:10.1287/mnsc.32.10.1231

Barney, J. B. (1991). Firms resources and sustained competitive advantage. *Journal of Management*, *17*(1), 191–210. doi:10.1177/014920639101700108

Barney, J. B., & Tyler, B. (1990). The attributes of top management teams and sustained competitive advantage. In M. Lawless & L. Gómez-Mejía (Eds.), *Managing the high technology firms* (pp. 33–48). Nueva York, NY: JAI Press.

Barney, J. B., Wright, M., & Ketchen, D. J. Jr. (2001). The resource-based view of the firm: Ten years after 1991. *Journal of Management*, *27*(6), 625–641. doi:10.1177/014920630102700601

Barney, J. B., & Wright, P. M. (1998). On becoming a strategic partner: The role of human resources in gaining competitive advantage. *Human Resource Management*, *37*(1), 31–47. doi:10.1002/(SICI)1099-050X(199821)37:1<31::AID-HRM4>3.0.CO;2-W

Barontini, R., & Caprio, L. (2006). The effect of family control on firm value and performance: Evidence from continental Europe. *European Financial Management*, *12*(5), 689–723. doi:10.1111/j.1468-036X.2006.00273.x

Barroso, A., Sanguino, R., & Bañegil, T. M. (2012). Diferentes criterios del concepto de empresa familiar. Una aportación desde Extremadura, España. *Ide@as. CONCYTEG*, *7*(83), 611–622.

Barry, B. (1975). The development of organization structure in the family firm. *Journal of General Management, otoño*, 42-60.

Basco, R. (2006). La investigación en la empresa familiar: Un debate sobre la existencia de un campo independiente. *Investigaciones Europeas*, *12*(1), 33–54.

Basco, R. (2014). Exploring the influence of the family upon firm performance: Does strategic behaviour matter? *International Small Business Journal*, *32*(8), 967–995. doi:10.1177/0266242613484946

Becattini, G. (1979). Del settore industriale al distretto industriale. Alcune considerazioni sull l'unita di indagine dell'economia industriale. *Rivista di Economia e Politica Industriale*, *1*, 7–21.

Becker, G. (1981). *A treatise on the family*. Cambridge, MA: Harvard University Press.

Benavides, C. A., Guzmán, V. F., & Quintana, C. (2011). Evolución de la literatura sobre empresa familiar como disciplina científica. *Cuadernos de Economía de la Empresa*, *14*(2), 78–90.

Berle, A., & Means, G. (1932). *The modern corporation and private property*. New York, NY: MacMillan.

Bhattacharya, U., & Ravikumar, B. (2001). Capital markets and the evolution of family business. *The Journal of Business*, *74*(2), 187–220. doi:10.1086/209670

Braun, M., & Sharma, A. (2007). Should the CEO also be chair of the board?: An empirical examination of family-controlled public firms. *Family Business Review*, *20*(2), 111–126. doi:10.1111/j.1741-6248.2007.00090.x

Brunninge, O., Nordqvist, M., & Wiklund, J. (2007). Corporate Governance and Strategic Change in SMEs: The Effects of Ownership, Board Composition and Top Management Teams. *Small Business Economics*, *29*(3), 295–308. doi:10.100711187-006-9021-2

Brusco, S. (1982). The Emilian Model: Productive decentralisation and social integration. *Cambridge Journal of Economics*, *6*, 167–184.

Bubolz, M. (2001). Family as source, user and builder of social capital. *Journal of Socio-Economics*, *30*(2), 129–131. doi:10.1016/S1053-5357(00)00091-3

Buchanan, J. M. (1975). The Samaritan's dilemma. In E. S. Phelps (Ed.), *Altruism, morality and economic theory* (pp. 71–75). New York, NY: Russell Sage Foundation.

Burack, E. H., & Calero, C. M. (1981). Seven perils of family business. *Nation's Business*, *69*(1), 62–64.

Cabrera, K., & García, J. M. (2000). Planteamiento multinivel para el estudio del proceso de sucesión en la empresa familiar. *Cuadernos de Economía y Dirección de la Empresa*, *6*, 187–212.

Calder, G. H. (1961). The peculiar problems of a family business. *Business Horizons*, *4*(3), 93–102. doi:10.1016/0007-6813(61)90029-5

Camisón, C. (1996). Dinámica de la competitividad de la PYME industrial española en la década 1984-94: Análisis del efecto país, efecto industria y efecto empresa. *Economía Industrial*, *310*, 121–140.

Camisón, C. (1997). *La competitividad de la PYME industrial española: estrategia y competencias distintivas*. Madrid, España: Civitas.

Camisón, C. (2001). *La competitividad de la empresa industrial de la Comunidad Valenciana: análisis del efecto del atractivo del entorno, los distritos industriales y las estrategias empresariales*. Valencia, España: Tirant lo Blanch.

Camisón, C. (2004). Shared, competitive and comparative advantages: A competence-based view of industrial-district competitiveness. *Environment & Planning A*, *36*(12), 2227–2256. doi:10.1068/a3759

Camisón, C. (2005). On how to measure managerial and organizational capabilities. *Management Research*, *3*(1), 27–48.

Camisón, C., & Cruz, S. (2008). La medición del desempeño organizativo desde una perspectiva estratégica: Creación de un instrumento de medida. *Revista Europea de Dirección y Economía de la Empresa*, *17*(1), 79–102.

Camisón, C., Forés, B., & Puig-Denia, A. (2016). Return on capital in Spanish tourism businesses: A comparative analysis of family vs non-family businesses. *European Journal of Management and Business Economics*, *25*(3), 91–110. doi:10.1016/j.redeen.2016.04.002

Camisón, C., & Monfort, V. (2011). *La empresa turística familiar en España: importancia, perfil y competitividad*. Madrid, España: Ministerio de Industria, Turismo y Comercio.

Canals, J. (1991). *Competitividad internacional y estrategia de la empresa*. Barcelona, España: Ariel.

Canals, J. (1995). Firm, industry and country specific advantages in international competition. In H. Thomas, D. O'Neal, & J. Kelly (Eds.), *Strategic Renaissance and Business Transformation* (pp. 107–134). Nueva York, NY: John Wiley & Sons.

Cannella, A. A. Jr, Jones, C. D., & Withers, M. C. (2015). Family- versus lone-founder-controlled public corporations: Social identity theory and boards of directors. *Academy of Management Journal, 58*(2), 436–459. doi:10.5465/amj.2012.0045

Capasso, A. (2004). Stakeholder theory and corporate governance: The role of intangible assets. *Working Paper Series, Social Sciencesearch Network SSRN.* Retrieved from http://papers.ssrn.com/sol3/papers.cfm?abstract_id:610661

Carney, M. (2005). Corporate governance and competitive advantage in family-controlled firms. *Entrepreneurship Theory and Practice, 29*(May), 249–265. doi:10.1111/j.1540-6520.2005.00081.x

Casillas, J., Moreno, A., & Barbero, J. (2010). A configurational approach of the relationship between entrepreneurial orientation and growth of family firms. *Family Business Review, 23*(1), 27–44. doi:10.1177/0894486509345159

Castanias, R. P., & Helfat, C. E. (1991). Managerial Resources and Rents. *Journal of Management, 17*(1), 155–171. doi:10.1177/014920639101700110

Cauffman, L. (1996). El desafío de la empresa familiar: Sus relaciones. In M. A. Gallo (Ed.), *La empresa familiar 5* (pp. 99–113). Barcelona, España: IESE, Publicaciones de la Cátedra de Empresa Familiar.

Caves, R. E., & Porter, M. E. (1977). From Entry Barriers to Mobility Barriers: Conjectural Decisions and Contrived Deterrence to New Competition. *The Quarterly Journal of Economics, 91*(2), 241–261. doi:10.2307/1885416

Chandler, A. D. (1990). *Scale and Scope: The Dynamics of Industrial Capitalism.* Cambridge: Harvard University Press.

Chrisman, J. J., Chua, J. H., & Sharma, P. (2003). Current trends and future directions in family business management studies: Toward a theory of the family firm. *Colerman White Paper Series.* Available at www.usabe.org/knowledge/whitepapers/index.asp

Chrisman, J. J., Chua, J. H., & Sharma, P. (2005). Trends and directions in the development of a strategic management theory of the family firm. *Entrepreneurship Theory and Practice, 29*(5), 555–576. doi:10.1111/j.1540-6520.2005.00098.x

Chrisman, J. J., Steier, L. P., & Chua, J. H. (2008). Toward a theoretical basis for understanding the dynamics of strategic performance in family firms. *Entrepreneurship Theory and Practice, 32*(6), 935–947. doi:10.1111/j.1540-6520.2008.00264.x

Chua, J. H., Chrisman, J. J., & Sharma, P. (1999). Defining the family business by behavior. *Entrepreneurship Theory and Practice, 23*(Summer), 19–39. doi:10.1177/104225879902300402

Claver, E., Rienda, L., Pertusa, E.M. (2004). Un marco teórico para la continuidad de la empresa familiar desde un punto de vista estratégico. *Esic Market, Mayo-Agosto*, 229-257.

Collis, D. J. (1994). Research note: How valuable are organizational capabilities? *Strategic Management Journal, 15*(S1), 143–152. doi:10.1002mj.4250150910

Conant, J. S., Mokwa, M. P., & Varadarajan, P. R. (1990). Strategic types, distinctive marketing competencies and organizational performance: A Multiple Measures-Based Study. *Strategic Management Journal, 11*(5), 365–383. doi:10.1002mj.4250110504

Cool, K., & Schendel, D. (1987). Strategic group formation and performance: The case of U.S. pharmaceutical industry, 1963-1982. *Management Science, 33*(9), 1102–1124. doi:10.1287/mnsc.33.9.1102

Cool, K., & Schendel, D. (1988). Performance differences among strategic group members. *Strategic Management Journal, 9*(3), 207–223. doi:10.1002mj.4250090302

Corbetta, G., Salvato, C. (2004). Self-serving or self-actualizing? Models of man and agency costs in different types of family firms: A commentary on 'comparing the agency costs of family and non-family firms: Conceptual issues and exploratory evidence. *Entrepreneurship Theory and Practice, summer*, 7-25.

Craig, J. B. L., & Moores, K. (2006). A 10 year longitudinal investigation of strategy, systems, and environment on innovation in family firms. *Family Business Review, 19*(1), 1–10. doi:10.1111/j.1741-6248.2006.00056.x

Cubbin, J. S., & Leech, D. (1983). The effeft of shareholding dispersion on the degree of control in British companies: Theory and measurement. *Economic Journal (London), 93*(37), 351–369. doi:10.2307/2232797

Cuervo, A. (1993). El papel de la empresa en la competitividad. *Papeles de Economía Española, 56*, 363-378.

Daily, C. M., & Dollinger, M. J. (1992). An empirical examination of ownership structure in family and professionally managed firms. *Family Business Review, 5*(2), 117–136. doi:10.1111/j.1741-6248.1992.00117.x

Daily, C. M., & Dollinger, M. J. (1993). Alternative methodologies for identifying family- versus nonfamily- managed business. *Journal of Small Business Management, 31*(2), 79–90.

Davis, J. H., Schoorman, R., Mayer, R., & Tan, H. (2000). The trusted general manager and business unit performance. *Strategic Management Journal, 21*(5), 563–576. doi:10.1002/(SICI)1097-0266(200005)21:5<563::AID-SMJ99>3.0.CO;2-0

Davis, P. (1983). Realizing the potential of the family business. *Organizational Dynamics, 12*(1), 47–56. doi:10.1016/0090-2616(83)90026-8

De Massis, A., Chirico, F., Kotlar, J., & Naldi, L. (2014). The temporal evolution of proactiveness in family firms: The horizontal S-curve hypothesis. *Family Business Review, 27*(1), 35–50. doi:10.1177/0894486513506114

Deephouse, D. L. (1999). To be different, or to be the same? It's a question (a theory) of strategic balance. *Strategic Management Journal, 20*(2), 147–166. doi:10.1002/(SICI)1097-0266(199902)20:2<147::AID-SMJ11>3.0.CO;2-Q

Demsetz, H., & Lehn, K. (1985). The structure of corporate ownership: Causes and consequences. *Journal of Political Economy, 93*(6), 1155–1177. doi:10.1086/261354

Demsetz, H., & Villalonga, B. (2001). Ownership structure and corporate performance. *Journal of Corporate Finance, 7*(3), 209–233. doi:10.1016/S0929-1199(01)00020-7

Denison, D., Lief, C., & Ward, J. (2004). Culture in family-owned enterprises: Recognizing and leveraging unique strengths. *Family Business Review, 17*(1), 61–70. doi:10.1111/j.1741-6248.2004.00004.x

Dierickx, I., & Cool, K. (1989). Asset stock accumulation and sustainability of competitive advantage. *Management Science, 35*(12), 1504–1513. doi:10.1287/mnsc.35.12.1504

Donckels, R., & Frölich, E. (1991). Are family businesses really different? European experiences from Stratos. *Family Business Review, 4*(2), 149–160. doi:10.1111/j.1741-6248.1991.00149.x

Donckels, R., & Lambrecht, T. (1999). Are family business really different? What we know from Western European business research that could be applied to the re-emergence of family-based. Enterprises in East Central Europe. *Family Business Review, 12*(2), 171–191. doi:10.1111/j.1741-6248.1999.00171.x

Donnelley, R. (1964). The family business. *Harvard Business Review, 42*(4), 93–105.

Dyer, W. G. (2006). Examining the family effect on firm performance. *Family Business Review, 19*(4), 253–273. doi:10.1111/j.1741-6248.2006.00074.x

Easterby-Smith, M., Lyles, M. A., & Peteraf, M. A. (2009). Dynamic capabilities: Current debates and future directions. *British Journal of Management, 20*, S1–S8. doi:10.1111/j.1467-8551.2008.00609.x

Eaton, C., Yuan, L., & Wu, Z. (2002). *Reciprocal altruism and the theory of the family firm.* Paper presented at the Second Annual Conference on Theories of the Family Enterprise, Philadelphia, PA.

Eisenhardt, K. M., & Martin, J. A. (2000). Dynamic Ccpabilities: What are they? *Strategic Management Journal, 21*(10-11), 1105–1121. doi:10.1002/1097-0266(200010/11)21:10/11<1105::AID-SMJ133>3.0.CO;2-E

Eshel, I., Samuelson, L., & Shaked, A. (1998). Altruists, egoists, and hooligans in a local interaction model. *The American Economic Review, 88*(1), 157–179.

Fahed-sreih, J., & Djoundourian, S. (2006). Determinants of longevity and success in Lebanese family businesses: An exploratory study. *Family Business Review, 19*(3), 225–234. doi:10.1111/j.1741-6248.2006.00071.x

Fama, E., & Jensen, M. (1983). Separation of ownership and control. *The Journal of Law & Economics, 26*(2), 301–325. doi:10.1086/467037

Fama, E. F., & Jensen, M. C. (1985). Organizational forms and investment decisions. *Journal of Financial Economics, 14*(1), 101–119. doi:10.1016/0304-405X(85)90045-5

Fernández, Z., & Nieto, M. J. (2005). La estrategia de internacionalización de la pequeña empresa familiar. *Cuadernos de Economía y Dirección de la Empresa, 22*, 107–126.

Fiegener, M. K., Brown, B. M., Prince, R. A., & File, K. M. (1996). Passing on strategic vision. *Journal of Small Business Management*, *34*(3), 15–26.

Fiol, C. M. (1991). Managing culture as a competitive resource: An identity-based view of sustainable competitive advantage. *Journal of Management*, *17*(1), 191–211. doi:10.1177/014920639101700112

Ford, C. M., & Gioia, D. A. (1995). *Creative action in organizations: Ivory tower visions and real world voices*. Newbury Park, MA: Sage Publications.

Friedman, M., & Friedman, S. (1994). How to run a family business. Cincinnati, OH: Better way Books.

Gallego, I. (2012). *La empresa familiar, su concepto y delimitación jurídica*. Universidad de Córdoba, España: Cuadernos de Reflexión de la Cátedra PRASA de Empresa Familiar, Cuaderno nº 14.

Gallo, M. A. (1995). *Empresa familiar: Textos y casos*. Barcelona, España: Praxis.

Gallo, M.A. (2002). Unidad y confianza en la empresa familiar. *Revista IESE, junio*, 28-35.

Gallo, M. A., & Melé, D. (1998). *Ética en la empresa familiar*. Barcelona, España: Praxis.

Gallo, M. A., & Sveen, J. (1991). Internationalizing the family business: Facilitating and restraining factors. *Family Business Review*, *4*(2), 181–190. doi:10.1111/j.1741-6248.1991.00181.x

Gallo, M. A., & Vilaseca, A. (1998). A financial perspective on structure, conduct, and performance in the family firms: An empirical study. *Family Business Review*, *11*, 35–47.

Galve, C. (2002). Propiedad y gobierno: La empresa familiar, *Ekonomiaz*, *50*(2), 158-181.

Galve, C., & Salas, V. (2003). *La empresa familiar en España. Fundamentos económicos y resultados*. Bilbao, España: Fundación BBVA.

Gedajlovic, E. R. (1993). Ownership, strategy and performance: Is the dichotomy sufficient? *Organization Studies*, *14*(5), 731–752. doi:10.1177/017084069301400507

Gedajlovic, E. R., & Shapiro, D. M. (1998). Management and ownership effects: Evidence from five countries. *Strategic Management Journal*, *19*(6), 533–553. doi:10.1002/(SICI)1097-0266(199806)19:6<533::AID-SMJ957>3.0.CO;2-#

Gersick, K. E., Davis, J. A., Hampton, M. M., & Lansberg, I. (1997). *Generation to generation: Life cycles of the family business*. Boston, MA: Harvard Business School Press.

Gilbert, N. (1989). Can a family business survive merger mania and divorce? *Management Review*, *78*(1), 38–42.

Gimeno, J., Folta, T., Cooper, A. C., & Woo, C. Y. (1997). Survival of the fittest? Entrepreneurial human capital. *Administrative Science Quarterly*, *42*(4), 750–784. doi:10.2307/2393656

Ginebra, J. (1997). *Las empresas familiares. Su dirección y su continuidad*. México: Panorama.

Goffee, R., & Scase, R. (1985). Proprietorial control in family firms: Some functions of quasi-organic management systems. *Journal of Management Studies*, *22*(1), 54–68. doi:10.1111/j.1467-6486.1985.tb00242.x

Gomez-Mejia, L. R., Nuñez-Nickel, M., & Gutierrez, I. (2001). The role of family ties in agency contracts. *Academy of Management Journal*, *44*, 81–95.

González, E., & Ventura, J. (2002). How much do strategic groups matter? *Review of Industrial Organization*, *21*(1), 55–71. doi:10.1023/A:1016001219134

Grant, R. M. (1991a). The resource-based theory of competitive advantages: Implications for strategy formulation. *California Management Review*, *33*(3), 114–135. doi:10.2307/41166664

Graves, C., & Thomas, J. (2006). Internationalization of Australian family business: A managerial capabilities perspective. *Family Business Review*, *19*(3), 207–224. doi:10.1111/j.1741-6248.2006.00066.x

Habbershon, T., & Williams, M. (1999). A resource-based framework for assessing the strategic advantage of family firms. *Family Business Review*, *12*(1), 27–39. doi:10.1111/j.1741-6248.1999.00001.x

Habbershon, T., Williams, M., & MacMillan, L. C. (2003). A unified systems perspective of family firm performance. *Journal of Business Venturing*, *18*(4), 451–465. doi:10.1016/S0883-9026(03)00053-3

Habbershon, T. G. (2006). Commentary: A framework for managing the familiness and agency advantages in family firms. *Entrepreneurship Theory and Practice*, *30*(6), 879–886. doi:10.1111/j.1540-6520.2006.00158.x

Hall, R. H. (1992). The strategic analysis of intangible resources. *Strategic Management Journal*, *13*(2), 135–144. doi:10.1002mj.4250130205

Hall, R. H. (1993). A framework linking intangible resources and capabilities to sustainable competitive advantage. *Strategic Management Journal*, *14*(8), 607–618. doi:10.1002mj.4250140804

Hambrick, D. C. (1988). *The executive effect: concepts and methods for studying top managers*. Greenwich, CT: JAI Press.

Hambrick, D. C., Cho, T. S., & Chen, M. J. (1996). The influence of top management team heterogeneity on firms competitive moves. *Administrative Science Quarterly*, *41*(4), 659–684. doi:10.2307/2393871

Hambrick, D. C., & Finkelstein, S. (1987). Managerial discretion: A bridge between polar views of organizational outcomes. In L. L. Cummings & B. Staw (Eds.), *Research in Organizational Behavior* (Vol. 9, pp. 369–406). Greenwich, CT: JAI Press.

Hamel, G. (2007). *The future of management*. Boston, MA: Harvard Business School Press.

Handler, W. C. (1989). Methodological issues and considerations in studying family businesses. *Family Business Review*, *2*(3), 257–276. doi:10.1111/j.1741-6248.1989.00257.x

Hansen, G., & Wernerfelt, B. (1989). Determinants of firm performance: The relative importance of economic and organizational factors. *Strategic Management Journal*, *10*(5), 399–411. doi:10.1002mj.4250100502

Hansmann, H. (1988). Ownership of the firm. *Journal of Law Economics and Organization*, *4*(2), 267–304.

Hansmann, H. (1996). *The ownership of enterprise*. Cambridge, MA: Belknap Press of the Harvard University Press.

Harris, R., Martinez, J., & Ward, J. (1994). Is strategy different for the family-owned business? *Family Business Review, VII*(2), 159–173. doi:10.1111/j.1741-6248.1994.00159.x

Harvey, M., & Evans, R. (1994). Family business and multiple levels of conflict. *Family Business Review, 7*(4), 331–347. doi:10.1111/j.1741-6248.1994.00331.x

Hawawini, G., Subramanian, V., & Verdin, P. (2003). Is performance driven by industry or firm-specific factors?: A new look at the evidence. *Strategic Management Journal, 24*(1), 1–16. doi:10.1002mj.278

Hayes, J. L. (1981). All in the family. *Management Review, 70*(7), 4–7. PMID:10310146

Helfat, C. E., & Peteraf, M. (2003). The dynamic resource-based view: Capability lifecycles. *Strategic Management Journal, 24*(10), 997–1010. doi:10.1002mj.332

Hernández-Linares, R., Sarkar, S., & López-Fernádez, M. C. (2017). How has the family firm literature addressed the heterogeneity through classification systems? An integrated analysis. *European Journal of family. Business (Atlanta, Ga.), 7*, 1–13.

Holland, J. (2001). Financial institutions, intangibles and corporate governance. *Accounting, Auditing & Accountability Journal, 14*(4), 497–529. doi:10.1108/EUM0000000005871

Holt, D. T., Pearson, A. W., Carr, J. C., & Barnett, T. (2017). Family firm(s) outcomes model: Structuring financial and nonfinancial outcomes across the family and firm. *Family Business Review, 30*(2), 182–202. doi:10.1177/0894486516680930

Hoopes, D. G., & Miller, D. (2006). Owner preferences, competitive heterogeneity and strategic capabilities. *Family Business Review, 19*(2), 89–101. doi:10.1111/j.1741-6248.2006.00064.x

Horton, T. P. (1986). Managing in a family way. *Management Review, 75*(2), 3.

Ibrahim, A. B., & Ellis, W. (1994). *Family business management. Concepts and practice*. Dubuque, IA: Kendall/Hunt Publishing Company.

Ibrahim, A. B., Soufani, K., & Lam, J. (2001). A study of succession in a family firm. *Family Business Review, 14*(3), 245–258. doi:10.1111/j.1741-6248.2001.00245.x

Itami, H., & Roehl, T. W. (1987). *Mobilizing Invisible Assets*. Cambridge, MA: Harvard University Press.

James, H. Jr. (1999). What can the family contribute to business? Examining contractual relationships. *Family Business Review, 12*(1), 61–71. doi:10.1111/j.1741-6248.1999.00061.x

Jensen, M. C. (1986). Agency costs of free cash flow, corporate finance and takeovers. *The American Economic Review, 76*(2), 323–329.

Jensen, M. C., & Meckling, W. H. (1976). Theory of the firm: Managerial behavior, agency costs, and ownership structure. *Journal of Financial Economics, 3*(4), 305–360. doi:10.1016/0304-405X(76)90026-X

Jorinsen, A., Laveren, E., Martens, R., & Reheul, A. (2001). *Planning and control practices in family firms versus non-family firms: empirical evidence from SMEs in the wholesale sector*. Antwerp, Belgium: Faculty of Applied Economics.

Judge, W. (2012). Owner type as emerging area of governance research. *Corporate Governance*, *20*(3), 231–232. doi:10.1111/j.1467-8683.2012.00908.x

Kellerman, F. W., Eddleston, K. A., Barnett, T., & Pearson, A. (2008). An exploratory study of family member characteristics and involvement effects on entrepreneurial behavior in the family firm. *Family Business Review*, *21*(1), 1–14. doi:10.1111/j.1741-6248.2007.00107.x

Kepner, E. (1983). The family and the firm: A coevolutionary perspective. *Organizational Dynamics*, *12*(1), 57–70. doi:10.1016/0090-2616(83)90027-X

Kets de Vries, M. F. R. (1993b). Lo bueno y lo malo de las empresas de titularidad familiar. *Harvard Business Review*, *4*, 32–44.

Kets de Vries, M. F. R. (1996). *Family business: Human dilemmas in the family firm*. London, UK: Thomson Business Press.

Khanna, T., & Rivkin, J. W. (2001). Estimating the performance effects of business groups in emerging markets. *Strategic Management Journal*, *22*(1), 45–74. doi:10.1002/1097-0266(200101)22:1<45::AID-SMJ147>3.0.CO;2-F

Kim, Y., & Gao, F. Y. (2013). Does family involvement increase business performance?: Family-longevity goals´ moderating role in Chinese family firms. *Journal of Business Research*, *66*(2), 265–274. doi:10.1016/j.jbusres.2012.08.018

Klein, B., Crawford, R. A., & Alchian, A. A. (1978). Vertical integration, appropriable rents, and the competitive contracting process. *The Journal of Law & Economics*, *21*(2), 297–326. doi:10.1086/466922

Klein, B., & Leffler, K. (1981). The role of market forces in assuring contractual performance. *Journal of Political Economy*, *89*(agosto), 615–641. doi:10.1086/260996

Kogut, B., & Zander, U. (1992). Knowledge of the firm, combinative capabilities, and the replication of technology. *Organization Science*, *3*(3), 383–397. doi:10.1287/orsc.3.3.383

Kosmidou, V., & Ahuja, M. K. (2019). A configurational approach to family firm innovation. *Family Business Review*, *32*(2), 154–173.

Lado, A. A., Boyd, N. G., & Wright, P. (1992). A competency-based model of sustainable competitive advantage: Toward a conceptual integration. *Journal of Management*, *18*(1), 77–91. doi:10.1177/014920639201800106

Lado, A. A., & Wilson, M. C. (1994). Human resource systems and sustained competitive advantage: A competency-based perspective. *Academy of Management Review*, *19*(4), 699–727. doi:10.5465/amr.1994.9412190216

Landes, D. S. (1951). French business and businessman in social and cultural analysis. In E. Mead (Ed.), *Modern France* (pp. 334–353). Princeton, NJ: Princeton University Press.

Lansberg, L., Perrow, E., & Rogolsky, S. (1988). Family business as an emerging field. *Family Business Review*, *4*(2), 1–8. doi:10.1111/j.1741-6248.1988.00001.x

Lazonick, W. (1991). *Business organization and the myth of the market economy*. Nueva York, NY: Cambridge University Press.

Leach, P. (1993). *La empresa familiar*. Barcelona, España: Granica.

Leonard-Barton, D. (1992). Core capabilities and core rigidities: A paradox in managing new product development. *Strategic Management Journal, 13*(special issue summer), 111-126.

Levin, S. G., & Levin, S. L. (1982). Ownership and control of large industrial firms. Some new evidence. *Review of Business and Economic Research, 18*(1), 37–49.

Levinson, H. (1971). Conflicts that plague family business. *Harvard Business Review, 49*(2), 90–98.

Lichtenthaler, U., & Muethel, M. (2012). Retracted: The impact of family involvement on dynamic innovation capabilities: Evidence from German manufacturing firms. *Entrepreneurship Theory and Practice, 36*(6), 1235–1253. doi:10.1111/j.1540-6520.2012.00548.x

Lubatkin, M., Schulze, W., Ling, Y., & Dino, R. (2005). The effects of parental altruism on the governance of family-managed firms. *Journal of Organizational Behavior, 26*(3), 313–330. doi:10.1002/job.307

Luhmann, N. (1996). *Introducción a la teoría de sistemas*. Universidad Iberoamericana.

Ly, M., & Simerly, R. L. (1998). The moderating effect of environmental dynamism on the ownership and performance relationship. *Strategic Management Journal, 19*(2), 169–179. doi:10.1002/(SICI)1097-0266(199802)19:2<169::AID-SMJ939>3.0.CO;2-2

Matlay, H. (2002). Training and HRD strategies in family and non-family owned small businesses: A comparative approach. *Education + Training, 44*(8/9), 357–369. doi:10.1108/00400910210449196

Mauri, A. J., & Michaels, M. P. (1998). Firm and industry effects within strategic management: An empirical examination. *Strategic Management Journal, 19*(3), 211–219. doi:10.1002/(SICI)1097-0266(199803)19:3<211::AID-SMJ947>3.0.CO;2-T

McConaughy, D. L., Matthews, C. H., & Fialko, A. S. (2001). Founding family controlled firms: Performance, risk, and value. *Journal of Small Business Management, 39*(1), 31–50. doi:10.1111/0447-2778.00004

McConnell, J. J., & Servaes, H. (1990). Additional evidence on equity ownership and Corporate value. *Journal of Financial Economics, 27*(2), 595–612. doi:10.1016/0304-405X(90)90069-C

McGahan, A. (1999). The performance of U.S. corporations: 1981-1994. *The Journal of Industrial Economics, 47*(4), 373–398. doi:10.1111/1467-6451.00105

McGahan, A., Porter, M. (1997): How much does industry matter, really? *Strategic Management Journal, 18*(special summer issue), 15-30.

McGahan, A., & Porter, M. (1998): *What do we know about variance in accounting profitability?* Working paper. Harvard Business School.

McGahan, A., & Porter, M. (1999). The persistence of shock to profitability. *The Review of Economics and Statistics, 81*(1), 143–153. doi:10.1162/003465399767923890

McKiernan, M. H., & Morris, C. (1994). Strategic planning and financial performance in UK SMEs: Does formality matter? *British Journal of Management*, *5*(special issue), 31–41. doi:10.1111/j.1467-8551.1994.tb00128.x

McNamara, G., Deephouse, D. L., & Luce, R. A. (2003). Competitive positioning within and across a strategic group structure: The performance of core, secondary, and solitary firms. *Strategic Management Journal*, *24*(2), 161–181. doi:10.1002mj.289

Miles, R. E., & Snow, C. C. (1978). *Organizational strategy, structure, and process.* McGraw-Hill.

Miller, D., & Le Breton-Miller, I. (2006). Family governance and firm performance: Agency, stewardship, and capabilities. *Family Business Review*, *19*(1), 73–87. doi:10.1111/j.1741-6248.2006.00063.x

Miller, D., Minichilli, A., & Corbetta, G. (2012). Is family leadership always beneficial? *Strategic Management Journal*, *34*(5), 553–571. doi:10.1002mj.2024

Miller, E. J., & Rice, A. K. (1988). The family business in contemporary society. *Family Business Review*, *1*(2), 193–210. doi:10.1111/j.1741-6248.1988.00193.x

Minichilli, A., Corbetta, G., & MacMillan, I. C. (2010). Top management teams in family-controlled companies: Familiness, fualtlines and their impact of financial performance. *Journal of Management Studies*, *47*(2), 205–222. doi:10.1111/j.1467-6486.2009.00888.x

Morck, R., Shleifer, A., & Vishny, R. (1988). Management ownership and market valuation: An empirical analysis. *Journal of Financial Economics*, *20*, 293–316. doi:10.1016/0304-405X(88)90048-7

Morck, R., & Yeung, B. (2004b), Special issues relating to corporate governance and family control. *World Bank Policy Research Working Paper 3406*.

Morris, M. H., Williams, R. O., Allen, J. A., & Avila, R. A. (1997). Correlates of success in family business transitions. *Journal of Business Venturing*, *12*(5), 358–401. doi:10.1016/S0883-9026(97)00010-4

Naldi, L., Nordqvist, M., Sjöberg, K., & Wiklund, J. (2007). Entrepreneurial orientation, risk taking and performance in family firms. *Family Business Review*, *23*(1), 33–47. doi:10.1111/j.1741-6248.2007.00082.x

Nelson, R.R. (1991): Why do firms differ and how does industry matter? *Strategic Management Journal*, *12* (special issue winter), 61-74.

Nelson, R. R., & Winter, S. (1982). *An evolutionary theory of economic change*. Cambridge, MA: Harvard University Press.

Neubauer, F., & Lank, A. G. (2003). *La empresa familiar: cómo dirigirla para que perdure*. Bilbao, España: Deusto.

Neubaum, D. O., Kammerlander, N., & Brigham, K. H. (2019). Capturing family firm heterogeneity: How taxonomies and typologies can help the field move forward. *Family Business Review*, *32*(2), 106–130.

Nickel, S., Nicolitsas, D., & Dryden, N. (1997). What makes firms perform well? *European Economic Review*, *41*(3-5), 783–796. doi:10.1016/S0014-2921(97)00037-8

Nieto, M. J., Fernández, Z., Casasola, M. J., & Usero, B. (2009). Impacto de la implicación familiar y de otros accionistas de referencia en la creación de valor, *Revista de Estudios Empresariales. Segunda Época, 2*, 5–20.

Nordqvist, M., Habbershon, T. G., & Melin, L. (2009). Transgenerational entrepreneurship: Exploring entrepreneurial orientation in family firms. In H. Landström, D. Smallbone, H. Crijns, & E. Laveren (Eds.), *Entrepreneurship, sustainable growth, and performance: Frontiers in European entrepreneurship research* (pp. 93–116). Londres, UK: Edward Elgar.

Nordqvist, M., Habbershon, T. G., & Melin, L. (2009). Transgenerational entrepreneurship: Exploring entrepreneurial orientation in family firms. In H. Landström, D. Smallbone, H. Crijns, & E. Laveren (Eds.), *Entrepreneurship, sustainable growth, and performance: Frontiers in European entrepreneurship research* (pp. 93–116). Londres, UK: Edward Elgar.

Nordqvist, M., & Melin, L. (2002). The dynamics of family firms: An institutional perspective on corporate governance and strategic change. In D. Fletcher (Ed.), *Understanding the small family business*. Londres: Routledge.

Ortín, P. (1998). El proceso de acumulación de capacidades directivas: Evidencia empírica a partir de una muestra de directivos españoles. *CEDE, 2*, 253–274.

Osterman, P. (1994). Supervision, discretion and work organization. *The American Economic Review, 84*(2), 380–384.

Oswald, S. L., & Janera, J. S. (1991). The influence of ownership on performance: An empirical study. *Strategic Management Journal, 12*(4), 321–326. doi:10.1002mj.4250120407

Pearson, A. W., Carr, J. C., & Shaw, J. C. (2008). Toward a theory of familiness: A social capital perspective. *Entrepreneurship Theory and Practice, 32*(6), 949–969. doi:10.1111/j.1540-6520.2008.00265.x

Pérez, M. J., Basco, R., García-Tenorio, J., Giménez, J., & Sánchez, I. (2007). *Fundamentos en la dirección de la empresa familiar. Emprendedor, empresa y familia*. Madrid, España: Thomson.

Peteraf, M. A. (1993). The cornerstone of competitive advantage: A resource-based view. *Strategic Management Journal, 14*(3), 179–191. doi:10.1002mj.4250140303

Pollak, R. (1985). A transaction cost approach to families and households. *Journal of Economic Literature, 23*, 581–608.

Porter, M. E. (1979). The Structure within Industries and Companies Performance. *The Review of Economics and Statistics, 61*(2), 214–227. doi:10.2307/1924589

Porter, M. E. (1980). *Competitive strategy. Techniques for analyzing industries and competitors*. Nueva York, NY: The Fress Press.

Porter, M. E. (1985). *Competitive advantage. Creating and sustaining superior performance*. Nueva York, NY: The Fress Press.

Porter, M. E. (1990a). *The competitive advantage of nations*. Nueva York, NY: The Fress Press. doi:10.1007/978-1-349-11336-1

Porter, M. E. (1990b). The competitive advantage of nations. *Harvard Business Review*, *68*(2), 73–93.

Porter, M.E. (1991). Towards a dynamic theory of strategy. *Strategic Management Journal, 12*(special issue winter), 95-117.

Poutziouris, P. Z. (2001). The views of family companies on venture capital: Empirical evidence from the UK small to medium-size enterprising economy. *Family Business Review*, *14*(3), 277–291. doi:10.1111/j.1741-6248.2001.00277.x

Poza, E. (1995). *A la sombra del roble: La empresa privada familiar y su continuidad*. Editorial Universitaria para la Empresa Familiar.

Rau, S. B., Schneider-Siebke, V., & Günther, C. (2019). Family firm values explaining family firm heterogeneity. *Family Business Review*, *32*(2), 195–215.

Roca Junyet, M. (2005). La empresa familiar en el ordenamiento jurídico interno y comunitario, en la obra El patrimonio familiar, profesional y empresarial. Sus protocolos, coordinado por M. Garrido Melero y J.M. Fugardo Estivill, tomo IV, Ordenamiento jurídico y empresa familiar (p.30). El protocolo familiar, coordinado por V.M. Garrido de Palma, Consejo General del Notariado. Barcelona, España: Bosch.

Roquebert, J., Phillips, R., & Westfall, P. (1996). Market vs management: What drives profitability? *Strategic Management Journal*, *17*(8), 653–664. doi:10.1002/(SICI)1097-0266(199610)17:8<653::AID-SMJ840>3.0.CO;2-O

Rosenblatt, P. C., deMik, L., Anderson, R. M., & Johnson, P. A. (1985). *The family in business: Understanding and dealing with the challenges entrepreneurial families face*. San Francisco: Jossey Bass.

Rumelt, R. P. (1984). Toward a strategic theory of the firm. In E. Lamb (Ed.), *Competitive Strategic Management* (pp. 556–570). Englewood Cliffs, NJ: Prentice-Hall.

Rumelt, R. P. (1991). How much does industry matter? *Strategic Management Journal*, *12*(3), 167–185. doi:10.1002mj.4250120302

Rumelt, R. P., Schendel, D., & Teece, D. (1991). Strategic management and economics. *Strategic Management Journal*, *12*(S2), 5–29. doi:10.1002mj.4250121003

Salas, V. (1992a). La empresa: un análisis económico frente a Europa. In *Albi, E. (coord.): Europa y la competitividad de la economía española* (pp. 233–250). Barcelona, España: Ariel.

Salas, V. (1992b). *Aspectos microorganizativos de la competitividad, Documento de Trabajo nº 9205*. Madrid, España: Fundación Empresa Pública.

Salas, V. (1993a). Factores de competitividad empresarial: Consideraciones generales. *Papeles de Economía Española*, *56*, 379–396.

Salas, V. (1993b). El papel de los mecanismos de asignación de capital en la competitividad a largo plazo de la economía española. In J. Velarde (Ed.), *Empresas y empresarios españoles en la encrucijada de los noventa. VII Jornadas de Alicante sobre Economía Española* (pp. 109–132). Madrid, España: Civitas.

Salvato, C., Chirico, F., Melin, L., & Seidl, D. (2019). Coupling family business research with organization studies: Interpretations, issues and insights. *Organization Studies*, *40*(6), 775–791. doi:10.1177/0170840619841402

Sánchez.Ruiz, P., Daspit, J. J., Holt, D. T., & Rutherford, M. W. (2019). Family social capital in the family firm: A taxonomic classification, relationships with outcomes, and directions for advancement. *Family Business Review*, *32*(2), 131–153.

Schmalensee, R. (1985). Do markets differ much? *The American Economic Review*, *75*, 341–351.

Schulze, W. S., Lubatkin, M. H., & Dino, R. N. (2003). Toward a theory of agency and altruism in family firms. *Journal of Business Venturing*, *18*(4), 473–490. doi:10.1016/S0883-9026(03)00054-5

Schulze, W. S., Lubatkin, M. H., Dino, R. N., & Buchholtz, A. K. (2001). Agency relationships in family firms: Theory and evidence. *Organization Science*, *12*(2), 99–116. doi:10.1287/orsc.12.2.99.10114

Schulze, W. S., Lubatkin, M. H., Dino, R. N., & Buchholtz, A. K. (2002). Altruism, agency and the competitiveness of family firms. *Managerial and Decision Economics*, *23*(4-5), 247–259. doi:10.1002/mde.1064

Shanker, M. C., & Astrachan, J. H. (1996). Myths and realities: Family businesses´ contribution to the US economy. A framework for assessing family business statistics. *Family Business Review*, *9*(2), 107–123. doi:10.1111/j.1741-6248.1996.00107.x

Sharma, P., Chrisman, J. J., & Chua, J. H. (1996). *A review and annotated bibliography of family business studies*. Boston: Kluwer. doi:10.1007/978-1-4419-8768-6

Sharma, P., Chrisman, J. J., & Chua, J. H. (1997). Strategic management of the family business: Past research and future challenges. *Family Business Review*, *10*(1), 1–36. doi:10.1111/j.1741-6248.1997.00001.x

Sharma, P., Christman, J., Pablo, A., & Chua, J. H. (2001). Determinants of initial satisfaction with the succession process in family firms: A conceptual model. *Entrepreneurship Theory and Practice*, *25*(3), 17–36. doi:10.1177/104225870102500302

Short, H. (1994). Ownership, control, financial structure and the performance of the firm. *Journal of Economic Surveys*, *8*(3), 203–249. doi:10.1111/j.1467-6419.1994.tb00102.x

Simon, H. A. (1993). Altruism and economics. *The American Economic Review*, *83*(2), 156–161.

Sirmon, D. G., & Hitt, M. A. (2003). Managing resources: Linking unique resources, management, and wealth creation in family firms. *Entrepreneurship Theory and Practice*, *27*(4), 339–358. doi:10.1111/1540-8520.t01-1-00013

Smith, A. (1796). An inquiry into the nature and causes of the wealth of nations (2nd ed.). Philadelphia: Thomas Dobson.

Snow, C. C., & Hrebiniak, L. G. (1980). Strategy, distinctive competence and organizational performance. *Administrative Science Quarterly*, *25*(2), 317–336. doi:10.2307/2392457

Stanley, L. J., Hernández-Linares, R., López-Fernández, M. C., & Kellermanns, F. W. (2019). A typology of family firms: An investigation of entrepreneurial orientation and performance. *Family Business Review*, *32*(2), 174–194.

Stinnett, N., & De Frain, J. (1985). *Secrets of strong families*. Nueva York, NY: Berkeley Books.

Tagiuri, R., & Davis, J. A. (1992). Bivalent attributes of the family firm. Family Business Review, 9(2), 199-208.

Teece, D. J. (2007). Explicating dynamic capabilities: The nature and microfoundations of (sustainable) enterprise performance. *Strategic Management Journal*, *28*(13), 1319–1350. doi:10.1002mj.640

Teece, D. J., & Pisano, G. (1998). The dynamic capabilities of the firm: An introduction. In Technology, organization, and competitiveness. Perspectives on industrial and corporate change (pp. 193-212). Oxford, UK: Oxford University Press.

Teece, D. J., Pisano, G., & Shuen, A. (1997). Dynamic capabilities and strategic management. *Strategic Management Journal*, *18*(7), 509–533. doi:10.1002/(SICI)1097-0266(199708)18:7<509::AID-SMJ882>3.0.CO;2-Z

Van Essen, M., Carney, M., Gedajlovic, E., & Heugens, P. (2015). How does family control influence firm strategy and performance: A meta-analysis of US publicly listed firms. *Corporate Governance*, *23*(1), 3–24. doi:10.1111/corg.12080

Villalonga, B., & Amit, R. (2006). How do family ownership, control and management affect firm value? *Journal of Financial Economics*, *80*(2), 385–417. doi:10.1016/j.jfineco.2004.12.005

Vives, X. (Ed.). (2000). Corporate governance: Theoretical and empirical perspectives. Nueva York, NY: Cambridge University Press.

Ward, J.L. (1986). How many will survive in 2046? *Family Enterprise, 9.*

Ward, J. L. (1987). *Keeping the family business healthy: How to plan for continuing growth, profitability, and family leadership*. San Francisco: Jossey-Bass.

Ward, J. L. (1988). The special role of strategic planning for family business. *Family Business Review*, *1*(2), 105–117. doi:10.1111/j.1741-6248.1988.00105.x

Welsh, J. H. M. (1993). The impact of family ownership and involvement on the process of management succession. *Family Business Review*, *6*(1), 31–45. doi:10.1111/j.1741-6248.1993.00031.x

Wernerfelt, B. (1984). A resource-based view of the firm. *Strategic Management Journal*, *5*(2), 171–180. doi:10.1002mj.4250050207

Westhead, P. (1997). Ambitions, 'external' environment and strategic factor differences between family and non-family companies. *Entrepreneurship and Regional Development*, *9*(2), 127–157. doi:10.1080/08985629700000007

Westhead, P., Cowling, M., & Storey, D. J. (1997). *The management and performance of unquoted family companies in the United Kingdom. Centre for Small and medium Sized Enterprises*. Warwick Business School.

Whipp, R., Rosenfeld, R., & Pettigrew, A. (1989). Culture and competitiveness: Evidence from two mature UK industries. *Journal of Management Studies, 26*(6), 561–585. doi:10.1111/j.1467-6486.1989.tb00745.x

Williamson, O. E. (1985). *The Economic Institutions of Capitalism. Firms, Markets, Relational Contracting*. Nueva York, NY: The Free Press.

Yu, A., Lumpkin, G. T., Sorenson, R. L., & Brigham, K. H. (2012). The landscape of family business outcomes: A summary and numerical taxonomy of dependent variables. *Family Business Review, 25*(1), 33–57. doi:10.1177/0894486511430329

Zahra, S. A. (2005). Entrepreneurial risk taking in family firms. *Family Business Review, 18*(1), 23–40. doi:10.1111/j.1741-6248.2005.00028.x

Zahra, S. A., Hayton, J. C., & Salvato, C. (2004). Entrepreneurship in family vs. non-family firms: A resource based analysis of the effect of organizational culture. *Entrepreneurship Theory and Practice, 28*(Summer), 363–381. doi:10.1111/j.1540-6520.2004.00051.x

Zahra, S. A., Neubaum, D. O., & Huse, M. (2000). Entrepreneurship in medium-size companies: Exploring the effects of ownership and governance systems. *Journal of Management, 26*(5), 947–976. doi:10.1177/014920630002600509

Zollo, M., & Winter, S. (2002). Deliberate learning and the evolution of dynamic capabilities. *Organization Science, 13*(3), 339–351. doi:10.1287/orsc.13.3.339.2780

Zucker, L. G. (1987). Normal change or risky business: Institutional effects of the hazard of change in hospital organizations, 1959-79. *Journal of Management Studies, 24*(6), 671–701. doi:10.1111/j.1467-6486.1987.tb00468.x

KEY TERMS AND DEFINITIONS

Capabilities: These are resource teams that are coordinated and organized to perform certain tasks.

Familiness: Designates the advantages and disadvantages in terms of resources and capacities that flow from the nature of the family business.

Family Effect: It is the effect that family control of capital and/or ownership of a company has on the strategy, structure, and organizational results.

Family Firm Heterogeneity: Expresses the variability in the nature of the family business due to causes such as its size, the dominant family generation, ownership and governance structures, or the family participation in work, management, and capital.

Governance Structures: These are the structures that detail a company's corporate governance model, including the organs of which it is composed, their composition, the representation assumed by the shareholders and stakeholders and the practices and rules that guide their behaviour.

Intangible Assets: They are assets made up of information or knowledge, that lack a material entity, that do not usually appear in the company's balance sheet and whose identification and measurement require specific methodologies.

Ownership and Control Structure: It is the structure that defines the nature of the capital owners and the organs of the companies' board of directors.

Typologies and Taxonomies of Family Firm: These are the configurations that can be distinguished within the population of family businesses and which expresses its strategic and organizational heterogeneity.

ENDNOTES

1 Assessments of the state of knowledge on this subject can be found in Bebchuk & Weisbach (2010), Hambrick, Werder & Zajac (2008) and Gillan (2006).

2 This literature follows the typical direction in the field of management research; it has moved on from the initial stage that got underway in the latter half of the 1970s (Wortman, 1994), which was dominated by purely descriptive studies. For a study of the evolution of the FF literature, see Basco (2006) and Casillas & Acedo (2007).

3 As can be seen, this is in contrast to how certain tax rules and even the Explanatory Statement on RD 171/2007 refer to blood relationships or kinship, while Article 2.1 refers to persons with "family ties".

4 In many cases, 100% of the capital is in the hands of the same family, though more than 50% would be enough. Moreover, in listed companies with dispersed share ownership, a company can be considered an FF if the family holds 25% of the share capital with voting rights, because said percentage of ownership ensures control over the firm.

5 Explanatory note: a typical feature of listed companies is their dispersed ownership. The largest shareholder (or block of shareholders) often holds less than 50% of the voting rights. In such companies, a shareholder, (or block of shareholders) can exert a decisive influence on fundamental aspects of corporate governance without having a majority of the voting rights. The fourth point of the definition refers to companies in which the family does not have the majority of the voting rights, but which, through its ownership interest, can exert a decisive influence.

6 Based on the concepts of Cohen et al. (1984), Salas (1993b: 111) y Puig (dir., 1996: 18).

7 The theoretical review carried out here is an extension of a preliminary conceptual framework presented in various previous studies (Camisón, 2009, 2001, 1997).

Chapter 2
The Role of Market Orientation and Organizational Capabilities of Family Businesses on Competitive Advantage

Özgür Atılgan
İstanbul Kültür Üniversitesi, Turkey

ABSTRACT

Family businesses are described as organizations owned by one or more members of the same family. Most of the business organizations in the world consists of family firms. However, although they constitute a larger share in almost all of the economies, in their first 5 years of operation, 90% of the family businesses disappear. Of the remaining 10%, 67% die or change ownership after first generation. Only 12% survive under current ownership past the third generation. Therefore, in order to maintain the continuity of the business, family businesses have to achieve competitive advantage. One way to achieve competitive advantage is through becoming market oriented. In this connection, the purpose of this chapter is to identify the role of market orientation and the four basic organizational capabilities (entrepreneurial ability, management ability, global ability, and building partnerships ability) on gaining competitive advantage by systematically reviewing relevant concepts, thereby contributing to the existing literature.

INTRODUCTION

Family businesses are described as organisations owned by one or more members of the same family (Litz, 1995). Most of the business organisations in the world consist of family firms. 75% of all the companies in OECD countries, 80%- 90% of the companies in U.S.A, 70% of all the firms in UK are family-owned enterprises. However, despite constituting the largest share in almost all economies, in their first five years of operation, 90% of family businesses disappear. Of the remaining 10%, 67% die or change ownership after the first generation and only 12% survive under the same ownership past the

DOI: 10.4018/978-1-7998-1655-3.ch002

third generation (Poza & Dougherty, 2014). Hence, in order to maintain the continuity of the operation, family businesses have to achieve competitive advantage (Zhou, Li, Zhou, & Su, 2008).

In this context, it is argued that one of the ways to achieve competitive advantage is to maintain market orientation with organisational capabilities. The focus of market orientation should be based on understanding the expectations and needs of customers, satisfying them and creating superior customer value. Becoming market oriented is important, because globalisation together with developing technologies and changing market conditions are pushing all companies into becoming more flexible and taking quick decisions (Ulrich & Smallwood, 2004). Hence, every company needs certain skills to ensure customer satisfaction and thus, acquire competitive advantage. In particualr, organisational capabilities, such as the entrepreneurial ability and management ability of family members are crucial for acquiring competitive advantage (Garces-Galdeano, Larraza-Kintana, Garcia-Olaverri, & Makri, 2016). Moreover, in today's business environment, the ability to support the development of the company's global capabilities and establish partnerships is also considered as an important organisational capability. In general, it is asserted that management and entrepreneurial abilities are considered as internal capabilities, while dynamic global and partnership abilities are considered as external organisational ones (McKelvie & Davidson, 2009).

The purpose of this chapter is probe market orientation and the four basic organisational capabilities (entrepreneurial ability, management ability, global ability and building partnerships ability), with the purpose of determining how these four basic organisational capabilities help family businesses to gain competitive advantage, which is lacking in the family businesses literature. By systematically reviewing the relevant concepts, the aim of this present chapter, is to fill this void. The chapter is composed as follows. First, the methodology of the literature review is presented and the characteristics of family businesses are identified. Second, the concepts of market orientation and the four organisational capabilities are explained. Finally, the role of market orientation and these capabilities in attaining competitive advantage will be specified.

METHODOLOGY OF THE LITERATURE REVIEW

What follows is an integrative type of literature review to provide a deeper understanding of the role of market orientation and organisational capabilities of family businesses in their attaining competitive advantage than has previously been presented. Accordingly, 84 documents in electronic databases, including JSTOR, EBSCOhost, ScienceDirect, Scopus, ProQuest, Springer and SAGE, which used any design, quantitative or qualitative, are scrutinised. These provide discussions about market orientation and the organisational capabilities of family firms relating to competitive advantage between 2001 and 2019. In identifying the studies, the following key words were utilised: family business, family business life cycle, market orientation, management abilities, entrepreneurial abilities, partnership abilities, dynamic global abilities and competitive advantage.

Table 1. Some definitions of family businesses

Author	Year	Definition
Donnelly	1964	A privately held company that will be inherited and controlled by one or more of the proprietor´s children upon that person's retirement.
Welsch	1993	Businesses where the majority of the shares are owned by family members.
Carsrud	1994	One in which ownership and policy making are dominated by members of an "emotional kinshipgroup".
Chua, Chrisman, & Sharma	1999	A family business is a business owned and managed by a nuclear family.
La Porta, Lopez-de-Silanes, & Schleifer	1999	Businesses where at least 20% of the shares belong to members from the same family.
Anderson & Reeb	2003	Businesses with high levels of family ownership, where the CEO is usually a family member and large numbers of family members dominate the company board.
Fernandez & Nieto	2005	Businesses with one or more family members occupying managerial positions.
Zahra	2005	Family firms are those businesses that reported some identifiable ownership share by at least one family and had multiple generations in leadership positions within them.
Miller, Miller, Lester & Cannella	2007	Businesses that are constituted by the merging of family and businesses and where family members affect firm policy by holding the majority of the shares.
Kontinen & Ojala	2010	A firm in which the family controls the largest block of shares or votes, has one or more of its members in key management positions, and has members of more than one generation actively involved with the business.
Banalieva & Eddleston	2011	Are those in which the family is the largest shareholder, controlling at least 20% of shares, although they may be led by family or nonfamily executives.
Calabro, Torchia, Pukall, & Mussolino	2013	Family businesses are those with an identifiable share of family ownership and having multiple generations in the firm's leadership positions.
Stanley, Kellermanns, & Zellweger	2016	Businesses where family members have an ownership stake of 20 to 25% are distinguished as family firms from non-family ones.
Carney & Nason	2018	A business, that is governed and/or managed with the intention of pursuing the vision of the business held by a dominant coalition controlled by members of the same family.

Family Businesses

Definition

Despite their hundreds of years history, there is still no consensus on the definiton of family businesses. The most important reason for this lies in the fact that the structural attributes of families and thus, family businesses differ across contexts (Neubauer & Lank, 2016). In addition to this, as the perspectives of scholars identifying family businesses differ, so do the definitions. Below in table 1, some of the definitions in the literature relating to family businesses are listed.

As it can be inferred from Table 1, whilst the definitions differ, the common ground is the focus on family ownership when defining family firms (Pindado & Requejo, 2015). For this chapter, we will present the role of market orientation and organisational capabilities of family firms for competitive advantage where 20 to 25% of shares are owned by a single family, as in most of the studies on family firms this cut off point has been used in defining such businesses (Stanley, Kellermanns, & Zellweger, 2017).In the following part, the general attributes of family businesses will be elaborated upon in further detail.

Attributes of Family Businesses

Today, accelerating competition together with globalisation and internationalisation have caused enterprises with an entrepreneurial sprit to draw the attention of many scholars. Since family firms are generally businesses with such a spirit, the characteristics of these firms has become a separate field of study (Teece, 2014). Whilst when the focus is on the characteristics of family businesses, small firms come to mind at first, some can also be large enterprises. Yet, a larger portion of family businesses are, indeed, enterprises that employ less than 20 workers (Memili, Fang, Chrisman, & De Massis, 2015). Even so, whether large or small, it can be argued that family businesses make a great contibution to national GDP and employ a great number workers. For example, nearly half of the U.S. GDP and 80% of the total employment are generated by family businesses (Miller, Steier, & Bretton-Miller, 2003). According to the Global Family Business Yearbook 2014 Report (Family Business Yearbook, 2014) prepared by Earnest & Young, the world's top ten family businesses in the United States have a revenue over 1 trillion dollars a year and employ 3.1 million people. Today, many well-known companies, such as Mariott International Inc., Hermes, Cargill, Heineken, Nordstrom, Ferragamo, Ford Motor Company and the Washington Post are family businesses (Ward, 2016).

Moreover, besides their contribution to national economies, family businesses have distinct attributes compared to non-family ones. Firstly, family members spend their entire careers in the family business and derive personal benefit from these companies (Aronoff & Ward, 2016). Second, the source of motivation for family members is usually internal factors, such as the pleasure of starting up as a business and achieving success. Unlike professional managers, family members are only accountable to themselves and to the family (Cohen & Sharma, 2016). Third, sometimes the nature of being family can contradict the essence of doing business. That is, families tend to be emotional, whilst businesses are rational organisations. Moreover, families usually protect their members no matter what they do, whereas business organisations do not tolerate unsuccessful employees (Jaskiewicz, Combs, Shanine, & Kacmar, 2017). Fourth, family businesses often have difficulties in abandoning existing habits and practices, i.e. resisting change. Moreover, they can adopt an authoritarian and centralised management style, which leads to disadvantages, such as lack of planning, arbitrary decision making and lack of institutionalisation (Cucculelli & Bettinelli, 2016). Fifth, family businesses can face difficulties in relation to succession across the generations. Even in family businesses where this is well planned, transfer of management is much more difficult when compared to non-family one. Today, it is report that only 20% to 30% can pass to the second generation, while only 12% of them are able to survive under the current ownership (Gilding, Gregory, & Cosson, 2015).

Given all the aforementioned attributes, family businesses are unique enterprises. This uniqueness originates from a system where the family and business are intertwined (Seaman, 2015). As the discussions between family members will directly affect firm management, the decision making process is indirectly affected by the intra-family conflict. Overall, it can be argued that, the merger of the family and business have some advantages and disadvantages (Hennart, Majocchi, & Forlani, 2019), which will be addressed more in detail next.

Advantages of Family Businesses

The advantages that family businesses have can be grouped in three categorie: financial, management and the organisational culture. In terms of financial advantages, it can be argued that family members are more likely to sacrifice their own savings compared to multiple owners in a joint stock company, when faced with an economic crisis (Xi, Kraus, Filser, & Kellermanns, 2015). In the context of the management, with the advantage of having a significant proportion of the ownership, family members can take decisions about applying new methods in technical and administrative issues and entering new businesses within a short period of time. Regarding the organisational culture, the coexistence of family members based on a common history leads to similar attitudes in communucation, values and beliefs (Sarbah & Xiao, 2015). Other advantages of family businesses are: solidarity of family members, dedication to work, quick decision making, easy access to domestic markets, stability in management, the continuity of management policies, ability to make long term business plans, employee loyality, autonomy, the ability to determine future, specialisation and dynamism and last but not least, trust based on familial relationships (Sundaramurthy, 2008; Goel, & Jones, 2016).

Recent work on family businesses has revealed that these enterprises are better than non-family ones in terms of implementing long lasting strategies. Moreover, they rate better on profitability and productivity measures compared to non-family enterprises. Family businesses also have high potential for reinvestment opportunities and thus, can show rapid growth during normal economic periods. Moreover, they are more likely to survive in times of economic crisis compared to non-family businesses (Carney, Van Essen, Gedajlovic, & Heugens, 2015) .

Disadvantages of Family Businesses

Whilst family businesses have many advantages that distinguish them from other types of enterprises, they also have some disadvantages that can be considered as weaknesses, which may lead to company failure. The common disadvantages are: nepotism, patriarchalism, competition among the family members, conservativeness, unbalanced work-family life, centralised management style, difficulties in the delegation of authority, difficulties in succession, the fear of losing authority, the fear of employing professional management, unavailability of job descriptions and non-alignment of business and family interests (Zellweger, 2017).

Considering the difficulties of managing a fast growing business with complex family relations, it is likely that in the long run the family business will disappear, if the succession of generations is not managed effectively. In this context, the biggest challenge for family businesses is the succession problem. The owner-managers of family businesses who are patriarchal, conservative and anxious about losing authority abnegate the responsibility of training the next generation for managerial positions and may even refuse to delegate authority to the younger generations (Mokhber, Gi Gi, Abdul Rasid, Vakilbashi, Mohd Zamil, & Woon Seng, 2017). Eventually, this may lead to the evaporation of the business after the first generation. However, under the assumption of a well planned succession, a family business goes thorugh the four phases of business life cycle: birth, growth, maturisation and continuity. Each of these phases will be explained in what follows (Le Breton-Miller, & Miller, 2015).

Family Business Life Cycle

Family businesses have a life-cycle like human beings. They are born, they slowly grow, mature and finally become a lasting business or in the worst case they die. This life-cycle process in family businesses may involve several successions across generations and similar to other businesses it depends on individuals as well as organisational and functional structure (Duh, 2015). Generally, the family business life-cycle is divided in four stages. The first, is the birth of the business by the first generation. The. second stage, is the growth and development of the business. Third, there is the maturation stage by the professional management and finally, comes the continuity stage, if we assume that the business does not go bankrupt (Basco, Calabro, & Campopiano, 2018).

The Birth Stage

In this stage, the founder of the enterprise starts up and shapes the business within the framework of his/her own culture and vision in order to keep the family together as well as creating job opportunities for the children. The mission and the vision of the company is determined according to the dreams and guidance of the owner. The founding owners usually, prefer a centralised management style and actively participate in every aspect of the business, including customer relations, without establishing any formal rules (Keasey, Martinez, & Pindado, 2015).

However, there might be some problems in this process. Firstly, the founder works incessantly, leading to a serious work-life balance conflict. Second, as the business is new in the market, expenditures are high, which can cause liquidity shortages and end up generating the need to borrow. Third,, the intimate relationships with employees which might seem an advantage at first glance, can however, hinder career development and the motivation of the employees in the long run. The businesses that can overcome the difficulties associated with the birth stage can enter the growth stage (Minola, Brumana, Campopiano, Garrett, & Cassia, 2016).

The Growth Stage

As the founder of the business achieves entrepreneurial success, his/her family is also positively affected. In the growth stage, the business is usually owned and controlled by the siblings. As second generation, the childeren of the founder start to manage the company. Growing family businesses usually have high market shares with well known goods or services, but as their development is not entirely finished, they will still lack some formalised systems and procedures (Arregle, Batjargal, Hitt, Webb, Miller, & Tsui, 2015). Moreover, the growth of the business leads the neccessity of professional management of the family business, as the family can not deal with all of its aspects. The future of the business is dependent on the transition between the family and professional management, with those family businesses capapble of employing such managers being able to enter the maturation stage (Stenholm, Pukkinen, & Heinonen, 2016).

Maturation Stage

In the maturation stage, the second and the third generation of family members work with the professional managers, participating in the management of the business and the number of employees increases as well. Since there are lots of interest groups, such as family members, non-family employees and external investors in the business, where the cultural structure of the family is no longer patriarchial, the probability of an outbreak of conflict of interest is quite high. This can arise from competition among family members, marriage disputes and the allocation of wealth among family members. Intrinsically, most of these conflicts affect business relations and sometimes even overshadow the problems associated with the work (Ward, 2016).

Despite these conflicts, the business usually continues to develop, but the speed of development is lower than during the growth stage. The family business's products and services find the maximum level of buyers in the market and the firm's ability to find financial leverage is also high. In this stage, the business achieves a good reputation in the existing market and it can even affect the market conditions. Accordingly, there is a high need for formalisation (Reddrop & Mapunda, 2015), with management trying to establish written job procedures, provide job descriptions, exercise division of labour, determine role and authority descriptions for family members and ensure coordination between the departments. Thus, the intention is to build up a business structure that will become independent from individuals (Craig & Moores, 2017). In addition, stragetic plans for the operation of the business, and/or emphasise on teamwork, quality management systems and corporate social responsibility policies are established in the maturation stage. The family business in this stage become more responsive to the needs of its stakeholders, including the government, society, suppliers and customers. Yet, as the business structures are more formalised, the management becomes more risk averse. In general, family businesses that can successfully manage firm growth are more likely to become continous (Ward, 2016).

Continuity Stage

Family businesses that manage to maintain their sustainability are those that place more importance on business values than family ones. These business are effectively managed, guided and controlled. In other words, the classical habits of ordinary family businesses, such as nepotism or arbitrary decision making, no longer exist in these corporations (Konopaski, Jack, & Hamilton, 2015). A sustainable business puts great emphasis on principles like fairness, transparency, accountability, responsibility, discipline and autonomy, which are important elements of institutionalisation. Hence, it can be argued that sustained family businesses are institutionalised corporations. In this last stage, the decisions taken by the management are not solely pursuing the interests of the family members, but rather, all the stakeholders as a whole (Merchant, Kumar, & Mallik, 2018). The performance evaluations and human resource planning are based on employees' abilities, skills and credentials, rather than informal relationships with the family and objective performance score cards are used. Business strategies, such as long-term goals, policies, the target market, performance management, compensation policies and career planning of employees, are systematically conducted by the professional management. However, it can also be the case that greater institutionalisation at this stage might cause family members to feel alienated, excluded from the work and kept away from the management of the business (Daspit, Holt, Chrisman, & Long, 2016).

Overall, it would papear reasonable to conclude that, the family and the business have to overcome all the difficulties in each phase of the whole life-cycle process to become a long surviving company. Inherently, no matter which stage the family business is in, one way to survive in a rapidly changing and complex environment is gaining competitive advantage and this can be attained through market orientation. The following section of the chapter is dedicated to the definition, dimensions and consequences of market orientation (Oudah, Jabeen, & Dixon, 2018).

Market Orientation

Market orientation is the ability to understand and satisfy the needs and wants of the customers in order to achieve a maximum level of profitability (Ozkaya, Droge, Hult, Calantone, & Ozkaya, 2015). An important point here is to distinguish the concept of "market orientation" from the concept of "marketing". Marketing is a business function that is confined to marketing department, which coordinates and combines all marketing activities to satisfy the customer's needs. "Market orientation", on the other hand, pertains to the neccessity that not only the marketing department but all business departments should have the responsibility to obtain market information, spread this information within the organisation and be responsive to customers' needs and wants (Wang & Miao, 2015). The existing literature on market orientation has focused on the dimensions, supplementary factors and the consequences of market orientation. The dimensions of market orientation are "customer orientation", "competitor orientation" and "interfunctional coordination". The supplementary factors of market orientation are "top management", "organisational culture", "coordination between the departments" and "organisational structure", while its consequences relate the employees, the business environment and firm performance (Zhang, Kara, Spillan, & Mintu-Wimsatt, 2017).

Dimensions of Market Orientation

Most of the existing research on market orientation suggests that it consists of three basic dimensions: customer orientation, competitor orientation and interfunctional coordination (Ho, Nguyen, Adhikari, Miles, & Bonney, 2018). Customer orientation pertains to the level to which a business organisation has maintained an understanding of its consumer base, being able to provide continuous and superior value to existing and potential customers, if it has done so. Moreover, customer orientation includes investigating and comprehending customer value chains to generate opportunities for further value creation (Wang, Zhao, & Voss, 2016).

Competitor orientation, on the other hand, refers to a business's understanding of the short-term strengths and weaknesses, long term capabilities as well as the strategies of competitors. Like customer orientation, competitor orientation involves considering the importance of comprehension of both the existing rivals and their potential operations as well as the potential future rivals and their operations (Jha & Bhattacharyya, 2017). Lastly, interfunctional coordination refers to the synchronised utilisation of resources in such a way to generate superior customer value. This neccessitates the participation of all of a business's structural components in the process of collection, allocation and utilisation of market information, not just merely the targeted marketing employees (Tajeddini, Altinay, & Ratten, 2017).

Customer orientation, competitor orientation and interfunctional coordination can only be effective when factors such as the support of the top management and an organisational cultural based on customer orientation are present. Below, these supporting factors are explained detailed (Frambach, Fiss, & Ingenbleek, 2016).

Supplementary Factors that Influence Market Orientation

Top management support can be considered as an important factor of market orientation in terms of helping its development within organisations. In the business organisations, customer-oriented values and principles are maintained under the leadership of top management. If it does not emphasise the importance of sensivity towards customer preferences loud and clear, it is less likely that an organisation will become market oriented (Cavusgil & Knight, 2015).

Organisational culture is another important antecedent of market orientation. Every business organisation has a unique culture, which is hard to change once it has been adopted by the members. In order to to delivermarket orientation, it is important to adopt a culture that emphasises the creation of value for customers. Recent studies have indicated that market orientation becomes an organisational culture when the organisation shows effective and efficient behaviours that enable it to respond better to the needs and wants of customers, thus engendering customer orientation. Some of the useful behaviours that positively foster market orientation are: emphasising the need for customer orientation, building consensus among organisation members, creating a vision and implementing a business plan accordingly, sharing the vision with organisation members, ensuring that the vision is adopted by every one, making a short term market plan and cash flow analysis, improving market performance and institutionalisation of constant learning for target customers (Slatten, Lien, & Svensson, 2018). As aforementioned, if the aim is to change the existing organisational culture towards market orientation, the support of top management is indispensible. Moreover, in order to create a market oriented organisational culture top management should have the responsibility of being a role model for all organisation members and mentor the subordinates (Jogaratnam, 2017).

The Consequences of Market Orientation

Market orientation combines the efforts of employees and different business departments for common organisational goals and thus, generally leads to better organisational performance in terms of higher employee satisfaction, better environment adaptation, higher customer satisfaction and higher customer loyality (Herhausen, 2016).

An important consequence of market orientation is the overall employee satisfaction. When the common organisational goals for customers are achieved, so does the employee satisfaction, which also yields higher levels of organisational commitment. Jaworski and Kohli (1996) asserted that market orientation will also provide social and psychological wellfare to employees, such as the satisfaction that there is congruence of the organisational and individual goals. Another consequence of market orientation is the fitting into business environmental. Check meaning The business environment is one of the factors that affects the market orientation of an organisation. It is expected that organisations operating in a harsh competitive business environment are more likely to become more market oriented, which results in increased performance as well (Pelham, 2015).

In addition, customer satisfaction is another consequence of market orientation. In order to establish this, market oriented companies change their attitudes towards customers by removing the classical buyer and seller perceptions, eventually placing the customers at the centre of their operations. Thus, market oriented companies should first learn the wants and needs of their customers and then, create customer value by providing benefits beyond their desires. This, in turn, will lead to satisfied customers, who will be loyal to the company and have positive effects on long term profitability (Pattanayak & Koilakuntla, & Punyatoya, 2017). Accordingly, the last consequence of market orientation is customer loyality, which can be described as the emotional commitment and continuous preference that the customer shows for a particular company, business, vendor, product or service in an environment where other alternatives are available. In this context, customer loyality refers to loyality towards both a company and its products or services. Considering the fact that today's customer profile is much more demanding, becoming market orientated is an indispensible strategy for every company. Companies with market orientation straegies are more likely to attract new customers and tend to keep existing ones (Pena, Jamilena, & Molina, 2017).

In the context of family businesses, market orientation may vary according to the management of different generations. Generations after the founding one can choose a more professional management style, which may bring more formal structures and higher levels of departmentalisation. As a result of formalisation, job descriptions, procedures and authority predominate the intra-organisation relationships. On the other hand, higher levels of departmentalisation may restrict the distribution of market information throughout the organisation, which will decrease the responsiveness to customer needs and changing preferences. Thus, family business owners have to be very careful with professionalisation of the business, needing to be aware of the contradictory nature of professionalisation and market orientation. Hence, they should ensure the organisational capabilities, including management abilities, entrepreneurial abilities, partnership abilities and dynamic global abilities are robust (Beck, Janssens, & Debruyne, 2011).

Organisational Capabilities

Organisational capabilities in order to establish market orientation within a company consist of: management abilities, entrepreneurial abilities, partnership abilities and dynamic global abilities (Grewal & Tansuhaj, 2001).

Management Abilities

Management of employees in family businesess, as in other companies, is a part of organisational culture. In general, management skills are not explicitly visible, being learned as they are performed and they are not easy to imitate. From a resource-based perspective, management skills play a critical role in organising the motivation and the abilities of employees within the organisational structures, processes and systems at the firm level. The resource-based perspective asserts that management skills are inimitable for the following two reasons. The first is the ambiguity of the relationship between the firm resources and how the firm attains its competitive advantage. The second is the fact that the managers of the competing firm do not know how to manage or exploit the resources of the imitatee company.Thus, in terms of managing family businesses, how the family members manage the non-family employees is very important (Prajogo, 2016).

On the other hand, some scholars consider managerial skills as dynamic skills and have asserted that managerial cognition underpins dyanamic managerial abilities. Robust managerial cognition ensures that managerial beliefs and mindsets are at the basis of the decision making process. Apart from managerial cognition, dynamic managerial skills are also influenced by the managerial human and social capital. While the former refers to the personal skills and managerial knowledge from training and professional experience, the latter pertains to the ability of managers to access possible resources through their relations and connections (Acquah & Agyapong, 2015).

Entrepreneurial Abilities

Entrepreneurship is described as the management attitude being within the scope of the strategy-making process, thus leading to entrepreneurial decisions being taken in organisations. When entrepreneurs create or develop new products or services with higher quality for niche markets they tend to charge lower prices compared to existing products or services with inferior quality. However, whilst most of the entrepreneurs can create excellent products or services, most of them are not commercialised since they fail to generate value for customers. In this context, entrepreneurship involves coordination of acquisition, exploitation and allocation of market knowledge. To be able to obtain and develop the market information, managers should be aware of the possibilities and should be able to disseminate this information in the most appropriate way, which is defined as entrepreneurial ability (Perez-Luno, Saparito, & Gopalakrishnan, 2016).

Companies run by managers with entrepreneurial ability are more likely to access external resources and adapt to environmental changes. This ability is distinguished from other abilities in three ways. First, entrepreneurial ability is usually characterised as the ability of managers to plan and implement the appropriate actions. Second, it is the combination of cognition and action. That is, it stimulates the managers to restructure the conditions inside and outside the organisations in accordance with their heterogeneous and collective mental models. Third, it involves both exploring and using opportunities as well as shaping and synchronising emerging internal and external conditions, which requires continuous identification, evaluation, recognition and creation of opportunities (Kajalo & Lindblom, 2015).

Partnership Abilities

Partnership can be defined as the inter-organisational relationships that arise between parties in order to achieve common goals. In the context of marketing, partnership can be explained through social exhange theory, which explains why organisations engage in closer relationships better than economic theories. Specifically, social exchange theory considers the interactions between partners and the relationships underpinning the exchange of resources as dynamic processes. Recent literature has suggested that social exchange theory should incorporate the concept of trust as this can help to explain the relationships of change between the parties. That is, according to this perspective trust plays an important role in long-term relationships between business organisations. Given the fact that, potential partners are generally reluctant to share their financial, social or human capital with emerging business organisations due to the uncertainity, the importance of trust is particullary vital for new enterprises. In sum, trust is one of the most important factors when aiming to establish long lasting and sound partnerships (Ku, Wu, & Chen, 2016).

Moreover, finding a reliable partner is also considered as an ability, since every business organisation is free to choose its partners. Forming partnerships is a fundamental ability, that paves the way for potential new ones and the development of existing partnerships is also important, both of which enable organisations to acquire new resources. As aforementioned, family businesses are generally small enterprises at the start-up stage, but their organsational boundaries will expand when they start to grow in a constantly changing business environment, which means that forming partnerships ability becomes particularly important for them. Moreover, globalisation, together with the advancements in information and communication technologies as well as free movement of capital in international markets, makes single-handed operations not possible for all kind of business organisations. Hence, the intention to form strategic alliances in a dynamic environment, both in international and national markets, will require the development of partnership formation capabilities (Hernandez-Espallardo & Arcas-Lario, 2003).

Dynamic Global Abilities

The globalisation of family businesses requires establishing new offices, the recruitment of skilled personnel, restructuring of the organisation and forging effective communication systems. Hence, the aim of the business should be creating international networks by developing its dynamic global capabilities that will guide its market selection within the cultural, political and legal framework. In general, the dynamic global capabilities of a firm consist of the following seven dimensions: vision and strategy, relying on core competence, efficient communication, innovation, appropriate organisation structure, organisational culture and technology management. These capabilities are very difficult to imitate and they provide competitive advantage to firms in global markets. In developing and constantly changing global markets, the ability of local family businesses to engage in cooperation with foreign companies will lead to their obtaining better locations, distribution channels, better suppliers and thus, it is expected that their profitability will increase accordingly (Monferrer, Blesa, & Ripolles, 2015).

Below each of these abilities and how they relate to market orientation and hence, competitive advantage in the context of family businesses, are further elaborated upon.

THE RELATIONSHIP BETWEEN MARKET ORIENTATION, ORGANISATION CAPABILITIES AND COMPETITIVE ADVANTAGE IN FAMILY BUSINESSES

In the extant literature, the relationship between market orientation and competitive advantage has drawn the attention of many scholars. While some have argue that family businesses are superior at achieving the competitive advantage compared to their non-family counterparts, others have challenged this view. Recent literature has emphasised the important role of organisational capabilities, such as management skills, entrepreneurial skills, establishing partnership skills and integrating with global market skills. Below, each organisational capability and its relation with market orientation and competitive advantage is explained in the context of family businesses (Martin & Javalgi, 2016).

Managerial ability to sustain a unique family culture is per se a management skill that can lead to the establishment of closer and informal ties with the customers, who may share similar values and beliefs as the family culture. OK? Recent research also suggests that family businesses with managers who are able to preserve the family culture through their dynamic managerial skills together with their with managerial human capital and managerial social capital, have unique advantages in terms of developing the assets and resources for business through informal ties. With their relational ties, family businesses are more likely to cultivate and nurture long lasting relationships accross generations compared to non-family ones, but this is dependent on the managers' ability to sustain these relational ties (Lonial & Carter, 2015).

Overall, the management abilites that put forward culture, reputation and loyality together with positive relations with employees, will provide customer satisfaction and interfunctional coordination, leading to enhanced market orientation and thus, superior customer value will be created. Eventually, since all of the aforementioned family management abilities are firm specific and hard to imitate, family businesses with skilled managers will exhibit higher superior competitive advantage compared to non-family ones (Rakthin, Calantone, & Wang, 2016).

On the other hand, entrepreneurial skill is possibly the most important ability to start-up an entire new family business. Entreprenurial ability emerges as a consequence of chasing market opportunities, recogniseing innovations in dynamic environmental conditions, taking advantage of the competitors by taking risk and developing entrepreneurial talent. Family firms with entrepreneurial ability are more likely to look for new products or services in order to satisfy the needs of their customers and for customer satisfaction their tendency for risk taking increases as well (Pratono & Mahmood, 2015). Check meaning

It could be argued that there is a common bond between market orientation and entrepreneurial ability. They both emphasise the importance of learning, which takes place more quickly in family businesses compared to their non-family counterparts with their minimal hierarchy, formalisation and standardisation. Quick learning about customers and markets seem to be a prerequisite for family businesses in order to have both a strong market orientation and entrepreneurial ability. The traits that are related with strong entrepreneurial ability, such as risk tolerance, proactiveness and receptivity to innovation also increase those associated with a strong market orientation, such as customer orientation, competitor orientation and interfunctional coordination. In the context of family businesses, thus, it can be contended that entrepreneurial skills will increase the market orientation of family firms, which will lead to competitive advantage by satisfying the needs of customers for innovative goods or services (Gruber-Muecke & Hofer, 2015).

In this vein, another important ability that every family business should have in order to generate market orientation and thus, create customer satisfaction, is building partnership skills. It is a fact that despite their innovativeness and quick decision making abilities, most of family businesses suffer from resource scarcity, such as insufficient human and financial capital. Hence, for the growth of family businesses collaboration with financially strong ones is vital. Strategic partnerships are not only a tool that is build by two businesses for long-term relations, for they can also be used to create long-term relationships between the focal firm, customers and suppliers. Thus, it can be asserted that establising partnership skills will increase the market orientation of a family business through increased competitor orientation, which will result in finding a successful partner(s) and hence, achieve competitive advantage (Kotabe, & Kothari, 2016).

The last ability that plays an important role in increasing the market orientation of family businesses is the ability to integrate with global markets, those that are successful in local markets need also be so in global markets for the growth of the business. The ability to integrate with global markets is maintained through the homogenisation of customer preferences, increasing product development and delivering effective positioning in foreign markets. It can be asserted that the ability to integrate with global markets is one of the required dynamic capabilities. Dynamic global capabilities allow family businesses to become aware of new market opportunities, enter new markets and thus, reach new customer groups which eventually will increase the customer orientation dimension of market orientation. It has been contended that family businesses that are successful in developing their dynamic global abilities will attain better competitive advantage through increased market orientation (Cacciolatti, & Lee, 2016).

To sum up, it is argued that the market orientation of family businesses can be enhanced by management abilites, entrepreneurial abilities, building partnership abilities and dynamic global abilities. These abilities will also provide competitive advantage to family businesses through their positive relations with market orientation. Below, solutions and recommendations on the relationship between market orientation, organisational capabilities and competitive advantage in family businesses are presented.

SOLUTIONS AND RECOMMENDATIONS

As aforementioned, despite family businesses having some potential difficulties, such as nepotism, patriarchalism, conservativeness and unbalanced work-family life, with their flat organisation structure, highly flexible strategic operations, family culture and quick decision making they are more likely to become market oriented. Yet, it should not be forgotten that these positive properties of family businesses do not guarantee a strong market orientation. Hence, it can be argued that, achieving a high level of market orientation in family businesses is contingent upon exploiting the following organisational abilities: management ability, entrepreneurial ability, establising partnership ability and global dynamic ability. In addition, factors such as the leadership and support of top management, and a strong family culture should also be deployed to support the organisational abilities in order to achieve a desired market orientation. Moreover, attaining a higher level of market orientation will help to achieve competitive advantage for family businesses, thus facilitating their survival when faced with fierce global competition.

FUTURE RESEARCH DIRECTIONS

This present chapter has been focused on the systematisation of the concepts relating to market orientation, organisational capabilities and competitive advantage by applying an integrative literature review. Future research would benefit from an empirical investigation into the relationship between market orientation and competitive advantage in family businesses in which organisational capabilities act as moderator variables.

CONCLUSION

Achieving competitive advantage in family businesses has for a long time been a subject of debate among scholars who work in the field of family business. Some have argued that family businesses are more likely to attain competitive advantage owing to their unique characteristics, such as being flexible, quick decisiion making, easy access to domestic markets, using owner's equity as financial leverage, stability in management and the continuity of management policies, ability to make long term business plans, employee loyality, autonomy, the ability to determine the future, specialisation and dynamism. Others have argued that family involvement in business can be problematic due to the fact that the nature of the family is contradictory with the essence of the business. Hence, it is important to identify which organisational capabilities in family businesses may lead to a higher market orientation and thus, superior competitive advantage. Accordingly, after an integrative literature review, in this chapter, the role of organisational capabilities as management ability, entrepreneurial ability, establising partnership ability and global dynamic ability has been emphasised. This, together with supporting mechanisms, such as top management support and family culture in the relationship between maket orientation and competitive advantage in family businesses.

Family businesses with management abilities that forge and protect a unique family culture are more likely to nurture long lasting relationships with their cutomers. Skilled managers contribute to the organisation with their with managerial human capital and social capital by providing the assets and resources for business through their informal ties with the customers and positively influence the market orientation through increased customer orientation. Moreover, skilled managers are more likely to exploit ""famili-ness", in other words, build positive relationships with employees and thus, increase the interfunctional coordination as a dimension of market orientation. Likewise, entreprenurial ability contributes to the family business by enabling the pursuit of market opportunities and the recognition of innovations in rapidly changing global market conditions. Quick learning about customers and competitors, as being a characteristic of entrepreneurial ability, will increase the traits such as risk tolerance, proactiveness and receptivity that are highly related with customer orientation and competitor orientation, thus leading to better market orientation and competitive advantage. Considering the fact that family businesses tend to loose their entrepreneurial sprit after the birth stage, it is important that they develop their entrepreneurial ablities as they are growing and concentrating on the market. If they fail to do so, they will fall behind in terms of such as technological developments and thus, their market orientation will be negatively affected. In a similar vein, taking into account that sometimes most of the family businesses suffer from resource scarcity, such as insufficient human and financial capital, establishing partnership ability is a crucial organisational ability for family businesses for enhancing market orientation. Partnerships not only with businesses from other sectors, but also with competitors when neccessary, can help family businesses to overcome the fierce competition in dynamic environments and facilitates the their entry to new markets, utilising the new technologies and analysing potential future investments. Thus, establishing partnership ability will increase customer orientation and competitor orientation, thereby enhancing market orientation, which will result in attaining competitive advantage. Further, regarding the fact that succeessful family businesses will not be satisfied operating just in local markets and hence, will soon want to expand their boundaries to global ones. Accordingly, the ability to integrate with global markets, which is defined as the ability to provide internal and external assets for the organisation against the competitors, engaging in international relations and the ability to coordinate operations quickly, is essential. Dynamic global capabilities enable family businesses to realise new market opportunities, enter new markets and thus, contact new customer groups, which eventualy yields stronger customer orientation and thereby, higher market orientation and better competitive advantage.

To sum up, it is contended that attaining competitive advantage for family businesses is not always easy due to the aforementioned difficulties. However, these businesses are unique enterprises that have also got some advantages and recent literature has suggested that, if they can succeessfully exploit their organisational capabilities together with the presence of supporting factors, such as leadership of top management and relying on family culture, they can attain better competitive advantage compared to their non-family counterparts.

REFERENCES

Acquaah, M., & Agyapong, A. (2015). The relationship between competitive strategy and firm performance in micro and small businesses in Ghana: The moderating role of managerial and marketing capabilities. *Africa Journal of Management, 1*(2), 172–193. doi:10.1080/23322373.2015.1025684

Aronoff, C., & Ward, J. (2016). *Family Business Governance*. London: Springer.

Arregle, J. L., Batjargal, B., Hitt, M. A., Webb, J. W., Miller, T., & Tsui, A. S. (2015). Family ties in entrepreneurs' social networks and venture growth. *Entrepreneurship Theory and Practice, 39*(2), 313–344. doi:10.1111/etap.12044

Banalieva, E. R., & Eddleston, K. A. (2011). Home-region focus and performance of family firms: The role of family vs. non-family leaders. *Journal of International Business Studies, 42*(8), 1060–1072. doi:10.1057/jibs.2011.28

Basco, R., Calabro, A., & Campopiano, G. (2018). Transgenerational entrepreneurship around the World: Implications for family business research and practice. *Journal of Family Business Strategy, 31*(3), 1–16.

Beck, L., Janssens, W., Debruyne, M., & Lommelen, T. (2011). A study of the relationships between generation, market orientation, and innovation in family firms. *Family Business Review, 24*(3), 252–272. doi:10.1177/0894486511409210

Cacciolatti, L., & Lee, S. H. (2016). Revisiting the relationship between marketing capabilities and firm performance: The moderating role of market orientation, marketing strategy and organisational power. *Journal of Business Research, 69*(12), 5597–5610. doi:10.1016/j.jbusres.2016.03.067

Calabro, A., Torchia, M., Pukall, T., & Mussolino, D. (2013). The influence of ownership structure and board strategic involvement on international sales: The moderating effect of family involvement. *International Business Review, 22*(3), 509–523. doi:10.1016/j.ibusrev.2012.07.002

Carney, M., & Nason, R. S. (2018). Family business and the 1%. *Business & Society, 57*(6), 1191–1215. doi:10.1177/0007650316661165

Carney, M., Van Essen, M., Gedajlovic, E. R., & Heugens, P. (2015). What do we know about private family firms? A Meta-Analytical Review. *Entrepreneurship Theory and Practice, 39*(3), 513–544. doi:10.1111/etap.12054

Carsrud, A. (1994). Meanderings of a resurrected psychologist, or lessons learned in creating a family business program. *Entrepreneurship Theory and Practice, 19*(1), 39–48. doi:10.1177/104225879401900103

Cavusgil, S., & Knight, G. (2015). The born global firm: An entrepreneurial and capabilities perspective on early and rapid internationalization. *Journal of International Business Studies, 46*(1), 3–16. doi:10.1057/jibs.2014.62

Chua, J. H., Chrisman, J. J., & Sharma, P. (1999). Defining the family business by behavior. *Entrepreneurship Theory and Practice, 23*(4), 19–39. doi:10.1177/104225879902300402

Cohen, A., & Sharma, P. (2016). *Entrepreneurs in every generation: How successful family businesses develop their next leaders*. Oakland, CA: Berrett-Koehler Publishers.

Craig, J. B., & Moores, K. (2017). *Leading a Family Business: Best Practices for Long-term Stewardship*. ABC-CLIO.

Cucculelli, M., & Bettinelli, C. (2016). Corporate governance in family firms, learning and reaction to recession: Evidence from Italy. *Futures*, *75*, 92–103. doi:10.1016/j.futures.2015.10.011

Daspit, J. J., Holt, D. T., Chrisman, J. J., & Long, R. G. (2016). Examining family firm succession from a social Exchange perspective: A multiphase, multistakeholder review. *Family Business Review*, *29*(1), 44–64. doi:10.1177/0894486515599688

Donnelly, R. G. (1964). The Family Business. *Harvard Business Review*, *42*(4), 93–105.

Duh, M. (2015). Succession process: A chance for rebirth or failure of a family business. *International Journal of Business and Management*, *10*(3), 45–52. doi:10.5539/ijbm.v10n3p45

Fernandez, Z., & Nieto, M. J. (2005). Internationalization strategy of small and medium-sized family businesses: Some influential factors. *Family Business Review*, *18*(1), 77–89. doi:10.1111/j.1741-6248.2005.00031.x

Frambach, R. T., Fiss, P. C., & Ingenbleek, P. T. (2016). How important is customer orientation for firm performance? A fuzzy set analysis of orientations, strategies and environments. *Journal of Business Research*, *69*(4), 1428–1436. doi:10.1016/j.jbusres.2015.10.120

Garces-Galdeano, L., Larazza-Kintana, M., Garcia-Olaverri, C., & Makri, M. (2016). Entrepreneurial orientation in family firms: The moderating role of technological intensity and performance. *The International Entrepreneurship and Management Journal*, *12*(1), 27–45. doi:10.100711365-014-0335-2

Gilding, M., Gregory, S., & Cosson, B. (2015). Motives and outcomes in family business succession planning. *Entrepreneurship Theory and Practice*, *39*(2), 299–312. doi:10.1111/etap.12040

Goel, S., & Jones, R. J. III. (2016). Entrepreneurial exploration and exploitation in family business: A systematic review and future directions. *Family Business Review*, *29*(1), 94–120. doi:10.1177/0894486515625541

Grewal, R., & Tansuhaj, P. (2001). Building organizational capabilities for managing economic crises: The role of market orientation and strategic flexibility. *Journal of Marketing*, *65*(2), 67–80. doi:10.1509/jmkg.65.2.67.18259

Gruber-Muecke, T., & Hofer, K. M. (2015). Market orientation, entrepreneurial orientation and performance in emerging markets. *International Journal of Emerging Markets*, *10*(3), 560–571. doi:10.1108/IJoEM-05-2013-0076

Hennart, J. F., Majocchi, A., & Forlani, E. (2019). The myth of the stay-at-home family firm: How family-managed SMEs can overcome internationalization limitations. *Journal of International Business Studies*, *50*(5), 758–782. doi:10.105741267-017-0091-y

Herhausen, D. (2015). Unfolding the ambidextrous effects of proactive and responsive market orientation. *Journal of Business Research*, *69*(7), 2585–2593. doi:10.1016/j.jbusres.2015.10.139

Hernandez-Espallardo, M., & Arcas-Lario, N. (2003). The effects of authoritative mechanisms of coordination on market orientation in asymmetrical channel partnerships. *International Journal of Research in Marketing*, *20*(2), 133–152. doi:10.1016/S0167-8116(03)00015-6

Ho, K. L. P., Nguyen, C. N., Adhikari, R., Miles, M. P., & Bonney, L. (2018). Exploring market orientation, innovation, and financial performance in agricultural value chains in emerging economies. *Journal of Innovation & Knowledge*, *3*(3), 154–163. doi:10.1016/j.jik.2017.03.008

Jaskiewicz, P., Combs, J. G., Shanine, K. K., & Kacmar, K. M. (2016). Introducing the family: A review of family science with implications for management research. *The Academy of Management Annals*, *11*(1), 309–341. doi:10.5465/annals.2014.0053

Jaworski, B. J., & Kohli, A. K. (1996). Market orientation: Review, refinement, and roadmap. *Journal of Market-Focused Management*, *1*(2), 119–135. doi:10.1007/BF00128686

Jha, S., & Bhattacharyya, S. S. (2017). Deveoplemt of model integrating determinants of job performance and competitor orientation. *International Journal of Indian Culture and Business Management*, *15*(3), 326–349. doi:10.1504/IJICBM.2017.087313

Jogaratnam, G. (2017). How organizational culture influences market orientation and business performance in the restaurant industry. *Journal of Hospitality and Tourism Management*, *31*, 211–219. doi:10.1016/j.jhtm.2017.03.002

Kajolo, S., & Lindblom, A. (2015). Market orientation, entrepreneurial orientation and business performance among small retailers. *International Journal of Retail & Distribution Management*, *43*(7), 580–596. doi:10.1108/IJRDM-04-2014-0044

Keasey, K., Martinez, B., & Pindado, J. (2015). Young family firms: Financing decisions and the willingness to dilute control. *Journal of Corporate Finance*, *34*, 47–63. doi:10.1016/j.jcorpfin.2015.07.014

Konopaski, M., Jack, S., & Hamilton, E. (2016). How family business members learn about continuity. *Academy of Management Learning & Education*, *14*(3), 347–364. doi:10.5465/amle.2014.0244

Kontinen, T., & Ojala, A. (2010). The internationalization of family businesses: A review of extant research. *Journal of Family Business Strategy*, *1*(2), 97–107. doi:10.1016/j.jfbs.2010.04.001

Kotabe, M., & Kothari, T. (2016). Emerging market multinational companies' evolutionary paths to building a competitive advantage from emerging markets to developed countries. *Journal of World Business*, *51*(5), 729–743. doi:10.1016/j.jwb.2016.07.010

Ku, E. C., Wu, W. C., & Chen, Y. J. (2016). The relationships among supply chain partnerships, customer orientation, and operational performance: The effect of flexibility. *Information Systems and e-Business Management*, *14*(2), 415–441. doi:10.100710257-015-0289-0

Le Breton-Miller, I., & Miller, D. (2015). Learning stewardship in family firms: For family, by family, across the life cycle. *Academy of Management Learning & Education*, *14*(3), 386–399. doi:10.5465/amle.2014.0131

Litz, R. A. (1995). The family business: Toward definitional clarity. *Family Business Review*, *8*(2), 71–81. doi:10.1111/j.1741-6248.1995.00071.x

Lonial, S. C., & Carter, R. E. (2015). The impact of organizational orientations on medium and small firm performance: A resource-based perspective. *Journal of Small Business Management*, *53*(1), 94–113. doi:10.1111/jsbm.12054

Martin, S. L., & Javalgi, R. R. G. (2016). Entrepreneurial orientation, marketing capabilities and performance: The moderating role of competitive intensity on Latin American International new ventures. *Journal of Business Research*, *69*(6), 2040–2051. doi:10.1016/j.jbusres.2015.10.149

McKelvie, A., & Davidsson, P. (2009). From Resource Base to Dynamic Capabilities: An Investigation of New Firms. *British Journal of Management*, *20*, 63–80. doi:10.1111/j.1467-8551.2008.00613.x

Memili, E., Fang, H., Chrisman, J. J., & De Massis, A. (2015). The impact of small-and medium sized family firms on economic growth. *Small Business Economics*, *45*(4), 771–785. doi:10.100711187-015-9670-0

Merchant, P., Kumar, A., & Malik, D. (2018). Factors Influencing Family Business Continuity in Indian Small and Medium Enterprises (SMEs). *Journal of Family and Economic Issues*, *39*(2), 177–190. doi:10.100710834-017-9562-3

Minola, T., Brumana, M., Campopiano, G., Garrett, R. P., & Cassia, L. (2016). Corporate venturing in family business: A developmental approach of the enterprising family. *Strategic Entrepreneurship Journal*, *10*(4), 395–412. doi:10.1002ej.1236

Mokhber, M., Gi Gi, T., Abdul Rasid, S. Z., Vakilbashi, A., Mohd Zamil, N., & Woon Seng, Y. (2017). Succession planning and family business performance in SMEs. *Journal of Management Development*, *36*(3), 330–347. doi:10.1108/JMD-12-2015-0171

Monferrer, D., Blesa, A., & Ripolles, M. (2015). Born global through knowledge-based dynamic capabilities and network market orientation. *BRQ Business Research Quarterly*, *18*(1), 18–36. doi:10.1016/j.brq.2014.04.001

Neubauer, F., & Lank, A. G. (2016). *The Family Business: Its governance for sustainability*. London: Springer.

Oudah, M., Jabeen, F., & Dixon, C. (2018). Determinants linked to family business sustainability in UAE: An AHP approach. *Sustainability*, *10*(1), 1–23. doi:10.3390u10010246 PMID:30607262

Ozkaya, H. E., Droge, C., Hult, G. T. M., Calantone, R., & Ozkaya, E. (2015). Market orientation, knowledge competence, and innovation. *International Journal of Research in Marketing*, *32*(3), 309–318. doi:10.1016/j.ijresmar.2014.10.004

Pattanayak, D., Koilakuntla, M., & Punyatoya, P. (2017). Investigating the influence of TQM, service quality and market orientation on customer satisfaction and loyality in the Indian banking sector. *International Journal of Quality & Reliability Management*, *34*(3), 362–377. doi:10.1108/IJQRM-04-2015-0057

Pelham, A. M. (2015). Strategy, Market Orientation, or Environment: Relative Influence on Small Manufacturing Firms. In *Proceedings of the 1998 Academy of Marketing Science (AMS) Annual Conference*. Cham: Springer. 10.1007/978-3-319-13084-2_107

Pena, A. I. P., Jamilena, D. M. F., & Molina, M. A. R. (2017). The effects of perceived value on loyality: The moderating effect of market orientation adoption. *Service Business*, *11*(1), 93–116. doi:10.100711628-016-0303-8

Perez-Luno, A., Saparito, P., & Gopalakrishnan, S. (2016). Small and Medium-Sized Enterprise's Entrepreneurial versus Market Orientation and the Creation of Tacit Knowledge. *Journal of Small Business Management*, *54*(1), 262–278. doi:10.1111/jsbm.12144

Pindado, J., & Requejo, I. (2015). Family business performance from a governance perspective: A review of empirical research. *International Journal of Management Reviews*, *17*(3), 279–331. doi:10.1111/ijmr.12040

Poza, E. J., & Daugherty, M. S. (2014). *Family Business*. Cengage Learning.

Prajogo, D. (2016). The Role of Human Capital and Market Orientation as Determinants of Service Innovation. *International Academy of Management and Business Conference*.

Pratono, A. H., & Mahmood, R. (2015). Mediating effect of marketing capability and reward philosophy in the relationship between entrepreneurial orientation and firm performance. *Journal of Global Entrepreneurship Research*, *5*(1), 5–15. doi:10.118640497-015-0023-x

Rakthin, S., Calantone, R. J., & Wang, J. F. (2016). Managing market intelligence: The comparative role of absorptive capacity and market orientation. *Journal of Business Research*, *69*(12), 5569–5577. doi:10.1016/j.jbusres.2016.03.064

Reddrop, A., & Mapunda, G. (2015). Family businesses: Seekers of advice. *Journal of Family Business Management*, *5*(1), 90–115. doi:10.1108/JFBM-08-2014-0018

Sarbah, A., & Xiao, W. (2015). Good corporate governance structures: A must for family businesses. *Open Journal of Business and Management*, *3*(1), 40–57. doi:10.4236/ojbm.2015.31005

Seaman, C. (2015). Creating space for the business family: Networks, social capital & family businesses in rural development. *Journal of Family Business Management*, *5*(2), 182–191. doi:10.1108/JFBM-08-2015-0032

Slatten, T., Lien, G., & Svensson, G. (2018). The value of cultivating norms for market orientation in Professional service firms. *International Journal of Quality and Service Sciences*, *10*(3), 316–330. doi:10.1108/IJQSS-09-2017-0086

Stanley, L., Kellermanns, F. W., & Zellweger, T. M. (2017). Latent profile analysis: Understanding family firm profiles. *Family Business Review*, *30*(1), 84–102. doi:10.1177/0894486516677426

Stenholm, P., Pukkinen, T., & Heinonen, J. (2016). Firm growth in family businesses-The role of entrepreneurial orientation and the entrepreneurial activity. *Journal of Small Business Management*, *54*(2), 687–713. doi:10.1111/jsbm.12166

Sundaramurthy, C. (2008). Sustaining trust within family businesses. *Family Business Review*, *21*(1), 89–102. doi:10.1111/j.1741-6248.2007.00110.x

Tajeddini, K., Altinay, L., & Ratten, V. (2017). Service innovativeness and the structuring of organizations: The moderating roles of learning orientation and inter-functional coordination. *International Journal of Hospitality Management, 65*, 100–114. doi:10.1016/j.ijhm.2017.06.010

Teece, D. J. (2014). A dynamic capabilities-based entrepreneurial theory of the multinational enterprise. *Journal of International Business Studies, 45*(1), 8–37. doi:10.1057/jibs.2013.54

Ulrich, D., & Smallwood, N. (2004). Capitalizing on capabilities. *Harvard Business Review, 82*(6), 119–127. PMID:15202293

Wang, G., & Miao, C. F. (2015). Effects of sales force market orientation on creativity, innovation implementation and sales performance. *Journal of Business Research, 68*(11), 2374–2382. doi:10.1016/j.jbusres.2015.03.041

Wang, Q., Zhao, X., & Voss, C. (2016). Customer orientation and innovation: A comparative study of manufacturing and service firms. *International Journal of Production Economics, 171*, 221–230. doi:10.1016/j.ijpe.2015.08.029

Ward, J. (2016). *Perpetuating the family business: 50 lessons learned from long lasting, successful families in business*. London: Springer.

Ward, J. (2016). *Keeping the family business healthy: How to plan for continuing growth, profitability and family leadership*. London: Springer.

Xi, J. M., Kraus, S., Filser, M., & Kellermanns, F. W. (2015). Mapping the field of family business research: Pats trends and future directions. *The International Entrepreneurship and Management Journal, 11*(1), 113–132. doi:10.100711365-013-0286-z

Zahra, S. A. (2005). Entrepreneurial risk taking in family firms. *Family Business Review, 18*(1), 23–40. doi:10.1111/j.1741-6248.2005.00028.x

Zellweger, T. (2017). *Managing the family business: Theory and Practice*. Cheltenham, UK: Edward Elgar Publishing.

Zhang, L., Kara, A., Spillan, J. E., & Mintu-Wimsatt, A. (2015). Exploring market orientation among Chinese small and medium-sized enterprises. *Chinese Management Studies, 11*(4), 617–636. doi:10.1108/CMS-08-2016-0158

Zhou, K. Z., Li, J. J., Zhou, N., & Su, C. (2008). Market orientation, job satisfaction, product quality and firm performance: Evidence from China. *Strategic Management Journal, 29*(5), 985–1000. doi:10.1002mj.700

ADDITIONAL READING

Martin, S. L., & Javalgi, R. R. G. (2016). Entrepreneurial orientation, marketing capabilities and performance: The moderating role of competitive intensity on Latin American International new ventures. *Journal of Business Research*, *69*(6), 2040–2051. doi:10.1016/j.jbusres.2015.10.149

Neubauer, F., & Lank, A. G. (2016). *The Family Business: Its governance for sustainability*. London: Springer.

Ward, J. (2016). *Perpetuating the family business: 50 lessons learned from long lasting, successful families in business*. London: Springer.

KEY TERMS AND DEFINITONS

Competitive Advantage: A condition that puts a company in a superior business condition compared to its competitors.

Dynamic Global Abilities: The capabilities of a firm that consists of vision and strategy, relying on core competence, efficient communication, innovation, appropriate organization structure, organizational culture and technology management.

Entrepreneurial Abilities: A management attitude within the scope of strategy-making process in order to take entrepreneurial decisions in organizations.

Family Business: Businesses where family members have a minimum ownership stake of 20-25% that are distinguished as family firms from non-family firms.

Family Business Life Cycle: The process that family businesses go through and includes birth, growth, maturation, and continuity stages.

Management Abilities: The capacity of the individuals to implement mental activities.

Market Orientation: Market orientation is the ability to understand and satisfy the needs and wants of the customers in order to achieve maximum level of profitability.

Partnership Abilities: The ability to build inter-organizational relationships that arise between the parties in order to achieve common goals.

Chapter 3
Family Firm Competitiveness and Organizational Ambidexterity

Montserrat Boronat-Navarro
https://orcid.org/0000-0002-9062-4161
Jaume I University, Spain

Alexandra García-Joerger
Jaume I University, Spain

ABSTRACT

Long-term survival is one of the main goals of family business. Nevertheless, very few firms survive to the third generation. The concept of organizational ambidexterity could add insights into the explanation of family firm (FF) survival. In the literature, organizational ambidexterity is defined as the capability to explore new knowledge, processes, and opportunities while exploiting current ones to achieve a greater competitive advantage and ensure the survival of the firm. The aim of this chapter is to review the literature that analyzes relationships between FF specificities and organizational ambidexterity to propose a framework of the antecedents of ambidexterity in this context. This could be a useful tool to better identify FF specificities that will support long-term survival through their influence on organizational ambidexterity.

INTRODUCTION

Long-term survival is one of the main goals of a family firm (FF). The firm's founder usually wants to maintain control for their successors. In fact, FF succession is common in these firms (Chrisman, Chua, Pearson, & Barnett, 2012; Hiebl, 2015). Nevertheless, fewer than 15% survive into the third generation (Hiebl, 2015; Ward, 1987).

DOI: 10.4018/978-1-7998-1655-3.ch003

The concept of organizational ambidexterity could add insights into the explanation of FF long-term survival (Hiebl, 2015; Stubner, Blarr, Brands, & Wulf, 2012). March (1991), from an organizational learning perspective, stated that to survive in the long term, firms should explore and exploit. In his seminal paper, March (1991) interpreted exploitation and exploration as different learning activities between which organizations should divide their attention. In his definition, exploitation refers to "refinement, efficiency, selection, and implementation," whereas exploration is interpreted as "search, variation, experimentation, and discovery" (March, 1991, p. 71).

Organizational ambidexterity is the capability to combine these two activities, explore new opportunities, processes and knowledge, and exploit current ones (Raisch, Birkinshaw, Probst, & Tushman, 2009; Simsek, 2009; Tushman & O'Reilly, 1996). This will achieve a greater competitive advantage and ensure the survival of the company. In other words, ambidextrous firms successfully manage short-term success while paying attention to their long-term success. Firms with high levels of exploration and exploitation achieve superior performance because they manage current business demands and adapt to future challenges to achieve long-term survival (Cao, Gedajlovic, & Zhang, 2009; Gibson & Birkinshaw, 2004; O'Reilly & Tushman, 2013). Higher levels of organizational ambidexterity lead to a better economic performance (Stubner et al. 2012). Consequently, ambidexterity promotes competitiveness. Nevertheless, difficulties of achieving ambidexterity are based on the fact that exploration and exploitation require different resources and processes, and therefore, they compete for scarce firm resources (Simsek, 2009).

Recently, the literature about the FF has recognized and analyzed the importance of organizational ambidexterity in this context. According to De Massis, et al. (2013), the topic of ambidexterity in FFs requires further development. There has been high importance set on organizational ambidexterity for the long-term survival of firms and the effect of ambidexterity on performance have been analyzed in some studies (e.g. Moss, Payne, & Moore, 2014). However, until now, knowledge about how family involvement and organizational factors interact with ambidexterity to influence performance in FFs is underdeveloped (Hughes, Filser, Harms, Kraus, Chang, & Cheng, 2018). Only six studies on this topic have been developed in the context of FFs until 2014 (Hiebl, 2015). After this date, a growing body of research has focused on this analysis (Dolz, Iborra. & Safón, 2019; Goel & Jones, 2016; Hiebl, 2015; Hughes et al., 2018).

According to Le Breton-Miller and Miller (2006), the specificities of FFs make them a benefiting arena for achieving continuity and focus, as well as reorienting and reinventing themselves when needed. Both, continuity and renewal are the essence of ambidexterity, since it implies managing current business demands while adapting to future challenges. The long-term vision and entrepreneurial spirit that characterize FFs are specific traits that could be beneficial in the achievement of ambidexterity (Hughes et al., 2018; Stubner et al., 2012). Although they do not exhibit homogeneous success regarding exploration and exploitation (Hughes et al., 2018), family involvement in ownership and management, are specificities of FFs that provide additional angle to analyze ambidexterity (Stubner et al., 2012).

Therefore, the aim of this proposal is to review the literature that analyzes relationships between FF specificities and organizational ambidexterity to propose a framework on how these characteristics influence ambidexterity in this context. The framework could be a useful tool to better identify FF specificities that help the long-term survival through their influence on organizational ambidexterity. The performance differences between FFs could be better explained considering these insights from the concept of organizational ambidexterity (Webb, Ketchen, & Ireland, 2010). The structure of the proposal includes a review of the ambidexterity concept and how it applies in FFs. Then, the proposal discusses the characteristics that could influence the development of ambidexterity.

THEORETICAL BACKGROUND

Ambidexterity Concept

Duncan (1976) was the first to use the term "organizational ambidexterity." However, March's (1991) landmark paper has been frequently cited as the catalyst for the current interest in exploration and exploitation. Building upon earlier work by Duncan (1976), Tushman and O'Reilly (1996) first presented a theory of organizational ambidexterity. They suggested that superior performance is expected from the ambidextrous organization, describing structural mechanisms to achieve ambidexterity.

From a strategic perspective, achieving long-term success requires firms to possess operational capabilities and competencies to compete in existing markets. In addition, they require the ability to recombine and reconfigure assets and organizational structures to adapt to emerging markets and technologies. In fact, Teece (2006) characterized dynamic capabilities as the distinct skills, processes, procedures, organizational structures, decision rules, and disciplines that enable senior leaders of a firm to identify threats and opportunities and reconfigure assets.

Organizational ambidexterity is a dynamic capability. It includes the ability of companies to handle the contradictions and paradoxes that arise from simultaneous exploration and exploitation activities, adjusting them to changes in the environment (O'Reilly & Tushman, 2011). As a dynamic capability, organizational ambidexterity emphasizes the management role in the adaptation, integration, and reconfiguration of the organization's skills and resources to adjust them in changing environments (Eisenhardt & Martin, 2000; Heavy & Simsek, 2010; O'Reilly & Tushman, 2008; Teece, Pisano, & Shuen, 1997).

Exploitation is associated with refinement, production, efficiency, and short-term orientation. Exploration is related with searching, variation, innovation, and long-term orientation (March, 1991). Exploration consists of experiments with new alternatives with distant, uncertain, and often negative returns. Conversely, exploitation is about the expansion of existing competencies, improvement, and technologies with positive, upcoming, and predictable returns (March, 1991). Ambidextrous organizations can develop both exploitation and exploration activities. They exploit their current knowledge, staying open to the exploration of new knowledge and opportunities (O'Reilly & Tushman, 2008).

Despite its importance for the success of companies, it is not easy to be ambidextrous. Thus, the literature links ambidexterity to the idea of conflict and tension, with a dilemma between enhancing innovation or focusing on efficiency. Difficulty exists in the reconciliation of the short and long term due to the complexity of choosing between the security of the known and the uncertain potentialities of the unknown while competing for the scarce resources of a company (March, 1991). The two activities require different structures, processes, strategies, capacities, and cultures. Therefore, they can have different impacts on the performance of an organization (He & Wong, 2004).

FFs and Ambidexterity

The study of FFs has been largely rooted on theoretical approaches that are also useful in this study. Two dominant paradigms are considered (Chua, Chrisman & Steier, 2003b). The first approach, which is based on the theory of agency, uses this paradigm to postulate a "dark side" of family ownership, emphasizing the risks of "agency transfers" within the family unit (Lubatkin, Schulze, Ling & Dino, 2005; Schulze, Lubatkin, & Dino, 2003). Nevertheless, the second approach suggests that altruism, as well as its consequences, complicates decision making in FFs (Schulze, Lubatkin, Dino, & Buchholtz, 2001). They argue that concentrated ownership may have a negative effect on firm performance:

1. Altruism of family chief executive officers (CEos) creates the opportunity for family members to act freely (Schulze, Lubatkin, & Dino, 2002).
2. When the CEO of the firm is a member of the family, nonfamily managers feel more excluded and identify less with the firm.
3. The combination of a family CEO with a subset of family executives reinforces the perception that nonfamily managers have limited opportunities for professional advancement (Chua, Chrisman & Sharma, 2003a).
4. The presence of a family CEO could aggravate tensions created by strong representation of both the family and nonfamily factions in the top management team (TMT).

If the altruism is moderate and the consequences of the joint utility are well managed, agency costs can be reduced considerably. This can lead to a superior performance of the company (Minichilli, Corbetta, & MacMillan, 2010).

The second approach uses the resource-based view (RBV) of the firm. It raises a "positive/bright side" of family ownership and management through the concept of "Familiness," stating that FFs differ from non-FFs due to unique resources and capabilities (Habbershon & Williams, 1999; Habbershon, Williams, & MacMillan, 2003). This approach also analyzes how such idiosyncratic resources can generate abnormal financial returns for the FF (Habbershon et al., 2003). Familiness has emerged from the resource-based view as a crucial idea to explain the complexity of resources and capabilities in this context. Specifically, familiness is "a resource unique to a FF because of the interactions between the family, its individual members, and the firm" (Habbershon & Williams, 1999, p.11). Increased ownership by family members can achieve better performance for different reasons:

1. When family members are owners and managers at the same time, the interest converges. Therefore, conflicts of interest decrease, having a positive effect on performance (Jensen & Meckling, 1976).
2. Even when controlling block holders are not involved in management, they are more capable of monitoring and controlling managers (Shleifer & Vishny, 1986).
3. Family-owned firms may make better investment decisions because they have more firm-specific knowledge, are less myopic, and have longer investment horizons (Stein, 1989).

Moreover, socioemotional wealth (SEW) states that the goals of family-oriented objectives can preserve or create socioemotional wealth (Berrone, Cruz, & Gomez-Mejia, 2012). Willingness, comprised goals, intentions, and motivations drive the family-controlled firm, influencing the company in directions that differ from those pursued by firms without family involvement (De Massis, Kotlar, Chua, & Chrisman, 2014). The possible causes of behavioral heterogeneity among FFs, as well as the integration of these noneconomic objectives into strategic decision-making, will be shaped by management configurations that allow for the alignment of pecuniary and nonpecuniary objectives (Corbetta & Salvato, 2004; Veider & Matzler, 2016).

FFs are based on the functional and dynamic interrelation between family and business subsystems. The traditional goals of these firms include the achievement of long-term survival of both, as well as the transmission of the business to future generations (Anderson & Reeb, 2003; Chua, Chrisman, & Sharma, 1999).

The most recent literature extends the theory of social capital to family construction (Arregle, Hitt, Sirmon, & Very, 2007). It studies how the unique resources and capabilities of FFs are created through interactions between the family and the firm (Pearson, Carr, & Shaw, 2008; Sharma, 2008). In this sense, some studies based on the theory of resources and capabilities suggest that FFs have superior skills to manage certain tensions and conflicts (Habbershon & Williams, 1999; Tokarczyk, Hansen, Green, & Down, 2007). This could represent an advantage to manage tensions to achieve ambidexterity.

Decisions in FFs are focused on meeting the objectives of both the family and the firm. These goals are often different from nonfamily companies (Yu, Lumpkin, Sorenson, & Brigham, 2012). In fact, some studies found evidence of the relationship between ambidexterity and family ownership (Lubatkin, Simsek, Ling, & Veiga, 2006). Others found positive results between family influence, especially related to family culture and family power, achievement of organizational ambidexterity, and components like innovation (Stubner et al., 2012; Tanewski, Prajogo, & Sohal, 2003). Still others analyzed the influence of variables that made a difference between FFs, like Sciascia, Mazzola, and Chirico (2013), who evaluated the influence of generational involvement on the entrepreneurial orientation of FFs. Nevertheless, the focus of the present chapter is on the characteristics of FFs that could benefit ambidexterity. Therefore, the next section discusses the specificities of FFs to achieve ambidexterity that have been outlined in the studies reviewed, that mainly are rooted on Agency, Resource, and Socioemotional arguments. The chapter reviews the literature and studies that measure ambidexterity in FFs. After reviewing these specificities, the following section outlines also different characteristics that appear in the studies reviewed about of how various degrees of family participation in the decision-making process and of diversity could affect the way in which these specificities influence ambidexterity.

SPECIFICITIES OF FFs AND THEIR RELATIONSHIP WITH AMBIDEXTERITY

Ownership and Management in FFs

Lubatkin et al. (2006) were the first to find a positive relationship between family ownership, TMT, and ambidexterity. The family who owns and manages the company generates a series of effects. For example, lower agency costs derived from the alignment of objectives of the main responsible parties contribute to better functioning. This effect is underlined by Jensen and Meckling (1976), for which it provides strong incentives for cost containment. In the same sense, Gedajlovic et al (2004) affirmed that companies managed by owners have the necessary incentives and discretion to exploit opportunities. In fact, ability is studied as the "discretion of the family to direct, allocate, add to, or dispose of a firm's resources" (De Massis et al., 2014, p. 346). This ability is achieved through the participation of family in the main governance dimensions, as well as membership in the TMT and board of directors (Carney, 2005; Chrisman, Chua, Pearson, A. & Barnett, 2012). This discretion provides freedom to choose between the range of strategic, tactical, and structural feasible options, giving family-controlled firms an unusual ability to behave idiosyncratically (Chrisman, Chua, De Massis, Frattini, & Wright, 2015). Veider and Matzler (2016) argued that the ability of FFs will be reflected in the idiosyncratic agency situation and endowment of company resources. These will determine the ability of the company to decide how to allocate resources for exploration and exploitation (Dolz et al., 2019) to become an ambidextrous organization.

The family power level (measured through a family's share of ownership, as well as the percentage of family members within the management and governance board) positively influences a firm's ambidextrous orientation (Stubner et al., 2012). Likewise, when the property participates in the management, it will have incentives to closely control the operations of the company and make decisions that ensure that costs are contained, production is efficient, and resources are allocated in a rational manner (Carney, 2005).

Family management facilitates the company's involvement in long-term innovation practices and the construction of internal knowledge structures to finding new opportunities (Patel & Fiet, 2011). Managers who hold the property of the company are usually well-rooted in it and are difficult to replace. Therefore, they will have a strong incentive to invest in activities and projects with good potential for long-term benefits. Professionalized management, which is less rooted, has a more short-term or exploitative orientation. Family members involved in the management are more willing to make investments of which they can obtain benefits beyond the duration of their professional career, favoring both the company and the family. This responds to the wish of continuity that defines these companies.

The presence of familiar managers increases the company's exploration capability by increasing the CEO's discretion, allowing him/her to make opportunistic investments or rely on intuition when making decisions. They will be more able to create products, enter new markets, and adapt to changes in the environment (Gedajlovic, Lubatkin, & Schulze, 2004; Schulze & Gedajlovic, 2010). This conjunction increases the ability of senior managers to set a strategic agenda and resist pressure from other interested parts who try to influence or change the company's direction (Gedajlovic et al., 2012).

TMT is usually divided between family and nonfamily members. Family members share common values, norms, and a culture inherited from their parents and relatives, including similar education. They generally feel satisfied and rewarded with their occupation in FFs (Chua et al., 2003a). Family members have a stronger emotional bond with the company. Emotional attachment increases the level of commitment and participation that people have with organizations because they identify with the organization (Sharma & Irving, 2005). Some papers discuss the importance of engaging nonfamily externals to the TMT to provide diversity in knowledge and backgrounds needed for achieving organizational ambidexterity (Gupta, Smith, & Shalley, 2006; Taylor & Greve, 2006; Veider & Matzler, 2016). For example, O'Reilly and Tushman (2011) remarked on the importance of having a common vision and value within the TMT to achieve ambidexterity.

Nevertheless, FFs tend to have an appearance of "schisms," which advances disagreements and tensions between family and nonfamily members. The existence of failures between family and nonfamily executives leads to behavioral interruptions and harm to the performance of the company (Li & Hambrick, 2005). When there are few members of a group, the minority group has less power to challenge decisions. Conflicts and interruptions between family and nonfamily factions increase as the proportion of both factions in the corporate elite increases. This supports the existence of a U-shaped relationship. Companies with TMT whose family-to-nonfamily relationship is high or low will perform better than companies with a solid representation of both factions. Hiebl (2015) also explains that risk aversion is a factor that appears in FFs with lower percentage of external investors and that the presence of non-family investors promotes riskier activities and enhance ambidexterity.

Long-Term Orientation

Long-term orientation is the propensity to prioritize long-term involvement, as well as the impact of decisions and actions resulting after a certain period (Lumpkin, Brigham & Moss, 2010). FFs have a long-term orientation, mainly due to their desire to pass the business to the next generation (Carney, 2005; Patel & Fiet, 2011). This long-term vision provides the desire to maintain the family heritage for future generations (Le-Breton Miller and Miller, 2006; Stubner et al., 2012). As a consequence, FFs in often surviving across two or three generations. The experience gained in the family in managing the firm is also beneficial in achieving ambidexterity (Stubner et al., 2012), with an orientation in protecting efficiency to overcome short term difficulties but also to preserving the long-term survival of the firm.

Le Breton-Miller and Miller (2011) noted the advantage of multitemporality in FFs due to the ability to achieve lasting success by balancing short- and long-term orientation. Thus, in these companies, ambidextrous orientation should prevail. The familiar nature of the companies gives them a greater concern to combine the requirements of different time periods, emphasizing issues like current incentives and dividends, employment security of family members, reputation of the company, and/or the legacy of a robust company for future generations (Gómez-Mejía, Núñez-Nickel, & Gutierrez, 2001). On the other side, owners who do not belong to the family (or professional managers) have a psychological and social distance from the larger company. Their relationship tends to be transitory, individualistic, and utilitarian.

Allison, McKenny, and Short (2014) showed that FFs can align their exploration and exploitation over time. Others suggest that these companies can reduce cognitive and affective conflict (Webb et al., 2010). Therefore, FFs must adopt a long-term vision in the decision-making process (Le Breton-Miller & Miller, 2006). There is a need to balance and align the family and company dimensions. FFs have the resources and family government influence in the decision-making process (Carney, 2005).

Due to these inherent characteristics, as compared to managers of non-FFs, family members who are involved in FFs have confidence in the networks and information channels built over generations. They involve the most effective combination of tacit and procedural knowledge, exploit and organize accumulated knowledge, and participate in investments that can generate benefits that extend beyond the individual career to support the company.

The lack of knowledge related to how temporary factors influence the ambidexterity of FFs generates a gap between what is known and what should be known about ambidexterity in these companies. The lack of knowledge is problematic because time plays an important role in the culture of the organization, innovation, and intragenerational succession of firms. In addition, the balance between exploitation and exploration can change over time (Craig & Moores, 2006).

Lumpkin and Brigham (2011) argued that the long-term orientations of FFs create stability and continuity. Companies with a short-term orientation tend to emphasize exploitation activities which result in a solid short-term performance and a long-term obsolescence (March, 1991). Given that companies with a long-term orientation make decisions and support them for long periods of time, those decisions are reviewed less frequently. This could, in turn, lead the company to make major adjustments when such decisions are re-examined.

Ambidexterity must be achieved through dynamic processes (Ketchen, Thomas, & Snow, 1993). This must be maintained by rebalancing exploration against exploitation in response to internal and external changes (Siggelkow, 2002). Managers should make conscious decisions about the allocation of resources to maintain ambidexterity (Raisch et al., 2009).

FFs, as compared to non-FFs, are better positioned to find and explore new opportunities in either static or dynamic environments (Patel & Fiet, 2011). This advantage is due to a combination of a long-term orientation in FFs along with low turnover, long manager durations, and predominant family ties (Chrisman, Kellermanns, Chan, & Liano, 2010).

Nevertheless, some disadvantages could be also linked to this long-term vision in some contexts when risk aversion appears. For example, Dolz et al. (2019) found a negative relationship in a context of economic crisis in which the goal of firm survival leads to FFs to prioritize efficiency.

Culture in FFs: Low Turnover and Family Ties

As proposed in the three-circle model by Tagiuri and Davis (1996), FFs are special in their context because they are made up of members of the family (property), the family itself, and business interaction (Chrisman, Chua, & Sharma, 2005). This interaction between the members of the family and the company allows for a higher level of trust, reciprocity, and exchange of information. The shared history and potential shared future creates a group identity between family workers (Gómez-Mejía et al., 2001; Mazzelli, De Massis, Petruzzelli, Del Giudice, & Khan, 2019). This notion of trust between relatives could be considered an advantage, especially in the accumulation of resources, the transfer of tacit knowledge, protection, the use of reputation, and the construction of solid relationships (Le Breton-Miller & Miller 2015; Habbershon & Williams 1999; Pearson et al., 2008).

Family power and culture have a positive influence on the ambidextrous orientation in FFs. When FFs show a high level of cultural alignment, the family is committed to the company. In addition, the family and firm goals are aligned (Klein, Astrachan, & Smyrnios, 2005). Some specific cultural traits affect organizations in an ambidextrous way.

Le Breton-Miller and Miller (2006) suggested how different characteristics of FFs play a key role in allowing managers to balance exploitation with exploration. Low levels of turnover and the presence of strong family ties suggest a management preference for the eventual change in ambidexterity (Chrisman et al., 2005).

Low levels of employee turnover suggest high levels of organizational inertia. If altering organizational premises dislocates, this should be clearly manifested in turnover, especially among the most senior employees within an organization. Turnover is an especially appropriate indicator of the disruptive effects of organizational change because retaining key human assets in firms is often viewed by senior management, investors, and other informed parties as a crucial requirement for organizational survival and success (Baron, Hannan, & Burton, 2001).

Family ties can facilitate the exchange of knowledge structures and innovation (Patel & Fiet, 2011). It can also make managers prefer less risky change trajectories. This option reduces the risk of losing socioemotional wealth, preserves the company for next generations, and maintains some free resources for family purposes (Gómez-Mejía et al. 2001).

Increased cooperation and communication stablished as a way in which family firms interact, acts as a facilitator in decision making processes, nurturing loyalty and commitment that in turn benefits ambidexterity (Veider & Matzler, 2016).

Family members are tied with bonds of affection, loyalty, and shared values (Gómez-Mejía, Cruz, Berrone, & De Castro, 2011). Their loyalty and affection are shown through high-quality performance in their companies as they set aside selfish motivation (Lubatkin et al., 2007). In fact, they are often willing to work for long hours with a minimum wage (Le Breton-Miller & Miller, 2015; Gómez-Mejía et al. 2011). In addition, family members feel more secure as they are enriched by experiences and the ability to explore opportunities (Sardeshmukh & Corbett, 2011).

The main studies that explicitly analyze these specificities of FFs and their relationship with ambidexterity are summarized in Table 1.

DEGREES OF FAMILY CONTROL AND DIVERSITY AND THEIR RELATIONSHIP WITH AMBIDEXTERITY

Apart from the previous FFs specificities, family firm are not a total homogeneous group. There are different degrees of family participation in the decision-making process and of diversity that literature have studied in their effect of ambidexterity. Specifically, in the present section we outline how some studies have proposed the participation in the council and the degree of diversity in different aspects can affect ambidexterity.

Table 1. Specificities of FFs and ambidexterity

Specificities	Authors	Theoretical approach	Arguments	Effect founded
Ownership and management	Lubatkin et al. (2006)	Ambidexterity Upper echelon view Group process theory	Family ownership and management (control variable) provides the ability to control decisions	Positive effect
	Dolz et al. (2015)	Upper echelon theory Agency theory arguments	Positive effect of having the same ownership and management in ability to assign resources and in agency costs reduction	Positive effect
	Dolz et al. (2019)	Ambidexterity Upper echelon view	Ability favors ambidexterity while willingness is restricted in a context of restrictions	Negative effect
	Stubner et al. (2012)	Ambidexterity	Power concentration facilitates decision making	Positive effect
	Hiebl (2015)	Agency theory	Different degrees of family involvement in ownership and management produces different levels of ambidexterity	(Conceptual paper)
	Veider and Matzler (2016)	Agency theory RBV	Ownership and management give FFs the ability to decide and produce agency advantages and disadvantages	(Conceptual paper)
Long-term perspective	Stubner et al. (2012)	Ambidexterity	Long term focus benefits exploration and exploitation	Positive effect
Culture	Mazzelli et al. (2019)	Behavioral theory of the firm Ambidexterity	Social interactions, communication and shared experiences affect how organizations search for solutions	Different effects founded on exploration and on exploitation
	Veider and Matzler (2016)	Agency theory Resource Based View SEW	The commitment of the family and the convergence of different goals provide a distinctive behavior to FFs	(Conceptual paper)

Source: Own elaboration

Family and Nonfamily Members in the Council

García-Castro and Sharma (2011) considered it relevant to capture the presence of family in the management council. It provides the formal link between owners and managers responsible for the daily operations of the company. This is described as "the top of the company's decision control system" (Fama & Jensen, 1983, p. 311).

The council focuses on monitoring executives and providing resources and competencies to top management (Hillman & Dalziel, 2003). Monitoring involves observing, measuring, and evaluating the behaviors and decisions of managers, avoiding that they use their position for their own benefit (Tosi & Gómez-Mejía, 1989). In FFs, family can use the management council to strengthen their control over the company and pressure managers to pursue family goals. Muskataillo, Autio, and Zahra (2002) found that most board positions in FFs are held by family members or their representatives. Gersick et al. (1997) pointed to the small number of nonfamily council members in FFs.

Le Breton-Miller, Miller, and Lester (2011) argued that a greater presence of family in the council increases the propensity to prioritize family issues, including controlling the business by the family, having family occupy executive positions, and ensuring security for future generations (Bertrand & Schoar, 2006; Chrisman et al. 2005; Gómez-Mejía et al. 2011). In contrast, FFs that incorporate external members often use the council as a form of strategic development (Fiegener, 2005). When not subjected to the routine of daily operations, they can think more freely about strategic alternatives for the company (Forbes & Miliken, 1999). Their experiences in different contexts help to generate new expectations and ideas that increase cognitive diversity, provide multiple sources of data (e.g., about markets or competitors), and offer different perspectives of analysis and interpretation styles. This allows them, at a strategic level, to participate in decision making, identify new directions, discover opportunities for change, and provide information and advice during the process (Brunninge, Nordqvist, & Wilklund, 2007). In other words, they provide an ambidextrous orientation.

Generational Diversity

Generally, founders are more entrepreneurs than their successors. Therefore, they are more likely to be emotionally linked to the business. It would be expected that companies managed by their founders are more oriented toward organizational growth, risk taking, and exploration of opportunities (Zhara, 2005). They encourage the expansion of the company because it provides personal benefits of power and prestige. They often view the company as an extension of themselves (Carney, 2005). Thus, exploring opportunities can contribute to both personal and corporate growth (Miller, Le Breton-Miller, & Scholnick, 2008).

On the other hand, the literature links family management with risk aversion in the case of second and subsequent generations (Pérez-González, 2006). These are less emotionally linked. The business becomes more important to the detriment of the family, losing vision of continuity and placing greater interest in the short term. Generational diversity incorporates knowledge diversity to the company due to the different competences and perspectives generated by the generations (Chirico, Sirmon, Sciascia, & Mazzola, 2011; Milliken & Martins, 1996).

Generational diversity is positively related to entrepreneurial behavior, expanding the range of strategic options to be considered by the TMT and increasing the novelty of strategic decisions (Kellermans & Eddleston, 2006; Salvato, 2004). As a result, multigenerational family TMTs perceive more aspects, do it differently, and are more likely to propose alternative actions. These factors foster debate and encourages long-term thinking, giving the TMT the cognitive flexibility to improve decision making, execution, and ability to take advantage of opportunities (O'Reilly & Tushman, 2008). This attitude is essential to create new businesses, renew operations, recombine resources, and build organizational capabilities that improve the efficiency of the company by compensating for short- and long-term decisions, exploration, and exploitation.

Regarding next generation operations, CEOs tend to transmute into a superior capability as they aim to achieve a broader exploitation and a more narrow exploration. In contrast, the founding CEOs were more capable of performing both an exploration and exploitation search or ambidexterity search (Mazzelli et al. 2019).

Age and Experience

In the same line, the literature discusses other diversity types that affect organizational ambidexterity. Diversity in the age and experience of TMT managers is related to their ability to perceive changes and assume different levels of risk for responding to changes in the environment. Neither seniority nor age have been negatively related to the TMT's ability to take risks. This influences the orientation toward efficiency (the known) and the capability to accept uncertainty associated with the search for alternatives through risk. FFs are characterized by a greater homogeneity of points of view in decision-making processes when sharing common roots, values, and beliefs (Webb et al., 2010). This hinders the enrichment of the information they handle and the use of alternative points of view. Therefore, diversity in the TMT can be beneficial from a decision-making perspective (Minichilli et al., 2010; Nielsen, 2010).

Diversity in age in the TMT has been related to its capacity to assume greater risks. Decision-making processes include managers with different career horizons and degrees of commitment to new projects. Older age has been linked to risk aversion and the search for alternatives with short-term results (exploitative behavior). The incorporation of young people, as well as the increase in diversity in age, can promote the TMT to take advantage of opportunities related to the environment and demanding changes in the company. Some studies suggest the influence of heterogeneity in age on the search for more proactive behaviors and assumption of risks (Wiersema & Bantel, 1992).

Age diversity in the TMT can also be a negative source of conflict as it can affect the capacity to reach consensus and increase conflict between its members. However, in FFs, family identity and trust between family members reduce the possibility that affective conflict affects decision-making processes, allowing them to take advantage of the functional benefits of cognitive conflict (Webb et al., 2010). Diversity in experience or seniority in the company are associated with the wealth of information sources and breadth and variety of analysis. Wiersema and Bantel (1992) argued that similar teams in antiquity will have had the same process of socialization, sharing the same managerial experiences and problems. However, heterogeneous TMTs will provide varied sources of information. Therefore, the points of view and alternatives will increase, favoring the exploration of ideas and compensating the tendency for exploitation. Diversity in seniority will be reduced, resulting in group thinking (Milliken & Martins, 1996).

Diversity in TMT provides different perspectives and criteria (Gedajlovic et al., 2012). Ambidexterity requires divergent thinking to identify and evaluate exploration opportunities and convergent thinking to identify and evaluate exploitation opportunities (Lubatkin et al., 2006). This implies carrying out exhaustive environmental analysis processes to discover, identify, and evaluate multiple opportunities and alternatives. The difference in experiences derived from the diversity in seniority provides the wealth of points of view and criteria to identify and evaluate alternatives, favoring the presence of more comprehensive processes. Ambidexterity requires the ability to take risks, be proactive, and reconfigure resources with the ability to perceive changes and signals from the environment (Lubatkin et al., 2006; O'Reilly & Tushman, 2008).

FUTURE RESEARCH DIRECTIONS

This study theoretically analyzes antecedents of ambidexterity. Future research could empirically study how these antecedents interact to achieve ambidexterity. Furthermore, to deeply understand how each of the antecedents contribute to the success of ambidexterity, future research should explain how to minimize the outlined disadvantages. To this end, case studies of successful FFs can offer a more complete vision of their evolution and the promotion of their positive role.

CONCLUSION

After reviewing the literature on ambidexterity in FFs, this chapter outlines the specificities these firms to achieve ambidexterity.

The effect of family control on organizational ambidexterity is not univocal. It depends on the ability and willingness of these firms to engage in specific demeanors (Veider & Matzler, 2016). The corresponding ability originating from FFs serves as a prerequisite to arriving at organizational ambidexterity. Heterogeneity among this type of company will depend on their willingness to face family-induced challenges with actions to mitigate associated deficiencies (Veider & Matzler, 2016).

Veider and Matzler (2016) remarked on the importance of incorporating both the ability and willingness of family-controlled firms to achieve organizational ambidexterity. A firm's ability and willingness allow for an exploration of how family structure and behavior affect the innovation process and drive the heterogeneity of FFs in the context of organizational ambidexterity (Chrisman et al., 2015; Lumpkin & Brigham, 2011).

The family character aligns incentives of managers with owners by benefiting from both short- and long-term financial impacts of strategic decisions. The combination of ownership and management gives greater power to launch the necessary actions to implement changes in the company. This allows for exploiting opportunities and an incentive to survive to realize the long-term results (Gedajlovic et al., 2012; Miller & Le Breton-Miller, 2005). Excessive family concentration in ownership or presence in a management team could negatively affect the firm's performance due to a schism or altruism.

The family character provides the necessary discretion to make a strategic agenda and avoid other interested parts from changing their course. In addition, this character permits monitoring and correcting of deviations (Gedajlovic et al., 2004). These companies have managerial elites with greater power and faculties to carry out their strategic agendas. Being multitemporal allows them to take advantage of opportunities and reconfigure resources. The joint diversity of age and experience of the management team reinforces ambidexterity (Fernández-Mesa et al., 2013). As there is diversity within the management team or the council, difficulties could be generated to achieve consensus among members.

Long-term value in FFs depends on the ability to dynamically recombine resources to balance exploration and exploitation. These firms tend to participate in long periods of exploitation interrupted by radical strategic exploration (Salvato & Melin, 2008). Changes in strategy over time are facilitated in

FFs where managers have greater social capital with employees. This facilitates faster acceptance among those who will implement these strategic changes (Salvato & Melin, 2008). Lack of knowledge could cause uncertainty in the firm. Family culture is also an important antecedent to promote ambidextrous orientation. A series of essential values and goals should be shared when working to attain ambidexterity. Family culture also create ties between the firm and its members, producing an exchange of knowledge.

Therefore, the positive aspects of FFs outlined in theories such as SEW or Resource-based View, have also a positive effect on ambidexterity. There is growing evidence of ambidextrous implications in business performance with the singular abilities of FFs to balance exploration with exploitation. Nevertheless, more research is needed to analyze how to minimize the negative effects of agency costs that arose when nepotism or negative altruism appears. For example, the question of which governance conditions trigger ambidexterity in FFs need deeper understanding. Moreover, more research is also needed to analyze how different degrees of involvement and diversity can enhance or hinder the positive aspects.

Managing diversity and various degrees of family involvement in ownership and management requires specific governance mechanisms and family governance mechanisms to positively direct the ability and willingness in FFs to the achievement of ambidexterity.

Practitioners could benefit of knowing the importance of achieving ambidexterity. This study also outlines how the specificities of FFs have a positive effect on ambidexterity if they are conveniently directed towards a positive willingness to ambidexterity.

Furthermore, ambidexterity represents a promising organizational construct to better understand the differences between FFs (Lubatkin et al., 2006; Stubner et al., 2012), and managers can promote the positive aspects of FFs that allow ambidexterity and long-term competitiveness.

ACKNOWLEDGMENT

This work was supported by the National Plan for R&D of the Spanish Ministry of Economy, Industry and Competitiveness –State Research Agency and FEDER (ECO2016-76796-P), and the Fundació Caixa Castelló-Bancaixa in the context of the Universitat Jaume I Annual Research Plan (UJI-A2017-04).

REFERENCES

Allison, T. H., McKenny, A. F., & Short, J. C. (2014). Integrating time into family business research: Using random coefficient modelling to examine temporal influences on family firm ambidexterity. *Family Business Review*, *27*(1), 20–34. doi:10.1177/0894486513494782

Anderson, R. C., & Reeb, D. M. (2003). Founding-family ownership and firm performance: Evidence from the S&P 500. *The Journal of Finance*, *58*(3), 1301–1328. doi:10.1111/1540-6261.00567

Arregle, J. L., Hitt, M. A., Sirmon, D. G., & Very, P. (2007). The development of organizational social capital: Attributes of family firms. *Journal of Management Studies*, *44*(1), 73–95. doi:10.1111/j.1467-6486.2007.00665.x

Baron, J. N., Hannan, M. T., & Burton, M. D. (2001). Labor pains: Change in organizational models and employee turnover in young, high-tech firms. *American Journal of Sociology*, *106*(4), 960–1012. doi:10.1086/320296

Berrone, P., Cruz, C., & Gomez-Mejia, L. R. (2012). Socioemotional wealth in family firms: Theoretical dimensions, assessment approaches, and agenda for future research. *Family Business Review*, *25*(3), 258–279. doi:10.1177/0894486511435355

Bertrand, M., & Schoar, A. (2006). The role of family in family firms. *The Journal of Economic Perspectives*, *20*(2), 73–96. doi:10.1257/jep.20.2.73

Brunninge, O., Nordqvist, M., & Wiklund, J. (2007). Corporate governance and strategic change in SMEs: The effects of ownership, board composition and top management teams. *Small Business Economics*, *29*(3), 295–308. doi:10.100711187-006-9021-2

Cao, Q., Gedajlovic, E., & Zhang, H. (2009). Unpacking organizational ambidexterity: Dimensions, contingencies, and synergistic effects. *Organization Science*, *20*(4), 781–796. doi:10.1287/orsc.1090.0426

Carney, M. (2005). Corporate governance and competitive advantage in family-controlled firms. *Entrepreneurship Theory and Practice*, *29*(3), 249–265. doi:10.1111/j.1540-6520.2005.00081.x

Chirico, F., Sirmon, D. G., Sciascia, S., & Mazzola, P. (2011). Resource orchestration in family firms: Investigating how entrepreneurial orientation, generational involvement, and participative strategy affect performance. *Strategic Entrepreneurship Journal*, *5*(4), 307–326. doi:10.1002ej.121

Chrisman, J. J., Chua, J. H., De Massis, A., Frattini, F., & Wright, M. (2015). The ability and willingness paradox in family firm innovation. *Journal of Product Innovation Management*, *32*(3), 310–318. doi:10.1111/jpim.12207

Chrisman, J. J., Chua, J. H., Pearson, A. W., & Barnett, T. (2012). Family involvement, family influence, and family-centered non-economic goals in small firms. *Entrepreneurship Theory and Practice*, *36*(2), 267–293. doi:10.1111/j.1540-6520.2010.00407.x

Chrisman, J. J., Chua, J. H., & Sharma, P. (2005). Trends and directions in the development of a strategic management theory of the family firm. *Entrepreneurship Theory and Practice*, *29*(5), 555–575. doi:10.1111/j.1540-6520.2005.00098.x

Chrisman, J. J., Kellermanns, F. W., Chan, K. C., & Liano, K. (2010). Intellectual foundations of current research in family business: An identification and review of 25 influential articles. *Family Business Review*, *23*(1), 9–26. doi:10.1177/0894486509357920

Chua, J. H., Chrisman, J. J., & Sharma, P. (1999). Defining the family business by behavior. *Entrepreneurship Theory and Practice*, *23*(4), 19–39. doi:10.1177/104225879902300402

Chua, J. H., Chrisman, J. J., & Sharma, P. (2003). Succession and nonsuccession concerns of family firms and agency relationship with nonfamily managers. *Family Business Review*, *16*(2), 89–107. doi:10.1111/j.1741-6248.2003.00089.x

Chua, J. H., Chrisman, J. J., & Steier, L. P. (2003b). Extending the theoretical horizons of family business research. *Entrepreneurship Theory and Practice*, *27*(4), 331–338. doi:10.1111/1540-8520.00012

Corbetta, G., & Salvato, C. (2004). Self-serving or self-actualizing? Models of man and agency costs in different types of family firms: A commentary on "comparing the agency costs of family and non-family firms: Conceptual issues and exploratory evidence.". *Entrepreneurship Theory and Practice*, *28*(4), 355–362. doi:10.1111/j.1540-6520.2004.00050.x

Craig, J. B., & Moores, K. (2006). A 10-year longitudinal investigation of strategy, systems, and environment on innovation in family firms. *Family Business Review*, *19*(1), 1–10. doi:10.1111/j.1741-6248.2006.00056.x

De Massis, A., Frattini, F., & Lichtenthaler, U. (2013). Research on technological innovation in family firms: Present debates and future directions. *Family Business Review*, *26*(1), 10–31. doi:10.1177/0894486512466258

De Massis, A., Kotlar, J., Chua, J. H., & Chrisman, J. J. (2014). Ability and willingness as sufficiency conditions for family-oriented particularistic behavior: Implications for theory and empirical studies. *Journal of Small Business Management*, *52*(2), 344–364. doi:10.1111/jsbm.12102

Dolz, C., Iborra, M., & Safón, V. (2015). Empresa familiar, equipos directivos, diversidad y ambidiestría en las Pymes. *Revista de Administração de Empresas*, *55*(6), 673–687. doi:10.1590/S0034-759020150606

Dolz, C., Iborra, M., & Safón, V. (2019). Improving the likelihood of SME survival during financial and economic crises: The importance of TMTs and family ownership for ambidexterity. *BRQ Business Research Quarterly*, *22*(2), 119–136. doi:10.1016/j.brq.2018.09.004

Duncan, R. B. (1976). The ambidextrous organization: Designing dual structures for innovation. *The Management of Organization*, *1*(1), 167-188.

Eisenhardt, K. M., & Martin, J. A. (2000). Dynamic capabilities: What are they? *Strategic Management Journal*, *21*(10-11), 1105–1121. doi:10.1002/1097-0266(200010/11)21:10/11<1105::AID-SMJ133>3.0.CO;2-E

Fama, E. F., & Jensen, M. C. (1983). Separation of ownership and control. *The Journal of Law & Economics*, *26*(2), 301–325. doi:10.1086/467037

Fernández-Mesa, A., Iborra, M., & Safón, V. (2013). CEO-TMT interaction: Do tenure and age affect ambidexterity dynamism? *European Journal of International Management*, *7*(1), 31–55. doi:10.1504/EJIM.2013.052098

Fiegener, M. K. (2005). Determinants of board participation in the strategic decisions of small corporations. *Entrepreneurship Theory and Practice*, *29*(5), 627–650. doi:10.1111/j.1540-6520.2005.00101.x

Forbes, D. P., & Milliken, F. J. (1999). Cognition and corporate governance: Understanding boards of directors as strategic decision-making groups. *Academy of Management Review*, *24*(3), 489–505. doi:10.5465/amr.1999.2202133

García-Castro, R. G., & Sharma, P. (2011). Family involvement-firm performance link: Winning configurations revealed by set-theoretic methods. *Universia Business Review*, (32): 54–69.

Gedajlovic, E., Cao, Q., & Zhang, H. (2012). Corporate shareholdings and organizational ambidexterity in high-tech SMEs: Evidence form a transitional economy. *Journal of Business Venturing*, *27*(6), 652–665. doi:10.1016/j.jbusvent.2011.06.001

Gedajlovic, E., Lubatkin, M. H., & Schulze, W. S. (2004). Crossing the threshold from founder management to professional management: A governance perspective. *Journal of Management Studies*, *41*(5), 899–912. doi:10.1111/j.1467-6486.2004.00459.x

Gersick, K., Davis, J., Hampton, M., & Lansberg, I. (1997). *Generation to generation: Life cycles of the family business*. Harvard Business Press.

Gibson, C. B., & Birkinshaw, J. (2004). The antecedents, consequences, and mediating role of organizational ambidexterity. *Academy of Management Journal*, *47*(2), 209–226.

Goel, S., & Jones, R. J. III. (2016). Entrepreneurial exploration and exploitation in family business: A systematic review and future directions. *Family Business Review*, *29*(1), 94–120. doi:10.1177/0894486515625541

Gómez-Mejía, L. R., Cruz, C., Berrone, P., & De Castro, J. (2011). The bind that ties: Socioemotional wealth preservation in family firms. *The Academy of Management Annals*, *5*(1), 653–707. doi:10.1080/19416520.2011.593320

Gómez-Mejía, L. R., Núñez-Nickel, M., & Gutierrez, I. (2001). The role of family ties in agency contracts. *Academy of Management Journal*, *44*(1), 81–95.

Gupta, A. K., Smith, K. G., & Shalley, C. E. (2006). The interplay between exploration and exploitation. *Academy of Management Journal*, *49*(4), 693–706. doi:10.5465/amj.2006.22083026

Habbershon, T. G., Williams, M., & MacMillan, I. C. (2003). A unified systems perspective of family firm performance. *Journal of Business Venturing*, *18*(4), 451–465. doi:10.1016/S0883-9026(03)00053-3

Habbershon, T. G., & Williams, M. L. (1999). A resource-based framework for assessing the strategic advantages of family firms. *Family Business Review*, *12*(1), 1–25. doi:10.1111/j.1741-6248.1999.00001.x

He, Z. L., & Wong, P. K. (2004). Exploration vs. exploitation: An empirical test of the ambidexterity hypothesis. *Organization Science*, *15*(4), 481–494. doi:10.1287/orsc.1040.0078

Heavy, C., & Simsek, Z. (2010). A dynamic capabilities model of organizational ambidexterity. *10th European Academy of Management Annual Conference*.

Hiebl, M. R. (2015). Family involvement and organizational ambidexterity in later-generation family businesses: A framework for further investigation. *Management Decision*, *53*(5), 1061–1082. doi:10.1108/MD-04-2014-0191

Hillman, A. J., & Dalziel, T. (2003). Boards of directors and firm performance: Integrating agency and resource dependence perspectives. *Academy of Management Review*, *28*(3), 383–396. doi:10.5465/amr.2003.10196729

Hughes, M., Filser, M., Harms, R., Kraus, S., Chang, M. L., & Cheng, C. F. (2018). Family firm configurations for high performance: The role of entrepreneurship and ambidexterity. *British Journal of Management, 29*(4), 595–612. doi:10.1111/1467-8551.12263

Jensen, M. C., & Meckling, W. H. (1976). Theory of the firm: Managerial behavior, agency costs and ownership structure. *Journal of Financial Economics, 3*(4), 305–360. doi:10.1016/0304-405X(76)90026-X

Kellermanns, F. W., & Eddleston, K. A. (2006). Corporate entrepreneurship in family firms: A family perspective. *Entrepreneurship Theory and Practice, 30*(6), 809–830. doi:10.1111/j.1540-6520.2006.00153.x

Ketchen, D. J. Jr, Thomas, J. B., & Snow, C. C. (1993). Organizational configurations and performance: A comparison of theoretical approaches. *Academy of Management Journal, 36*(6), 1278–1313.

Klein, S. B., Astrachan, J. H., & Smyrnios, K. X. (2005). The F-PEC scale of family influence: Construction, validation, and further implication for theory. *Entrepreneurship Theory and Practice, 29*(3), 321–339. doi:10.1111/j.1540-6520.2005.00086.x

Le Breton–Miller, I., & Miller, D. (2006). Why do some family businesses out–compete? Governance, long–term orientations, and sustainable capability. *Entrepreneurship Theory and Practice, 30*(6), 731–746. doi:10.1111/j.1540-6520.2006.00147.x

Le Breton-Miller, I., & Miller, D. (2011). Commentary: Family firms and the advantage of multitemporality. *Entrepreneurship Theory and Practice, 35*(6), 1171–1177. doi:10.1111/j.1540-6520.2011.00496.x

Le Breton–Miller, I., & Miller, D. (2015). Article Commentary: The Arts and Family Business: Linking Family Business Resources and Performance to Industry Characteristics. *Entrepreneurship Theory and Practice, 39*(6), 1349–1370. doi:10.1111/etap.12177

Le Breton-Miller, I., Miller, D., & Lester, R. H. (2011). Stewardship or agency? A social embeddedness reconciliation of conduct and performance in public family businesses. *Organization Science, 22*(3), 704–721. doi:10.1287/orsc.1100.0541

Li, J., & Hambrick, D. C. (2005). Factional groups: A new vantage on demographic faultlines, conflict, and disintegration in work teams. *Academy of Management Journal, 48*(5), 794–813. doi:10.5465/amj.2005.18803923

Lubatkin, M. H., Durand, R., & Ling, Y. (2007). The missing lens in family firm governance theory: A self-other typology of parental altruism. *Journal of Business Research, 60*(10), 1022–1029. doi:10.1016/j.jbusres.2006.12.019

Lubatkin, M. H., Schulze, W. S., Ling, Y., & Dino, R. N. (2005). The effects of parental altruism on the governance of family-managed firms. *Journal of Organizational Behavior: The International Journal of Industrial. Occupational and Organizational Psychology and Behavior, 26*(3), 313–330. doi:10.1002/job.307

Lubatkin, M. H., Simsek, Z., Ling, Y., & Veiga, J. F. (2006). Ambidexterity and performance in small- to medium-sized firms: The pivotal role of top management team behavioral integration. *Journal of Management, 32*(5), 646–672. doi:10.1177/0149206306290712

Lumpkin, G. T., & Brigham, K. H. (2011). Long-term orientation and intertemporal choice in family firms. *Entrepreneurship Theory and Practice*, *35*(6), 1149–1169. doi:10.1111/j.1540-6520.2011.00495.x

Lumpkin, G. T., Brigham, K. H., & Moss, T. W. (2010). Long-term orientation: Implications for the entrepreneurial orientation and performance of family businesses. *Entrepreneurship and Regional Development*, *22*(3-4), 241–264. doi:10.1080/08985621003726218

March, J. G. (1991). Exploration and exploitation in organizational learning. *Organization Science*, *2*(1), 71–87. doi:10.1287/orsc.2.1.71

Mazzelli, A., De Massis, A., Petruzzelli, A. M., Del Giudice, M., & Khan, Z. (in press). Behind ambidextrous search: The microfoundations of search in family and non-family firms. *Long Range Planning*.

Miller, D., & Le Breton-Miller, I. (2005). Management insights from great and struggling family business. *Long Range Planning*, *38*(6), 517–530. doi:10.1016/j.lrp.2005.09.001

Miller, D., Le Breton-Miller, I., & Scholnick, B. (2008). Stewards vs. stagnation: An empirical comparison of small family and non-family businesses. *Journal of Management Studies*, *45*(1), 51–78. doi:10.1017/S0021875807004379

Milliken, F., & Martins, L. L. (1996). Searching for common threads: Understanding the multiple effects of diversity in organizational groups. *Academy of Management Review*, *21*(2), 402–433. doi:10.5465/amr.1996.9605060217

Minichilli, A., Corbetta, G., & MacMillan, I. C. (2010). Top management teams in family-controlled companies: 'Familiness', 'Faultiness', and their impact on financial performance. *Journal of Management Studies*, *47*(2), 205–222. doi:10.1111/j.1467-6486.2009.00888.x

Moss, T. W., Payne, G. T., & Moore, C. B. (2014). Strategic consistency of exploration and exploitation in family businesses. *Family Business Review*, *27*(1), 51–71. doi:10.1177/0894486513504434

Muskataillo, M., Autio, E., & Zahra, S. A. (2002). Relational and contractual governance in family firms: Effects on strategic decision making. *Family Business Review*, *15*(3), 205–222. doi:10.1111/j.1741-6248.2002.00205.x

Nielsen, S. (2010). Top management team diversity: A review of theories and methodologies. *International Journal of Management Reviews*, *12*(3), 301–316.

O'Reilly, C. A. III, & Tushman, M. L. (2008). Ambidexterity as a dynamic capability: Resolving the innovator's dilemma. *Research in Organizational Behavior*, *28*, 185–206. doi:10.1016/j.riob.2008.06.002

O'Reilly, C. A. III, & Tushman, M. L. (2011). Organizational ambidexterity in action: How managers explore and exploit. *California Management Review*, *53*(4), 5–22. doi:10.1525/cmr.2011.53.4.5

O'Reilly, C. A. III, & Tushman, M. L. (2013). Organizational ambidexterity: Past, present, and future. *The Academy of Management Perspectives*, *27*(4), 324–338. doi:10.5465/amp.2013.0025

Patel, P. C., & Fiet, J. O. (2011). Knowledge combination and the potential advantages of family firms in searching for opportunities. *Entrepreneurship Theory and Practice*, *35*(6), 1179–1197. doi:10.1111/j.1540-6520.2011.00497.x

Pearson, A. W., Carr, J. C., & Shaw, J. C. (2008). Toward a theory of Familiness: A social capital perspective. *Entrepreneurship Theory and Practice*, *32*(6), 949–969. doi:10.1111/j.1540-6520.2008.00265.x

Pérez-González, F. (2006). Inherited control and firm performance. *The American Economic Review*, *96*(5), 1559–1588. doi:10.1257/aer.96.5.1559

Raisch, S., Birkinshaw, J., Probst, G., & Tushman, M. L. (2009). Organizational ambidexterity: Balancing exploitation and exploration for sustained performance. *Organization Science*, *20*(4), 685–695. doi:10.1287/orsc.1090.0428

Salvato, C. (2004). Predictors of entrepreneurship in family firms. *Journal of Private Equity*, *7*(3), 68–76. doi:10.3905/jpe.2004.412339

Salvato, C., & Melin, L. (2008). Creating value across generations in family-controlled businesses: The role of family social capital. *Family Business Review*, *21*(3), 259–276. doi:10.1177/08944865080210030107

Sardeshmukh, S. R., & Corbett, A. C. (2011). The duality of internal and external development of successors: Opportunity recognition in family firms. *Family Business Review*, *24*(2), 111–125. doi:10.1177/0894486510391783

Schulze, W. S., & Gedajlovic, E. R. (2010). Whither family business? *Journal of Management Studies*, *47*(2), 191–204. doi:10.1111/j.1467-6486.2009.00887.x

Schulze, W. S., Lubatkin, M. H., & Dino, R. N. (2002). Altruism, agency and the competitiveness of family firms. *Managerial and Decision Economics*, *23*(4-5), 247–259. doi:10.1002/mde.1064

Schulze, W. S., Lubatkin, M. H., & Dino, R. N. (2003). Exploring the agency consequences of ownership dispersion among the directors of private family firms. *Academy of Management Journal*, *46*(2), 179–194.

Schulze, W. S., Lubatkin, M. H., Dino, R. N., & Buchholtz, A. K. (2001). Agency relationships in family firms: Theory and evidence. *Organization Science*, *12*(2), 99–116. doi:10.1287/orsc.12.2.99.10114

Sciascia, S., Mazzola, P., & Chirico, F. (2013). Generational involvement in the top management team of family firms: Exploring nonlinear effects on entrepreneurial orientation. *Entrepreneurship Theory and Practice*, *37*(1), 69–85. doi:10.1111/j.1540-6520.2012.00528.x

Sharma, P. (2008). Commentary: Familiness: Capital stocks and flows between family and business. *Entrepreneurship Theory and Practice*, *32*(6), 971–977. doi:10.1111/j.1540-6520.2008.00266.x

Sharma, P., & Irving, P. G. (2005). Four bases of family business successor commitment: Antecedents and consequences. *Entrepreneurship Theory and Practice*, *29*(1), 13–33. doi:10.1111/j.1540-6520.2005.00067.x

Shleifer, A., & Vishny, R. W. (1986). Large shareholders and corporate control. *Journal of Political Economy*, *94*(3, Part 1), 461–488. doi:10.1086/261385

Siggelkow, N. (2002). Evolution toward fit. *Administrative Science Quarterly*, *47*(1), 125–159. doi:10.2307/3094893

Simsek, Z. (2009). Organizational ambidexterity: Towards a multilevel understanding. *Journal of Management Studies*, *46*(4), 597–624. doi:10.1111/j.1467-6486.2009.00828.x

Stein, J. C. (1989). Efficient capital markets, inefficient firms: A model of myopic corporate behavior. *The Quarterly Journal of Economics*, *104*(4), 655–669. doi:10.2307/2937861

Stubner, S., Blarr, W. H., Brands, C., & Wulf, T. (2012). Organizational ambidexterity and family firm performance. *Journal of Small Business and Entrepreneurship*, *25*(2), 217–229. doi:10.1080/08276331.2012.10593570

Tagiuri, R., & Davis, J. (1996). Bivalent attributes of the family firm. *Family Business Review*, *9*(2), 199–208. doi:10.1111/j.1741-6248.1996.00199.x

Tanewski, G. A., Prajogo, D., & Sohal, A. (2003, January). Strategic orientation and innovation performance between family and non-family firms. In *ICSB 2003: 48th World Conference Proceedings* (pp. 1-22). International Council for Small Business.

Taylor, A., & Greve, H. R. (2006). Superman or the fantastic four? Knowledge combination and experience in innovative teams. *Academy of Management Journal*, *49*(4), 723–740. doi:10.5465/amj.2006.22083029

Teece, D. J. (2006). Reflections on "profiting from innovation". *Research Policy*, *35*(8), 1131–1146. doi:10.1016/j.respol.2006.09.009

Teece, D. J., Pisano, G., & Shuen, A. (1997). Dynamic capabilities and strategic management. *Strategic Management Journal*, *18*(7), 509–533. doi:10.1002/(SICI)1097-0266(199708)18:7<509::AID-SMJ882>3.0.CO;2-Z

Tokarczyk, J., Hansen, E., Green, M., & Down, J. (2007). A resource-based view and market orientation theory examination of the role of "familiness" in family business success. *Family Business Review*, *20*(1), 17–31. doi:10.1111/j.1741-6248.2007.00081.x

Tosi, H. L., & Gómez-Mejía, L. R. (1989). The decoupling of CEO pay and performance: An agency theory perspective. *Administrative Science Quarterly*, *34*(2), 169–189. doi:10.2307/2989894

Tushman, M. L., & O'Reilly, C. A. III. (1996). Ambidextrous organizations: Managing evolutionary and revolutionary change. *California Management Review*, *38*(4), 8–29. doi:10.2307/41165852

Veider, V., & Matzler, K. (2016). The ability and willingness of family-controlled firms to arrive at organizational ambidexterity. *Journal of Family Business Strategy*, *7*(2), 105–116. doi:10.1016/j.jfbs.2015.10.001

Ward, J. L. (1987). *Keeping the family business healthy: How to plan for continuing growth, profitability and family leadership*. San Francisco, CA: Jossey-Bass.

Webb, J. W., Ketchen, D. J. Jr, & Ireland, R. D. (2010). Strategic entrepreneurship within family-controlled firms: Opportunities and challenges. *Journal of Family Business Strategy*, *1*(2), 67–77. doi:10.1016/j.jfbs.2010.04.002

Wiersema, M., & Bantel, K. (1992). Top management team demography and corporate strategic change. *Academy of Management Journal*, *35*(1), 91–121.

Yu, A., Lumpkin, G. T., Sorenson, R. L., & Brigham, K. H. (2012). The landscape of family business outcomes: A summary and numerical taxonomy of dependent variables. *Family Business Review*, *25*(1), 33–57. doi:10.1177/0894486511430329

Zahra, S. A. (2005). Entrepreneurial risk taking in family firms. *Family Business Review*, *18*(1), 23–40. doi:10.1111/j.1741-6248.2005.00028.x

ADDITIONAL READING

Chrisman, J. J., Sharma, P., & Taggar, S. (2007). Family influences on firms: An introduction. *Journal of Business Research*, *60*(10), 1005–1011. doi:10.1016/j.jbusres.2007.02.016

Escribá-Esteve, A., Sánchez-Peinado, L., & Sánchez-Peinado, E. (2008). The influence of top management teams in the strategic orientation and performance of small and medium-sized enterprises. *British Journal of Management*, *20*(4), 581–597. doi:10.1111/j.1467-8551.2008.00606.x

Miller, D., & Le Breton-Miller, I. (2006a). Family governance and firm performance: Agency, stewardship, and capabilities. *Family Business Review*, *19*(1), 73–87. doi:10.1111/j.1741-6248.2006.00063.x

Miller, D., & Le Breton-Miller, I. (2006b). The best of both worlds: Exploitation and exploration in successful family businesses. In *Ecology and Strategy* (pp. 215–240). Bingley: Emerald Group Publishing Limited. doi:10.1016/S0742-3322(06)23007-9

Sharma, P. (2004). An overview of the field of family business studies: Current status and directions for the future. *Family Business Review*, *17*(1), 1–36. doi:10.1111/j.1741-6248.2004.00001.x

Sharma, P., Chrisman, J. J., & Chua, J. H. (1996). *A review and annotated bibliography of family business studies*. Boston: M.A. Kluwer Academic. doi:10.1007/978-1-4419-8768-6

Sharma, P., & Salvato, C. (2011). Commentary: Exploiting and exploring new opportunities over life cycle stages of family firms. *Entrepreneurship Theory and Practice*, *35*(6), 1199–1205. doi:10.1111/j.1540-6520.2011.00498.x

Zellweger, T., & Sieger, P. (2012). Entrepreneurial orientation in long-lived family firms. *Small Business Economics*, *38*(1), 67–84. doi:10.100711187-010-9267-6

KEY TERMS AND DEFINITIONS

Ambidexterity: Ambidexterity is the firm capability to simultaneously excel in both, exploration and exploitation finding the appropriate way of balancing the trade-offs that arose in his management.

Diversity: Diversity refers to different characteristics that integrate a variety in the participation in management, ownership or employment in a family firms, for example regarding diversity in family generations in the firms.

Exploitation: Exploitation defines the firm capability of improving practices, processes, tools or techniques that allow firm the application or improvement of previous existing knowledge.

Exploration: Exploration defines the firm capability of searching and experimenting with new practices, processes, tools or techniques that integrate new knowledge.

Family Firm Ability and Willingness: The family possibility in influencing the firm decisions and actions.

Ownership: Ownership in family firms refer to the degree in which family members has property rights of the firm.

Section 2

Family Firm and Competitiveness

Chapter 4
The Accumulation of Distinctive Competences in Family Firms

César Camisón
University of Valencia, Spain

Alba Puig-Denia
Jaume I University, Spain

ABSTRACT

Taking as its basis the resource- and capability-based view of the firm, this study provides an in-depth exploration of the ability of the family tourism firm to accumulate and develop the distinctive competences that are key to its success. Specifically, the analysis centres on how the family tourism firm acquires distinctive competences through the development of managerial capabilities. Using structural equation modelling (SEM), the empirical analysis focuses on a sample of 1,019 Spanish tourism firms. The results of the study suggest that family businesses face certain problems in accumulating distinctive competences. Moreover, the study indicates that such problems are due in part to the difficulties of developing efficient managerial capabilities in this type of company, which is an obstacle to the accumulation and management of other distinctive competences.

INTRODUCTION

In recent decades, there has been unprecedented growth in world tourism demand, fuelled by the population explosion and the rise in global income (Pedreño & Ramón, 2009). In Spain, tourism is one of the main drivers of growth in the economy, and it is a key sector in terms of its contribution to GDP and employment (Vera & Marchena, 1996; Larrinaga & Vallejo, 2013; Cuadrado Roura & López Morales; 2015). Certain characteristics of many tourist activities facilitate the entry and growth of family firms in this sector. As such, the tourism sector in Spain has traditionally been dominated by this type of company (Camisón, Forés & Puig-Denia, 2016). This sector offers a wide range of opportunities for family firms; the small size of various tourism businesses (cafés, bars, restaurants, etc.) along with the link between tourism and certain preferences in terms of leisure, lifestyle or location (Ateljevic & Doorne,

DOI: 10.4018/978-1-7998-1655-3.ch004

2000; Getz & Carlsen, 2000) make this an appealing sector for setting up a family business. In addition, the tourism sector is conducive to host-guest interactions in the family property (Getz & Carlsen, 2005); moreover, the families from the family firms can even form part of the tourist experience (Wanhill, 1997, 2000), thereby enhancing the value of the service. Despite the important role played by family firms in the Spanish tourism sector, family control of firms has only been studied incidentally in the context of tourism (Andersson, Carlsen & Getz, 2002; Getz & Carlsen, 2005); hence the interest and relevance of analysing it within this sector.

The characteristic features of family firms set them apart from non-family firms and shape their strategic and competitive behaviour (Esparza et al., 2009). Some authors suggest that these family-firm-specific characteristics make them unique (Tokarczyk et al., 2007) and rich in intangible resources (Habbershon & Williams, 1999). The family/business combination fosters the creation of relationships and elements that are unique to each company. In turn, these enable the development of intangible capabilities and resources that would be unthinkable in another type of organization and, in many cases, practically impossible to measure or quantify. Most of the studies that analyse these specific features of the family firm are based on the concept of "familiness" (Habbershon & Williams, 1999). Inspired by the resource-based view (RBV), such studies hold that familiness is a key concept to consider in the analysis of the relationship between the competitive advantages derived from a family firm's resources and capabilities, and its performance outcomes (Habbershon, Williams & MacMillan, 2003; Habbershon, 2006; Pearson, Carr & Shaw, 2008). Familiness refers to the unique set of resources and capabilities that a family business develops through the interaction of different systems: the family as a whole, the individual family members, and the business. In this regard, previous studies focusing on the concept of familiness highlight how the elements born of the nexus between family and business represent a source of advantage that influences family firms' success.

However, this subject has attracted a good deal of controversy, as not all the resources and capabilities generated by the interaction of these two systems have a direct or even a positive impact on the development and maintenance of a competitive advantage that genuinely influences the success of the company. In fact, they may even be an obstacle at times. That is, although a firm may have certain unique elements due to its status as a family business, these do not necessarily contribute positively and significantly to its competitiveness or organizational performance. Rather, the combination of family and business involves a myriad of distinctive characteristics; while some of these may have a positive impact, others can have a negative effect on the company. Indeed, while some authors argue that family businesses are rich in intangible resources, and that the characteristics specific to this type of company make them unique, inimitable entities and can thus be a source of competitive advantage (e.g., Habbershon & Williams, 1999, 2000; Cabrera et al., 2001; Habbershon et al., 2003, Hoffman et al., 2006; Eddleston et al., 2008), it is practically impossible to determine whether the unique set of resources generated internally due to the family nature of the firm will overall be an advantage or a disadvantage.

Taking that into consideration, it may be worth focusing on elements that the literature highlights as key to achieving a competitive advantage, regardless of whether or not the company is family-owned: distinctive competences. Distinctive competences have been held up as the most important determinants of business competitiveness (Barney, 1991, 1997; Amit & Schoemaker, 1993; Peteraf, 1993; Barney et al., 2001). Despite the complementarity and interrelationships between external and internal aspects, the only ones that the company can to some extent control are the internal elements. In this regard, the RBV (Barney, 1991; 1997, Amit & Schoemaker, 1993; Peteraf, 1993; Barney et al., 2001) emphasizes that the roots of competitive advantage lie in the acquisition and maintenance of an organization's core competences. A firm enjoys a sustainable competitive advantage when it implements a value-creation strategy that is not developed simultaneously by any current or potential competitor and when the firm's competitors are unable to replicate the advantage based on said strategy (Barney, 1991).

Despite the important role played by a family firm's core competences in its competitiveness, this subject has not been explored in great depth. Moreover, there are very few studies that analyse how the family nature of a business affects the accumulation and development of these competences. Bearing in mind that family firms make up a substantial share of the economy in all countries, and that a large number of companies throughout the world are run by families (Cucculelli & Micucci, 2008, Bigliardi & Dormio, 2009), it is interesting to analyse how being a family business affects the achievement of these competences. Such an analysis would help us to understand the real internal drivers of the competitiveness of the family firm. Therefore, ***the first objective of this chapter is to explore the ability of family firms to create and develop key distinctive competences.***

On the other hand, in order to manage and foster the development of their distinctive competences, firms need other capabilities; namely, managerial capabilities. Managerial resources are crucial for the generation and maintenance of business success (e.g., Penrose, 1959; Child, 1972; Katz, 1974; Anderson & Paine, 1975; Hambrick & Mason, 1984; Andrews, 1987; Castanias & Helfat, 1991, 2001; Lado & Wilson, 1994; Pickett, 1998; Landeta et al., 2007). Managers must have the skills to understand, describe and evaluate the potential that the company's resources and capabilities offer for driving economic performance (Martínez et al., 2010). In fact, there is strong empirical evidence for the positive influence of managerial capabilities on business performance (Hitt & Ireland, 1985; Finkelstein & Hambrick, 1990; Thomas, Clark & Gioia, 1993; Markides & Williamson, 1994; Robins & Wiersema, 1995; Mehra, 1996; Russo & Fouts, 1997; Boeker, 1997; Carmeli, 2001, Lerner & Almor, 2002; Acquaah, 2003; Kor, 2003; Carmeil & Tishler, 2006). In this respect, managerial capabilities are essential for the appropriate management of the organization as well as for the proper development and use of its other competences (Lado & Wilson, 1994; Mahoney, 1995; Martínez et al., 2010). They provide the foundations on which the rest of the competences can be developed (Lado & Wilson, 1994). Thus, ***the second objective of this chapter is to analyse family firms' ability to achieve suitable managerial capabilities, which in turn allow them to create and develop key distinctive competences.***

Therefore, in light of the above ideas, and based on the RBV, this study explores family firms' ability to accumulate and develop key distinctive competences that are critical to their success. Specifically, this study analyses how being a family business affects the accumulation of distinctive competences, through the development of managerial capabilities. In order to test the proposed hypothesis, the present empirical study applies the structural equation modelling (SEM) method to a sample of 1,019 family tourism companies. The results of the study suggest that family firms face certain problems when accumulating distinctive competences, and that these problems are due, in part, to the difficulties this type of firm faces in developing efficient management capabilities. Indeed, it is shown that a lack of efficient management capabilities represents an obstacle to the creation, growth and management of the firm's other distinctive competences.

THEORETICAL FRAMEWORK

Distinctive Competences in the Family Firm

A Resource-and Capabilities-Based Approach and Distinctive Competences

A strategy perspective on competitiveness centres on explaining why certain companies are able to achieve a competitive advantage over other firms that are located in the same environment, industry, destination and that use the same strategy. This complex task requires an in-depth analysis of the company itself and the resources and capabilities it possesses. This approach underlines the fact that the responsibility for a firm's competitiveness ultimately lies with the firm itself. Thus, analyses of business competitiveness should primarily focus on the firms themselves and, only in a complementary way, on firms as an element of the markets or inhabitants of a certain environment.

Systematic observation of successful competitive companies has revealed that the key to their competitiveness is innovative capacity based on the accumulation of resources (mainly intangible) and, above all, capabilities that are difficult for their competitors to reproduce or imitate. The RBV (Barney, 1991, 1997; Amit & Schoemaker, 1993; Peteraf, 1993; Barney et al., 2001) is the most widely-applied theory for identifying the mechanisms underlying a firm's generation of competitive advantages.

While various perspectives have been applied to the analysis of the family business, including agency theory, stewardship theory, and the resource-based view (RBV) of the firm (Siebels & zu Knyphausen-Aufseß, 2012), the approach that will serve as the theoretical framework for this study is the RBV. This approach emphasizes that the roots of competitive advantage lie in an organization's acquisition and maintenance of core competences. A firm enjoys a sustainable competitive advantage when it implements a value-creation strategy that is not developed simultaneously by any current or potential competitor and when the firm's competitors are unable to replicate the advantage based on said strategy (Barney, 1991). This approach predicts the existence of significant and persistent differences in intra-industry competitive success due to firm-specific factors, which are even greater than inter-industrial differences (Schmalensee, 1985; Rumelt, 1991).

In this regard, it has been argued that the specific, internal characteristics of each company—that is, its distinctive competences—are the most important determinants of business competitiveness (Barney, 1991, 1997; Amit & Schoemaker, 1993; Peteraf, 1993; Barney et al., 2001). Some of the distinctive competences which are most relevant to competitiveness, and which because of their key role are analysed in this chapter, are the capabilities in innovation and technology; in human resources and organizational culture; in marketing; and in quality. Managerial capabilities are viewed as necessary for coordinating and managing the other distinctive competences, and will therefore be analysed separately. The following subsection analyses these distinctive competences.

The Generation of Distinctive Competences in the Family Firm

Generally speaking, the literature has shown that family and non-family firms possess different resources and capabilities, and generate or obtain them in a different way. For example, Sirmon & Hitt (2003) suggest that family and non-family firms differ in the way they evaluate, acquire, shed, bundle and leverage human capital, social capital, patient capital and survivability capital, along with the governance structure attribute. Similarly, Tokarczyk et al. (2007) state that family firms differ from non-family firms in terms of the deployment of available resources and capabilities, and how advantages are created and sustained. For this reason, the study of the generation of distinctive competences in family businesses merits special attention. These specific characteristics that shape their performance are primarily determined by the source of capital, the involvement of the family, the governance structure and ownership, and the management system. In addition, these distinctive features are determined by the existence of two different forces within the firm: the family and the business.

The combination of family and business leads to the creation of a series of firm-specific relationships and elements that enable the creation of intangible resources and capabilities that would be unthinkable in another type of organization. In many cases, these are practically impossible to measure or quantify: for example, the advice a parent gives to their child; the informal relationships derived from family contacts that can help expand the client base; closer relations with suppliers; or informal interactions between family members who share a common culture, which can lead to improved work efficiency (Basco, 2006). However, the mere existence of specific resources and capabilities derived from its family status will not necessarily represent an advantage for the firm. Indeed, they may sometimes become an obstacle. For this reason, the study of distinctive competences within the family firm is not entirely free of controversy; it is not easy to determine whether the resources and capabilities inherent to family firms represent advantages or disadvantages, or whether family firms have a greater or lesser ability to create competitive advantages than non-family firms do (Tokarczy et al., 2007).

In this regard, not all the elements that are unique to family firms necessarily contribute positively and significantly to competitiveness or organizational performance; moreover, most of these mechanisms are generated unconsciously, without the intention of creating and sustaining a competitive advantage. The combination of family and business leads to the emergence of multiple objectives; these may not always be aimed at improving the firm's performance or competitive position, but may instead be linked to the well-being of the family.

Thus, some authors argue that family businesses are rich in intangible resources and that their firm-specific factors make them unique, inimitable entities and can thus be a source of competitive advantage (e.g., Habbershon & Williams, 1999, 2000; Cabrera, Saá & Garcia, 2001; Habbershon et al., 2003; Hoffman, Hoelscher & Sorenson, 2006; Eddleston, Kellermanns & Sarathy, 2008). Similarly, characteristics such as long-term relationships (James, 1999), the intergenerational transfer of tacit knowledge (Cabrera et al., 2001) or the interactions between the family unit, the business unit and individual family members, create rare, complex and dynamic resources and capabilities (Habbershon, et al., 2003), which may give rise to competitive advantages for the family business (Basco, 2006). The term "familiness" has been used to describe the unique bundle of resources which can be used to establish a competitive advantage, and which family businesses have as a result of their specific systems, family interactions, individual family members and the business itself (Habbershon & Williams, 1999; Cabrera et al., 2001). Hoffman et al. (2006) argue that family capital is a rare, inimitable and irreplaceable resource for each family business. It provides the family firm with efficiencies that cannot be replicated by non-family firms, and can therefore be considered a strategic resource.

However, it is practically impossible to capture all the distinguishing features stemming from the business-family link, so it cannot be ascertained whether all the intangible resources generated within the family business are beneficial. Moreover, these resources and capabilities may not necessarily represent an advantage when it comes to competing against non-family firms or indeed other family firms. In short, as noted by Sharma et al. (1997), in strategic terms the family can act both as a resource and as a constraint; therefore, determining whether the family status of a firm is beneficial or harmful will largely depend on the specific characteristics of the family firm in question and/or on the objectives to be assessed. Therefore, we focus on the aspects that the literature has identified as relevant to the competitiveness of companies, both family and non-family; that is, their stock of resources and capabilities.

Despite the fact that most of the related literature holds these resources and capabilities as key to achieving a competitive advantage regardless of whether or not the company is family-owned, few studies have analysed in detail how being a family business influences their acquisition. Some studies emphasize that the differentiating characteristics of the family business may facilitate the development of certain types of capabilities (Ward, 1988, 1997; Levring & Moskowitz, 1993; Aronoff & Ward, 1995; Tagiuri & Davis, 1996; Pervin, 1997; Bannò & Sgobbi, 2016): for example, some authors argue that family firms tend to be more creative and devote more attention to R&D (Pervin, 1997; Ward, 1997); that family relationships generate more motivation and greater loyalty, improve confidence and enable more efficient communication (Tagiuri & Davis, 1996); that family firms have tend to have a reputation for greater reliability and lower transaction costs (Aronoff & Ward, 1995; Tagiuri & Davis, 1996); or that their employee-centred working environment inspires loyalty and thus leads to lower hiring and human resources costs (Ward, 1988; Levring & Moskowitz, 1993). Nevertheless, there is more support for arguments to the contrary, which hold that family businesses are inferior in terms of the resources and capabilities that determine competitiveness. In this study, we focus specifically on the capabilities in innovation and technology, human resources and organizational culture, marketing, and quality, all of which are discussed below.

Innovation and Technology Capabilities

As far as **innovation and technology capabilities** are concerned, a firm's technological know-how and its innovative capacity are considered to be among its most important resources (Galende, 2006); indeed, the ability to innovate is a critical source of competitive advantage (Galende & Suárez, 1998).

In the case of family businesses, some authors point out that family-firm characteristics shape their innovative behaviour (Bennedsen and Foss, 2015). The internal orientation that some authors point to as characteristic of the family firm entails conservative behaviour (Donckels & Frölich, 1991). As a result, many family businesses are resistant to change (Beckhard & Dyer, 1983; Ward, 1987; Vago, 2004), since they believe it may cause conflict, be expensive or simply that it is not necessary to modernize (Beckhard & Dyer, 1983; Handler, 1989; Stavrou, 1999). A willingness to change is linked to innovation (Karagozoglu & Brown, 1988), so the conservative behaviour of family firms can constrain the generation of capabilities in innovation and technology. Donckels & Fröhlich (1991) conclude that most family businesses believe innovation entails too much risk, and that both creativity and innovation are considered less important in family firms than in non-family firms. Family firms thus tend to be less innovative than non-family firms (e.g., Gómez-Mejía, Larrazar-Kintana & Makril, 2003; Kellermanns & Eddleston, 2006; Chin et al., 2009), which is why they tend to be less concerned with and to put less of an emphasis on innovation and technology-related aspects compared to non-family firms (Westhead, 1997).

In addition, family firms are ambivalent towards technology: they are interested in its potential benefits but are not sure that these will offer a competitive advantage (Andersen, 1997; Mariussen, Wheelock & Baines, 1997). In addition, Nieto et al. (2015) point out that family firms use fewer external sources of innovation such as technological collaborations. Equally, the desire of the family firm's owners to protect their socioemotional wealth (Gómez-Mejía, Haynes, Núñez-Nickel, Jacobson & Moyano-Fuentes, 2007) can dampen their willingness to participate in collaborative innovation projects (De Massis, Frattini &

Lichtenthaler, 2012; Nieto, Santamaria & Fernandez, 2015). In addition, some authors also point out that family firms usually invest less in R&D (Chen & Hsu, 2009; Munari Oriani & Hat, 2010; Chrisman & Patel, 2012; Block, 2012; Acosta-Prado, Longo-Somoza, & Lozano, 2017) and tend to have poorer innovation performance outcomes in terms of patents (Decker & Günther, 2017). As such, there is likely to be limited internal development of knowledge through R&D&I since innovative attitudes are not promoted internally. Furthermore, the acquisition and absorption of valuable external knowledge will also be difficult for family firms if they maintain a "closed" attitude towards the outside.

Human Resources and Organizational Culture Capabilities

Regarding **human resources and organizational culture capabilities**, RBV research underscores the importance of human resources to the organization (e.g., Wright, McMahan & McWilliams, 1994; Kamoche, 1996; Becker & Gerhart, 1996; Barney & Wright, 1998; Amit & Belcourt, 1999; Bayo & Merino, 2002; Aragon, Beard & Sanz, 2003; Landeta, Barrutia, Araujo & Hoyos, 2007). Both human resources and organizational culture are among the most difficult elements to imitate or replicate; therefore capabilities that enable their efficient management are vital in order to transform them into core elements that generate sustainable competitive advantages.

Family firms are characterized as having a greater concern for their employees (Ward, 1988), which may also result in their employees showing greater commitment to the company. Moreover, if we consider that maintaining the independence of the family and the internal orientation of this type of company makes them more likely to hire family members as employees, the feeling of belonging to and collaboration with the company is likely to be even stronger. At the same time, however, these features can be dangerous.

While the owners of the family firm may prefer to hire family members (Barach, Ganitsky, Carson & Doochin., 1988; Dyer & Handler, 1994; Cromie, Stevenson & Montieth, 1995), bringing family members in as employees can be a double-edged sword. The resulting dual nature of the relationships (family and business) increases the complexity of the company's human resources and creates a unique human capital context that can be both positive and negative (Sirmon & Hitt, 2003). Thus, despite the fact that such employees may feel a greater sense of belonging and a stronger commitment to the company (Donnelley, 1964; Horton, 1986), studies reveal a degree of controversy regarding the appropriateness of hiring family members as employees. Arguments against are based on the results of studies on topics such as family employees' productivity, or their pay and bonuses (Rosenblatt, DeMik, Anderson & Johnson, 1985; Kirchhoff & Kirchhoff, 1987; Heck & Walker, 1993; Dunn, 1995). Family ties can also lead to other problems: for example, conflicts within the family may transfer over into the business; it is more difficult to get rid of unwanted employees as feelings are involved; or there may be conflicts with other, non-family employees if they feel they are being treated differently. Also, family firms often use more informal human resources mechanisms, based on trust and personal relationships (Basco & Perez Rodriguez, 2009).

With regard to staff qualifications, many family businesses do not emphasize experience and training (Fiegener, Brown, Prince & File, 1996), such that the hiring and promotion of staff tends to be based more on sentimental reasons or family membership than on suitability for the position. The lack of trust in the abilities of non-family staff along with the desire to maintain family control and power (Hayward, 1992) can also result in the family-owners choosing managers on the basis of their family ties instead of their specific skills, knowledge or competence (Westhead, 1997). Thus, the staff and mangers of this type of firm are often not very highly qualified due to the propensity to employ family members—especially in managerial positions—even if they do not have sufficient training or experience.

Marketing Capabilities

Marketing capabilities are also highly relevant to the organization, as shown by a number of authors who have found a positive effect of the possession of marketing resources and capabilities on performance (e.g., Hunt & Morgan, 1995; Vorhies, Harker & Rao, 1999; Dutta, Narasimhan & Rajiv, 1999; Hooley, Greenley, Cadogan & Fahy, 2005; Milfelner, Gabrijan & Snoj, 2008). Marketing academics have adopted the RBV to analyse the effects of marketing on performance and the creation of competitive advantage (e.g., Webster, 1992; Day, 1994; Hooley, Broderick & Möller, 1998; Srivastava, Shervani & Fahey, 1998, 1999; Hunt, 2000), acting as a link between the RBV and marketing concepts such as value to the customer, the marketing resources capable of generating sustainable competitive advantages or competitive positioning (Martínez, Charterina & Araujo, 2010). Aspects such as brand reputation, client relations or market orientation play a role in creating and sustaining a competitive advantage (Martínez et al., 2010).

While some recent studies have shown the importance of marketing capabilities for family firms (e.g., Pérez-Cabañero, González-Cruz & Cruz-Ros, 2012), in general, this type of capability has not been widely explored within the context of the family business.

In family firms, the family and the business are so interwoven that their identities merge into one (Kabbach De Castro, Aguilera & Crespí-Cladera, 2017). The family name often engenders a sense of credibility and trust, so many companies use it directly to differentiate themselves and champion their products and services (Bradburd & Ross, 1989). However, simply using the family name as a brand requires the backing of years of reputation or an appropriate communications strategy, as well as a wide range of quality products/services, which in turn requires a major effort on the part of the company management.

Furthermore, Westhead (1997) found that family firms tend to be much less likely to use product/service differentiation advertising techniques in comparison with non-family firms. Miller, McLeod & Oh (2001) claim that the most problematic area in family businesses is marketing. Furthermore, Cooper, Upton & Seaman (2005) conclude that executives of family firms show less interest in customer relationship management (CRM) and place less emphasis on its role in the firm's success, despite feeling that they have a similar level of knowledge on the subject to non-family firms. However, the implementation of CRM in family firms relies on much more traditional and less risky versions of such techniques.

Quality Capabilities

Lastly, the RBV holds quality to be a basic strategic asset, with multiple studies demonstrating its importance for success (Reed, Lemak & Montgomery, 1996; Rubio & Aragón, 2002, 2006, 2008; Lerner & Almor, 2002; Calvo & López, 2003; Rogoff, Lee & Suh, 2004). Thus, proper management of this capability can make quality a key strategic competence and a competitive weapon that should not be overlooked by any organization (Eldridge, Balubaif & Barber, 2006).

Family firms do not appear to effectively develop **quality capabilities** either. Although it is true that family businesses tend to be concerned with quality and customer service (Rubenstein, 1990; Tagiuri & Davis, 1992; Westhead, 1997; Backes-Gellner, 2001), this concern is not reflected in the use of practices related to these types of issues. In this regard, Backes-Gellner (2001) observes in her study that, in comparison with non-family firms, family firms are less likely to use quality improvement mechanisms such as quality circles.

For their part, Ellington, Jones & Deane (1996) show that, while the adoption of a more holistic and comprehensive Total Quality Management (TQM) model is related to better performance in family firms, these companies are characterized as being less likely to adopt TQM practices. A reputation for quality tied to the family name is an interesting element to exploit; however, effort and investment are required to achieve a real impact and transform it into a competitive advantage.

Family firms are aware of the importance of quality in upholding the family name, but they are not committed to growth and evolution (Gallo, Tàpies & Cappuyns, 2004); therefore, if the family firm's commitment to quality is not focused towards achieving a competitive advantage, it will be hard to develop quality capabilities that prove advantageous for the company.

As can be seen from the review thus far, the intrinsic characteristics of the family firm influence its key capabilities for achieving competitiveness. The success of the family firm will largely depend on the effective management of the overlap between the family system and the business system, and less so on the resources or processes that can be found in one system or the other (Olson, Zuiker, Danes, Stafford, Heck & Duncan, 2003). As such, the family firm could better position itself if it could make its distinctive features work in its favour. However, the above review indicates that, in general, family firms do not manage these opportunities effectively, leading to a negative influence on its stock of distinctive competences. Thus, the first hypothesis of the present study is the following:

H1. Being a family firm has a negative effect on its set of distinctive competences.

Managerial Capabilities in the Family Firm

The Importance of Managerial Capabilities for the Development of Distinctive Competences

Managerial resources are a highly relevant group when it comes to generating and maintaining business success (e.g., Penrose, 1959; Child, 1972; Katz, 1974; Anderson & Paine, 1975; Hambrick & Mason, 1984; Andrews, 1987; Castanias & Helfat, 1991, 2001; Lado & Wilson, 1994; Pickett, 1998; Landeta et al., 2007). This group must have the ability to understand, describe and evaluate the potential that the company's endowment of resources offers for driving economic performance (Martínez et al., 2010). In this respect, the elements studied in the previous section require other capabilities in order to manage them and promote their development: namely, managerial capabilities. Managerial capabilities stem from the tacit knowledge assets held by managers and therefore show notable heterogeneity (Hambrick et al., 1996). They include the individual skills and knowledge of those in managerial positions, as well as the competences derived from the relationships between them. The empirical evidence overwhelmingly supports the positive impact of managerial capabilities on business performance (Hitt & Ireland, 1985; Finkelstein & Hambrick, 1990; Thomas, Clark & Gioia, 1993; Markides & Williamson, 1994; Robins & Wiersema, 1995; Mehra, 1996; Russo & Fouts, 1997; Boeker, 1997; Carmeli, 2001; Lerner & Almor, 2002; Acquaah, 2003; Kor, 2003; Carmeil & Tishler, 2006).

Managerial capabilities enable the coordination of functional and dynamic capabilities. They can be used to create the mission that shapes the formulation and implementation of company strategy, on the basis of which the rest of the organizational competences can be developed. These capabilities are based on aspects such as strategic vision, support for change and learning, the fostering of a spirit of dialogue, an entrepreneurial orientation, business management expertise and leadership. As such, these capabilities are essential for the proper management of the organization and for the appropriate development and exploitation of the rest of the capabilities.

The literature underscores the link between the firm's competitiveness and the managerial ability to fully develop and utilize the experience and talent of all members of the organization, integrating and encouraging the efforts of a complex team of people (Osbaldeston & Barham, 1992). According to Lado & Wilson (1994), managerial competences provide the basis for developing the rest of the competences, while Mahoney (1995) points out that the key to resource management is the management resource. Using a sample of 861 Basque companies, Martínez et al. (2010) show that managerial capabilities act as a catalyst for other firm capabilities, demonstrating that their real source of competitiveness stems from managerial capabilities and not from the mere possession of capabilities or resources. Training and experience, along with other, innate qualities, are often identified as highly relevant traits for managers to have (Barney, 1991; Fondas & Wiersema, 1997; Kor, 2003).

As with the other distinctive competences, it is to be expected that managerial capabilities will be influenced by the specific characteristics of the family firm. Sharma, Chrisman & Chua (1997) underline how the family influences the choice of company objectives through the strategic planning process; they argue that the firm must address the family's demands in order to tailor its plans and action towards achieving those objectives. Therefore, the owning family, their specific characteristics, and their thoughts about the business will inevitably influence the way the business is run, regardless of whether the management of the business is in the hands of the family or not.

The Development of Managerial Capabilities in the Family Firm

The characteristics of the family firm, derived essentially from its specific structure of governance, ownership and control, can significantly affect the development of managerial capabilities and, therefore, the accumulation and management of other distinctive competences. Carney (2005) suggests that the governance structure of the family firm places constraints on managerial capabilities, which causes problems when it comes to the acquisition of resources and capabilities, thereby generating a competitive disadvantage. Specifically, when family firms limit participation in decision-making roles to a restricted insider group (Chandler, 1990; Demsetz & Lehn, 1985)—usually family members—this hinders their ability to accumulate intangible capabilities and to develop the routines and organizational systems required to coordinate various functions and a large number of people (Kogut & Zander, 1992).

Many of the characteristics and the mentality of the family business mask aspects that may represent obstacles to the effective development of managerial capabilities. Aspects that can hinder the development of the appropriate capabilities required to properly manage and run the family business include nepotistic or altruistic practices, conflicts and misunderstandings, informal structures, overlapping roles, and the pursuit of personal vs. business goals. Below we present some of the main features that may impede the development of this type of capability.

Family members often feel bonded to the company, making it very difficult for them to have the flexibility to adapt to changing situations (Duncan, 1973) or even to leave the company in difficult times (Brown, 1987). Similarly, family firms are often characterized by their conservative behaviour (Donckels & Frölich, 1991), their risk aversion, (Morris, 1998) and their resistance to change (Levinson, 1987), all of which underscores their rigidity in the face of changing environments and reinforces their inward orientation. These traits represent an obstacle to developing and maintaining an entrepreneurial orientation and a positive attitude towards change, and thus repress the growth of an open organizational culture.

Furthermore, managers of family firms often do not attribute enough importance to training, and their educational level is often lower than that of managers in non-family firms (Jorissen, Laveren, Martens & Reheul, 2001; Matlay, 2002). The staff and managers of family businesses often have a lower level of qualifications, primarily because such companies are more likely to employ family members, especially in managerial positions, even if they do not have the right training (Gallo & García, 1996). They also hire fewer professional managers (Chandler, 1990). The desire to keep company management in the hands of family members may explain why the level of training or experience can at times be inadequate, even though management's tasks and responsibilities are complex and require the possession of special knowledge and skills. According to Fernández & Nieto (2005) family firms' managerial staff tend to have a lower level of qualifications for two reasons: first, to avoid losing control of the organization, the firm will tend to employ family members to occupy managerial positions, whether or not they have the necessary training; and second, these firms have trouble attracting qualified professional managers due to the unstructured nature of the firm and, in terms of career development, the difficulty of competing on equal terms with family members, who are favoured by the systems of incentives and promotion (Lansberg, 1983; Gallo & Sveen, 1991; James, 1999). Similarly, the most highly-qualified family members often seek the opportunity to develop their career elsewhere, while those who are less competent are the ones that join the company (Gallo & Melé, 1998).

Regarding the management of the company, Duréndez, García & Madrid (2007), based on a sample of 436 Spanish SMEs, find that family firms make less use of management tools than non-family firms. Equally, family firms will tend to use more financial mechanisms than strategic ones to control their assets (Carney, 2005), thus hindering the development of a strategic vision for the business. Similarly, Ateljevic (2007) indicates that most owner-managers are more concerned with day-to-day operational management, paying little attention to strategic issues. These problems represent some of the obstacles to acquiring expertise in business management principles and methods. This lack of a strategic vision will have a negative impact when it comes to fostering the key capabilities for competitiveness; without such a vision it is impossible to strategically manage and exploit the aspects that can steer the company towards success, such as quality, human resources, technology and marketing.

Effective leadership and an entrepreneurial orientation are also critical for fostering managerial capabilities. While the founder of the company is likely to have such qualities, and they are common features of many family businesses (Hall, Melin & Nordqvistl, 2001; Steier, 2003; Zahra, Hayton & Salvato, 2004; Zahra, 2005), the same may not necessarily be true of future company executives. Opinions on this issue vary. Some authors argue that a strong corporate culture related to the family could influence the ability to create and sustain entrepreneurial capabilities (Casillas, Moreno, & Barbero, 2010). As such, we may find innovative, proactive and entrepreneurial family businesses, as opposed to other family companies that are conservative, traditional, inward-looking and risk-averse (Naldi, Nordqvist, Sjöberg & Wiklund, 2007). But in fact, Naldi et al. (2007) find that there is less risk-taking in family firms than in non-family firms and that, for family firms, risk-taking is negatively related to their performance; these results may indicate that family firms do not have a sufficiently well-developed entrepreneurial orientation to enable them to take risks and manage them properly.

On the other hand, when the recruitment of family members is not carried out from a business perspective, this can lead to conflicts in the family-business sphere and the emergence of far more informal structures and agreements. Relationships will develop more spontaneously and, in many cases, there will be no rules or regulations governing certain behaviour. Altruism fosters greater communication and cooperation in the family business, which will encourage this use of more informal agreements (Daily &

Dollinger, 1992). Although these poorly defined and informal structures can be advantageous to some extent, in some cases there is no clear differentiation between the roles of certain family employees and those of other, higher-ranking employees. Thus, family members tend to take advantage of management when there is an overlap between the responsibilities of management and of the family member (Lindbeck & Weibull, 1988), thereby reducing the effectiveness of management's supervisory role. Such situations present a problem for management when it comes to exercising strong leadership, and at the same time they pose an obstacle to strategic visions in which the interests of the firm prevail over those of the individuals. In addition, the unstructured nature of these firms prevents them from attracting professional managers (family members or external) who are actually competent to do the job (Fernández & Nieto, 2005), which directly affects the firm's managerial capabilities. On the other hand, non-family employees may feel unfairly treated (Schulze et al., 2002) if they perceive favouritism towards others. In this regard, altruistic behaviour towards the family could lead to an inability to discipline or dismiss family employees who actually deserve it (Schulze et al., 2003). Similarly, such altruistic conduct will entail treating different members of the same family equally, even if their contributions are not equal (Schulze et al., 2002). At the same time, a situation in which there are too many family members involved in the business opens the door for conflicts arising within the family to cross over into the business. These aspects have a negative impact on managerial capabilities as they hinder the objectivity and acceptance of diverse ideas and complicate the decision-making process,

In terms of future successors, there are also different positions regarding leadership and entrepreneurship. If the children of the controlling family or other family members that are potential successors feel involved in the running of the company, this may prompt them to develop the skills and attitudes of entrepreneurship and leadership; conversely, exposure to the hard work and other negative aspects typical of the tourism sector may be off-putting to potential successors (Getz & Carlsen, 2005). Moreover, in order to develop leadership skills, not only must the successor be influenced by the family's attitude towards the business, but he/she must also have undergone training before joining the business and to continue training over the course of his/her career in the family business (Fiegener, Brown, Prince & File, 1994). On the other hand, family firms are often inward-looking, influenced by long-held traditions, inflexible and resistant to change (Kets de Vries, 1993; Dyer, 1994; Gersick, Davis, Hampton & Lansberg, 1997). Thus, even if the founders of the family business were entrepreneurs, this capability seems to wane as the firm matures: on the one hand, once the business is successfully established, many founder-entrepreneurs lose that entrepreneurial capability; on the other hand, subsequent generations run the business in line with traditional practices and past values (Hall et al., 2001), without considering new requirements or orientations that may be key to the success of the company. Some studies have found evidence that subsequent generations of family members often lack clarity about their abilities, talents, goals and professional interests (Eckrich & Loughead, 1996). According to some authors (García-Álvarez et al. 2002), this confusion may be due to the socialization processes aimed at instilling potential successors with a sense of obligation to pursue a professional career within the family firm.

Therefore, family firms do not appear to possess sufficient qualities to successfully develop managerial capabilities. Without the appropriate managerial capabilities, it is hard for family firms to foster and develop the other distinctive competences needed to build a strong competitive advantage. Thus, the second hypothesis is that being a family firm has a negative effect on its managerial capabilities, while the third hypothesis concerns the mediating effect of the managerial capabilities:

Figure 1. Effects of the family tourism firm on the stock of distinctive competences

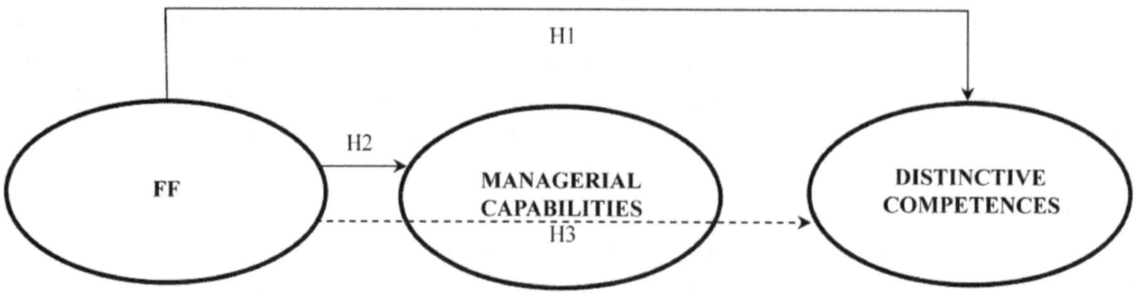

H2. Being a family firm has a negative effect on its managerial capabilities.
H3. The negative effect of being a family firm on its stock of distinctive competences is mediated by managerial capabilities.

Effects of Being a Family Firm on the Stock of Distinctive Competences: Theoretical Models to Test

Figure 1 graphically represents the model to be tested. It shows how being a family tourism firm affects the stock of capabilities, with managerial capabilities as a mediator variable.

METHODOLOGY

Database

The empirical research uses a database constructed from a primary study of Spanish tourism firms. Data were collected using a questionnaire. The fieldwork was carried out through personal interviews arranged in advance by telephone. This method offers significant advantages, especially in a case with the complexity and characteristics of the present study, where we sought a high response rate, flexibility, knowledge of the respondent's identity, control over the distribution of the sample and the ability to capture higher quality information thanks to the counselling of the interviewer. It was decided that the owner, managing director or general manager of the company were the appropriate people to provide their responses to the questionnaire. In order to address the problems associated with questionnaires as a data collection method, and in an attempt to improve the response rate and the quality of the information, a set of recommended procedures for questionnaire-based research was used. This was essentially a modified version of the Dillman's Total Design Method (1978). The field work was carried out between December 2009 and March 2010.

The final sample includes 1,019 companies, which over the entire sector represents a statistical margin of error of ±3.1% (confidence interval of 95.5%). The sample is distributed as follows: 62.71% micro-enterprises, 25.22% small enterprises, 9.62% medium-sized enterprises and 2.45% large enterprises. Of the 1,019 companies included in the final sample, 748 are family firms, while 271 are non-family firms. Although we focus on family firms, the complete sample must be used to test the proposed models.

As suggested by Armstrong & Overton (1977), we used the time trend extrapolation test to check for the possible existence of non-response bias. This test is based on a comparison of the first and last survey respondents. This test assumes that the last respondents (those who responded only after receiving a second questionnaire and a follow-up phone call) better resemble the non-respondents, as they themselves would have been non-respondents if they had not completed the second questionnaire. The results of the t-tests show that no significant differences are observed in any of the explanatory or dependent variables.

Measurement of the Variables

The theoretical model to be empirically tested analyses the different effects of being a family firm on its stock of competitive capabilities. The final dependent construct is termed "distinctive competences" and comprises the different dimensions corresponding to the firm's capabilities in innovation and technology, human resources and organizational culture, marketing, and quality. The construct "managerial capabilities", which is introduced as a mediator variable, includes items linked to management's strategic vision and its ability to support change and learning, the fostering of a spirit of dialogue, an entrepreneurial orientation, managerial expertise in business management principles and methods, and effective leadership.

The items that make up each of these constructs are measured through a multi-item Likert scale, specifically a 7-point semantic differential scale with scores reflecting the managers' perception of the strength of their company compared to competitors in the industry (1 = "much worse", 2 = "worse", 3 = "slightly worse", 4 = "at the average", 5 = "slightly better", 6 = "better", 7 = "much better"). The managerial self-evaluation scales allow us to translate key individuals' judgement, knowledge, and experience into subjective multi-item scales. The literature documents the use of this method for measuring a firm's resources and capabilities (Camisón, 2005, 2004), and several studies have demonstrated its convergent validity with objective measurements (e.g., Camisón, 2005).

The concept of the family firm is difficult to measure due to the large number of related definitions and measurements that have emerged (Miller, Le Breton-Miller, Lester & Cannella, 2007). Some authors leave it to the respondent to decide whether or not theirs should be considered a family firm (e.g. Gallo et al., 2004; Dibrell & Moeller, 2011; Neubaum, Dibrell, & Craig, 2012). This criterion is also used in studies on family tourism firms: Getz & Carlsen (2000) argue in favour of this method and use it in their study for the advantages it offers; namely, it is easy for the respondent to understand this question and it does not impose a restrictive definition. Thus, we apply this criterion in our study and introduce the independent variable "family firm (FF)" as a dichotomous variable.

Table 1 summarizes the characteristics of the instruments used to measure the variables.

Multi-item scales offer the advantage of reducing measurement error, as the use of multiple indicators reduces uncertainty and measurement errors associated with a single response (Hair, Anderson, Tatham & Black, 1998). In addition, in order to prevent a "robot effect" in responses, a control process was implemented, consisting of formulating certain items in reverse order.

For the SEM analysis, the variable "distinctive competences" is created as a second-order construct from the dimensions explained above; in turn, each dimension is made up of its constituent items. The variable "managerial capabilities", on the other hand, is operationalized as a first-order construct formed by the items described above. The multi-item measurement scales used have already been validated in previous studies (Camisón, 2002). However, in this study it has been considered appropriate to carry out a reliability analysis, to ensure the internal consistency of the scales. To that end, two statistical

Table 1. Measurements of model variables

Variable	Nº items	Cronbach's Alpha	Main attributes	Source
DISTINCTIVE COMPETENCES	4	0.765	Capabilities in innovation and technology, marketing, human resources and organizational culture, and quality	Adapted from Camisón (2002)
INNOVATION AND TECHNOLOGY CAPABILITIES	5	0.933	Items related to the innovation of products/services and processes, the ability of the company to develop internally through R&D&I and to acquire external knowledge and capabilities to exploit and apply to developing innovations	Adapted from Camisón (2002)
HR AND ORGANIZATIONAL CULTURE CAPABILITIES	5	0.941	Items related to staff qualifications and satisfaction, employee commitment to the company, encouragement of teamwork and commitment to continuous improvement and quality	Adapted from Camisón (2002)
MARKETING CAPABILITIES	7	0.849	Items related to the price of the services, company reputation, brand image, marketing channel, communication policy, range of services and customer satisfaction	Adapted from Camisón (2002)
QUALITY CAPABILITIES	3	0.945	Items related to reputation for quality, total quality and service quality	Adapted from Camisón (2002)
MANAGERIAL CAPABILITIES	6	0.942	Items linked to management's strategic vision and its ability to support change and learning, the fostering of a spirit of dialogue, an entrepreneurial orientation, managerial expertise in business management principles and methods, and effective leadership.	Adapted from Camisón (2002)
FAMILY FIRM	1	-	Dichotomous variable that equals 1 for a family firm and 0 for a non-family firm	--

tools are used: Cronbach's Alpha coefficient and combined reliability analysis. The combined reliability analysis will be introduced later when analysing the corresponding measurement models. With regard to Cronbach's Alpha coefficient, the value should exceed a minimum threshold of around 0.7. As can be seen in the table, all the instruments used far exceed this level. As FF is a dichotomous variable, the scale reliability analyses are not applied.

Analysis Techniques

The complete model with the mediator variables will be tested using structural equation modelling (SEM). The proposed theoretical model is derived from a review of the specialized literature on the topic under study, which allows to affirm that the proposed SEM model is correctly specified when studying the theoretically grounded causal relationships. Both the measurement and the causal model are estimated using the maximum likelihood with robust standard errors (MLR) estimation procedure, which provides unbiased and consistent estimators when the variables used are continuous, with multivariate normal distribution and when the sample used is large. The statistical package used is EQS 6.1. In addition, linear regression analysis is used to test the direct effect of FF on the stock of distinctive competences, through the SPSS 15.0 program for Windows. Table 2 shows the descriptive statistics and correlations of the variables under study. The dimensions of capabilities in innovation and technology, human resources and organizational culture, marketing, and quality form part of the construct of distinctive competences.

Table 2. Descriptive statistics and correlations of study variables

	μ	σ^2	1	2	3	4	5	6
1.DISTINCTIVE COMPETENCES	**4.71**	**0.83**						
2. INNOVATION AND TECHNOLOGY CAPABILITIES	***3.72***	***1.36***	*.766***					
3. HR AND ORGANIZATIONAL CULTURE CAPABILITIES	***5.13***	***1.03***	*.714***	*.273***				
4. MARKETING CAPABILITIES	***4.76***	***0.79***	*.811***	*.524***	*.464***			
5. QUALITY CAPABILITIES	***5.20***	***1.04***	*.834***	*.450***	*.551***	*.668***		
6. MANAGERIAL CAPABILITIES	**4.83**	**0.99**	.659**	.489**	.499**	.545**	.517**	
7.FAMILY FIRM	**0.73**	**0.44**	-.068*	-.053	-.070*	-.067*	-.020	-.067

(**) Significant at 1%
(*) Significant at 5%

RESULTS AND DISCUSSION

Measurement Models

A number of procedures are required to verify the adequacy of structural models. To that end, the dimensionality, reliability and validity of the measurement models must be checked by means of an overall Confirmatory Factor Analysis (CFA), which includes all the proposed scales and dimensions without the causal relationships.

Dimensionality

The CFA allows us to observe how well the data fit the proposed model, and to verify that the model has sufficient degrees of freedom to ensure the model is not overidentified. The EQS 6.1 offers a series of measures that allow us to check the fit of the model.

First, the absolute fit measures show whether the matrix estimated by the model fits the initial data matrix. A suitable indicator in this respect is the Root Mean Square Error of Approximations (RMSEA), which measures the distance between the initial data matrix and the matrix estimated by the model, indicating whether the model is a good fit for the population. In addition, Chi-Square measures the distance between the initial data matrix and the matrix estimated by the model (the Satorra-Bentler Chi-Square is similar but for robust estimation methods). However, the latter indicator is not used here as it has been criticized for its sensitivity to large samples (Camisón, 2005).

Second, incremental fit measures compare the proposed model with a baseline model, or the worst possible model that stipulates no association between indicators. EQS 6.1 provides two indexes of this type. The first is the Bentler-Bonett Normed Fit Index (BB-NFI), which measures the proportional reduction in the model fit function when moving from the baseline model to the proposed one. However, in this study we use the Incremental Fit Index (IFI), which overcomes some of the disadvantages of the NFI by incorporating the degrees of freedom of the proposed model. EQS 6.1 also provides the Bentler-Bonett Non-Normed Fit Index (BB-NNFI), which compares the degree of freedom fit of the proposed model and the null model; it will also be used here, along with the Comparative Fit Index (CFI).

Table 3. Measures of fit for the measurement models

INDEX	MINIMUM LEVELS OF FIT	FAMILY FIRM MODEL
	Absolute measure	
RMSEA	Below 0.08	0.067
	Incremental measure	
IFI	Close to 1	0.918
BB-NNFI	Equal to or higher than 0.9	0.910
CFI	Close to 1	0.918
	Measure of parsimony	
Normed Chi-Square	Between 1 and 5	4.218

Finally, we use measures of parsimony, which indicate the fit for each coefficient or parameter estimated, to prevent overfitting. In this case, the measure used is the Normed Chi-Square, which is obtained by dividing the Chi-Square statistic by the degrees of freedom. Table 3 shows the fit measures obtained.

All the statistics meet the minimum thresholds, allowing us to affirm that the proposed model is an adequate representation of the causal relationship between the variables considered.

Reliability

An assessment of reliability must take into account two essential elements. The first of these is internal consistency, which means that the observed operational variables measure the underlying concept; and the second element is stability, which refers to the ability of the scale to generate consistent results for the same measurement. Stability is usually measured using the test-retest method, which consists of administering the same scale twice to the same group of firms and comparing the results (Camisón, 2005). Regarding internal consistency, Cronbach's Alpha is a good indicator; its value should be higher than 0.5. As observed above, this minimum threshold is exceeded in all cases. In addition to Cronbach's Alpha, there is another very useful measure for checking internal consistency: the Composite Reliability Index (Werts, Linn & Jöreskog, 1974), which generally requires values greater than 0.7. Table 4 shows the values obtained for each construct and each dimension.

All the constructs have a composite reliability value of more than 0.7. Taken together with the values for Cronbach's Alpha, this confirms that the scales used are reliable.

Validity

The validity of the measurement model indicates whether the model actually measures what the researcher is attempting to measure. First, content validity indicates whether the scales used reflect the competences being measured. There is no quantitative measure to assess this validity, so it is essential to carry out a thorough review of the literature on scale construction methodology and techniques. The scales used in this study can be considered valid because they are based on existing theory. Second, criterion validity indicates whether the scale or items are useful for predicting other concepts or criteria; it is verified by checking the fit of the causal model and the assumptions made. Third, convergent validity tells us whether different measures used to evaluate the same concept are correlated with each other. It can be

Table 4. Factor loadings and composite reliability

DIMENSION	ITEM	FACTOR LOADING	MEASUREMENT ERROR	R^2	COMPOSITE RELIABILITY
INNOVATION AND TECHNOLOGY CAPABILITIES	INN_1	0.848	0.53	0.719	**0.885**
	INN_2	0.863	0.505	0.745	
	INN_3	0.801	0.599	0.641	
	INN_4	0.901	0.433	0.812	
	INN_5	0.924	0.383	0.854	
HR AND ORGANIZATIONAL CULTURE CAPABILITIES	RRHH_1	0.776	0.631	0.602	**0.891**
	RRHH_2	0.861	0.508	0.742	
	RRHH_3	0.908	0.419	0.824	
	RRHH_4	0.921	0.390	0.848	
	RRHH_5	0.918	0.395	0.844	
MARKETING CAPABILITIES	MK_1	0.863	0.505	0.745	**0.812**
	MK_2	0.466	0.885	0.217	
	MK_3	0.841	0.542	0.707	
	MK_4	0.577	0.816	0.333	
	MK_5	0.544	0.839	0.296	
	MK_6	0.640	0.769	0.409	
	MK_7	0.728	0.685	0.531	
QUALITY CAPABILITIES	CAL_1	0.933	0.361	0.870	**0.875**
	CAL_2	0.932	0.362	0.869	
	CAL_3	0.923	0.384	0.853	
DISTINCTIVE COMPETENCES	INN	0.570	0.821	0.325	**0.770**
	RRHH	0.595	0.804	0.354	
	MK	0.888	0.459	0.789	
	CAL	0.876	0.481	0.768	
MANAGERIAL CAPABILITIES	DIR_1	0.861	0.509	0.741	**0.901**
	DIR_2	0.899	0.438	0.808	
	DIR_3	0.824	0.566	0.679	
	DIR_4	0.855	0.518	0.732	
	DIR_5	0.877	0.481	0.768	
	DIR_6	0.882	0.471	0.778	

measured through the BB-NNFI, which, as stated above, is higher than 0.9. The magnitude of the factor loadings is another important measure, which ideally should exceed the value of 0.4; as can be observed in Table 4, all the coefficients exceed this value. Lastly, discriminant validity shows the degree to which two different constructs are unrelated, and is assessed through the correlation matrix. This condition is met when the coefficients of correlation do not exceed the value of 0.9 and are statistically significant. In Table 2, we can check that these values, which have been obtained using the SPSS 15.0 program, meet requirements.

Table 5. Measures of fit for causal models

INDEX	MINIMUM LEVELS OF FIT	FAMILY FIRM MODEL
Absolute measure		
RMSEA	Below 0.08	0.060
Incremental measure		
IFI	Close to 1	0.934
BB-NNFI	Equal to or higher than 0.9	0.927
CFI	Close to 1	0.934
Measure of parsimony		
Normed Chi-Square	Between 1 and 5.	3.604

Therefore, the requirements in terms of Dimensionality, Reliability and Validity are met, showing that the model is properly specified. Below we analyse the structural model estimated using EQS 6.1.

Structural Models

As with the measures analysed to confirm the fit of the measurement model, there are other mechanisms that demonstrate the adequacy of the structural model. These conditions are shown below.

Analysis of Overall Model Fit

The overall model reflects the relationships proposed in the theoretical model. A perfect fit exists when the matrix estimated by the model and the observed matrix show a perfect match. To measure this fit, the indicators explained above are used for the causal model. The results obtained are presented in Table 5.

As can be seen, once again all the statistics meet the minimum thresholds, allowing us to affirm that the proposed model is an adequate representation of the causal relationship between the variables considered.

Analysis of Measurement Model Fit

To analyse the goodness of fit of the measurement model, we check the significance of each loading obtained, which must exceed 0.4 in order to confirm a good fit. Also, internal consistency is evaluated, as before, through the combined reliability of the construct.

Adequate values can be seen for both the factor loadings and R^2, as well as for the composite reliability of the constructs. We can therefore confirm the goodness of fit of the measurement model.

Analysis of Structural Model Fit

In this case, we have to assess the statistical significance of the coefficients. As shown in Table 6, all coefficients are significant at the 1% level. Likewise, the R^2 values are very high. It can therefore be concluded that the structural model meets the established requirements for goodness of fit.

Table 6. Factor loadings and composite reliability

DIMENSION	ITEM	FACTOR LOADING	MEASUREMENT ERROR	R^2	COMPOSITE RELIABILITY
INNOVATION AND TECHNOLOGY CAPABILITIES	INN_1	0.848**	0.531	0.718	**0.885**
	INN_2	0.863**	0.506	0.744	
	INN_3	0.800**	0.600	0.640	
	INN_4	0.902**	0.432	0.813	
	INN_5	0.924**	0.382	0.854	
HR AND ORGANIZATIONAL CULTURE CAPABILITIES	RRHH_1	0.776**	0.631	0.602	**0.891**
	RRHH_2	0.861**	0.508	0.742	
	RRHH_3	0.907**	0.420	0.823	
	RRHH_4	0.921**	0.390	0.848	
	RRHH_5	0.919**	0.395	0.844	
MARKETING CAPABILITIES	MK_1	0.855**	0.519	0.731	**0.813**
	MK_2	0.470**	0.883	0.221	
	MK_3	0.836**	0.549	0.699	
	MK_4	0.584**	0.812	0.341	
	MK_5	0.555**	0.832	0.308	
	MK_6	0.652**	0.758	0.425	
	MK_7	0.726**	0.687	0.527	
QUALITY CAPABILITIES	CAL_1	0.932**	0.363	0.868	**0.875**
	CAL_2	0.932**	0.363	0.868	
	CAL_3	0.925**	0.381	0.855	
DISTINCTIVE COMPETENCES	INN	0.604**	0.797	0.364	**0.773**
	RRHH	0.612**	0.791	0.374	
	MK	0.890**	0.456	0.792	
	CAL	0.852**	0.524	0.725	
MANAGERIAL CAPABILITIES	DIR_1	0.863**	0.506	0.744	**0.901**
	DIR_2	0.898**	0.440	0.807	
	DIR_3	0.826**	0.564	0.682	
	DIR_4	0.855**	0.519	0.731	
	DIR_5	0.876**	0.482	0.768	
	DIR_6	0.881**	0.472	0.777	

(**) Significant at 1%

RESULTS

After analysing the fit of the model and verifying its adequacy, the results obtained for each of the models are shown below, indicating whether or not these results support the hypotheses proposed. First, we analysed how being a family firm affects the stock of intangibles, finding a negative and significant

Figure 2. Effects of being a family tourism firm on the stock of distinctive competences

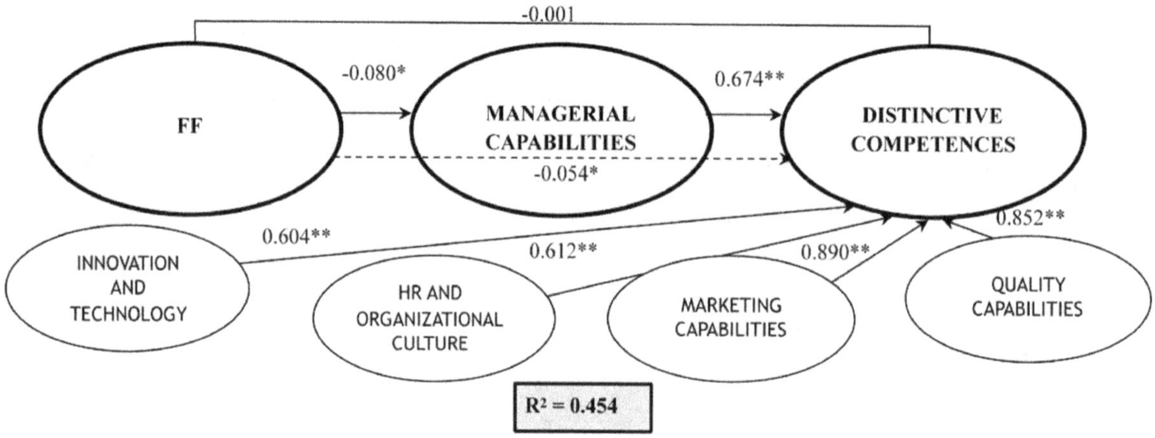

influence (β=-0.068; p>5%). Thus, we observe a direct negative and significant effect of being a family firm on its distinctive competences, thereby supporting H1.

Second, we estimated the complete model (see Figure 2), which includes managerial capabilities as a mediator variable of the former relationship.

The results obtained confirm H2 and H3, demonstrating that the effect of being a family firm on distinctive competences is fully mediated by the managerial capabilities, with the direct effect disappearing. Thus, on the one hand, it is shown that being a family firm negatively and significantly affects the development of its managerial capabilities, which is in line with H2; we can therefore accept that hypothesis. While it is true that the factor loading for this effect is not particularly high (-0.080), the analysis considers family firms as a whole, without specifying which specific characteristics influence managerial capabilities. It is reasonable to suppose that not all the characteristics of the family firm will have a negative affect; however, given the significance and the sign of the effect, it does seem clear that, in general, being a family firm hinders the development of managerial capacities.

On the other hand, it can be seen that managerial capabilities contribute to the development of distinctive competences, as suggested in the theoretical review. This confirms that appropriate managerial capabilities are required in order to be able to develop and manage the distinctive competences that contribute to the success of the company. We also note that when we include managerial capabilities in the model, the characteristics of the family firm no longer have a significant effect on distinctive competences. This indicates that managerial capabilities have a mediating effect between the characteristics of the family firm and its stock of distinctive competences, thus confirming H3. Therefore, the negative effect of being a family firm on its stock of competences is indirect and mediated by managerial capabilities.

SOLUTIONS AND RECOMMENDATIONS

The difficulties involved in developing distinctive competences may make it hard for a firm to achieve a strong competitive position or good organizational performance. Family tourism firms must therefore attempt to address this issue. As has been examined in this chapter one of the principal roots of the problem lies in the negative effect of family-firm characteristics on managerial capabilities. Those in charge of running a family business must therefore be aware of the need to develop appropriate managerial capabilities in order for the company to thrive.

The process of professionalization is a powerful lever for developing resources and capabilities (Qureshi, Chen & Wang, 2017). In this regard, many authors highlight the need for family firms to "professionalize" (e.g., Stewart & Hitt, 2012), a process which is usually understood as including non-family managers in the management of the family business. However, the process of professionalization in family firms can take many other forms, as suggested, for example, by Stewart & Hitt (2012) or Dekker, Lybaert, Steijvers & Depaire (2015).

For their part, Lansberg & Gersick (2015) point to the importance of training in the context of the family business so that those responsible can plan the company succession and implement an effective continuity process. Thus, these authors emphasize that training the owners of the family business can be considered as an ongoing process of capability-building, which should be strategically designed in order to be able to continuously anticipate the needs of both the firm and the family.

In this regard, the specific characteristics of the family firm should be managed from a different perspective. As such, we believe that it would be of particular interest to incorporate specific courses on managing family firms into business education programmes, as some authors have already suggested (e.g., Chrisman et al., 2003; Peters & Buhalis, 2004). Specific knowledge relating to family firms would contribute to a better understanding of the particular managerial capabilities required to manage this type of business and how such skills can be developed.

Therefore, the improvement of managerial capabilities in family firms through professionalization and/or training for company managers is key to developing and managing distinctive competences that effectively contribute to the success of the company; it is also key to the proper use of the specific features of family firms, which fall under the concept of *familiness*.

FUTURE LINES OF RESEARCH

With regard to future lines of research, it is important to stress the need for further research in the field of family business. While it is true that we are witnessing a growing number of studies in this area, empirical contributions are still scarce and there are some important aspects that should be explored in greater detail to gain an understanding of the characteristics, challenges and needs of the family business. Similarly, despite the importance of family firms in the tourism sector, there have been few contributions in this context (Getz & Carlsen, 2005), so it would be interesting to carry out more research in this sector.

It also seems reasonable to look at the characteristics of managers or those in charge of family firms in order to analyse the source of the problems in developing managerial capabilities.

Furthermore, the authors consider it significant to study the family firm in the context of the RBV, highlighting not only the importance of accumulating certain resources and capabilities for the family business, but also analysing the problems that may arise if the family's involvement in the business is not properly managed. On the other hand, it is important to highlight the need for a more in-depth study focusing on certain specific characteristics of family firms, since an overall analysis does not allow us to capture the distinctive characteristics of the family business (Bannò & Sgobbi, 2016).

Lastly, the specific characteristics of the family firm should be managed from a different perspective. As such, the authors believe that it would be of particular interest to incorporate specific courses on managing family firms into business education programmes, as some authors have already suggested (e.g., Chrisman, Chua & Sharma, 2003; Peters & Buhalis, 2004; De Massis & Kotlar, 2015). Specific knowledge relating to family firms would contribute to a better understanding of the particular managerial capabilities required to manage this type of business and how such skills can be developed.

As for the limitations of this study, the authors should first comment that there has been used a cross-sectional research design, which influences the conclusions obtained, with it thus being necessary to qualify the prediction of causality. Furthermore, the study focuses on the Spanish tourism sector, so its applicability to other sectors or territories should be approached with caution. In addition, while the effects of being a family firm have been assessed in light of such firms' overall intrinsic characteristics, the authors have not identified which specific features hinder the proper development of their capabilities. The characteristic features of family firms arising from the relationship between the family and the business translate into structures of governance, ownership and control that differ from those of non-family firms. It is these structures that would ultimately affect the development of their capabilities. Future studies should therefore attempt to analyse these elements in depth, in order to examine their implications for the success of the family business.

CONCLUSION

This chapter has focused on studying family tourism firms and how being a family firm affects their key capabilities, and thus their ability to achieve a sustainable competitive advantage. It also explores possible problems that may arise from their status as a family firm.

To this end, a theoretical review has first been carried out in order to discover how the characteristic features of the family firm influence the accumulation and development of capabilities that can influence its success. Although there are some contradictory findings, our review of the literature shows that most related studies hold that the family firm—due to its special characteristics derived from the relationship between family and business— will have problems achieving a sustainable competitive advantage through the development of its capabilities in innovation and technology, human resources and organizational culture, marketing, and quality.

On the other hand, the review of various previous studies has prompted us to consider managerial capabilities alongside other capabilities, because of their importance in managing and coordinating the other distinctive competences. Managerial capabilities drive the development of the firm's distinctive competences; and as with all the other capabilities, the literature largely supports the idea that the family firm may have problems developing this type of capability.

The empirical evidence reported here highlights the difficulties faced by the family tourism firm in accumulating key competences. Moreover, the findings point to managerial capabilities as the source of the problem. These results lead to the conclusion that family-firm characteristics impede the proper development of managerial capabilities, possibly due to the specific structure of governance and ownership derived from family influence. This corroborates previous studies that suggest that family firms tend to use fewer professional managers (Chandler, 1990; Lubatkin Schulze, Ling, & Dino, 2005) and therefore their management methods and company vision are not aligned with purely strategic and competitive interests. Family values and wishes may act as a block against managerial positions being occupied by qualified, genuinely suitable candidates, causing problems in developing and managing the rest of the firm's competences, and thereby undermining its competitive capacity.

ACKNOWLEDGMENT

This study has been funded by the Ministry of Science, Innovation and Universities and the Agencia Estatal de Investigación (the Spanish State Research Agency), with co-financing from the European Regional Development Fund (ERDF). Reference [ECO2016-26796-P].

REFERENCES

Acosta-Prado, J. C., Longo-Somoza, M., & Lozano, M. B. (2017). Does family ownership affect innovation activity? A focus on the biotechnological industry. *Innovar (Universidad Nacional de Colombia)*, *27*(65), 11–23. doi:10.15446/innovar.v27n65.64886

Acquaah, M. (2003). Corporate management, industry competition and the sustainability of firm abnormal profitability. *The Journal of Management and Governance*, *7*(1), 57–85. doi:10.1023/A:1022489324208

Amit, R., & Belcourt, M. (1999). Human resources management processes: A value-creating source of competitive advantage. *European Journal of Management*, *71*(2), 174–181. doi:10.1016/S0263-2373(98)00076-0

Amit, R., & Schoemaker, P. (1993). Strategic assets and organizational rent. *Strategic Management Journal*, *14*(1), 33–46. doi:10.1002mj.4250140105

Andersen, A. (1997). Research findings: Amercian family business survey 1997. Arthur Andersen.

Anderson, C. R., & Paine, F. T. (1975). Managerial perceptions and strategic behavior. *Academy of Management Journal*, *18*(4), 811–823.

Andersson, T., Carlsen, J., & Getz, D. (2002). Family business goals in the tourism and hospitality sector: Case studies and cross-case analysis from Australia, Canada, and Sweden. *Family Business Review*, *15*(2), 89–106. doi:10.1111/j.1741-6248.2002.00089.x

Andrews, K. R. (1987). *The concept of corporate strategy* (3rd ed.). Homewood, IL: Richard D. Irwin.

Aragón, A., Barba, M. I., & Sanz, R. (2003). Efectos de la formación de directivos en las PYMES españolas. Estudios Financieros. *Revista de Trabajo y Seguridad Social*, *243*, 103–134.

Armstrong, J. S., & Overton, T. S. (1977). Estimating non response bias in mail surveys. *JMR, Journal of Marketing Research*, *16*(3), 396–402. doi:10.1177/002224377701400320

Aronoff, C. E., & Ward, J. L. (1995). Family-owned business. A thing of the past or a model of the future? *Family Business Review*, *8*(2), 121–130. doi:10.1111/j.1741-6248.1995.00121.x

Ateljevic, I., & Doorne, S. (2000). Staying within the fence: Lifestyle entrepreneurship in tourism. *Journal of Sustainable Tourism*, *8*(5), 378–392. doi:10.1080/09669580008667374

Ateljevic, J. (2007). Small tourism firms and management practices in New Zeland: The Centre Stage Macro Region. *Tourism Management, 28*(1), 307–316. doi:10.1016/j.tourman.2006.07.004

Backes-Gellner, U. (2001). *Das insdustrielle Familienunternehmen – Kontinuität im Wandel.* Bonn: Institut für Mittelstandforschung.

Bannò, M., & Sgobbi, F. (2016). Family business characteristics and the approach to HRM in overseas ventures. *Journal of Small Business Management, 54*(2), 640–658. doi:10.1111/jsbm.12162

Barach, J. A., Ganitsky, J. B., Carson, J. A., & Doochin, B. A. (1988). Entry of the next generation: Strategic challenge for family business. *Journal of Small Business Management, 26*, 49–56.

Barney, J. B. (1991). Firms resources and sustained competitive advantage. *Journal of Management, 17*(1), 191–210. doi:10.1177/014920639101700108

Barney, J. B. (1997). *Gaining and sustaining competitive advantage.* Aldershot, UK: Addison-Wesley Publishing.

Barney, J. B., Wright, M., & Ketchen, D. J. Jr. (2001). The resource-based view of the firm: Ten years after 1991. *Journal of Management, 27*(6), 625–641. doi:10.1177/014920630102700601

Barney, J. B., & Wright, P. M. (1998). On becoming a strategic partner: The role of human resources in gaining competitive advantage. *Human Resource Management, 37*(1), 31–47. doi:10.1002/(SICI)1099-050X(199821)37:1<31::AID-HRM4>3.0.CO;2-W

Basco, J. T. (2006). La investigación en la empresa familiar: Un debate sobre la existencia de un campo independiente". *Investigaciones Europeas, 12*(1), 33–54.

Basco, R., & Perez Rodríguez, M. J. (2009). Studying the family enterprise holistically evidence for integrated family and business systems. *Family Business Review, 22*(1), 82–95. doi:10.1177/0894486508327824

Bayo, A., & Merino, J. (2002). Las prácticas de recursos humanos de alto compromiso: Un estudio de los factores que influyen sobre su adopción en la industria española. *Cuadernos de Economía y Dirección de la Empresa, 12*, 227–246.

Becker, B., & Gerhart, B. (1996). The impact of human resource management on organizational performance: Progress and prospects. *Academy of Management Journal, 39*(4), 779–801.

Beckhard, R., & Dyer, W. G. Jr. (1983). SMR forum: Managing change in the family firm – Issues and strategies. *Sloan Management Review, 24*, 59–65.

Bennedsen, M., & Foss, N. (2015). Family assets and liabilities in the innovation process. *California Management Review, 58*(1), 65–81. doi:10.1525/cmr.2015.58.1.65

Bigliardi, B., & Ivo Dormio, A. (2009). Successful generational change in family business. *Measuring Business Excellence, 13*(2), 44–50. doi:10.1108/13683040910961207

Block, J. H. (2012). R&D investments in family and founder firms: An agency per-spective. *Journal of Business Venturing, 27*(2), 248–265. doi:10.1016/j.jbusvent.2010.09.003

Boeker, W. (1997). Strategic change: The influence of managerial characteristics and organizational growth. *Academy of Management Journal*, *40*(1), 152–170.

Bradburd, R. M., & Ross, D. R. (1989). Can small firms find and defend strategic niches? A test of the Porter Hypotheses. *The Review of Economics and Statistics*, *71*(2), 258–262. doi:10.2307/1926971

Brown, B. (1987). Recent tourism research in South East Dorset. In Tourism and development: Overviews and Case Studies of the UK and the South West Region (pp. 57-66). Department of Geography, University of Exeter.

Cabrera, K., De Saá, P., & Garcia, D. (2001). The succession process from a resource -and knowledge- based view of the family firm. *Family Business Review*, *14*(1), 37–46. doi:10.1111/j.1741-6248.2001.00037.x

Calvo, A. R., & López, V. A. (2003). Modelo RBV y rendimiento empresarial: Análisis discriminante en PYMEs gallegas. *Boletín de Estudios Económicos*, *59*(180), 503–521.

Camisón, C. (2002). *Las competencias distintivas basadas en activos intangibles. In Nuevas claves para la dirección estratégica* (pp. 117–151). Barcelona: Editorial Ariel.

Camisón, C. (2004). Shared, competitive and comparative advantages: A competence-based view of industrial-district competitiveness. *Environment & Planning A*, *36*(12), 2227–2256. doi:10.1068/a3759

Camisón, C. (2005). On how to measure managerial and organizational capabilities: Multi-Item models for measuring distinctive competences. *Management Research*, *3*(1), 27–48.

Camisón, C., Forés, B., & Puig-Denia, A. (2016). Return on capital in Spanish tourism businesses: A comparative analysis of family vs non-family businesses. *European Journal of Management and Business Economics*, *25*(3), 91–110. doi:10.1016/j.redeen.2016.04.002

Carmeli, A. (2001). High -and low- performance firms: Do they have different profiles of perceived core intangible resources and business environment? *Technovation*, *21*(10), 661–671. doi:10.1016/S0166-4972(01)00050-5

Carmeli, A., & Tishler, A. (2006). The relative importance of the top management team's managerial skills. *International Journal of Manpower*, *27*(1), 9–36. doi:10.1108/01437720610652817

Carney, M. (2005). Corporate governance and competitive advantage in family-controlled firms. *Entrepreneurship Theory and Practice*, *29*(May), 249–265. doi:10.1111/j.1540-6520.2005.00081.x

Casillas, J., Moreno, A., & Barbero, J. (2010). A configurational approach of the relationship between entrepreneurial orientation and growth of family firms. *Family Business Review*, *23*(1), 27–44. doi:10.1177/0894486509345159

Castanias, R. P., & Helfat, C. E. (1991). Managerial resources and rents. *Journal of Management*, *17*(1), 155–171. doi:10.1177/014920639101700110

Castanias, R. P., & Helfat, C. E. (2001). The managerial rents model: Theory and empirical analysis. *Journal of Management*, *27*(6), 661–678. doi:10.1177/014920630102700604

Chandler, A. D. (1990). *Scale and Scope: The dynamics of industrial capitalism.* Cambridge, MA: Harvard University Press.

Chen, H. L., & Hsu, W. T. (2009). Family ownership, board independence, and R&D investment. *Family Business Review*, *22*(4), 347–362. doi:10.1177/0894486509341062

Child, J. (1972). Organization structure, environment and performance: The role of strategic choice. *Sociology*, *6*(January), 1–22. doi:10.1177/003803857200600101

Chin, C. L., Chen, Y. J., Kleinman, G., & Lee, P. (2009). Corporate ownership struc-ture and innovation: Evidence from Taiwan's electronics industry. Journal ofAccounting. *Auditing & Finance*, *24*(1), 145–175. doi:10.1177/0148558X0902400108

Chrisman, J. J., Chua, J. H., & Sharma, P. (2003). *Current trends and future directions in family business management studies: Toward a theory of the family firm*. Colerman White Paper Series. Disponible en www.usabe.org/knowledge/whitepapers/index.asp

Chrisman, J. J., & Patel, P. C. (2012). Variations in R&D investments of family and non-family firms: Behavioral agency and myopic loss aversion perspectives. *Academy of Management Journal*, *55*(4), 976–997. doi:10.5465/amj.2011.0211

Cooper, M. J., Upton, N., & Seaman, S. (2005). Customer relationship management: A comparative analysis of family and nonfamily business practices. *Journal of Small Business Management*, *43*(3), 242–256. doi:10.1111/j.1540-627X.2005.00136.x

Cromie, S., Stevenson, B., & Montieth, D. (1995). The management of family firms: An empirical investigation. *International Small Business Journal*, *13*(4), 11–34. doi:10.1177/0266242695134001

Cuadrado Roura, J. R., & López Morales, J.M. (2015). *El turismo, motor del crecimiento y de la recuperación de la economía española*. Documentos de trabajo. IAES- Instituto Universitario de Análisis Económico y Social, Universidad de Alcalá, No. 04/15.

Cucculelli, M., & Micucci, G. (2008). Family succession and firm performance: Evidence from Italian family firms. *Journal of Corporate Finance*, *14*(1), 17–31. doi:10.1016/j.jcorpfin.2007.11.001

Daily, C. M., & Dollinger, M. J. (1992). An empirical examination of ownership structure in family and professionally managed firms. *Family Business Review*, *5*(2), 117–136. doi:10.1111/j.1741-6248.1992.00117.x

Day, G. S. (1994). The capabilities of market-driven organizations. *Journal of Marketing*, *58*(4), 37–52. doi:10.1177/002224299405800404

De Massis, A., Frattini, F., & Lichtenthaler, U. (2012). Research on technological innovation in family firms: Present debates and future directions. *Family Business Review*, *26*(1), 10–31. doi:10.1177/0894486512466258

De Massis, A., & Kotlar, J. (2015). Learning resources for family business education: A review and directions for future developments. *Academy of Management Learning & Education*, *14*(3), 415–422. doi:10.5465/amle.2014.0246

Decker, C., & Günther, C. (2017). The impact of family ownership on innovation: Evidence from the German machine tool industry. *Small Business Economics*, *48*(1), 199–212. doi:10.100711187-016-9775-0

Dekker, J., Lybaert, N., Steijvers, T., & Depaire, B. (2015). The effect of family business professionalization as a multidimensional construct on firm performance. *Journal of Small Business Management, 53*(2), 516–538. doi:10.1111/jsbm.12082

Demsetz, H., & Lehn, K. (1985). The structure of corporate ownership: Causes and consequences. *Journal of Political Economy, 93*(6), 1155–1177. doi:10.1086/261354

Dibrell, C., & Moeller, M. (2011). The impact of a service-dominant focus strategy and stewardship culture on organizational innovativeness in family-owned businesses. *Journal of Family Business Strategy, 2*(1), 43–51. doi:10.1016/j.jfbs.2011.01.004

Dillman, D.A. (1978). *Mail and telephone surveys: The Total Design Method.* John Wiley & Sons.

Donckels, R., & Frölich, E. (1991). Are family businesses really different? European experiences from Stratos. *Family Business Review, 4*(2), 149–160. doi:10.1111/j.1741-6248.1991.00149.x

Donnelley, R. (1964). The family business. *Harvard Business Review, 42*(4), 93–105.

Duncan, R. (1973). Multiple decision making structures in adapting to the environmental uncertainty: The impact of organizational effectiveness. *Human Relations, 26*(3), 273–291. doi:10.1177/001872677302600301

Dunn, B. (1995). Success themes in Scottish family enterprises: Philosophies and practices through the generations. *Family Business Review, 8*(1), 17–28. doi:10.1111/j.1741-6248.1995.00017.x

Duréndez, A., García, D., & Madrid, A. (2007). *Culture management control systems and performance in SME family firms. VII International Family Enterprise Research Academy Conference*, June, Germany.

Dutta, S., Narasimhan, O., & Rajiv, S. (1999). Success in high-technology markets: Is marketing capability critical. *Marketing Science, 18*(4), 547–568. doi:10.1287/mksc.18.4.547

Dyer, W. G. Jr. (1994). Potential contributions of organizational behaviour to the study of family-owned businesses. *Family Business Review, 7*(2), 109–131. doi:10.1111/j.1741-6248.1994.00109.x

Dyer, W. G. Jr, & Handler, W. (1994). Entrepreneurship and family business: Exploring the connections. *Entrepreneurship Theory and Practice, 19*(Fall), 71–83. doi:10.1177/104225879401900105

Eckrich, C. J., & Loughead, T. A. (1996). Effects of family business membership and psychological separation on the career development of late adolescents. *Family Business Review, 9*(4), 369–386. doi:10.1111/j.1741-6248.1996.00369.x

Eddleston, K. A., Kellermanns, F. W., & Sarathy, R. (2008). Resource configuration in family firms: Linking resources, strategic planning and technological opportunities to performance. *Journal of Management Studies, 45*, 26–50.

Eldridge, S., Balubaif, M., & Barber, K. D. (2006). Using a knowledge management approach to support quality costing. *International Journal of Quality & Reliability Management, 23*(1), 81–101. doi:10.1108/02656710610637569

Ellington, E. P., Jones, R. T., & Deane, R. (1996). TQM adoption practices in the family-owned business. *Family Business Review, 9*(1), 5–14. doi:10.1111/j.1741-6248.1996.00005.x

Esparza, J. L., García, D., & Duréndez, A. (2009). Gestión estratégica y competitiva de las empresas familiares turísticas mexicanas: Un estudio empírico. *Revista EAN*, *66*(Mayo-Agosto), 5–30.

Fernández, Z., & Nieto, M. J. (2005). La estrategia de internacionalización de la pequeña empresa familiar. *Cuadernos de Economía y Dirección de la Empresa*, *22*, 107–126.

Fiegener, M., Brown, B., Prince, R., & File, K. (1994). A comparison of successor development in family and non-family businesses. *Family Business Review*, *7*(4), 313–329. doi:10.1111/j.1741-6248.1994.00313.x

Fiegener, M. K., Brown, B. M., Prince, R. A., & File, K. M. (1996). Passing on strategic vision. *Journal of Small Business Management*, *34*(3), 15–26.

Finkelstein, D., & Hambrick, D. C. (1990). Top management team tenure and organizational outcomes: The moderating role of managerial discretion. *Administrative Science Quarterly*, *35*(3), 484–503. doi:10.2307/2393314

Fondas, N., & Wiersema, M. (1997). Changing of the guard: The influence of CEO socialization on strategic change. *Journal of Management Studies*, *34*(4), 561–584. doi:10.1111/1467-6486.00063

Galende, J. (2006). Analysis of technological innovation from business economics and management. *Technovation*, *26*(3), 300–311. doi:10.1016/j.technovation.2005.04.006

Galende, J., & Suárez, I. (1998). Los factores determinantes de las inversiones empresariales en I+D. *Economía Industrial*, *319*, 63–76.

Gallo, M. A., & Melé, D. (1998). *Ética en la empresa familiar*. Barcelona: Praxis.

Gallo, M. A., & Pont, C. G. (1996). Important factors in family business internationalization. *Family Business Review*, *9*(1), 45–59. doi:10.1111/j.1741-6248.1996.00045.x

Gallo, M. A., & Sveen, J. (1991). Internationalizing the family business: Facilitating and restraining factors. *Family Business Review*, *4*(2), 181–190. doi:10.1111/j.1741-6248.1991.00181.x

Gallo, M. A., Tàpies, J., & Cappuyns, K. (2004). Comparison of family and nonfamily business: Financial logic and personal preferences. *Family Business Review*, *17*(4), 303–318. doi:10.1111/j.1741-6248.2004.00020.x

García-Álvarez, E., López-Sintas, J., & Saldaña Gonzalvo, P. (2002). Socialization patterns of successors in first-to second-generation family businesses. *Family Business Review*, *15*(3), 189–203.

Gersick, K. E., Davis, J. A., Hampton, M., & Lansberg, I. (1997). *Generation to generation - Life cycles of the family business*. Harvard Business School Press.

Getz, D., & Carlsen, J. (2000). Characteristics and goals of family and owner-operated business in the rural tourism and hospitality sectors. *Tourism Management*, *21*(6), 547–560. doi:10.1016/S0261-5177(00)00004-2

Getz, D., & Carlsen, J. (2005). Family business in tourism. State of the art. *Annals of Tourism Research*, *32*(1), 237–258. doi:10.1016/j.annals.2004.07.006

Gómez-Mejía, L. R., Haynes, K. T., Núñez-Nickel, M., Jacobson, K. J., & Moyano-Fuentes, J. (2007). Socioemotional wealth and business risks in family-controlled firms: Evidence from Spanish olive oil mills. *Administrative Science Quarterly*, *52*(1), 106–137. doi:10.2189/asqu.52.1.106

Gómez-Mejía, L. R., Larrazar-Kintana, M., & Makri, M. (2003). The determinants of executive compensation in family- controlled public corporations. *Academy of Management Journal*, *46*(2), 226–237.

Habbershon, T., & Williams, M. (1999). A resource-based framework for assessing the strategic advantage of family firms. *Family Business Review*, *12*(1), 27–39. doi:10.1111/j.1741-6248.1999.00001.x

Habbershon, T., & Williams, M. (2000). A model for understanding the competitiveness of family-controlled companies. In P. Poutziouris (Ed.), *Tradition or entrepreneurship in the New Economy* (pp. 94–115). Manchester, UK: Manchester Business School.

Habbershon, T., Williams, M., & MacMillan, L. C. (2003). A unified systems perspective of family firm performance. *Journal of Business Venturing*, *18*(4), 451–465. doi:10.1016/S0883-9026(03)00053-3

Habbershon, T. G. (2006). Commentary: A framework for managing the familiness and agency advantages in family firms. *Entrepreneurship Theory and Practice*, *30*(6), 879–886. doi:10.1111/j.1540-6520.2006.00158.x

Hair, J. F., Anderson, R. E., Tatham, R. L., & Black, W. C. (1998). *Multivariate data analysis.* Prentice Hall.

Hall, A., Melin, L., & Nordqvist, M. (2001). Entrepreneurship as radical change in family business: Exploring the role of cultural patterns. *Family Business Review*, *14*(3), 193–208. doi:10.1111/j.1741-6248.2001.00193.x

Hambrick, D. C., Cho, T. S., & Chen, M. J. (1996). The influence of top management team heterogeneity on firms' competitive moves. *Administrative Science Quarterly*, *41*(4), 659–684. doi:10.2307/2393871

Hambrick, D. C., & Mason, P. (1984). Upper echelons: The organization as a reflection of its top managers. *Academy of Management Review*, *9*(2), 193–206. doi:10.5465/amr.1984.4277628

Handler, W. C. (1989). Methodological issues and considerations in studying family business. *Family Business Review*, *2*(3), 257–276. doi:10.1111/j.1741-6248.1989.00257.x

Hayward, S. (1992). *Managing the family business in the UK: A Stoy Hayward survey in conjunction with the London Business School.* London: Stoy Hayward.

Heck, R. K. Z., & Walker, R. (1993). Family-owned home-business: Their employees and unpaid helpers. *Family Business Review*, *6*(4), 397–415. doi:10.1111/j.1741-6248.1993.00397.x

Hitt, M. A., & Ireland, R. D. (1985). Corporate distinctive competence, strategy, industry, and performance. *Strategic Management Journal*, *6*(3), 273–293. doi:10.1002mj.4250060307

Hoffman, J., Hoelscher, M., & Sorenson, R. (2006). Achieving sustained competitive advantage: A family capital theory. *Family Business Review*, *19*(2), 135–145. doi:10.1111/j.1741-6248.2006.00065.x

Hooley, G. J., Broderick, A., & Möller, K. (1998). Competitive positioning and the resource-based view of the firm. *Journal of Strategic Marketing*, *6*(2), 97–115. doi:10.1080/09652549800000003

Hooley, G. J., Greenley, G. E., Cadogan, J. W., & Fahy, J. (2005). The performance impact of marketing resources. *Journal of Business Research, 58*(1), 18–27. doi:10.1016/S0148-2963(03)00109-7

Horton, T. P. (1986). Managing in a family way. *Management Review, 75*(2), 3.

Hunt, S. D. (2000). *A general theory of competition*. Thousand Oaks, CA: Sage Publications.

Hunt, S. D., & Morgan, R. M. (1995). The comparative advantage theory of competition. *Journal of Marketing, 59*(2), 1–15. doi:10.1177/002224299505900201

James, H. Jr. (1999). What can the family contribute to business? Examining contractual relationships. *Family Business Review, 12*(1), 61–71. doi:10.1111/j.1741-6248.1999.00061.x

Jorissen, A., Laveren, E., Martens, R., & Reheul, A. (2001). *Planning and control practices in family firms versus non-family firms: empirical evidence from SMEs in the wholesale sector*. Antwerp, Belgium: Faculty of Applied Economics.

Kabbach de Castro, L. R., Aguilera, R. V., & Crespí-Cladera, R. (2017). Family firms and compliance: Reconciling the conflicting predictions within the socioemotional wealth perspective. *Family Business Review, 30*(2), 137–159. doi:10.1177/0894486516685239

Kamoche, K. (1996). Strategic human resource management within a resource-capability view of the firm. *Journal of Management Studies, 33*(2), 213–233. doi:10.1111/j.1467-6486.1996.tb00158.x

Karagozoglu, N., & Brown, W. B. (1988). Adaptive responses by conservative and entrepreneurial firms. *Journal of Product Innovation Management, 5*(4), 269–281. doi:10.1111/1540-5885.540269

Katz, R. L. (1974). Skills of and effective administrator. *Harvard Business Review, 52*(September-October), 90–102.

Kellermanns, F. W., & Eddleston, K. A. (2006). Corporate entrepreneurship in family firms: A family perspective. *Entrepreneurship Theory and Practice, 30*(November), 809–830. doi:10.1111/j.1540-6520.2006.00153.x

Kets de Vries, M. F. R. (1993). The dynamics of family controlled firms: The good and the bad news. *Organizational Dynamics, 21*(3), 59–71. doi:10.1016/0090-2616(93)90071-8

Kirchhoff, B. A., & Kirchhoff, J. J. (1987). Family contributions to productivity and profitability in small business. *Journal of Small Business Management, 25*(4), 25–31.

Kogut, B., & Zander, U. (1992). Knowledge of the firm, combinative capabilities, and the replication of technology. *Organization Science, 3*(3), 383–397. doi:10.1287/orsc.3.3.383

Kor, Y. Y. (2003). Experience-based Top management team competence and sustained growth. *Organization Science, 14*(6), 707–719. doi:10.1287/orsc.14.6.707.24867

Lado, A. A., & Wilson, M. C. (1994). Human resource systems and sustained competitive advantage: A competency-based perspective. *Academy of Management Review, 19*(4), 699–727. doi:10.5465/amr.1994.9412190216

Landeta, J., Barrutia, J., Araujo, A., & Hoyos, J. (2007). *Claves del comportamiento de la empresa respecto a la formación continua de sus directivos*. Thomson Cívitas, Navarra.

Lansberg, I., & Gersick, K. (2015). Educating family business owners: The fundamental intervention. *Academy of Management Learning & Education*, *14*(3), 400–413. doi:10.5465/amle.2014.0254

Lansberg, I. S. (1983). Managing human resources in family firms: The problem of institutional overlap. *Organizational Dynamics*, *12*(1), 39–46. doi:10.1016/0090-2616(83)90025-6

Larrinaga, C., & Vallejo, R. (2013). El turismo en el desarrollo español contemporáneo. *TST: Transportes. Servicios y Telecomunicaciones*, *24*, 12–29.

Lerner, M., & Almor, T. (2002). Relationships among strategic capabilities and the performance of women-owned small ventures. *Journal of Small Business Management*, *40*(2), 109–125. doi:10.1111/1540-627X.00044

Levinson, R. E. (1987). Problems in managing a family-owned business. In C. E. Aronoff & J. L. Ward (Eds.), *Family business sourcebook* (pp. 169–174). Detroit, MI: Omnigraphics.

Levring, R., & Moskowitz, M. (1993). The ten best companies to work for in *America. Business and Society Review*, *85*(1), 26–38.

Lindbeck, A., & Weibull, J. W. (1988). Altruism and time consistency: The economics of fait accompli. *Journal of Political Economy*, *96*(6), 1165–1182. doi:10.1086/261582

Lubatkin, M. H., Schulze, W. S., Ling, Y., & Dino, R. N. (2005). The effects of parental altruism on the governance of family-managed firms. *Journal of Organizational Behavior*, *26*(3), 313–330. doi:10.1002/job.307

Mahoney, J. T. (1995). The management of resources and the resource of management. *Journal of Business Research*, *33*(2), 91–101. doi:10.1016/0148-2963(94)00060-R

Mariussen, A., Wheelock, J., & Baines, S. (1997). The family business Tradition in Britain and Norway. *International Studies of Management & Organization*, *27*(3), 64–85. doi:10.1080/00208825.1997.11656713

Markides, C.C., Williamson, P.J. (1994). Related diversification, core competences and corporate performance. *Strategic Management Journal 15*(special issue, summer), 149-165.

Martínez, R., Charterina, J., & Araujo, A. (2010). Un modelo causal de competitividad empresarial planteado desde la VBR: Capacidades directivas, de innovación, marketing y calidad. *Investigaciones Europeas de Dirección y Economía de la Empresa*, *16*(2), 1135–2523.

Matlay, H. (2002). Training and HRD strategies in family and non-family owned small businesses: A comparative approach. *Education + Training*, *44*(8/9), 357–369. doi:10.1108/00400910210449196

Mehra, A. (1996). Resource and market based determinants of performance in the US banking industry. *Strategic Management Journal*, *17*(4), 307–322. doi:10.1002/(SICI)1097-0266(199604)17:4<307::AID-SMJ820>3.0.CO;2-2

Milfelner, B., Gabrijan, V., & Snoj, B. (2008). Can marketing resources contribute to company performance? *Organizacija*, *14*(1), 3–13.

Miller, D., Le Breton-Miller, I., Lester, R. H., & Cannella, A. A. Jr. (2007). Are family firms really superior performers? *Journal of Corporate Finance*, *13*(5), 829–858. doi:10.1016/j.jcorpfin.2007.03.004

Miller, N. J., McLeod, H., & Oh, K. Y. (2001). Managing family business in small communities. *Journal of Small Business Management*, *39*(1), 73–87. doi:10.1111/0447-2778.00007

Morris, M. H. (1998). *Entrepreneurial intensity*. Westport, CT: Quorum Books.

Munari, F., Oriani, R., & Sobrero, M. (2010). The effects of owner identity and external governance systems on R&D investments: A study of Western European firms. *Research Policy*, *39*(8), 1093–1104. doi:10.1016/j.respol.2010.05.004

Naldi, L., Nordqvist, M., Sjöberg, K., & Wiklund, J. (2007). Entrepreneurial orientation, risk taking and performance in family firms. *Family Business Review*, *23*(1), 33–47. doi:10.1111/j.1741-6248.2007.00082.x

Neubaum, D. O., Dibrell, C., & Craig, J. B. (2012). Balancing natural environmental con-cerns of internal and external stakeholders in family and non-family businesses. *Journal of Family Business Strategy*, *3*(1), 28–37. doi:10.1016/j.jfbs.2012.01.003

Olson, P. D., Zuiker, V. S., Danes, S. M., Stafford, K., Heck, R. K. Z., & Duncan, K. A. (2003). The impact of the family and the business on family business sustainability. *Journal of Business Venturing*, *18*(5), 639–666. doi:10.1016/S0883-9026(03)00014-4

Osbaldeston, M., & Barham, K. (1992). Using management development for competitive advantage. *Long Range Planning*, *25*(6), 18–24. doi:10.1016/0024-6301(92)90165-X

Pearson, A. W., Carr, J. C., & Shaw, J. C. (2008). Toward a theory of familiness: A social capital perspective. *Entrepreneurship Theory and Practice*, *32*(6), 949–969. doi:10.1111/j.1540-6520.2008.00265.x

Pedreño, A., & Ramón, A. (2009). El turismo: Globalización, competitividad y sostenibilidad. *Colección Mediterráneo Económico*, *16*, 227–256.

Penrose, E. (1959). *The Theory of the growth of the firm*. New York: John Wiley & Sons.

Pérez-Cabañero, C., González-Cruz, T., & Cruz-Ros, S. (2012). Do family SME managers value marketing capabilities' contribution to firm performance? *Marketing Intelligence & Planning*, *30*(2), 116–142. doi:10.1108/02634501211211948

Pervin, A. (1997). A conversation with Henry Mintzberg. *Family Business Review*, *10*(2), 1985–198. doi:10.1111/j.1741-6248.1997.00185.x

Peteraf, M. A. (1993). The cornerstone of competitive advantage: A resource-based view. *Strategic Management Journal*, *14*(3), 179–191. doi:10.1002mj.4250140303

Peters, M., & Buhalis, D. (2004). Family hotel business: Strategic planning and the need for education and training. *Education + Training*, *46*(8/9), 406–415. doi:10.1108/00400910410569524

Pickett, L. (1998). Competencies and managerial effectiveness: Putting competencies to work. *Public Personnel Management, 27*(1), 103–115. doi:10.1177/009102609802700110

Qureshi, S., Chen, C., & Wang, M. (2017). A multi-dimensional professionalisation construct for UK family businesses–building internal capabilities and improving business performance. In *ICSB World Conference Proceedings* (pp. 1-10). International Council for Small Business (ICSB).

Reed, R., Lemak, D. J., & Montgomery, J. C. (1996). Beyond process: TQM content and firm performance. *Academy of Management Review, 12*(1), 173–202. doi:10.5465/amr.1996.9602161569

Robins, J., & Wiersema, M. F. (1995). A resource-based approach to the multibusiness firm: Empirical analysis of portfolio interrelationships and corporate financial performance. *Strategic Management Journal, 16*(4), 277–299. doi:10.1002mj.4250160403

Rogoff, E. G., Lee, M., & Suh, D. (2004). Who done it? Attributions by entrepreneurs and experts of the factors that cause and impede small business success. *Journal of Small Business Management, 42*(4), 374–376. doi:10.1111/j.1540-627X.2004.00117.x

Rosenblatt, P. C., DeMik, L., Anderson, R. M., & Johnson, P. A. (1985). *The family in business: Understanding and dealing with the challenges entrepreneurial families face.* San Francisco: Jossey-Bass.

Rubenstein, C. (1990). Power and priorities. *Family Business Magazine, 2*(2), 37.

Rubio, A., & Aragón, A. (2002). Factores explicativos del éxito competitivo. Un estudio empírico en la PYME. *Cuadernos de Gestión, 2*(1), 49–63.

Rubio, A., & Aragón, A. (2006). Competitividad y recursos estratégicos en las PYMEs. *Revista de Empresa, 17*, 32–47.

Rubio, A., & Aragón, A. (2008). Recursos estratégicos en las PYMEs. *Revista Europea de Dirección y Economía de la Empresa, 17*(1), 103–126.

Rumelt, R. P. (1991). How much does industry matter? *Strategic Management Journal, 12*(3), 167–185.

Russo, M., & Fouts, P. (1997). A resource-based perspective on corporate environmental performance and profitability. *Academy of Management Journal, 40*(3), 534–559.

Schmalensee, R. (1985). Do markets differ much? *The American Economic Review, 75*, 341–351.

Schulze, W. S., Lubatkin, M. H., & Dino, R. N. (2002). Altruism, agency, and the competitiveness of family firms. *Managerial and Decision Economics, 23*(4-5), 247–259. doi:10.1002/mde.1064

Schulze, W. S., Lubatkin, M. H., & Dino, R. N. (2003). Toward a theory of agency and altruism in family firms. *Journal of Business Venturing, 18*(4), 473–490. doi:10.1016/S0883-9026(03)00054-5

Sharma, P., Chrisman, J. J., & Chua, J. H. (1997). Strategic management of the family business: Past research and future challenges. *Family Business Review, 10*(1), 1–36. doi:10.1111/j.1741-6248.1997.00001.x

Siebels, J. F., & zu Knyphausen-Aufseß, D. (2012). A review of theory in family business research: The implications for corporate governance. *International Journal of Management Reviews, 14*(3), 280–304. doi:10.1111/j.1468-2370.2011.00317.x

Sirmon, D., & Hitt, M. (2003). Managing resources: Linking unique resources, management and wealth creation in family firms. *Entrepreneurship Theory and Practice, 27*(Summer), 339–358. doi:10.1111/1540-8520.t01-1-00013

Srivastava, R. K., Shervani, T. A., & Fahey, L. (1998). Market-based assets and shareholder value: A framework for analysis. *Journal of Marketing, 62*(1), 2–18. doi:10.1177/002224299806200102

Srivastava, R. K., Shervani, T. A., & Fahey, L. (1999). Marketing business process, and shareholder value: An organizationally embedded view of marketing activities and the discipline of marketing. *Journal of Marketing, 63*(special issue), 168–179. doi:10.1177/00222429990634s116

Stavrou, E. T. (1999). Succession in family business: Exploring the effects of demographic factor on offspring intentions to join and take over the business. *Journal of Small Business Management, 37*(3), 43–61.

Steier, L. (2003). Variants of agency contracts in family-financed ventures as a continuum of familial altruistic and market rationalities. *Journal of Business Venturing, 18*(5), 597–618. doi:10.1016/S0883-9026(03)00012-0

Stewart, A., & Hitt, M. A. (2012). Why can't a family business be more like a nonfamily business? Modes of professionalization in family firms. *Family Business Review, 25*(1), 58–86. doi:10.1177/0894486511421665

Tagiuri, R., & Davis, J. A. (1992). On the Goals of Successful Family Companies. *Family Business Review, 5*(1), 263–281. doi:10.1111/j.1741-6248.1992.00043.x

Tagiuri, R., & Davis, J. A. (1996). Bivalent attributes of the family firm. *Family Business Review, IX*(2), 199–208. doi:10.1111/j.1741-6248.1996.00199.x

Thomas, J. B., Clark, S. M., & Gioia, D. A. (1993). Strategic sensemaking and organizational performance: Linkages among scanning, interpretation, action and outcomes. *Academy of Management Journal, 36*(2), 239–270.

Tokarczyk, J., Hansen, E., Green, M., & Down, J. (2007). A resource-based view and market orientation theory examination of the role of familiness in family business success. *Family Business Review, XX*(1), 17–31. doi:10.1111/j.1741-6248.2007.00081.x

Vago, M. (2004). Integrating change management: Challenges for family business clients and consultants. *Family Business Review, 17*(1), 71–80. doi:10.1111/j.1741-6248.2004.00005.x

Vera, F., & Marchena, M. (1996). *El modelo turístico español. In Introducción a la economía del turismo en España* (pp. 327–364). Madrid: Civitas.

Vorhies, D. W., Harker, M., & Rao, C. P. (1999). The capabilities and performance advantages of market-driven firms. *European Journal of Marketing, 33*(11-12), 1171–1202. doi:10.1108/03090569910292339

Wanhill, S. (1997). Peripheral area tourism: A European perspective. *Progress in Tourism and Hospitality Research, 3*(1), 47–70. doi:10.1002/(SICI)1099-1603(199703)3:1<47::AID-PTH38>3.0.CO;2-F

Wanhill, S. (2000). Small and medium tourism enterprises. *Annals of Tourism Research, 27*(1), 132–147. doi:10.1016/S0160-7383(99)00072-9

Ward, J. L. (1987). *Keeping the family business healthy: How to plan for continuing growth, profitability, and family leadership*. San Francisco: Jossey-Bass.

Ward, J. L. (1988). The special role of strategic planning for family business. *Family Business Review*, *1*(2), 105–117. doi:10.1111/j.1741-6248.1988.00105.x

Ward, J. L. (1997). Growing the family business: Special challenges and best practices. *Family Business Review*, *10*(4), 323–337. doi:10.1111/j.1741-6248.1997.00323.x

Webster, F. E. Jr. (1992). The changing role of marketing in the corporation. *Journal of Marketing*, *56*(4), 1–17. doi:10.1177/002224299205600402

Werts, C. E., Linn, R. L., & Jöreskog, K. G. (1974). Interclass reliability estimates: Testing structural assumptions. *Educational and Psychological Measurement*, *34*(1), 25–33. doi:10.1177/001316447403400104

Westhead, P. (1997). Ambitions, external environment and strategic factor differences between family and non-family companies. *Entrepreneurship and Regional Development*, *9*(2), 127–157. doi:10.1080/08985629700000007

Wright, P. M., McMahan, G. C., & McWilliams, A. (1994). Human resources and sustained competitive advantage: A resource-based perspective. *International Journal of Human Resource Management*, *5*(2), 301–326. doi:10.1080/09585199400000020

Zahra, S. A. (2005). Entrepreneurial risk taking in family firms. *Family Business Review*, *18*(1), 23–40. doi:10.1111/j.1741-6248.2005.00028.x

Zahra, S. A., Hayton, J. C., & Salvato, C. (2004). Entrepreneurship in family vs. non-family firms: A resource based analysis of the effect of organizational culture. *Entrepreneurship Theory and Practice*, *28*(Summer), 363–381. doi:10.1111/j.1540-6520.2004.00051.x

ADDITIONAL READING

Ahluwalia, S., Mahto, R. V., & Walsh, S. T. (2017). Innovation in small firms: Does family vs. non-family matter? *Journal of Small Business Strategy*, *27*(3), 39–49.

Bello-Pintado, A., & Garcés-Galdeano, L. (2017). Bundles of HRM practices in family and non-family firms: The impact on enhancing performance. *International Journal of Human Resource Management*, 1–22. doi:10.1080/09585192.2017.1391311

Camisón, C., & Forés, B. (2015). Is tourism firm competitiveness driven by different internal or external specific factors?: New empirical evidence from Spain. *Tourism Management*, *48*, 477–499. doi:10.1016/j.tourman.2015.01.001

Chrisman, J. J., Steier, L. P., & Chua, J. H. (2008). Toward a theoretical basis for understanding the dynamics of strategic performance in family firms. *Entrepreneurship Theory and Practice*, *32*(6), 935–947. doi:10.1111/j.1540-6520.2008.00264.x

Dyer, W. G. (2018). Are family firms really better? Reexamining "examining the 'family effect'on firm performance". *Family Business Review*, *31*(2), 240–248. doi:10.1177/0894486518776516

Forcadell, F. J., Ubeda, F., & Zúñiga-Vicente, J. Á. (2018). Initial resource heterogeneity differences between family and non-family firms: Implications for resource acquisition and resource generation. *Long Range Planning*, *51*(5), 693–719. doi:10.1016/j.lrp.2017.11.003

Le Breton-Miller, I., Miller, D., & Bares, F. (2015). Governance and entrepreneurship in family firms: Agency, behavioral agency and resource-based comparisons. *Journal of Family Business Strategy*, *6*(1), 58–62. doi:10.1016/j.jfbs.2014.10.002

Zahra, S. A. (2018). Entrepreneurial risk taking in family firms: The wellspring of the regenerative capability. *Family Business Review*, *31*(2), 216–226. doi:10.1177/0894486518776871

KEY TERMS AND DEFINITIONS

Distinctive Competences: Specific and internal characteristics unique in a company on which their competitive advantage is based. Some of the most relevant to competitiveness are capabilities in innovation and technology, human resource and organizational culture, marketing, quality, and management.

Family Firms: Firms where the business and the family are interrelated. Firms that are owned and managed by a family who has the interest in passing its ownership from generation to generation.

Managerial Capabilities: Necessary skills and abilities for an adequate management of the business and for a correct development and use of the rest of competences.

Structural Equations: Statistical technique of a multivariate nature that is used for testing causal relationships from statistical data.

Tourism Sector: Set of firms and other agents belonging to different industries that produce consumer goods and services demanded by visitors. It encompasses activities such as hotel, catering or transportation, among others.

Chapter 5
Which Competitive Strategy Fits Better to Different Family-Business Profiles?
A Configurational Approach

Tomás F. González-Cruz
https://orcid.org/0000-0001-7479-7268
University of Valencia, Spain

Norat Roig-Tierno
ESIC Business and Marketing School, Spain

ABSTRACT

This chapter belongs to the vein of research that analyses family firms from a configurational approach. This survey explores which combination of competitive strategy, environmental turbulence, family complexity, and family firm management and governance arrangements are present when firm performance is present. This research follows Le Breton-Miller and Miller's call to gain a better understanding of the interaction between competitive strategy, environmental conditions, and family firm features. Literature reports controversial results with regard to family-business strategic preferences and firm performance, and recent research shows that this relationship needs considering both industry and family context. This chapter analyses a sample of 129 Spanish SME-Family-Business that belong to the tourism industry. Using fuzzy-set qualitative comparative analysis, the authors find seven configurations to firm performance presence and one recipe for performance absence.

INTRODUCTION

Understanding family-firm preferences in terms of strategic choice remains and open and relevant question in the field of family-business research. There is a generalized assumption that family-firms with high degree of family involvement are prone to conservatism and strategic stagnation. However, Miller

DOI: 10.4018/978-1-7998-1655-3.ch005

& Le-Breton Miller (2005), as well as Van Gils et al (2004), report that family-business do not show any specific preference toward any specific competitive strategy. If anything, the last paper reports a high percentage of family-firms 'stuck in the middle'. In a conceptual paper Le-Breton Miller & Miller (2008), argues that *'there are important differences in the priorities and risk preferences of individual or unrelated founder vs family owners and managers'* (p.43). That is, they state that family-business strategic preferences will depend on family-firm involvement, firm governance and CEO profile.

The evidence that family-business do not behave in an homogeneous way call for turning attention toward gaining understanding of family-business heterogeneity, analyzing firm behavior in a contextualized way and paying attention to the set of circumstances where decisions are made and enacted. This configurative approach requires specific research methodologies recently incorporated to the family-business research literature, as latent profile analysis or fuzzy-set qualitative comparative analysis. However, despite this call to a contextualized understanding of family-firm strategic behavior, to date the amount of research devoted to the topic remains limited:

Basco (2014), proposes a typology based on decision-making –'business first'; 'family-business first'; and 'family first'– and Porter (1985) competitive strategies. Through a cluster-analysis looks for fit between decision-making style and competitive strategy. Results show that high performance occurs in those family-firms that follow a differentiation strategy and balance family and firm priorities and to family-firms that chose a low cost strategy and follow a 'business first' decision-making logic.

The same year, Moss et al. (2014) run a longitudinal research over 94 high-tech family-business, and consider firm size, environmental dynamism and munificence. They analyze strategic consistency –refers to the intensity of both, exploration and exploitation activities together and along time– and its impact on performance. Results show that the relationship between strategic consistency and financial performance is stronger in family-business that in non-family business. Alike they report that environmental dynamism positively moderates the relationship between strategic consistency and financial performance. On the contrary, firm size moderates negatively this relationship.

Recently, Stanley et al (2019) analyze the presence of entrepreneurial orientation and firm performance in a sample of Spanish and Portuguese family-firms. They consider family-firm features related to family influence in ownership –percentage of stock in family hands– and management –family CEO–; and life cycle stage: generation in charge, firm governance –Board of Directors– and firm size. This paper proposes a family-firm typology using a 2X2 matrix based on the degree of family influence and the family-firm life-cycle stage. Using latent profile analysis, the survey finds out four profiles and report that family-firms profiles with a board of directors and a family CEO present superior traits of entrepreneurial orientation. Alike, small and closely held family firms that have a board of directors and a family CEO, present superior performance than small, first generation, closely held family-firms that do not have board of directors but have a family CEO.

In order to continue this emergent vein of research, this chapter analyses a sample of 129 family-firms. In order to reduce the source of heterogeneity, all of they are SME closely held family-business that belong to the Spanish tourism industry. Applying fuzzy set comparative analysis the survey takes performance as the outcome, and considers as conditions: competitive strategy, environmental turbulence, family complexity –generations and number of shareholders–, the presence of Board of Directors and a Family CEO.

The contributions are several: first, this survey considers environmental turbulence, a more comprehensive measure of environmental conditions, given that turbulence is a mix of hostility, dynamism, uncertainty and complexity. Second, even when the initial sample was much larger, the research strategy of this chapter looks for limiting the potential sources of heterogeneity, and really focusing on the condition variables under research. Last, but not least, the survey uses an alternative methodology to those applied in previous pieces of research: cluster and latent profile analysis. Fuzzy set comparative analysis is a technique applied in recent research in the field of family-business (González-Cruz & Cruz-Ros, 2016; Kosmidou & Ahuja, 2019; Rojas, 2019), that results proper to explore configurations of equifinal sets of conditions that are present when an outcome is present. Following an exploratory approach, the paper analyzes core and peripheral conditions that appear in the combinations that have presence of firm performance, as well on the recipe for performance absence.

The remainder of the chapter structures as follows: Next paragraph presents a concise review of family-firm's state of the art regarding strategic preferences. Given that there is wide consensus about its relevance to explain family-firm's strategic behavior, the chapter considers some family firm features related to family-firm complexity, governance and management. Alike, the paper reviews past research analyzing family-firm behavior under dynamic and uncertain environments. Next, data collection and methodology paragraphs present sample main features, how variables are measured and calibration criteria. Results show seven recipes for performance presence and one recipe for performance absence. The chapter closes with conclusion and a set of propositions for future research.

FAMILY-FIRM STRATEGIC PREFERENCES AND PERFORMANCE

Mainstream literature in family-business sustains that this type of ownership is conducive to specific strategic preferences and different levels of tolerance to uncertainty (Anderson & Reeb, 2003; Maury, 2006; Miller et al., 2007; Villalonga & Amit, 2006), and consequently, to different strategic choices and performance levels. However, when analyzing such differences, results are inconclusive and even contradictory. To address this issue Le Breton-Miller & Miller (2008) state that understanding family choices and outcomes requires considering the exact nature of the family-business. This paragraph briefly presents main contributions that describe family-business strategic preferences and some environmental factors and family-firm circumstances that circumscribe these strategic preferences and behaviors.

Family-Firm Strategic Preferences

Two main veins of research sustain contradictory family-business strategic preferences and behavior. On one hand, those that state that closely held family-business have and orientation toward exploration, risk-taking, growth and value creation (Arrègle et al., 2007; Miller & Le Breton-Miller, 2005; James, 2009; Ward, 2004). On the other hand, those that report that family-business are oriented to serve family interest. In consequence, they favor ownership control and value extraction to satisfy the family dominant coalition, at a cost of long term investment, risk taking, growth and value creation (Bertrand & Schoar (2006; Claessens et al., 2002; Gómez-Mejía et al., 2007; Morck et al., 2005; Pérez-González, 2006).

The first one are family-business that maintain the entrepreneurial spirit of the founder generation. They are oriented toward value creation and growth. These family-firms focus on developing and absorbing the specific knowledge needed to sense new ventures, as well as the discretion to remain quick in seizing transient opportunities. They tolerate uncertainty and dynamic environments, and take risk in long-term investments, addressed to explore new challenges, developing new capabilities and reconfiguring resources to seize such opportunities (James, 2009; Kang, 1998; Miller & Le Breton-Miller, 2005; Weber et al.; 2003). In terms of strategic behavior, these family-firms focus on making a difference through new products and services addressed to untapped markets (Covin & Selvin, 2002). As a result, these family-firms generate superior performance and growth (Gómez-Mejía et al., 2007; Moss et al., 2014).

The second one are owner-families that consider that the firm is a means to satisfy present and future family's aspirations and needs in terms of wealth, social status, reputation, etc. Consequently, they focus on minimizing chances of losses, maintaining ownership control, sustaining family´s income flow, at the same time that keeping family's wealth safe. Therefore, this family-business are risk averse and present low tolerance levels to uncertainty and turbulent environments. In terms of strategic behavior, these family-firms focus on reaping form the business looking for value capture. In order to keep ownership control they avoid debt at a cost of reducing investment and sacrificing firm growth (Bloom & van Reenen, 2007). The result is that firm performance constrains in favor of other family's non-financial outcomes (Miller et al., 2007). The positive side is that financial performance becomes less risky and more predictable, satisfying family needs (Le Breton-Miller & Miller, 2008).

Family Complexity as a Conditioning of Strategic Preferences

Family complexity refers to the family size, number of generations and family branches that comprise the owner family. Frequently this complexity leads also to ownership dilution between family members. The most common outcomes of the increasing in family complexity are: reduced emotional commitment to the firm (Vilaseca, 2002); less cohesion and more divergences due to heterogeneous views, intentions and needs (Gnan et al., 2005); and reduces management discretion to made strategic decisions (James, 2009). With regard performance, published research reports a negative and significant impact (De Massis et al., 2013, 2015; Mazzola et al., 2013; Miller et al., 2013).

In terms of strategic preferences, family complexity and ownership dilution bring to the fore front family interests at a cost of firm interest. In addition, later generations sometimes lack the necessary competences to make the business grow (Lubatkin et al., 2007; Pérez-González, 2006; Villalonga & Amit, 2006). Similarly, when the number of generations in the business increases, the risk of conflict grows because of disparity of identities and intents (Bertrand & Schoar, 2006). Therefore, conservatism –to protect family wealth– and value extraction –to satisfy diverse family expectations and needs– emerge. Alike, ownership dilution reduces family discretion to take risk an engage in new ventures that require exploration activities and investing in specific resources. These family-firms behave as price acceptance players, which exploit the present firm's endowment of resources and capabilities. Given that the lack of entrepreneurial action reduces firm's offer attractiveness, they embark on a price reduction at a cost of a mix of renewal investments and profit, behaving as apparent low cost players.

On the contrary, low family complexity reduces agency cost and the risk of owner-owner conflicts (Le Breton-Miller & Miller, 2009), leaving room to entrepreneurial behavior. Alike, low ownership complexity –a few number of shareholder– results in more discretion and agility to make decisions. These features favor exploratory strategies that look for differentiation –based on product, marketing or service– (Basco, 2014; Moss et al., 2014).

Family-Firm Government and Management as a Conditioning of Strategic Preferences

With regard family involvement in government and management, this chapter considers the existence of a board of directors and a CEO belonging to the owner family.

For the case of family-business, the board of directors becomes a key government device to balancing business and family goals (Addae-Boateng et al., 2014). The board of directors also gives room to family that is not in managerial post to contribute with their personal expertise, provide alternative perspectives, and bring information and relational capital to the family-business (Addae-Boateng et al., 2014; Johannisson & Huse 2000). In addition, those boards that include non-family directors, and especially outside directors, can also serve as more objective monitors of executives, help in locating and hiring new managers, improve resource-allocation decisions, and avoiding that family members expropriate the firm's wealth (Bammens et al., 2011; Brenes et al., 2011; Lai et al., 2014; Voordeckers et al., 2007).

In terms of strategic behavior, the board of directors can be a double-edged sword, depending on its composition. In complex owner families, the board of directors can become the scenario in which differences are aired, and conflicts are staged. Family directors not involved in management may lack knowledge of the business, inclining the board to be risk averse and thus to favor conservative strategies, becoming an impediment to the development of the firm and the exploration of new opportunities. In these situations, non-family directors and especially outside directors are a necessary condition to convert the board in a dynamic forum that supports managers in their process of exploring, sensing and creating new business opportunities.

The origin of the CEO, family vs non-family CEO, is another question that has impact on family business strategic behavior. A CEO that belongs to the owner family shares owners' interest, reducing traditional agency cost (Jensen & Meckling, 1976; McConaughy, 2000), alike, CEO's closeness to the business may provide them with information, specific knowledge and experience that reduce decision making uncertainty and afford greater risk tolerance. Finally, compared to a non-family CEO, a family CEO is more apt to have the personal status and the job- and financial-security to resist pressures from other family owners for conservatism or for gratuitous benefits from the business. In terms of outcomes, Minichilli et al. (2010) and Miller et al. (2013) report that family business, especially SME, with a family CEO present better financial performance than those with a non-family CEO.

Environmental Turbulence and Family-Firm Strategic Preferences

The perception of a turbulent competitive environment occurs when the management coalition labels it as dynamic, hostile and uncertain. Dynamism implies high rates of change both in market factors and in technology factors, as well as changes in customer preferences. Firms that face dynamic environments should focus on sensing new opportunities for value creation. On the contrary, in stable environments, firms ought to focus on efficiency and resource exploitation.

There is plenty of evidence that reactive strategic behavior in dynamic environments lead to underperformance. For the case of family-firms, it is foreseeable that no-executive family owners, that do not understand the industry's dynamic, will fear the risk associated to the needed strategic changes. If this group has a dominant position, they will delay changes and block management initiatives. On the contrary, a family-firm focused on value creation will be first in responding to changes, taking advantage of their long-standing industry knowledge and reputation (Moss et al., 2014).

Environmental hostility refers to the abundance or scarcity of resources, as well as the rate of market growth of the industry (Castrogiovanni, 1991). In munificent environments, firms will focus on exploiting its market positon and its resource endowment, given that there is no pressure to make any changes. On the contrary, hostile environments require strategic changes to survive. The way family-firms react to, well a hostile well a munificent environment, depends on family orientation toward value creation or toward wealth preservation. In hostile environments, value creation, plus family-firm survival, will act as strong motivation to trigger strategic changes and face the associated investment (Dyer & Mortensen, 2005). Alike, family-business driven by value creation, will adopt a more innovation-oriented strategic behavior when they perceive their environment to be munificent (Dess & Lumpkin, 2005). However, family firms that fear wealth dissipation will entrench in conservative positions, blocking changes and focusing in known activities and markets. Alike in munificent environments, with no change pressure, they will focus on exploiting current resources and market propositions.

Uncertainty that the business faces has major impact on how the firm prospects, develops and exploits new ventures (Navis & Ozbek, 2016). Alike, uncertainty increases the perceived risk associated to the firm activity. For the case of family business, specialized literature states that risk-taking propensity is lower in family-firms than in non-family firms (Naldi et al., 2007), and that the degree of risk aversion depends on the degree of family involvement in the business (Li & Daspit, 2016). Given that uncertainty is a subjective environment feature that depends on the judgment of the dominant coalition (Ahsan, 2017; Boyd, Dess, & Rasheed, 1993; Navis & Ozbek, 2017), the way in which uncertainty will affect family-firm strategic preferences, will depend on family-firm government and management. A family-firm with high risk-taking propensity, tolerates uncertainty, encourages personal initiative within the family group (Isaksen & Tidd, 2007), and boosts strategic changes. Conversely, a family-firm with low risk-taking propensity prefers to preserve wealth and competitive position. Therefore, they will be reluctant to embark on new strategies (De Massis, Minin & Frattini, 2015).

METHODOLOGY

Sample and Data Collection

We use a database from a primary study on Spanish tourism industry, the economic activity considered in the definition of Tourism set by the Instituto de Estudios Turísticos. This definition follows the recommendations of international institutions such as the World Tourism Organization (UNWTO) and the United Nation Statistic Commission. The survey corresponds to a wider research project supported by the Spanish Instituto de Estudios Turísticos, a public institution depending on the central government. The sample comes from the entire population of Spanish tourism companies presented in the 2009 Central Companies Directory (DIRCE) compiled by the Spanish National Institute of Statistics. According to this census, there was a total population of approximately 140,900 tourism businesses. The initial sample of 8,148 companies was selected using a stratified random sampling procedure with proportional allocation to ensure the representativeness of the sample in terms of activity (considering four groups), size (taking the number of employees as a measure of the size of the company) and location. The result of the fieldwork, after various data cleansing processes, was a sample of 1,019 companies with a confidence level of 95% and an error interval of ± 3.1%. This final sample represents a response rate of 25.6%.

Table 1. Sample distribution by activity

Activity	Frequency	Valid Percentage	Accumulated Percentage
Hospitality	71	55,03	55,03
Restaurants & Cafeterias	35	27,13	82,16
Travel Ag	14	10,85	93,01
Passenger Transport	5	3,87	96,88
Sport & Wellness	4	3,1	100
Total	129	100,0	

For data collection, we use a questionnaire, conducted through personal interviews with the firms' CEO or general manager in 2010. The original questionnaire ask for a wide range of questions dealing with: situation of the industry; level of digitalization; strategic choice; capabilities development –technological, organizational, managerial, marketing, innovation–; performance. The survey, when possible, collects both, subjective and objective data from third sources. In order to correct potential problems regarding questionnaires as a data collection method, the project team follow a set of recommended procedures; based on the Dillman's Total Design Method (1978) for questionnaire-based research. The data collection process lasted from December 2009 to March 2010. We got a total sample of 165 non-family-business and 378 family-business.

Due to the extended length of the questionnaire, we work only with family-firms that give complete and reliable answers. Alike, given the small number of large firms and the research goals, authors remove large firms. Because the survey includes a limited number of conditions to form configurations, the research team decide limiting the sample in order to increase homogeneity in those factors that could affect the output, like firm size –removing micro-firms–, too young firms –removing firms with less than 10 years– and some subsectors that behave differently to the main industry. So the final sample was made of 129 SME family-firms. Figure 1 presents the sample distribution by activity.

With regard to other sample features, 72,87% of the firms are founded in the early 80`s, so they are in the transition between the first and second generation with a few older firms founded between the 60,s and the 70's. In fact, the generation in charge is: 43,4% first generation; 39,5% second generation; and 17,05% third or later generation. Of course, all of them are non-listed and closely held family-business, where the family holds over 70% of the share in all cases.

Measures

Outcome Variables

Performance

To measure firm performance, this survey includes financial and non-financial items. Using a subjective instrument, this research asks respondents to rate their firm's performance in comparison to competitors on a 7-point response scale running from 1 = worsen to 7 = much better. Respondents measured fourteen items: Net profit, profit sales ratio, sales growth, cash flow, market share, return on investment, product development, market development, R&D activities, costs efficiency, labor productivity, environmental protection, customer satisfaction, and employee satisfaction (Basco, 2014). The reliability of this scale shows a Cronbach's alpha of 0.87. Subjective self-reported performance measures are common in the literature (Basco, 2014; Eddleston & Kellermanns, 2007; Kim & Gao, 2013; Kim & Gray, 2008; Love et al., 2002; Sciascia & Mazzola, 2008; Stanley et al., 2019). Some studies indicate that subjective financial performance is generally quite consistent with objective performance data (Covin et al., 1994; Ling & Kellermanns, 2010; Venkatraman, 1990; Wall et al., 2004). Furthermore, subjective financial performance is appropriate when studying small and medium-size firms (Dess & Robinson, 1984; Venkatraman & Ramanujam, 1987; Wallace et al., 2010).

Condition Variables

This survey considers five condition variables regarding family-firm ownership complexity, government and management, as well as environmental turbulence.

Competitive Strategy

This research follows the competitive strategy typology from Porter (1985), table 2 shows the items' statement that this survey uses to measure this condition variable.

Environmental Turbulence

To measure environmental turbulence, the survey uses a 17-item scale asking for dynamism, uncertainty, hostility and complexity issues on a 7-point response scale running from 1 = very low to 7 = very high. Table 3 shows the 17 items' statement.

Family Complexity Index

Following a similar criteria than González-Cruz & Cruz-Ros, (2016), this measure arises from the multiplication of ordinal number of the generation in charge and the number of family shareholders.

Board of Directors

Respondents indicate if the firm has a board of directors (1 = yes, 0 = no).

Family CEO

Respondents indicated if the CEO is a family member (1 = yes, 0 = no).

Table 2. Competitive strategy

Item statement
1. This firm tries to do the best job possible. It pursues efficiency and low cost. The organization tends to offer a more limited range of services than its competitors do.
2. The firm's motto is "to be the first" in new products and markets, even if you are not sure that these innovations are profitable.
3. This type of firm tries to maintain a stable and limited range of products or services, while at the same time betting on some innovative developments.

Table 3. Industry Turbulence Scale

Item statement
1. Unpredictability of the challenges arising from changes in the environment
2. Frequency of change in relevant environment area
3. Demand instability (difficulty to be predicted)
4. The cost that adaptation to changes entails for firms
5. Amount of time the firm needs to respond to changes
6. Frequency and degree of novelty of changes in the market and demand
7. Frequency and degree of novelty of social, political or cultural changes
8. Usefulness of experience to face the challenges of the future
9. Scarcity of resources that the industry needs
10. Industry sales growth
11. Degree of risk implicit in the activity that the firm develops
12. Degree of hostility of the environment towards the activity that the firm develops
13. Diversity of competitors in the activity
14. Diversity of consumers by their shopping habits
15. Diversity of suppliers
16. Degree of presence of differentiated products within the activity
17. Diversity of viable technologies to develop the activity

Calibration of Variables Into Fuzzy Sets

Following Ragin (2008), the calibration requires an anchoring of three qualitative breakpoints: Full membership (1), full non-membership (0) and the ambiguous crossover point (0.5). Table 4 shows the calibration criteria.

RESULTS

Analysis of Necessary Conditions

Necessary conditions are especially important because the outcome (performance) cannot occur without their presence (Dul, 2016). In other words, a necessary condition must always be present for the outcome to take place (Fiss 2007; Schneider & Eggert, 2014). Thus, Table 5 presents an analysis of necessary conditions using the fsQCA 3.0 software (Ragin & Sean, 2016).

Conventionally, a condition, or a combination of conditions, is "necessary" or "almost always necessary" if the consistency score exceeds the threshold of 0.9 (Schneider et al., 2010, p. 254). As table 5 shows, any variable alone reaches the category of necessary condition. The two last rows show that, the absence of environmental turbulence and family complexity is not a necessary condition for performance. On the contrary, a turbulent environment and family complexity become near necessary conditions to the absence of performance.

Table 4. Calibration criteria for outcome and condition variables

Variable	Max	Min	Ave (SD)	Fully In	Cross Over Point	Fully Out
Performance	6.600	1.000	4.068 (0.974)	5	3.5	2.5
Turbulence	6.400	2.100	4.384 (0.763)	5	4.5	3.5
Competitive Strategy	3.000	1.000	2.281 (0.896)	Dichotomous condition. 1 means differentiation strategy (2 and 3) and 0 means non-differentiation strategy (1)		
Familiar Complexity	1.000	0.000	0.471 (0.321)	Dichotomous condition. 1 means Familiar Complexity[1] and 0 Non-Familiar Complexity[2] (1st gg & and all FB with one shareholder)		
FamilyCEO	1.000	0.000	0.781 (0.415)	Dichotomous condition. 1 means the CEO is member of the family and 0 the CEO is not Familiar member		
Board of Directors	1.000	0.000	0.445 (0.499)	Dichotomous condition. 1 means the firm has an extern advisory board and 0 the firm do not have.		

[1] second or later generation in charge and two or more shareholders.
[2] first generation and two or less shareholders; one shareholder independently of the generation.

Table 5. Analysis of necessary conditions

	Performance_fs		~Performance_fs	
Conditions	**Consistency**	**Coverage**	**Consistency**	**Coverage**
Turbulence_fs	0,565	0,774	0,630	0,412
~Turbulence_fs	0,571	0,764	0,654	0,418
Differentiation Strategy_cs	0,736	0,709	0,633	0,291
~Differentiation Strategy_cs	0,264	0,601	0,367	0,399
Family Complexity_fs	0,550	0,792	0,685	0,470
~Family Complexity_fs	0,631	0,808	0,697	0,425
Family CEO_cs	0,778	0,674	0,789	0,326
~ Family CEO _cs	0,222	0,688	0,211	0,312
Board of Directors_cs	0,457	0,694	0,422	0,306
~Board of Directors_cs	0,543	0,663	0,578	0,337
~Turbulence + ~Fam Complex	0.789	0.758	---	---
Turbulence + Fam Complex	---	---	0.843	0.406

In any case, and in line with literature, family-firms' strategic choice and performance, depends on a set of conditions related to government (Le Breton-Miller & Miller (2008) and environmental conditions (Moss et al., 2014; Van Gils et al., 2004).

Analysis of Sufficient Conditions

A sufficient condition implies that a condition or combination of conditions can reach the outcome by itself. On the contrary, a necessary condition must always be present for the outcome to take place (Fiss 2007; Schneider and Eggert 2014).

One of the main characteristics of comparative qualitative analysis is that the result or outcome can be achieved through different paths or causal configurations— equifinality (Ragin 2000). In this line, Table 6 shows seven configurations that determine the presence of performance. This chapter presents results following the notation used by Ragin & Fiss (2008) and Fiss (2011), where large circles indicate core conditions and small circles indicate peripheral conditions. In addition, black circles indicate the presence and white circles the absence of a condition.

As stated by Fiss (2011, p. 403): *'core conditions are those that are part of both parsimonious and intermediate solutions, and peripheral conditions are those that are eliminated in the parsimonious solution and thus only appear in the intermediate solution. Accordingly, this approach defines causal coreness in terms of the strength of the evidence relative to the outcome, not connectedness to other configurational elements'.*

The results for presence of performance are both adequate and suitable as the overall solution consistency is greater than 0.75 (Fiss 2011). More specifically, it reveals the presence of two main core conditions: environmental turbulence and competitive strategy. As table 6 shows, when family-firms perceive a turbulent environment and choose a differentiation strategy –both global and niche– performance is present. Alike, performance is present when the family-firm perceives a non-turbulent environment and chooses a low cost strategy. As peripheral conditions, when family-firm perceives turbulence and follows a differentiation strategy, are the presence either a family CEO, or the presence of a board of directors *–recipes 1 & 2–*.

Recipe 3 shows the presence of family complexity and the absence of board of directors as core conditions and a family CEO that chooses a differentiation strategy as peripheral conditions. In this case, a complex owner-family trust a family CEO to run the family-firm and deploy its managerial capabilities to value creation.

Recipe 4 shows a non-family CEO as core condition, and a mix of peripheral conditions that have to do with a firm that perceives a non-turbulent environment and follows a differentiation strategy, and a complex owner-family not formally involved in firm government through a board of directors. That is, the owner family decides to keep aside the business and trust a non-family CEO.

R*ecipes 5 & 6* correspond to family-firms perceiving a non-turbulent environment and following a low cost strategy, as core conditions for performance presence. These configurations show as peripheral conditions the presence of either a family CEO –when family complexity is absent–, or a family CEO plus a board of directors.

Last, but not least, recipe 7 shows a simple owner-family, a non-turbulent environment perception and the presence of a board of directors as core conditions, and the presence of a family CEO as a peripheral condition. This description fit the profile of a family-firm that relies on the board of directors to gain additional knowledge and relational capital as a powerful mean to gain competitiveness.

With regard sufficient conditions to performance absence, only one recipe is both adequate and suitable as the overall solution consistency is 0,756 –greater than 0.75 (Fiss 2011)– and coverage is equal to 0,114. This recipe shows presence of owner family-complexity, board of directors and a low cost strategy, and seems to adhere to the misfit described by Basco (2014), a family-firm following a low cost strategy without a 'firm first' decision-making style.

Table 6. Analysis of sufficient conditions

	Performance						
	1	2	3	4	5	6	7
Turbulence	●	●		○	○	○	○
Differentiation Strategy	●	●	●	●	○	○	
Familiar Complexity			●	○	○		○
Family CEO		●	●	○	●	●	●
Board of Advisors	●		○	○		●	●
Consistency (incl.)	0.844	0.829	0.784	0.849	0.887	0.832	0.915
Raw coverage (cov.r)	0.213	0.316	0.148	0.029	0.098	0.073	0.108
Unique coverage (cov.u)	0.083	0.099	0.062	0.029	0.059	0.034	0.035
Overall solution consistency	0.825						
Overall solution coverage	0.656						

NOTE: As in Fiss (2011), ● means presence of the condition and ○ means absence of the condition; Large circle means core conditions and small circles means peripheral conditions.
Consistency cutoff: 0.80; Frequency cutoff: 3; Assumptions (0, -, 0, -, -). Calculated as Ragin and Sean (2016).

CONCLUSION

The strategic behavior associated to family firm is the research goal of a large stream of research that advocates for contradictory statements. While some sustain that family firms benefit from long term view and entrepreneurial behavior orientated to create value, others contend that family business are risk averse and prone to stagnation and harvest strategies focuses on exploitation and value appropriation.

In an intermediate position, Miller & Le Breton-Miller (2006) and Le Breton-Miller & Miller (2008) suggest that there is no *per se* family-film strategic behavior and that this depends on a set of circumstances related to family firm involvement and government.

Closing this research gap requires the adoption of a configurational approach, which main axioms are that: first, outcomes depend on a set of coherent intentions, practices and circumstances that lead to *'fit'*; second, different combinations of conditions can lead to the same output –*'equifinality'*–. This approach requires specific research methods like cluster analysis, latent profile analysis or fuzzy set qualitative analysis. In recent years, some papers answer to this call from different approaches and methodologies: Basco (2014) through cluster analysis, Moss et al. (2014) using panel data, and Stanley et al (2019) running a latent profile analysis.

The present paper swells this vein of research analyzing a sample of 129 Spanish SME family-firms that belong to the tourism industry. This research is original because: first, it works on a deliberately homogenous sample for those factors that are not included in the research model; second, combines family-firm variables with environmental variables, and is the first paper to consider turbulence. In any case, this paper has an exploratory intention that looks for providing complementary evidence to the published research.

The survey, through fuzzy set qualitative analysis, shows that no one condition alone is a necessary one to performance presence or absence. Alike, the absence of turbulence and family complexity in not a necessary condition for the presence of performance. However, the presence of turbulence and family complexity becomes a near necessary condition for the absence of performance, suggesting that in such conditions performance is not impossible but becomes much harder. In any case, the analysis supports the main statement of this vein of research: *outcomes depend on a coherent set of factors and circumstances.*

In general, results show that performance is present for those firms that follow a differentiation strategy in turbulent environments and a low-cost strategy in non-turbulent environments.

The analysis throws seven combinations for performance presence: Recipes 1 to 4 seem to fit Basco (2014) *'Quadrant A'* where family involvement lead to an equilibrium between family and firm priorities, and does not suppose the prevalence of family interests. There is a proper mix of family participation in government and management, that leaves room to growth orientation (Le Breton-Miller & Miller, 2008), strategic orientation (Escribá-Esteve et al., 2009), and entrepreneurial orientation (Stanley et al., 2019) needed to succeed in turbulent environments. Even in complex owner-families, a recipe for success is leaving discretion to an entrepreneurial family CEO that chooses a differentiation strategy. Alike, under non-turbulent competitive environment, other family-firms trust in a non-family CEO to run a differentiation strategy, keeping the family aside from the firm.

In line with Moss et al. (2014), less dynamic environments are associated to harvest (Le Breton-Miller & Miller, 2008) and exploitation strategic behaviors, that focus on operational efficiency and low-cost strategies. In these cases, owner-family complexity should be compensated by a proper mix of government and management devices, that make possible managing such complexities in order to keep family issues out of the business operations, in line with Basco (2014) *'Quadrant C'*.

Alike, and in accordance to Gimeno-Sanding et al. (2010), even in non-turbulent competitive environments, family complexity requires a suitable set of government and management devices to counterbalance negative consequences associated to family complexity.

One recipe shows the combination of conditions to performance absence. A complex owner family, a firm governed by a board and a low-cost strategy. In line with previous research (Basco, 2014) this configuration suggest a family firm where family issues and preferences become barriers to achieve the operational efficiency required for a successful low-cost strategy.

Overall, this results show that this is not a closed vein of research, on the contrary, it requires additional efforts. The main one has to do with the combination of what Basco (2014) calls the *demographic approach* –this survey and González-Cruz & Cruz-Ros (2016) are examples of this approach– based on proxies to measure family involvement and its consequences, and the *essential approach* that directly measures behavioral outcomes –i.e. Basco (2014)–. Instead of being considered as alternative approaches, new research need to properly combine both, demographic proxies and behavioral outcome un line with Stanley et al. (2019). Last, but not least, this chapter disagrees with Stanley et al (2017), which claims for the superiority of one methodology over other. Cluster Analysis, Latent Profile Analysis and Fuzzy Set Qualitative Comparative analysis are alternative and complementary tools to better understanding family-business heterogeneity and its consequences from a configurational approach.

This chapter is no without limitations. First data come from one informant, even when test to prevent common method bias show no problems in this regard, this kind of data collection remains a drawback that call for alternative research strategies. Second, the sample is deliberately homogenous in order to focus on variables analyzed in the research model, but this feature goes against results generalizability. Lastly but important, this demographic approach obliges the researcher to make an interpretation of the data, following a logic attributed to the observed results.

ACKNOWLEDGMENT

This research was supported by the Spanish Ministry of Science, Innovation and Universities, co-financed with FEDER funds [grant number ECO2016-26796-P]

REFERENCES

Addae-Boateng, S., Xiao, W., & Brew, Y. (2014). Governance Issues in Family Businesses. International *Journal of Economics. Commerce and Management*, *2*(12), 1–28.

Ahsan, M. (2017). The right people at the right time—The place does not matter. *Academy of Management Review*, *42*(1), 145–148. doi:10.5465/amr.2015.0276

Anderson, R. C., & Reeb, D. M. (2003). Founding-family ownership, corporate diversification, and firm leverage. *The Journal of Law & Economics*, *46*(2), 653–684. doi:10.1086/377115

Arregle, J. L., Hitt, M. A., Sirmon, D. G., & Very, P. (2007). The development of organizational social capital: Attributes of family firms. *Journal of Management Studies*, *44*(1), 73–95. doi:10.1111/j.1467-6486.2007.00665.x

Bammens, Y., Voordeckers, W., & Van Gils, A. (2011). Boards of directors in family businesses: A literature review and research agenda. *International Journal of Management Reviews*, *13*(2), 134–152. doi:10.1111/j.1468-2370.2010.00289.x

Basco, R. (2014). Exploring the influence of the family upon firm performance: Does strategic behaviour matter? *International Small Business Journal*, *32*(8), 967–995. doi:10.1177/0266242613484946

Basco, R., & Pérez Rodríguez, M. J. (2009). Studying the family enterprise holistically: Evidence for integrated family and business systems. *Family Business Review*, *22*(1), 82–95. doi:10.1177/0894486508327824

Bertrand, M., & Schoar, A. (2006). The role of family in family firms. *The Journal of Economic Perspectives*, *20*(2), 73–96. doi:10.1257/jep.20.2.73

Bloom, N., & Van Reenen, J. (2007). Measuring and explaining management practices across firms and countries. *The Quarterly Journal of Economics*, *122*(4), 1351–1408. doi:10.1162/qjec.2007.122.4.1351

Boyd, B. K., Dess, G. G., & Rasheed, A. M. (1993). Divergence between archival and perceptual measures of the environment: Causes and consequences. *Academy of Management Review*, *18*(2), 204–226. doi:10.5465/amr.1993.3997514

Brenes, E. R., Madrigal, K., & Requena, B. (2011). Corporate governance and family business performance. *Journal of Business Research*, *64*(3), 280–285. doi:10.1016/j.jbusres.2009.11.013

Castrogiovanni, G. J. (1991). Environmental munificence; a theoretical assessment. *Academy of Management Review*, *16*(3), 542–565.

Claessens, S., Djankov, S., Fan, J. P., & Lang, L. H. (2002). Disentangling the incentive and entrenchment effects of large shareholdings. *The Journal of Finance*, *57*(6), 2741–2771. doi:10.1111/1540-6261.00511

Covin, J. G., & Slevin, D. P. (2002). The entrepreneurial imperatives of strategic leadership. In M. A. Hitt (Ed.), *Strategic Entrepreneurship: Creating a New Mindset* (pp. 309–327). Oxford, UK: Blackwell Publishing.

Covin, J. G., Slevin, D. P., & Schultz, R. L. (1994). Implementing strategic missions: Effective strategic, structural and tactical choices. *Journal of Management Studies*, *31*(4), 481–506. doi:10.1111/j.1467-6486.1994.tb00627.x

De Massis, A., Di Minin, A., & Frattini, F. (2015). Family-driven innovation: Resolving the paradox in family firms. *California Management Review*, *58*(1), 5–19. doi:10.1525/cmr.2015.58.1.5

De Massis, A., Kotlar, J., Campopiano, G., & Cassia, L. (2013). Dispersion of family ownership and the performance of small-to-medium size private family firms. *Journal of Family Business Strategy*, *4*(3), 166–175. doi:10.1016/j.jfbs.2013.05.001

De Massis, A., Kotlar, J., Campopiano, G., & Cassia, L. (2015). The Impact of Family Involvement on SME s′ Performance: Theory and Evidence. *Journal of Small Business Management*, *53*(4), 924–948. doi:10.1111/jsbm.12093

Dess, G. G., & Lumpkin, G. T. (2005). The role of entrepreneurial orientation in stimulating effective corporate entrepreneurship. *The Academy of Management Perspectives*, *19*(1), 147–156. doi:10.5465/ame.2005.15841975

Dess, G. G., & Robinson, R. B. Jr. (1984). Measuring organizational performance in the absence of objective measures: The case of the privately-held firm and conglomerate business unit. *Strategic Management Journal*, *5*(3), 265–273. doi:10.1002mj.4250050306

Dillman, D. A. (1978). *Mail and telephone surveys: The total design method* (Vol. 19). New York: Wiley.

Dul, J. (2016). Identifying single necessary conditions with NCA and fsQCA. *Journal of Business Research*, *69*(4), 1516–1523. doi:10.1016/j.jbusres.2015.10.134

Dyer Jr, W. G., & Panicheva Mortensen, S. (2005). Entrepreneurship and family business in a hostile environment: The case of Lithuania. *Family Business Review*, *18*(3), 247–258. doi:10.1111/j.1741-6248.2005.00045.x

Eddleston, K. A., & Kellermanns, F. W. (2007). Destructive and productive family relationships: A stewardship theory perspective. *Journal of Business Venturing*, *22*(4), 545–565. doi:10.1016/j.jbusvent.2006.06.004

Escribá-Esteve, A., Sánchez-Peinado, L., & Sánchez-Peinado, E. (2009). The influence of top management teams in the strategic orientation and performance of small and medium-sized enterprises. *British Journal of Management*, *20*(4), 581–597. doi:10.1111/j.1467-8551.2008.00606.x

Fiss, P. C. (2007). A set-theoretic approach to organizational configurations. *Academy of Management Review*, *32*(4), 1180–1198. doi:10.5465/amr.2007.26586092

Fiss, P. C. (2011). Building better causal theories: A fuzzy set approach to typologies in organization research. *Academy of Management Journal*, *54*(2), 393–420. doi:10.5465/amj.2011.60263120

Gimeno, A., Baulenas, G., & Coma-Cros, J. (2010). Family business models. In *Family business models* (pp. 57–77). London: Palgrave Macmillan. doi:10.1057/9780230282148_4

Gnan, L., Montemerlo, D., & Sharma, P. (2005). Ownership and governance structures: towards a typology of Italian family firms. *The Family business network: annual world conference.*

Gómez-Mejía, L. R., Haynes, K. T., Núñez-Nickel, M., Jacobson, K. J., & Moyano-Fuentes, J. (2007). Socioemotional wealth and business risks in family-controlled firms: Evidence from Spanish olive oil mills. *Administrative Science Quarterly*, *52*(1), 106–137. doi:10.2189/asqu.52.1.106

González-Cruz, T. F., & Cruz-Ros, S. (2016). When does family involvement produce superior performance in SME family business? *Journal of Business Research*, *69*(4), 1452–1457. doi:10.1016/j.jbusres.2015.10.124

Isaksen, S., & Tidd, J. (2006). *Meeting the innovation challenge: Leadership for transformation and growth.* Hoboken, NJ: John Wiley & Sons.

James, H. (2009). *Family capitalism: Wendels, Haniels, Falcks, and the continental European model.* Harvard University Press. doi:10.2307/j.ctvjz811m

Jensen, J., & Meckling, W. H. (1976). Theory of the firm: Managerial behavior, agency costs and ownership structure. *Journal of Financial Economics*, *3*(4), 305–360. doi:10.1016/0304-405X(76)90026-X

Johannisson, B., & Huse, M. (2000). Recruiting outside board members in the small family business: An ideological challenge. *Entrepreneurship and Regional Development*, *12*(4), 353–378. doi:10.1080/08985620050177958

Kang, D. (1998). *The impact of ownership type on performance in public corporations: a study of the US textile industry 1983-1992.* Available at SSRN 10592.

Kim, Y., & Gao, F. Y. (2013). Does family involvement increase business performance? Family-longevity goals' moderating role in Chinese family firms. *Journal of Business Research*, *66*(2), 265–274. doi:10.1016/j.jbusres.2012.08.018

Kim, Y., & Gray, S. J. (2008). The impact of entry mode choice on foreign affiliate performance: The case of foreign MNEs in South Korea. *Management International Review*, *48*(2), 165–188. doi:10.100711575-008-0010-3

Kosmidou, V., & Ahuja, M. K. (2019). A configurational approach to family firm innovation. *Family Business Review*, *32*(2), 154–173.

Lai, J. H., Chen, L. Y., & Chen, I. J. (2014). The value of outside director experience to firm strategies: Evidence from joint ventures. *Journal of Management & Organization*, *20*(3), 387–409. doi:10.1017/jmo.2014.18

Le Breton-Miller, I., & Miller, D. (2008). To grow or to harvest? Governance, strategy and performance in family and lone founder firms. *Journal of Strategy and Management*, *1*(1), 41–56. doi:10.1108/17554250810909419

Le Breton-Miller, I., & Miller, D. (2009). Agency vs. stewardship in public family firms: A social embeddedness reconciliation. *Entrepreneurship Theory and Practice*, *33*(6), 1169–1191. doi:10.1111/j.1540-6520.2009.00339.x

Le Breton-Miller, I., & Miller, D. (2013). Socioemotional wealth across the family firm life cycle: A commentary on "Family Business Survival and the Role of Boards". *Entrepreneurship Theory and Practice*, *37*(6), 1391–1397. doi:10.1111/etap.12072

Li, Z., & Daspit, J. J. (2016). Understanding family firm innovation heterogeneity: A typology of family governance and socioemotional wealth intentions. *Journal of Family Business Management*, *6*(2), 103–121. doi:10.1108/JFBM-02-2015-0010

Ling, Y., & Kellermanns, F. W. (2010). The effects of family firm specific sources of TMT diversity: The moderating role of information exchange frequency. *Journal of Management Studies*, *47*(2), 322–344. doi:10.1111/j.1467-6486.2009.00893.x

Love, L. G., Priem, R. L., & Lumpkin, G. T. (2002). Explicitly articulated strategy and firm performance under alternative levels of centralization. *Journal of Management*, *28*(5), 611–627. doi:10.1177/014920630202800503

Lubatkin, M. H., Ling, Y., & Schulze, W. S. (2007). An organizational justice-based view of self-control and agency costs in family firms. *Journal of Management Studies*, *44*(6), 955–971. doi:10.1111/j.1467-6486.2006.00673.x

Maury, B. (2006). Family ownership and firm performance: Empirical evidence from Western European corporations. *Journal of Corporate Finance*, *12*(2), 321–341. doi:10.1016/j.jcorpfin.2005.02.002

Mazzola, P., Sciascia, S., & Kellermanns, F. W. (2013). Non-linear effects of family sources of power on performance. *Journal of Business Research*, *66*(4), 568–574. doi:10.1016/j.jbusres.2012.01.005

McConaughy, D. L. (2000). Family CEOs vs. nonfamily CEOs in the family-controlled firm: An examination of the level and sensitivity of pay to performance. *Family Business Review*, *13*(2), 121–131. doi:10.1111/j.1741-6248.2000.00121.x

Miller, D., & Le Breton-Miller, I. (2005). Management insights from great and struggling family businesses. *Long Range Planning*, *38*(6), 517–530. doi:10.1016/j.lrp.2005.09.001

Miller, D., & Le Breton-Miller, I. (2005). *Managing for the long run: Lessons in competitive advantage from great family businesses*. Harvard Business Press.

Miller, D., & Le Breton-Miller, I. (2006). Priorities, practices and strategies in successful and failing family businesses: An elaboration and test of the configuration perspective. *Strategic Organization*, *4*(4), 379–407. doi:10.1177/1476127006069575

Miller, D., Le Breton-Miller, I., Lester, R. H., & Cannella, A. A. Jr. (2007). Are family firms really superior performers? *Journal of Corporate Finance*, *13*(5), 829–858. doi:10.1016/j.jcorpfin.2007.03.004

Miller, D., Minichilli, A., & Corbetta, G. (2013). Is family leadership always beneficial? *Strategic Management Journal*, *34*(5), 553–571. doi:10.1002mj.2024

Minichilli, A., Corbetta, G., & MacMillan, I. C. (2010). Top management teams in family-controlled companies: 'familiness', 'faultlines', and their impact on financial performance. *Journal of Management Studies, 47*(2), 205–222. doi:10.1111/j.1467-6486.2009.00888.x

Morck, R., Wolfenzon, D., & Yeung, B. (2005). Corporate governance, economic entrenchment, and growth. *Journal of Economic Literature, 43*(3), 655–720. doi:10.1257/002205105774431252

Moss, T. W., Payne, G. T., & Moore, C. B. (2014). Strategic consistency of exploration and exploitation in family businesses. *Family Business Review, 27*(1), 51–71. doi:10.1177/0894486513504434

Naldi, L., Nordqvist, M., Sjöberg, K., & Wiklund, J. (2007). Entrepreneurial orientation, risk taking, and performance in family firms. *Family Business Review, 20*(1), 33–47. doi:10.1111/j.1741-6248.2007.00082.x

Navis, C., & Ozbek, O. V. (2016). The right people in the wrong places: The paradox of entrepreneurial entry and successful opportunity realization. *Academy of Management Review, 41*(1), 109–129. doi:10.5465/amr.2013.0175

Navis, C., & Ozbek, O. V. (2017). Why context matters: Overconfidence, narcissism, and the role of objective uncertainty in entrepreneurship. *Academy of Management Review, 42*(1), 148–153. doi:10.5465/amr.2016.0208

Pérez-González, F. (2006). Inherited control and firm performance. *The American Economic Review, 96*(5), 1559–1588. doi:10.1257/aer.96.5.1559

Porter, M. E. (1985). *Competitive Advantages*. New York: Free Press.

Ragin, C. (2000). *Fuzzy-set social science*. Chicago: University of Chicago Press.

Ragin, C. C. (2008). *Redesigning social inquiry: Fuzzy sets and beyond*. Chicago, IL: University of Chicago Press. doi:10.7208/chicago/9780226702797.001.0001

Ragin, C. C., & Fiss, P. C. (2008). Net effects analysis versus configurational analysis: An empirical demonstration. *Redesigning social inquiry: Fuzzy sets and beyond, 240*, 190-212.

Ragin, C. C., & Sean, D. (2016). *Fuzzy-set/qualitative comparative analysis 3.0*. Irvine, CA: University of California.

Rojas, A. (2019). *Conditions for innovation in family firms. A configurational approach*. XXIX Conference ACEDE, Globalization under complexity and uncertainty environments.

Schneider, M. R., & Eggert, A. (2014). Embracing complex causality with the QCA method: An invitation. *Journal of Business Market Management, 7*(1), 312–328.

Schneider, M. R., Schulze-Bentrop, C., & Paunescu, M. (2010). Mapping the institutional capital of high-tech firms: A fuzzy-set analysis of capitalist variety and export performance. *Journal of International Business Studies, 41*(2), 246–266. doi:10.1057/jibs.2009.36

Sciascia, S., & Mazzola, P. (2008). Family involvement in ownership and management: Exploring nonlinear effects on performance. *Family Business Review, 21*(4), 331–345. doi:10.1177/08944865080210040105

Stanley, L., Kellermanns, F. W., & Zellweger, T. M. (2017). Latent profile analysis: Understanding family firm profiles. *Family Business Review*, *30*(1), 84–102. doi:10.1177/0894486516677426

Stanley, L. J., Hernández-Linares, R., López-Fernández, M. C., & Kellermanns, F. W. (2019). A Typology of Family Firms: An Investigation of Entrepreneurial Orientation and Performance. *Family Business Review*.

Van Gils, A., Voordeckers, W., & van den Heuvel, J. (2004). Environmental uncertainty and strategic behavior in Belgian family firms. *European Management Journal*, *22*(5), 588–595. doi:10.1016/j.emj.2004.09.015

Venkatraman, N. (1990). Performance implications of strategic coalignment: A methodological perspective. *Journal of Management Studies*, *27*(1), 19–41. doi:10.1111/j.1467-6486.1990.tb00751.x

Venkatraman, N., & Ramanujam, V. (1987). Measurement of business economic performance: An examination of method convergence. *Journal of Management*, *13*(1), 109–122. doi:10.1177/014920638701300109

Vilaseca, A. (2002). The shareholder role in the family business: Conflict of interests and objectives between nonemployed shareholders and top management team. *Family Business Review*, *15*(4), 299–320. doi:10.1111/j.1741-6248.2002.00299.x

Villalonga, B., & Amit, R. (2006). How do family ownership, control and management affect firm value? *Journal of Financial Economics*, *80*(2), 385–417. doi:10.1016/j.jfineco.2004.12.005

Voordeckers, W., Van Gils, A., & Van den Heuvel, J. (2007). Board composition in small and medium-sized family firms. *Journal of Small Business Management*, *45*(1), 137–156. doi:10.1111/j.1540-627X.2007.00204.x

Wall, T. D., Michie, J., Patterson, M., Wood, S. J., Sheehan, M., Clegg, C. W., & West, M. (2004). On the validity of subjective measures of company performance. *Personnel Psychology*, *57*(1), 95–118. doi:10.1111/j.1744-6570.2004.tb02485.x

Wallace, J. C., Little, L. M., Hill, A. D., & Ridge, J. W. (2010). CEO regulatory foci, environmental dynamism, and small firm performance. *Journal of Small Business Management*, *48*(4), 580–604. doi:10.1111/j.1540-627X.2010.00309.x

Ward, J. L. (2004). *Perpetuating the Family Business: 50 Lessons Learned from Long Lasting, Successful Families in Business*. Marietta, GA: Family Enterprise Publishers. doi:10.1057/9780230505995

Weber, J., Lavelle, L., Lowry, T., Zellner, W., & Barrett, A. (2003). Family Inc. *Business Week*, *3857*, 100-110.

KEY TERMS AND DEFINITIONS

Closely Held Family Business: A family firm whose stock is held by a small number of people pertaining to the same kin group.

Configurational Approach: A systemic understanding of organizations coherent and mutually dependent set of intentions, practices and structural arrangements.

Demographic Approach: A research strategy that analyses the outcomes of family involvement through objective, directly observable proxies.

Environmental Turbulence: A turbulent environment exists when changes are unexpected and unpredictable. The key environmental issues concern the nature of the pressure for change and the speed at which the organization must be able to respond an act.

Equifinality: Is a feature of open systems that means that an outcome can be reached by many potential paths or combinations of conditions and circumstances.

Essence Approach: A research strategy that explores the outcomes of family involvement through the subjective measurement of behavioural outputs.

Fit: Is the coherent combination of the element that belong to a system, enabling positive synergies and goal attainment.

Section 3
Family Firm Strategic Behavior

Chapter 6
Factors Determining the Internationalization of Spanish Family SMEs:
A Resource-Based Approach

Marta Fernández-Olmos
University of Zaragoza, Spain

ABSTRACT

This chapter examines the factors determining international expansion for a group of Spanish family SMEs. Internationalization is modelled taking into account both the decision to enter foreign markets and the degree of internationalization. This chapter uses the information provided by the Survey on Business Strategies in Spain, including 1,519 observations. The results indicate that the presence of the second generation in the family firm, the establishment of alliances with other firms, and some intangible resources (in particular, product innovations, and human resources) all positively influence the degree of internationalization. The results also indicate that the size and age of family firms are important factors in determining their international expansion.

INTRODUCTION

Nowadays, family SMEs face a new competitive situation in that their survival depends on their capacity to grow internationally (Chen, 2011; Patel, Pieper & Hier, 2012). Since the internationalization of family SMEs has been restrained by shortages of both long-term financial assets and intangible assets, export plays a vital role, being regarded as the simplest and quickest way to access foreign markets (Sacristán, Rico & Lafuente, 2011).

As a consequence, a growing body of empirical research has been aimed at understanding the factors that have led family SMEs to develop international markets over the last decade (Pukall & Calabrò, 2014; Alayo, Maseda, Iturralde & Arzubiaga, 2019). However, previous literature has provided mixed evidence concerning the factors that impact on the internationalization of family SMEs and these need

DOI: 10.4018/978-1-7998-1655-3.ch006

further clarification (Benavides-Velasco, Quintana-García & Guzmán-Parra, 2013; Fernández & Nieto, 2006; Kontinen & Ojala, 2010). Several reasons could explain this lack of consensus. First, previous studies have mostly focused on the reluctance of different types of family firm to internationalize in comparison with their non-family counterparts (e.g., Banalieva & Eddleston, 2011; Claver, Rienda & Quer, 2009; Fernández & Nieto, 2006; Gomez-Mejia, Makri & Larraza-Kintana, 2010), although there are exceptions such as Zahra (2003) and Fernández and Nieto (2005). However, family firms are heterogeneous (Arregle, Naldi, Nordqvist & Hitt, 2012; Banalieva & Eddleston, 2011) and therefore, rather than comparing family and non-family firms, this chapter examines the specific determining factors of internationalization in family businesses. Another reason for the mixed results may be the lack of uniformity in the conceptualization and measurement of the construct of internationalization. For example, the export intensity ratio is by far the most widely used indicator in empirical international family business research (e.g., Almódovar, 2012; Lu & Beamish, 2006), but other measures of the degree of internationalization have included the number of countries in which the family firm sold its products (e.g., Zahra, 2003) and the ratio of foreign assets to total assets (e.g., Tsao & Lien, 2013). Finally, another reason for these inconsistent empirical findings that several scholars have highlighted is the lack of consensus on the exact definition of family business (Benavides-Velasco et al., 2013; Graves & Thomas, 2008; Sacristán et al., 2011).

The objective of this research is to fill that gap by investigating the factors determining the internationalization process undertaken by the family firm. To do so, this chapter uses the resource-based view (RBV) as the theoretical foundation to develop hypotheses that relate resource-based factors to expansion into international markets. This research focuses on export activities, because most family firms' international expansion efforts are likely to take the form of exports (Fernández & Nieto, 2005; Okoroafo, 1999).

This paper first contributes to extending previous research by focusing on differences between family firms, these being defined as firms in which there is a family identity in the ownership and control of the business.

Secondly, most papers on the internationalization of family businesses have not modelled internationalization behaviour in a dual manner, i.e., as both the decision to internationalize and the degree of internationalization. This chapter analyses whether the process underlying a family SME's decision to internationalize is a separate one from that determining the degree of internationalization by applying a well-established methodology, i.e., a two-stage dynamic model.

Finally, the empirical application of the analysis of the export behaviour of Spanish family SMEs is very limited and most empirical studies are descriptive and cross-sectional (Sacristán et al., 2011). This chapter adds to previous literature by studying a large sample of Spanish manufacturing family SMEs that includes nearly 3,000 observations from the period 2006-2012.

This paper is structured as follows: in the next section this chapter presents the theoretical framework forming the basis for the empirical hypotheses the authors propose to test. The third section describes the empirical results. Finally, this chapter considers their implications and suggest directions for future research.

BACKGROUND

When family firms choose to go international, they must be able to identify international business opportunities through their managerial capabilities, alliances and other resources (Liang, Wang and Cui, 2013). The resource-based view suggests that a lack of strategic resources and capabilities to exploit their local competitive advantages in foreign markets usually has a negative influence on the decision to internationalize (Hitt et al., 1997; Peng, 2001).

Family businesses are seen as one of the most complex forms of business (Neubauer and Lank, 1998) and thus internationalization researchers have to deal with this specific group separately.

According to the resource-based view, the board of directors in a family SME's governance structure is likely to play a key role in its process of internationalization, since it increases the amount of information available to the operational management when expanding its activities to new countries (Chrisman, Chu & Sharma, 2005). In particular, the board members provide a source of strategic initiative and relevant information and also a source of know-how, counsel and control (Basly, 2007; Pfeffer & Salancik, 2003).

But the role of the board of directors is bound by the number of family members in the management team. Due to a bias towards family members, with a view to avoiding loss of control, family SME management tends to limit external managerial involvement, even if it would be valuable to undertake international activities (Basly, 2007).

Previous literature has suggested that the more the family is involved, the less decisive the role of the board will be (Arregle et al., 2012; Mustakallio & Autio, 2001). The reason is that the pursuit of managerial independence by the family firm inhibits internationalization from the human point of view. Family SMEs have been associated with negative characteristics such as paternalistic management and nepotism, which tend to foster organizational rigidity and a failure to recruit able and competent family directors and managers (Yeung, 2000). A number of empirical studies have thus found a negative relationship between the presence of family members in managerial positions in family businesses and the internationalization process of the family firm (Cerrato & Piva, 2012; Fernández & Nieto, 2006; Westhead & Howorth, 2006).

However, the presence of family members in managerial positions in family businesses provides a clear advantage when they advance the internationalization process by expediting decision making.

Not all research supports the above view. Some papers posit that the presence of family members in the management team is positively related to the internationalization of family SMEs, because they support better risk taking (Aldrich & Cliff, 2003; Zahra, 2003).

Overall, studies emphasise that recruiting external board members may facilitate the internationalization strategy of family SMEs. Although research yields contrasting results, the theory that tends to prevail is that the family nature of a business is reflected in the defence of a stronger presence of family members in governance. Consequently, the following hypothesis can be formulated:

Hypothesis 1: In family SMEs, family involvement in managerial positions has a negative effect on internationalization.

Generational change in the family business is another key factor influencing internationalization (Claver, Rienda & Quer, 2007). It is well known that the attitudes and behaviours of family businesses can vary by generation (Swinth & Vinton, 1993; Welch, 1992), as they may have different interests, styles of management and objectives (Okoroafo, 1999). While the founding generation mostly concentrates on consolidating the family firm's position in the domestic market, the new generation of leadership brings new strategic ideas that build on long-held competencies developed for earlier strategies (Nagy, 2013; Ward, 1998). Later generations can then be expected to be more independent and more predisposed to expand into international markets (Brush, 1992; Fernández & Nieto, 2006).

There are thus some benefits associated with the second and subsequent generations, particularly regarding the decision to internationalize. First, the second generation has more information and is usually more qualified and, therefore, more predisposed to expand into international markets (Gallo & García-Pont, 1996). Secondly, family successors (e.g., son, daughter, nephew, grandson) share the same values and interests, being more closely linked to the business than an external successor. Consistent with this view, they are probably less manipulative, opportunistic and self-serving. So it is easier for family successors to establish international expansion proposals and for them to be accepted. Finally, a successful succession provides a good opportunity for the family business, which may encourage the internationalization process (Ibrahim, Soufani & Lam, 2001; Menéndez-Requejo, 2005; Ward, 1987).

Therefore, this chapter can argue that the influence of second and subsequent generations on the internationalization process of family SMEs is positive:

Hypothesis 2: In family SMEs, the presence of the second and subsequent generations has a positive effect on internationalization.

Alliances and cooperative arrangements are strategically important to the internationalizing family SME (Fernández & Nieto, 2005; Gallo & García- Pont, 1996; Swinth & Vinton, 1993). In particular, they are believed to facilitate the internationalization of family SMEs in several ways.

First, through stable cooperation with other companies, these being either customers or vendors in the domestic market, a family SME can develop a high awareness of opportunities and threats pertaining to its activities, since it is strongly exposed to the environment, and the perceived risk is reduced as a result (Bonaccorsi, 1992). Thus, Olivares-Mesa and Cabrera-Suárez (2006) state that through their involvement in a network, family businesses may enjoy a "learning advantage" and find it easier to go abroad than firms without network ties.

Secondly, through a system of alliances, family SMEs may be able to share some of the fixed costs and risks associated with international expansion, which would otherwise be too high for them to face on their own (Fernández & Nieto, 2005).

Finally, the network could also be a way to improve the international performance of family SMEs, as it allows a direct transfer of knowledge between participants (Johanson & Mattsson, 1993).

Overall, previous research shows that collaborative relationships and network ties are positively associated with international growth among family SMEs. For this reason the authors hypothesize that:

Hypothesis 3: In family SMEs, the establishment of alliances with other firms has a positive effect on internationalization.

According to the RBV, family SMEs are heterogeneous in the resources they control, and these resources can lead to a sustainable competitive advantage when they are rare, valuable, difficult to imitate or irreplaceable.

In an international context, for family SMEs, access to resources is critical for exporting to foreign markets, as international expansion is costly and often requires significant resource commitment (Buckley, 1989; Westhead, Wrigth & Ucbasaran, 2004; Zahra, 2003). For example, internationalization is a complex process that requires one to develop international supplier and customer bases, to deal with cultural and linguistic differences between the home and foreign countries, and to face the increasing competition within foreign markets (Hill, Hwang & Kim, 1990).

Intangible resources, such as technological, marketing and human resources, are pivotal for the internationalization of family firms (Fernández & Nieto, 2006; Gallo & García-Pont, 1996; Graves & Thomas, 2006; Hitt, Tihanyi, Miller & Connelly., 2006).

With an increasing commitment to foreign markets, the level of technology, such as the use of internet, also increases. The pursuit of international development strategies by family SMEs therefore brings the role of technological resources into the foreground (Gallo & García-Pont, 1996; Koopman & Sebel, 2009). In this respect, a study by Davis and Harverston (2000) concluded that the presence of significant capacity for technological innovation has a significant positive influence on the internationalization process of family businesses.

Marketing-based resources also play a key role in internationalizing family businesses (Leonidou, 2004). A vast number of studies (e.g., Durán & Úbeda, 2003; Durán, 2008; Plá, 1999; Rialp, 1999) have obtained empirical evidence that for Spanish firms operating in international markets, marketing-based resources (publicity expenses, after-sales service, and an international brand) are valuable for their internationalization efforts.

Specialized human resources are considered to be crucial to the recognition and exploitation of international business opportunities. For this reason, operating in foreign markets makes it necessary for family SMEs to have a greater supply of qualified personnel compared to purely domestic family SMEs (Gómez-Mejía, 1988). In line with this postulation, Davis and Harveston (2000) found that when the founder of the family business had a higher educational level it had a positive impact on internationalization.

For all these reasons the authors hypothesize that:

Hypothesis 4: Intangible (technological, marketing-based and human) resources have a positive effect on the internationalization of family SMEs.

Although some authors have posited that business size is not a constraint for competing globally (Davis & Harveston, 2000; Roida & Sunarjanto, 2012), most previous literature has suggested that it may affect the internationalization process of the family firm (Claver et al., 2007). The family firm's size is associated with a family firm's ability to gain financial resources (Olivares-Mesa & Cabrera-Suárez, 2006). Thus, a smaller size may mean that family SMEs have fewer market-servicing options, and fewer opportunities to invest in manufacturing facilities and to create economies of scale. These restrictions may prevent or discourage family SMEs from entering and expanding in international markets (Benito & Welch, 1994; Deardoff, 1984; Moen, 1999; Zahra, Matherne & Carleton, 2003). This suggests that:

Hypothesis 5: Larger family SMEs are more likely to have a greater degree of internationalization.

Finally, age has traditionally been considered as another main predictor of a family firm's international activities (Andersson, Gabrielsson & Wictor, 2004; Axinn, Savitt, Sinkula & Thatch, 1995; Chen & Martin 2001; Claver et al., 2007; Fernández & Nieto 2006; Reuber & Fischer 1997). By means of an incremental process, the number of years the family SME has been operating in business generates experience and knowledge of markets that turn into key capabilities for its international strategy (Reuber

& Fischer, 1997). Previous research (e.g., Cerrato & Piva, 2012; Liang et al., 2013; Zahra, 2003) has found that age is positively related to the internationalization of family SMEs. The following hypothesis can therefore be formulated:

Hypothesis 6: Older family SMEs are more likely to have a greater degree of internationalization.

Several studies have examined the effect of industry sector on internationalization (Fernández & Nieto, 2005; Liang et al., 2013). The authors accordingly monitor the effect of sector in our research. Figure 1 provides the summary of this model.

EMPIRICAL ANALYSIS

Data Set and Variables

Sample

The data used in this paper are drawn from the Survey on Business Strategies (SBS), an annual survey of Spanish firms' strategies sponsored by the SEPI Foundation, a government institution, with the support of the Spanish Ministry of Industry.

Figure 1. Summary of the model

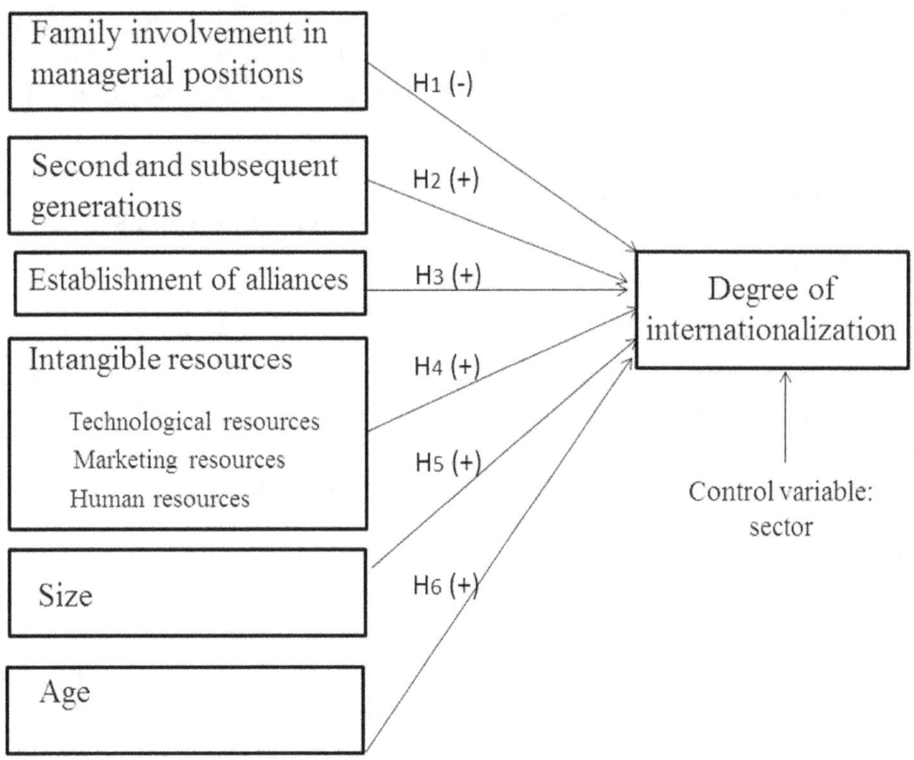

The authors chose this survey for several reasons. First, the literature which refers to the internationalization of family businesses has recognized that there is a lack of longitudinal studies (Benavides-Velasco et al., 2013). This database offers information on Spanish firms´ strategies for the 1990-2012 period. Secondly, the SEPI Foundation applies a series of criteria to maintain the representativity[1] of the reference population. Finally, many other researchers have used the SBS to study the export activity of Spanish firms (e.g. Fernández & Nieto, 2005; Merino & Salas, 2002).

Initially, to select the sample, the authors identified Spanish manufacturing firms that are SMEs and family firms. Although the upper limit for an SME is 250 employees according to the European Commission, this chapter sets the limit at 200 employees, as had previous research[2] (Chandra, Styles & Wilkinson, 2009; Muñoz-Bullón & Sánchez-Bueno, 2011).

While family firms represent a significant economic force worldwide (IFERA, 2003; DeMassis et al., 2018), there is a lack of consensus on the exact definition of family business (Abdellatif, Amann & Jaussaud, 2010; Benavides-Velasco et al., 2013). Nevertheless, Allouche, Amann, Jaussaud & Kurashina (2008) recognizes that a consensus definition may not represent a pertinent research goal because, by nature, family businesses are contingent on the institutional legal context, which differs from country to country.

The sample obtained includes 702 family business groups defined according to two criteria: (1) they are businesses owned and managed by a nuclear family (Abdellatif et al., 2010; Chua, Chrisman & Sharma, 1999; Graves and Thomas, 2008); and (2) they self-classify themselves as family business. Since this latter variable is only available from 2006 onwards, our analysis covers the 7 years from 2006.

Dependent Variable

The dependent variable used in the study is a well-established measure that combines the geographical scale and scope of foreign operations to reflect the living reality of family SMEs in the process of exporting (Fernández-Olmos, 2011; Grant, Jammine & Thomas, 1988; Pangarkar, 2008). It is calculated as follows:

$$DOI = \frac{\text{proportion of foreign sales}}{\sum_{i=1}^{n}\left(\text{proportion of sales in region}_i^2\right)} x100 \qquad \text{n = number of regions}$$

Following previous literature (Delgado-Gómez, Ramírez-Alesón & Espitia-Escuer, 2004; Hitt, Hoskisson & Kim, 1997; Kim, Hwang & Burges, 1989), the authors grouped the world environment into six homogenous regions based on political and economic conditions: the European Union, North America, Tax Havens, other Developed Countries, Latin America, and other Developing Countries.

Independent Variables

Family involvement. This is the number of family members occupying managerial positions.

Second generation. Following Fernández and Nieto (2005), the authors use a binary dummy that equals 1 if a firm is more than 30 years old (second and subsequent generation family SMEs) and 0 when it is less than 30 years old (first generation business).

Alliances. The authors measured these by using a dichotomous variable to represent the establishment of alliances, indicating whether the family SME has commercial agreements with wholesalers and retailers (Fernández & Nieto, 2005).

Intangible Resources

Technological resources: The traditional indicator (R&D expenditure in relation to total sales) is not adequate for studying technological resources in non-R&D intensive industries and small firms (Sterlacchini, 1999). For this reason, technological resources were measured by two dummies (product innovations and process innovations), i.e. whether the firm has introduced a product or process innovation (Basile, 2001; Cohen & Klepper, 1996; Lachenmaier & Wößmann, 2006).

Marketing resources: By including the proportion of advertising and promotional expenditures over total sales, this chapter reflects marketing-based resources (Morgan & Rego, 2009).

Human resources: Human capital can be defined as consisting of education, experience and skills (Boxall & Steeneveld, 1999; Rauch, Frese & Utsch, 2005). Although skilled work does not automatically imply having a specific qualification (Devins, 2008), employees' education is considered an important attribute of human capital (Hambrick & Mason, 1984). Consistent with this view, the authors used the proportion of employees in the firm with university degrees as a proxy for human capital. Fernández-Olmos (2011) has also adopted this measurement.

Size: The authors adopt the natural log of full-time employees as the measure of firm size, following past research (e.g., Davis & Harveston, 2000; Díez & Fernández, 2013; Zahra, 2003).

Age: This is measured as the logarithm of the number of years (plus one3) since the year of establishment (Anderson & Reeb, 2003).

Control Variables

Sector: Following previous studies such as Fernández and Nieto (2005), the authors used the mean export intensity by industry and year as a proxy for sector.

Descriptive Analysis

Table 1 provides summary statistics for the whole dataset of family SMEs and for exporters and non-exporters separately. Table 2 shows Spearman's correlations4 for each of the independent variables used.

SOLUTIONS AND RECOMMENDATIONS

Table 3 presents the regression results. A pooled regression model is presented in the first column of the table. However, the techniques used in the estimation of linear panel data models are inappropriate, because of the censoring nature of the dependent variable, the degree of internationalization.

In the second column the authors presents a random[5] effect Tobit. In order to relax the restrictions imposed by the Tobit model, the chapter estimated in the last two columns a dynamic Heckman probit model to allow the variables which characterize the decision whether or not to export to be separated from the variables which determine the decision regarding how much internationalization there is, given that the firm exports. But the inverse of the Mills ratio appears to be insignificant, which indicates that the

Table 1. Sample characteristics

Variable	All-SME family firms	Exporting- SME family firms	Non exporting- SME family firms	t-test
Family involvement	1.743 (0.021)	1.754 (0.021)	1.49 (0.083)	-2.591***
Second generation	0.381 (0.012)	0.382 (0.013)	0.359 (0.060)	-0.373
Alliances	0.299 (0.011)	0.396 (0.011)	0.152 (0.043)	-2.786***
Product innovations	0.223 (0.010)	0.228 (0.010)	0.109 (0.037)	-2.383**
Process innovations	0.322 (0.011)	0.327 (0.012)	0.205 (0.048)	-2.181**
Marketing resources	1.328 (0.060)	1.353 (0.062)	0.763 (0.177)	-2.004**
Human resources	5.972 (0.159)	6.059 (0.164)	4.076 (0.576)	-2.544**
Size	54.395 (1.137)	55.722 (1.174)	25.082 (2.214)	-5.531***
Age	30.952 (0.563)	30.902 (0.573)	32.078 (3.033)	-0.419
Sector	0.498 (0.005)	0.502 (0.005)	0.429 (0.021)	-2.944***

For comparison purposes, the authors take the anti-log of the variables Size and Age
Standard errors in parentheses. ** Significant at the 1%, * at the 5%,
Source: Own elaboration

Table 2. Spearman correlations

	1	2	3	4	5	6	7	8	9	10
Family involvement	1									
Second generation	0.004	1								
Alliances	0.076**	0.031	1							
Product innovations	0.040*	0.069**	0.149**	1						
Process innovations	0.057**	0.003	0.113**	0.336**	1					
Marketing resources	0.056**	0.043*	0.218**	0.156**	0.091**	1				
Human resources	0.114**	0.177**	0.111**	0.185**	0.168**	0.183**	1			
Size	0.182**	0.131**	0.266**	0.200**	0.268**	0.153**	0.245**	1		
Age	0.050**	0.801**	0.068**	0.055**	-0.009	0.088**	0.175**	0.170**	1	
Sector	0.054**	0.013	-0.042*	0.140**	0.038*	0.023	0.140**	0.062**	0.022	1

The authors take the anti-log of the variables Size and Age
** Significant at the 1%, * at the 5%,
Source: Own elaboration

authors do not need to control for sample selection bias in our study. All of this indicates that the random effects Tobit model is adequate for our data and this chapter therefore explains the results of this model.

The results and tests reported in the random effects Tobit model clearly support hypothesis 1 regarding the negative effect of family involvement in internationalization.

Hypothesis 2, that internationalization is encouraged when family firms survive into the second and subsequent generations, is supported.

Our results are also consistent with hypothesis 3 which proposes the positive effect on internationalization of establishing alliances with other firms.

This chapter advances hypothesis 4 to determine whether intangible resources have a positive effect on internationalization, as expected by the literature. Our model validates this hypothesis for human resources, and partially validates it for technological resources. The product innovations variable is positively and significantly related to internationalization, while the process innovations variable is not significant. Finally, the effect is not significant in the case of marketing resources.

As mentioned previously, most empirical studies find that the size of the family firm affects its internationalization positively. The authors corroborated this relationship, supporting hypothesis 5.

Studying the age of the family firm, the authors observe the significant positive effect that it exerts on its internationalization (hypothesis 6).

Finally, there is a positive significant sector effect.

FUTURE RESEARCH DIRECTIONS

Although this paper advances the understanding of the factors that influence the internationalization of Spanish family SMEs, the current findings should be understood in the light of several inherent limitations that provide directions for future research.

First, because of limitations in the second-hand data, our findings are based on a limited set of variables to identify what type of resources provide support for internationalization. While our study is a first step, future studies could take account of other variables that have also been identified in the literature, such as the CEO characteristics (Ramón-Llorens et al., 2017), the regional environment in which they operate (Gajewski & Tchorek, 2017) or the role of networks (Kampouri et al., 2017). As a

Table 3. The determinants of the degree of internationalisation

Independent variable	(1) Pooled regression	(2) Random Effects Tobit	Dynamic Hekman Probit Model	
			(3) Selection equation	(4)Regression equation
Family involvement	-0.004 (0.015)	-0.034 (0.013)**	0.057 (0.154)	-0.010 (0.017)
Second generation	0.017 (0.040)	0.062 (0.032)**	0.082 (0.377)	0.025 (0.038)
Alliances	-0.014 (0.029)	0.049 (0.023)**	0.492 (0.342)	0.036 (0.031)
Product innovations	0.068 (0.033)**	0.062 (0.018)***	0.042 (0.303)	0.058 (0.023)**
Process innovations	-0.043 (0.029)	-0.024 (0.015)	-0.122 (0.249)	-0.031 (0.018)*
Marketing resources	-0.003 (0.005)	-0.002 (0.005)	0.211 (0.105)**	-0.002 (0.005)
Human resources	0.011 (0.002)***	0.003 (0.002)*	0.027 (0.023)	0.010 (0.003)***
Size	0.156 (0.016)***	0.076 (0.020)***	0.756 (0.202)***	0.119 (0.025)***
Age	0.086 (0.032)***	0.092 (0.037)**	-0.181 (0.304)	0.079 (0.037)**
Sector	77.501 (6.353)***	52.070 (6.492)***	67.930 (67.526)	66.051 (7.773)***
Constant	-0.874 (0.113)***	-0.428 (0.142)***	0.039 (1.092)	-0.663 (0.142)***
Inverse Mills				0.008 (0.413)
Fit of the model	Prob > F=0.000	Prob > X^2=0.000	Prob > X^2=0.01 Prob > X^2=0.000	

Standard errors in parentheses. *** Significant at the 1%, ** at the 5%, * at the 10% level. The dependent variable is the internationalisation degree.

Source: Own elaboration

consequence, in order to further clarify how family businesses go about their internationalization, future research could use in-depth interviews to examine factors such as the perceptions of managers about the benefits of internationalization.

Another limitation is our specification of family business: even if the authors apply a dichotomous measure, like previous studies of family SMEs (e.g., Abdellatif et al., 2010; Chua et al., 1999; Graves & Thomas, 2008), it only captures a specific type of family business. While this approach is acceptable in a Spanish context (Merino et al., 2015), such as ours, future research might also analyse continuous measurements of family business, such as the F-PEC scale (Abdellatif et al., 2010; Klein, Shapiro & Young, 2005).

Thirdly, there is the matter of the geographical scope of this study. Although the Survey on Business Strategies guarantees the representativeness of the sample, data were collected exclusively in Spain, introducing a potential cultural bias and limiting the generalizability of our findings to other countries (Abdellatif et al., 2010). Future research should replicate our study for countries other than Spain to assess the internationalization strategies of family SMEs there.

CONCLUSION

The high volatility of environments and globalization of markets has increased the importance of internationalization strategies for all firms, including family ones. Therefore, our understanding of the international expansion of family firms and how to increase it needs to be improved (Merino, Monreal-Pérez & Sánchez-Marín, 2015).

The primary purpose of this article was to analyse the international involvement of Spanish Family SMEs, for which the authors have relevant and reliable data. In particular, this chapter uses the information provided by a representative sample of the SBS from 2006 to 2012, including 1,519 observations.

This study offers a number of contributions. Theoretically, building on resource dependency theory, our framework aims to identify key distinguishing features that characterize the internationalization of family businesses. While most previous research has focused on investigating the internationalization strategies of family businesses compared with those of non-family businesses (Banalieva & Eddleston, 2011), this study uncovers the importance of the heterogeneity of family firms in connection with their internationalization strategy.

The chapter extends previous academic literature that aims to address the existing conflicting findings regarding the internationalization of family firms by focusing on family-controlled firms, a specific type of family firm in which the business is owned and managed by a nuclear family.

Given the inconsistent results regarding the measures used to assess the degree of internationalization (Fernández-Olmos, 2011), our study includes the two dimensions of scale and scope of international involvement to provide a richer perspective of internationalization strategies.

Finally, little empirical research has been conducted to identify the variables that affect Spanish family SMEs' internationalization decisions with panel data (some exceptions are Fernández & Nieto, 2005 and Merino et al., 2015). The existing evidence on family SMEs focuses on studying whether family-controlled firms achieve superior performance when compared with their non-family counterparts (Graver and Shan, 2014).

The authors believe our study is timely because about 85% of the companies in Spain are family businesses and exporting is becoming an increasingly important strategy for them. In particular, at the level of international trade, family businesses account for almost 60% of Spanish exports (Instituto de la Empresa familiar, www.iefamiliar.com).

Identifying the factors that lead family SMEs to international expansion has important managerial implications.

It is crucial that managers understand the negative effect of family involvement in managerial positions on the degree of internationalization. As supported by previous literature (Banalieva & Eddleston, 2011, Cerrato & Piva, 2012), family firms striving to internationalize should consider hiring non-family members because international expansion strategies require managerial talent often not found within the family.

The succession of members in top senior positions is an essential event for the internationalization process of family SMEs. This is consistent with the arguments presented in other studies (Basly, 2007; Nonaka & Takeuchi, 1998; Tsang, 1999), which have argued that family firms could implement a deliberate strategy of knowledge transfer through generations in order to encourage the internationalization process.

As supported by our research, the establishment of alliances plays a crucial role in the international development of family SMEs. This is a consequence of the growth of the firm's knowledge base thanks to the development and maintenance of such contacts, which is beneficial for internationalization.

Our results suggest that family SMEs should exploit product innovations (i.e., products with superior characteristics to those offered by the competition) in developing their internationalization strategy. However, process innovations (e.g., reducing the costs of production) do not result in more overseas activity.

Our model does not provide statistical support for the influence of marketing resources on the international commitment of family SMEs. This result suggests that resources of this type, such as advertising, are more effective in domestic than foreign markets due to communication and language barriers (Salomon & Shaver, 2005). Therefore, managers should develop marketing strategies for products that meet the needs of customers in the international markets targeted.

The positive link between human resources and the degree of internationalization implies that managers and policy makers should focus on fostering this (i.e., exploiting the skills of management and staff in developing their export strategy) in order to stimulate export expansion by family SMEs.

The positive effect of size is consistent with many studies, which have highlighted its importance in the internationalization of family firms (e.g., Fernández & Nieto, 2005; Merino et al., 2015).

The analysis of our results suggests that age represents one of the most important factors in increasing the international competitiveness of firms. It could provide support for the incremental view of internationalization suggested by stage theory (Johanson & Vahlne, 1977): as a family firm gains experience, it develops new knowledge and capabilities in order to increase its presence in international markets.

In conclusion, this article increases our understanding of the heterogeneity of family SMEs through an examination of their international expansion. Moreover, it contributes to the RBV theory of internationalization by providing empirical support for the positive association between the resources of some family SMEs and the degree of internationalization. Hence, the authors encourage fellow researchers to further investigate the heterogeneous nature of family firms and the contexts in which they operate, which will make a valuable contribution to understanding their strategic behaviour in the global marketplace.

ACKNOWLEDGMENT

This research was supported by the AEI/FEDER, UE [project grant ECO2016-77-P]; and the Government of Aragón-Spain and FEDER 2014-2020 "Construyendo Europa desde Aragón [COMPETE S52_17R research group].

REFERENCES

Abdellatif, M., Amann, B., & Jaussaud, J. (2010). Family versus nonfamily business: A comparison of international strategies. *Journal of Family Business Strategies*, *1*(2), 108–116. doi:10.1016/j.jfbs.2010.04.004

Alayo, M., Maseda, A., Iturralde, T., & Arzubiaga, U. (2019). Internationalization and entrepreneurial orientation of family SMEs: The influence of the family character. *International Business Review*, *28*(1), 48–59. doi:10.1016/j.ibusrev.2018.06.003

Aldrich, H. E., & Cliff, J. E. (2003). The Pervasive Effects of Family on Entrepreneurship: Toward a Family Embeddedness Perspective. *Journal of Business Venturing*, *18*(5), 573–596. doi:10.1016/S0883-9026(03)00011-9

Allouche, J., Amann, B., Jaussaud, J., & Kurashina, T. (2008). The Impact of Family Control on the Performance and Financial Characteristics of Family Versus Nonfamily Businesses in Japan: A Matched-Pair Investigation. *Family Business Review*, *21*(4), 315–329. doi:10.1177/08944865080210040104

Almodóvar, P. (2012). The International performance of standardizing and customizing Spanish firms. The M curve relationships. *Multinational Business Review*, *20*(4), 306–330. doi:10.1108/15253831211286246

Almodóvar, P., & Rugman, A. M. (2014). The M Curve and the Performance of Spanish International New Ventures. *British Journal of Management*, *2*, S6–S23. doi:10.1111/1467-8551.12022

Anderson, R., & Reeb, D. (2003). Founding family ownership and firm performance: Evidence from the S&P 500. *The Journal of Finance*, *58*(3), 1301–1328. doi:10.1111/1540-6261.00567

Andersson, S., Gabrielsson, J., & Wictor, I. (2004). International Activities in Small Firms: Examining Factors Influencing the Internationalisation and Export Growth of Small Firms. *Canadian Journal of Administrative Sciences*, *21*(1), 22–34. doi:10.1111/j.1936-4490.2004.tb00320.x

Arregle, J.-L., Naldi, L., Nordqvist, M., & Hitt, M. A. (2012). Internationalization of family-controlled firms: A study of the effects of external involvement in governance. *Entrepreneurship Theory and Practice*, *36*(6), 1115–1143. doi:10.1111/j.1540-6520.2012.00541.x

Axinn, C. N., Savitt, R., Sinkula, J. M., & Thatch, S. V. (1995). Export Intention, Beliefs, and Behaviors in Smaller Industrial Firms. *Journal of Business Research*, *32*(1), 49–55. doi:10.1016/0148-2963(94)00009-4

Banalieva, E. R., & Eddeleston, K. (2011). Home-region focus and performance of family firms: The role of family vs non-family leaders´. *Journal of International Business Studies*, *42*(8), 1060–1072. doi:10.1057/jibs.2011.28

Basile, R. (2001). Export behaviour if Italian manufacturing firms over the nineties: The role of innovation. *Research Policy*, *30*(8), 1185–1201. doi:10.1016/S0048-7333(00)00141-4

Basly, S. (2007). The internationalization of family SME. An organizational learning and knowledge development perspective. *Baltic Journal of Management*, *2*(2), 154–180. doi:10.1108/17465260710750973

Benavides-Velasco, C. A., Quintana-García, C., & Guzmán-Parra, V. F. (2013). Trends in family business research. *Small Business Economics*, *40*(1), 41–57. doi:10.100711187-011-9362-3

Benito, G. R. G., & Welch, L. S. (1994). Foreign market servicing: Beyond choice of entry mode. *Journal of International Marketing*, *2*(2), 7–28. doi:10.1177/1069031X9400200202

Bonaccorsi, A. (1992). On the relationship between firm size and export intensity. *Journal of International Business Studies*, *23*(4), 605–635. doi:10.1057/palgrave.jibs.8490280

Boxall, P., & Steeneveld, M. (1999). Human resource strategy and competitive advantage: A longitudinal study of engineering consultancies. *Journal of Management Studies*, *36*(4), 443–463. doi:10.1111/1467-6486.00144

Brush, C. (1992). *Factors motivating small firms to internationalize: The effect of firm age* (Doctoral dissertation). Boston University.

Buckley, P. J. (1989). Foreign investment by small-and-medium-sized enterprises: The theoretical background. *Small Business Economics*, *1*(2), 89–100. doi:10.1007/BF00398627

Cerrato, D., & Piva, M. (2012). The internationalization of small and medium-sized enterprises: The effect of family management, human capital and foreign ownership. *The Journal of Management and Governance*, *16*(4), 617–644. doi:10.100710997-010-9166-x

Chandra, Y., Styles, C., & Wilkinson, I. (2009). The recognition of first time international entrepreneurial opportunities: Evidence from firms in knowledge-based industries. *International Marketing Review*, *26*(1), 30–61. doi:10.1108/02651330910933195

Chen, H. (2011). Internationalization in Taiwanese family firms. *Global Journal of Business Research*, *5*(4), 15–23.

Chen, R., & Martin, J. M. (2001). Foreign expansion of small firms: The impact of domestic alternatives and prior foreign business involvement. *Journal of Business Venturing*, *16*(6), 557–574. doi:10.1016/S0883-9026(99)00058-0

Chrisman, J. J., Chua, J. H., & Sharma, P. (2005). Trends and directions in the development of strategic management theory of the family firm. *Entrepreneurship Theory and Practice*, *29*(5), 555–575. doi:10.1111/j.1540-6520.2005.00098.x

Chua, J. H., Chrisman, J. J., & Sharma, P. (1999). Defining family business by behavior. *Entrepreneurship Theory and Practice*, *23*(4), 19–39. doi:10.1177/104225879902300402

Claver, E., Rienda, L., & Quer, D. (2007). The internationalisation process in family firms: Choice of market entry strategies. *Journal of General Management*, *33*(1), 1–14. doi:10.1177/030630700703300101

Claver, E., Rienda, L., & Quer, D. (2009). Family firms´ international commitment: The influence of family-related factors. *Family Business Review*, *22*(2), 25–135. doi:10.1177/0894486508330054

Cohen, W. M., & Klepper, S. (1996). Firm size and the nature of innovation within industries: The case of product and process R&D. *The Review of Economics and Statistics*, *78*(2), 232–243. doi:10.2307/2109925

Davis, P. S., & Harveston, P. D. (2000). Internationalization and organizational grow: The impact of internet usage and technology involvement among entrepreneur-led family businesses. *Family Business Review*, *18*(2), 107–120. doi:10.1111/j.1741-6248.2000.00107.x

De Massis, A., Frattini, F., Majocchi, A., & Piscitello, L. (2018). Family firms in the global economy: Toward a deeper understanding of internationalization determinants, processes, and outcomes. *Global Strategy Journal*, *8*(1), 3–21. doi:10.1002/gsj.1199

Deardorff, A. (1984). Testing Trade Theories and Predicitng Trade Flows´. In R. Jones & P. Kenen (Eds.), *Handbook of International Economics I*. Amsterdam: Elsevier Science Publishers. doi:10.1016/S1573-4404(84)01013-3

Delgado-Gómez, J. M., Ramírez-Alesón, M., & Espitia-Escuer, M. A. (2004). Intangible Resource as a key factor in the internationalisation of Spanish firms. *Journal of Economic Behavior & Organization*, *53*(4), 477–494. doi:10.1016/j.jebo.2002.11.001

Devins, D. (2008). Encouraging skills acquisitions and SMEs. In R. Barret & S. Mayson (Eds.), International Handbook of Entrepreneurship and HRM, (pp. 420–433). Cheltenham, UK: Elgar.

Díez Vial, I., & Fernández-Olmos, M. (2013). Internal resources, local externalities and export performance: An application in the Iberian ham cluster in Spain. *Journal of Management & Organization*, *19*(4), 478–497. doi:10.1017/jmo.2013.32

Duran, J., & Úbeda, F. (2003). A Dynamic Analysis of the Inward and Outward Direct Investment of the Newly Developed Countries. *29th Annual Conference of the European International Business Academy*.

Durán Herrera, J. J. (2008). La Geografía de la Empresa Multinacional Española. *Boletín de Estudios Económicos*. *63*, *193*, 15–44.

Farinas, J. C., & Jaumandreu, J. (1999). *La empresa industrial en la década de los noventa*. Madrid: Fundación Argentaria/ Visor Dis.

Fernández, Z., & Nieto, M. J. (2005). Internationalization strategy of small and medium-sized family businesses: Some influential factors. *Family Business Review*, *18*(1), 77–89. doi:10.1111/j.1741-6248.2005.00031.x

Fernández, Z., & Nieto, M. J. (2006). Impact of ownership on the international involvement of SMEs. *Journal of International Business Studies*, *37*(3), 340–351. doi:10.1057/palgrave.jibs.8400196

Fernández-Olmos, M. (2011). The determinants of internationalization: Evidence from the wine industry. *Applied Economic Perspectives and Policy*, *33*(3), 384–401. doi:10.1093/aepp/ppr017

Gajewski, P., & Tchorek, G. (2017). What drives export performance of firms in Eastern and Western Poland? *European Planning Studies*, *25*(12), 2250–2271. doi:10.1080/09654313.2017.1355890

Gallo, M. A., & Garcia Pont, C. (1996). Important factors in family business internationalization. *Family Business Review*, *9*(1), 45–60. doi:10.1111/j.1741-6248.1996.00045.x

Gómez-Mejia, L. (1988). The Role of Human Resources Strategy in Export Performance: A Longitudinal Study. *Strategic Management Journal*, *9*(5), 493–505. doi:10.1002mj.4250090508

Gómez-Mejia, L. R., Makri, M., & Larraza-Kintana, M. (2010). Diversification decisions in family-controlled firms. *Journal of Management Studies*, *47*(2), 223–252. doi:10.1111/j.1467-6486.2009.00889.x

Grant, R. M., Jammine, A. P., & Thomas, H. (1988). Diversity, diversification, and profitability among British manufacturing companies, 1972–1984. *Academy of Management Journal*, *31*(4), 771–801.

Graves, C., & Shan, Y. G. (2014). An Empirical Analysis of the Effect of Internationalization on the Performance of Unlisted Family and Nonfamily Firms in Australia. *Family Business Review*, *27*(2), 142–160. doi:10.1177/0894486513491588

Graves, C., & Thomas, J. (2006). Internationalization of Australian family businesses: A managerial capabilities perspective. *Family Business Review*, *19*(3), 207–224. doi:10.1111/j.1741-6248.2006.00066.x

Graves, C., & Thomas, J. (2008). Determinants of the Internationalization Pathways of Family Firms: An Examination of Family Influence. *Family Business Review*, *21*(2), 151–167. doi:10.1111/j.1741-6248.2008.00119.x

Hambrick, D. C., & Mason, P. A. (1984). Upper echelons: The organization as a reflection of its top managers. *Academy of Management Review*, *9*(2), 193–206. doi:10.5465/amr.1984.4277628

Hill, C. W. L., Hwang, P., & Kim, C. (1990). An eclectic theory of the choice of international entry mode. *Strategic Management Journal*, *11*(2), 117–128. doi:10.1002mj.4250110204

Hitt, M. A., Hoskisson, R. E., & Kim, H. (1997). International diversification: Effects on innovation and firm performance in product-diversified firms. *Academy of Management Journal*, *40*, 767–798.

Hitt, M. A., Tihanyi, L., Miller, T., & Connelly, B. (2006). International diversification: Antecedents, outcomes, and moderators. *Journal of Management*, *32*(6), 831–867. doi:10.1177/0149206306293575

Ibrahim, A., Soufani, K., & Lam, J. (2001). A Study of Succession in a Family Firm. *Family Business Review*, *14*(3), 245–258. doi:10.1111/j.1741-6248.2001.00245.x

Johanson, J., & Mattsson, L. G. (1993). Internationalization in industrial systems – a network approach, strategies in global competition´. In P. J. Buckley & P. N. Ghauri (Eds.), *The Internationalization of the Firm: A Reader* (pp. 303–322). London: Academic Press.

Johanson, J., & Vahlne, J. E. (1977). The internationalization process of the firm: A model of knowledge development and increasing market commitment. *Journal of International Business Studies*, *8*(1), 23–32. doi:10.1057/palgrave.jibs.8490676

Kampouri, K., Plakoyiannaki, E., & Leppäaho, T. (2017). Family business internationalisation and networks: Emerging pathways. *Journal of Business and Industrial Marketing*, *32*(3), 357–370. doi:10.1108/JBIM-04-2015-0066

Kim, W. C., Hwang, P., & Burgers, W. P. (1989). Global Diversification Strategy and Corporate Profit Performance. *Strategic Management Journal, 10*(1), 45–57. doi:10.1002mj.4250100105

Klein, P., Shapiro, D., & Young, J. (2005). Corporate governance, family ownership and firm value: The Canadian evidence. *Corporate Governance, 13*(6), 769–784. doi:10.1111/j.1467-8683.2005.00469.x

Kontinen, T., & Ojala, A. (2010). The Internationalization of Family Businesses: A Review of Extant Research. *Journal of Family Business Strategy, 1*(2), 97–107. doi:10.1016/j.jfbs.2010.04.001

Koopman, M., & Sebel, K. (2009). *The internationalization of family firms: Facilitating and Constraining Features*. Jönköping: Jönköping University.

Lachenmaier, S., & Wößmann, L. (2006). Does Innovation Cause Export? Evidence from Exogenous Innovation Impulses and Obstacles Using German Micro Data. Oxford Economic Press.

Leonidou, L. C. (2004). An analysis of the barriers hindering small business export development. *Journal of Small Business Management, 42*(3), 279–302. doi:10.1111/j.1540-627X.2004.00112.x

Liang, X., Wang, L., & Cui, Z. (2014). Chinese Private Firms and Internationalization: Effects of Family Involvement in Management and Family Ownership. *Family Business Review, 1*, 259–274.

Lu, J. W., & Beamish, P. W. (2006). SME internationalization and performance: Growth vs. profitability. *Journal of International Entrepreneurship, 4*(1), 27–48. doi:10.100710843-006-8000-7

Menéndez-Requejo, S. (2005). Growth and internationalization of family businesses. *International Journal of Globalisation and Small Business, 1*(2), 122–133. doi:10.1504/IJGSB.2005.008009

Merino, F., Monreal-Pérez, J., & Sánchez-Marín, G. (2015). Family SMEs´ internationalization: Disentangling the Influence of Familiness on Spanish Firms´ Export Activity. *Journal of Small Business Management, 53*(4), 1164–1184. doi:10.1111/jsbm.12111

Merino, F., & Salas, V. (2002). Causes and consequences of exports´ channel integration. *Spanish Economic Review, 4*(4), 239–259. doi:10.1007101080200056

Moen, O. (1999). The relationship between firm size, competitive advantage and export performance revisited. *International Small Business Journal, 18*(1), 53–72. doi:10.1177/0266242699181003

Morgan, N. A., & Rego, L. L. (2009). Brand Portfolio Strategy and Firm Performance. *Journal of Marketing, 73*(1), 59–74. doi:10.1509/jmkg.73.1.59

Muñoz-Bullón, F., & Sánchez-Bueno, M. J. (2011). The impact of family involvement on the R&D intensity of publicly traded firms. *Family Business Review, 24*(1), 62–70. doi:10.1177/0894486510396870

Mustakallio, M., & Autio, E. (2001). *Optimal governance in family firms*. Paper presented at the Babson Entrepreneurship Conference.

Nagy, S. (2013). The internationalisation of the Spanish SME sector. *Society and Economy, 35*(1), 71–86. doi:10.1556/SocEc.2012.0005

Neubauer, F., & Lank, A. G. (1998). *The family business: it's governance for sustainability*. New York: Routledge. doi:10.1007/978-1-349-14465-5

Nonaka, I., & Takeuchi, H. (1998). A Theory of the Firm's Knowledge-Creation Dynamics., In A. Chandler, P. Hagström & Ö. Sölvell (Eds.), The Dynamic Firm, The Role of Technology, Strategy, Organization, and Regions. Oxford University Press.

Okoroafo, S. (1999). Internationalization of family businesses: Evidence from Northwest Ohio, USA. *Family Business Review*, *21*, 147–158.

Olivares-Mesa, A., & Cabrera-Suárez, K. (2006). Factors affecting the timing of the export development process: Does the family influence on the business make a difference? *International Journal of Globalisation and Small Business*, *1*(4), 326–339. doi:10.1504/IJGSB.2006.012183

Pangarkar, N. (2008). Internationalization and performance of small- and medium sized enterprises. *Journal of World Business*, *43*(4), 475–485. doi:10.1016/j.jwb.2007.11.009

Patel, V. K., Pieper, T. M., & Hair, J. F. Jr. (2012). The global family business: Challenges and drivers for cross-border growth. *Business Horizons*, *55*(3), 231–239. doi:10.1016/j.bushor.2012.01.002

Peng, M. W. (2001). The resource-based view and international business. *Journal of Management*, *27*(6), 803–829. doi:10.1177/014920630102700611

Pfeffer, J., & Salancik, G. R. (2003). *The External Control of Organizations: A Resource Dependence Perspective*. Stanford, CA: Stanford University Press.

Plá Barber, J. (1999). Filiales de Entrada en los Mercados Internacionales: Factores Determinantes. *Revista de Economía Aplicada*, *20*, 29–51.

Pukall, T. J., & Calabrò, A. (2014). The Internationalization of family firms: A critical review and integrative model. *Family Business Review*, *27*(2), 323–332. doi:10.1177/0894486513491423

Ramón-Llorens, M. C., García-Meca, E., & Duréndez, A. (2017). Influence of CEO characteristics in family firms internationalization. *International Business Review*, *26*(4), 786–799. doi:10.1016/j.ibusrev.2017.01.007

Rauch, A., Frese, M., & Utsch, A. (2005). Effects of human capital and long-term human resources development and utilization on employment growth of small-scale businesses: A causal analysis. *Entrepreneurship Theory and Practice*, *29*(6), 681–698.

Reuber, A. R., & Fischer, E. (1997). The influence of the management team's international experience on the internationalization behaviors of SMEs. *Journal of International Business Studies*, *28*(4), 807–825. doi:10.1057/palgrave.jibs.8490120

Rialp, A. (1999). Los Enfoques Micro-organizativos de la Internacionalización de la Empresa: Una Revisión y Síntesis de la Literatura. *ICE: Revista de Economía*, *781*, 117–128.

Roida, H. Y., & Sunarjanto, N. A. (2012). Family ownership type and the international involvement of SMEs: Empirical study of agency theory in East Java Indonesia. *The China Business Review*, *11*, 224–232.

Sacristán, M., Rico, G. & Lafuente, C. (2011). Spanish SMEs and Family Firms export behavior: are there differences in their incremental approach? *Revista de Empresa Familiar, 1*(1), 7-21.

Salomon, R., & Shaver, M. (2005). Export and domestic sales: Their interrelationship and determinants. *Strategic Management Journal, 26*(9), 855–871. doi:10.1002mj.481

Sterlacchini, A. (1999). Do innovative activities matter to small firms in non R&D intensive industries? An application to export performance. *Research Policy, 28*(8), 819–832. doi:10.1016/S0048-7333(99)00023-2

Swinth, R., & Vinton, K. (1993). Do Family-Owned Businesses have a Strategic Advantage in International Joint Ventures? *Family Business Review, 4*(1), 19–30. doi:10.1111/j.1741-6248.1993.00019.x

Tsang, E. W. K. (1999). Internationalization as a learning process: Singapore MNCs in China. *The Academy of Management Executive, 13*(1), 91–101. doi:10.5465/ame.1999.1567359

Tsao, S., & Lien, W. (2013). Family management and internationalization: The impact on firm performance and innovation. *Management International Review, 53*(2), 189–213. doi:10.100711575-011-0125-9

Ward, J. L. (1987). *Keeping the Family Business Healthy: How to plan for continuing growth, profitability, and family leadership*. San Francisco, CA: Jossey-Bass.

Ward, J. L. (1998). Growing the family business: Special challenges and best practices. *Family Business Review, 10*(4), 323–337. doi:10.1111/j.1741-6248.1997.00323.x

Welch, L. (1992). The use of alliances by small firms in achieving internationalization. *Scandinavian International Business Review, 1*(2), 21–37. doi:10.1016/0962-9262(92)90019-3

Westhead, P., & Howorth, C. (2006). Ownership and Management Issues Associated with Family Firm Performance and Company Objectives. *Family Business Review, 19*(4), 301–316. doi:10.1111/j.1741-6248.2006.00077.x

Westhead, P., Wright, M., & Ucbasaran, D. (2004). Internationalization of private firms: Environmental turbulence and organizational strategies and resources. *Entrepreneurship and Regional Development, 16*(6), 501–522. doi:10.1080/0898562042000231929

Yeung, H. W. (2000). Limits to the growth of family owned business? The case of Chinese transnational corporations from Hong Kong. *Family Business Review, 13*(1), 55–70. doi:10.1111/j.1741-6248.2000.00055.x

Zahra, S. A. (2003). `International expansion of US manufacturing family businesses: The effect of ownership and involvement´. *Journal of Business Venturing, 18*(4), 495–512. doi:10.1016/S0883-9026(03)00057-0

Zahra, S. A., Matherne, B. P., & Carleton, J. M. (2003). `Technological resource leveraging and the internationalization of new ventures´. *Journal of International Entrepreneurship, 1*(2), 163–186. doi:10.1023/A:1023852201406

KEY TERMS AND DEFINITIONS

Alliance: An arrangement or relationship among independent businesses with corresponding goals, established for a specific purpose.

Export: Send goods or services to another country for sale.

Family Business: A business actively owned and/or managed by more than one member of the same family.

Family Involvement: This is the number of family members occupying managerial positions.

Intangible Resources: Intangible assets are the long-term resources of an entity, but have no physical existence.

International Expansion: The planned expansion of a company's business activities into countries in several regions throughout the world.

Survey on Business Strategies: A panel survey of manufacturing firms located in Spain.

ENDNOTES

1 See Fariñas and Jaumandreu (1999) and www.funep.es for further details.

2 The Survey on Business Strategies uses this threshold when sampling the Spanish manufacturing sector (Almodóvar & Rugman, 2014)

3 The authors add one year to avoid ages of zero (Fukugawa, 2006).

4 The Kolmogorov-Smirnov test determined that the variables are not normally distributed. The authors therefore cannot use Pearson correlations.

5 The authors apply the random effect specification because it allows unobserved heterogeneity, first order state dependence and serial correlation in the error components.

Chapter 7
Technological Innovation in Family Firms

Mario Ossorio
University of Campania Luigi Vanvitelli, Italy

ABSTRACT

This chapter illustrates the main issues with respect to innovation process within family firms. In the first part, it describes the main theories underlying the innovation process of family firms (agency theory, altruism, portfolio theory, stewardship theory, socioemotional wealth perspective). In the second part, it exposes the R&D underinvestment problem in large companies with a focus on the effect of the family ownership on the R&D investments. In the third part, it describes the effect of family ownership on the innovation output with a focus on the kind of innovation (radical vs. incremental). In the fourth section, studies exploring the innovation strategies of family firms (prospectors, analysers, defenders, reactors) are examined. In the fifth section, it sheds light on the innovation management process of family firms. In this part, it explores the issues of internal innovation process (functional vs. cross-functional structure) and of the partnerships with external actors aimed to generate innovation.

INTRODUCTION

Over the last years, technological innovation within family firm context is receiving an increasing attention (Calabrò et al., 2019; De Massis et al., 2012a). Although family firms are recognized more conservative and less incline to innovation, the majority of the most innovative firms around the world are family firms (Calabrò et al., 2018; Rondi et al., 2018). According to the consolidated process based conceptualization (Tidd & Bessant, 2009), technological innovation can be conceived as the set of activities through which a firm identifies, designs, produces, and introduces a new product, technology, system, or technique (Freeman, 1976). Literature indicates that innovation represents a key driver for firms' competitiveness and technologically innovative companies are more likely to achieve an enduring competitive advantage (Geroski et al.,1993). Scholars have widely investigated innovation process in small and medium firms so as with respect to large companies. Anyway, only recently an emerging strand of literature has focused on innovation activities within a family firm context, emphasizing the scant

DOI: 10.4018/978-1-7998-1655-3.ch007

attention paid referring this theme. This is surprising considering that family firms are characterized by an interaction between family, individual family members and the business (Habbershon & Williams, 1999) that generates a unique bundle of idiosyncratic resources and capabilities with an intangible and tacit nature favouring the achievement of long-lasting competitive advantage. Technological innovation issue represents a great potential research area "... *because there are strong theoretical reasons to believe that the antecedents and effects of technological innovation*" (De Massis et al., 2012b p. 1). Family firms may differ from nonfamily counterparts with respect to risk aversion, investment horizons, return aspiration, climate organization and so on (Carney, 2005; Zellweger et al., 2012). These aspects inevitably influence firms' propensity to invest in innovation and in managing innovation activities. While some research portrays family firms as reluctant to undertake R&D investments (Chen & Hsu, 2009), and assume risk (Morris, 1998), other research suggests that family firms show a high innovation productivity rate (Matzler et al., 2015).

The aim of this chapter is to review and systematize literature referring to technological innovation in family firms, separating the different phases of family firms' innovation process (De Massis et al., 2012b), and emphasizing the role of family-related antecedents. The discussion of the main issues regarding family firms' innovation allows to illustrate the research areas where scholars find a consensus and other areas where literature manifests different results and therefore the consequent debate is still open. In order to explore family firms' innovation process, empirical studies will be examined and the interpretation of the relative results will leverage on the main theoretical frameworks used within family business literature.

The chapter is articulated in the following sections:

1. The first section illustrates the theoretical frameworks used in the most of the family firms' innovation studies, which are agency theory, altruism, portfolio theory, stewardship theory, and socio-emotional wealth perspective;
2. The second section explores studies on direct effects of family involvement on technological innovation inputs and on the moderating effect of some factors (such as aspirational gap, Ceo duality, growth opportunities) on the relationship between family involvement and innovation inputs. Starting by the R&D underinvestment problem, the chapter highlights some factors featuring family firms, such as risk aversion and the agency conflicts between controlling family and minority shareholders, may negatively affect the propensity to invest in R&D;
3. The third section highlights the influence of family involvement on technological innovation management; more specifically, studies in this research area focus on how the innovation process is managed and favoured inside the firm (e. g.: the choice of type organization that handles the innovation process) and outside it (propensity to interact with external stakeholders, their number and kind);
4. The fourth section sheds light on family firms' strategic behaviour with respect to the innovation. These studies, on one hand, emphasize family firms approach towards product R&D activities and development of new products/markets; on the other hand, they emphasize how some family antecedents, such as succession process and ownership dispersion, affect the above mentioned strategic behaviour;
5. The fifth section describes the innovation output of family firms, focusing on the number of innovative output, the choice on incremental vs disruptive innovation and the generational involvement effect on the output.

BACKGROUND

Studies on the effect of family ownership on innovation input, activities and output have been conducted using many theoretical frameworks. This chapter will consider articles using mainly the following perspectives: 1) agency theory (Jensen & Meckling, 1976), with special emphasis on relationships between family controlling owner and minority shareholders, 2) altruism, described as an utility function that positively links the welfare of a parent to the welfare of his children (Stark, 1995; Lubatkin et al., 2005), 3) portfolio theory, that highlights the concentration of family members' wealth on the family business and their following risk-averse behavior (Carney, 2005), 4) stewardship theory, that views individual as a steward, driven also by nonfinancial motivation, and 5) socio-emotional wealth perspective (Gómez-Mejía et al., 2007) that considers the impact of the strategic choices on the family members' affective endowment.

Agency Theory

This theoretical framework derives from financial economics studies and constitutes one of the main blocks in the corporate governance literature. The work of Jensen and Meckling (1976) represents a seminal paper of agency theory and examines the interest conflicts following the separation of ownership and control in public companies. Agency relationship can be viewed as a contract where one part (principal) delegates work to another part (the agent). To be effective, this relationship requires that the principal has to concede to agent a certain degree of decisional autonomy. Jensen and Meckling (1976) use this kind of framework to explore the dynamics characterizing the relationship between shareholders and managers in public companies, that are respectively principal and agent of the agency relationship. Agency theorists point out that manager has motivation to consume non pecuniary personal benefits (perquisites), because he will take entirely the connected advantages while he will sustain only a part of the relative costs, being the rest of them in charge to shareholders. More specifically, agency costs are constituted by monitoring costs - such as that linked to the use of board of directors and auditors -, bonding costs - e.g.: contractual limitations to managerial decision-making and golden parachutes - and residual loss.

There are some relevant postulates basing agency theory. The first one is relative to bounded rationality of the individuals, that do not allow them to forecast every potential situations and, consequently, to sign complete contracts. Thus, managers shall deal with some unforeseen events, not regulated by the contracts. The second postulate is relative to the "model of man", that is represented by a self-interested, individualistic actor aimed to maximise his own personal economic gain. *The model is individualistic and is predicated upon the notion of an in-built conflict of interest between owner and manager* (Donaldson & Davis 1991, p. 51). The third assumption is relative to the information asymmetry between principal and agent, that can generate problems of moral hazard that arises when the action undertaken by the agent is unobservable and has a different value to the agent as compared to the principal. Taking into account these assumptions entails that shareholders have no guarantee that managers achieve their task without emerging any agency costs.

In family firms agency conflicts between owners and managers do not appear a critical issue because largely an overlapping between managers and family members occurs and the latter possess adequate information to supervise nonfamily managers (Munoz-Bullòn & Sanchez-Bueno, 2011). Nevertheless, agency problem can emerge because controlling shareholders may expropriate value from minority shareholders (Dharwadkar et al., 2000; La Porta et al., 1999). "*In a family business, the agency cost associated with major and minor shareholders could be important when the divergence between cash flow rights and voting rights created through the pyramid structures and cross-holdings of a family group becomes significant .....When family shareholders hold more voting rights than cash flow rights, they have effective control over the investment decisions, and may use a firm's resources for their own interests while other stakeholders bear the costs*" (Chang et al., 2010, p. 157).

Altruism

Another important feature of family ownership is represented by altruism, which is considered a powerful factor which leads parents to look after their children's interests and stimulates thoughtfulness between family members (Lubatkin et al., 2005). This trait causes family members to consider themselves as residual claimants of the family estate (Corbetta & Salvato, 2004), producing an alignment of growth strategy and risk-taking objectives between family and firm (Chang et al., 2010). In addition, altruism is one of the main drivers of noneconomic goals of family firms through which family members tend to defend socioemotional wealth of the firm (Berrone et al., 2012) and press managers to pursue long-term strategies, even despite poor short-term performance (Carney, 2005). The focus on the long-term inevitably promotes investments in innovative activities (Miller & Le Breton-Miller, 2006). Altruism can have a positive effect on trust and communication, reducing risks associated to opportunistic behaviour (Memili et al., 2011; Tsai et al., 2006).

Portfolio theory

Scholars have emphasized that the desire of family owners to keep the business in the family for future generations leads them to invest their wealth in the firm for the long-term (Miller *et al.*, 2010). In order to avoid diluting family ownership, family firms use limited sources of outside financial capital and are reluctant to sell their shares (Sirmon & Hitt, 2003). The strong ownership position permits family members to enjoy control over strategic decisions (Chua et al., 1999). Family firms encounter certain difficulties in diversifying their investment because most of their "eggs" lie in the family business, as a means of avoiding opening equity capital to third parties and thus losing control of their business. The necessity of investing the entirety of their wealth in the business stimulates family members to avoid to undertake investment that may increase the firm overall risk degree (Miller et al., 2010).

Stewardship Theory

Scholars adopt a stewardship view to interpret organizational culture and leadership in family-owned firms (Chrisman et al. 2007; Corbetta & Salvato 2004). Under this perspective, a steward is an individual stimulated by a need to achieve to gain intrinsic satisfaction through excellent performance at work (Donaldson & Davis, 1991). The model of man described by stewardship theory adopts a pro-organizational and collectivistic behaviour and "*...far from being an opportunistic shirker, essentially wants to do a good job, to be a good steward of the corporate assets*" (Donaldson & Davis, 1991, p.3). Because, whether he can choose between self-serving behaviour and pro-organizational behaviour, he will not give up to the interest of his or her organization (Davis et al. 1997). He always will prefer cooperation than defection. He will place higher value to organization's objectives, such as sales growth or profitability, because through the achievement of those, shareholders' wealth is maximized and, in turn, steward's utility function is maximized.

Socioemotional Wealth

When family managers take a strategic decision they evaluate not only the effects on financial wealth but also the effects on affective wealth, so called socio-emotional wealth (henceforth, SEW). "*Using a socioemotional reference point, family firms are likely to place a high priority on maintaining family control even if this means accepting an increased risk of poor firm performance, yet because they must also keep the firm from failing, they may also act more conservatively by avoiding business decisions that may increase performance variability*" (Gómez-Mejía et al., 2007, p. 106). The family members' control over strategic decisions, their identification with the firm, their social ties within and beyond the firm, their emotional attachment to the firm, and their sense of dynasty, represent the five main components of SEW (Berrone et al., 2012). According to Gómez-Mejía et al. (2011): "*Therefore major managerial choices will be driven by a desire to preserve and enhance the family's socioemotional wealth apart from efficiency or economic instrumentality considerations.*" The preservation of this wealth represents an end in itself, and it is linked to a deep psychological level among family owners whose identity is strictly intermeshed to the organization.

FAMILY OWNERSHIP AND INNOVATION INPUTS

Literature on the propensity of family firms to undertake investments aimed to develop technological innovation within family firms context roots in the studies exploring the relationship between firms' ownership and R&D investments. These studies investigated the effect of ownership concentration and identity on firms' R&D strategies. The starting point of this stream of literature is the acknowledgment that managers may show a disincentive to adopt innovative investments. Therefore, the next paragraphs will explore the R&D underinvestment problem and then the effect of special kind of firm owner, a controlling family.

R&D Underinvestment Problem

Research & Development (R&D) expenditures are investments with specific features. In fact, they are characterized by uncertain payoffs, their potential profit is generated only in the long-run and have a high rate of failure (Baysinger et al., 1991). Beside, scholars highlight that R&D productivity is unpredictable: higher R&D investments do not imply necessearly higher innovation performance (Bebchuck & Stole, 1993). In addition, accounting rules allow firms operating in certain countries to consider innovation activities as costs rather than as investments, therefore, their cutting fictitiously increase earnings (Bushee, 1998) and balance stock return (Chakravarty & Grewal, 2011). Anyway, investments in innovation are essential for reaching a long-term competitive advantage (Porter, 1985). These investments are crucial for firms operating in high-tech industries, such as pharmaceutical and biotechnological. Their traits and their importance for firms' survival and competitiveness make very effortful decisions concerning these types of investments.

Particularly, R&D investments show characteristics that may discourage public companies' managers to choice them. In fact, the information gap between investors and managers (Stein, 1988) constitutes a key issue to shed light the management motivation to invest in R&D, and, therefore, the relationship between ownership structure and innovation. Indeed, managers may have not the propensity to communicate R&D programs, because in this way they disclose relevant details to rival firms and push firms they run in a competitive disadvantage (Bhattacharya & Ritter, 1983). Therefore, managers may renounce to reveal information about firms' R&D strategies. Consequently, investors may encounter several obstacles to understand management's long-term objectives and, thus, they will value the effects of management decisions observing quarterly earnings (Lee & O'Neill, 2003). The shareholder's short-termism may be detrimental for firm's R&D strategies. In fact, R&D expenditures contract current earnings and lead short-term stockholders to sell their shares (Froot et al., 1992). If stockholders massively sell their shares, they may provoke a drop of stock price and external investors - attracted by low prices - may be stimulated to launch a hostile takeover in order to remove incumbent management and run the firm. Therefore, R&D underinvestment problem may arise because of the short termism caused by the threat of takeovers (Stein, 1988). Put differently, the short-termism of investors influences management behaviour, and, in turn their long-term strategic decisions.

Family Ownership and R&D Investments

By a corporate governance perspective, family shareholders often represent large shareholders. Literature on ownership structure has pointed out how a shareholder with a relevant stake in a firm may play an important role to limit the R&D under-investment problem. In fact, a small stockholder generally is not stimulated to control top managers' activities because while he should bear the full cost (in term of money and time), the rest of investors will benefit of its activity, and a free riding problem may emerge (Grossman & Hart, 1980). In addition, small investors may not have the adequate competences and capabilities to evaluate the appropriateness of the managerial decisions within short-time (Zona et al., 2011).

Differently, large shareholder has an adequate percentage of firms' shares and therefore the sufficient motivation to gather more detailed information on firms' investments projects and to analyse managerial choices relative to firm's innovation. A large shareholder may provide at least a partial solution to the free riding problem because it has financial incentive to verify whether management decisions are aligned with their own preferences or not (Anderson & Reeb, 2003).

Considering institutional investor as large shareholder, empirical findings show a positive relationship between concentrated ownership and R&D investments. Focusing on the effect of a controlling family as large investor, there is an ample body of literature that highlights a negative effect on R&D investment. In this sense, the seminal study of Morck, et al. (2000) in this field points out that families controlling business groups are less incline to finance R&D investments.

Chen and Hsu (2009) compare family business with non-family counterparts and find that family ownership is negatively correlated with R&D intensity and this negative relationship is stronger in presence of CEO duality and weakened by the presence of an independent board of directors. Munari, et al. (2010) shed light that family ownership is negatively associated with R&D intensity, while Munoz-Bullon and Sanchez-Bueno (2011) argue that family-owned firms are less apt to undertake innovation activities and tend to have lower R&D intensity compared to non-family businesses. Liu et al. (2017) highlight that a higher percentage of shares controlled by family is associated with low R&D investments. Sanchez-Famoso et al. (2017) emphasize that, because of inadequate professional experience of family managers, family involvement in the Top Management Team (henceforth, TMT) is detrimental to innovation. Arzubiaga et al. (2018) confirm previous results and find that family involvement in the board of directors negatively affects family firms' ability to turn EO into innovation. More recently, Alayo et al. (2019) state "*.... involving non-family members in family firms' managerial positions increases the diversity among TMT members, which tends to generate creativity, innovation....*" (p. 51).

These studies highlight several reasons underlying the negative relationship between family ownership and R&D investments.

One of most largely used perspective in analysing the relationship between family ownership and R&D investments is the agency theory. In fact, the divergence of cash flow and voting rights may permit the family controlling owner to extract monetary and nonmonetary private benefits, such as *i)* "*special dividends or (....) business relationships with the companies they control*" (Shleifer & Vishny, 1997), *ii)* related party transactions (Cheung et al., 2006; Friedman et al., 2003), *iii)* empire building, *iv)* assignment of family members to management roles (Bjuggren & Palmberg, 2010). Such behaviours may allow family members to allocate improperly firms' resources, using them to maximize family welfare at the expense of R&D investments, jeopardizing in turn family firms' enduring competitive advantage (Chen & Hsu, 2009).

A second reason is connected to the altruistic bond between parent and child, that shows two sides in family firms (Eddlestone & Kellermans, 2007): a positive side, above mentioned, and a negative side, stemming from an economic perspective, described as an utility function that positively links the welfare of a parent to the welfare of their children (Lubatkin et al., 2005). Altruism and the lack of self-control by principals can create different kinds of agency costs. A first kind is linked to adverse selection problem: since the hire of a family agent is based on family status as well as on their professional competencies, altruism can generate a deficiency of ability (Schulze et al., 2003), which, in turn, can cause low performance (Eddleston & Kidwell, 2012). Secondly, the generosity of parent to his/her child can distort the perceptions of a parent regarding their children, which, in turn, hinders their activity of monitoring and disciplining them. As a consequence, parental altruism may produce free-riding behaviour and shirking in their children (Schulze et al., 2003). Incompetent family members protected by altruism may not have the appropriate competencies to allocate resources into innovation projects (Chang et al., 2010).

A third reason is represented by the effect of the lack of wealth diversification: the portfolio view contends that investors may only be concerned with systematic risks, such as political and economic risks, when they possess diversified portfolios (Wright et al., 2002). While atomistic investors can reduce specific risk by creating diversified portfolios, family members invest high fractions of their wealth in the family firm or are deeply involved in the management and are not so able to diversify their investment in financial assets or human capital (Thomsen & Pedersen, 2000). This could lead family shareholders to avoid risky investments (Zellweger & Sieger, 2012) because the consequences of negative returns are more crucial than the perks of potential gains. In addition, the lack of diversification could push family members "*.....to oppose certain projects with inherent risks, and thus creativity and innovation are usually considered less important in family firms*" (Chang et al., 2010, p. 157).

Another reason is represented by the emotional attachment of the family to the firm: family members do not perceive the firm like any other financial investment because of the family heritage and tradition represented by the firm (Tagiuri & Davis, 1992; Berrone et al., 2012). Using a socioemotional wealth perspective, when family members are called to take a decision on R&D strategies, they consider not only the effects on the financial wealth, but also those on the affective endowment (Gomez-Mejia et al., 2007). Requiring R&D strategies specialized human capital investments and family business may suffer from the lack of adequate managerial competencies (Fernandez & Nieto, 2006). This may imply the hire of nonfamily managers with technical backgrounds and experience (Daellenbach et al., 1999), but family could be reluctant to recruit nonfamily managers. In fact, the direct and the indirect control over strategic decisions is one of the main blocks of socio-emotional wealth (Berrone et al., 2012). Therefore, family members may be reluctant to engage nonfamily managers in order to avoid the dilution of their control over decision process, which, in turn, diminishes socioemotional wealth (Gomez-Mejia et al. 2010).

In order to undertake R&D investments, firms may need additional financial funds. However, if, on one side, external capital providers would confer additional resources, on the other side they would affect the decision-making process, thus diluting the influence and the control of the family over the firm. The dilution of influence and control would generate a loss in terms of affective endowment (Berrone et al., 2012).

While many empirical findings point out a negative relationship between family ownership and R&D investments, some scholars have explored factors able to moderate this relationship. The negative relationship between family ownership and innovation is weaker if family firms possess unabsorbed organizational slack (Liu et al., 2017). Brinkerink and Bammens (2018) highlight that SEW concerns and reputational issues represent mediator factors into the relationship between family status and R&D spending.

FAMILY FIRMS' INNOVATION MANAGEMENT

Some studies focus on structures, processes and capabilities that may stimulate or hamper the generation of new products or new process within family firms.

Two main issues are the organizational structures adopted because they may influence innovation process, affecting consequently the ability to produce innovation output, and the choice relative to the interaction with external stakeholder, because it influences open innovation strategies.

With respect to the first issue, one of the more interesting debate within family firms' innovation management is relative to the choice on cross-functional team versus functional organization.

Empirical findings of De Massis et al. (2015) point out that family firms usually adopt functional structures, whereas nonfamily ones largely prefer cross-functional teams, constituted of employees belonging to different functions and temporarily separated from these (e.g., R&D, marketing, operations). This difference may be explained with higher motivation and commitment (Fukuyama 1995; Lyman 1991), the closer relationships between individuals (Horton 1986), that represent unique features of family firms and that allow to overcome communication problems - characterizing functional structures - and to solve conflicts between the functional heads, making easier the information exchange (Tagiuri & Davis, 1996). Therefore, family firms may adopt this form of structural solution to manage innovation process without sustaining high costs and resources duplication (De Massis et al., 2015).

Anyway, when the attention is focused on the patent management, empirical evidence is quite different. The study of Jell et al. (2015) on family firms' patent management highlights that family firms prefer a cross-functional patent management to a higher degree than in non-family-owned firms. The cross-functional approach implies that employees joining to several corporate function areas, such as, marketing, production, R&D, distribution, establish an interaction process in order to take a decision relative to patent management (Kahn, 1996). In cross-functional meetings, firms decide which patent approve for out-licensing and which abandon. Some of long-term benefits of cross-functional patent management are the positive impact on the effectiveness of product development and patent exploitation, through an improved communication between the functions involved (Faems et al., 2005), widespread awareness of patent-related issues within the firm, and a management of human resources more flexible.

Apart the benefits, cross function patent management generates some short time costs such as those relative to tear down barriers to cross-functional integration (Griffin & Hauser, 1996) and to the emerging conflicts related to the distribution of the workload and licensing revenues.

Anyway, short-term costs may emerge in an inferior extent within family firms compared to nonfamily firms because of the stewardship culture of the former (Jell et al., 2015). Consequently, members of different functions will emphasize the importance to the performance of the firm as a whole than of their own function performance.

Within the literature investigating the innovation management process within family firms context, another relevant topic is relative to the relationships between family firms and external actors in order to promote innovation. The diversity of cooperation partners used by family firms for innovation-related activities and how widely they leverage external knowledge are crucial points in the study of Classen et al. (2012), Nieto et al. (2015) and De Massis et al. (2015). In fact, scholars have constantly pointed out the interactive feature of the innovation process, signalling that innovators lean on their interaction with customers, suppliers, competitors, universities, public agencies and a range of stakeholders inside the innovation system. More specifically, firms rely on different types of R&D partners for different scopes. For example, companies interacting with customers mainly look for new insights to overcome uncertainty connected with market introduction of innovations (Von Hippel, 1988). Conversely, collaborations with suppliers generally focus on input quality improvements or cost reductions from process innovations (Hagedoorn, 1993).

The debate on the family firms' propensity to partnership with external stakeholders is still open. In fact, Classen et al. (2012) point out that family SMEs have a lower search breadth than nonfamily counterparts. In other words, the number of external actors or search channels that family SMEs interact in their innovative activities is inferior to nonfamily SMEs. This result can be interpreted using the behavourial agency theory, and consequently, considering the effect of strategic decisions on family firm's socioemotional wealth (Gomez-Mejia et al., 2007). Therefore, when a family firm involves several partners in order to improve their innovation potential, family members perceive a loss of freedom because externals will influence the decision-making processes, generating a decrease of socioemotional wealth (Gomez-Mejia et al., 2010). Therefore, this fear will discourage family firms from utilizing mechanisms, such as a broad portfolio of innovation collaborations (Classen et al., 2012; Nieto et al., 2015).

Anyway, De Massis et al. (2015) find that family firms are more likely to exploit external sources of knowledge whereas nonfamily firms largely prefer to implement a closed and inward-looking approach. The authors go a step further in order to investigate the identity of external stakeholders that family firms interact with. From a deeper investigation of the sample used in the study, the authors highlight that family firms mainly establish vertical collaborations - especially with suppliers - and partnership with university and public research centres, that represent a low threat to socioemotional wealth, if compared with horizontal collaborations with competing firms.

Focusing on the factors influencing family firms' search breadth, it is positively affected by:

1. Family CEO university education, that confers him a more rational approach to managerial decision-making (Papadakis & Barwise 2002). Put differently, graduated CEOs might be more able to conciliate the socioemotional and financial objectives of family firms (Distelberg & Sorenson 2009);
2. The percentage of nonfamily managers in the TMT, that may increase the cognitive diversity of a family firm by bringing new views not possessed by the family (Zahra, 2012). A wider managerial set of competencies and expertise improves family firm's absorptive capacity, that in turn increases the firm's entrepreneurial orientation (Jennings & Lumpkin 1989; Cruz & Nordqvist 2012) and its innovativeness.

FAMILY FIRMS' INNOVATION STRATEGIES

In order to investigate family firm's general orientation towards innovation some authors have used the Miles and Snow's configurational model (1978), that views the organisation as composed of a set of elements highly interrelated. This holistic approach permits to shed light on the effect of "*familiness*" (Habbershon & Williams, 1999) on firms' strategic behaviours with respect to innovation process.

Following Miles and Snow's model (1978), these studies identify the following categories:

1. *Prospectors*, which are represented by firms focused on product innovation and flexible/prototypical process; they adopt a "*first to market*" strategy implying strengths in product R&D activities and establishment of communication channel with external actors;
2. *Analysers*, which are represented by firms adopting a follower strategy but they invest in the development of new products/markets whether they identify new opportunities; this category is constituted also by firms that expand existing knowledge base to new market segments and/or groups of customers;
3. *Defenders*, that operate in a very limited product/market development path and prefer controlling stable niches within their industry;
4. *Reactors*, that are firms with passive and un-focused behaviours with respect to innovation and their innovative behaviours represent a short-term response to external pressures; this category does not show any distinct profile in term of competitive advantage.

Using the above mentioned categories, the seminal study of McCann et al. (2001) examines a sample of family firms and find that prospector and defender strategies constitute the main behaviors adopted by family firms and firms adopting prospector behavior attribute a greater importance to innovation based growth than other categories, are younger and smaller than defender.

The four categories of strategic behaviours are the focal point in the study of Pittino and Visintin (2009). The authors find that 1) founders managed family firms exhibit a greater propensity to adopt *prospector* or *analyser* strategies than non-founder led family firms, and 2) as generational stage increases, family firms are likely to adopt defender or reactor strategy than founder led family firms.

The authors go a step further and highlight that the adoption of a *defender* or *reactor* strategy is more likely when:

a) The succession process occurs. In fact, the process is very complex because it implies the involvement of many stakeholders surrounding the family and produces several implications, psychological, financial and behavioural. Consequently, "….*the entrepreneurial leadership copes with the uncertainty of the process by reducing the environmental complexity. Organizational theory suggests that one strategy to reduce uncertainty and environmental complexity is the simplification of strategic goals*" (Pittino & Visintin, 2009, p. 267). In order to implement this behaviour, firms tend to adopt defender or a reactor strategy, pursuing continuity or passive adaptation in their strategic actions.
b) There is a higher proportion of ownership dispersed among family members not involved in the management: in fact, they are more likely to prefer investments preserving their wealth and to avoid risky strategies, generating *strategic impasse* (Schulze et al., 2003). In addition, scholars highlight a positive relationship between the presence of family owners not involved in the management and conflict situations in first and second generation family firms (Davis & Harveston, 2001). Conservative or unclear strategic action may be the consequence of the divergence of goals among several categories of owners.

The adoption of *prospector or analyser* strategy is more likely when dominant coalitions are more specialized in R&D and marketing. In fact, "*managers from output functions (marketing, sales and product R&D) emphasize growth and the search for new domain opportunities*", while "*managers from throughput functions (production, process engineering, accounting) emphasize increased efficiency*" (Hambrick & Mason, 1984, p. 199). In addition, top managers with a specialization in production, engineering and R&D are more able to asses potential value of the technologies than top managers whose background is in financial and legal areas (Daellenbach et al., 1999). Furthermore, *prospector* strategies are positively affected by the presence of venture capitalists or private equity in the family firm's ownership structure: these investors are more incline to risk, provide resources, relational networks, competences and solve the parsimony problem that features family firms.

More recently, Rondi et al. (2018) drawing on the concept of innovation posture, identify four ideal types of innovative FFs. More specifically, innovation posture is conceived as the strategic orientation the owning family confers to the family business, forging the firm's innovation climate, philosophy and practices and the authors, considering the different degree of risk-taking propensity and attachment to tradition, develop the following ideal types: *Seasoner, Re-enactor, Digger, Adventurer*. These ideal types emphasize the different propensity to take risks and attachment to tradition that differentiate innovation behaviours of family firms.

FAMILY FIRMS' INNOVATION OUTPUTS

The final step of technological innovation process is represented by the innovation output, that may be represented by new ways of doing things or new products, services, or techniques. Investment in R&D, human resources management, strategic behaviour, organizational structures and the rest of innovation process activities influence innovation output.

Because of a large amount of contradictory and inconsistent findings, the propensity of family firms to generate innovative output is a debate still open (Urbinati et al., 2017). Decker and Gunther (2017) point out that family ownership negatively influences the innovation output, measured as number of patents.

A high percentage of shares owned by the family exposes her in great extant to company performances (Carney, 2005). Family members' desire to transfer the business in good health to offspring furnishes disincentives to adopt hazardous actions and discourage innovation (Gomez-Mejia et al., 2010). Consequently, a negative family ownership-company's innovation output relationship occurs.

Anyway, the study of Matzler et al. (2015) finds that family participation in management positively affects both firm's number of patents and quality of its innovation, measured by forward citation intensity, while family governance only influences number of patents. More specifically, findings highlight that family firms invest less in innovation but they exhibit a greater rate of conversion of innovation input in innovation output, that in turn generates a higher innovation output than nonfamily counterparts. These results are in line with family firms' lower agency costs and inferior exposure of family managers to unemployment risk, that allow them to focus on the long term performance. Leal-Rodriguez et al. (2017) confirm Matzler's results, pointing out that family ownership positively moderates the relationship between organizational unlearning and firms' innovation output, measured through top managers' self-evaluation on technological innovation in firms' products and processes.

Measuring innovativeness through self-evaluation and self-perceived external appraisals of the firm's capacity to innovate, Filser et al. (2018) find that it is positively affected by two main dimensions of socioemotional wealth, that are the family's binding social ties and the renewal of family bonds through intra family succession.

A study of De Massis et al. (2018) on German family firms highlights that some characteristics, such as niche focus and customer collaboration, globalization strategy, preference for self-financing, long-run mindset, superior employee relations and community embeddedness, stimulate innovation, despite resource constraints.

Furthermore, studies point out that family firms concentrate their efforts toward incremental product innovations, whereas nonfamily firms are more likely focused in radically new product development programs, which propose completely new functionalities to customers and are selected to unknown market segments (De Massis et al., 2015; Nieto et al., 2015). This family firms' behaviour may be explained through their propensity toward parsimony (Carney 2005) that implies a careful preservation of resources that discourages their propensity to exploit costly and radically new venture opportunities because they require resources needed for successful experimentation (Nohria & Gulati 1996). In addition, the experimentation in radically new products leads to investments more expensive than incremental innovations, and consequently ceding shares to outside parties, such as venture capitalists or institutional investors, could be an obliged choice (Gomez-Mejia et al., 2011). The presence of external funders would reduce the control of family members on the firm and a SEW loss would occur (Gomez-Mejia et al., 2007). Therefore, family firms prefer incremental innovation investments over radical innovation ones.

Innovative output is also affected by the generational involvement. Empirical findings point out a negative relationship between generational stage and the number of patents (Decker & Gunther, 2017). In fact, as generational stage increases, the ownership becomes dispersed and the number of decision makers and of family members involved in ownership increases. This may cause the disappointment of some family members with respect to strategic decision or their role in the company and emotionally devastating conflicts between emerging factions, creating problems of coordination that negatively influence innovation. In addition, the increasing number of family members nurturers problems with succession and nepotism that hinders investment in innovation.

SOLUTIONS AND RECOMMENDATIONS

By analyzing the literature on technological innovation in family firms, some suggestions will emerge. Firstly, family firms should acknowledge the relevant role of technological innovation and, consequently, they should not renounce to the connected investments. This is a crucial point because it often implies the recruitment of nonfamily managers that may bring to the family firms new competencies, capabilities, know how, expertise, networking. All these intangible assets are essential to evaluate, on one hand, the potential of innovation investments, and, on the other hand, the exploration and the exploitation of some scientific discovery. Anyway, family firms may suffer from lack of managerial skills, so they could be lead to recruit nonfamily human resources. Consequently, they should leverage external managers only when particular conditions permit to defend their affective wealth, for example, when protection on proprietary technologies is available (De Massis et al., 2012c). In order not to compromise their socioemotional wealth, family firms should use best practice aimed to improve communication and relationship between family and nonfamily members.

Beside, managers of family firms should not apply management principles valid for all firms regardless their ownership nature. The unique interaction between family, individual family members and the business make family firms organizational entities very different from nonfamily counterparts. Therefore, organizational or managerial solutions that are considered as best practices for innovation process in management research (Ernst, 2002), should not be used for family firms because they do not exploit their unique resources and therefore may represent barriers to technological innovation. Management of innovation project through a structured process, which is considered one of the most critical success factors of innovation (Ernst, 2002), might be not aligned with parsimony and personalism featuring family firms (De Massis et al., 2012b).

FUTURE RESEARCH DIRECTIONS

Studies analysed in the chapters highlight the possibility to conduct deeper analysis with respect both to innovation input and innovation output. Over the last years, corporate governance literature has emphasized the role of board of directors in achieving firms' competitive advantage. "*Boards of directors play an important part in the management of the firm, as they take an active role in the choice and implementation of strategic decisions, advising management and observing the consequences of those decisions*" (Barroso, 2011, p. 355). More specifically, directors that bring new knowledge, expertise and experience may increase the role of advice and counsel of the board and strengthen long-term competitiveness of firms. Attributes of board members, such as level of academic achievement, industry-specific experience, past experience as Ceos or general managers, board tenure, could affect the propensity of family firms to undertake R&D investments and the types of innovation output realized. Further research could investigate further the relationships above mentioned.

Although family firms are reluctant to cede their shares to third parties, under some circumstances external finance is needed in order to take some investments, such as R&D. While some studies highlighted the effect of institutional investors on innovation input (Gomez-Mejia et al., 2014; Cirillo et al., in press), deeper analysis could be conduct on the effect of institutional investors on innovation activities and innovation output. In fact, when an institutional investor (e.g.: venture capital) buys firms shares, it will ask to influence firm's strategy and management and, in addition, it brings not just financial capital but also intangible assets, such as competencies, know-how, networking, expertise and so on. Therefore, institutional investor's presence in family firm's ownership structure may deeply affect firm's innovation management process and output and this issue deserves to be better explored.

CONCLUSION

Nowadays, the integration of different geographic areas, fast changes, hyper-competition and consumer needs variations within the actual context push firms to a constant search of new products, new markets and new processes in order to survive in long-term and to achieve and defend an enduring competitive advantage. Investments in R&D, innovative output, an organizational climate that favour innovation process and a strategic behaviour that stimulates effective approaches to innovation issues are essential activities. While management literature has widely investigate these topics regardless firm's ownership structure, only recently scholars have been investigating this topic within family firms context, leveraging family business and innovation management literatures. Although family firms' innovation studies are still at an infant stage, there are already many studies sufficient to point out some relevant results. In fact, empirical findings show a reluctance of family members to undertake innovation investments, confirming previous literature highlighting family members' risk aversion, due to the entire wealth invested into the business, their fear to dilute the control over firm's strategic decision, the tendency to distract firm's resources transferring wealth from minority shareholders to controlling family and so on. The effect of family involvement on innovation inputs is also enriched by several studies regarding to moderating factors, such as previous performance, aspirational gaps, industry growth opportunities, independent board, that may affect the relationship above mentioned.

Literature regarding family firms' innovation activities shows some different results. As pointed out in previous pages, for instance, studies on the relationships between family firm and external stakeholders and the organizational structure adopted by family firm to favour innovation process often do not show perfectly consistent results. Anyway, it is worthwhile noting that some of these studies have an exploratory nature and, more specifically, they use the multiple case study as an empirical research strategy. This circumstance may show some problems with respect to their degree of generalization. Therefore, further research on this topic is encouraged to permit to statistically generalize the results. In addition, future studies could use different variable to measure some phenomena in order to disentangle the issue and shed light on the effect of family-related antecedents on innovation management activities.

REFERENCES

Alayo, M., Maseda, A., Iturralde, T., & Arzubiaga, U. (2019). Internationalization and entrepreneurial orientation of family SMEs: The influence of the family character. *International Business Review*, *28*(1), 48–59. doi:10.1016/j.ibusrev.2018.06.003

Amabile, T., Conti, R., Coon, H., Lazenby, J., & Herron, M. (1996). Assessing the work environment for creativity. *Academy of Management Journal*, *39*, 1154–1184.

Anderson, R., & Reeb, D. (2003). Founding family ownership and firm performance: Evidence from the S&P 500. *The Journal of Finance*, *58*(3), 1301–1328. doi:10.1111/1540-6261.00567

Arzubiaga, U., Kotlar, J., De Massis, A., Maseda, A., & Iturralde, T. (2018). Entrepreneurial orientation and innovation in family SMEs: Unveiling the (actual) impact of the Board of Directors. *Journal of Business Venturing*, *33*(4), 455–469. doi:10.1016/j.jbusvent.2018.03.002

Bammens, Y., Notelaers, G., & Gils, A. (2015). Implications of family business employment for employees' innovative work involvement. *Family Business Review*, *28*(2), 123–144. doi:10.1177/0894486513520615

Barroso, C., Villegas, M. M., & Pérez-Calero, L. (2011). Board influence on a firm's internationalization. *Corporate Governance*, *19*(4), 351–367. doi:10.1111/j.1467-8683.2011.00859.x

Baysinger, B. D., Kosnik, R. D., & Turk, T. A. (1991). Effects of board and ownership structure on corporate R&D strategy. *Academy of Management Journal*, *34*, 205–214.

Bebchuk, L. A., & Stole, L. A. (1993). Do short-term objectives lead to under- or overinvestment in long-term projects? *The Journal of Finance*, *48*(2), 719–729. doi:10.1111/j.1540-6261.1993.tb04735.x

Berrone, P., Cruz, C., & Gomez-Mejia, L. R. (2012). Socioemotional wealth in family firms: Theoretical dimensions, assessment approaches, and agenda for future research. *Family Business Review*, *25*(3), 253–279. doi:10.1177/0894486511435355

Berrone, P., Cruz, C., & Gomez-Mejia, L. R. (2012). Socioemotional wealth in family firms: Theoretical dimensions, assessment approaches, and agenda for future research. *Family Business Review*, *25*(3), 253–279. doi:10.1177/0894486511435355

Bhattacharya, S., & Ritter, J. R. (1983). Innovation and communication: Signalling with partial disclosure. *The Review of Economic Studies*, *50*(2), 331–346. doi:10.2307/2297419

Bjuggren, P. O., & Palmberg, J. (2010). The impact of vote differentiation on investment performance in listed family firms. *Family Business Review*, *23*(4), 327–340. doi:10.1177/0894486510379001

Brinkerink, J., & Bammens, Y. (2018). Family influence and R&D spending in Dutch manufacturing SMEs: The role of identity and socioemotional decision considerations. *Journal of Product Innovation Management*, *35*(4), 588–608. doi:10.1111/jpim.12428

Bushee, B. (1998). The influence of institutional investors on myopic R&D investment behavior. *The Accounting Review*, *73*(3), 305–333.

Calabrò, A., Minichilli, A., Amore, M. D., & Brogi, M. (2018). The courage to choose! Primogeniture and leadership succession in family firms. *Strategic Management Journal*, *39*(7), 2014–2035. doi:10.1002mj.2760

Calabrò, A., Vecchiarini, V., Gast, J., Campopiano, G., De Massis, A., & Kraus, S. (2019). Innovation in Family Firms: A Systematic Literature Review and Guidance for Future Research. *International Journal of Management Reviews*, *21*(3), 317–355. doi:10.1111/ijmr.12192

Carney, M. (2005). Corporate governance and competitive advantage in family¬ controlled firms. *Entrepreneurship Theory and Practice*, *29*(3), 249–265. doi:10.1111/j.1540-6520.2005.00081.x

Chakravarty, A., & Grewal, R. (2011). The stock market in the driver's seat! Implications for R&D and marketing. *Management Science*, *57*(9), 1594–1609. doi:10.1287/mnsc.1110.1317

Chang, S., Wu, W., & Wong, Y. (2010). Family control and stock market reactions to innovation announcements. *British Journal of Management*, *21*(1), 152–170. doi:10.1111/j.1467-8551.2008.00618.x

Chen, H. L., & Hsu, W. T. (2009). Family ownership, board independence, and R&D investment. *Family Business Review*, *22*(4), 347–362. doi:10.1177/0894486509341062

Cheung, Y. L., Rau, P. R., & Stouraitis, A. (2006). Tunneling, propping and expropriation: Evidence from connected party transactions in Hong Kong. *Journal of Financial Economics*, *82*(2), 343–386. doi:10.1016/j.jfineco.2004.08.012

Chua, J. H., Chrisman, J. J., & Sharma, P. (1999). Defining the family business by behavior. *Entrepreneurship Theory and Practice*, *23*(4), 19–39. doi:10.1177/104225879902300402

Cirillo, A., Ossorio, M. & Pennacchio, L. (in press). Family ownership and R&D investment: the moderating role of banks and private equity. *Management Decision*, *57*(7), 1675-1694.

Classen, N., Van Gils, A., Bammens, Y., & Carree, M. (2012). Accessing resources from innovation partners: The search breadth of family SMEs. *Journal of Small Business Management*, *50*(2), 191–215. doi:10.1111/j.1540-627X.2012.00350.x

Corbetta, G., & Salvato, C. (2004). Self-serving or self-actualizing? Models of man and agency costs indifferent types of family firms. *Entrepreneurship Theory and Practice*, *28*(4), 355–362. doi:10.1111/j.1540-6520.2004.00050.x

Cruz, C., & Nordqvist, M. (2012). Entrepreneurial Orientation in Family Firms: A Generational Perspective. *Small Business Economics*, *38*(1), 33–49. doi:10.100711187-010-9265-8

Daellenbach, U. S., McCarthy, A. M., & Schoenecker, T. S. (1999). Commitment to innovation: The impact of top management characteristics. *Strategic Management Journal*, *29*, 199–209.

Davis, J. H., Schoorman, F. D., & Donaldson, L. (1997). Toward a stewardship theory of management. *Academy of Management Review*, *22*(1), 20–47. doi:10.5465/amr.1997.9707180258

Davis, P., & Harveston, P. D. (2001). The Phenomenon of Substantive Conflict in the Family Firm: A Cross-Generational Study. *Journal of Small Business Management*, *39*(1), 14–30. doi:10.1111/0447-2778.00003

De Massis, A., Audretsch, D., Uhlaner, L., & Kammerlander, N. (2018). Innovation with limited resources: Management lessons from the German Mittelstand. *Journal of Product Innovation Management*, *35*(1), 125–146. doi:10.1111/jpim.12373

De Massis, A., Frattini, F., & Lichtenthaler, U. (2012b). Research on Technological Innovation in Family Firms: Present Debates and Future Directions. *Family Business Review*, *20*(10), 1–22.

De Massis, A., Frattini, F., Pizzurno, E., & Cassia, L. (2015). Product innovation in family versus nonfamily firms: An exploratory analysis. *Journal of Small Business Management*, *53*(1), 1–36. doi:10.1111/jsbm.12068

De Massis, A., Kotlar, J., & Cassia, L. (2012c). How do entrepreneurs of family firms perceive their competitive advantages and disadvantages compared to non-family companies? Empirical evidence from the transportation industry. *International Journal of Entrepreneurship and Small Business, 51*(1).

De Massis, A., Sharma, P. A., Chua, J. H., & Chrisman, J. J. (2012a). *Family business studies: An annotated bibliography*. Northhampton, MA: Edward Elgar. doi:10.4337/9781781002988

Decker, C., & Gunther, C. (2017). The impact of family ownership on innovation: Evidence from the German machine tool industry. *Small Business Economics, 48*(1), 199–212. doi:10.100711187-016-9775-0

Dharwadkar, R., Gerard, G., & Brandes, P. (2000). Privatization in emerging economies: An agency theory perspective. *Academy of Management Review, 25*(3), 650–669. doi:10.5465/amr.2000.3363533

Distelberg, B., & Sorenson, R. L. (2009). Updating Systems Concepts in Family Businesses. *Family Business Review, 22*(1), 65–81. doi:10.1177/0894486508329115

Donaldson, L., & Davis, J. H. (1991). Stewardship theory or agency theory: CEO governance and shareholder returns. *Australian Journal of Management, 16*(1), 49–64. doi:10.1177/031289629101600103

Eddleston, K. A., & Kellermanns, F. W. (2007). Destructive and productive family relationships: A stewardship theory perspective. *Journal of Business Venturing, 22*(4), 545–565. doi:10.1016/j.jbusvent.2006.06.004

Eddleston, K. A., & Kidwell, R. E. (2012). Parent-child relationships: Planting the seeds of deviant behavior in the family firm. *Entrepreneurship Theory and Practice, 36*(2), 369–386. doi:10.1111/j.1540-6520.2010.00403.x

Eisenberger, R., Armeli, S., Rexwinkel, B., Lynch, P., & Rhoades, L. (2001). Reciprocation of perceived organizational support. *The Journal of Applied Psychology, 86*(1), 42–51. doi:10.1037/0021-9010.86.1.42 PMID:11302232

Ernst, H. (2002). Success factors of new product development: A review of the empirical literature. *International Journal of Management Reviews, 4*(1), 1–40. doi:10.1111/1468-2370.00075

Faems, D., Van Looy, B., & Debackere, K. (2005). Interorganizational collaboration and innovation: Toward a portfolio approach. *Journal of Product Innovation Management, 22*(3), 238–250. doi:10.1111/j.0737-6782.2005.00120.x

Fernandez, Z., & Nieto, M. J. (2006). Impact of ownership on the international involvement of SMEs. *Journal of International Business Studies, 37*(3), 340–351. doi:10.1057/palgrave.jibs.8400196

Filser, M., De Massis, A., Gast, J., Kraus, S., & Niemand, T. (2018). Tracing the roots of innovativeness in family SMEs: The effect of family functionality and socioemotional-wealth. *Journal of Product Innovation Management, 35*(4), 609–628. doi:10.1111/jpim.12433

Freeman, C. (1976). *Economics of industrial innovation*. London, UK: Pinter.

Friedman, E., Johnson, S., & Mitton, T. (2003). Propping and tunneling. *Journal of Comparative Economics, 31*(4), 732–750. doi:10.1016/j.jce.2003.08.004

Froot, K. A., Perold, A. F., & Stein, J. C. (1992). Shareholder trading practices and corporate investment horizons. *Journal of Applied Corporate Finance*, *5*(2), 42–58. doi:10.1111/j.1745-6622.1992.tb00489.x

Fukuyama, F. (1995). *Trust: The Social Virtues and the Creation of Prosperity*. New York: Free Press.

Gagne, M., & Deci, E. (2005). Self-determination theory and work motivation. *Journal of Organizational Behavior*, *26*(4), 331–362. doi:10.1002/job.322

Geroski, P., Machin, S., & Van Reenen, J. (1993). The profitability of innovating firms. *The Rand Journal of Economics*, *24*(2), 198–211. doi:10.2307/2555757

Gomez-Mejía, L. R., Campbell, J. T., Martin, G., Hoskisson, R. E., Makri, M., & Sirmon, D. G. (2014). Socioemotional wealth as a mixed gamble: Revisiting family firm R&D investments with the behavioural agency model. *Entrepreneurship Theory and Practice*, *38*(6), 1351–1374.

Gomez-Mejia, L. R., Cruz, C., Berrone, P., & De Castro, J. (2011). The bind that ties: Socioemotional wealth preservation in family firms. *The Academy of Management Annals*, *5*(1), 653–707. doi:10.1080/19416520.2011.593320

Gomez-Mejia, L. R., Haynes, K., Nunez-Nickel, M., Jacobson, K. J. L., & Moyano-Fuentes, J. (2007). Socioemotional wealth and business risks in family controlled firms: Evidence from Spanish olive oil mills. *Administrative Science Quarterly*, *52*(1), 106–137. doi:10.2189/asqu.52.1.106

Gomez-Mejia, L. R., Makri, M., & Larraza-Kintana, M. (2010). Diversification decisions in family-controlled firms. *Journal of Management Studies*, *47*(2), 223–252. doi:10.1111/j.1467-6486.2009.00889.x

Griffin, A., & Hauser, J. R. (1996). Integrating R&D and marketing: A review and analysis of the literature. *Journal of Product Innovation Management*, *13*(3), 191–215. doi:10.1111/1540-5885.1330191

Gudmundson, D., Tower, C. B., & Hartman, E. A. (2003). Innovation in small businesses: Culture and ownership structure do matter. *Journal of Developmental Entrepreneurship*, *8*, 1–17.

Habbershon, T. G., & Williams, M. L. (1999). A resourcebased framework for assessing the strategic advantages of family firms. *Family Business Review*, *12*(1), 1–25. doi:10.1111/j.1741-6248.1999.00001.x

Hagedoorn, J. (1993). Understanding the rationale of strategic technology partnering: Interorganizational modes of cooperation and sectoral differences. *Strategic Management Journal*, *14*(3), 371–385. doi:10.1002mj.4250140505

Hambrick, D. C. (1983). Some tests of the effectiveness and functional attributes of Miles and Snow's strategic types. *Academy of Management Journal*, *26*, 5–25. PMID:10299037

Hillman, A. J., & Dalziel, T. (2003). Boards of directors and firm performance: Integrating agency and resource dependence perspectives. *Academy of Management Review*, *28*(3), 383–396. doi:10.5465/amr.2003.10196729

Horton, T. (1986). Managing in a Family Way. *Management Review*, *75*(2), 3.

Jell, F., Block, J., Henkel, J., Spiegel, F., & Zischka, H. (2015). Cross-functional patent management in family firms. *Journal of Business Economics*, *85*(2), 181–203. doi:10.100711573-014-0732-6

Jennings, R., & Lumpkin, G. T. (1989). Functioning Modeling Corporate Entrepreneurship: An Empirical Integrative Analysis. *Journal of Management*, *15*(3), 485–502. doi:10.1177/014920638901500310

Jensen, M. C., & Meckling, W. H. (1976). Theory of the firm: Managerial behaviour, agency costs and ownership structure. *Journal of Financial Economics*, *3*(4), 305–360. doi:10.1016/0304-405X(76)90026-X

Kahn, K. B. (1996). Interdepartmental integration: A definition with implications for product development performance. *Journal of Product Innovation Management*, *13*(2), 137–151. doi:10.1111/1540-5885.1320137

La Porta, R., Lopez-De-Silanes, F., & Shleifer, A. (1999). Corporate ownership around the world. *The Journal of Finance*, *54*(2), 471–514. doi:10.1111/0022-1082.00115

Leal-Rodrìguez, A. L., Peris-Ortiz,M. & Leal-Mill´an, A.G. (2017). Fostering entrepreneurship by linking organizational unlearning and innovation: the moderating role of family business. *Management International/International Management/Gestion Internacional*, *21*, 86-94.

Lee, P. M., & O'Neill, H. M. (2003). Ownership structures and R&D investments of U.S. and Japanese firms: Agency and stewardship perspectives. *Academy of Management Journal*, *46*(2), 212–225.

Lichtenthaler, U., & Muethel, M. (2012). The impact of family involvement on dynamic innovation capabilities: Evidence from German manufacturing firms. *Entrepreneurship Theory and Practice*, *36*(6), 1235–1253. doi:10.1111/j.1540-6520.2012.00548.x

Liu, Y., Chen, Y.-J., & Wang, L. C. (2017). Family business, innovation and organizational slack in Taiwan. *Asia Pacific Journal of Management*, *34*(1), 193–213. doi:10.100710490-016-9496-6

Lubatkin, M. H., Schulze, W. S., Ling, Y., & Dino, R. N. (2005). The effects of parental altruism on the governance of family-managed firms. *Journal of Organizational Behavior*, *26*(3), 313–330. doi:10.1002/job.307

Lyman, A. R. (1991). Customer Service: Does Family Ownership Make a Difference? *Family Business Review*, *4*(3), 303–324. doi:10.1111/j.1741-6248.1991.00303.x

Matzler, K., Veider, V., Hautz, J., & Stadler, C. (2015). The impact of family ownership, management, and governance on innovation. *Journal of Product Innovation Management*, *32*(3), 319–333. doi:10.1111/jpim.12202

McCann, J. E. III, Leon-Guerrero, A., & Haley, J. D. (2001). Strategic goals and practices of innovative family businesses. *Journal of Small Business Management*, *39*(1), 50–59. doi:10.1111/0447-2778.00005

Memili, E., Chrisman, J. J., & Chua, J. H. (2011). Transaction Costs and Outsourcing Decisions in Small- and Medium-Sized Family Firms. *Family Business Review*, *24*(1), 47–61. doi:10.1177/0894486510396706

Miles, R. E., & Snow, C. C. (1978). *Organisational Strategy, Structure and Process*. New York: McGraw-Hill.

Miller, D., & Le Breton-Miller, I. (2006). Family Governance and Firm Performance: Agency, Stewardship, and Capabilities. *Family Business Review*, 19.

Miller, D., Le Breton-Miller, I., & Lester, R. H. (2010). Family ownership and acquisition behavior in publicly-traded companies. *Strategic Management Journal, 31*(2), 201–223.

Morck, R., Stangeland, D. A., & Yeung, B. (2000). Inherited wealth, corporate control, and economic growth: The Canadian disease. In R. Morck (Ed.), *Concentrated Corporate Ownership* (pp. 319–369). Chicago: University of Chicago Press. doi:10.7208/chicago/9780226536828.001.0001

Morris, M. H. (1998). *Entrepreneurial Intensity*. Westport, CT: Quorum.

Munari, F., Oriani, R., & Sobrero, M. (2010). The effects of owner identity and external governance systems on R&D investments: A study of Western European firms. *Research Policy, 39*(8), 1093–1104. doi:10.1016/j.respol.2010.05.004

Munoz-Bullon, F., & Sanchez-Bueno, M. J. (2011). The Impact of family involvement on the R&D intensity of publicly traded firms. *Family Business Review, 24*(1), 62–70. doi:10.1177/0894486510396870

Nieto, M. J., Santamaria, L., & Fernandez, Z. (2015). Understanding the innovation behaviour of family firms. *Journal of Small Business Management, 53*(2), 382–399. doi:10.1111/jsbm.12075

Nohria, N., & Gulati, R. (1996). Is Slack Good or Bad for Innovation? *Academy of Management Journal, 39*(5), 1245–1264. doi:10.5465/256998

Papadakis, V. M., & Barwise, P. (2002). How Much Do CEOs and Top Managers Matter in Strategic Decision- Making? *British Journal of Management, 13*(1), 83–95. doi:10.1111/1467-8551.00224

Pittino, D., & Visintin, F. (2009). Innovation and strategic types of family SMEs – a test and extension of Miles and Snow's configurational model. *Journal of Enterprising Culture, 17*(03), 257–295. doi:10.1142/S0218495809000382

Porter, M. E. (1985). *Competitive Advantage: creating and sustaining superior performance*. New York: Free Press.

Rhoades, L., & Eisenberger, R. (2002). Perceived organizational support: A review of the literature. *The Journal of Applied Psychology, 87*(4), 698–714. doi:10.1037/0021-9010.87.4.698 PMID:12184574

Rondi, E., De Massis, A. & Kotlar, J. (2018). Unlocking innovation potential: a typology of family business innovation postures and the critical role of the family system. *Journal of Family Business Strategy*. DOI: doi:10.1016/j.jfbs.2017.12.001

Sanchez-Famoso, V., Maseda, A., & Iturralde, T. (2017). Family involvement in top management team: Impact on relationships between internal social capital and innovation. *Journal of Management & Organization, 23*(1), 136–162. doi:10.1017/jmo.2016.2

Schulze, W., Lubatkin, M. H., & Dino, R. N. (2003). Toward a theory of agency and altruism in family firms. *Journal of Business Venturing, 18*(4), 473–490. doi:10.1016/S0883-9026(03)00054-5

Shleifer, A., & Vishny, R. W. (1997). A survey of corporate governance. *The Journal of Finance, 52*(2), 737–783. doi:10.1111/j.1540-6261.1997.tb04820.x

Sirmon, D. G., & Hitt, M. A. (2003). Managing resources: Linking unique resources, management, and wealth creation in family firms. *Entrepreneurship Theory and Practice, 27*(4), 339–358. doi:10.1111/1540-8520.t01-1-00013

Somech, A., & Drach-Zahavy, A. (2013). Translating team creativity to innovation implementation: The role of team composition and climate for innovation. *Journal of Management, 39*(3), 684–708. doi:10.1177/0149206310394187

Stark, O. (1995). *Altruism and beyond: An economic analysis of transfers and exchanges within families and groups*. New York: Cambridge University Press. doi:10.1017/CBO9780511493607

Stein, J. (1988). Takeover threats and managerial myopia. *Journal of Political Economy, 96*(1), 61–80. doi:10.1086/261524

Tagiuri, R., & Davis, J. (1996). Bivalent Attributes of the Family Firm. *Family Business Review, 9*(2), 199–208. doi:10.1111/j.1741-6248.1996.00199.x

Tagiuri, R., & Davis, J. A. (1992). On the goals of successful family companies. *Family Business Review, 5*(1), 43–62. doi:10.1111/j.1741-6248.1992.00043.x

Thomsen, S., & Pedersen, T. (2000). Ownership structure and economic performance in the largest European Companies. *Strategic Management Journal, 21*(6), 689–705. doi:10.1002/(SICI)1097-0266(200006)21:6<689::AID-SMJ115>3.0.CO;2-Y

Tidd, J., & Bessant, J. R. (2009). *Managing innovation: Integrating technological, market and organizational change*. New York, NY: John Wiley.

Tsai, W. H., Hung, J. H., Kuo, Y. C., & Kuo, L. (2006). CEO tenure in Taiwanese family and nonfamily firms: An agency theory perspective. *Family Business Review, 19*(1), 11–28. doi:10.1111/j.1741-6248.2006.00057.x

Urbinati, A., Franzo, S., DeMassis, A., & Frattini, F. (2017). Innovation in family firms: a review of prior studies and a framework for future research. In A. Brem & E. Viardot (Eds.), *Revolution of Innovation Management*. London, UK: Palgrave Macmillan. doi:10.1057/978-1-349-95123-9_8

Von Hippel, E. (1988). *Sources of Innovation*. Oxford, UK: Oxford University Press.

Wayne, S., Shore, L., & Liden, R. (1997). Perceived organizational support and leader-member exchange: A social exchange perspective. *Academy of Management Journal, 40*, 82–111.

Wright, P., Kroll, M., Load, A., & Van, B. (2002). The structure of ownership and corporate acquisition strategies. *Strategic Management Journal, 23*(1), 41–53. doi:10.1002mj.208

Zahra, S. A. (2012). Organizational Learning and Entrepreneurship in Family Firms: Exploring the Moderating Effect of Ownership and Cohesion. *Small Business Economics, 38*(1), 51–65. doi:10.100711187-010-9266-7

Zellweger, T., Nason, R., & Nordqvist, M. (2012). From longevity of firms to transgenerational entrepreneurship of families: Introducing family entrepreneurial orientation. *Family Business Review, 25*(2), 136–155. doi:10.1177/0894486511423531

Zellweger, T., & Sieger, P. (2012). Entrepreneurial orientation in long-lived family firms. *Small Business Economics*, *38*(1), 67–84. doi:10.100711187-010-9267-6

Zona, F., Minichilli, A., & Zattoni, A. (2011). Boards of Directors and Firm Innovation: An Empirical Analysis on Large Italian Companies. In The Value Creating Board. Corporate Governance and Organizational Behaviour. Routledge, Taylor & Francis Group.

ADDITIONAL READING

Block, J. H. (2011). How to pay a non-family manager in a family business: A multi-task principal agent model. *Family Business Review*, *24*(1), 9–27. doi:10.1177/0894486510394359

Block, J. H. (2012). R&D investments in family and founder firms: An agency perspective. *Journal of Business Venturing*, *27*(2), 248–265. doi:10.1016/j.jbusvent.2010.09.003

Choi, Y. R., Zahra, S. A., Yoshikawa, T., & Han, B. H. (2015). Family ownership and R&D investment: The role of growth opportunities and business group membership. *Journal of Business Research*, *68*(5), 1053–1061. doi:10.1016/j.jbusres.2014.10.007

Chrisman, J. J., & Patel, P. C. (2012). Variations in R&D investments of family and nonfamily firms: Behavioral agency and myopic loss aversion perspectives. *Academy of Management Journal*, *55*(4), 976–997. doi:10.5465/amj.2011.0211

David, P., Hitt, M. A., & Gimeno, J. (2001). The influence of activism by institutional investors on R&D. *Academy of Management Journal*, *44*(1), 144–157.

Kor, Y. Y. (2006). Direct and interactive effects of top management team and board compositions on R&D investment strategy. *Strategic Management Journal*, *27*(11), 1081–1099. doi:10.1002mj.554

Kotlar, J., Fang, H., De Massis, A., & Frattini, F. (2014). Profitability goals, control goals, and the R&D investment decisions of family and nonfamily firms. *Journal of Product Innovation Management*, *31*(6), 1128–1145. doi:10.1111/jpim.12165

Patel, P. C., & Chrisman, J. J. (2014). Risk abatement as a strategy for R&D investments in family firms. *Strategic Management Journal*, *35*(4), 617–627. doi:10.1002mj.2119

Wu, H. L. (2008). When does internal governance make firms innovative? *Journal of Business Research*, *61*(2), 141–153. doi:10.1016/j.jbusres.2007.06.010

KEY TERMS AND DEFINITIONS

CEO Duality: It refers to the situation of the CEO that simultaneously wears the hat of the chairperson of the board of directors.

Cross-Functional Team: It is a group made up of employees from different functional areas (finance, marketing, production, etc.) that interact in order to reach a common goal.

Family Ownership: It represents the percentage of shares owned by controlling family and is measured as the number of shares of all classes held by the family divided by total shares outstanding.

Large Shareholder: It is an owner that has a sizable percentage of voting shares and therefore has a great incentive to gather information about firm investments.

R&D Investments: They represent the economic effort made by the firm and they are generally calculated as R&D expenditures scaled by total sales.

Socioemotional Wealth: It represents the nonfinancial aspects of the firm and may come in a variety of related forms, such as the family members' control over strategic decisions and their identification with the firm.

Underinvestment Problem: Within R&D decisions, it represents the choice of management to undertake investment in R&D below their optimal level.

Chapter 8
Leverage and Family Firms: A Multi-Theoretical Approach

Sergio Camisón-Haba
Universitat de València, Spain

José Antonio Clemente
Universidad Internacional de La Rioja, Spain

Beatriz Forés
Universitat Jaume I, Spain

Melanie Grueso-Gala
Universitat de València, Spain

ABSTRACT

This chapter analyses the relationship between ownership structure and leverage, providing an integrated theoretical approach that combines traditional financial theories, agency theory, and recently developed theories relating to non-financial preferences. The results show that, after controlling for endogeneity, being a family firm has a positive effect on the propensity to incur debt. These findings add to the existing body of literature and underline the need for a multi-theoretical approach when explaining the capital structure of family firms. The authors apply panel data methodology to control for individual heterogeneity of family firms. The chapter uses a sample of Spanish firms operating in the tourism industry.

INTRODUCTION

Despite intense research efforts to analyse the capital structure of family firms, the empirical results have not been entirely conclusive (Schmid, 2013). Although the literature has striven to uncover the inherent causes of the use of debt or equity capital in family firm financing, it reports contradictory effects. While some authors have pointed to a negative effect (Margaritis and Psillaki, 2010; Ampenberger, Schmid,

DOI: 10.4018/978-1-7998-1655-3.ch008

Achleitner and Kaserer, 2013), others have found positive (González et al., 2013; Croci et al., 2011) or non-significant relationships (Bjuggren, Duggal, and Giang, 2012).

This diversity of empirical results may arise from the fact that classical theories of finance cannot deal with the heterogeneity in family firms. Family firm research is underpinned by agency theory (Jensen & Meckling, 1976) and stewardship theory (Davis et al., 1997), with the supposition that there is closer alignment between owners and managers in family firms, and lower agency costs. The main implication of this hypothesis is that family firms have less need to use debt and dividends as part of their corporate governance systems.

On the other hand, pecking-order theory (Myers, 1984; Myers & Majluf, 1984), as well as new theories based on motivations and preferences—including the theory of preferences (Hutchinson, 1995; Romano, Tanewski & Symyrnios, 2001), the SEW perspective (Wiseman & Gómez-Mejía, 1998; Gómez-Mejía et al., 2007), and the theory of planned behaviour (Koropp et al., 2014; Ajzen, 1985)—point in the opposite direction. Specifically, they hold that in family firms, the desire to maintain control, along with the socioemotional wealth and the social capital invested in the firm, make family firms more oriented towards higher leverage levels.

In order to shed light on the debate about the capital structure of family firms, and in line with the growing academic interest in this subject (Le Breton-Miller & Miller, 2014), this study combines the abovementioned theories to construct an explanatory theoretical framework for the relationships between ownership, financial considerations, non-financial preferences and leverage. In a second stage, the theoretical framework is empirically tested in order to gain a better understanding of the relationship between family firms and leverage. This model is tested using data from 1019 Spanish tourist firms.

This study contributes to the literature on the relationship between ownership structure and financing decisions regarding the use of leverage. Specifically, it shows that, after controlling for endogeneity, being a family firm has a positive effect on the propensity to incur debt. This finding is to be expected given family firms' intense desire to maintain social control and socioemotional wealth.

The system GMM estimator is used to deal with the potential endogeneity problem in the analysis. Additionally, a panel data approach is used to avoid biased coefficients due to unobservable heterogeneity; this is a particularly relevant issue in in family firm research because of specific unobservable characteristics that may affect the models (Chi, 2005).

BACKGROUND

There is no universal theory that can explain the diversity of factors affecting firms' financial structure (Myers, 2001). According to Michiels and Molly (2017: 371), the predominant theoretical framework in the current study of financial decisions in family firms is agency theory, followed by traditional theories of capital structure, such as pecking-order theory and trade-off theory.

Pecking-order theory (Myers, 1984; Myers & Majluf, 1984) highlights the costs and problems stemming from information asymmetries as the key factor determining imperfections in the capital structure. Information asymmetries between managers and investors create uncertainty in all financing negotiations. This results in increased costs (for example, arising from the demand for more information) or a higher rate of return required by the financier. In this context, managers prefer to draw on internal financing to prevent information asymmetries and their associated costs, applying maximum managerial discretion in the use of these funds. Thus, they only resort to the capital market when the firm has insufficient financial resources of its own. However, if it becomes necessary to secure external financing, managers also tend to prioritize the different possibilities. In this case, they first opt for debt, which, although affected by adverse selection, is less problematic than a share issue. Thus, the theory entirely rejects the existence of an optimum capital structure; rather, it holds that managers apply a hierarchy of preferences when planning new investments and designing the firm's financial structure.

In turn, **trade-off theory** (Brennan & Schwartz, 1978; DeAngelo & Masulis, 1980; Bradley, Jarrell & Kim, 1984) combines arguments from the previous approach with an analysis of the tax advantages associated with debt repayment, in order to predict the optimum debt-equity ratio. The advantages of debt lie in the deductibility of interest and in the disciplinary role it plays in preventing liquidity problems (Modigliani & Miller, 1963). Thus, the higher the effective tax rate, the more attractive the debt option (Haugen & Senbet, 1986). However, high levels of leverage also entail high costs in terms of financial stress and potential bankruptcy (Kraus & Litzenberger, 1973), costs relating to information asymmetries between shareholders and lenders (Jensen & Meckling, 1976) and underinvestment problems due to the expropriation of wealth from potential investors by lenders (Stulz, 1990). Given the tax advantages of debt interest, value maximization is achieved when the benefits derived from the debt are equal to its marginal costs.

Although pecking-order theory and trade-off theory draw their inspiration from **agency theory**, the latter has its own unique profile. The institutional approach has been used to carry out a comparative analysis of the efficiency of various organizational forms (Fama & Jensen, 1985), by studying the competitiveness factors related to the firm's internal organization and ownership structure. This structure underpins the major decisions that determine the volume and composition of the available productive resources; thus it plays a key role in mobilizing the volume and composition of productive investment required in the future. In addition, it enables the identification of critical resources needed to improve the firm's competitive position, mobilize the required financing, and optimize the coordination of human resources with which it interacts.

Agency theory is based on the managerial model of the firm characterized by the separation of ownership and control, whereby the shareholder-owners delegate the task of running the firm to a professional manager, who is not a member (or at least not a significant one) of that group. This seems to be the most satisfactory solution given the more detached behaviour of a dispersed share ownership and in order to access specialized managerial knowledge. Nevertheless, this managerial model of the firm has been subject to criticism, based on the notion of the financial structure as a reflection of the degree of convergence between managers' and shareholders' incentives and utility functions, or between those of shareholders and lenders, and the information asymmetry between these parties. Information asymmetry arises when one of the parties has more or better information; for example, when shareholders hire a manager to run the company on their behalf because they themselves do not have the necessary qualifications to do so, and thus are uncertain as to whether they have made the right choice. However, such asymmetry also stems from the different positions held by each party. It may be the case that managers have privileged access to the organization's internal and external information flows, receiving information that they may not share with the principal.

Within this context, agency problems can arise due to the separation of ownership and control, as well as the potential conflicts of interest if the managers set a strategy oriented towards serving their own interests through opportunistic behaviour. Another problem that can emerge in an agency relationship stems from the principal and the agent having different attitudes to risk, as a result of which they show different preferences for action. The design of the financial structure is understood as a means of minimizing these conflicts of interest and preferences (Fama & Jensen, 1983; Jensen & Meckling, 1976).

The literature also proposes alternative theories that explain financial decisions in terms of risk preferences and business objectives that are not exclusively driven by financial motives. Of these, Michiels and Molly (2017) highlight stewardship theory, the socioemotional wealth (SEW) perspective and the more recent theory of planned behaviour. **Stewardship theory** (Davis et al., 1997) stands in direct contrast to agency theory regarding the underlying principle guiding the behaviour of individuals in organizations. Whereas agency theory contends that people are driven by an extrinsic motivation to look after their own interests, stewardship theory emphasizes the intrinsic motivation that goes beyond economic objectives and leads individuals to behave in ways that serve the organization's aims (Zahra et al., 2008).

The **socioemotional wealth** (SEW) **perspective** (Wiseman & Gómez-Mejía, 1998; Gómez-Mejía et al., 2007) highlights the importance of non-financial aspects in explaining the behaviour of family firms. These include emotional needs, identity, exercising influence as family owners, and the desire to continue the family dynasty. According to this theoretical approach, financial decisions in family firms tend to be oriented towards preserving family control, with such firms being reluctant to select options that could threaten their socioemotional wealth.

The **theory of planned behaviour**, when applied to the analysis of managerial decisions in family firms, centres on explanatory factors such as the family's attitudes, values, preferences and standards (Koropp et al., 2014; Ajzen, 1985).

Finally, **the theory of preferences** encompasses a diverse set of studies (e.g., Hutchinson, 1995, Romano et al., 2001) which highlight the role of managers'/owners' preferences in explaining the capital structure of family firms. Under these preferences, maintaining social control, risk aversion, and other non-financial aims and values are prioritized above maximizing value for the shareholders. These criteria lead to a hierarchy of financial decisions, in line with that proposed by pecking-order theory: an overall preference for self-financing; and when it comes to external financing, a preference for debt over a capital increase.

This study adopts the behavioural arguments underlying these related theories to extend the traditional agency perspective in explaining financing behaviour.

MAIN FOCUS OF THE CHAPTER

Family Ownership and Leverage

The empirical literature is inconclusive about the nature of the relationships between family ownership of firms and debt levels (Schmid, 2013). In a study based on a US database of small firms, Coleman and Carski (1999) find no significant differences between family and non-family firms, in either the type of credit products used or the degree of leverage. Anderson and Reeb (2003) analyse listed US firms and find no evidence of a systematic difference between family and non-family firms in terms of debt levels.

By contrast, Margaritis and Psillaki (2010) find evidence that French family firms have lower debt ratios than their non-family counterparts. The same negative effect is reported by Ampenberger et al. (2012) for German firms. Schmid (2013) finds differences between German family firms and those in East Asia and Western Europe; specifically, German family firms are shown to have lower leverage than their non-family counterparts, whereas the opposite is found to be the case for the international dataset.

Furthermore, the author reports that whether family firms use more or less leverage depends on the level of creditor monitoring (or the creditors' ability to exert influence on the firms that they finance) in a specific institutional environment.

These authors base their analyses on the theory of agency costs and stewardship theory, arguing that in family firms there are fewer agency conflicts between owners and managers, thus invalidating the free cash flow hypothesis (Jensen & Meckling, 1976) regarding the use of debt to minimize the costs of financial slack and discipline managers. This alignment of interest between owners and managers can also reduce the firm's willingness to pay out dividends, thereby increasing the potential for internal financing.

There is, however, robust empirical evidence to show that when family firms need external financing, in accordance with pecking-order theory, they prefer debt to equity financing, so as to avoid diluting or relinquishing control (González et al., 2013; Croci et al., 2011). The new theories on the motivations and preferences of family firm manager-owners provide further support for this evidence by factoring in the desire to maintain family and social control (Hutchinson, 1995; Romano et al., 2001), to safeguard the socioemotional wealth accumulated during the development of the family business (Wiseman & Gómez-Mejía, 1998; Gómez-Mejía et al., 2007) and to promote the family's values and objectives in the organization's behaviour. (Koropp et al., 2014). These theories suggest that non-financial preferences and objectives will prevail over financial considerations in the trade-off between the firm's desire to maintain control, which fosters the use of debt, and the firm's risk aversion, which encourages a prudent attitude towards debt.

The preference for financing through internally-available funds means that the reinvestment of profits plays a more important role in the capitalization of family firms. Therefore, the debt-equity ratio of family firms could be expected to be lower than that of non-family firms. However, internal financing places excessive constraints on family firm growth and wealth accumulation in the case of succession processes, which require considerable funds to buy the capital of heirs who want to leave the business. The use of debt stabilizes the family's capital base in the operational dynamics of the business and in situations when family partners leave the firm, and also helps maintain family control. This latter point is crucial in 'insider' cultures such as that of Spain, where there are significant problems involved in securing capital from external investors (Franks et al., 2012) due to the underdevelopment of the financial markets, a more restricted corporate control market and weaker legal protection of investors.

Access to debt also enables family firms to cope with the capital constraints that could hinder them from investing in innovation (Carney, 2005). According to the EU Industrial R&D Investment Scoreboard (European Commission, 2017) the world's top 2500 R&D-investing companies have substantially increased their R&D investments whereas their revenue growth has stagnated; this reveals the difficulties of financing innovation output internally, especially output that matches or exceeds the average in the specific industry and country in which the firm competes. It can therefore be seen that, in the interests of competitiveness and financial health, family firm leverage will inevitably increase.

Among the non-financial factors relating to family firm leverage, stewardship theory highlights the need to evaluate the alignment of interests between equity and debt providers (Anderson et al., 2003). The family firm's long-term survival objective is reflected in a long investment horizon that gives rise to a relationship of trust between family firms and their debt providers. This "patient capital" (Lumpkin & Brigham, 2011) brings down the agency costs of debt (Anderson et al., 2003) by reducing the family's incentives to expropriate debt providers through risk-shifting (Boubakri & Ghouma, 2010; Yen et al., 2015; Schmid, 2013). In addition, in many cases, family owners can offer their personal wealth as collateral, thus facilitating their access to debt (Margaritis & Psillaki, 2010), particularly long-term debt

(Croci et al., 2011), and reducing their reliance on internal financing (Pindado et al., 2015; Chrisman, Chua, & Litz, 2004).

Another strength that allows the family firm to increase its leverage is its social reputation, linked to the family's prestige and financial success, and its desire to survive from one generation to the next (Arregle et al., 2007). Aspects such as the family name being associated with the business name, the family's pride in seeing itself reflected in the corporate image, and its concern for maintaining its good reputation in its social environment are all distinctive values of family firms. These values instil confidence that the firm will meet its contractual obligations. This family social capital (Chua et al., 2011) is especially important in countries where there is a social sanction for business failure (Edelman, 2006). It could be assumed that ownership will be more concentrated in these countries, and the tendency to use debt to grow will therefore be stronger.

In this context and despite the contradictory theoretical predictions, most empirical evidence supports a positive relationship between family control and debt. For example, in a sample of Canadian firms, King and Santor (2008) show that family-owned firms have higher debt ratios than non-family firms. Similar results for Australian firms are found by Brav (2009), for UK private firms by Setia-Atmaja et al. (2009), and in transnational studies conducted by Ellul (2009) and Croci et al. (2011) in Europe. The inconsistency of empirical findings about the effect of family control on leverage can therefore be resolved by considering the non-financial preferences and objectives prevailing in family firms. This leads to the following hypothesis:

Hypothesis One: There is a positive relationship between family control and the firm's leverage.

A number of other variables are also used in the financial literature, which could a priori be considered determinants of the firm's capital structure. These variables—profitability, endowment of tangible assets, growth, average leverage in the industry, firm size—are included in our model as control variables.

The potential agency problems that can arise from information asymmetries between the firm and its financiers could prompt the latter to demand guarantees from the firm, usually in the form of collateral assets. Tangible assets best meet the required conditions to serve as collateral, because their value can be assessed by comparison with a real market (Van Caneghem & Van Campenhout, 2010); thus, firms with a larger endowment of tangible collateral assets will have higher levels of leverage. There is abundant empirical evidence to support this claim (Myers, 1977; Myers & Majluf, 1984; Williamson, 1988; Sogorb, 2005; Heyman et al., 2008; Van Caneghem & Van Campenhout, 2010).

The relationship between leverage and economic profitability has been systematically analysed in the literature, with different theories making contradictory predictions. Modigliani and Miller (1963), as well as trade-off theory (Jensen, 1986), predict that the most profitable firms will tend to have higher levels of leverage so as to take advantage of the tax deductions on debt expenses and the disciplinary role played by debt in preventing problems of liquidity and bankruptcy. In contrast, pecking-order theory predicts a negative relationship between economic profitability and financial leverage, as firms with greater capacity to self-finance will be able to avoid debt costs (Myers, 2001, Fama & French, 2002, Van Caneghem & Van Campenhout, 2010).

When the need for resources driven by firm growth exceeds the resources available from self-financing, the firm's leverage may increase (e.g., Michaelas et al. 1999; López-Gracia & Sogorb-Mira, 2008; Céspedes, González, & Molina, 2009). The barrier to higher leverage that can arise from the aversion to loss of control will be moderated by the perception that the firm must expand in order to ensure its survival (Berggren et al., 2000).

The literature reports empirical evidence that largely supports a direct relationship between size and level of financial leverage (Holmström & Tirole, 1998; Michaelas et al., 1999; Fama & French, 2002; Sogorb, 2005). According to trade-off theory, the higher debt capacity of large companies can be explained by fewer information asymmetries (Van Caneghem & Van Campenhout, 2010; Cole, 2008), lower income volatility due to more diversification, which leads to a lower likelihood of bankruptcy (Pettit & Singer, 1985), and higher investments in tangible assets (Céspedes, González, & Molina, 2009).

Research Method

Data

The final result of the field work, after various data cleansing processes consists of 1019 Spanish tourism industry firms, with a confidence level of 95% and a margin of error of ± 3.1%. This represents, prior to the cleansing processes, a response rate of 25.6% from the initial sample of 8148 firms, sourced from the entire population of Spanish tourism companies listed in the 2008 Central Companies Directory (DIRCE). The initial sample was selected using a stratified random sampling procedure with proportional allocation to ensure the representativeness of the sample in terms of activity, size and location.

The data contained in the database were obtained from a questionnaire conducted in 2009 through personal interviews with the CEO or general manager of selected firms. Dillman's Total Design Method (1978) was used to mitigate the problems associated with questionnaires as a data collection method, and to improve the response rate and the quality of the information. The fieldwork was carried out between December 2009 and March 2010.

In order to complete the financial information from 2008 to 2016, additional data were sourced from the Sistema de Análisis de Balances Ibéricos (SABI), a database managed by Bureau Van Dijk and Informa D&B, S.A. Since SABI does not provide information for all the companies interviewed, the final database contained 543 companies, 378 of which were family firms.

Variables

This section defines the dependent and independent variables used in the model, all of which have been winsorized at 0.5% in each tail of the distribution in order to deal with outliers.

Dependent Variable

LEV: the dependent variable in the model is leverage, defined as the ratio of long-term plus short-term debt (with the exclusion of trade credit and other non-debt liabilities) to total assets (Miller et al., 2007; Van Caneghem & Van Campenhout, 2010; Molly, et al., 2010; Cole, 2013).

Independent Variables

FF: the family firm variable is a dummy variable, equal to 1 if the company is considered a family firm, and 0 otherwise. In the present study, family firms are identified under the broad concept of ownership structure (Shanker & Astrachan, 1996); namely, a business is considered a family firm if the founder and/or their descendants hold majority ownership and have control over strategic decisions.

Control Variables

Five variables are included in the model as control variables, using commonly-employed proxies (Van Caneghem & Van Campenhout, 2010; Molly et al., 2010).

SIZE: firm size is measured as the natural logarithm of total assets.
TANG: tangibility is defined as the ratio of tangible assets (net fixed assets) to total assets.
AGE: firm age is defined as the number of years since the creation of the firm.
PROF: firm profitability is measured as earnings before interest and taxes (EBIT) divided by total assets.
GROWTH: firm growth is measured as current sales less sales from 2008, divided by sales from 2008.

A year dummy is also included to control for any temporary effects arising from macroeconomic conditions that could influence leverage decisions. The descriptive statistics and correlations for the variables in the model are shown in Tables 1 and 2, respectively. The mean leverage is 53.8%, which is not substantially above the average leverage reported for the tourism sector in Spain (Camisón & Monfort, 2011: 286-288).

Table 2 shows the correlation matrix. The highest correlations are obtained between the variables size and leverage, and between profitability and leverage, which yielded negative coefficients of -0.244 and -0.28, respectively. These results coincide with those obtained in the regression (Table 3). However, the fact that the levels of correlation between the variables are below 0.6, together with the multicollinearity test performed using the Variance Inflation Factor (VIF), confirm the absence of collinearity between the variables under study (Table 2).

Empirical Models

To test hypothesis 1, we use the following Equation [1]:

$$LEV_{it} = \beta_0 + \beta_1 \cdot FF_{it} + \beta_2 \cdot TANG_{it} + \beta_3 \cdot SIZE_{it} + \beta_4 \cdot PROF_{it} + \beta_5 \cdot GROWTH_{it} + \beta_6 \cdot AGE_{it} + \varepsilon_{it}$$

Table 1. Descriptive statistics

Variables	Obs.	Mean	S.D.	Min.	Max.
LEV	1,993	0.538	0.692	0.001	7.230
FF	4,887	0.696	0.459	0	1
TANG	3,441	0.444	0.317	0.000	0.989
SIZE	3,598	14.187	2.224	8.775	20.944
AGE	3,582	25.889	21.687	7	174
PROF	3,584	-0.007	0.229	-1.994	0.558
GROWTH	3,100	0.299	2.526	-0.983	27.001

*Table 2. Correlation Matrix and Variance Inflation Factors**

	LEV	*FF*	*SIZE*	*TANG*	*PROF*	*GROWTH*	*AGE*
LEV	1.000						
FF	0.002 (0.929)	1.000					
SIZE	-0.244 (0.000)	-0.087 (0.000)	0.064 (0.000)	1.000			
TANG	0.024 (0.285)	0.125 (0.000)	0.065 (0.000)	1.000			
PROF	-0.283 (0.000)	0.034 (0.042)	0.185 (0.000)	-0.006 (0.722)	1.000		
GROWTH	0.089 (0.000)	0.048 (0.008)	0.032 (0.073)	-0.069 (0.000)	0.039 (0.030)	1	
AGE	-0.123 (0.000)	0.124 (0.000)	0.190 (0.000)	0.065 (0.001)	0.054 (0.007)	0.074 (0.000)	1
VIF		1.11	1.04	1.05	1.06	1.03	1.01

*Significance levels in brackets

In order to allay concerns about endogeneity in Equation [1], the system GMM (Generalized Method of Moments) estimator is applied, using the lagged values of the explanatory variables as instruments (Molina, 2005; Clemente & Sogorb, 2018). However, since the system GMM estimator cannot deal with the endogeneity problem for variables that are stable over time, as is the case with the family firm variable, to ensure that the findings regarding the impact of the family firm variable on leverage are not affected by reverse causality, an instrumental variable is used to replace the family firm variable in Equation [1] (Schmid, 2013). The instrument is the probability of the business being a family firm. The probabilities are obtained by running a logit regression model for each year of the research period, where the dependent variable is the initial family firm dummy variable. The following explanatory variables are used: size, growth, the Altman (1968) Z-Score for specific firms' risk of bankruptcy, ownership concentration, and the control mechanism of the family firm (Pindado et al., 2011).

Research Results

Results from Equation [1] are reported in Table 3.

Notes: GMM regression coefficients from Equation [1] with standard errors—adjusted using the finite sample correction proposed by Windmeijer (2005)—shown in parentheses. AR(2) is a second-order serial correlation test. The Hansen test is a test of over-identifying restrictions in a statistical model, asymptotically distributed as $\chi 2$ under the null hypothesis that the instruments are uncorrelated with the error term. Superscript asterisks indicate statistical significance at 0.01(***), 0.05(**) and 0.10(*) levels. FF is the probability of being a family firm. TANG is tangible assets to total assets. SIZE is the natural logarithm of total assets. AGE is the number of years since the creation of the firm. PROF is earnings before interest, taxes and depreciation and amortization (EBITDA) divided by total assets. GROWTH is current sales less sales from 2008, divided by sales from 2008. Time dummies are not included in the table.

Table 3. Estimation results Equation [1]

Explanatory Variables	*Dependent Variable: LEV*
FF	4.875***(1.752)
TANG	1.047 (1.196)
SIZE	-0.749** (0.329)
PROF	-2.069*** (0.787)
GROWTH	0.021 (0.047)
AGE *Intercept*	0.015 (0.080) 4.879 (4.723)
Observations AR(2) Prob > z Hansen Prob > chi2	763 0.379 0.367

The AR(2) test does not reject the null hypothesis of no autocorrelation of the residuals (Arellano & Bond, 1991). The Hansen test is far from rejecting the null hypothesis, indicating that the instruments used are appropriate (Baum, Schaffer, & Stillman, 2007).

Coefficients for the variables in Equation [1] have the predicted signs, lending support to hypothesis 1 on the positive effect of the family firm on leverage.

As for the control variables, the only variable that is negative and significant in both estimations is size, whereas profitability shows a negative and significant effect only in the first estimation. Although a positive effect was expected between the variable size and leverage, this study endorses the findings of previous research such as that of Van Caneghem and Van Campenhout (2010), who noted the ambiguity of empirical studies analysing this effect. In addition, the significance of the negative effect of profitability on leverage is in line with the findings of previous studies by Van Caneghem and Van Campenhout (2010), Ampenberger et al. (2013), and López-Gracia and Sánchez-Andújar (2007), thus lending support to the pecking-order theory.

SOLUTIONS AND RECOMMENDATIONS

This study sheds light on the interactions between different effects of managerial discretion: on the one hand, the managerial preference for restricting the distribution of profits as dividends (rather than allocating them to reserves) in order to have access to internally-available funds; and on the other, a preference for curbing the propensity for greater leverage motivated by external information. A potential conflict thus emerges between managerial preferences for internal financing and the family owners' desire to maintain social control through debt capital. The design of the financial structure can be understood as a means of reducing conflicts of interest between different actors (Hart et al., 1997; Fama & Jensen, 1983; Jensen & Meckling, 1976). For example, a potential conflict of interests between managers and shareholders could be alleviated by opting for a higher level of debt: since more resources would have to be allocated to paying interest, it would reduce the flow available to managers for possible bonuses or for remunerating shareholders through dividends. Jensen (1986) and Stulz (1990) argue that debt plays a preventive role, discouraging managers from building empires in firms with high levels of free cash flow.

Due to information asymmetry between managers and investors, the financial structure becomes a means of signalling or transmitting information to capital markets. It is the managers who know most about the expected return on investment projects, while the investors (aware that the managers know something they do not) tend to underestimate said return. This information asymmetry generates uncertainty in financing negotiations, which ultimately drives up costs (for example, those arising from the demand for more information) or the rate of return required by the financier (Myers, 1977; Myers & Majluf, 1984). In this context, pecking-order theory posits a hierarchy of managerial preferences when it comes to deciding how to finance a new investment. This hierarchy is governed by an overarching objective: to minimize the costs of information asymmetries; that is, to select sources of financing that are less exposed to the risk of underestimation caused by information asymmetries. Managers prefer to use internal financing as it does not entail information asymmetries or the associated costs, and allows them maximum managerial discretion in the use of that financing. They only resort to the capital market when the firm has insufficient financial resources of its own. Managers also follow a hierarchy in the choice of external financing; they first opt for debt, which although affected by adverse selection is less problematic than shares in this regard. A new share issue would be the last option, as investors would require a higher expected rate of return to offset the higher risk involved.

It is worth considering these factors as determinants of financial decisions because it enables a comprehensive understanding of the behaviour of family firms when designing their financial structure. Family firms' desire to retain control (Hutchinson, 1995; Romano et al., 2001) and safeguard the socioemotional wealth (Gómez-Mejía et al., 2007) residing in the firm, leads them to adopt financial structures that are more oriented towards debt. Although not always financially optimal, such structures also support the desire of family owners and managers to keep external investors out of the company.

The results of this study contribute empirical evidence to the literature analysing the capital structure of family firms, confirming the assumptions of pecking-order theory, the socioemotional wealth perspective, and the theories of planned behaviour and preferences.

FUTURE RESEARCH DIRECTIONS

This study provides relevant conclusions for family firm owners and managers, offering them an understanding of how financial interests and other non-economic variables interact to determine the leverage and the capital structure of this type of organization.

However, the conclusions are equally pertinent at an academic level. Classical theories of finance and agency theory, which are often used in isolation to explain the family firm capital structure, yield poor results as a result of this incomplete analysis. The family firm must be understood as a specific type of organization in which financial interests converge with others intrinsic to family ownership. New theories based on non-economic perspectives should be helpful in explaining the leverage (among other phenomena) of family firms. In short, a multi-theoretical approach is required in order to construct a successful explanatory model of the family firm.

Nevertheless, the present study is not without its limitations. First, the model omits certain variables that have strong explanatory power for family firm leverage. One of the most relevant of these is the generation that controls the family firm (Bennedsen et al., 2007; Schmid et al., 2015; Michiels & Molly, 2017); this is especially important when analysing the differences between the first generation, i.e. that of the founding family member, and subsequent generations, principally composed of the founder's descendants. However, the empirical evidence is once again inconclusive. The underlying conditions in each generation, in terms of strategic positioning, competences, ownership dispersion and general behaviour, represent a future line of research for the authors.

In addition, the authors recognize the geographical and sectoral limitations of the sample. Despite the vital importance of the tourism sector in Spain, in reality the findings from this study should be extrapolated to other sectors or regions with caution.

CONCLUSION

The theoretical frameworks presented here have provided the basis for identifying another set of variables that may determine firms' level of leverage; in other words, their choice between debt and internal financing. These include the family's desire to maintain control of social capital, managerial discretion, the family's financial wealth and the family's socioemotional wealth. The empirical analysis in this chapter is limited to studying the variable capturing firms' leverage, showing how the family firm tends to develop a capital structure with a higher level of leverage.

This chapter highlights the need to combine classical theories of finance with other more recent approaches based on socioemotional and often non-financial preferences. This multi-theoretical approach becomes essential for the study of family firms' financial decisions and capital structure.

ACKNOWLEDGMENT

This research has been funded by the Ministry of Science, Innovation and Universities and the State Research Agency (AEI), and co-funded by the European Regional Development Fund (FEDER), project reference [ECO2016-76796-P], and [FPU17/04804]. Support was also provided by Universitat Jaume I, [reference+UJI-A2017-04].

REFERENCES

Ajzen, I. (1985). From intentions to actions: A theory of planned behavior. In J. Kuhl & J. Beckmann (Eds.), *Action Control* (pp. 11–39). Berlin: Springer. doi:10.1007/978-3-642-69746-3_2

Altman, E. I. (1968). Financial ratios, discriminant analysis and the prediction of corporate bankruptcy. *The Journal of Finance*, *23*(4), 589–609. doi:10.1111/j.1540-6261.1968.tb00843.x

Ampenberger, M., Bennedsen, M., & Zhu, H. (2012). The capital structure of family firms. In D. Cumming (Ed.), *Oxford Handbook of Entrepreneurial Finance* (pp. 167–191). Oxford, UK: Oxford University Press.

Ampenberger, M., Schmid, T., Achleitner, A., & Kasere, C. (2013). Capital structure decisions in family firms: Empirical evidence from a bank-based economy. *Review of Managerial Science*, *7*(3), 247–275. doi:10.100711846-011-0077-2

Anderson, R. C., Mansi, S. A., & Reeb, D. M. (2003). Founding family ownership and the agency cost of debt. *Journal of Financial Economics*, *68*(2), 263–285. doi:10.1016/S0304-405X(03)00067-9

Anderson, R. C., & Reeb, D. M. (2003). Founding-family ownership, corporate diversification, and firm leverage. *The Journal of Law & Economics*, *46*(2), 653–684. doi:10.1086/377115

Arellano, M., & Bond, S. (1991). Some tests of specification for panel data: Monte Carlo evidence and an application to employment equations. *The Review of Economic Studies*, *58*(2), 277–297. doi:10.2307/2297968

Arregle, J. L., Hitt, M. A., Sirmon, D. G., & Very, P. (2007). The development of organizational social capital: Attributes of family firms. *Journal of Management Studies*, *44*(1), 73–95. doi:10.1111/j.1467-6486.2007.00665.x

Baum, C. F., Schaffer, M. E., & Stillman, S. (2007). Enhanced routines for instrumental variables/generalized method of moments estimation and testing. *The Stata Journal*, *7*(4), 465–506. doi:10.1177/1536867X0800700402

Bennedsen, M., Nielsen, K. M., Pérez-González, F., & Wolfenzon, D. (2007). Inside the family firm: The role of families in succession decisions and performance. *The Quarterly Journal of Economics*, *122*(2), 647–691. doi:10.1162/qjec.122.2.647

Berggren, B., Olofsson, C., & Silver, L. (2000). Control Aversion and The Search for External Financing in Swedish SMEs. *Small Business Economics*, *15*(3), 233–242. doi:10.1023/A:1008153428618

Bjuggren, P. O., Duggal, R., & Giang, D. T. (2012). Ownership dispersion and capital structures in family firms: A study of closed medium-sized enterprises. *Journal of Small Business and Entrepreneurship*, *25*(2), 185–200. doi:10.1080/08276331.2012.10593568

Boubakri, N., & Ghouma, H. (2010). Control/ownership structure, creditor rights protection, and the cost of debt financing: International evidence. *Journal of Banking & Finance*, *34*(10), 2481–2499. doi:10.1016/j.jbankfin.2010.04.006

Bradley, M., Jarrell, G., & Kim, E. (1984). On the Existence of an Optimal Capital Structure: Theory and Evidence. *The Journal of Finance*, *39*(3), 857–878. doi:10.1111/j.1540-6261.1984.tb03680.x

Brav, O. (2009). Access to capital, capital structure, and the funding of the firm. *The Journal of Finance*, *64*(1), 263–308. doi:10.1111/j.1540-6261.2008.01434.x

Brennan, M. J., & Schwartz, E. S. (1978). Corporate income taxes, valuation and the problem of optimal capital structure. *The Journal of Business*, *51*(1), 103–114. doi:10.1086/295987

Camisón, C., & Monfort, V. M. (2011). *La empresa turística familiar en España: importancia, perfil y competitividad*. Madrid: Ministerio de Industria, Energía y Turismo.

Carney, M. (2005). Corporate Governance and Competitive Advantage in Family-Controlled Firms. *Entrepreneurship Theory and Practice*, *29*(3), 249–265. doi:10.1111/j.1540-6520.2005.00081.x

Céspedes, J., González, M., & Molina, C. (2009). Ownership and capital structure in Latin America. *Journal of Business Research*, *63*(3), 248–254. doi:10.1016/j.jbusres.2009.03.010

Chi, J. (2005). Understanding the Endogeneity between Firm Value and Shareholder Rights. *Financial Management*, *34*(4), 65–76. doi:10.1111/j.1755-053X.2005.tb00118.x

Chrisman, J. J., Chua, J. H., & Litz, R. A. (2004). Comparing the agency costs of family and non-family firms: Conceptual issues and exploratory evidence. *Entrepreneurship Theory and Practice*, *28*(4), 335–354. doi:10.1111/j.1540-6520.2004.00049.x

Chua, J., Chrisman, J. J., Kellermanns, F., & Wu, Z. (2011). Family Involvement and New Venture Debt Financing. *Journal of Business Venturing*, *26*(4), 472–488. doi:10.1016/j.jbusvent.2009.11.002

Clemente, J. A., & Soborg, F. (2018). Costs of debt, tax benefits and a new measure of non-debt tax shields: Examining debt conservatism in Spanish listed firms. *Spanish Accounting Review*, *21*(2), 162–175.

Cole, R. A. (2013). What Do We Know about the Capital Structure of Privately Held US Firms? Evidence from the Surveys of Small Business Finance. *Financial Management*, *42*(4), 777–813. doi:10.1111/fima.12015

Coleman, S., & Carski, M. (1999). Sources of capital for small family-owned businesses: Evidence from the National Survey of Small Business Finances. *Family Business Review*, *12*(1), 73–86. doi:10.1111/j.1741-6248.1999.00073.x

Croci, E., Doukas, J., & Gonenc, H. (2011). Family Control and Financing Decisions. *European Financial Management*, *17*(5), 860–897. doi:10.1111/j.1468-036X.2011.00631.x

Davis, J., Schoorman, F., & Donaldson, L. (1997). Toward a stewardship theory of management. *Academy of Management Review*, *22*(1), 20–47. doi:10.5465/amr.1997.9707180258

De Angelo, H., & Masulis, R. W. (1980). Optimal capital structure under corporate and personal taxation. *Journal of Financial Economics*, *8*(1), 3–29. doi:10.1016/0304-405X(80)90019-7

Dillman, D. A. (1978). *Mail and telephone surveys: The total design method (Vol. 19)*. New York: Wiley.

Edelman. (2006). *La imagen de la empresa familiar en España*. Madrid: Instituto de Empresa Familiar.

Ellul, A. (2009). *Control Motivations and Capital Structure Decision*. Working Paper, Indiana University.

European Commission. (2017). *2017 EU Industrial R&D Investment Scoreboard*. Luxembourg: European Commission.

Fama, E. F., & French, K. R. (2002). Testing trade-off and pecking order predictions about dividends and debt. *Review of Financial Studies*, *15*(1), 1–33. doi:10.1093/rfs/15.1.1

Fama, E. F., & Jensen, M. C. (1983). Separation of Ownership and Control. *The Journal of Law & Economics*, *26*(2), 301–325. doi:10.1086/467037

Fama, E. F., & Jensen, M. C. (1985). Organizational forms and investment decisions. *Journal of Financial Economics*, *14*(1), 101–119. doi:10.1016/0304-405X(85)90045-5

Franks, J., Mayer, C., Volpin, P., & Wagner, H. F. (2012). The life cycle of family ownership: International evidence. *Review of Financial Studies*, *25*(6), 1675–1712. doi:10.1093/rfs/hhr135

Gómez-Mejía, L. R., Haynes, K. T., Núñez-Nickel, M., Jacobson, K. J. L., & Moyano-Fuentes, H. (2007). Socioemotional wealth and business risk in family-controlled firms: Evidence from Spanish olive oil mills. *Administrative Science Quarterly*, *52*(1), 106–137. doi:10.2189/asqu.52.1.106

González, M., Guzmán, A., Pombo, C., & Trujillo, M. A. (2013). Family firms and debt: Risk aversion versus risk of losing control. *Journal of Business Research*, *66*(11), 2308–2320. doi:10.1016/j.jbusres.2012.03.014

Hart, O., Shleifer, A., & Vishny, R. W. (1997). The Proper Scope of Government: Theory and an Application to Prisons. *The Quarterly Journal of Economics*, *112*(4), 1127–1161. doi:10.1162/003355300555448

Haugen, R. A., & Senbet, I. W. (1986). Corporate finance and taxes: A review. *Financial Management*, *15*(3), 5–21. doi:10.2307/3664840

Heyman, D., Deloof, M., & Ooghe, H. (2008). The financial structure of private held Belgian firms. *Small Business Economics*, *30*(3), 301–313. doi:10.100711187-006-9031-0

Holmström, B., & Tirole, J. (1998). Private and public supply of liquidity. *Journal of Political Economy*, *106*(1), 1–40. doi:10.1086/250001

Hutchinson, R. (1995). The capital structure and investment decisions of the small owner-managed firm: Some exploratory issues. *Small Business Economics*, *7*(3), 231–239. doi:10.1007/BF01135368

Jensen, M., & Meckling, W. (1976). Theory of the firm: Managerial behavior, agency costs and ownership structure. *Journal of Financial Economics*, *3*(4), 305–360. doi:10.1016/0304-405X(76)90026-X

Jensen, M. C. (1986). Agency costs of free cash flow, corporate finance and takeovers. *The American Economic Review*, *76*(2), 323–329.

Jensen, M. C., & Meckling, W. H. (1994). The nature of man. *Journal of Applied Corporate Finance*, *7*(2), 4–19. doi:10.1111/j.1745-6622.1994.tb00401.x

King, M., & Santor, E. (2008). Family values: Ownership structure, performance and capital structure of Canadian firms. *Journal of Banking & Finance*, *32*(11), 2423–2432. doi:10.1016/j.jbankfin.2008.02.002

Koropp, C., Kellermanns, F., Grichnik, D., & Stanley, L. (2014). Financial Decision Making in Family Firms. *Family Business Review*, *27*(4), 307–327. doi:10.1177/0894486514522483

Kraus, A., & Litzenberger, R. (1973). A State-Preference Model of Optimal Financial Leverage. *The Journal of Finance*, *28*(4), 911–922. doi:10.1111/j.1540-6261.1973.tb01415.x

López-Gracia, J., & Sánchez-Andújar, S. (2007). Financial Structure of the Family Business: Evidence From a Group of Small Spanish Firms. *Family Business Review*, *20*(4), 269–287. doi:10.1111/j.1741-6248.2007.00094.x

López-Gracia, J., & Sogorb-Mira, F. (2008). Testing trade-off and pecking order theories financing SMEs. *Small Business Economics*, *31*(2), 117–136. doi:10.100711187-007-9088-4

Lumpkin, G. T., & Brigham, K. H. (2011). Long-Term Orientation and Intertemporal Choice in Family Firms. *Entrepreneurship Theory and Practice*, *35*(6), 1149–1169. doi:10.1111/j.1540-6520.2011.00495.x

Margaritis, D., & Psillaki, M. (2010). Capital structure, equity ownership and firm performance. *Journal of Banking & Finance*, *34*(3), 621–632. doi:10.1016/j.jbankfin.2009.08.023

Michaelas, N., Chittenden, F., & Poutziouris, P. (1999). Financial policy and capital structure choice in U.K. SMEs: Empirical evidence from company panel data. *Small Business Economics, 12*(2), 113–130. doi:10.1023/A:1008010724051

Michiels, A., & Molly, V. (2017). Financial decisions in family businesses: A review and suggestions for developing the field. *Family Business Review, 30*(4), 369–399. doi:10.1177/0894486517736958

Modigliani, F., & Miller, M. (1963). Corporate income taxes and the cost of capital: A correction. *The American Economic Review, 53*(3), 433–443.

Molina, C. A. (2005). Are firms underleveraged? An examination of the effect of leverage on default probabilities. *The Journal of Finance, 60*(3), 1427–1459. doi:10.1111/j.1540-6261.2005.00766.x

Molly, V., Laveren, E., & Deloof, M. (2010). Family business succession and its impact on financial structure and performance. *Family Business Review, 23*(2), 131–147. doi:10.1177/089448651002300203

Myers, S. C. (1977). Determinants of corporate borrowing. *Journal of Financial Economics, 5*(2), 147–175. doi:10.1016/0304-405X(77)90015-0

Myers, S. C. (1984). The capital structure puzzle. *The Journal of Finance, 39*(3), 574–592. doi:10.1111/j.1540-6261.1984.tb03646.x

Myers, S. C. (2001). Capital structure. *The Journal of Economic Perspectives, 15*(2), 81–102. doi:10.1257/jep.15.2.81

Myers, S. C., & Majluf, N. (1984). Corporate financing and investment decisions when firms have information that investors do not have. *Journal of Financial Economics, 13*(2), 187–221. doi:10.1016/0304-405X(84)90023-0

Pettit, R. R., & Singer, R. F. (1985). Small business finance: A research agenda. *Financial Management, 14*(3), 47–60. doi:10.2307/3665059

Pindado, J., Requejo, I., & de la Torre, C. (2011). Family control and investment-cash flow sensitivity: Empirical evidence from the Euro zone. *Journal of Corporate Finance, 17*(5), 1389–1409. doi:10.1016/j.jcorpfin.2011.07.003

Pindado, J., Requejo, I., & la Torre, C. (2015). Does family control shape corporate capital structure? An empirical analysis of eurozone firms. *Journal of Business Finance & Accounting, 42*(7-8), 965–1006. doi:10.1111/jbfa.12124

Romano, C., Tanewski, G., & Smyrnios, K. (2001). Capital structure decision making. *Journal of Business Venturing, 16*(3), 285–310. doi:10.1016/S0883-9026(99)00053-1

Schmid, T. (2013). Control considerations, creditor monitoring, and the capital structure of family firms. *Journal of Banking & Finance, 37*(2), 257–272. doi:10.1016/j.jbankfin.2012.08.026

Setia-Atmaja, L., Tanewski, G. A., & Skully, M. (2009). The role of dividends, debt and board structure in the governance of family controlled firms. *Journal of Business Finance & Accounting, 36*(7-8), 863–898. doi:10.1111/j.1468-5957.2009.02151.x

Shanker, M. C., & Astrachan, J. H. (1996). Myths and realities: Family businesses' contribution to the US economy. A framework for assessing family business statistics. *Family Business Review*, *9*(2), 107–123. doi:10.1111/j.1741-6248.1996.00107.x

Sogorb, F. (2005). How SME uniqueness affects capital structure: Evidence from a 1994-1998 Spanish data panel. *Small Business Economics*, *25*(5), 447–457. doi:10.100711187-004-6486-8

Stulz, R. M. (1990). Managerial discretion and optimal financing policies. *Journal of Financial Economics*, *26*(1), 3–27. doi:10.1016/0304-405X(90)90011-N

Van Caneghem, T., & Van Campenhout, G. (2012). Quantity and quality of information and SME financial structure. *Small Business Economics*, *39*(2), 341–358. doi:10.100711187-010-9306-3

Voordeckers, W., Le Breton-Miller, I., & Miller, D. (2014). In search of the best of both worlds: Crafting a finance paper for the Family Business Review. *Family Business Review*, *27*(4), 281–286. doi:10.1177/0894486514552175

Williamson, O. E. (1988). Corporate finance and corporate governance. *The Journal of Finance*, *43*(3), 567–591. doi:10.1111/j.1540-6261.1988.tb04592.x

Wiseman, R., & Gomez-Mejia, L. (1998). A Behavioral Agency Model of Managerial Risk Taking. *Academy of Management Review*, *23*(1), 133–153. doi:10.5465/amr.1998.192967

Yen, J. F., Lin, C. Y., Chen, Y. S., & Huang, Y. C. (2015). Founding family firms and bank loan contracts. *Journal of Financial Services Research*, *48*(1), 53–82. doi:10.100710693-014-0199-1

Zahra, S., Rawhouser, H., Bhawe, N., Neubaum, D., & Hayton, J. (2008). Globalization of Social Entrepreneurship. *Strategic Entrepreneurship Journal*, *2*(2), 117–131. doi:10.1002ej.43

ADDITIONAL READING

Blanco-Mazagatos, V., de Quevedo-Puente, E., & Castrillo, L. (2007). The Trade-Off Between Financial Resources and Agency Costs in the Family Business: An Exploratory Study. *Family Business Review*, *20*(3), 199–213. doi:10.1111/j.1741-6248.2007.00095.x

Burgstaller, J., & Wagner, E. (2015). How do family ownership and founder management affect capital structure decisions and adjustment of SMEs? *The Journal of Risk Finance*, *16*(1), 73–101. doi:10.1108/JRF-06-2014-0091

Carney, M., Van Essen, M., Gedajlovic, E. R., & Heugens, P. P. (2015). What Do We Know About Private Family Firms? A Meta-Analytical Review. *Entrepreneurship Theory and Practice*, *39*(3), 513–544. doi:10.1111/etap.12054

Chua, J. H., Chrisman, J. J., Steier, L. P., & Rau, S. B. (2012). Sources of Heterogeneity in Family Firms: An Introduction. *Entrepreneurship Theory and Practice*, *36*(6), 1103–1113. doi:10.1111/j.1540-6520.2012.00540.x

Croci, E., Doukas, J., & Gonenc, H. (2011). Family Control and Financing Decisions. *European Financial Management*, *17*(5), 860–897. doi:10.1111/j.1468-036X.2011.00631.x

Koropp, C., Grichnik, D., & Kellermanns, F. (2013). Financial attitudes in family firms: The moderating role of family commitment. *Journal of Small Business Management*, *51*(1), 114–137. doi:10.1111/j.1540-627X.2012.00380.x

Mishra, C., & Mcconaughy, D. (1999). Founding Family Control and Capital Structure: The Risk of Loss of Control and the Aversion to Debt. *Entrepreneurship Theory and Practice*, *23*(4), 53–64. doi:10.1177/104225879902300404

Sánchez-Vidal, J., & Martín-Ugedo, J. F. (2006). Determinantes del conservadurismo financiero de las empresas españolas. *Revista de Economía Financiera*, *9*, 47–66.

Titman, S., & Wessels, R. (1988). The determinants of capital structure choice. *The Journal of Finance*, *43*(1), 1–19. doi:10.1111/j.1540-6261.1988.tb02585.x

Zahra, S. (2005). Entrepreneurial Risk Taking in Family Firms. *Family Business Review*, *18*(1), 23–40. doi:10.1111/j.1741-6248.2005.00028.x

KEY TERMS AND DEFINITIONS

Agency Theory: Theory used to explain the relationships between business principals and their agents, especially those between owners and managers.

Capital Structure: The distribution of debt and equity on a firm's balance sheet.

Family Firm: Status in which a family has a controlling interest in a particular firm.

Leverage: Use of debt capacity, defined as the accounting ratio between debt and total assets.

Managerial Discretion: Level of autonomous decision-making in the governance of a firm by a qualified group of employees who are responsible for managing the firm.

Ownership Structure: Internal organization of a firm that defines the rights and duties of the people that have legal interest or stake in it.

Section 4

Family Firm Financial Behavior

Chapter 9
Ownership and Operating Performance of Spanish Family IPO Firms

Fuencisla Martínez Lobato
University of Valencia, Spain

C. José García Martín
University of Valencia, Spain

José Emilio Farinós Viñas
University of Valencia, Spain

ABSTRACT

Previous studies have shown the existence of a relationship between the ownership structure of a company and its operational performance. In this context, the empirical evidence reveals that after an initial public offering (IPO), companies experience a decline in their operational performance. In this research, the authors investigate whether the characteristics of Spanish family firms led to a different operating behavior with respect to non-family companies when they go public through an IPO. The results show that the particularities of the family firm do not turn into significant differences in operational performance after the listing process.

INTRODUCTION

Ever since the work of Berle & Means (1932), various studies have attempted to explain the effects of ownership on a firm's results and value. The ownership structure of a firm is not a static feature; rather, it changes over the lifespan of the firm as a result of various operations that must be undertaken to ensure its survival or to respond to demands stemming from the complexity of the environment. These include mergers, Initial Public Offerings (IPOs), takeover bids and capital increases, among others. Of all these, the decision to go public through an IPO represents an important step in the trajectory of a firm, entail-

DOI: 10.4018/978-1-7998-1655-3.ch009

ing substantial changes to the nature of the firm and in the operational relationships with the different actors involved in its activity. In particular, the IPO produces a change in the ownership structure, which leads to greater dispersion and separation between ownership and managerial control. This may in turn reduce the incentives for the owners to exercise a supervisory role over the managers. Consequently, such a change of ownership may have a significant impact on the functioning and performance of the firm.

Empirical evidence shows that companies suffer a decline in their operating performance levels after they begin trading on the stock market through an IPO (Jain & Kini, 1994; Pagano *et al.*, 1998; Mikkelson *et al.*, 1997; Cai & Wei, 1997; Kim *et al.*, 2004; Álvarez & González, 2005). Some of these studies report that the decline in firms' post-IPO operating performance is accompanied by increased sales and capital investments, so the drop cannot be explained by a lack of investment opportunities or problems of demand. Therefore, related research has focused on analysing the greater dispersion of ownership resulting from going public as the root cause of this decline in firms' efficiency. As discussed in the next section, empirical evidence relating to this phenomenon is inconclusive.

According to Galve & Salas (1993), compared to shareholder dispersion in US firms, European firms—particularly Spanish firms—are essentially characterized as having very concentrated control, even in large companies. This leads to the controlling group exercising greater vigilance over management's behaviour and decisions. Given this feature of Spanish companies, studies of their ownership and control should primarily focus on examining the implications for firm's efficiency of the nature of the controlling group (families, banks, other companies...), rather than on analysing the effects of separation between ownership and control stemming from a dispersed shareholding without taking into account the nature of the controlling group. In particular, it is worth noting the key role played by family businesses in the Spanish economy, where they account for 85% of total firms. Furthermore, in line with agency theory (Berle & Means, 1932; Jensen & Meckling, 1976; Fama & Jensen, 1983a, 1983b), the characteristics of family firm's objectives and relationships could be seen as contributing to the reduction of certain agency costs, but these same features may give rise to others.[1]

Within this area, there is little previous research on the Spanish market, and existing studies do not analyse the possible differences between family and non-family firms. In this regard, the aim of this study is to provide new evidence of the post-IPO operating performance behaviour for samples of family and non-family firms in the period 1994-2012.

Thus, this chapter is organized as follows. Section 1 outlines the theoretical foundations provided by agency theory, which can explain the decline observed in firms' operating performance after listing the firm on the stock exchange, the previous empirical evidence and the hypotheses to be tested. Section 2 details the methodology. Section 3 sets out the results of the analysis of the levels and changes in the operating performance of all Spanish IPO firms in the period 1994-2012, distinguishing between family and non-family firm sub-samples. Lastly, the main conclusions of the study are presented.

OWNERSHIP STRUCTURE AND POST-IPO OPERATING PERFORMANCE. HYPOTHESES TO BE TESTED

The theoretical foundations underpinning existing research on how a firm's ownership affects its performance come from the contributions of the Organization Theory and, in particular, from one of its key branches, Agency Theory. According to the Organization Theory, the productive efficiency of a company depends on, among other factors, the firm's ownership structure and control and its internal organizational design. Agency theory seeks to resolve the various conflicts that affect the functioning of a firm by viewing it as a set of contractual relationships between participants who are attempting to serve their own interests. This conception of the firm attributes different efficiency to firms with concentrated ownership—where ownership and control coincide—compared to firms with a dispersed ownership structure, in which the owners therefore have less control over management.

Based on the work of Berle & Means (1932) on the separation between share ownership and control over management, and the contributions of authors such as Jensen & Meckling (1976) and Fama & Jensen (1983a, 1983b), Agency Theory holds that ownership concentration should have a positive effect on firm value because it reduces conflicts of interest between owners and managers. These authors describe the classic agency problem that arises when managers of a company make decisions that serve their own objectives and interests to the detriment of those of the owners. Jensen & Meckling (1976) suggest that shareholders can reduce the firm-specific risk they face by diversifying their investment portfolios; as such, shareholders may be unconcerned by this risk, whereas the managers, who are in fact affected by it, may try to prevent it by adopting decisions that are potentially detrimental to the shareholders' objectives. Such behaviour goes against shareholders' objectives and entails a series of agency costs relating to control, the agent's guarantee of loyalty and/or residual loss. In firms with a concentrated ownership structure, shareholders have a greater incentive to monitor managerial activity and thus ensure that their ultimate goal of maximizing firm value is pursued. In addition, in this type of firm, the main owners are involved in the administration and/or senior management level of the business, such that there is an alignment of interests between owners and managers. As a result, firms with concentrated and managerial ownership are expected to face fewer agency problems and costs stemming from the conflict between owners and managers (*Hypothesis on monitoring and alignment of interests*). Thus, Shleifer & Vishny (1986) show a positive relationship between ownership concentration and firm value in USA Agrawal & Mandelker (1990) provide further support for this finding, especially when ownership is concentrated in institutional investors. However, the studies of Leech & Leahy (1991) and Mudambi & Nicosia (1998) on the British market report a negative relationship between ownership concentration and firm value. These conflicting results suggest a possible non-linear relationship and the existence of ownership concentration factors that have a negative impact on firm value.

In this regard, in firms with concentrated and managerial ownership a second type of agency problem may arise. This new conflict arises from the possibility that the majority shareholders, who also control the decisions, may use their position of power to take advantage of the private benefits of control, and thereby extract wealth from minority shareholders who are not involved in the management of the firm (*Hypothesis of expropriation*). In this respect, Shleifer & Vishny (1986) argue that when the degree of ownership concentration reaches a certain level, such that large shareholders have a high level of control over the company, they may be more interested in using that control to generate private profits they will not share with minority shareholders. This expropriation of the wealth from the external minority shareholders by the large owners who control the company generates an agency conflict that can outweigh the benefits stemming from increased monitoring (Villalonga & Amit, 2006). In addition, another source of agency costs may arise in these firms: namely, *managerial entrenchment*. That is, high levels of managerial ownership can enable the owner-managers take decisions that run counter to the aim of maximizing firm value, without adversely affecting their job permanence and/or salary (*Hypothesis of entrenchment*).

Therefore, the presence of large shareholders can have a positive effect on firm value if they use their supervisory power to monitor managers and/or derive benefits from the control shared with the rest of the owners. Conversely, they may have a negative effect if they take advantage of their control to obtain private profits from the company (Lemmon & Lins, 2003) and/or entrench themselves in their post for longer than appropriate in terms of efficiency.

The relationship between ownership and performance is likely to differ according to the type of shareholder. Regarding family-owned businesses, as Galve & Salas (2003) point out, they represent the anti-paradigm of the separation between ownership and control described by Berle & Means (1932) in large US companies. Family firms are characterized by high ownership concentration, with the family having the highest percentage of ownership in the business and usually being involved in the management of the business, such that ownership, control and management all coincide. In addition, family firms have a particular contract structure, in which economic and family relationships overlap. It is therefore appropriate to apply the tenets of agency theory to analyse the effects of these overlapping relationships on the performance of these firms.

Fama & Jensen (1983a) also point out, however, that firms with concentrated managerial ownership sacrifice the benefits stemming from the specialization of decision functions; thus, inefficient decisions are taken that adversely impact the competitiveness of the firm, such as rejecting risky yet profitable investment projects.

The agency benefits that a family is assumed to contribute to a business derive from the fact that in some family firms the role of principal owner and CEO are sometimes held by the same person, while in others, these positions are held by family members who trust one another, share the same values and pursue common interests and objectives. In both cases, the classic owner-manager conflict is eliminated or mitigated, so that the principal does not have to spend time and resources controlling the agent's behaviour; nor are there any marginal or residual costs that could result from the agent acting counter to the principal's goal of utility maximization. Moreover, for family firms, one of their main objectives is to maintain control over the company over time, thereby ensuring sound, stable relationships with customers, suppliers, workers and financial creditors, and helping to reduce other types of agency conflicts. Several authors have found evidence to support the greater efficiency of family firms compared to non-family firms (Jensen & Meckling, 1976; Fama & Jensen, 1983a; Daily & Dollinger, 1992; Harvey,1999).

Nevertheless, family relationships are not always as harmonious as needed for the efficient running of the business. In this respect, conflicts of interest, opportunistic behaviour, laziness and adverse selection problems arising from altruism may emerge; these negatively affect the professionalism required in business decision-making and can therefore lead to high agency costs. This type of problem primarily occurs as the company is passed on to successive generations. Likewise, family firms can suffer from agency problems as a consequence of the family owners using their position of control in the company to gain benefits at the expense of minority shareholders through expropriation mechanisms. This in turn requires minority shareholders to exercise greater control, with a resulting increase in agency costs.

Consequently, being a family firm can have positive or negative effects on performance through agency relations, among other factors. Various empirical studies on this topic have tried to draw conclusions as to which of these effects predominates. Notable examples include McConnaughy *et al.* (1998, 2001), Anderson & Reeb (2003) and Villalonga & Amit (2006) focusing on the USA; Maury (2006) and Barontini & Caprio (2006) focusing on Western Europe; Westhead & Cowling (1997) focusing on the UK; Sraer & Thesmar (2007) on France; and Menéndez-Requejo (2006) and Sacristán & Gómez (2006) on Spain. However, the empirical research to date has not produced conclusive results, so the issue of whether or not family firms create more value than non-family firms remains unresolved.

Within the context of the studies that examine the relationship between firm ownership structure and performance, there is relatively little research focusing on the changes in the ownership structure due to the decision to go public and how this affects firms' operating performance. Table 1 presents a list of studies that provide empirical evidence in this regard. Among other contributions, Jain & Kini (1994) find a positive and significant relationship between a firm's operating performance and the ownership share retained by the original shareholders after the IPO. However, Mikkelson *et al.* (1997), Cai & Wei (1997), and Álvarez & González (2005) find no evidence of a significant relationship between firms' ownership structure and operating performance after they go public. For their part, Kim *et al.* (2004) provide evidence of a non-linear relationship between managerial ownership and changes in the operating performance of Thai IPO firms. In summary, all these studies confirm a decline in firms' post-IPO operating performance, but they do not report conclusive results as to whether this variation in operating performance is due to the change in firms' ownership structure occurring as a result of their IPO.

On the other hand, there is practically no existing research on the differences between family firms and non-family firms in terms of the effects of going public on their operating performance. With the aim of highlighting the advantages of IPOs in terms of business growth, Mazzola & Marchisio (2002) provide a descriptive analysis of the evolution of different performance characteristics of 36 companies that floated on the Italian stock market in the period 1995-1998, distinguishing between family (26 cases) and non-family firms (10 cases). These authors observe that family firms double their revenue in the period from three years before their IPO to three years after, and that the revenue growth rate is slightly higher in non-family firms. In terms of profitability (measured as *ROA* and *ROE*), they found similar trends for family and non-family firms: that is, they both show significant growth prior to the IPO and a decline in the year following the flotation, with growth restarting two years after the IPO.

Ferreira (2008) studies why family firms experience a significant post-IPO drop in their levels of profitability, efficiency, employment and activity, but register an increase in sales and capital investment. To this end, Ferreira (2008) analyses a sample of 25 family firms that floated on the Portuguese stock market during the period 1989-2004, concluding that the post-IPO decline in performance is significantly higher when one or several of the following situations occur: there are no owners in management, which means an increase in agency costs; there is a low level of ownership concentration after going public; the founder retains only a small ownership share; the economic situation at the time of the IPO is poor; or the former CEO is replaced. Ferreira (2016) updates the sample period of his former study to 1999-2010, finding similar results.

Kartika (2012) studies the post-IPO performance of 121 companies that floated on the Malaysian stock exchange in the period 2005-2008, comparing family and non-family firms. The descriptive analysis shows that family firms do not achieve better post-IPO performance than non-family firms. However, the multivariate analysis reveals that the composition of the board of directors and the ownership influences firms' post-IPO performance.

Chahine & Goergen (2013), basing their analysis on the tenets of agency theory, examine the contrasting effects (an increase or decrease in agency costs depending on whether or not the positive effect of the alignment of interests prevails over the negative effect of the expropriation of minority shareholders) of both family ties and social ties between board members and top management on firms' post-IPO operating performance. To that end, they study a sample of 500 IPOs in USA during the period 1997-2008. They find that post-IPO operating performance is positively related to the strength of social ties, but

Table 1. Empirical evidence on post-IPO operating performance and ownership structure

Authors	Market	Sample	Results
Jain & Kini (1994)	USA	682 IPOs in 1976-1988	✓ Significant decline in operating performance in the five years following the IPO. ✓ Significantly smaller in firms where the initial owner-managers continue to hold an important position in the company. ✓ It cannot be determined whether this positive relationship is the result of reduced agency conflicts or other reasons, such as the fact that retaining ownership sends a signal as to the quality of the firm.
Cai & Wei (1997)	Japan	180 IPOs in 1971-1992	✓ Significant decline in operating performance in the five years following the IPO. ✓ Explained by the managers exploiting a window of opportunity when choosing the time to go public.
Mikkelson *et al.* (1997)	USA	283 IPOs in 1980-1983	✓ Significant decline in operating performance, especially in the year following the IPO. ✓ Post-IPO changes in shareholder ownership are not the cause of this decline; rather, it is better explained by firm age and size of the company, and by the old shares offered in the IPO.
Pagano *et al.* (1998)	Italy	69 IPOs in 1982-1992	✓ Post-IPO drop in profitability, which becomes greater over time from the first to the third year after going public. ✓ The median percentage of voting rights held by the controlling group falls by 30% when the firm goes public, and by 5% in the following three years.
Kim *et al.* (2004)	Thailand	133 IPOs in 1987-1993	✓ Significant decline in operating performance following the IPO. ✓ Non-linear relationship between post-IPO performance change and managerial ownership. ✓ The positive effects in terms of monitoring and alignment of interests of an increase in managerial ownership prevails for low and high levels of management, but at intermediate levels the negative effect of entrenchment predominates.
Álvarez & González (2005)	Spain	111 IPOs in 1985-1997	✓ Significant decline in operating performance in the three years following the IPO. ✓ No significant relationship found between this variation and changes in ownership structure; as such, the decline cannot be explained by an increase in agency costs after the IPO.
Khurshed *et al.* (2005)	UK	411 IPOs in 1995-1999	✓ Permanent and significant decline in operating performance after going public.
Wang (2005)	China	747 IPOs in 1994-1999	✓ Marked decline in post-IPO operating performance ✓ Neither the ownership concentration nor ownership by the State or individuals are related to the changes in performance. ✓ However, companies with low and high levels of non-State ownership (intermediate levels) show a positive (negative) relationship between this ownership and performance changes.
Farinós *et al.* (2007)	Spain	44 IPOs in 1993-2001	✓ For IPOs of both private companies and state-owned companies being privatized, significant increases found in post-IPO sales, capital investment, employment and efficiency, but no significant change observed in their profitability.
Atinc *et al.* (2017)	USA	185 IPOs in 2001-2005	✓ In the case of young IPO companies, changes are observed in the board of directors but not in the top management teams. ✓ Negative impact of changes in the board of directors on post-IPO operating performance.
Pereira & Sousa (2017)	Europe	555 IPOs in 1995-2006	✓ Decline in post-IPO operating performance ✓ Greater in European companies located in emerging markets than in those located in developed markets. ✓ This can be explained by greater use of creative accounting techniques and taking advantage of a window of opportunity in choosing the timing of the IPO.

negatively to the strength of family ties. They also find that, controlling for social ties, the independence of the board of directors boosts post-IPO operating performance.

Based on the theoretical approaches that relate the ownership structure of a firm to its operating performance, and the existing empirical evidence on firms' post-IPO operating performance, our aim is to analyse whether our data support the following hypotheses:

H1: Spanish firms experience a significant post-IPO decline in their operating performance.
H2: Family firms, characterized by their desire to retain control of the company in the hands of the family, experience a smaller drop in their post-IPO operating performance than non-family firms.

SAMPLE AND METHODOLOGY

The sample under study consists of 56 Spanish IPOs in the period 1994-2012.

The data on the IPOs have been obtained from the prospectuses that firms are legally required to produce when they go public. These prospectuses are available through the website of Spain's National Securities Market Commission (CNMV by its initials in Spanish) for public offerings registered in or after the second half of 1998.[2] In addition, the authors have accessed relevant information related to these offerings and the financial and audit reports annually submitted to the CNMV by the firms that are the subject of our study. Accounting and financial data come from the SABI database and the stock market data were sourced from the company Bolsas y Mercados Españoles S.A. (BME).

The total sample is split into two groups according to whether the company is a family firm or not. According to Steiger *et al.* (2015), there is still a lack of consensus on what defines the family firm. Current research tends to emphasize family firm typology. However, given the size of the sample, it is not possible to split it into different types of family firm. The authors have thus chosen to work with two definitions of family firms—a strict and a broad definition—both based on the involvement of the family in the company through its influence on ownership, control and/or management. The first criterion, which it can be referred to as *lax* or *weak*, is that used by Galve & Salas (2011). Under this criterion, a company is considered to be a family firm when the sum of the (direct or indirect) interests in the company's share capital held by one or more families is greater than the sum of those held by the other significant shareholders.[3] When this criterion is applied, our sample of 56 IPO firms can be broken down into 31 family firms (FF) and 25 non-family firms (NFF). According to the second criterion, which it can be referred to as *strict* or *strong*, a company is defined as a family firm if the members of one or several families hold at least a 50 percent in the ownership and control rights of the firm. When this criterion is applied, the total sample can be broken down into 23 FF and 33 NFF. Anyway, in both cases the family must exercise significant control over the firm in order to be considered a family firm. Furthermore, although the authors did not stipulate it as a requirement, all the companies in the sample deemed family firms under either one of these criteria have family members on the board and/or in senior management positions.

Table 2 exhibits some descriptive statistics of the two subsamples (family and non-family firms) for the weak and the strong classification criteria. In brief, Table 2 shows that family firms appear to be older, smaller and less indebted than non-family firms regardless the classification criterion used to split the sample.

Table 2. Descriptive statistics of the family and non-family firm subsamples for the weak and the strong classification criteria

	Age	Total Assets	EBIT	Leverage
Panel A: Family Firms (weak criterion)				
Average	22.76	609,080,423	53,363,911	0.56
Standard Deviation	18.11	1,314,735,743	84,489,836	0.22
Min	2.52	3,031,070	83,060	0.06
Median	17.97	141,280,310	16,120,000	0.59
Max	67.59	7,191,390,000	320,843,000	0.93
N	31	31	31	31
Panel B: Non Family Firms (weak criterion)				
Average	19.65	1,126,643,143	83,907,410	0.65
Standard Deviation	20.28	1,585,611,383	148,343,437	0.22
Min	0.36	18,645,830	-84,270,000	0.21
Median	11.26	563,427,500	47,448,000	0.73
Max	66.64	5,561,886,000	549,509,000	1.05
N	25	20	21	20
Panel C: Family Firms (strong criterion)				
Average	22.37	779,405,755	68,271,233	0.57
Standard Deviation	16.34	1,493,914,391	93,878,318	0.24
Min	2.52	3,031,070	96,980	0.06
Median	18.90	319,986,000	20,537,540	0.59
Max	60.96	7,191,390,000	320,843,000	0.93
N	23	23	23	23
Panel D: Non Family Firms (strong criterion)				
Average	21.05	838,857,986	63,658,569	0.62
Standard Deviation	20.88	1,410,774,463	129,806,006	0.21
Min	0.36	18,645,830	-84,270,000	0.15
Median	11.98	306,673,805	23,670,000	0.70
Max	67.59	5,561,886,000	549,509,000	1.05
N	33	28	29	28

The researchers estimate operating performance through three measures: *ROA*, return on assets, calculated as the ratio between Earnings Before Interest and Taxes (EBIT) and total assets; *ROE*, return on equity, calculated as the ratio between net income and equity; and *cash flow*, calculated as EBIT plus fixed asset depreciation, divided by total assets (hereafter *cash flow* or *CF/A*). Economic profitability or *ROA* provides a measure of a firm's efficiency in its use of assets, regardless of how it is financed. Financial profitability or *ROE* assesses the efficiency of the firm's activity, taking into account its financing, for the owners of the firm. The *cash flow* measure offers an alternative to *ROA* for assessing operating performance which allows us to eliminate any discretionary actions by managers when calculating the depreciation of fixed assets.

For each firm in the sample, the levels of each of the abovementioned variables are measured in a seven-year window: the three years before the IPO, the year of the IPO (year 0) and the three years following the IPO. The authors also calculate the changes in these variables for each firm as the percentage difference of the values in years 0, 1, 2 and 3, compared to the value in year -1, or the year prior to the IPO. Below, the mean and median values of both the level and the variation in operating performance are obtained. These values are calculated for both the full sample and for the sub-samples of family and non-family firms.

Furthermore, in order to confirm that negative variations in firms' operating performance in the years after they go public are not due to demand problems or a lack of investment opportunities, the values of variations in firms' sales and capital investment are calculated and included in the analysis.

When analysing the evolution of firms' post-IPO operating performance, it is appropriate to exclude the part of it caused by factors specific to the industries in which firms are operating. For this reason, as suggested by Barber & Lyon (1996), the calculations of the three measures of operating performance adjusted for industry are computed. To that end, the following procedure is applied. First, for each IPO firm and for each year in the seven-year window analysed, the corresponding median value for firms in the same industry in the same year have been subtracted from each ratio (*ROA*, *ROE* and *cash flow*), which gives us the firm's industry-adjusted operating performance level in each of those seven years. Second, the variation in each firm's industry-adjusted level for the years 0, 1, 2 and 3 is calculated relative to the value for year -1, the year prior to the IPO. Lastly, the mean and median values of firms' industry-adjusted levels and the changes they experience after going public are computed.

Therefore, in order to adjust the data by industry a sample of control firms has been selected. To that end, all the firms registered between 1995 and 2012 that met the following criteria are extracted from the SABI database:[4]

- They are legally constituted as a public limited company.
- They are active
- They have a firm size, measured as total assets, of at least 12 million euros if they report stand-alone financial statements, 48 million euros in the case of consolidated financial statements, and 69 million euros if they provide consolidated accounts in accordance with IAS.[5]
- They are not financial institutions or state-owned enterprises. Governments and public authorities do not hold more than a 50% ownership interest in the company.
- Their parent company is not a foreign company; in other words, foreign shareholders do not hold more than a 50% interest in the firm.

As a result of this search 92,615 cases or firm-year observations have been obtained. From this number, firms with consolidation code U2 in SABI have been eliminated, since they have already been included with their consolidated accounts. In this way, it is ensured that in each year there are no duplicate firms. Besides, all firms whose Classification of Economic Activities (CNAE by its initials in Spanish) code is 7415 (holding companies) have been excluded, as well as the IPO firms that are our focus of study. This gives us a total of 85,091 cases available.

In order to adjust the data of IPO firms with those of their respective industries, their CNAE codes, taking the first two digits, are identified. Thus, Table 3 shows the industries of the Spanish IPO firms in the period 1994-2012, as well as the number of firms that went public and the number of firm-year observations in each of these industries.

Table 3. Distribution by activity code (CNAE-93 Rev. 1) of the sample of IPO firms and control firms (excluding financial companies and state-owned companies that have been privatized) in the period 1994-2012

Activity codes (CNAE-93 rev.1)	Number of IPOs	Number of firm-year control sample
15 Food and beverage industry	4	5,736
17 Textile industry	1	943
21 Paper industry	3	973
22 Publishing, printing and reproduction of recorded media	2	1,390
24 Chemical industry	2	2,299
28 Manufacture of fabricated metal products, except machinery and equipment	1	2,169
31 Manufacture of electrical machinery and material	1	592
37 Recycling	1	133
40 Production and distribution of electricity, gas, steam and hot water	1	1,800
45 Construction	3	8,277
51 Wholesale trade and intermediaries, except motor vehicles and motorcycles	3	9,185
52 Retail trade, except motor vehicles and motorcycles; repair of personal and household effects	6	1,497
55 Hospitality	2	3,337
60 Land transport; pipeline transport	1	1,168
62 Air and space transport	1	170
63 Activities associated with transport; travel agency activities	3	2,207
64 Post and telecommunications	2	498
70 Real estate activities	7	17,193
71 Rental of machinery and equipment without operator, personal effects and household goods	1	493
72 IT activities	1	422
74 Other business activities*	2	4,266
85 Health and veterinary activities, social services	1	836
92 Leisure, culture and sports activities	5	2,018
93 Miscellaneous personal services	2	210

* Excluding companies with CNAE code 7415 (holding companies)

Parametric and non-parametric tests are performed in order to determine whether there is a significant change in firms' operating performance after they go public, and to compare the possible differences in this variation between family firms and non-family firms.

Specifically, the parametric Student-*t* test is used to analyse whether or not the mean values are significantly different from zero, and to compare whether or not there are significant differences between the mean values for family and non-family firms. Given the small size of the samples and in order to ensure the robustness of our results, the *bootstrap* method (Efron, 1982) is also used to generate the empirical distribution of performance under the null hypothesis, thus relaxing the assumptions of normality, stationarity and time independence of the observations.[6]

Also, since it is not possible to ensure symmetric data and, therefore, the measurement of the mean may not be appropriate, the Wilcoxon signed-rank test and the Kruskal-Wallis test for the median values are performed.

RESULTS

Below the results obtained are discussed for the family firm and non-family firm sub-samples classified according to the *weak* criterion. As a matter of robustness analysis, results obtained according to the *strong* criterion are briefly discussed.

Family vs. Non-Family Firms Classification With the Weak Criterion

Table 4 shows that there is an increase in operating performance in the years running up to the IPO and a decline in this performance in the following three years.

Specifically, regarding the evolution of the median gross operating performance of family firms as a result of going public (Table 4), the median *ROA* value in gross terms decreases from 9.4% in the year before the IPO to 8% three years after the event; the median *ROE* value in gross terms falls from 18.3% to 11.5%; and the median *cash flow* in gross terms falls from 12.4% to 11.4%.

However, when considering the industry-adjusted measures (Table 4), different patterns between the operating performance measured by *ROA* and *cash flow*, and that measured by *ROE*, are found. Thus, in the case of *ROA* and *cash flow*, the upturn occurs not in the year prior to the IPO but in the same year, followed by a decline in the two years following the IPO, and a recovery in the third year. However, in the case of *ROE,* the peak occurs in the year prior to the IPO, and the largest fall occurs in the year of the IPO.

Furthermore, the industry-adjusted mean and median levels of operating performance measured by *ROA* and *cash flow* are significantly different from zero, but this is not the case when measured by *ROE*. Therefore, these levels are a result of factors other than those specific to the industry in question. Thus, when taking into account the effects of the industry, family firms' post-IPO operating performance is not the same regardless of the operating performance measure used. It should be recalled that while *ROA* and *cash flow* can be considered alternative measures, with the only difference being depreciation, *ROE* is influenced by other items, such as outperformance and financial expenses.

When non-family firms go public, they follow the same pattern of operating performance—in both gross and industry-adjusted terms—as the full sample, regardless of the measure used. Furthermore, the industry-adjusted mean and median levels of operating performance are not significantly different from zero for any of the three measures, so it seems that non-family firms' operating performance more closely corresponds to that of the industry in which they operate.

Table 5 exhibits the mean and median values of the variations in operating performance for the family firm and non-family firm sub-samples, measured through the three ratios: *ROA* (panel A), *ROE* (panel B) and *cash flow* (panel C), in both gross and industry-adjusted terms, in years 0, 1, 2 and 3, relative to the value in year -1, the year prior to the IPO. The results of the mean and median tests are also shown.

After decomposing the sample into the family firm and non-family firm sub-samples, a general decline in firms' post-IPO operating performance relative to the value in the year prior to the IPO is still observed. This decline is mainly significant in the third year after going public.

Table 4. Mean and median values of operating performance using the Weak Criterion to split the IPO sample firms

	Year -3	Year -2	Year -1	Year 0	Year 1	Year 2	Year 3
Panel A: ROA (%)							
FF							
Mean	8.56	8.47	13.29	13.92	11.37	9.46	10.53
Median	6.88	7.34	9.40	10.62	9.21	7.91	8.04
N	21	26	31	31	31	30	28
Adjusted mean	2.81 [c]	1.51	7.68 [b]	8.30 [a]	5.50 [a]	4.64 [a]	5.64 [c]
Adjusted median	0.46	0.03	2.95 [a]	5.59 [a]	3.81 [a]	3.21 [a]	4.78 [b]
N	18	22	29	30	31	30	28
NFF							
Mean	10.90	7.72	7.45	7.91	6.71	6.59	8.10
Median	9.24	7.29	9.04	6.17	7.68	6.47	5.66
N	16	19	20	25	25	25	23
Adjusted mean	5.93 [c]	1.94	1.50	2.63	1.42	1.98	3.07
Adjusted median	3.63	2.86	4.36	2.04	1.32	1.65	-0.08
N	14	18	18	23	25	25	22
Panel B: ROE (%)							
FF							
Mean	13.45	11.19	21.74	19.11	16.15	10.45	6.69
Median	12.89	11.68	18.35	16.45	15.14	11.81	11.50
N	21	26	31	31	31	30	28
Adjusted mean	-0.17	-3.24	8.98 [b]	6.04 [b]	3.72	1.41	-1.60
Adjusted median	2.08	0.60	3.81 [b]	0.87	2.24	3.54	3.78
N	18	22	29	30	31	30	28
NFF							
Mean	18.49	17.53	9.33	15.55	5.36	0.12	11.19
Median	18.60	19.13	18.28	12.43	11.61	10.15	10.74
N	16	19	20	25	25	25	24
Adjusted mean	8.19	4.01	-5.49	2.43	-6.43	-8.70	2.82
Adjusted median	10.44	6.56	8.18	2.30	0.63	0.59	-1.01
N	14	18	18	23	25	25	23
Panel C: CF/A (%)							
FF							
Mean	11.38	10.93	16.32	16.88	14.72	12.50	11.52
Median	10.46	9.20	12.41	14.01	13.67	11.74	11.43
N	21	25	29	31	30	29	27
Adjusted mean	2.65	1.30	7.33 [b]	7.81 [a]	5.39 [a]	4.16 [a]	3.03 [b]
Adjusted median	1.04	-0.36	1.81 [b]	4.51 [a]	3.77 [a]	2.10 [b]	3.39 [c]
N	18	22	27	30	30	29	27
NFF							
Mean	17.05	12.87	12.97	12.41	10.47	10.96	12.31
Median	14.43	11.19	14.96	10.12	11.63	10.36	9.51
N	16	19	20	25	25	25	23
Adjusted mean	8.47 [c]	3.11	3.73	3.09	1.59	2.03	2.78
Adjusted median	6.06 [c]	1.23	4.36 [c]	2.27	2.74	2.76	0.94
N	14	18	18	23	25	25	22

[a, b, c] denote significant at 1%, 5% and 10%, respectively.

Thus, with respect to family firms, Table 5 shows a significant reduction of 22.4% in *ROA*, in median and in gross terms, three years after the IPO relative to the values in the year prior to the IPO, and a 36.3% decline in industry-adjusted terms, although this drop is not significant. There is also a significant decline in median *ROE*, in gross terms, of 39.7%, and an industry-adjusted decline of 72%, which is not significant. Median *cash flow* in gross terms falls by 12.5%, but this decline is not significant, while the equivalent industry-adjusted reduction is 79.8%, which is statistically significant. Therefore, when using industry-adjusted data, family firms' decline in operating performance observed in the three years after the IPO compared to the year prior to the IPO is not statistically significant, except when measured by *cash flow*. When the *bootstrap* method is applied, the mean industry-adjusted variations are also found to be not significant. Consequently, as mentioned above, the significant decline in gross measures would be better explained by changes in industry-specific aspects than by the greater dispersion of ownership in family firms after going public.

On the other hand, Table 5 shows that non-family firms experience a significant reduction in the median gross and industry-adjusted *ROA* of 58.5% and 81.1%, respectively, in the three years after the IPO compared to the year prior to it; they also register a statistically significant decline in the median industry-adjusted *ROE* of 97.8%; and, finally, a significant decline in the median *cash flow* in gross terms of 29.8%. When applying the *bootstrap* method, the mean variations in gross and industry-adjusted terms are significant, except when the measure is *cash flow*, in which case this value is not significant in industry-adjusted terms.

There are significant post-IPO increases in both sales and capital investments compared to the year prior to the IPO in both family firm and non-family firm sub-samples. Consequently, the significant decline in these firms' operating performance cannot be explained as a result of a drop in demand or lack of profitable investment opportunities in these periods. Conversely, they can again be attributed to a rise in agency costs due to post-IPO increases in ownership dispersion. Thus, Table 6 shows the evolution of the mean and median ownership dispersion in family and non-family firms, classified according to the *weak* criterion, in the year prior to the IPO, at the end of the year in which they went public, and three years later. Table 6 exhibits that there is an increase in the ownership dispersion in the year in which they went public in both family and non-family firms, and this dispersion level remains fairly stable in the following three years.

Table 7 shows the mean and median variation in family firms' and non-family firms' ownership dispersion as a result of their IPO, in the year of flotation and three years after, relative to their pre-IPO level of dispersion. As can be seen, there are significant increases in the mean and median dispersion of the ownership structure in all the periods considered and for both family and non-family sub-samples. In particular, there is a significant increase in the median value of the dispersion that family firms undergo three years after the IPO, with respect to the year prior to the IPO, of 34.97%, while for non-family firms, the equivalent figure is 27.79%. No significant differences are observed between family and non-family firms in terms of the change in ownership structure.

When variations in operating performance in family and non-family firms are compared (see Table 5), in general, non-family firms suffer a greater decline in operating performance than family firms. However, this difference between family and non-family firms is only significant for variations in *ROA* in median and in adjusted terms, one year and three years after the IPO, relative to the year prior to the IPO. Thus, the industry-adjusted *ROA* of non-family firms one year after the IPO, relative to the year prior to the IPO, falls significantly, by a median of 32.3 percentage points more than the industry-adjusted *ROA* of family firms (panel A). The equivalent significant decline three years after the IPO is 44.8 percentage

Table 5. Mean and median values of variations in operating performance (Weak Criterion)

	Variation -1 to 0	Variation -1 to 1	Variation -1 to 2	Variation -1 to 3
Panel A: ROA (%)				
FF				
Mean	**18.70	10.19	-10.88	**-26.12 [c]
Median	3.36	1.15	-17.09	-22.43 [c]
N	30	30	29	27
Adjusted mean	**108.95	**83.83	61.43	4.51
Adjusted median	-0.73	-12.06	-24.51	-36.29
N	28	28	27	25
NFF				
Mean	-9.04	-4.84	-24.43	**-44.41 [b]
Median	-10.73	-4.93	-18.49	-58.52 [b]
N	19	19	19	19
Adjusted mean	-30.85	-34.00	-29.72	***-134.68 [a]
Adjusted median	-33.03	-24.46	-43.36	-81.10 [a]
N	17	17	18	16
DIFFERENCE *(FF-NFF)*				
Mean	*27.74	15.03	13.55	18.29
Median	14.09	6.08	1.40	36.09
Adjusted mean	**139.80	**117.83	91.15	*139.19
Adjusted median	32.30 [b]	12.40	18.85	44.81 [c]
Panel B: ROE (%)				
FF				
Mean	**60.22	*57.92	-29.99	**-49.32 [c]
Median	-2.67	-14.19	-28.92	-39.70 [b]
N	30	30	29	27
Adjusted mean	58.26	***-84.63 [a]	50.19	157.60
Adjusted median	-51.59 [a]	-59.23 [a]	-47.22	-71.99
N	28	27	27	25
NFF				
Mean	**-32.77	-22.83	**-48.81 [b]	-19.17
Median	-17.60	-24.29	-66.16 [b]	-60.28
N	19	19	19	19
Adjusted mean	-13.67	*-40.79	*-51.97	***-175.33 [b]
Adjusted median	-23.96	-27.50	-37.64	-97.78 [a]
N	17	17	17	16

continued on following page

Table 5. Continued

	Variation -1 to 0	Variation -1 to 1	Variation -1 to 2	Variation -1 to 3
DIFFERENCE ***(FF-NFF)***				
Mean	***92.99	**80.75	18.82	-30.15
Median	14.93	10.10	37.24	20.58
Adjusted mean	71.93	-43.84	102.16	332.93
Adjusted median	-27.63	-31.73	-9.58	25.79
Panel C: CF/A (%)				
FF				
Mean	**17.31	11.53	-1.53	-13.97
Median	1.43	10.54	-2.57	-12.48
N	28	27	26	24
Adjusted mean	**-82.33	*-90.91	*-297.44	-261.44
Adjusted median	-14.33 [c]	-46.58	-57.95 [c]	-79.84 [b]
N	26	25	27	27
NFF				
Mean	-2.69	-1.87	-12.81	*-29.54 [c]
Median	-2.59	-10.95	-8.44	-29.77 [c]
N	19	19	19	19
Adjusted mean	23.99	-51.11	-29.06	15.63
Adjusted median	-27.23	-5.79	-13.44	-5.33
N	17	17	17	17
DIFFERENCE ***(FF-NFF)***				
Mean	*20.00	13.40	11.28	15.57
Median	4.02	21.49	5.87	17.29
Adjusted mean	**-106.32	-39.80	-268.38	-277.07
Adjusted median	12.90	-40.79	-44.51	-74.51
Panel D: **Sales (%)**				
FF				
Mean	***188.57 [c]	***235.69 [c]	**254.91	***318.02 [c]
Median	25.95 [a]	51.06 [a]	55.48 [a]	74.36 [a]
N	30	30	29	27
NFF				
Mean	***64.24	***102.94 [b]	***122.93 [a]	***108.53 [b]
Median	23.42 [a]	47.86 [a]	78.24 [a]	42.73 [a]
N	20	20	20	20
DIFFERENCE ***(FF-NFF)***				
Mean	*124.33	*132.75	131.98	*209.49
Median	2.53	3.20	-22.76	31.63

continued on following page

Table 5. Continued

	Variation -1 to 0	Variation -1 to 1	Variation -1 to 2	Variation -1 to 3
Panel E: Capital investment (%)				
FF				
Mean	***88.86 [b]	***335.75	***426.21 [c]	***217.82 [a]
Median	30.71 [a]	63.43 [a]	103.24 [a]	96.70 [a]
N	29	29	28	27
NFF				
Mean	***104.26 [c]	***71.47 [a]	***80.19 [a]	***106.89 [b]
Median	37.82 [a]	58.60 [a]	61.96 [a]	58.22 [a]
N	19	19	19	19
DIFFERENCE *(FF-NFF)*				
Mean	-15.40	**264.28	***346.02	*110.93
Median	-7.11	4.83	41.28	38.48

[a, b, c] denote significant at 1%. 5% and 10%, respectively.
***, **, * denote significant at 1%, 5% and 10%, respectively, using *bootstrapping*.

Table 6. Mean and median of ownership dispersion (Weak Criterion)

	Year -1	Year 0	Year 1	Year 2	Year 3
FF					
Mean	11.99%	48.01%	48.13%	48.05%	47.69%
Median	5.50%	45.58%	43.88%	45.78%	43.27%
N	28	28	25	25	23
NFF					
Mean	14.56%	45.77%	48.92%	45.53%	42.82%
Median	7.85%	44.70%	49.29%	42.33%	43.25%
N	23	23	23	23	23

points greater in non-family firms than in family firms. When the *bootstrap* method is used, positive and significant differences between family and non-family firms are observed in the mean industry-adjusted variation in *ROA* in 0 and 1, and in year 3, relative to the year prior to the IPO. However, when the measure is the *ROE* (panel B), the positive and significant differences are found in the mean variation in gross terms in years 0 and 1 relative to year -1. Moreover, when *cash flow* is calculated (panel C), there is a positive and significant difference in the gross mean variation but a negative one in the adjusted mean variation, and only in the year of the IPO relative to the year prior to it. Therefore, it cannot be stated that, regardless of the measure used, the post-IPO operating performance of family firms differs from that of non-family firms. While family firms are characterized as seeking to retain control in the hands of family owners, our findings seem to indicate that when they make the decision to go public, they are

Table 7. Mean and median variation in ownership dispersion (Weak Criterion)

	Variation Dispersion -1 to 0	Variation Dispersion -1 to 1	Variation Dispersion -1 to 2	Variation Dispersion -1 to 3
FF				
Mean	34.76%[a]	35.17% [a]	35.09% [a]	34.85% [a]
Median	37.97% [a]	37.02% [a]	36.76% [a]	34.97% [a]
N	27	25	25	23
NFF				
Mean	31.21% [a]	34.36% [a]	30.96% [a]	28.26% [a]
Median	28.41% [a]	33.58% [a]	29.73% [a]	27.79% [a]
N	23	23	23	23
DIFFERENCE (*FF-NFF*)				
Mean	3.55%	0.81%	4.13%	6.59%
Median	9.56%	3.44%	7.03%	7.18%

[a, b, c]denote significant at 1%, 5% and 10%, respectively.

governed by the same criteria as other firms. As shown in Table 6, there are no significant differences between these two types of firms in terms of the changes in ownership structure stemming from their introduction on the stock market.[7]

In summary, when family and non-family firms classified according to the *weak* criterion are compared, whether or not there are significant differences between family and non-family firms, and with different signs, depends on the measure used to assess operating performance and whether parametric or non-parametric tests are applied. Therefore, it cannot be stated that the characteristic features of family firms compared to non-family firms translate into different patterns in their post-IPO operating performance; as such, our results do not support hypothesis H2. Nor are significant differences observed between these two types of firms in terms of the change in ownership structure as a result of the aforementioned strategic decision. Thus, although family firms are characterized as seeking to retain control in the hands of family owners, our findings seem to indicate that when they make the decision to go public, they are governed by the same criteria as other firms, and they experience the same changes in their ownership structure and operating performance.

Analysis of the Robustness of the Results

When the family and non-family firm sub-samples classified according to the *strong* criterion are analysed, the results do not notably differ from those obtained with sub-samples classified according to the *weak* criterion. That is, the pre- and post-IPO operating performance levels show an upturn in the year prior to that event and a decline in the following three years. Regarding variations, they are not always significant, regardless of the measure and methodology used. In addition, significant differences in terms of median variations in operating performance experienced are not found by the two groups of firms, for any of the measures calculated or for any of the periods considered. When the *bootstrap* method is applied, significant differences appear between family and non-family firms in the mean variation they experience three years after the IPO, relative to the year prior to it. These differences are positive when the measure used is the gross and industry-adjusted *ROA*, but negative when the measure used is the gross and industry-adjusted *ROE*.

CONCLUSION

Previous empirical evidence from other markets has shown that companies suffer a decline in their operating performance levels after their flotation on the stock market. Part of the literature has attempted to explain this fact on the basis of the tenets of agency theory: going public entails greater ownership dispersion, which may in turn lead to higher agency costs by reducing monitoring and alignment of interests between owners and managers. The objective of this chapter has been to provide new evidence from the Spanish market; moreover, since the existing studies have not addressed the possible differences in IPO outcomes depending on whether or not firms are family-owned, the authors have attempted to contribute to filling this gap. Thus, the researchers have analysed the operating performance of Spanish IPO firms in the period 1994-2012, differentiating between family and non-family firms according to their ownership structure.

The results of the analysis carried out reflect that, when the sample is split into the family and non-family firm sub-samples according to two different classification criteria–one relatively *lax* and the other stricter–the results reveal similar operating performance to that shown by the full sample, there is an increase in operating performance in the years running up to the IPO, and a decline in the following three years. However, in this case, the specific profile of the operating performance levels is more influenced by the measure used to calculate said performance. Furthermore, when calculating variations in the family firm and non-family firm groups, although there is a post-IPO decline in these values, this decline is not always significant, regardless of the measure used.

In addition, when the sample is split into family and non-family firms according to the *strong* criterion, the mean and median values of industry-adjusted operating performance, when measured with *ROA* or *cash flow,* are significantly different from zero for some of the years under analysis. This indicates that firms' post-IPO operating performance is independent of the performance in the industry and, therefore, attributable to the event itself. However, when firms are classified according to the *weak* criterion, this result is found for family firms but not for non-family firms.

The results show that, under both classification criteria, non-family firms tend to suffer a greater decline in operating performance than family firms. This could be the consequence of the greater monitoring and alignment of interests between owners and managers in the family firm compared to the non-family firm, since one of the characteristic features of the former is its desire to retain control of the business within the family. However, these observed differences between family and non-family firms in terms of changes in post-IPO operating performance are not always statistically significant; the result depends on the criterion used to define a family firm, the measure used to assess operating performance, and whether parametric or non-parametric tests are applied. Therefore, this seems to indicate that when they make the decision to go public, family firms are governed by the same criteria as other firms, and they experience the same consequences.

In the period in which the significant decline in IPO firms' operating performance occurs, significant increases are registered in sales and capital investments. As such, the decline in performance cannot be explained by a fall in demand or lack of investment opportunities. However, the study reveals that going public effectively leads to a change in firms' ownership structure, which entails a significant increase in shareholder dispersion. That said, significant differences are not found between family and non-family firms with respect to this change in ownership structure.

As in any empirical study, the results are conditional on the sample size and sample period. In our case—and generally in studies concerning the Spanish market—the small sample size means that the results should be taken with caution. Future research could attempt to shed more light on this and other IPO-related phenomena, accounting for family firm typologies.

ACKNOWLEDGMENT

The authors thank the financial support of the University of Valencia (UV–INV–PRECOMP12–80505) and the Ministry of Economy and Competitiveness of Spain (ECO2016-76796-P).

REFERENCES

Agrawal, A., & Mandelker, G. (1990). Large shareholders and the monitoring of managers: The case of antitakeover charter amendments. *Journal of Financial and Quantitative Analysis*, *25*(2), 143–161. doi:10.2307/2330821

Álvarez, S., & González, V. (2005). Performance of Spanish firms going public: Windows of opportunity and the informative effect. *Applied Financial Economics*, *15*(18), 1283–1297. doi:10.1080/09603100500391479

Anderson, R. C., & Reeb, D. M. (2003). Founding-family ownership and firm performance: Evidence from the S&P 500. *The Journal of Finance*, *58*(3), 1301–1328. doi:10.1111/1540-6261.00567

Atinc, G., Kroll, M., & Walters, B. (2017). Detrimental effects of post-IPO corporate governance changes: The case of young entrepreneurial firms. *Management Decision*, *55*(2), 234–247. doi:10.1108/MD-02-2016-0084

Barber, B. M., & Lyon, J. D. (1996). Detecting abnormal operating performance: The empirical power of specification of test-statistics. *Journal of Financial Economics*, *41*(3), 359–399. doi:10.1016/0304-405X(96)84701-5

Barontini, R., & Caprio, L. (2006). The effect of family control on firm value and performance: Evidence from continental Europe. *European Financial Management*, *12*(5), 689–723. doi:10.1111/j.1468-036X.2006.00273.x

Berle, A. & Means, G. (1932). *The modern corporation and private property*. Nueva York: McMillan.

Cai, J., & Wei, K. C. (1997). The investment and operating performance of Japanese initial public offerings. *Pacific-Basin Finance Journal*, *5*(4), 289–417. doi:10.1016/S0927-538X(97)00021-8

Chahine, S., & Goergen, M. (2013). The effects of management-board ties on IPO performance. *Journal of Corporate Finance*, *21*, 153–179. doi:10.1016/j.jcorpfin.2013.02.001

Daily, C. M., & Dollinger, M. J. (1992). An empirical examination of ownership structure and family and professionally managed firms. *Family Business Review*, *5*(2), 117–136. doi:10.1111/j.1741-6248.1992.00117.x

Duréndez, A., García-Pérez-de-Lema, D., & Mariño, T. (2015). The behaviour of family firms in relation to the Alternative Stock Market (MAB): Empirical evidence. *Spanish Journal of Finance and Accounting*, *44*(2), 208–237.

Efron, B. (1982). *The jackknife, bootstrap, and other resampling plans. Society for industrial and Applied Mathematics monograph 38*. CBMS-NSF. doi:10.1137/1.9781611970319

Fama, E., & Jensen, M. (1983a). Separation of ownership and control. *The Journal of Law & Economics*, *26*(2), 301–325. doi:10.1086/467037

Fama, E., & Jensen, M. (1983b). Agency problems and residual claims. *The Journal of Law & Economics*, *26*(2), 327–349. doi:10.1086/467038

Farinós, J. E., García, C. J., & Ibáñez, A. M. (2007). Operating and stock market performance of state-owned enterprise privatizations: The Spanish experience. *International Review of Financial Analysis*, *16*(4), 367–389. doi:10.1016/j.irfa.2007.01.001

Ferreira, J. V. (2008). Determinants of performance of closely-held (family) firms after going public: The role of the ownership structure, economy, changes in top management, partial sale, equity concentration after the IPO and shareholders in management. *Corporate Ownership & Control*, *5*(2), 55–67. doi:10.22495/cocv5i2p5

Ferreira, J. V. (2016). *The Performance of Family Firms after Going Public*. Working paper available at SSRN: https://ssrn.com/abstract=2906411

Galve, C., & Salas, V. (1993). Propiedad y resultados de la gran empresa española. *Investigacion Economica*, *17*(2), 207–238.

Galve, C., & Salas, V. (2003). *La empresa familiar en España. Fundamentos económicos y resultados*. Bilbao: Fundación BBVA.

Galve, C., & Salas, V. (2011). ¿Determina la propiedad familiar diferencias en las relaciones entre preferencias, comportamiento y resultados en las empresas españolas cotizadas? *Revista de Economía Aplicada*, *19*(57), 5–34.

Harvey, S. (1999). Owner as a manager, extended horizons and the family firm. *International Journal of the Economics of Business*, *6*(1), 41–55. doi:10.1080/13571519984304

Jain, B. A., & Kini, O. (1994). The post-issue operating performance of IPO firms. *The Journal of Finance*, *49*(5), 1699–1726. doi:10.1111/j.1540-6261.1994.tb04778.x

Jensen, M. C., & Meckling, W. (1976). Theory of the firm: Managerial behavior, agency costs and ownership structure. *Journal of Financial Economics*, *3*(4), 305–360. doi:10.1016/0304-405X(76)90026-X

Kartika, R. (2012). *Family ownership and post-IPO performance: evidence in Malaysia* (Unpublished doctoral dissertation). Universiti Utara, Malaysia.

Khurshed, A., Paleari, S., & Vismara, S. (2005). *The Operating Performance of Initial Public Offerings: The UK Experience*. Università di Bergamo Working Paper. Available at SSRN: https://ssrn.com/abstract=439240 or doi:10.2139srn.439240

Kim, K. A., Kitsabunnarat, P., & Nofsinger, J. R. (2004). Ownership and operating performance in an emerging market: Evidence from Thai IPO firms. *Journal of Corporate Finance, 10*(3), 355–381. doi:10.1016/S0929-1199(02)00019-6

Leech, D., & Leahy, J. (1991). Ownership structure, control type classifications and the performance of large British companies. *The Economical Journal, 101*, 1418–1437.

Lemmon, M., & Lins, K. (2003). Ownership Structure, Corporate Governance, and Firm Value: Evidence from the East Asian Financial Crisis. *The Journal of Finance, 58*(4), 1445–1468. doi:10.1111/1540-6261.00573

Loughran, T., & Ritter, J. R. (1997). The operating performance of firms conducting seasoned equity offerings. *The Journal of Finance, 52*(5), 1823–1850. doi:10.1111/j.1540-6261.1997.tb02743.x

Maury, B. (2006). Family ownership and firm performance: Empirical evidence from Western European corporations. *Journal of Corporate Finance, 12*(2), 321–341. doi:10.1016/j.jcorpfin.2005.02.002

Mazzola, P., & Marchisio, G. (2002). The role of going public in family businesses' long-lasting growth: A study of Italian IPOs. *Family Business Review, 15*(2), 133–148. doi:10.1111/j.1741-6248.2002.00133.x

McConaughy, D. L., Matthews, C., & Fialko, A. (2001). Founding family controlled firms: Performance, risk and value. *Journal of Small Business Management, 39*(1), 31–49. doi:10.1111/0447-2778.00004

McConaughy, D. L., Walker, M., Henderson, G. V. Jr, & Mishra, C. S. (1998). Founding family controlled firms: Efficiency and value. *Review of Financial Economics, 7*(1), 1–19. doi:10.1016/S1058-3300(99)80142-6

Menéndez-Requejo, S. (2006). Ownership structure and firm performance: evidence from Spanish family firms. In P. Z. Poutziouris, K. X. Smyrnios, & S. B. Klein (Eds.), *Handbook of Research on Family Business* (pp. 575–593). Edward Elgar Publishing Limited.

Mikkelson, W. H., Partch, M. M., & Shah, K. (1997). Ownership and operating performance of companies that go public. *Journal of Financial Economics, 44*(3), 281–307. doi:10.1016/S0304-405X(97)00006-8

Mudambi, R., & Nicosia, C. (1998). Ownership structure and firm performance: Evidence from the UK financial services industry. *Applied Financial Economics, 8*(2), 175–180. doi:10.1080/096031098333159

Pagano, M., Panetta, F., & Zingales, L. (1998). Why do companies go public? An empirical analysis. *The Journal of Finance, 53*(1), 27–64. doi:10.1111/0022-1082.25448

Pereira, T., & Sousa, M. (2017). Is there still a Berlin Wall in the post-issue operating performance of European IPOs? *International Journal of Finance & Economics, 22*(2), 139–158. doi:10.1002/ijfe.1573

Sacristán, M., & Gómez, S. (2006). Family ownership, corporate governance and firm value: evidence from the Spanish market. In P. Z. Poutziouris, K. X. Smyrnios, & S. B. Klein (Eds.), *Handbook of Research on Family Business* (pp. 593–613). Edward Elgar Publishing Limited.

Shleifer, A., & Vishny, R. (1986). Large shareholders and corporate control. *Journal of Political Economy*, *94*(3, Part 1), 461–488. doi:10.1086/261385

Sraer, D., & Thesmar, D. (2007). Performance and behaviour of family firms: Evidence from the French stock market. *Journal of the European Economic Association*, *5*(4), 709–751. doi:10.1162/JEEA.2007.5.4.709

Steiger, T., Duller, C., & Hiebl, M. R. W. (2015). No consensus in sight: An analysis of ten years of family business definitions in empirical research studies. *Journal of Enterprising Culture*, *23*(01), 36. doi:10.1142/S0218495815500028

Villalonga, B., & Amit, R. (2006). How do family ownership, control and management affect firm value? *Journal of Financial Economics*, *80*(2), 385–417. doi:10.1016/j.jfineco.2004.12.005

Wang, C. (2005). Ownership and operating performance of Chinese IPOs. *Journal of Banking & Finance*, *29*(7), 1835–1856. doi:10.1016/j.jbankfin.2004.07.003

Wehrens, R., Putter, H., & Buydens, L. M. (2000). The bootstrap: A tutorial. *Chemometrics and Intelligent Laboratory Systems*, *50*(1), 35–53. doi:10.1016/S0169-7439(00)00102-7

Westhead, P., & Cowling, M. (1997). Performance contrasts between family and non-family unquoted companies in the UK. *International Journal of Entrepreneurial Behaviour & Research*, *3*(1), 30–52. doi:10.1108/13552559710170892

ADDITIONAL READING

Álvarez-Otero, S., & López-Iturriaga, F. J. (2018). Does corporate governance affect the valuation of Spanish IPOs? The role of ownership structure and the board of directors. *Spanish Journal of Finance and Accounting. Revista Española de Financiación y Contabilidad*, *47*(2), 214–241. doi:10.1080/02102412.2018.1429556

Chrisman, J. J., Chua, J. H., & Litz, R. (2004). Comparing the agency costs of family and non-family firms: Conceptual issues and exploratory evidence. *Entrepreneurship Theory and Practice*, *28*(4), 335–354. doi:10.1111/j.1540-6520.2004.00049.x

Dawson, A., & Mussolino, D. (2014). Exploring what makes family firms different: Discrete or overlapping constructs in the literature? *Journal of Family Business Strategy*, *5*(2), 169–183. doi:10.1016/j.jfbs.2013.11.004

Pindado, J., & Requejo, I. (2015). Family Business Performance from a Governance Perspective: A Review of Empirical Research. *International Journal of Management Reviews*, *17*(3), 279–311. doi:10.1111/ijmr.12040

Poutziouris, P. Z., Smyrnios, K. X., & Klein, S. B. (Eds.), *Handbook of Research on Family Business*. Edward Elgar Publishing Limited. doi:10.4337/9781847204394

Röell, A. (1996). The decision to go public: An overview. *European Economic Review*, *40*(3-5), 1071–1081. doi:10.1016/0014-2921(95)00114-X

Rydqvist, K., & Hoghölm, K. (1995). Going public in the 1980s: Evidence from Sweden. *European Financial Management*, *1*(3), 287–315. doi:10.1111/j.1468-036X.1995.tb00021.x

Steiger, T., Duller, C., & Hiebl, M. R. W. (2015). No consensus in sight: An analysis of ten years of family business definitions in empirical research studies. *Journal of Enterprising Culture*, *23*(1), 25–62. doi:10.1142/S0218495815500028

Yu, A., Lumpkin, G. T., Sorenson, R. L., & Brigham, K. H. (2012). The landscape of family business outcomes: A summary and numerical taxonomy of dependent variables. *Family Business Review*, *25*(1), 35–57. doi:10.1177/0894486511430329

KEY TERMS AND DEFINITIONS

Agency Costs: Costs that occur in an organization as a result of a conflict of interests between the different groups (stakeholders) that participate in it.

Agency Theory: Theory used to explain the relationships between the different groups (stakeholders) that participate in an organization.

Family Firm: A firm in which a family has the control on the business decision making.

Initial Public Offering (IPO): A common way to go public, that is, to be a listed company in a stock market, through an offer of equity to the public.

Operating Performance: The measure of the efficiency of a company's assets in the achieving results.

Ownership Structure: It is the structure that define how the ownership and control of a company is distributed.

Stakeholder: A party that has an interest in a company and can either affect or be affected by the business, like shareholders, employees, customers and suppliers.

Stock Market: A market in which a company's securities can be bought and sold at a market price after the issuance.

ENDNOTES

1. In this sense, Duréndez *et al.* (2015) find that under certain circumstances family firms are more reluctant than non-family firms to go public into the Spanish Alternative Stock Market (MAB), due to their conservatism and resistance to change.
2. IPO prospectuses from before the second half of 1998 are not available.
3. Galve & Salas (2011) refer only to a family group.
4. The choice of this time horizon for the analysis was determined by the availability of data in the SABI database at the time of the data collection.

5 As there are firms that go public without meeting the size or earnings requirements stipulated by the regulations, the criterion used to select the control sample is firm size, measured as total assets, equal to or greater than that of the smallest firm in the group that went public in the period under analysis. Firms have been also distinguished according to the type of financial statements they present.

6 Specifically, a similar procedure to that in Wehrens *et al.* (2000) is followed.

7 Likewise, Table 5 shows no significant differences between family and non-family firms in terms of median increases in sales and capital investment after going public.

Chapter 10
Keys to the Survival of the Family Firm:
Long-Lived Family Firms

César Camisón
University of Valencia, Spain

José Antonio Moreno
EDEM University, Spain

ABSTRACT

The purpose of this research is to carry out an in-depth exploration of the causes of the family firm's success over short and long term, analysing which capabilities are the most valuable sources of sustainable competitive advantage in every time horizon. The results confirm only functional capabilities have a positive and significant effect on short-term economic performance, whereas dynamic capabilities are the only ones that have a positive and significant impact on long-term economic performance.

INTRODUCTION

Family firm research has attracted a great deal of interest due to the importance of this type of business in the worldwide economy. In fact, they are the most common form of organization among small and medium-sized enterprises (Gersick et al., 1997; Westhead & Howorth, 2007), and they represent the majority of businesses in many countries (Ifera, 2003). While their crucial role in global wealth creation makes these firms an important focus of study, their long-term survival is made more difficult by certain aspects that are intrinsic to family firms. However, some have managed to sustain themselves over several generations, achieving an enviable long-term success (Miller & Le Breton-Miller, 2005). There is, in fact, a debate in the literature about the real internal causes of family firm competitiveness, in both the short and long term.

DOI: 10.4018/978-1-7998-1655-3.ch010

The matter of how firms create value cannot be analysed in isolation from how they create and sustain competitive advantages. This is one of the main issues that the field of strategic management has attempted to resolve (Teece, Pisano & Shuen, 1997). Internal analysis of the firm is key to shedding light on how it creates value; indeed, the resource-based view, along with subsequent related developments such as the dynamic capabilities view (Teece et al., 1997) have proven critical to gaining an understanding of this value creation (Barney, 1997). The dynamic capabilities view analyses how the firm's resources are generated, renewed and combined to yield new capabilities that can create value over time (Teece et al., 1997). These theories are therefore crucial to understanding the sources of family firms' competitiveness (Chirico & Salvato, 2008). In fact, these approaches have given rise to the concept of *familiness*, which captures how the specific interaction between the family and the business produces its specific set of resources and capabilities (Habbershon & Williams, 1999). In turn, these resources and capabilities can contribute positively or negatively to the family firm's sources of competitive advantage (Habbershon et al., 2003; Habbershon, 2006).

The purpose of this research is to carry out an in-depth exploration of the causes of the family firm's success over different time horizons, analysing which capabilities are key to its development. Specifically, the objective is to determine the different short-and long-term effects of the family firms' capabilities, in order to identify the most valuable sources of sustainable competitive advantage. To that end, the study compares the relative importance of the three types of business capabilities: functional, coordination and cohesion, and dynamic.

The wide variety of family firm definitions in the academic literature has given rise to a broad range of concepts and measures (Miller et al., 2007; Sharma et al., 1996). In particular, Handler (1989) identified three basic dimensions underlying the definitions of the family firm: the family having an ownership interest; the family and the business being considered interdependent subsystems; and the desire for continuity through intergenerational transfer. Based on these dimensions, Shanker & Astrachan (1996) classify family firms according to three concepts—broad, middle and narrow definitions—referring to an increasing level of family involvement in the organization. Influential authors such as Gallo et al. (2004) and Chua et al. (1999) argue that when it comes to defining the concept of a family firm it is more reasonable to use broad definitions that are inclusive, rather than exclusive ones. This criterion is also applied in other works (e.g., Gallo, Tàpies & Cappuyns, 2004; Dibrell & Moeller, 2011; Neubaum, Dibrell, & Craig, 2012). Along the same lines, this study takes the position that a family firm is one in which majority ownership and control of strategic decisions lie with the founder or his/her descendants; there must be family capital in the firm's capital structure and the family must hold a majority of the voting capital, endowing family members with sufficient power over the firm to influence and determine the strategy.

Following this introduction, the rest of this chapter is structured in three additional sections. The first section presents the theoretical framework and the hypotheses to be tested, analysing the different types of firm capabilities that the literature identifies as sources of competitive advantage, and how these affect performance in both the short and long term. The second section presents the methodological considerations that have guided the empirical research. The third section details the results of the empirical analysis carried out to test the hypotheses. Finally, the fourth section explains the main conclusions drawn from the analysis of the results, notes the limitations of the study and suggests future lines of research.

THEORETICAL FRAMEWORK AND HYPOTHESES

The resource-based view (RBV) (Barney, 1991, 1997; Amit & Schoemaker, 1993; Peteraf, 1993; Barney et al., 2001) emphasizes the fact that there are marked differences between firms that make them unique entities capable of achieving a competitive advantage over their competitors. In particular, the RBV points out that firms can achieve a sustainable competitive advantage through its resources and capabilities, which should have the attributes of being valuable, rare, inimitable and non-substitutable (Barney 1991; Teece et al. 1997). The availability and accumulation of distinctive competences will be key to defining the firm's strategy, achieving a sustainable competitive advantage and generating revenue.

Complementary to the RBV, the dynamic capabilities view (DCV) (Nelson & Winter, 1982; Dosi, 1982; Teece, 1986; Dosi et al., eds. 1988; Nelson, 1991, 1995; Mahoney & Pandian, 1992; Winter, 1995; Helfat, 1997; Teece et al., 1990, 1997; Teece & Pisano, 1998; Eisenhardt & Martin, 2000) enables an analysis from a more dynamic perspective; this approach highlights innovation as a key strategic action whereby firms can sustain their competitive advantage by reconfiguring their base of resources and capabilities. Rather than focusing on the resources and capabilities available at any given time, the DCV centres on the process of generating new capabilities, emphasizing the importance of the asset development process that helps sustain and renew the competitive advantage.

These approaches are very useful for identifying the resources and capabilities that make family firms unique and that help to differentiate between family and non-family firms (Chrisman, Chua, & Sharma, 2005). This approach has yielded one of the most fruitful lines of family firm analysis: *familiness*. This concept serves to define the specific resources and capabilities of the family firm that stem from the family-business interaction, in turn resulting from the owning family's involvement in the business (its capital, governance structure and management system). In other words, this concept refers to the interactions between the systems comprised of the family as a whole, individual family members, and the business (Habbershon & Williams, 1999). This term therefore describes the availability and development of unique resources created within family firms as a result of the interaction between the business and the family (Habbershon & Williams, 1999; Cabrera et al., 2001).

When managed efficiently, these resources can create a competitive advantage and improve performance (Hitt et al., 2001; Sirmon & Hitt, 2003). These resources and capabilities include the organizational culture; the reputation of the firm based on the trajectory of the family over generations; its long-term orientation; the increased level of trust between family members and stakeholders; and the greater willingness to share information among members of the company, among others (Whiteside, Aronoff & Ward, 1993; Barney et al., 2002; Miller & Le Breton-Miller, 2005; Gallo & Amat, 2003; Audretsch, Hülsbeck, & Lehmann, 2013).

However, not all the specific aspects of family firms are positive. Indeed, some of them can even adversely affect firm performance, the acquisition of resources or the development of a competitive advantage: for example, the inability to dismiss certain employees or get rid of some resources; the difficulties of maintaining strong social bonds outside of the family circle; or certain aspects of family firm culture or structure (Sirmon & Hitt, 2003; Sharma & Manikutty, 2005; Kellermanns, 2005). Therefore, in the case of the family firm, the RBV and the DCV can help to analyse how the possession of certain resources, such as those related to *familiness*, may contribute to gaining a competitive advantage, and how these resources can be developed through family involvement (Chrisman, Chua & Sharma, 2005).

Resources are all the assets that the company owns and controls; they differ from capabilities in that they are individual resources and can be characterized as stock. While resources that are considered strategic assets can be a source of competitive advantage, such resources tend not to persist over time and thus are not a source of *sustainable* competitive advantage (Wang & Ahmed, 2007). Ketchen et al. (2007) stress that, in fact, resources will only have value for firms when they develop the appropriate capabilities to be able to use and manage those resources in order to improve their performance. Resources are the basis for capability building and development (Wang & Ahmed, 2007). Thus, the distinctive critical characteristics that will result in a competitive advantage for the firm can be found in different types of capabilities.

One of the most interesting, clear and consistent criteria for classifying distinctive capabilities is based on the idea that they are structured hierarchically. As such, any criterion used to classify capabilities should take this hierarchy into account (Grant, 1991; Collis, 1991; Teece et al., 1994; Fuchs, Mifflin, Miller & Whitney, 2000; Lawson & Samson, 2001). Thus, firm capabilities can be classified as follows:

1. The first level contains the **functional or static capabilities**, associated with the different functional activities of the firm. They can thus be identified according to the standard classification of the different functional activities of the firm (Snow & Hrebiniak, 1980); examples include marketing, operations or finance. This type of capabilities reflects the use of management capabilities in different parts of the value chain (Camisón, 2005). This first level includes the least versatile capabilities, related to the operation and management of tangible resources.

According to Camisón Zornoza and Monfort-Mir (eds., 2012), marketing capabilities include skills in interacting with agents external to the firm, such as customers or distributors. They also include all the skills that enable the design and implementation of the various marketing policies: namely, the ability to develop communication campaigns; aptitude in selecting target markets; ability to set prices; sales and distribution skills; and quality post-sale customer service, among others. Also included here is the ability to create a reputation for the firm that translates into a prestigious, widely-recognized company image and brand, and a satisfied customer base. With respect to production capabilities, these refer to the firm's ability to compete on costs, product differentiation, quality, time and flexibility. They can all be considered a source of success since a competitive position can be built on either the company's ability to specialize or its ability to diversify its product offer. Thus, it can harness vertical integration strategies to gain a competitive advantage, seeking economies of scale, or implement decentralized production strategies, seeking economies of scope. With respect to financial capabilities, they refer to the capabilities in managing the firm's capital, which include financial reputation; the trust and information networks with financial intermediaries that may give rise to, among others, a reduced cost of capital, better financial terms, or an increase in the organization's financial potential; skill in cost-containment and reduction; capacity for reducing the cost of stock; and investment management know-how. These capabilities are also relevant because they determine the attributes incorporated into the product and into the intangible assets. Moreover, they are key to laying the foundations for the appropriate management of divergences between shareholders and creditors seeking to exercise their rights over the company, which also has an effect on the process of accumulating intangible assets. The capital allocation mechanisms that underlie firms' ownership structure support the decisions that determine the volume and composition of the available productive resources, as well as the internal and external activities and processes involved in production and sales.

2. The second level contains **coordination and cohesion capabilities or interfunctional coordination capabilities.** These capabilities include those related to the integration of functional activities and organizational cohesion. They help to create an appropriate environment for the efficient activation and management of functional capabilities (Kogut & Zander, 1996). Camisón (2005), who also frames coordination capabilities as second-level capabilities, suggests that managerial and organizational capabilities should be included to support the content of coordination and cohesion capabilities .

Managerial capabilities include the skills needed to create and communicate a strategic vision, as well as to identify and explore asymmetries in strategic factor markets. They are also key to developing and managing the other capabilities (Westley & Mintzberg, 1989; Lado, Boyd & Wright, 1992; Camisón & Boronat, 2004). Furthermore, organizational capabilities include having a mission and culture that reinforces cooperation, commitment and the generation of ideas that can lead to innovations (Lado, Boyd & Wright, 1992; Camisón & Boronat, 2004). Specifically, there are two components that make up managerial capabilities: specialized, technical know-how relating to management tasks; and a more cognitive component, reflecting the manager's personal attributes, personality profile and values (Nonaka & Konno, 1998: 42).

Therefore, according to Camisón (2005), this conceptualization includes: (i) the ability to solve problems that call for creativity and creation of opportunities in the allocation of resources; (ii) the manager's accumulated experience in the field and decision-making expertise; (iii) the manager's influence over the company due to his/her position of power; (iv) his/her leadership ability, inspiring other employees to fulfil the company mission by working collectively; (v) the creation of an environment that encourages change and learning, guiding other employees in developing a creative, innovative spirit.

These skills thus play an essential role in firm competitiveness by contributing to employee talent development and collaborative work (Osbaldeston & Barham, 1992). They help transform resources and capabilities in order to generate value (Lado et al., 1992). Thanks to their experience and know-how, managers can interpret environmental signals to create opportunities. The value of these managerial capabilities stems from a number of factors: they are tacit, rare, complex to construct, and based on a complex set of interactions with key stakeholders, thus making them difficult to imitate (Castanias & Helfat, 1991).

With regard to organizational capabilities, these refer to the culture and routines that foster employees' emotional commitment to the organization, their acceptance of and involvement in the strategy, mission and values of the company, interactions between individuals and teamwork, and the creation of an organizational culture that promotes cohesion (Camisón, 2005). It should also be a culture that fosters an orientation towards quality and encourages the participation of all involved. Various organizational design mechanisms should also be used to build this participatory culture, in terms of defining roles, organizing teamwork, and setting up communication channels to ensure that information flows in all directions within the company. Therefore, these capabilities are built on the basis of social interactions within the organization; as such, they are idiosyncratic and difficult to imitate. For these reasons, they are also key to the success of the firm.

3. The third level contains the **dynamic capabilities.** These capabilities enable the renewal of the firm's resources and capabilities, as well as the construction, renewal, and management of different capabilities (Henderson & Cockburn, 1994; Kogut & Zander, 1992; Lawson & Samson, 2001; Fuchs et al., 2000). They are thus sometimes referred to as higher-order integration capabilities (Lawson & Samson, 2001; Fuchs et al., 2000). Dynamic capabilities include those related to change, knowledge management and development, learning and innovation. These capabilities highlight the importance of strategic management in responding to environmental changes and in developing new value-creating competencies by exploring different combinations of resources and capabilities (Pisano, 1994; Grant, 1996).

This type of capabilities is precisely what will enable the firm's renewal of its existing resources and capabilities (Kogut & Zander, 1992; Henderson & Cockburn, 1994), since it reflects the ability to build, renew and manage multiple capabilities. Capability building and renewal are both fundamental to the firm's competitive advantage.

These dynamic capabilities refer to competences in knowledge management and development as well as in learning. Knowledge management and development encompasses a range of dimensions concerning the capabilities and skills relating to the knowledge management system, the internal capacity for increasing the stock of knowledge, capabilities and skills in the transfer and application of knowledge, and lastly, a dimension relating to the stock of knowledge. The dimensions that relate to learning competences reflect leadership's commitment to change and learning, a culture of innovation and learning, the development of competences, and the degree to which organizational design is open to learning. The measurement scales used in this study (Camisón, 2002a) are based on items extracted from a wide range of relevant work in the field (Goh & Richards, 1997; Eisenhardt & Brown, 1998; Helfat & Raubitschek, 2000; Schulz, 2001; Takeishi, 2001).

According to the literature, dynamic capabilities are those related to sustaining a long-term competitive advantage (Teece, 2007). Dynamic capabilities act as catalysts in the processes of generating and renewing the firm's other distinctive capabilities (p.78). In terms of Schumpeterian competition, this enables the firm to sustain and renew its competitive advantage of imitation. Dynamic capabilities emphasize the key role of strategic management in exploring new combinations of resources and capabilities to generate new value-creating competencies, as well as in consistently responding to changing environmental situations (Pisano, 1994; Grant, 1996).

The capabilities outlined above are key to achieving and sustaining a competitive advantage (Penrose 1959; Rothwell, 1977; Dosi 1988a,b; Dierickx & Cool, 1989; Nelson & Winter, 1982; Pavitt, 1991; Dosi & Marengo, 1993). In addition, although some studies state that there is a cost involved in managing capabilities (Helfat et al., 2007), in general, the theoretical and empirical evidence tends to support the idea that these capabilities usually improve firm performance, positively affecting performance by increasing revenue or reducing costs (Wernerfelt, 1984; Barney, 1991; Peteraf, 1993; Maijoor & Witteloostuijn, 1996; Miller & Shamsie, 1996; Makadok, 1999; Combs & Ketchen, 1999; Yeoth & Roth, 1999; Henderson & Cool, 2003; Barua et al., 2004; Wang & Ang, 2004; Newbert, 2007; Arend & Bromiley, 2009). In fact, the RBV points out that the heterogeneous distribution of capabilities across firms is the cause of differences in their performance (Peteraf, 1993; Felin et al., 2012).

However, not all types of capabilities have the same impact when it comes to achieving a competitive advantage and improving organizational performance (Hoopes & Madsen, 2008; Leiblein & Madsen, 2009; Drnevich & Kriauciunas, 2011). Thus, while capabilities that allow existing resources and capabilities to be harnessed and exploited are often seen as more important for achieving better performance in the short term, those that enable the exploration of new resources and capabilities are considered crucial for improving performance over the long term.

The authors Dosi, Teece and Winter (1992) proposed a distinction between static and dynamic capabilities. Similarly, Lado, Boyd and Wright (1992), albeit using different terminology, addressed this idea of dynamic capabilities and long-term renewal; they denote these capabilities "transformation-based competencies". Henderson and Cockburn (1994) also allude to this distinction when they put forward the importance of architectural competence. Whereas static capabilities represent the organizational skills required for the distinctive performance of tasks that have already been developed, dynamic capabilities are understood as the ability of the organization to integrate, build, adapt and reconfigure its endowment of resources and capabilities in order to respond to changes in the environment, adjust to the market or generate change. They are thus explicitly geared towards learning and the development of new products and processes (Teece et al., 1994; Teece, Pisano & Shuen, 1997; Eisenhardt & Martin. 2000). As such, dynamic capabilities emphasize the key role of strategic management in exploring new combinations of resources and capabilities to generate new capabilities, as well as in responding to changing environmental situations (Grant, 1996).

In the same vein, but using alternative nomenclature, some studies refer to ordinary capabilities and dynamic capabilities (Drnevich & Kriauciunas, 2011). In this regard, ordinary capabilities can be seen as those that allow the firm to "make a living" in the short term (Winter, 2003); on the other hand, dynamic capabilities are those that allow ordinary capabilities to be developed, created or modified (Collis, 1994; Dosi, Nelson & Winter, 2000; Winter, 2003; Hoopes & Madsen, 2008).

Ordinary capabilities tend to contribute to improving the quality of processes and products, to increasing revenues or to reducing costs associated with the provision of services, which can boost firm performance both directly and indirectly (Porter, 1980; 1985; Barney 1991; Williamson, 1991; Brush & Artz, 1999; Peng & York, 2001; Kaleka, 2002; Zhu & Kraemer, 2002; Barua et al., 2004; Piccoli & Ives, 2005; Lai et al., 2008; Makadok, 2010).

On the other hand, dynamic capabilities are recognized as a source of sustainable competitive advantage and crucial to long-term financial performance (Blyler & Coff, 2003; Hsu & Wang, 2010; Teece et al., 1997; Schenkel & Teigland, 2016). The DCV highlights the strategic value of dynamic capabilities as catalysts in the processes of generation and renewal of distinctive capabilities (Nelson & Winter, 1982; Dosi, 1982; Teece, 1986; Dosi et al., eds. 1988; Nelson, 1991, 1995; Mahoney & Pandian, 1992; Winter, 1995; Helfat, 1997; Teece et al., 1990, 1997; Teece & Pisano, 1998; Eisenhardt & Martín, 2000). The capabilities related to innovation and the regeneration and strengthening of firm capabilities help the firm adapt to external factors, ensuring its long-term competitiveness (Mascarenhas et al., 1998).

Thus, dynamic capabilities (also known as third-order capabilities) are targeted at the constant renewal and reconfiguration of both resources and capabilities, in order to recognize and respond to threats and opportunities in the business environment (Eisenhard & Martin, 2000; Drnevich & Kriauciunas, 2011). As such, they are not just a sub-set of the firm's capabilities, they are those that will ultimately determine its long-term performance (Collis, 1994; Teece et al. 1997; Wang & Ahmed, 2007).

These capabilities can boost revenue and performance by enabling the identification of opportunities in the business environment and the response to these opportunities through the development of new processes, products and/or services (Makadok, 2001, 2010; Zou, Fang & Zhao, 2003; Chmielewski & Paladino, 2007) or by improving the speed, efficiency, and effectiveness of responses to changes in the environment (Hitt et al., 2001; Chmielewski & Paladino, 2007; Tallon, 2008).

In this regard, the empirical evidence indicates that these capabilities play an essential role in firms' long-term survival and success. Given their importance in the long run, there are a large number of longitudinal studies on dynamic capabilities (Athreye, 2005; Helfat, 1997; Majumdar, 1999; Pisano, 2000; Rindova & Kotha, 2001; Lampel & Shamsie, 2003), as noted by Wang & Ahmed, 2007. Thus, some longitudinal studies conclude that the capabilities relating to absorbing new information, internal adaptation and innovation are key to long-term survival and business success (Rindova & Kotha, 2001; Lampel & Shamsie, 2003).

Firms' competitiveness can be explained by both their ability to use their existing capabilities and their talent for exploring new combinations of resources and capabilities (Wernerfelt, 1984; Madhok, 1997) reflected in their dynamic capabilities, though it is necessary to strike a balance between the two (Levinthal & March, 1993). The development of new resources and capabilities is a lengthy process (Hamel & Prahalad, 1994) and so the effects of dynamic capabilities will be seen over the long term. Conversely, the effects of functional and cohesion capabilities should be evident in the short term, enabling the firm to achieve day-to-day success by doing what it knows works regarding its principal activity. Coordination and cohesion capabilities thus underpin the functional capabilities; these so-called second-order capabilities facilitate the integration of functional capabilities in order to ensure their coordinated action. It can therefore be assumed that their effects should also emerge in the short term, along with those of the functional capabilities.

Teece, Pisano & Shuen (1997) argued that the most valuable capabilities for firm success are dynamic capabilities. It is precisely the imbalance created by the new combinations and renewal of resources and capabilities that can generate long-term advantages. Teece (2007) argues that operational capabilities, insofar as they relate to technical aspects, can help achieve positive performance in a short time frame, but if the company does not develop dynamic capabilities, the positive effect will not extend past the short term. Operational capabilities are those that enable the firm to sell its current products to its current customers. Without them, the firm cannot secure a return on the activities it carries out (Winter, 2003). However, dynamic capabilities are necessary for the firm to generate value in the long term. Dynamic capabilities link management's ability to sense opportunities and address threats with the ability to combine and reconfigure the firm's resources and capabilities.

In light of the above discussion of the literature, the first hypotheses of this thesis can be proposed as follows:

H1. Functional capabilities are positively related to family firm performance in the short term.
H2. Coordination and cohesion capabilities are positively related to family firm performance in the short term.
H3. Dynamic capabilities are positively related to family firm performance over the long term.

The above hypotheses are represented in Figures 1 and 2.

Figure 1. Model 1: influence of the family firm's portfolio of capabilities on its short-term performance

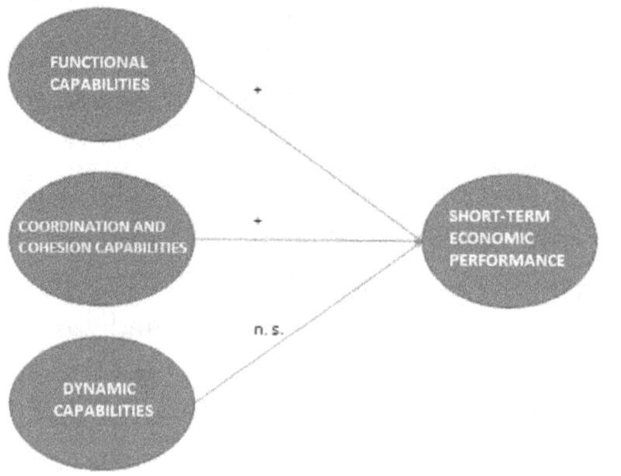

Figure 2. Model 2: influence of the family firm's portfolio of capabilities on its long-term performance

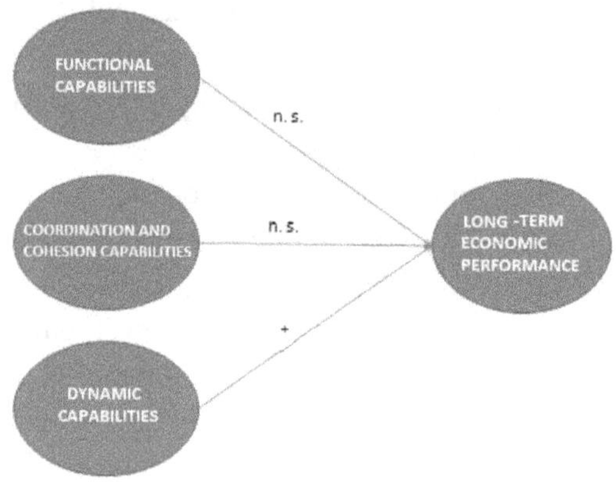

METHODOLOGY OF THE EMPIRICAL RESEARCH

Database

The empirical research is based on a database of 748 family firms in the Spanish tourism sector. The sample was selected according to information provided in the Central Companies Directory. A random stratified sampling procedure was used, with proportional allocation criteria based on size and activity. The component units of the sample were identified by checking whether the selected firm was included in the Sistema de Análisis de Balances Ibérico (SABI) database, since this source provides complete management information on companies. For companies in the sample not included in SABI, the directories of various sectoral associations and public registers were consulted; also, certain data were obtained from the information that the hotels provided online, (on their own website, on the website of the chain or group, or on other websites that referred to them) or from the information offered by the Spanish Yellow Pages and Dun & Bradstreet.

In terms of size, the sample was distributed as follows: 62.71% micro-enterprises (of which 54.8% were micro-enterprises with at least one salaried employee along with the owner, and another 7.9% operating on a self-employed basis); 25.22% small enterprises, 9.62% medium-sized enterprises and 2.45% large enterprises. In terms of the type of tourist activity carried out, 30.03% were accommodation providers, 37.88% were food and beverage companies, almost 11% were intermediaries (travel agencies, tour operators, etc.), 3.93% were transport organizations, and 17.17% represented the so-called complementary offer .

Data were collected using a questionnaire—a commonly-used tool in studies of competitiveness (Camisón, 1997, 2001)—administered through personal interviews. All this fieldwork was carried out by a company specializing in market research, in close collaboration with the research team responsible for the project. This method offers significant advantages, especially in a case with the complexity and characteristics of the present study, which sought a high response rate, flexibility, knowledge of the respondent's identity, control over the distribution of the sample and the ability to capture higher quality information through the counselling of the interviewer.

In addition, a set of recommended procedures for questionnaire-based research was used. This was essentially a modified version of the Dillman's Total Design Method (1978). The final questionnaire design took into account various instruments used for similar objectives in this field of research. It was refined over several stages to ensure its complete comprehensibility and efficiency in obtaining the desired information, as well as to make it as short as possible.

The data cleansing process was jointly carried out by the lead researchers and the professionals from the company hired to carry out the field work. In order to avoid the risk of respondents giving their answers on "auto-pilot", the order of the possible responses was altered so that they were sometimes listed in ascending order and other times in descending order. Control items were also included, in which the question was stated in the opposite way to the others. With regard to the interviewees, it was decided that the owner, managing director or general manager of the company were the appropriate people to provide their responses to the questionnaire.

As suggested by Armstrong & Overton (1977), the time trend extrapolation test was used to check for the possible existence of non-response bias. This test is based on a comparison of the first and last survey respondents. It assumes that the last respondents (those who responded only after receiving a second questionnaire and a follow-up phone call) better resemble the non-respondents, as they themselves would have been non-respondents if they had not completed the second questionnaire. The results of the t-tests show that no significant differences are observed in any of the explanatory or dependent variables.

Telephone conversations were also used to confirm the accuracy of the data on each of the selected establishments. On the one hand, these calls were used to verify the characteristics of each of the selected establishments drawn from external sources, thereby ensuring the random distribution of firms in sample (with respect to size, location and age). On the other hand, the calls were made to ensure that the person contacted matched the selected respondent profile. The field work was carried out between December 2009 and March 2010.

Data Analysis Techniques

This study uses multiple linear regression analysis, a technique that allows the researcher to estimate the relative importance of the different explanatory variables discussed above, in terms of their effect on the firm's competitive position. The SPSS 21.0 program for Windows has been used for the statistical analysis of the data drawn from the primary source. Having verified that the assumptions of regression analysis are met, the estimated results are statistically robust.

Measurement of the Variables

The firm's portfolio of capabilities is measured through a multi-item Likert scale, specifically a 7-point semantic differential scale with scores reflecting the manager's perception of the strength of their firm's endowment compared to competitors in the industry (1 = "much worse", 2 = "worse", 3 = "slightly worse", 4 = "about average", 5 = "slightly better", 6 = "better", 7 = "much better"). The use of this type of managerial self-evaluation scale allows key individuals' judgement, knowledge, and experience to be translated into subjective multi-item scales. The literature documents the use of this method for assessing a firm's resources and capabilities (Camisón, 2005b, 2004), and several studies have demonstrated its convergent validity with objective measurements (e.g., Camisón, 2005). Equally, multi-item scales offer the advantage of reducing measurement error, as the use of multiple indicators reduces uncertainty and measurement errors associated with a single response (Hair et al., 1998).

Specifically, the **functional capabilities** cover items related to *human resources,* specifically staff's satisfaction with and commitment to the firm; *financial capability*; *marketing capabilities*, linked to marketing and customer satisfaction, and *quality capabilities*, related to the firm's reputation, quality of service, certification, and total quality.

The **coordination and cohesion capabilities** include items related to management's ability to support change and learning, entrepreneurial orientation, and managerial expertise in the methods and principles of business management.

Dynamic capabilities cover the items related to service and process innovation, and the internal and external capabilities required to accumulate and exploit new knowledge.

Since the models are tested using regression analysis, the items that make up each scale are introduced into the model as arithmetic means of the item scores. This is a well-established procedure in strategic research, offering advantages over alternatives (such as factor scores after summarizing the information through an exploratory factor analysis of each of the scale items) as it maintains the exhaustive definition of the construct domains.

The firm's **economic performance** is measured using the objective variable economic profitability sourced from SABI, taking data for 2010 and 2014 as short- and long-term measures, respectively. In order to analyse both these objective performance variables, two empirical models have to be tested to assess what capabilities are necessary to ensure the firm's economic performance.

Table 1. Measurements of model variables

Variable	Number of items	Cronbach's alpha	Main attributes	Source
FUNCTIONAL CAPABILITIES	9	0.857	Items related to human resources, financial capabilities, and marketing and quality capabilities	Adapted from Camisón (2002)
COORDINATION AND COHESION CAPABILITIES	3	0.890	Items related to management's ability to support change and learning, entrepreneurial orientation, and expertise in business management methods	Adapted from Camisón (2002)
DYNAMIC CAPABILITIES	5	0.931	Items related to innovation, and the capabilities required to accumulate and exploit new knowledge	Adapted from Camisón (2002)
SHORT-TERM ECONOMIC PERFORMANCE	1	----	Economic profitability 2010 (SABI)	
LONG-TERM ECONOMIC PERFORMANCE	1	----	Economic profitability 2014 (SABI)	
AGE	1		Logarithm of the number of years the company has been operating, taking 2017 as base year	
SIZE	1		Logarithm of the number of employees in the company	
CORPORATE GROUP	1		Dichotomous variable where 1 indicates that the management of the company is in the hands of the owners	

The age and size of the firm, as well as whether it belongs to a corporate group, are included as control variables. Table 1 summarizes the main characteristics of the instruments used to measure the variables included in the model.

The consistency of the items is verified through composite reliability; specifically, Cronbach's Alpha is used as an indicator. Table 1 shows that the value of Cronbach's Alpha is above 0.7 for all factors (Cronbach, 1971; Nunnally, 1978; Hair et al., 1998).

Discriminant validity is assessed through the correlation matrix. Levels of correlation between variables are below 0.6 (Churchill, 1979), as shown by the analysis in Table 3. The highest correlation (0.570) is found among the endowment of capabilities, specifically, between functional capabilities and the coordination and cohesion capabilities. This is to be expected given how they closely interact in order for the potential of functional capabilities to be realized in company practices.

Table 2, below, presents the descriptive statistics and correlations for the variables.

The estimated results of the two models are statistically robust; residual analysis as well as other graphs and statistics provided by the SPSS program have been used to ensure that the basic assumptions for linear regression analysis (linearity, independence, homoscedasticity, normality and no collinearity) are met.

Table 2. Descriptive statistics and correlations for study variables

	Mean	Standard deviation	Pearson correlation	1	2	3	4	5	6	7	8
1. FUNCTIONAL CAPABILITIES	4.818	0.832	Pearson correlation	1	.570	.534	- .016	.200	.041	.129	.153
			Sig.		.000	.000	.775	.001	.350	.001	.000
2. COORDINATION AND COHESION CAPABILITIES	4.737	1.069	Pearson correlation	.570	1	.494	-.010	.124	-.067	.167	.080
			Sig.	.000		.000	.861	.036	.135	.000	.047
3. DYNAMIC CAPABILITIES	3.677	1.368	Pearson correlation	.534	.494	1	.191	.144	- .027	.117	.102
			Sig.	.000	.000		.001	.015	.549	.003	.011
4. S-T PERFORMANCE	2.713	119.371	Pearson correlation	- .016	-.010	.191	1	- .369	- .035	- .001	- .087
			Sig.	.775	.861	.001		.000	.566	.978	.099
5. L-T PERFORMANCE	-2.110	22.262	Pearson correlation	.200	.124	.144	- .369	1	.092	.042	.085
			Sig.	.001	.036	.015	.000		.167	.451	.128
6. AGE	26.618	22.777	Pearson correlation	.041	-.067	- .027	- .035	.092	1	.068	.012
			Sig.	.350	.135	.549	.566	.167		.092	.776
7. SIZE	28.566	127.996	Pearson correlation	.129	.167	.117	- .001	.042	.068	1	.199
			Sig.	.001	.000	.003	.978	.451	.092		.000
8. CORPORATE GROUP	0.205	0.404	Pearson correlation	.153	.080	.102	- .087	.085	.012	.199	1
			Sig.	.000	.047	.011	.099	.128	.776	.000	

RESULTS

The results of the two models show the difference between the effect of the control variables and the effect of the explanatory variables. To that end, the models are tested in two stages in order to check the increase in R^2 after adding the explanatory variables (second model) to the control variables (first model). The results shown below reveal fairly significant changes in R^2 when the explanatory variables are included. The significance of the F statistic is adequate for all estimated models. Tables 3 and 4 present the results obtained when testing the three hypotheses regarding the effect of the set of capabilities on short-and long-term economic performance, respectively.

The results indicate that the classic control variables of size and age have no effect on performance in either the short or the long term ($p>0.01$). Nor does belonging to a corporate group—a fairly commonly-used variable in tourism sector studies—have any effect on economic performance ($p>0.01$).

Regarding the impact of the portfolio of capabilities on short-term economic performance, the results indicate that only the functional capabilities (0.164, $p<0.1$) affect economic performance in the short term, confirming hypothesis 1; however, it was not possible to confirm hypothesis 2 concerning the impact of the coordination and cohesion capabilities (0.000, $p>0,1$).

Table 3. Results of the effect of capabilities on short-term performance

		Model I		Model II	
		(1)	**(2)**	**(1)**	**(2)**
	Constant	942.845 (3)	1012.131	1080.737 (3)	1020.059
Control Variables					
1	**Age**	-0.065	-0.938	-0.076	-1.087
2	**Size**	0.084	1.158	0.031	0.408
3	**Corporate group**	0.061	0.881	0.050	0.722
Explanatory Variables					
4	**Functional capabilities**			0.164*	1.952
5	**Coordination and cohesion capabilities**			0.000	0.005
6	**Dynamic capabilities**			0.050	0.616
	F	1.622		2.165**	
	R	0.146		0,236	
	R^2	0.021		0.056	
	Adjusted R^2	0.008		0.03	
	Δ adjusted R^2	--		0.034**	
(1) Standardized coefficients				(2) *t*	
(3) Non-standardized Beta					
* p < 0.1		** p < 0.05		*** p < 0.01	

Table 4. Results of the effect of capabilities on long-term performance

		Model I		Model II	
		(1)	**(2)**	**(1)**	**(2)**
	Constant	-2399.661 (3)	-0.476	-505.748 (3)	-0.101
Control Variables					
1	**Age**	0.031	0.478	0.007	0.108
2	**Size**	-0.008	-0.119	-0.064	-0.920
3	**Corporate group**	-0.084	-1.307	-0.080	-1.273
Explanatory Variables					
4	**Functional capabilities**			-0.109	-1.423
5	**Coordination and cohesion capabilities**			-0.080	-1.031
6	**Dynamic capabilities**			0.312***	4.232
	F	0.764		3.393**	
	R	0.093		0,27	
	R^2	0.009		0.073	
	Adjusted R^2	-0.003		0.051	
	Δ adjusted R^2	--		0.064***	
(1) Standardized coefficients				(2) *t*	
(3) Non-standardized Beta					
* p < 0.1		** p < 0.05		*** p < 0.01	

Conversely, long-term economic performance is explained only by dynamic capabilities, as postulated in hypothesis 3 (0.312, p<0.01), thereby confirming that hypothesis.

CONCLUSION

The results of this study represent a significant contribution to the understanding of the sources of family firm competitiveness. Moreover, they make an interesting contribution to the ongoing debate about the relationship between family firms and performance, opening up new ways to uncover the sources of sustainable competitive advantage. In particular, this study has shown which internal sources— in terms of the firm's capabilities—are most relevant to the family-firm's long-term performance, while also considering the effects of all its capabilities in a shorter time frame.

The literature has shown intangible resources and capabilities to be the main determinants of family tourism firms' competitiveness (Camisón & Forés, 2015). Along with certain static capabilities such as organizational routines, these include dynamic capabilities such as an organizational culture and architecture oriented towards innovation and learning (Henderson & Cockburn, 1994). One of the main objectives of this chapter has been to gain an understanding of the principal capabilities that determine the competitiveness of family tourism firms, in both the short and the long term. To that end, capabilities are first classified in levels, distinguishing between functional capabilities, coordination and cohesion capabilities, and dynamic capabilities.

According to the literature, the first level includes those capabilities relating to the use of existing knowledge and resources, which enable short-term economic profitability (Teece, 2007). The functional or operational capabilities are those that enable the firm to sell its current products to its current customers. Without them, the firm cannot secure a return on the activities it carries out (Winter, 2003). Functional capabilities tend to contribute to improving the quality of processes and products, to increasing revenues or to reducing costs associated with the provision of services, which can boost firm performance both directly and indirectly (Porter, 1980; 1985; Barney 1991; Williamson, 1991; Brush & Artz, 1999; Peng & York, 2001; Kaleka, 2002; Zhu & Kraemer, 2002; Barua et al., 2004; Piccoli & Ives, 2005; Lai et al., 2008; Makadok, 2010). The results of the present study confirm the findings of this literature for the specific field of the family firm, revealing that only functional capabilities have a positive and significant effect on short-term economic performance.

The results obtained in this study regarding the impact of the firm's set of capabilities on its long-term economic performance are in line with the tenets of the dynamic capabilities view; they show that, in a family business environment, these capabilities act as catalysts in the processes of generation and renewal of the firm's distinctive competences (Nelson & Winter, 1982; Teece et al., 1997; Teece, 2007). Therefore, the results confirm that dynamic capabilities are the only ones that have a positive and significant impact on long-term economic performance.

Teece (2007) argues that functional or operational capabilities, insofar as they relate to technical aspects, can help achieve positive performance in a short period of time, but if the company does not develop dynamic capabilities, the positive effect will not extend past the short term. However, dynamic capabilities are necessary for the firm to generate value in the long term. Functional capabilities can be seen as those that allow the firm to "make a living" in the short term (Winter, 2003); while dynamic capabilities are those that allow the functional capabilities to be developed, created or modified (Collis, 1994; Dosi, Nelson & Winter, 2000; Winter, 2003; Hoopes & Madsen, 2008).

Dynamic capabilities cover both the processes of internal knowledge generation as well as the absorption of external knowledge (Camisón & Forés, 2010; Chakravarthy, McEvily, Doz, & Devaki, 2003). These two dimensions make it possible to mitigate the obstacles of exogenous change and take advantage of new opportunities. As such, dynamic capabilities are considered a vital underpinning for change and innovation processes, and key to ensuring that the organization responds strategically to its environment; that is, they allow the firm to secure a sustainable competitive advantage by reconfiguring its base of resources and capabilities (Barney, 1991; Hambrick, ed., 1988).

Family firms should therefore understand that in a changing market the capabilities needed to renew their base of resources and capabilities are essential to their survival over the generations (Chirico & Nordqvist, 2010). Family members should support open relationships to foster creativity; in fact, when the older generation does not allow the new generation to participate in decision-making, this blocks change and leads to inertia. Hall et al. (2001: 205-206) argue that "in turbulent and changing environments, traditional ways of thinking and acting will not be of much help to the organization." To encourage change, "it is, instead, essential to question old patterns of strategic action and to explore new ones in a process of continuous learning".

The literature points out that the greater family involvement in management, the family's high level of ownership interest in the firm and the lack of separation between ownership and management are variables that negatively affect family firms' accumulation of dynamic capacities. This may be due to the more conservative behaviour and greater risk aversion that inevitably result from the link between family wealth and the business. This kind of attitude hampers the creation of an entrepreneurial orientation and strategic vision needed to boost dynamic capabilities. Given the proven importance of dynamic capabilities for family firm competitiveness over the long term, the top managers of family firms should seek to put in place a series of mechanisms that foster and transmit an innovative culture. Moreover, this culture must persist beyond the first two generations, which is where the entrepreneurial spirit of the founder seems to lie. Just as important as innovative values are the mechanisms that offer a certain degree of discretion and objectivity in managing them.

Coordination and cohesion capabilities—which are linked to the establishment of an appropriate environment for the efficient activation and management of functional capabilities through managerial and organizational components—were not found to have a significant effect on this performance. Given that these capabilities reflect the existence of a managerial and organizational environment that is conducive to the firm carrying out its different functions, future research should analyse whether they exert a moderating or even a mediating effect on the relationships between other levels of capabilities and firm performance. The results of such analysis may also provide support for the findings of some previous studies which have shown that functional capabilities exert a mediating effect on the relationship between higher-order capabilities and economic performance (e.g., Zahra et al., 2006).

The main limitations of this study stem from the nature of the research itself, which centres on a network of relationships between highly complex concepts. For this reason, the study involves a partial empirical test, limiting the aspects under analysis, their concept and scope, and the possible range of relationships. The aim is to reduce the complexity of the study and obtain initial results that can provide the basis for further analysis and new lines of research.

Using multiple regression models to test the hypotheses meant that it was not possible to examine the richness of certain constructs, such as functional capabilities and coordination and cohesion capabilities, which are by nature multidimensional. This limitation regarding the measurement of the portfolio of capabilities can explain the low fit index values obtained for the first two models, regarding the effects of the different types of capabilities on economic performance. Future studies should thus apply new methodologies that can incorporate the richness of these latent constructs, such as structural equation modelling. However, in comparison with previous studies that introduce the effects of subjective variables on objective variables, the results obtained are reasonable, especially taking into account that said studies do not report corrected R^2 (e.g. Berchicci, 2013).

Linked to the above limitation, subsequent studies should examine why certain capabilities are not found to be significant in terms of performance, especially in the long term. This would involve opening the 'black box' of capabilities, further exploring the type of causal relationship between them. For this type of analysis, structural equation modelling is once again needed. On the other hand, adopting a cross-sectional research design influences the conclusions drawn, making it necessary to refine the prediction of causality. It would therefore be interesting to develop longitudinal studies that offer a more complete, objective view of the subject. Likewise, although the focus on the Spanish tourism sector has enabled a clear, specific approach, it may limit the applicability of these conclusions to other sectors and territories. As such, it is important to study the family firm in other areas, in order to confirm whether or not the findings can be replicated.

ACKNOWLEDGMENT

This study has been funded by the Ministry of Science, Innovation and Universities and the Agencia Estatal de Investigación (the Spanish State Research Agency), with co-financing from the European Regional Development Fund (ERDF). Reference ECO2016-26796-P.

REFERENCES

Amit, R., & Schoemaker, P. (1993). Strategic assets and organizational rent. *Strategic Management Journal*, *14*(1), 33–46. doi:10.1002mj.4250140105

Arend, R. J., & Bromiley, P. (2009). Assessing the dynamic capabilities view: Spare change, everyone? *Strategic Organization*, *7*(1), 75–90. doi:10.1177/1476127008100132

Armstrong, J. S., & Overton, T. S. (1977). Estimating non response bias in mail surveys. *JMR, Journal of Marketing Research*, *16*(3), 396–402. doi:10.1177/002224377701400320

Athreye, S. S. (2005). The Indian software industry and its evolving service capability. *Industrial and Corporate Change*, *14*(3), 393–418. doi:10.1093/icc/dth056

Audretsch, D. B., Hülsbeck, M., & Lehmann, E. E. (2013). Families as active monitors of firm performance. *Journal of Family Business Strategy*, *4*(2), 118–130. doi:10.1016/j.jfbs.2013.02.002

Barney, J. B. (1991). Firms resources and sustained competitive advantage. *Journal of Management*, *17*(1), 191–210. doi:10.1177/014920639101700108

Barney, J. B. (1997). *Gaining and sustaining competitive advantage*. Aldershot: Addison-Wesley Publishing.

Barney, J. B., Clark, C., & Alvarez, S. (2002). *Where does entrepreneurship come from: Network models of opportunity and resource acquisition with application to the family firm*, Second Annual Conference on Theories of the Family Enterprise, Philadelphia, PA.

Barney, J. B., Wright, M., & Ketchen, D. J. Jr. (2001). The resource-based view of the firm: Ten years after 1991. *Journal of Management*, *27*(6), 625–641. doi:10.1177/014920630102700601

Barua, A., Konana, P., Whinston, A. B., & Yin, F. (2004). An empirical investigation of net-enabled business value. *Management Information Systems Quarterly*, *28*(4), 585–620. doi:10.2307/25148656

Berchicci, L. (2013). Towards an open R&D system: Internal R&D investment, external knowledge acquisition and innovative performance. *Research Policy*, *42*(1), 117–127. doi:10.1016/j.respol.2012.04.017

Blyler, M., & Coff, R. W. (2003). Dynamic capabilities, social capital, and rent appropriation: Ties that split pies. *Strategic Management Journal*, *24*(7), 677–686. doi:10.1002mj.327

Brush, T. H., & Artz, K. W. (1999). Toward a contingent resource-based theory: The impact of information asymmetry on the value of capabilities in veterinary medicine. *Strategic Management Journal*, *20*(3), 223–250. doi:10.1002/(SICI)1097-0266(199903)20:3<223::AID-SMJ14>3.0.CO;2-M

Cabrera, K., De Saá, P., & Garcia, D. (2001). The succession process from a resource -and knowledge- based view of the family firm. *Family Business Review*, *14*(1), 37–46. doi:10.1111/j.1741-6248.2001.00037.x

Camisón, C. (1997). *La competitividad de la PYME industrial española: estrategia y competencias distintivas*. Madrid, España: Civitas.

Camisón, C. (2001). *La competitividad de la empresa industrial de la Comunidad Valenciana: análisis del efecto del atractivo del entorno, los distritos industriales y las estrategias empresariales*. Valencia, España: Tirant lo Blanch.

Camisón, C. (2002). Las competencias distintivas basadas en activos intangibles. In Nuevas claves para la dirección estratégica. Barcelona, España: Editorial Ariel.

Camisón, C. (2004). Shared, competitive and comparative advantages: A competence-based view of industrial-district competitiveness. *Environment & Planning A*, *36*(12), 2227–2256. doi:10.1068/a3759

Camisón, C. (2005). On how to measure managerial and organizational capabilities: Multi-Item models for measuring distinctive competences. *Management Research*, *3*(1), 27–48.

Camisón, C., & Boronat, M. (2004). Factores determinantes del desempeño organizativo: Efecto industria, incertidumbre y competencias distintivas. *Investigaciones Europeas de Dirección y Economía de la Empresa*, *10*(3), 127–143.

Camisón, C., & Forés, B. (2010). Knowledge absorptive capacity: New insights for its conceptualization and measurement. *Journal of Business Research*, *63*(7), 707–715. doi:10.1016/j.jbusres.2009.04.022

Camisón, C., & Forés, B. (2015). Is tourism firm competitiveness driven by different internal or external specific factors?: New empirical evidence from Spain. *Tourism Management*, *48*(1), 477–499. doi:10.1016/j.tourman.2015.01.001

Camisón, C., & Monfort, V. M. (2012). La empresa turística familiar en España: importancia, perfil y competitividad. Madrid: Ministerio de Industria, Energía y Turismo (Estudios del IET).

Castanias, R. P., & Helfat, C. E. (1991). Managerial Resources and Rents. *Journal of Management*, *17*(1), 155–171. doi:10.1177/014920639101700110

Chakravarthy, B., McEvily, S., Doz, Y., & Devaki, R. (2003). Knowledge management and competitive advantage. In M. Easterby-Smith & M. A. Lyles (Eds.), *Handbook of Organizational Learning and Knowledge Management* (pp. 305–323). New York: Blackwell Publishing.

Chirico, F., & Nordqvist, M. (2010). Dynamic capabilities and trans-generational value creation in family firms: The role of organizational culture. *International Small Business Journal*, *28*(5), 487–504. doi:10.1177/0266242610370402

Chirico, F., & Salvato, C. (2008). Knowledge integration and dynamic organizational adaptation in family firms. *Family Business Review*, *21*(2), 169–181. doi:10.1111/j.1741-6248.2008.00117.x

Chmielewski, D. A., & Paladino, A. (2007). Driving a resource orientation: Reviewing the role of resource and capability characteristics. *Management Decision*, *45*(3), 462–483. doi:10.1108/00251740710745089

Chrisman, J. J., Chua, J. H., & Sharma, P. (2005). Trends and directions in the development of a strategic management theory of the family firm. *Entrepreneurship Theory and Practice*, *29*(5), 555–576. doi:10.1111/j.1540-6520.2005.00098.x

Chua, J. H., Chrisman, J. J., & Sharma, P. (1999). Defining the family business by behavior. *Entrepreneurship Theory and Practice*, *23*(Summer), 19–39. doi:10.1177/104225879902300402

Churchill, G. Jr. (1979). A paradigm for developing better measures of marketing constructs. *JMR, Journal of Marketing Research*, *16*(1), 64–73. doi:10.1177/002224377901600110

Collis, D. J. (1991). A resource-based analysis of global competition: The case of bearings industry. *Strategic Management Journal*, *12*(S1), 49–68. doi:10.1002mj.4250120906

Collis, D. J. (1994). Research note: How valuable are organizational capabilities? *Strategic Management Journal*, *15*(S1), 143–152. doi:10.1002mj.4250150910

Combs, J. G., & Ketchen, D. J. Jr. (1999). Explaining interfirm cooperation and performance: Toward a reconciliation of predictions. *Strategic Management Journal*, *20*(9), 867–888. doi:10.1002/(SICI)1097-0266(199909)20:9<867::AID-SMJ55>3.0.CO;2-6

Cronbach, L. J. (1951). Coefficient alpha and the internal structure of tests. *Psychometrika*, *16*(3), 297–334. doi:10.1007/BF02310555

Dibrell, C., & Moeller, M. (2011). The impact of a service-dominant focus strategy and stewardship culture on organizational innovativeness in family-owned businesses. *Journal of Family Business Strategy*, *2*(1), 43–51. doi:10.1016/j.jfbs.2011.01.004

Dierickx, I., & Cool, K. (1989). Asset stock accumulation and sustainability of competitive advantage. *Management Science*, *35*(12), 1504–1511. doi:10.1287/mnsc.35.12.1504

Dillman, D. A. (1978). *Mail and Telephone Surveys: The Total Design Method*. New York: John Wiley & Sons.

Dosi, G. (1982). Technological paradigms and technological trajectories. A suggested interpretation of the determinants and directions of technical change. *Research Policy*, *11*(3), 147–162. doi:10.1016/0048-7333(82)90016-6

Dosi, G. (1988a). Sources, procedures, and microeconomic effects of innovation. *Journal of Economic Literature*, *26*, 1120–1171.

Dosi, G. (1988b). The nature of the innovative process. In G. Gosi, C. Freeman, R. Nelson, G. Silverberg, & L. Soete (Eds.), *Technical Change and Economic Theory*. London: Pinter.

Dosi, G., Freeman, C., Nelson, R. R., Silverberg, G., & Soete, L. (Eds.). (1988). Technical change and economic theory. Pinter Publishers.

Dosi, G., & Marengo, L. (1993). Some elements of an evolutionary theory of organisational competences. In R. W. England (Ed.), *Evolutionary Concepts in Contemporary Economics*. Ann Arbor, MI: University of Michigan Press.

Dosi, G., Nelson, R., & Winter, S. (2000). Introduction: the nature and dynamics of organizational capabilities. In G. Dosi, R. Nelson, & S. G. Winter (Eds.), *Nature and Dynamics of Organizational Capabilities* (pp. 1–21). New York: Oxford University Press.

Dosi, G., Teece, D. J., & Winter, S. (1992). Towards a theory of corporate coherence: Preliminary remarks. In G. Dosi, R. Giannetti, & P. A. Toninelli (Eds.), *Technology and Enterprise in a Historical Perspective* (pp. 185–211). Oxford, UK: Clarendon Press.

Drnevich, P. L., & Kriauciunas, A. P. (2011). Clarifying the conditions and limits of the contributions of ordinary and dynamic capabilities to relative firm performance. *Strategic Management Journal*, *32*(3), 254–279. doi:10.1002mj.882

Eisenhardt, K. M., & Brown, S. L. (1998). Competing on the edge: Strategy as structured chaos. *Long Range Planning*, *31*(5), 786–789. doi:10.1016/S0024-6301(98)00092-2

Eisenhardt, K. M., & Martin, J. A. (2000). Dynamic Capabilities: What are they? *Strategic Management Journal*, *21*(10-11), 1105–1121. doi:10.1002/1097-0266(200010/11)21:10/11<1105::AID-SMJ133>3.0.CO;2-E

Felin, T., Foss, N. J., Heimeriks, K. H., & Madsen, T. L. (2012). Microfoundations of routines and capabilities: Individuals, processes, and structure. *Journal of Management Studies*, *49*(8), 1351–1374. doi:10.1111/j.1467-6486.2012.01052.x

Fuchs, P. H., Mifflin, K. E., Miller, D., & Whitney, J. O. (2000). Strategic integration: Competing in the age of capabilities. *California Management Review*, *42*(3), 118–147. doi:10.2307/41166045

Gallo, M. A., & Amat, J. A. (2003). *Los secretos de las empresas familiares centenarias*. Barcelona: Deusto.

Gallo, M. A., Tàpies, J., & Cappuyns, K. (2004). Comparison of family and nonfamily business: Financial logic and personal preferences. *Family Business Review*, *XVII*(4), 303–318. doi:10.1111/j.1741-6248.2004.00020.x

Gersick, K. E., Davis, J. A., Hampton, M., & Lansberg, I. (1997). *Generation to generation—Life cycles of the family business*. Boston: Harvard Business School Press.

Goh, S., & Richards, G. (1997). Benchmarking the learning capability of organizations. *European Management Journal*, *15*(5), 575–583. doi:10.1016/S0263-2373(97)00036-4

Grant, R. M. (1991). *Contemporary Strategy Analysis: Concepts, Techniques, Applications*. Cambridge: Blackwell Publishers.

Grant, R.M. (1996). Toward a knowledge-based theory of the firm. *Strategic Management Journal*, *17*(winter special issue), 109–122.

Habbershon, T., & Williams, M. (1999). A resource-based framework for assessing the strategic advantage of family firms. *Family Business Review*, *12*(1), 27–39. doi:10.1111/j.1741-6248.1999.00001.x

Habbershon, T., Williams, M., & MacMillan, L. C. (2003). A unified systems perspective of family firm performance. *Journal of Business Venturing*, *18*(4), 451–465. doi:10.1016/S0883-9026(03)00053-3

Habbershon, T. G. (2006). Commentary: A framework for managing the familiness and agency advantages in family firms. *Entrepreneurship Theory and Practice*, *30*(6), 879–886. doi:10.1111/j.1540-6520.2006.00158.x

Hair, J. F., Anderson, R. E., Tatham, R. L., & Black, W. C. (1998). *Multivariate data analysis*. Prentice Hall.

Hall, A., Melin, L., & Nordqvist, M. (2001). Entrepreneurship as radical change in family business: Exploring the role of cultural patterns. *Family Business Review*, *14*(3), 193–208. doi:10.1111/j.1741-6248.2001.00193.x

Hambrick, D. C. (Ed.). (1988). The executive effect: concepts and methods for studying top managers. JAI Press.

Hamel, G., & Prahalad, C. K. (1994). *Competing for the future*. Cambridge, MA: Harvard Business School Press.

Handler, W. C. (1989). Methodological issues and considerations in studying family business. *Family Business Review*, *2*(3), 257–276. doi:10.1111/j.1741-6248.1989.00257.x

Helfat, C. E. (1997). Know-how and asset complementarity and dynamic capability accumulation: The case of R&D. *Strategic Management Journal*, *18*(5), 339–360. doi:10.1002/(SICI)1097-0266(199705)18:5<339::AID-SMJ883>3.0.CO;2-7

Helfat, C. E., Finkelstein, S., Mitchell, W., Peteraf, M., Singh, H., Teece, D., & Winter, S. G. (2007). *Dynamic Capabilities: Understanding Strategic Change in Organizations*. Malden, MA: Wiley-Blackwell.

Henderson, J., & Cool, K. (2003). Learning to time capacity expansions: An empirical analysis of the worldwide petrochemical industry, 1975–1995. *Strategic Management Journal*, *24*(5), 393–413. doi:10.1002mj.309

Henderson, R., & Cockburn, I. (1994). Measuring competence? Exploring firm effects in pharmaceutical research. *Strategic Management Journal*, *15*(S1), 63–84. doi:10.1002mj.4250150906

Hitt, M. A., Ireland, R. D., & Hoskisson, R. E. (2001). *Strategic Management: Competitiveness and Globalization*. Cincinnati, OH: Southwestern College Publishing Company.

Hoopes, D. G., & Madsen, T. L. (2008). A capability-based view of competitive heterogeneity. *Industrial and Corporate Change*, *17*(3), 393–426. doi:10.1093/icc/dtn008

Hsu, L. C., & Wang, C. H. (2012). Clarifying the effect of intellectual capital on performance: The mediating role of dynamic capability. *British Journal of Management*, *23*(2), 179–205. doi:10.1111/j.1467-8551.2010.00718.x

Ifera. (2003). Family business dominate. *Family Business Review, 16*(4), 235-9.

Kaleka, A. (2002). Resources and capabilities driving competitive advantage in export markets: Guidelines for industrial exporters. *Industrial Marketing Management*, *31*(3), 273–283. doi:10.1016/S0019-8501(00)00148-6

Kellermanns, F. W. (2005). Family firm resource management: Comments and extensions. *Entrepreneurship Theory and Practice*, *29*(3), 313–319. doi:10.1111/j.1540-6520.2005.00085.x

Ketchen, D. J., Hult, G. T. M., & Slater, S. F. (2007). Toward greater understanding of market orientation and the resource-based view. *Strategic Management Journal*, *28*(9), 961–964. doi:10.1002mj.620

Kogut, B., & Zander, U. (1992). Knowledge of the firm, combinative capabilities, and the replication of technology. *Organization Science*, *3*(3), 383–397. doi:10.1287/orsc.3.3.383

Kogut, B., & Zander, U. (1996). What firms do? Coordination, learning, and learning. *Organization Science*, *7*(5), 502–518. doi:10.1287/orsc.7.5.502

Lado, A. A., Boyd, N. G., & Wright, P. (1992). A competency-based model of sustainable competitive advantage: Toward a conceptual integration. *Journal of Management*, *18*(1), 77–91. doi:10.1177/014920639201800106

Lai, F., Li, D., Qiang, Q., & Zhao, X. (2008). The information technology capability of third party logistics providers: A resource-based view and empirical test from China. *The Journal of Supply Chain Management*, *9*(1), 21–36.

Lampel, J., & Shamsie, J. (2003). Capabilities in motion: New organizational forms and the reshaping of the Hollywood movie industry. *Journal of Management Studies*, *40*(8), 2189–2210. doi:10.1046/j.1467-6486.2003.00417.x

Lawson, B., & Samson, D. (2001). Developing innovation capability in organisations: A dynamic capabilities approach. *International Journal of Innovation Management*, *5*(3), 377–400. doi:10.1142/S1363919601000427

Leiblein, M. J., & Madsen, T. L. (2009). Unbundling competitive heterogeneity: Incentive structures and capability influences on technological innovation. *Strategic Management Journal*, *30*(7), 711–735. doi:10.1002mj.746

Levinthal, D. A., & March, J. G. (1993). The myopia of learning. *Strategic Management Journal*, *14*(S2), 95–112. doi:10.1002mj.4250141009

Madhok, A. (1997). Cost, value, and foreign market entry mode: The transaction and the firm. *Strategic Management Journal*, *18*(1), 39–61. doi:10.1002/(SICI)1097-0266(199701)18:1<39::AID-SMJ841>3.0.CO;2-J

Mahoney, J. T., & Pandian, J. R. (1992). The resource-based view within the conversation of strategic management. *Strategic Management Journal*, *13*(5), 363–380. doi:10.1002mj.4250130505

Maijoor, S., & Witteloostuijn, A. V. (1996). An empirical test of the resource-based theory: Strategic regulation in the Dutch audit industry. *Strategic Management Journal*, *17*(7), 549–569. doi:10.1002/(SICI)1097-0266(199607)17:7<549::AID-SMJ827>3.0.CO;2-R

Majumdar, S. K. (1999). Sluggish giants, sticky cultures, and dynamic capability transformation. *Journal of Business Venturing*, *15*(1), 59–78. doi:10.1016/S0883-9026(98)00010-X

Makadok, R. (1999). Interfirm differences in scale economies and the evolution of market shares. *Strategic Management Journal*, *20*(10), 935–952. doi:10.1002/(SICI)1097-0266(199910)20:10<935::AID-SMJ56>3.0.CO;2-G

Makadok, R. (2001). Toward a synthesis of the resource-based and dynamic-capability views of rent creation. *Strategic Management Journal*, *22*(5), 387–401. doi:10.1002mj.158

Makadok, R. (2010). The interaction effect of rivalry restraint and competitive advantage on profit: Why the whole is less than the sum of the parts. *Management Science*, *56*(2), 356–372. doi:10.1287/mnsc.1090.1102

Mascarenhas, B., Baveja, A., & Jamil, M. (1998). Dynamics of Core Competencies in Leading Multinational Companies. *California Management Review*, *40*(4), 117–132. doi:10.2307/41165967

Miller, D., & Le Breton-Miller, I. (2005). *Managing for the long run: Lessons in competitive advantage from great family businesses*. Harvard Business Press.

Miller, D., Le Breton-Miller, I., Lester, R. H., & Cannella, A. A. Jr. (2007). Are family firms really superior performers? *Journal of Corporate Finance*, *13*(5), 829–858. doi:10.1016/j.jcorpfin.2007.03.004

Miller, D., & Shamsie, J. (1996). The resource-based view of the firm in two environments: The Hollywood film studios from 1936 to 1965. *Academy of Management Journal*, *39*(3), 519–543.

Nelson, R.R. (1991). Why do firms differ and how does industry matter?, *Strategic Management Journal*, *12*(special issue winter), 61-74.

Nelson, R. R. (1995). Recent evolutionary theorizing about economic change. *Journal of Economic Literature*, *33*(March), 48–90.

Nelson, R. R., & Winter, S. (1982). *An evolutionary theory of economic change*. Cambridge, MA: Harvard University Press.

Neubaum, D. O., Dibrell, C., & Craig, J. B. (2012). Balancing natural environmental concerns of internal and external stakeholders in family and non-family businesses. *Journal of Family Business Strategy*, *3*(1), 28–37. doi:10.1016/j.jfbs.2012.01.003

Newbert, S. L. (2007). Empirical research on the resource-based view of the firm: An assessment and suggestions for future research. *Strategic Management Journal*, *28*(2), 121–146. doi:10.1002mj.573

Nonaka, I., & Konno, N. (1998). The concept of Ba: Building a foundation for knowledge creation. *California Management Review*, *40*(3), 40–54. doi:10.2307/41165942

Nunnally, J. C. (1978). *Psychometric theory*. New York: McGraw-Hill.

Osbaldeston, M., & Barham, K. (1992). Using management development for competitive advantage. *Long Range Planning*, *25*(6), 18–24. doi:10.1016/0024-6301(92)90165-X

Pavitt, K. (1991). Key characteristics of the large innovating firm. *British Journal of Management*, *2*(1), 41–50. doi:10.1111/j.1467-8551.1991.tb00014.x

Peng, M. W., & York, A. S. (2001). Behind intermediary performance in export trade: Transactions, agents, and resources. *Journal of International Business Studies*, *32*(2), 327–346. doi:10.1057/palgrave.jibs.8490955

Penrose, E. (1959). *The Theory of the Growth of the Firm*. New York: John Wiley & Sons.

Peteraf, M. A. (1993). The cornerstone of competitive advantage: A resource-based view. *Strategic Management Journal*, *14*(3), 179–191. doi:10.1002mj.4250140303

Piccoli, G., & Ives, B. (2005). IT-dependent strategic initiatives and sustained competitive advantage: A review and synthesis of the literature. *Management Information Systems Quarterly*, *29*(4), 747–776. doi:10.2307/25148708

Pisano, G.P. (1994). Knowledge, integration, and the locus of learning: An empirical analysis of process development. *Strategic Management Journal*, *15*(winter special issue), 85-100.

Pisano, G. P. (2000). In search of dynamic capabilities: the origins of R&D competence in biopharmaceuticals. In G. Dosi, R. R. Nelson, & S. G. Winter (Eds.), *The Nature and Dynamics of Organizational Capabilities*. Oxford, UK: Oxford University Press.

Porter, M. E. (1980). *Competitive strategy. Techniques for analyzing industries and competitors*. New York: The Free Press.

Porter, M. E. (1985). *Competitive advantage. Creating and sustaining superior performance*. New York: The Free Press.

Rindova, V. P., & Kotha, S. (2001). Continuous morphing: Competing through dynamic capabilities, form, and function. *Academy of Management Journal*, *44*, 1263–1280.

Rothwell, R. (1977). The characteristics of successful innovators and technically progressive firms. *R & D Management*, *7*(3), 191–206. doi:10.1111/j.1467-9310.1977.tb01334.x

Schenkel, A., & Teigland, R. (2016). Why doesn't downsizing deliver? A multi-level model integrating downsizing, social capital, dynamic capabilities, and firm performance. *International Journal of Human Resource Management*.

Shanker, M. C., & Astrachan, J. H. (1996). Myths and realities: Family businesses´ contribution to the US economy. A framework for assessing family business statistics. *Family Business Review*, *9*(2), 107–123. doi:10.1111/j.1741-6248.1996.00107.x

Sharma, P., Chrisman, J. J., & Chua, J. H. (1996). *A review and annotated bibliography of family business studies*. Boston: Kluwer. doi:10.1007/978-1-4419-8768-6

Sharma, P., & Manikutty, S. (2005). Strategic divestments in family firms: Role of family structure and community culture. *Entrepreneurship Theory and Practice*, *29*(3), 293–311. doi:10.1111/j.1540-6520.2005.00084.x

Sirmon, D., & Hitt, M. (2003). Managing resources: Linking unique resources, management and wealth creation in family firms. *Entrepreneurship Theory and Practice*, *27*(Summer), 339–358. doi:10.1111/1540-8520.t01-1-00013

Snow, C. C., & Hrebiniak, L. G. (1980). Strategy, distinctive competence and organizational performance. *Administrative Science Quarterly*, *25*(2), 317–336. doi:10.2307/2392457

Tallon, P. P. (2008). Inside the adaptive enterprise: An information technology capabilities perspective on business process agility. *Information Technology Management*, *9*(1), 21–36. doi:10.100710799-007-0024-8

Teece, D. J. (1986). Profiting from technological innovation: Implications for integration, collaboration, licensing and public policy. *Research Policy*, *15*(6), 285–305. doi:10.1016/0048-7333(86)90027-2

Teece, D. J. (2007). Explicating dynamic capabilities: The nature and microfoundations of (sustainable) enterprise performance. *Strategic Management Journal*, *28*(13), 1319–1350. doi:10.1002mj.640

Teece, D. J., & Pisano, G. (1998). The dynamic capabilities of the firm: An introduction. In G. Dosi, D. J. Teece, & J. Chytry (Eds.), *Technology, organization, and competitiveness. Perspectives on industrial and corporate change* (pp. 193–212). Oxford, UK: Oxford University Press. doi:10.1093/0198290969.003.0006

Teece, D. J., Pisano, G., & Shuen, A. (1997). Dynamic capabilities and strategic management. *Strategic Management Journal*, *18*(7), 509–533. doi:10.1002/(SICI)1097-0266(199708)18:7<509::AID-SMJ882>3.0.CO;2-Z

Teece, D. J., Pisano, G. P., & Shuen, A. (1990). *Firm capabilities, resources, and the concept of strategy*. Working Paper, Berkeley, University of California.

Teece, D. J., Rumelt, R., Dosi, G., & Winter, S. (1994). Understanding corporate coherence. Theory and evidence. *Journal of Economic Behavior & Organization*, *23*(1), 1–30. doi:10.1016/0167-2681(94)90094-9

Wang, C. K., & Ang, B. L. (2004). Determinants of venture performance in Singapore. *Journal of Small Business Management*, *42*(4), 347–363. doi:10.1111/j.1540-627X.2004.00116.x

Wang, C. L., & Ahmed, P. K. (2007). Dynamic capabilities: A review and research agenda. *International Journal of Management Reviews*, *9*(1), 31–51. doi:10.1111/j.1468-2370.2007.00201.x

Wernerfelt, B. (1984). A resource-based view of the firm. *Strategic Management Journal*, *5*(2), 171–180. doi:10.1002mj.4250050207

Westhead, P., & Howorth, C. (2007). 'Types' of private family firms: An exploratory conceptual and empirical analysis. *Entrepreneurship and Regional Development*, *19*(5), 405–431. doi:10.1080/08985620701552405

Westley, F., Mintzberg, H. (1989). Visionary leadership and strategic management. *Strategic Management Journal, 10*(summer special issue), 17-32.

Whiteside, M. F., Aronoff, C. E., & Ward, J. L. (1993). *How families work together*. Marietta, GA: Business Owner Resources.

Williamson, O. E. (1991). Strategizing, economizing, and economic organization. *Strategic Management Journal*, *12*(S2), 75–94. doi:10.1002mj.4250121007

Winter, S. G. (1995). Four Rs of profitability: Rents, resources, routines and replication. In C. A. Montgomery (Ed.), *Resource-based and evolutionary theories of the Firm: Toward a Synthesis* (pp. 147–178). Boston: Kluwer Academic Publishers. doi:10.1007/978-1-4615-2201-0_7

Winter, S. G. (2003). Understanding dynamic capabilities. *Strategic Management Journal*, *24*(10), 991–995. doi:10.1002mj.318

Yeoth, P. L., & Roth, K. (1999). An empirical analysis of sustained advantage in the U.S. pharmaceutical industry: Impact of firm resources and capabilities. *Strategic Management Journal*, *20*(7), 637–653. doi:10.1002/(SICI)1097-0266(199907)20:7<637::AID-SMJ42>3.0.CO;2-Z

Zahra, S. A., Sapienza, H. J., & Davidsson, P. (2006). Entrepreneurship and dynamic capabilities. A review, model and research agenda. *Journal of Management Studies*, *43*(4), 917–955. doi:10.1111/j.1467-6486.2006.00616.x

Zhu, K., & Kraemer, K. L. (2002). E-commerce metrics for net-enhanced organizations: Assessing the value of e-commerce to firm performance in the manufacturing sector. *Information Systems Research*, *13*(3), 275–295. doi:10.1287/isre.13.3.275.82

Zou, S., Fang, E., & Zhao, S. (2003). The effect of export marketing capabilities on export performance: An investigation of Chinese exporters. *Journal of International Marketing*, *11*(4), 32–55. doi:10.1509/jimk.11.4.32.20145

KEY TERMS AND DEFINITIONS

Dynamic Capabilities: They are the capacities that a company possesses to renew its capacities and to develop others new skills. It can be understood as a synonym for innovative skills.

Economic Performance Over Short and Long term: The economic performance of the company expresses its economic efficiency, that is, the capacity to generate economic rents by harnessing resources and capacities to develop and implement marketing goods or services. It can be measured in the short and long term, without there being any a commonly accepted criterion for separating the two time horizons.

Family Firm Success: The success of a family business depends on the degree to which the company satisfies the expectations and needs of its founders and current owners and, at the same time, meets the conditions of economic logic required for competition in the markets.

Functional Capabilities: Functional capacities are those that the company has to manage resource teams in each functional area (production, marketing, resources, etc.).

Long-Lived Family Firm: Indicates the existence of long-lived family businesses. Despite recurrent criticism of the mortality of the family business, it is an indisputable fact that the most important companies are existing in the world are almost exclusively familiar.

Survival: Survival is one of the aspects that measure the success of a family business, since it is usually typified by a will to remain and to be relieved that guarantees business continuity.

Sustainable Competitive Advantage: A competitive advantage is sustainable when it is protected from imitation and replication by other competitors.

Section 5

Family Firm Survival and Resilience

Chapter 11
The Role of Family Ownership in Survival and Bouncing Back:
Good and Bad News?

María Iborra
https://orcid.org/0000-0001-7140-799X
University of Valencia, Spain

Vicente Safón
University of Valencia, Spain

Consuelo Dolz
University of Valencia, Spain

ABSTRACT

The latest global economic and financial crisis has been a litmus test for companies, especially for SMEs. These companies have had to demonstrate their ability to be resilient, surviving first and then recovering. This chapter studies the role of family ownership in the survival and recovery of SMEs during a stressful event. From a perspective based on the complementarity or substitutability of goals that family firms pursue, the authors propose that family ownership has a positive effect on survival but a negative effect on recovery. Furthermore, they propose that the risk of bankruptcy before a crisis moderates the relationship between family ownership and survival. Hypotheses have been tested with a dataset of 3,133 Spanish manufacturing MEs finding evidence for the positive role of family ownership in survival and for the moderating effect of previous bankruptcy risk. The empirical data confirms good news for family-owned firms.

DOI: 10.4018/978-1-7998-1655-3.ch011

INTRODUCTION

Family-owned SMEs (small and medium-sized enterprises) account for a large part of the world economy. Thus, it seems logical that the effect of family ownership on different dimensions of firm performance remains a core area of research (Chua, Chrisman, De Massis & Wang, 2018; Dyer, 2018; Wagner, Block, Miller & Schwens, 2015) and that specific advances have been made to understand its role in SMEs (De Massis, Kotlar, Campopiano & Cassia, 2013). In this regard, several studies focus on how family ownership affects classical indicators of performance and highlight its positive effect on SME profitability, while its effects on other dimensions such as SME innovation or growth are far from being clearly positive.

However, during a threatening and stressful external event, such as the most recent world financial and economic crisis, new dimensions of performance have emerged as being relevant. Under this kind of pressure, whereas some firms survive and recover, demonstrating resilience, a large number of other SMEs disappear or are incapable of regaining their previous level of activity because they cannot adapt to the challenges of the environment (McGuinness, Hogan & Powell, 2018). In business and management research, resilience is a well-known area of interest (for reviews, see Linnenluecke, 2017; Williams et al. 2017). Throughout their existence, organizations are exposed to stressful disruptions, abrupt changes and extreme events – both internal and external – from which some firms are able to recover quickly, while for others it takes longer to bounce back, and some never recover and eventually disappear. Therefore, understanding which type of firms become resilient and how they do so is a relevant topic.

SMEs have particular difficulties or weaknesses when it comes to achieving resilience; first, because the strain and disruption caused by internal or external disturbances is greater for these firms than for large firms (Linnenluecke, 2017)[1]; and secondly, because they do not have complex and costly systems to prevent crises (Harries, McEwen & Wragg, 2018; van der Vegt, Essens, Walshtröm, & George, 2015).

Thus, in an SME context, the close relationship, involvement and position of family members in family-owned-firms can be crucial for decision making when dealing with a stressful external event. The researchers of this chapter argue that, during these events, in the case of SMEs, the characteristics related to family ownership shape the actions and behaviors of the firm; the authors of this manuscript base their arguments on the socioemotional wealth (SEW) theory. As Carney (2005) highlights, this form of governance implies that family owners enjoy certain control rights over the firm's assets and may use these rights to influence decision-making. Family research states that family firms consider both financial and emotional goals in their actions and behaviors. Following Chua et al. (2018), the authors of this chapter state that SMEs will benefit from family ownership when survival is at stake, because the financial and emotional goals of the family-owned firm become complementary; however, when focusing on recovery, both goals (financial and emotional) may have a substitute relationship, and a negative effect can be expected from family ownership.

This study makes several contributions. First, it contributes to family firm research by offering a theoretical explanation for the complementary and substitute effect between financial and non-financial family goals proposed by Chua et al. (2018) in a context of financial and economic crisis, providing strong empirical support for the complementary effect. Second, this research contributes to the growing literature on organizational resilience by investigating its antecedents, a topic that demands researchers' attention (Linnenluecke, 2017), in particular, the role of SMEs' family ownership in resilience (survival and recovery).

In the next section, the literature is reviewed and hypotheses are presented. The authors examine the relationship of family ownership with survival and recovering in SMEs under an economic and financial crisis. Additionally, they analyze the relationship between the likelihood of bankruptcy of family-owned firms and their survival. After describing the research method, the empirical findings are presented, which derive from data on 3,133 Spanish manufacturing MEs. The chapter concludes with a discussion of the results, their implications, and some suggestions for further research.

THE ROLE OF SME FAMILY OWNERSHIP IN RESILIENCE: SURVIVAL AND RECOVERY

Organizational resilience, a term coined by Meyer (1982), is a metaphor borrowed from material science and used in strategic management research regarding the ability of a person, unit or organization, to absorb, strain and maintain its shape through its actions and behaviors (Hamel & Välikangas, 2003; Sutcliffe & Vogus, 2003). Interest in organizational resilience has been growing over the last few years because it is an essential characteristic for the success of modern organizations in today's world (DesJardine, Bansal & Yang, 2019; Rodriguez-Sánchez et al., 2019). Resilient organizations are able to anticipate, cope with and adapt to stressful and disruptive unexpected events that threaten the achievement of strategic goals (Duchek, 2019). SMEs may face even greater challenges when dealing with disruptions and disasters since they have fewer resources for anticipating and diversifying risks, being insured against disasters or preventing disruptive events.

The literature usually identifies two different dimensions of resilience: (a) a system's ability to endure a major disruption (i.e. surviving) and (b) its capacity to bounce back (i.e. recovering) (Buyl, Boone & Wade, 2019). Both dimensions reflect different SMEs' goals under a crisis, which authors argue may be influenced by the family ownership of the firm.

Family-owned SMEs differ from non-family-owned ones because they have different goals, financial and family-oriented, i.e. non-financial objectives (Chua et al. 2018). As Chua et al. (2018) propose in their theoretical model, family-owned firms may perform better than non-family firms when both goals, financial and family-oriented, are complementary and provide a synergistic effect. In contrast, when these financial and family-oriented goals are substitutes, non-family firms will perform better than family-owned firms.

Following this line of reasoning, the authors propose that SME family-ownership goals have different effects on both dimensions of resilience.

A Complementary Effect of SME Family Ownership Goals on Survival

The last financial and economic crisis threatened the chances of firms' survival (Gottardo & Moisello, 2017; Wilson, Wright & Scholes, 2013). Especially in the case of SMEs, there were huge restrictions on the access to financial credit that led to an increase in bankruptcy rates (McGuinness et al., 2018).

Against this background of increased bankruptcy rates, it is here argued that survival is an overriding goal in which family-owned firms outperform non-family firms because the financial goals of survival are complementary to the family-oriented non-financial ones (Chua et al., 2018). In this sense, bankruptcy may end with a loss of family patrimony (owners are the last creditors to be remunerated during bankruptcy) to the detriment of their financial goals. But, from a SEW perspective, bankruptcy may damage the family's reputation, their emotional endowments and the likelihood of dynastic succession (Berrone,

Cruz, & Gómez-Mejía, 2012; Casillas, Moreno-Menéndez, Barbero & Clinton, 2019). Consequently, the loss of value that bankruptcy generates for family firms is greater than for non-family firms.

As developed further below, there are different arguments that can explain why family-owned SMEs may outperform other firms when facing the likelihood of not surviving. Some of these arguments focus on financial superiority while others concern emotional superiority.

With respect to financial superiority, during the last crisis, credit was rationed and finance suppliers and banks tightened credit conditions for firms. In some cases, access to funding was even stopped (Crespí & Martín-Oliver, 2015; McGuinness et al., 2018). As a result, firms found it very difficult to finance their activities, whether they were current projects or new ones. And, thus, gaining access to financial resources became crucial for survival, as McGuiness et al. (2018) evidence in a sample of 202,696 non-financial unlisted EU SMEs. Crespí and Martín-Oliver (2015), using a panel of more than 14,000 private family firms, found strong evidence of better access to external finance for family firms during the last economic crisis. Due to their long-term commitment and reputation, family-owned firms may access credit more easily since lenders perceive that their interests coincide with those of the family. In a similar line, Wilson et al. (2013) suggest that family firms set up stronger boards, with committed members who have greater human and social capital, and that these features are related to their higher survival rates.

As regards to emotional superiority, research has revealed that one of the main factors that enhances the ability to endure a major disruption is having caring and supportive relationships which offer encouragement and reassurance (American Psychological Association, 2018). In the case of employees, the well-known research by Gittel et al. (2006), conducted on the US airline industry after the terrorist attacks on September 11th, 2001, found that one determining factor which enables resilience in firms is strong employee relationships that improve relational reserves and ensure commitment. In a stressful and threatening environment, where large-scale redundancies are common practice, the importance of a shared project and vision, which characterize family-owned firms, will enhance the psychological sense of safety through the sense of belonging to a community (Amman & Jaussaud, 2012). Family-owned firms will try to preserve their relationship with employees, but also with family members and, moreover, will try to maintain their social capital and reputation (Casillas et al., 2019).

Additionally, in a study of 700,000 UK family-owned firms regarding the first period of the crisis, 2007-2010, Wilson et al. (2013) found that family firms had stronger boards, i.e. their boards enjoyed greater stability, lower resignation rates and fewer past failures than non-family ones, and that these characteristics are associated with lower failure rates. In this sense, stronger and more stable boards may reinforce the argument for better access to financial support because lenders tend to have greater trust in boards that are stable and are made up of well-known directors. Furthermore, under uncertainty, older and more experienced boards of directors, and thus more stable ones, will provide stakeholders with stronger emotional support.

Therefore, in an environment of economic and financial crisis, the effect of family ownership on SME survival will be positive due to their greater access to financial credit, their stronger emotional commitment and their loss aversion (not only financial losses but also emotional ones) in comparison to non-family-owned firms. Hence, as this study argues above,

Hypothesis One: Family ownership has a positive effect on SME survival in a financial and economic crisis context

Recent research states that strategies followed by family firms during a financial and economic crisis may depend on their perception of the survival risk (Casillas et al., 2019). Thus, it can be expected that the complementary effect between the financial goals and the non-financial family-oriented goals for SMEs will vary according to their perception of the pre-crisis SME risk of bankruptcy. In this regard, the authors of this chapter claim that the complementary effect, through which financial superiority is combined with emotional superiority, is moderated negatively for those firms that had already gone bankrupt before the crisis or those that were not at risk of bankruptcy at all.

In the first case, the financial superiority of family-owned SMEs will be reduced if they have to face financial restrictions together with the worst outcome of financial distress (i.e. high risk of bankruptcy). This research argues that, while family-owned firms may access credit more easily, since lenders perceive that their interests coincide with those of the family, their negative profile causes them to have worse access to financing facilities. As McGuinness et al. (2018) state, loans of less than €1 million to Spanish SMEs declined, on average, by 66% against pre-crisis peaks in Spain, greatly restricting access to external finance. In addition, Crespí & Martín-Oliver (2015) show in a sample of more than 19,400 private firms that more than 50% of their firms reduce their leverage and debt during the period of crisis. Furthermore, Crespí & Martín-Oliver (2015) found that the leverage ratio during the last financial crisis was better for family firms not at risk of bankruptcy (Altman Z-score >1.23) than for those which were nearing bankruptcy.

In the latter case, the emotional superiority of family-owned firms is reduced because as they enter the crisis with the best outcome of financial distress (i.e. low risk of bankruptcy), the real risk of losing family reputation or of failure in the preservation of dynastic succession will not take place (Berrone et al., 2012).

In this sense, in the case of medium-level risk of bankruptcy, it is possible to expect the maximum level of high complementarity between the financial and non-financial goals. In such a situation, exit would be seen as a family failure that would increase the likelihood of family financial losses, as well as the loss of family reputation and of preservation of dynastic succession (Chrisman & Patel, 2012). In this regard, Casillas et al. (2019) maintain that the family will become more involved in order to develop quicker and effective strategies to be able to survive.

This leads to the second hypothesis,

Hypothesis Two: The SME risk of bankruptcy before the crisis moderates the relationship between family ownership and SME survival in an environment of financial and economic crisis. This moderation effect has an inverted U shape.

A Substitute Effect of SME Family Ownership on Recovery

Financial and economic crises, like the last recession, are characterized by a large and long-lasting reduction in gross domestic product. The global financial crisis severely hit the demand of SME products and services, leading to a reduction in revenues and in the workforce employed by firms.

In such an environment of decreased demand rates, this study argues that bouncing back and recovering will be a difficult goal to achieve for family-owned firms because in these companies, the family-oriented non-financial goals will counteract (substitute effect) the financial goals of recovery (Chua et al., 2018). In other words, and from the SEW perspective, the effort of investing in recovery may substitute the loss aversion that is typical of family firms (Berrone et al., 2012). And thus, for family firms, their aversion to a loss of value will counteract the goal of financial recovery.

There are different arguments related to socioemotional characteristics that can explain why these firms do not perform well when facing the likelihood of recovering.

Turnaround strategies involve retrenchment and recovery activities, which researchers view differently regarding the balance between them. For some authors, an initial focus only on retrenchment may decrease the firm's innovation capacity, and restrict or inhibit effective recovery activities (Schmitt & Raisch, 2013). Therefore, firms undergoing turnarounds could initiate retrenchment activities and use their savings to overlap recovery activities; that is, to be able to recover, firms must work to efficiently identify and capture new opportunities to prevent organizational inertia and the negative effects of path dependence (Simsek, Heavey, Veiga, & Souder, 2009). Additionally, in the resilience literature, some authors highlight that recovery after a disrupting and stressful event relies on the role of novelty, thinking outside of the box, finding unique solutions, and responding to adversity by increasing innovation and experimentation (Williams et al., 2017).

In regard to efficiently identifying and capturing new opportunities, family business scholars agree that, due to their loss aversion attitude, family-owned firms will be more concerned with avoiding losses than with obtaining gains in order to preserve their SEW, making them risk averse to business opportunities (Chrisman & Patel, 2012). According to SEW researchers, family members wish to preserve and reinforce their socioemotional wealth and those non-economic goals may have a negative effect on the family's innovation behavior (König, Kammerlander, & Enders, 2013).

In this chapter it is argued that under an economic and financial crisis, family-owned SMEs may be especially concerned with the SEW priorities of family members, concentrating mainly on goals related to the firm's survival in which increased efficiency is prioritized through controlling costs, while avoiding the uncertainty of novelty, experimentation and innovation (Block, Miller, Jaskiewicz & Spiegel, 2013). In this line, in a study of 126 firms listed on the Spanish Stock Exchange from 2008 to 2012, Casillas et al. (2019) find evidence of the effect of family involvement (family board members) on the intensity of the retrenchment strategy. Moreover, they find that those adjustment measures were more intense when survival was at risk. This leads to the last hypothesis,

Hypothesis Three: Family ownership has a negative effect on SME recovery under an economic and financial crisis

METHODS

Sample and Data Collection

Geographical and Temporal Context

This study is carried out on Spanish companies that faced the recent recession. The last international economic and financial crisis offers a unique context for analyzing the survival and recovery of family SMEs. During this period, the global economic crisis also struck Europe and was characterized by a simultaneous decrease in demand, together with a significant reduction in available financial credit for firms. These were the main problems faced by euro area SMEs, particularly in countries such as Spain

(European Central Bank, 2013 and 2019; see Figure 1). On the other hand, in many European countries, the impact of the crisis on SMEs (e.g. European Central Bank, 2019), especially Spanish SMEs, increased their vulnerability and failure rates (see Figures 2 and 3). This makes Spain a good environment in which to test the hypotheses of this study.

Spain went into recession in 2009 and came out of it in 2013. The authors take 2015 as the year for dependent variables measurement because that year showed a stabilization in the proportion of companies with difficulties and also in those making profits (Figure 2), which means that the system (economy) had returned to a new state of equilibrium after the perturbation (crisis), in terms of the systems theory. And it was in the last quarter of that year that the Spanish GDP virtually reached its 2008 level, as can be seen in Figure 4.

Sample of the Study

In this study the Bureau Van Dijk ORBIS® database was used to extract a sample which included all Spanish firms with 50 to 250 employees, reporting sales of 10 to 50 million euros in 2006 (three years

Figure 1. The most important problems faced by Spain and Euro Area SMEs. 2010-2017
Source: European Central Bank (2019)

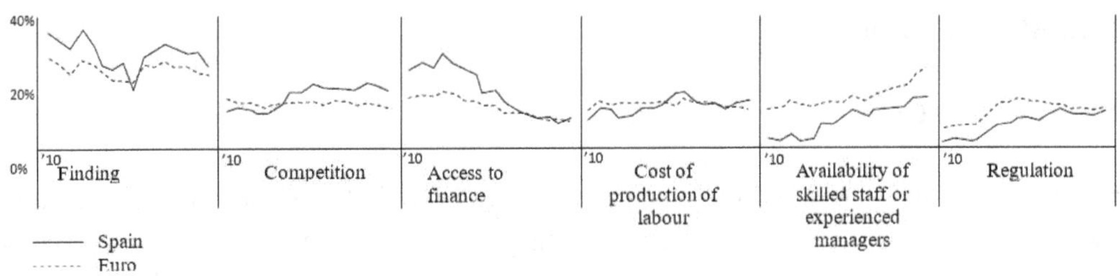

Figure 2. Distressed and profitable firms: Spain vs Euro Area. Percentage of total firms (weighted averaged). 2010-2017
Source: European Central Bank (2019)

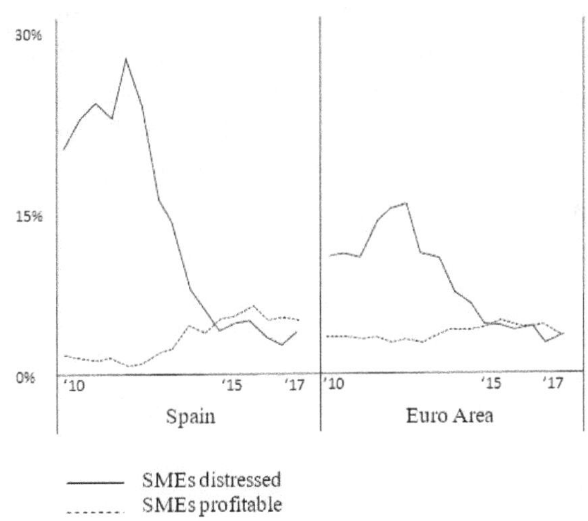

Figure 3. Number of Spanish firms going bankrupt each year
Source: INE (Spanish statistics office) database (www.ine.es)

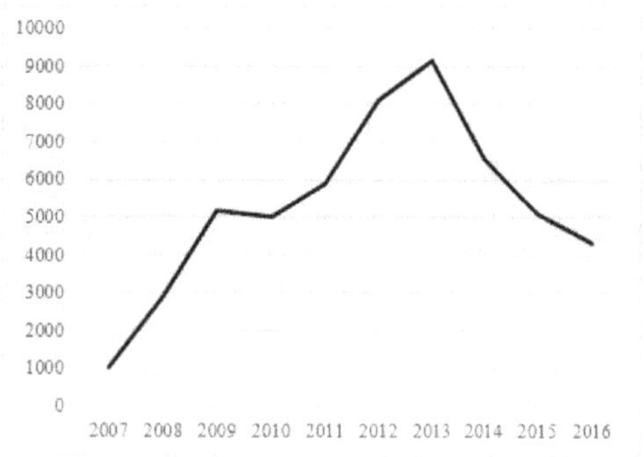

Figure 4. Spanish GDP at current prices (Q4, Euro)
Source: INE (Spanish statistics office) database (www.ine.es).

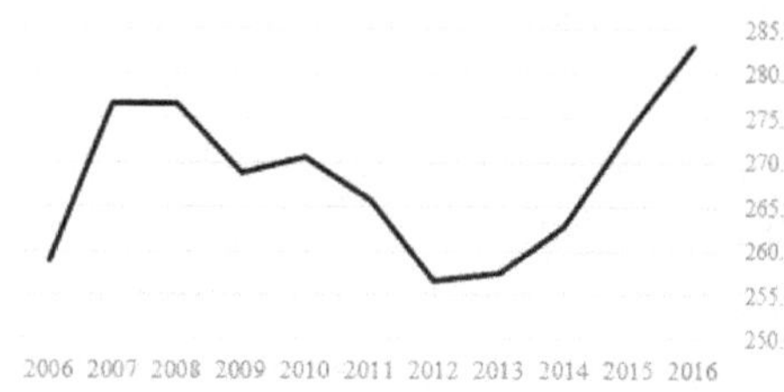

before the financial and economic crisis had started in this country). The authors chose only medium-sized firms given that smaller companies in Spain are exempted from an external audit of their annual accounts and, thus, their accounting information is quite often unreliable. Furthermore, the sample included only manufacturing SMEs that were active from 2006 to 2008. Complete data for 3,133 firms was obtained.

Variables and Measures

Dependent Variables

In this study *recovery* was measured with the ratio of sales in FY2015 to sales in FY2008, and *survival* was measured with a dichotomous variable, depending on whether the company was alive and active (=1) in December 2015 or not (=0). Josefy, Harrison, Sirmon and Carnes (2017) observe that previous scholars operationalized survival with various measures of mortality, such as market exit, bankruptcy or discontinuation of operations, rather than measures such as the number of years a company survived after a baseline or the overall life span of a firm. Thus, in this research, the classification of surviving and failed firms was based on the classification of firms according to their active status marker and firm bankruptcy/liquidation status marker in 2015, taken from ORBIS© database. The companies that appeared as bankrupt were classified as failed firms, since the rehabilitation rate of companies in the focal area that had filed for bankruptcy is less than 6%, according to national statistics. The companies that appeared as liquidated or in liquidation were also marked as failed. On the other hand, the authors verified that no company had ceased its activity because another company had acquired it. On December 31st 2015, 78.61% of the companies in the sample had survived and, on average, surviving firms recovered 103% of their level of sales obtained in 2008.

Independent Variables

Bankruptcy risk was measured with Altman Z-score for private firms in 2008, a procedure previously used for models of bankruptcy and financial distress of SMEs by specialized literature (Altman & Sabato, 2007; McGuinness et al., 2018).

For *family ownership,* this chapter adopted a dichotomous, objective ownership measure based on the Spanish Institute of Family Firm (IEF[2]) studies. The database generated by the IEF (2015) takes into account only firms that were active in 2013. In order to complete the database and classify firms that were active in 2008 but not in 2013, the same process used by IEF (2015) was carried out. The first step of this process follows an automatic classification procedure that allows three categories of firms to be defined: family, non-family and doubtful firms, using a similar process to the one in Rojo, Dieguez and Lopez (2011) and in Pindado and Requejo (2014). For this automatic process, and following the above researchers, the study distinguished between concentrated ownership firms (based on the independence indicator from the ORBIS database, C or D), dispersed ownership firms (independence indicator A or B) and unknown ownership firms (independence indicator U). For independence indicators C and D, family firms were those where a family owned 50.01%; and for the A and B indicators, family firms were firms in which an individual owned more than 5%, or a family owned more than 20% of the firm, and where these family members were also the CEOs. A second step took into account additional information about the boards of directors, and through webpages and professional knowledge it was possible to complete information for the doubtful cases. Firms that belonged to a multinational corporation were automatically excluded.

Control Variables

Taking into consideration the literature on survival, recovery and resilience (Pal, Torstensson, & Mattila, 2014; Parker & Ameen, 2018; Tognazzo, Gubitta, & Favaron, 2016; van Essen, Strike, Carney, & Sapp, 2015), for this study, the authors also included k-1 *industry*, *prior performance* (Altman Z-score in 2008, in the case of recovery analysis) and *firm size* (log of sales in 2008) as control variables.

ANALYSES AND RESULTS

In order to perform hypotheses contrast, here two studies were carried out. The first one dealt with the contrast of hypotheses 1 and 2, both of which are linked to the survival DV, and the second study analyzed hypothesis 3, which predicts a negative relationship between family ownership and recovery.

Previously the authors had made an approximation to the study of the relationship between the independent (IV) and the dependent variables (DV) by means of ANOVA. Figure 5 shows the average of survival and sales recovery by family and non-family-owned firms. The total sample in the survival study is 3,133 firms, 47% of which are family-owned companies, while the total sample in the sales recovery study is 2,339 firms, of which 53% are family-owned companies. According to the ANOVA test, the differences are only significant ($p<.001$) in the case of the survival variable.

The first study was carried out with binary logistic regression, given the binary nature of the DV. Table 1 shows the means, standard deviations and correlations of the variables. Table 2 shows the results of the regressions performed. The first regression (Model 1a) introduces the control variables and is significant (Wald $\chi^2= 118.96, p<.001$) with a pseudo R^2 of 5.77%. It can be observed that there are several industries with significant parameters, and that firm size is significant. The second regression (Model 1b) adds the IV, *family ownership*. The regression is significant and there is an increase in pseudo R^2 up to 12.06%, which is also significant ($\Delta\chi^2_{[1]} >10.82, p<.001$). The parameter associated with family ownership has a significant coefficient, and takes the predicted direction, which supports hypothesis 1.

Figure 5. Survival and recovery of sales in 2015 by type of ownership

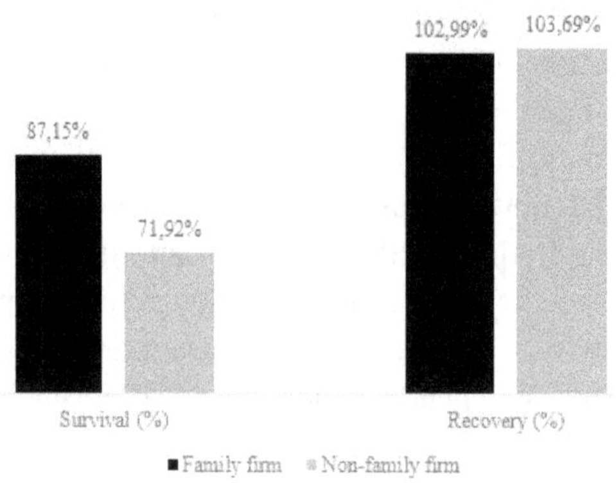

Hypothesis 2 predicts an inverted U-shape interaction effect of bankruptcy risk (Altman Z-score) on the relationship between family ownership and survival. The linear interaction effect between family ownership and bankruptcy risk (Model 1b) is positive and significant (b=.60, p<.001), and the quadratic term is negative and significant (b= –.05, p<.001). The regression shown in Model 1d is also significant (Wald χ^2= 412.49, p<.001), with an increase in pseudo R^2 up to 19.10%, and significantly different from the control model shown in Model 1c ($\Delta\chi^2_{[2]}$ >13.81, p<.001). Thus, the results support hypothesis 2.

Figure 6 illustrates the quadratic moderating effect of bankruptcy risk. The Altman Z-score sets two critical levels: below 1.23, companies are considered at risk of bankruptcy (red zone), and above 2.9, they are considered out of danger (green zone). The grey zone is established between these two levels. Figure 6 shows the difference between the percentage of survival in 2015 of family-owned firms and non-family-owned firms. In the red zone there is no difference in survival rate. In the grey zone, family-owned businesses survive longer than non-family-owned businesses, exceeding their survival rate by almost 20%. In the green zone the differences remain above 10%.

In the second study, hypothesis 3 was tested using ordinary least squares. Here the DV is the *recovery of sales* in 2015. Given that failed or inactive companies were not considered, the sample was reduced to 2,339 companies. In this sample, 53% of the companies are family firms, and the average of sales recovery for all firms in 2015 versus sales in 2008 is 102.99%. Table 3 shows the means, standard deviations and correlations of the variables, and Table 4 shows the results of the regressions performed. The first regression (Model 2a) introduces the control variables (size, industry and performance before the crisis) and is significant with an adjusted R^2 of 8.80%. It can be observed that there are several industries with significant parameters, and that firm size and past performance, measured by a Z-score, are negative and significant. These results are contrary to expectations. Regarding the Z-score, one possible explanation is that companies with low levels of solvency and profitability were already implementing survival strategies, specifically retrenchment strategies. In order to check this point out, a new analysis was carried out where the dependent variable was the recovery of sales in 2015 with respect to 2007. It was verified that the Z-score is no longer significant. The results regarding size are also surprising, although they should be relativized as the bivariate correlation with the dependent variable is not significant (see Table 3). In the second regression (Model 2b) the IV is added. The regression is not significant and there is no increase in pseudo R^2. The parameter associated to family ownership has a non-significant coefficient, which does not support hypothesis 3. This result reinforces the one obtained with ANOVA and illustrated in Figure 5.

Table 1. Study 1: Descriptive statistics

Variable	Median	S.D.	1	2	3	4	5	6	7	8	9	10	11	12	13	14	15	16	17	18	19	20	21	22	23	24	25	26	27	28	29	30
1. Firm survival	.79	.41																														
2. Size (ln 2008 sales)	9.86	.61	.11																													
3. Industry NACE-10	.13	.33	.04	.06																												
4. Industry NACE-11	.02	.14	.03	.01	-.06																											
5. Industry NACE-12	.00	.03	-.01	-.03	-.01	.00																										
6. Industry NACE-13	.03	.17	.01	-.06	-.06	-.02	-.01																									
7. Industry NACE-14	.01	.11	-.05	-.04	-.04	-.02	.00	-.02																								
8. Industry NACE-15	.01	.11	.02	-.05	-.04	-.02	.00	-.02	-.01																							
9. Industry NACE-16	.02	.15	-.04	-.05	-.06	-.02	.00	-.03	-.02	-.02																						
1. Industry NACE-17	.04	.19	.02	.04	-.07	-.03	-.01	-.03	-.02	-.02	-.03																					
11. Industry NACE-18	.03	.17	.00	-.03	-.06	-.02	-.01	-.03	-.02	-.02	-.03	-.03																				
12. Industry NACE-19	.00	.04	.00	.01	-.02	-.01	.00	-.01	.00	.00	-.01	-.01	-.01																			
13. Industry NACE-20	.07	.25	.04	.07	-.10	-.04	-.01	-.04	-.03	-.03	-.04	-.05	-.05	-.01																		
14. Industry NACE-21	.02	.14	.03	.05	-.05	-.02	.00	-.02	-.02	-.02	-.02	-.03	-.02	-.01	-.04																	
15. Industry NACE-22	.07	.25	.04	.01	-.10	-.04	-.01	-.05	-.03	-.03	-.04	-.05	-.05	-.01	-.07	-.04																
16. Industry NACE-23	.11	.31	-.07	-.07	-.13	-.05	-.01	-.06	-.04	-.04	-.05	-.07	-.06	-.01	-.09	-.05	-.09															
17. Industry NACE-24	.04	.19	.01	.07	-.07	-.03	-.01	-.03	-.02	-.02	-.03	-.04	-.03	-.01	-.05	-.03	-.05	-.07														
18. Industry NACE-26	.02	.14	-.04	.00	-.05	-.02	.00	-.02	-.02	-.02	-.02	-.03	-.02	-.01	-.04	-.02	-.04	-.05	-.03													

continued on following page

Table 1. Continued

Variable	Median	S.D.	1	2	3	4	5	6	7	8	9	10	11	12	13	14	15	16	17	18	19	20	21	22	23	24	25	26	27	28	29	30
19. Industry NACE-27	.04	.19	-.02	.01	-.08	-.03	-.01	-.03	-.02	-.02	-.03	-.04	-.03	-.01	-.05	-.03	-.05	-.07	-.04	-.03												
20. Industry NACE-28	.07	.26	.01	-.01	-.10	-.04	-.01	-.05	-.03	-.03	-.04	-.05	-.05	-.01	-.07	-.04	-.07	-.09	-.05	-.04	-.05											
21. Industry NACE-29	.05	.23	.02	.08	-.09	-.03	-.01	-.04	-.03	-.03	-.04	-.05	-.04	-.01	-.06	-.03	-.06	-.08	-.05	-.03	-.05	-.07										
22. Industry NACE-30	.01	.11	-.02	.03	-.04	-.02	.00	-.02	-.01	-.01	-.02	-.02	-.02	.00	-.03	-.02	-.03	-.04	-.02	-.02	-.02	-.03	-.03									
23. Industry NACE-31	.03	.17	-.07	-.10	-.07	-.03	-.01	-.03	-.02	-.02	-.03	-.03	-.03	-.01	-.05	-.02	-.05	-.06	-.03	-.02	-.03	-.05	-.04	-.02								
24. Industry NACE-32	.01	.11	.02	.00	-.04	-.02	.00	-.02	-.01	-.01	-.02	-.02	-.02	.00	-.03	-.01	-.03	-.04	-.02	-.01	-.02	-.03	-.03	-.01	-.02							
25. Industry NACE-33	.01	.09	.01	.01	-.03	-.01	.00	-.02	-.01	-.01	-.01	-.02	-.02	.00	-.02	-.01	-.02	-.03	-.02	-.01	-.02	-.02	-.02	-.01	-.02	-.01						
26. Industry NACE-35	.01	.08	-.04	.05	-.03	-.01	.00	-.01	-.01	-.01	-.01	-.02	-.01	.00	-.02	-.01	-.02	-.03	-.02	-.01	-.02	-.02	-.02	-.01	-.01	-.01	-.01					
27. Industry NACE-36	.02	.14	.04	.01	-.05	-.02	.00	-.02	-.02	-.02	-.02	-.03	-.02	-.01	-.04	-.02	-.04	-.05	-.03	-.02	-.03	-.04	-.03	-.02	-.02	-.02	-.01	-.01				
28. Industry NACE-37	.00	.04	-.03	-.01	-.02	-.01	.00	-.01	.00	.00	-.01	-.01	-.01	.00	-.01	-.01	-.01	-.02	-.01	-.01	-.01	-.01	-.01	-.01	-.01	.00	.00	.00	-.01			
29. Industry NACE-38	.01	.12	.01	.01	-.05	-.02	.00	-.02	-.01	-.01	-.02	-.02	-.02	.00	-.03	-.02	-.03	-.04	-.02	-.02	-.02	-.03	-.03	-.01	-.02	-.01	-.01	-.01	-.02	-.01		
30. Family firm	.47	.50	.19	-.05	.13	.01	-.03	-.01	.03	.03	.04	-.02	-.02	-.01	-.03	-.04	.00	-.02	-.01	-.01	-.02	.01	.00	-.02	.03	-.01	.01	-.05	-.09	.00	-.03	
31. 2008 Altman Z-score	2.35	1.42	.21	.12	.04	.00	-.01	-.03	-.01	.03	.00	-.01	-.05	-.01	.00	.02	-.02	-.05	.04	.03	.05	.02	.00	-.03	.01	.01	.02	.01	-.06	.01	-.02	.14

Notes: N=3,133. All correlations that are equal to or greater than |.04| are significant at $p<0.05$.

Table 2. Study 1: Analysis of firm survival via binary logistic regression

	Dependent Variable = survival in FY2015											
	Model 1a			Model 1b			Model 1c			Model 1d		
Variables	**B**	**Exp(B)**	*p-value*	**B**	**Exp(B)**	*p-value*	**B**	**Exp(B)**	*p-value*	**B**	**Exp(B)**	*p-value*
Constant	-2.57	.08	.000	-3.49	**.03**	.000	-3.34	.04	.000	-3.25	.04	.000
Size (*ln* 2008 sales)	.37	1.45	.000	.43	**1.53**	.000	.30	1.35	.000	.32	1.38	.000
Industry NACE-10	.46	1.59	.010	.27	**1.31**	.148	.38	1.46	.045	.35	1.42	.068
Industry NACE-11	.83	2.29	.036	.82	**2.27**	.041	.99	2.70	.015	.97	2.63	.018
Industry NACE-12	-.21	.81	.867	.25	**1.28**	.845	.42	1.52	.747	.37	1.45	.772
Industry NACE-13	.49	1.62	.109	.52	**1.69**	.092	.63	1.88	.053	.58	1.79	.069
Industry NACE-14	-.56	.57	.108	-.74	**.48**	.042	-.70	.50	.067	-.75	.47	.058
Industry NACE-15	.88	2.41	.075	.76	**2.14**	.133	.69	1.99	.183	.62	1.85	.234
Industry NACE-16	-.26	.77	.342	-.42	**.66**	.137	-.40	.67	.167	-.42	.66	.149
Industry NACE-17	.48	1.61	.086	.52	**1.68**	.067	.62	1.87	.033	.60	1.82	.040
Industry NACE-18	.30	1.35	.300	.35	**1.42**	.233	.51	1.67	.084	.52	1.68	.080
Industry NACE-19	.24	1.27	.833	.30	**1.34**	.796	.35	1.42	.762	.34	1.40	.769
Industry NACE-20	.58	1.79	.011	.64	**1.90**	.006	.74	2.10	.002	.67	1.96	.005
Industry NACE-21	.85	2.34	.045	1.01	**2.76**	.019	1.01	2.76	.019	1.01	2.75	.019
Industry NACE-22	.64	1.90	.005	.64	**1.90**	.005	.77	2.16	.001	.74	2.09	.002
Industry NACE-23	-.22	.80	.190	-.23	**.80**	.189	-.11	.90	.549	-.12	.88	.478
Industry NACE-24	.30	1.35	.269	.32	**1.37**	.249	.30	1.35	.283	.29	1.34	.299
Industry NACE-26	-.37	.69	.225	-.36	**.70**	.246	-.42	.66	.194	-.41	.67	.207
Industry NACE-27	-.05	.95	.844	-.01	**.99**	.980	-.11	.90	.664	-.13	.88	.603
Industry NACE-28	.25	1.29	.217	.22	**1.25**	.288	.23	1.26	.281	.22	1.24	.307
Industry NACE-29	.32	1.38	.166	.31	**1.37**	.187	.42	1.52	.088	.35	1.42	.150
Industry NACE-30	-.16	.85	.667	-.09	**.92**	.817	.13	1.14	.739	.09	1.10	.810
Industry NACE-31	-.53	.59	.028	-.68	**.51**	.007	-.75	.47	.004	-.78	.46	.003
Industry NACE-32	.68	1.97	.171	.72	**2.04**	.156	.83	2.30	.106	.80	2.23	.119
Industry NACE-33	.53	1.70	.343	.49	**1.63**	.396	.31	1.37	.587	.27	1.31	.639
Industry NACE-35	-.89	.41	.051	-.65	**.52**	.163	-.61	.55	.222	-.70	.50	.161
Industry NACE-36	1.11	3.02	.013	1.41	**4.10**	.002	1.69	5.43	.000	1.64	5.13	.000
Industry NACE-37	-1.09	.34	.188	-1.21	**.30**	.163	-1.36	.26	.150	-1.61	.20	.110
Industry NACE-38	.42	1.52	.303	.56	**1.75**	.176	.73	2.07	.085	.69	1.99	.101
Family firm				1.10	**3.01**	.000	.98	2.67	.000	.04	1.04	.879
2008 Altman Z score							.55	1.73	.000	.30	1.34	.000
2008 Altman Z score (squared) (SQR_ ZAltman08							-.02	.98	.002	.02	1.02	.120
Family firm x 2008 Altman Z score										.60	1.83	.000
Family firm x 2008 Altman Z score (squared)										-.05	.95	.000
Wald chi-square	118.96		.000	254.04		.000	391.51		.000	412.49		.000
Nagelkerke R square	5.77%			12.06%			18.19%			19.10%		
-2 Log likelihood	3133.20			2998.12			2860.64			2839.67		
Note: N = 3133.												

Table 3. Study 2: descriptive statistics

Variable	Median	S.D.	1	2	3	4	5	6	7	8	9	10	11	12	13	14	15	16	17	18	19	20	21	22	23	24	25	26	27	28	29	30
1. Recovery	1,03	.68																														
2. Size (ln 2008 sales)	9,91	.55	-.02																													
3. Industry NACE-10	.13	.34	.15	.07																												
4. Industry NACE-11	.02	.15	.01	.01	-.06																											
5. Industry NACE-12	.00	.02	-.02	-.05	-.01	.00																										
6. Industry NACE-13	.03	.17	-.03	-.04	-.07	-.03	.00																									
7. Industry NACE-14	.01	.10	-.02	-.03	-.04	-.02	.00	-.02																								
8. Industry NACE-15	.01	.12	.03	-.06	-.05	-.02	.00	-.02	-.01																							
9. Industry NACE-16	.02	.14	-.03	-.05	-.06	-.02	.00	-.03	-.02	-.02																						
1. Industry NACE-17	.04	.20	.03	.03	-.08	-.03	.00	-.04	-.02	-.02	-.03																					
11. Industry NACE-18	.03	.16	-.04	-.04	-.06	-.03	.00	-.03	-.02	-.02	-.02	-.03																				
12. Industry NACE-19	.00	.04	-.01	.01	-.02	-.01	.00	-.01	.00	.00	-.01	-.01	-.01																			
13. Industry NACE-20	.07	.26	.09	.07	-.11	-.04	-.01	-.05	-.03	-.03	-.04	-.06	-.05	-.01																		
14. Industry NACE-21	.02	.14	.10	.07	-.06	-.02	.00	-.03	-.02	-.02	-.02	-.03	-.02	-.01	-.04																	
15. Industry NACE-22	.07	.26	.02	.00	-.11	-.04	-.01	-.05	-.03	-.03	-.04	-.06	-.05	-.01	-.08	-.04																
16. Industry NACE-23	.09	.29	-.16	-.07	-.13	-.05	-.01	-.06	-.03	-.04	-.05	-.07	-.05	-.01	-.09	-.05	-.09															
17. Industry NACE-24	.04	.19	-.04	.08	-.08	-.03	.00	-.03	-.02	-.02	-.03	-.04	-.03	-.01	-.06	-.03	-.06	-.06														
18. Industry NACE-26	.02	.13	.03	-.02	-.05	-.02	.00	-.02	-.01	-.02	-.02	-.03	-.02	-.01	-.04	-.02	-.04	-.04	-.03													
19. Industry NACE-27	.03	.18	-.03	-.01	-.07	-.03	.00	-.03	-.02	-.02	-.03	-.04	-.03	-.01	-.05	-.03	-.05	-.06	-.04	-.03												
20. Industry NACE-28	.07	.26	-.05	-.01	-.11	-.04	-.01	-.05	-.03	-.03	-.04	-.06	-.05	-.01	-.08	-.04	-.08	-.09	-.06	-.04	-.05											
21. Industry NACE-29	.06	.23	.08	.09	-.10	-.04	-.01	-.04	-.03	-.03	-.04	-.05	-.04	-.01	-.07	-.04	-.07	-.08	-.05	-.03	-.05	-.07										

continued on following page

Table 3. Continued

Variable	Median	S.D.	1	2	3	4	5	6	7	8	9	10	11	12	13	14	15	16	17	18	19	20	21	22	23	24	25	26	27	28	29	30
22. Industry NACE-30	.01	.11	.00	.01	-.04	-.02	.00	-.02	-.01	-.01	-.02	-.02	-.02	.00	-.03	-.02	-.03	-.04	-.02	-.01	-.02	-.03	-.03									
23. Industry NACE-31	.02	.15	-.03	-.09	-.06	-.02	.00	-.03	-.02	-.02	-.02	-.03	-.02	-.01	-.04	-.02	-.04	-.05	-.03	-.02	-.03	-.04	-.04	-.02								
24. Industry NACE-32	.01	.11	.00	-.02	-.04	-.02	.00	-.02	-.01	-.01	-.02	-.02	-.02	.00	-.03	-.02	-.03	-.03	-.02	-.01	-.02	-.03	-.03	-.01	-.02							
25. Industry NACE-33	.01	.09	-.03	.01	-.04	-.01	.00	-.02	-.01	-.01	-.01	-.02	-.02	.00	-.03	-.01	-.03	-.03	-.02	-.01	-.02	-.03	-.02	-.01	-.01	-.01						
26. Industry NACE-35	.00	.07	-.06	.04	-.03	-.01	.00	-.01	-.01	-.01	-.01	-.01	-.01	.00	-.02	-.01	-.02	-.02	-.01	-.01	-.01	-.02	-.02	-.01	-.01	-.01	-.01					
27. Industry NACE-36	.02	.15	.02	.00	-.06	-.02	.00	-.03	-.02	-.02	-.02	-.03	-.03	-.01	-.04	-.02	-.04	-.05	-.03	-.02	-.03	-.04	-.04	-.02	-.02	-.02	-.01	-.01				
28. Industry NACE-37	.00	.04	.01	.01	-.01	-.01	.00	-.01	.00	.00	-.01	-.01	-.01	.00	-.01	-.01	-.01	-.01	-.01	.00	-.01	-.01	-.01	.00	-.01	.00	.00	.00	-.01			
29. Industry NACE-38	.01	.12	-.03	-.01	-.05	-.02	.00	-.02	-.01	-.01	-.02	-.03	-.02	-.01	-.03	-.02	-.03	-.04	-.02	-.02	-.02	-.03	-.03	-.01	-.02	-.01	-.01	-.01	-.02	.00		
30. Family firm	.53	.50	.01	-.13	.14	.00	-.02	-.02	.06	.04	.06	-.04	-.02	.00	-.06	-.06	.00	.01	-.02	-.02	.00	-.01	-.01	-.01	.08	.00	.01	-.05	-.12	.03	-.07	
31. 2008 Altman Z-score	2,52	1,38	-.09	.03	.05	-.02	-.03	-.01	.00	.03	.02	-.03	-.06	-.01	-.02	-.01	-.02	-.02	.04	.03	.05	.01	.00	-.02	.02	.02	.02	-.01	-.08	.03	-.04	.12

Notes: N=2,339. All correlations that are equal to or greater than |.04| are significant at $p<0.05$.

Table 4. Study 2: Analysis of recovery via OLS.

Dependent Variable = sales recovery in FY2015							
	Model 2a				Model 2b		
Variables	**B**	**Beta**	**p-value**		**B**	**Beta**	**p-value**
Constant	1.78		.000		1.77		.000
Size (*ln* 2008 sales)	-.08	-.06	.002		-.08	-.06	.002
2008 Altman Z-score	-.05	-.10	.000		-.05	-.10	.000
Industry NACE-10	.41	.21	.000		.41	.21	.000
Industry NACE-11	.17	.04	.078		.17	.04	.079
Industry NACE-12	-.56	-.02	.387		-.56	-.02	.389
Industry NACE-13	.01	.00	.874		.01	.00	.874
Industry NACE-14	.02	.00	.904		.02	.00	.909
Industry NACE-15	.28	.05	.022		.28	.05	.022
Industry NACE-16	.01	.00	.924		.01	.00	.929
Industry NACE-17	.22	.06	.004		.22	.06	.004
Industry NACE-18	-.04	-.01	.627		-.04	-.01	.628
Industry NACE-19	-.09	-.01	.782		-.09	-.01	.782
Industry NACE-20	.36	.14	.000		.36	.14	.000
Industry NACE-21	.61	.13	.000		.61	.13	.000
Industry NACE-22	.17	.07	.006		.17	.07	.006
Industry NACE-23	-.23	-.10	.000		-.23	-.10	.000
Industry NACE-24	.04	.01	.622		.04	.01	.622
Industry NACE-26	.28	.05	.009		.28	.05	.009
Industry NACE-27	.06	.02	.487		.06	.02	.487
Industry NACE-28	.02	.01	.743		.02	.01	.744
Industry NACE-29	.37	.12	.000		.37	.12	.000
Industry NACE-30	.11	.02	.392		.11	.02	.392
Industry NACE-31	-.01	.00	.915		-.01	.00	.910
Industry NACE-32	.16	.03	.220		.16	.03	.221
Industry NACE-33	-.03	.00	.832		-.03	.00	.831
Industry NACE-35	-.40	-.04	.046		-.40	-.04	.047
Industry NACE-36	.19	.04	.050		.19	.04	.050
Industry NACE-37	.33	.02	.388		.32	.02	.390
Industry NACE-38	-.07	-.01	.574		-.06	-.01	.579
Family firm					.00	.00	.918
Adjusted R^2	8.78%				8.74%		
ΔAdjusted R^2					-.04		.918

Note: N=2,339.

Figure 6. Family vs non-family-owned firms' rate of survival in 2015 by Altman Z-score's zones

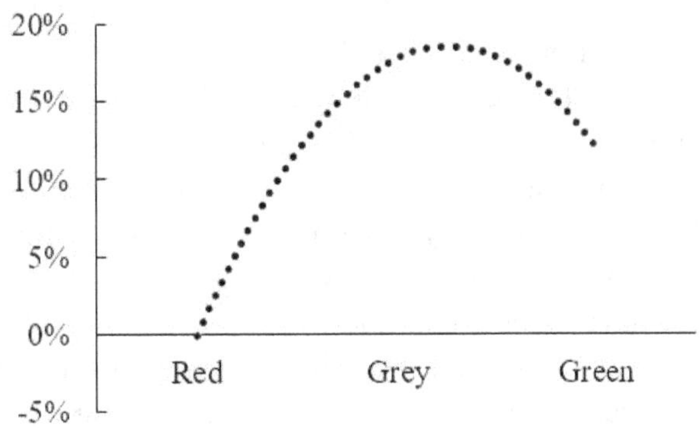

CONCLUSION

This chapter uses the context of the last economic and financial crisis to analyze the effect of family ownership on SME resilience. After an external disturbing event like the recent crisis, many companies must change their goals. In this respect, it is particularly interesting to study the behavior of family firms. Most family business researchers seem to agree that the goals of family-owned companies include obtaining family-oriented non-financial benefits as well as satisfying the family's affective needs, such as identity, safety, or the family's influence (Chua et al., 2018). Yet, while these goals are sometimes also considered relevant for non-family firms, they are of utmost importance for family-owned firms.

Recent interest in the role of the multiplicity of goals in family firm performance has increased the understanding of their risk-taking propensities (Chua et al., 2018; Patel & Chrisman, 2014). This study extends the understanding by proposing that not only do family-owned SMEs have higher survival rates than non-family firms, but also that they have greater difficulties in recovering than non-family firms given the nature – complementary or substitute – of their goals. Additionally, this study finds evidence of a moderating effect of SMEs' risk of bankruptcy, before the crisis, on the complementarity between financial and non-financial goals.

This study examined how family ownership influences survival and recovery in SMEs. The results show that family ownership has a positive effect on the survival of family-owned firms, which is the first good news. Furthermore, in line with other recent studies (Gottardo & Moisello, 2017), this chapter highlights that these firms' idiosyncrasy helps them to outperform non-family firms when facing the likelihood of not surviving.

However, the authors found no evidence regarding the possible negative effect of family ownership on recovery, as proposed. Thus, there is good news for family firms once again. Indeed, the results exhibit that recovery in family firms is similar to that of non-family owned firms. The authors assumed that the loss aversion attitude of family-owned firms undermines their capacity to perceive and seize new opportunities, which is needed to recover. From the point of view of the substitute effect of goals, this chapter confirms the trade-off between growth and risk shrinking objectives, or between retrenchment and recovery activities in family-owned SMEs. Nevertheless, in a hostile environment, when the continuity of the family firm is at stake, i.e., when their socioemotional wealth is at risk, loss-averse family-firm owners may be motivated to adopt innovative behaviors, simply to make the risk disappear. Therefore, the findings of the study are more in line with the behavioral agency theory which suggests that, in this situation, the motivation to seize new opportunities for experimentation and innovation, to be able to rectify the trajectory, should be strong among family owners who put both their economic and socioemotional wealth at risk (Carney, 2005; Gómez-Mejía et al., 2011; Wiseman & Gómez-Mejía, 1998).

Lastly, the results also confirm the moderating effect of previous bankruptcy risk on the relationship between family ownership and survival. This implies that the complementary effect generated by combining the emotional and financial superiority of family-owned firms diminishes in those cases where the previous risk of bankruptcy was very high or very low.

To summarize, this study offers several contributions. First, it contributes to the literature by illustrating that family-owned firms are able to reconcile their financial and non-financial goals – the latter yielding family-oriented intangible benefits – when trying to survive during recession. Their risk-taking propensity to pursue financial and non-financial goals is in the same direction when the continuity of the company is in danger. In other words, the findings of the study suggest that family-owned firms make decisions aimed at preserving the family's financial and socioemotional wealth. The evidence found of complementarity between goals goes beyond previous studies, which presumed incompatibility between financial and non-financial goals (Gómez-Mejía, Makri & Larraza-Kintana, 2010).

Second, this chapter also contributes to the literature of organizational resilience by investigating family ownership as an antecedent of resilience (survival and recovery) in SMEs, a topic that researchers have demanded be given more attention (Linnenluecke, 2017). By identifying firm ownership as a key factor in SME resilience, this study adds a new finding to the scarce research on the antecedents of resilience at an organizational level and sheds some light on the sources of resilience in SMEs.

In addition to the contributions described, certain limitations must also be acknowledged that could lead to interesting lines of further research. This chapter compared family-owned SMEs with non-family firms in terms of their resilience during times of distress. However, here the focus was only on one of the main characteristics of family firms, their ownership, while other family firm features could also help explain the complementary and substitute relationships between financial and family-oriented goals for achieving resilience. In this sense, it would be interesting to examine other family firm features, specifically those related to their emotional wealth, in order to analyze the differences in SME firms in terms of resilience (survival and recovery).

ACKNOWLEDGMENT

This research was supported by the Spanish Ministry of Science, Innovation and Universities [grant number ECO2016-80002-R].

REFERENCES

Altman, E. I., & Sabato, G. (2007). Modelling credit risk for SMEs: Evidence from the US market. *Abacus*, *43*(3), 332–357. doi:10.1111/j.1467-6281.2007.00234.x

Amann, B., & Jaussaud, J. (2012). Family and non-family business resilience in an economic downturn. *Asia Pacific Business Review*, *18*(2), 203–223. doi:10.1080/13602381.2010.537057

American Psychological Association. (2018). Retrieved from https://www.apa.org

Berrone, P., Cruz, C., & Gomez-Mejia, L. R. (2012). Socioemotional wealth in family firms: Theoretical dimensions, assessment approaches, and agenda for future research. *Family Business Review*, *25*(3), 258–279. doi:10.1177/0894486511435355

Block, J., Miller, D., Jaskiewicz, P., & Spiegel, F. (2013). Economic and technological importance of innovations in large family and founder firms: An analysis of patent data. *Family Business Review*, *26*(2), 180–199. doi:10.1177/0894486513477454

Buyl, T., Boone, C., & Wade, J. B. (2019). CEO narcissism, risk-taking, and resilience: An empirical analysis in US commercial banks. *Journal of Management*, *45*(4), 1372–1400. doi:10.1177/0149206317699521

Carney, M. (2005). Corporate governance and competitive advantage in family-controlled firms. *Entrepreneurship Theory and Practice*, *29*(3), 249–265. doi:10.1111/j.1540-6520.2005.00081.x

Casillas, J. C., Moreno-Menéndez, A. M., Barbero, J. L., & Clinton, E. (2019). Retrenchment strategies and family involvement: The role of survival. *Family Business Review*, *32*(1), 58–75.

Chrisman, J. J., & Patel, P. C. (2012). Variations in R&D investments of family and nonfamily firms: Behavioral agency and myopic loss aversion perspectives. *Academy of Management Journal*, *55*(4), 976–997. doi:10.5465/amj.2011.0211

Chua, J. H., Chrisman, J. J., De Massis, A., & Wang, H. (2018). Reflections on family firm goals and the assessment of performance. *Journal of Family Business Strategy*, *9*(2), 107–113. doi:10.1016/j.jfbs.2018.02.001

Crespí, R., & Martín-Oliver, A. (2015). Do family firms have better access to external finance during crises? *Corporate Governance*, *23*(3), 249–265. doi:10.1111/corg.12100

De Massis, A., Kotlar, J., Campopiano, G., & Cassia, L. (2013). Dispersion of family ownership and the performance of small-to-medium size private family firms. *Journal of Family Business Strategy*, *4*(3), 166–175. doi:10.1016/j.jfbs.2013.05.001

DesJardine, M., Bansal, P., & Yang, Y. (2019). Bouncing Back: Building resilience through social and environmental practices in the context of the 2008 global financial crisis. *Journal of Management*, *45*(4), 1434–1460. doi:10.1177/0149206317708854

Duchek, S. (2019). Organizational resilience: a capability-based conceptualization. *Business Research, 1-32, https://doi.org/10.1007/s40685-019-0085-7.*

Dyer, W. G. (2018). Are family firms really better? Reexamining "examining the 'family effect'on firm performance". *Family Business Review*, *31*(2), 240–248. doi:10.1177/0894486518776516

European Central Bank. (2013). *Survey on the Access to Finance of Enterprises in the euro area – October 2012 to March 2013*. Author.

European Central Bank. (2018). *Survey on the Access to Finance of Enterprises in the euro area – October 2018 to March 2019*. Author.

Gittell, J. H., Cameron, K., Lim, S., & Rivas, V. (2006). Relationships, layoffs, and organizational resilience: Airline industry responses to September 11. *The Journal of Applied Behavioral Science*, *42*(3), 300–329. doi:10.1177/0021886306286466

Gomez-Mejia, L. R., Cruz, C., Berrone, P., & De Castro, J. (2011). The bind that ties: Socioemotional wealth preservation in family firms. *The Academy of Management Annals*, *5*(1), 653–707. doi:10.1080/19416520.2011.593320

Gomez-Mejia, L. R., Makri, M., & Kintana, M. L. (2010). Diversification decisions in family-controlled firms. *Journal of Management Studies*, *47*(2), 223–252. doi:10.1111/j.1467-6486.2009.00889.x

Gottardo, P., & Moisello, A. M. (2017). Family Firms, Risk-taking and Financial Distress. *Problems and Perspectives in Management*, *15*(2), 168–177. doi:10.21511/ppm.15(2-1).2017.01

Hamel, G., & Välikangas, L. (2003). The Quest for Resilience 2003. *Harvard Business Review*, (Sept), 52–62. PMID:12964393

Harries, T., McEwen, L., & Wragg, A. (2018). Why it takes an 'ontological shock' to prompt increases in small firm resilience: Sense making, emotions and flood risk. *International Small Business Journal*, *36*(6), 712–733. doi:10.1177/0266242618765231

Instituto de Empresa Familiar. (2015). *La empresa Familiar en España*. Barcelona: Author.

Josefy, M. A., Harrison, J. S., Sirmon, D. G., & Carnes, C. (2017). Living and dying: Synthesizing the literature on firm survival and failure across stages of development. *The Academy of Management Annals*, *11*(2), 770–799. doi:10.5465/annals.2015.0148

König, A., Kammerlander, N., & Enders, A. (2013). The family innovator's dilemma: How family influence affects the adoption of discontinuous technologies by incumbent firms. *Academy of Management Review*, *38*(3), 418–441. doi:10.5465/amr.2011.0162

Linnenluecke, M. K. (2017). Resilience in business and management research: A review of influential publications and a research agenda. *International Journal of Management Reviews*, *19*(1), 4–30. doi:10.1111/ijmr.12076

Lubatkin, M. H., Simsek, Z., Ling, Y., & Veiga, J. F. (2006). Ambidexterity and performance in small-to medium-sized firms: The pivotal role of top management team behavioral integration. *Journal of Management*, *32*(5), 646–672. doi:10.1177/0149206306290712

McGuinness, G., Hogan, T., & Powell, R. (2018). European trade credit use and SME survival. *Journal of Corporate Finance*, *49*, 81–103. doi:10.1016/j.jcorpfin.2017.12.005

Meyer, A. D. (1982). Adapting to environmental jolts. *Administrative Science Quarterly*, *27*(4), 515–537. doi:10.2307/2392528 PMID:10257768

O'Reilly, C. A. III, & Tushman, M. L. (2008). Ambidexterity as a dynamic capability: Resolving the innovator's dilemma. *Research in Organizational Behavior*, *28*, 185–206. doi:10.1016/j.riob.2008.06.002

Pal, R., Torstensson, H., & Mattila, H. (2014). Antecedents of organizational resilience in economic crises—An empirical study of Swedish textile and clothing SMEs. *International Journal of Production Economics*, *147*, 410–428. doi:10.1016/j.ijpe.2013.02.031

Parker, H., & Ameen, K. (2018). The role of resilience capabilities in shaping how firms respond to disruptions. *Journal of Business Research*, *88*, 535–541. doi:10.1016/j.jbusres.2017.12.022

Pindado, J., & Requejo, I. (2015). Family business performance from a governance perspective: A review of empirical research. *International Journal of Management Reviews*, *17*(3), 279–311. doi:10.1111/ijmr.12040

Raisch, S., & Birkinshaw, J. (2008). Organizational ambidexterity: Antecedents, outcomes, and moderators. *Journal of Management*, *34*(3), 375–409. doi:10.1177/0149206308316058

Rodríguez-Sánchez, A., Guinot, J., Chiva, R., & López-Cabrales, Á. (2019). How to emerge stronger: Antecedents and consequences of organizational resilience. *Journal of Management & Organization*, 1–18. doi:10.1017/jmo.2019.5

Rojo, A., Diéguez, J., & López, P. (2011). Importancia del concepto de Empresa Familiar en investigación: Utilización de la base de datos SABI para su clasificación. *Revista de Empresa Familiar*, *1*(1), 53–67.

Sarkees, M., Hulland, J., & Chatterjee, R. (2014). Investments in exploitation and exploration capabilities: Balance versus focus. *Journal of Marketing Theory and Practice*, *22*(1), 7–24. doi:10.2753/MTP1069-6679220101

Schmitt, A., & Raisch, S. (2013). Corporate turnarounds: The duality of retrenchment and recovery. *Journal of Management Studies*, *50*(7), 1216–1244.

Simsek, Z., Heavey, C., Veiga, J. F., & Souder, D. (2009). A typology for aligning organizational ambidexterity's conceptualizations, antecedents, and outcomes. *Journal of Management Studies*, *46*(5), 864–894. doi:10.1111/j.1467-6486.2009.00841.x

Sutcliffe, K. M., & Vogus, T. J. (2003). Organization for resilience. In K. Cameron, J. E. Dutton, & R. E. Quinn (Eds.), Positive Organizational Scholarship (pp. 94–110). San Francisco: Academic Press.

Tognazzo, A., Gubitta, P., & Favaron, S. D. (2016). Does slack always affect resilience? A study of quasi-medium-sized Italian firms. *Entrepreneurship and Regional Development*, *28*(9-10), 768–790. doi:10.1080/08985626.2016.1250820

van der Vegt, G. S., Essens, P., Walshtröm, M., & George, G. (2015). Managing Risk and Resilience. *Academy of Management Journal*, *59*(4), 971–980. doi:10.5465/amj.2015.4004

van Essen, M., Strike, V. M., Carney, M., & Sapp, S. (2015). The resilient family firm: Stakeholder outcomes and institutional effects. *Corporate Governance*, *23*(3), 167–183. doi:10.1111/corg.12087

Wagner, D., Block, J. H., Miller, D., Schwens, C., & Xi, G. (2015). A meta-analysis of the financial performance of family firms: Another attempt. *Journal of Family Business Strategy*, *6*(1), 3–13. doi:10.1016/j.jfbs.2015.01.001

Williams, T. A., Gruber, D. A., Sutcliffe, K. M., Shepherd, D. A., & Zhao, E. Y. (2017). Organizational response to adversity: Fusing crisis management and resilience research streams. *The Academy of Management Annals*, *11*(2), 733–769. doi:10.5465/annals.2015.0134

Wilson, N., Wright, M., & Scholes, L. (2013). Family Business Survival and the Role of Boards. *Entrepreneurship Theory and Practice*, *37*(Nov), 1369–1389. doi:10.1111/etap.12071

Wiseman, R. M., & Gomez-Mejia, L. R. (1998). A behavioral agency model of managerial risk taking. *Academy of Management Review*, *23*(1), 133–153. doi:10.5465/amr.1998.192967

KEY TERMS AND DEFINITIONS

Economic and Financial Crisis: A situation in which a country's economy suffers a downturn caused by a financial crisis.

Family-Owned Firm: Any business in which two or more family members are involved and the majority of the property or control is within a family.

Organizational Resilience: The ability of an organization to absorb, compel and recover its form through its actions and behaviors after a disruptive shock.

Recovery: To return to a natural or original state.

Risk of Bankruptcy: The probability that a company will not be able to satisfy its debt commitments. The Altman Z-Score is a simple method of analyzing its likelihood.

SMEs: Small and medium-sized enterprises. Companies with 10 to 250 employees, reporting sales of 2 to 50 million euros and/or a balance sheet total of 2 to 43 million euros.

Survival: Refers to the duration of the company. The state or fact of continuing a firm to exist despite challenging conditions.

ENDNOTES

1 Large diversified companies have different markets and products; and thus the adverse effects of an unexpected shock on one of their environments will be offset by other products or markets of their global or diversified scope.

2 The Institute of Family Firms generated this database through the Family Firm Chair Network to which 36 public and private universities from all Spanish regions belong.

Chapter 12
The Quadruple Sustainability: Economic, Social, Environmental, and Family

Beatriz Forés
Universitat Jaume I, Spain

José Antonio Clemente Almendros
Universidad Internacional de La Rioja, Spain

José María Fernández Yáñez
Universitat Jaume I, Spain

ABSTRACT

This chapter analyzes the relationship between ownership structure and sustainability performance adopting the socioemotional wealth approach. This work extends previous literature on the topic by considering the three dimensions of sustainability performance: economic, social, and environmental. Analysis with the matching technique revealed that being a family firm has a positive effect on economic profitability, growth sales, employees training and commitment, investment in R&D, environmental commitment, and cooperation agreements with external partners. The authors use a sample of Spanish firms operating in the tourism industry.

INTRODUCTION

As social and environmental pressures have increased in recent decades, motivated by various scandals and illicit practices, corporate responsibility and sustainability have received growing attention in the literature. In this context, firms are called to act not only as economic agents, but also as important contributors to the solution to social and environmental global issues (Matten & Crane, 2005).

Despite the interest these issues have attracted in recent decades, academia tends to focus on the analysis of large corporations (Collier & Fuller, 2005), while the role of family business (FB) is relatively sidelined and still deserves more study (Bergamaschi & Randerson, 2016). The authors conceive fam-

DOI: 10.4018/978-1-7998-1655-3.ch012

ily firms as those in which multiple members of the same family serve jointly as owners and managers (Miller & Le Breton-Miller, 2005).

The prominence and contribution of FBs to the global economy (Chua et al., 2003; Samara et al., 2018), and specifically in the tourism sector (Memili et al., 2015; Memili et al., 2018), where FBs are clearly predominant, only serves to heighten this need for analysis.

Though still in its infancy, research has begun to unravel with increasing interest the diffusion of sustainability in FB (Lamb & Butler, 2018; Nekhili et al., 2017). The sustainability approach (Brown et al., 1987) encompasses business efforts towards the longer-term benefit to stakeholders of all internal and external organizations (Le Breton-Miller & Miller, 2016; Porter & Kramer, 2006), in economic, social, and environmental terms, and all with equal relevance (Elkington, 2004).

In this vein, the extant literature suggests that the antecedents, results, and triggers underlying sustainable FB patterns differ from those manifested in non-family businesses (NFB) (Campopiano & De Massis, 2014).

The tourism sector is an economic activity with a broadly positive impact on growth and employment (Juul, 2015). However, the concentration of tourists in a set geographical area can also result in a higher risk of damage to natural ecosystems (Aall, 2011). Therefore, considering these tourism firms' dependence on the natural resources of the destination, sustainability is posited as a key condition for both the competitiveness of firms' and destinations alike (Prud'homme & Raymond, 2016).

Specifically, diagnosis of economic, social, and environmental performance of tourism businesses and the factors determining their progress is vital for helping private agents develop the differentiation capacity to place themselves competitively on a level with global competition, thereby ensuring their continuity. Public agents also need to be involved in creating an atmosphere of cooperation and engagement of these businesses in public goods problems and necessities (Bergamaschi & Randerson, 2016).

However, despite the importance of FBs in tourism, research in this area has only been carried out incidentally (Getz & Carlsen, 2005). The aim of this research lies precisely in determining the sustainability performance of the tourism sector based on an analysis of its economic-financial results, comparing FB with NFB. The authors consider that an FB is a firm where a family exerts power over the organization and its strategic direction through ownership, management, or board positions (Pieper, Klein, & Jaskiewicz, 2008).

FBs have peculiarities that lend another dimension to the sustainability construct because they include an additional specific group of stakeholders: the family. In this vein, the presence of family members affects values and culture, governance mechanisms, and strategic positioning. In order to explain the FB attitude to sustainability, the authors ground this analysis in socioemotional wealth (SEW) (Gómez-Mejía et al., 2007; Marques et al., 2014) and, specifically, in the FIBER model by Berrone et al. (2012). The five dimensions included in their model enable the description of both positive and negative effects of family involvement in ownership and management on economic, social, and environmental performance, building on previous studies by Kellermanns et al. (2012), Breton-Miller & Miller (2016), and Samara et al. (2018).

Among the most important characteristics and values integrated in these dimensions, it is important to emphasize long-term orientation (e.g., Le Breton-Miller & Miller, 2006) and the desire to keep the family dynasty in the business across generations (Kim et al., 2017); family cohesion; altruism linked to employee protection and welfare (e.g., Arregle et al., 2007; Bjuggren, 2015); community embeddedness (e.g. Berrone et al., 2012); and concern for public reputation (e.g. Corbetta & Salvato, 2004) deriving from quality relationships with both internal and external stakeholders (e.g., De La Cruz Déniz & Suárez,

2005; Cennamo et al., 2012). Therefore, though they are not considered an additional dimension of sustainability, the family does have important connotations in the three classical spheres described above.

Although there is increasing interest in the impact of FBs on sustainability performance in comparison to NFBs, gaps in the literature prevail because of the lack and controversial nature of empirical studies on FB sustainability (Fang et al., 2016; Samara et al., 2018), and more specifically tourism FBs (Memili et al., 2018), despite their importance over the past decade.

These contradictory results can be explained by a number of interplaying factors, the most significant being differences in the definition of family firms, approaches to measuring sustainability performance and to identifying determinant factors and triggers, sampling techniques, methodologies, study periods, and institutional settings considered by authors (Miller et al., 2007; Sacristán-Navarro et al., 2011; Wagner et al., 2015).

Most empirical literature seems to be dominated by an economic and instrumental approach to sustainability, with social and environmental dimensions being sidelined (Bergamaschi & Randerson, 2016), thereby limiting exploration of the role of the family firm in society.

Furthermore, when social and environmental issues are considered, sustainability performance has been measured both in terms of output and practices, and by mixing outputs with values as an aggregated concept in the literature (e.g., Memili et al., 2018; Le Breton-Miller & Miller, 2016), which does not clarify the comparative positioning between FB and NFB in each of the dimensions that compose the construct of sustainability performance.

Interest in this research is not merely descriptive. Indeed, the idea is to use the results to improve the understanding of the values, governance mechanisms, and practices deployed by FB, compared with NFB, and to suggest lines of action which both tourism authorities and Spanish tourism FBs might develop to improve their medium- and long-term performance in economic, social, and environmental terms.

The authors' proposed empirical models were estimated using a final sample of 543 firms taken from an initial study of the Spanish tourism industry. Data was gathered from Sistema de Análisis de Balances Ibéricos (SABI), a database managed by Bureau van Dijk and Informa D&B S.A., to complete financial information from 2008 to 2016.

In order to analyze which factors underlie the sustainability performance of FBs compared to NFBs, the authors use the propensity score matching method (Neckebrouck et al., 2018; Ampenberger et al., 2013; Rosenbaum & Rubin, 1983). Propensity score matching builds a comparison group based on the probabilities of being treated, using observed characteristics. Treated and non-treated observations are then matched on the basis of this probability. The average treatment effect is then estimated as the mean difference in outputs between the two groups (Khandker, Koolwal, & Samad, 2010). As a robustness test, the authors conducted a different matching technique and applied direct nearest-neighbour matching (Khandker et al., 2010; Dehejia & Wahba, 2002; Dehejia & Wahba, 1999). Although propensity score matching supposes a successful methodological development to control for endogeneity, to the authors' knowledge, there is no prior empirical evidence on this issue. The results of this study show that FBs have a greater sustainability performance in economic, social, and environmental terms.

BACKGROUND

The Sustainability Approach

In recent decades, various economic and institutional agents have become increasingly concerned about sustainability problems (Benito-Hernández et al., 2016). In this context, sustainability stands as a fundamental paradigm capable of addressing economic, social, and environmental issues (WCED, 1987).

The sustainability approach (Brown et al., 1987) encompasses business efforts towards the longer-term benefit of all internal and external organizational stakeholders (Le Breton-Miller & Miller, 2016; Porter & Kramer, 2006), in economic, social, and environmental terms, all the dimensions having equal relevance (Elkington, 2004). Thus, managing sustainability involves reducing and alleviating the effects of business activity (Wood, 2010) under this triple bottom line (Elkington, 2004).

The literature on the tourism sector has highlighted the need to analyze the achievement of objectives related to sustainability (e.g., Memili et al., 2018; Kallmuenzer et al., 2018; Blancas et al., 2016; Font et al., 2016; Pace, 2016). However, sustainability concerns in these studies have been approached from two incomplete perspectives, lacking a clear definition and operationalization of the construct under research (Memili et al., 2018).

On the one hand, literature on the tourism sector has emphasized the concept of sustainability as a practice rather than an output (e.g., Memili et al., 2018; Le Breton-Miller & Miller, 2016), introducing a certain level of complexity when it comes to defining the results from the factors themselves.

On the other hand, this empirical literature seems to be dominated by an instrumental approach to sustainability, the social and environmental dimensions being overshadowed by the economic dimension (Bergamaschi & Randerson, 2016).

Within research on sustainability, analysis of the relevant role played by the family in attaining this goal has gained prominence (Samara et al., 2018; Le Breton-Miller & Miller, 2016). FBs have specific peculiarities such as values and culture, government mechanisms and strategic positioning (Anderson & Reeb, 2003; Chrisman et al., 2012) that influence the achievement of economic, social, and environmental objectives, which will be examined in the following section (Chrisman et al., 2015).

However, if studies analyzing sustainability in the tourism sector are scarce, they are even more limited when the effect of FBs is compared with NFBs, in terms of economic, social, and environmental performance.

Family Firm Sustainability Through the Lens of the Socioemotional Wealth Approach

FBs pursue the accumulation and conservation of wealth for future family generations (Zellweger et al., 2012), for the family name and, therefore, its reputation (Lumpkin et al., 2010). Both goals are indicative of the long-term orientation of FBs (Le Breton-Miler & Miler, 2006) compared with that of their NFB counterparts (Doluca et al., 2018).

The SEW approach is gaining attention in explaining sustainability (López-Pérez et al., 2018; Marques et al., 2014). SEW is defined as "the stock of affect-related value that the family has invested in the firm" (Berrone et al., 2010, p. 82). The basic argument is that family members govern the firm in order to preserve the socioemotional values deriving from their involvement in the business (Gómez-Mejía et al., 2007).

When the SEW approach is used to analyze internal relationships between managers and shareholders (usually one and the same), it highlights the importance of non-financial aims and values that are prioritized over value maximization for owners in explaining the behaviour of FBs (Kotlar & De Massis, 2013). Thus, FBs are more likely to act in the interest of their stakeholders (Hernández-Perlines & Rung-Hoch, 2017).

Specifically, Berrone et al. (2012) identify five SEW dimensions related to non-economic goals in their FIBER model: a desire for family influence and control, close identification with the business, binding social ties, an emotional attachment to the firm, and a desire for renewal of family bonds through dynastic succession.

In the early stages of its development, SEW was considered as a stimulus that enhances FB sustainability. However, recent studies show it as a double-edged sword (Samara et al., 2018; Le Breton-Miller & Miller, 2016; Kim et al., 2016).

On the basis of the identification of these dimensions, following is an outline of specific governance, and managerial and related psychological characteristics that can trigger or reduce FB sustainability performance, taking into consideration economic, social, and environmental dimensions. Social actions and benefits for internal and external stakeholders are differentiated, with the protection of the natural environment as one of the most important societal objectives (Samara et al., 2018).

Economic Performance

The **alignment of the interests of owners and managers, or even their shared identity,** reduces agency costs and boosts performance, in terms of economic profitability (Anderson & Reeb, 2003; Andrés, 2008) and sales growth (Chrisman, Chua, & Litz, 2004).

In addition, family ownership and management are characterized by lengthy job tenures (between 15 and 25 years) (Miller & Le Breton-Miller, 2006), which provide the security needed in the job to operate with a long investment time horizon. In this vein, some evidence reveals that FBs invest more in R&D (Cassia et al., 2011; Kammerlander & Ganter, 2015) and equipment (Kang, 2000), which may generate important strategic outcomes that bring higher economic returns (Miller & Le Breton-Miller, 200).

The **involvement of family members** also fosters the pursuit of organizational objectives, even at the expense of personal sacrifice, which engender distinctive capabilities and economic returns (Miller & Le Breton-Miller, 2006). Moreover, FBs invest more resources in employee training and salaries (Allouche & Amann, 1997), which can also contribute to capabilities development and economic performance (Miller & Le Breton-Miller, 2006).

The **long-term orientation of FBs** fosters investment in the development of an endurable reputation, differentiation, and marked positioning (Orlitzky et al., 2011), which have an important impact on economic performance (Rindova et al., 2005; Turban & Cable, 2003). Specifically, López-Pérez et al. (2018) show that FBs positively moderate the relationship between corporate reputation and financial value.

Owner intentions to keep a business in the family may also lead to more conservative financial strategies, related to less debt, more liquidity, and sounder balance sheets (Anderson & Reeb, 2003; Gallo & Vilaseca, 1996).

According to the above arguments, the authors' first hypothesis is:

Hypothesis One*:* Economic performance is higher in FBs than in NFBs.

Social and Environmental Performance

Internal Stakeholders

FBs promote **the identification of family members with the firm**, that is, an enduring relationship with its employees, a sense of responsibility among them, the business itself (Neckebrouck et al., 2018), and its social and environmental performance (Sharma & Sharma, 2011). To this end, FBs empower employees and invest in their development through training and an inclusive work culture (Neckebrouck et al., 2018; Kachaner, Stalk, & Bloch, 2012; Miller et al., 2008).

The **emotional attachment of family members to the firm** blurs boundaries between family and corporation in FB (Berrone et al., 2010), allowing emotions to infiltrate the organization and influence the FB decision-making process (Baron, 2008). These emotions are not static and emerge and evolve through more or less critical events in each FB system (succession, divorce, illness, family or business loss, economic downturn, etc.) (Wiklund et al., 2009; Dunn, 1999). By their very nature, families are characterized by a wide range of emotions, some of which are positive for enhancing social concerns of internal and external shareholders alike, such as warmth, tenderness, love, consolation, and happiness (Epstein et al., 1993; Berrone et al., 2012).

Arregle et al. (2007) pointed out that FBs support the development of loyalty and reciprocity among employees, thereby reinforcing identification with the family and the firm. This engagement with the organization fosters cooperative and altruistic behaviours, and not merely self-interest among employees (Jaskiewicz et al., 2017).

In addition, family desires for **renewing family bonds and preserving transgenerational control** of the firm can foster financial and employment security for the family (Madison et al., 2016; Block, 2010), which can benefit both family and non-family employees, as well as reduce employment risk (Neckebrouck et al., 2018). FBs' willingness to invest in reaching a sustainable position should also encourage investment in the professionalization and development of their human capital because of the importance of employee satisfaction, motivation, and empowerment to take new initiatives (Neckebrouck et al., 2018; Bammens et al., 2015), thereby leading to reduced recruitment and training costs (Memili et al., 2018).

In light of the previous arguments, the authors expect family firms to exhibit higher labour productivity, as a critical indicator of workforce performance. This prediction is rooted in SEW arguments, which suggest that labour productivity is a function of alignment interests between owners and managers (Kruse et al., 2010; Davis et al., 1997), and the strong social bonds between employees and the business, which increase their commitment to work for the business objectives. Higher job security in family firms also encourages employees to extract more output with fewer resources (Sraer & Thesmar, 2007). Moreover, FBs are associated with more flexible structures and decision-making processes and are less likely to use formal control instruments than NFBs (Daily & Dollinger, 1992), which spurs innovation (Craig & Dibrell, 2006). Specifically, Sraer and Thesmar (2007) found that labour productivity of the workforce is high in FBs because they provide employees with long-term contracts and higher job security.

Nevertheless, the excessive level of **family ownership of business equity** can also result in *nepotism* and *entrenchment* problems (Lubatkin et. 2007) associated with the employment of family members without considering their previous training, experience, or competences (Breton-Miller & Miller, 2016). Along these lines, previous literature has pointed out the importance of recruiting external directors to provide an objective view of stakeholder needs and opportunities (Bammens, Voordeckers, & Van Gils, 2011; Le Breton-Miller & Miller, 2016), including needs relating to environmental topics.

In light of the previous arguments, the authors hypothesize that:

Hypothesis Two: Employee involvement in organization is higher in FBs than in NFBs.
Hypothesis Three: Investment in employee training is higher in FBs than in NFBs.
Hypothesis Four: Labour productivity is higher in FBs than in NFBs.

External Stakeholders and the Environment

Family involvement in ownership and management is positively related to the pursuit of non-economic goals (Berrone et al., 2012; Chrisman et al., 2012; Gómez-Mejía et al., 2007). In addition, family firms are more likely to perpetuate direct or indirect owner control and influence over the firm's affairs, regardless of financial considerations (Gómez-Mejía et al., 2007). Along these lines, some authors suggest that FBs are associated with greater investment in new products and R&D that help to sustain business competitiveness for future generations (Le Breton-Miller et al., 2011; Cassia et al., 2011; Kammerlander & Ganter, 2015). The alignment of interests in FBs with high rates of ownership can also foster effective decision-making to invest in social and environmentally friendly activities (Samara et al., 2018).

The family sense of belonging, self-esteem, and identity are often shared by non-family employees, promoting a sense of stability and commitment to the business (Miller & Le Breton-Miller, 2005). Ties among members of the extended family are also likely to give rise to **strong social ties** with the community at large (Berrone et al., 2012). As Brickson (2005; 2007) argued, given the reciprocal bonds in FBs, these firms would be expected to pursue the welfare of those around them, even when these acts have no obvious economic gains.

Berrone et al. (2010) pointed out that FBs are deeply embedded in their community, through charities, special events, and local sports teams, for example. FBs might do this for altruistic reasons, for the enjoyment of receiving recognition for generous actions (Schulze et al., 2003), or for both. Accordingly, Berrone et al. (2012) suggest that FBs exhibit greater values in variables such as human interest, cooperation, and collectives. Deephouse and Jaskiewicz (2013) also demonstrate the positive effect of family ownership on reputation.

In addition, **the identification of family members with the firm** fosters the preservation of a good family image. Family members are quite sensitive about the external image they project to their external stakeholders (Micelotta & Raynard, 2011) and are keen to be seen as involved in environmental actions, rather than greenwashing (Kim et al., 2016).

Because public condemnation could be emotionally damaging for family members (Westhead, Cowling, & Howorth, 2001), family firms also exhibit higher levels of corporate social responsibility and community citizenship (Berrone et al., 2010; Craig & Dibrell, 2006). Specifically, Berrone et al. (2010) reported that FBs in polluting industries tend to contaminate less than NFBs, so as to enhance the family image.

Controlling owners' desire **to transfer the business to future generations** can also boost the firm's social performance through the enhancement of family reputation and image (López-Pérez et al., 2018; Campopiano et al., 2015; Dyer & Whetten, 2006) and the design of new products that show a commitment to the environment (Memili et al., 2018). Because protecting the natural environment is also part of the values that FBs are interested in safeguarding for future generations, more emphasis is placed on developing an environmental policy (Craig & Dibrell, 2006).

Concern for long-term prosperity encourages FBs to build customer loyalty through continuous investment in branding, quality, and customer service (Zellweger et al., 2012; Miller & Le Breton-Miller, 2006). FBs seeking to accommodate future family generations are also concerned with developing social capital through enduring associations with external resource providers (Gómez-Mejía et al., 2001). These associations can take the form of long-term alliances with partners, suppliers, and customers (Miller & Le Breton-Miller, 2006).

In sum, the theories posited here suggest the following three hypotheses:

Hypothesis Five: Investment in R&D is higher in FBs than in NFBs.
Hypothesis Six: Environmental commitment is higher in FBs than in NFBs.
Hypothesis Seven: Cooperation agreements are higher in FBs than in NFBs.

RESEARCH METHOD

Data

The database used consists of 1,019 firms operating in the Spanish tourism industry, with a confidence level of 95% and an error interval of ±3.1%. This final sample represents a response rate of 25.6% over the initial sample of 8,148 firms, selected from the entire population of Spanish tourism companies listed in the 2008 Central Companies Directory (DIRCE). This initial sample was selected using a stratified random sampling procedure with proportional allocation to ensure the representativeness of the sample, in terms of activity (considering four groups), size (taking the number of employees as a measure of the size of the company), and location.

The initial data to create the database were obtained from a questionnaire conducted in 2009 through personal interviews with the CEO or general manager. We applied a modified version of Dillman's Total Design Method (1978) to mitigate the problems associated with questionnaires as a data collection method, and to improve the response rate and quality of the information.

The fieldwork was carried out between December 2009 and March 2010. Data from the SABI, a database managed by Bureau van Dijk and Informa D&B, S.A., was also added to complete the financial information from 2008 to 2016. Since SABI does not provide information for all the companies interviewed, the final database contained 543 companies, 378 of which were FBs.

Variables

Independent Variable

Family Business (FB), the "broad concept", was used to classify a company as an FB, only taking into account "ownership structure" (Shanker & Astrachan 1996), that is, if the founder and/or descendants hold majority ownership and control strategic decisions. If the company can be included in the previous definition or not, the dummy variable takes the value of 1, and 0, respectively.

Dependent Variables

Economic Performance

ROA (Return on Assets) is measured as the ratio between EBIT (Earnings before interests and taxes) and Total Assets (Anderson & Reeb, 2003; Andrés, 2008).

Social Performance For Internal Stakeholders

Employees' involvement in the organization (EMPL_INV) is accounted for by the number of improvement suggestions from employees (p60_5).

Employees' formation (EMPL_FOR) refers to the number of training hours (divided by the total number of employees) (p58/divided by number of employees).

Employee productivity (EBIT_NE) represents EBIT divided by the number of employees.

Social and Environmental Performance For External Stakeholders

R&D Investment (RD) measures the internal investment in research and development activities (P106_1).

Environmental commitment (ENV) takes into account the number of quality standards met by the company (p37_7_8s) (ISO 14000 and EMAS).

Cooperation agreements (COOP) is measured by the number of years of business collaborations and partnerships with other companies (P95).

The propensity-based matched pair method was used with specific covariates, commonly used in the literature for estimating the probabilities of being an FB (Pindado et al., 2011; Schmid, 2013). The covariates are risk (RISK), according to the Altman (1968) Z-Score, size (size), as in the log of Total Assets, sales growth (GROWTH), control mechanism of the FB (CONTROL), and ownership concentration (CONC). The descriptive statistics and correlations for the variables in the model are shown in Tables 1 and 2, respectively.

The correlations shown in Table 2, together with the multicollinearity test performed using the Variance Inflation Factor (VIF), reveal no problems of collinearity among the variables considered.

RESEARCH RESULTS

Following Neckebrouck al. (2018), a propensity-based matched pair method was used to test the hypotheses. This method reduces the impact of unobserved heterogeneity and matches company-years rather than companies, thereby providing a relatively bias-free, conservative test. This technique requires comparing the sample means of all the variables used in the matching process between the first and following generation groups. Table 3 shows the results of the propensity-based matched pair method, together with a different matching technique conducted as a robust test, nearest-neighbour matching (Khandker et al., 2010; Dehejia & Wahba, 2002; Dehejia & Wahba, 1999).

As shown in Table 3, the variable ROA is higher for FB, which confirms the first hypothesis. The second hypothesis is also confirmed, since the difference of the variable EMPL_INV between FB and NFB is positive and significant. However, the third hypothesis is not confirmed, as the variable EMPL_FOR

Table 1. Descriptive statistics

All firms			
Variables	**Obs.**	**Mean**	**SD**
FB	4,887	0.696	0.459
ROA	3,584	-0.007	0.229
EMPL_INV	3,249	23.243	66.461
EMPL_FOR	882	10.712	49.759
EBIT_NE	3,444	5.081	65.852
RD	2,403	5,472.44	35,754.34
ENV	4,131	0.204	0.5000
COOP	2,250	14.976	13.042
RISK	3,598	1.388	2.718
SIZE	3,598	14.178	2.224
GROWTH	3,100	0.299	2.526
CONTROL	4,887	0.147	0.354
CONC	3,672	81.230	26.777

Source: *Own preparation*

Table 2. Correlation Matrix and Variance Inflation Factors

	1	*2*	*3*	*4*	*5*	*6*	*7*	*8*	*9*	*10*	*11*	*12*	*13*
1.FB	1.000												
2.ROA	0.034 (0.042)	1.000											
3.EMPL_INV	0.060 (0.001)	0.001 (0.976)	1.000										
4.EMPL_FOR	-0.097 (0.004)	0.087 (0.025)	-0.088 (0.042)	1.000									
5.EBIT_NE	0.001 (0.938)	0.139 (0.000)	0.055 (0.008)	0.002 (0.958)	1.000								
6.RD	0.082 (0.000)	0.003 (0.908)	-0.002 (0.945)	-0.070 (0.156)	0.059 (0.015)	1.000							
7.ENV	0.003 (0.863)	0.013 (0.453)	0.125 (0.000)	0.183 (0.000)	0.015 (0.408)	0.002 (0.921)	1.000						
8.COOP	0.145 (0.000)	0.012 (0.997)	0.081 (0.002)	-0.165 (0.000)	0.016 (0.512)	0.043 (0.120)	0.087 (0.000)	1.000					
9.RISK	-0.087 (0.000)	0.600 (0.000)	-0.029 (0.151)	0.011 (0.754)	0.056 (0.001)	-0.045 (0.062)	0.010 (0.557)	-0.029 (0.231)	1.000				
10.SIZE	-0.087 (0.000)	0.185 (0.000)	0.057 (0.005)	-0.163 (0.000)	0.108 (0.000)	0.248 (0.000)	0.093 (0.000)	0.186 (0.000)	-0.051 (0.002)	1.000			
11.GROWTH	0.048 (0.007)	0.039 (0.030)	-0.008 (0.702)	-0.011 (0.762)	0.088 (0.000)	0.560 (0.000)	-0.008 (0.663)	0.078 (0.003)	0.048 (0.014)	0.032 (0.072)	1.000		
12.CONTROL	0.263 (0.000)	-0.002 (0.865)	-0.010 (0.567)	-0.047 (0.162)	-0.001 (0.981)	0.149 (0.000)	0.050 (0.001)	-0.004 (0.831)	-0.042 (0.0148)	0.010 (0.549)	0.018 (0.312)	1.000	
13.CONC	0.050 (0.002)	-0.035 (0.066)	0.036 (0.072)	-0.036 (0.364)	-0.028 (0.156)	-0.140 (0.000)	0.002 (0.891)	-0.059 (0.011)	0.004 (0.826)	-0.173 (0.000)	-0.065 (0.001)	-0.060 (0.000)	1.000
VIF		**1.53**	**1.01**	**1.03**	**1.05**	**1.69**	**1.04**	**1.06**	**1.05**	**1.04**	**1.01**	**1.01**	**1.00**

Source: *Own preparation*

Table 3. Propensity-based matched tests

Variables	Family Business	Non-Family Business	Propensity based-matched difference			Direct nearest-neighbour matching
	Mean	Mean	Mean	S.E.	t-test	Z statistic
ROA	-0.001	-0.435	0.434	0.054	7.95***	1.79*
EMPL_INV	31.525	22.927	8.597	4.607	1.87*	1.77*
EMPL_FOR	6.101	79.348	-73.24	22.994	-3.19***	-2.20**
EBIT_NE	3.894	-3.812	7.707	6.587	1.17	6.984**
RD	10,111.85	923.54	9,188.30	2,027.51	4.53***	5.01***
ENV	0.204	0.138	0.065	0.094	0.70	2.24**
COOP	17.599	10.793	6.86	2.859	2.38**	6.496***

Source: *Own preparation*

shows a negative and significant difference. Hypotheses four, five, six, and seven are also confirmed, though four and six are only confirmed with the second matching method.

DISCUSSION

The results, using data from 543 tourism firms, are revealing. Propensity score matching suggests that FBs obtain greater economic performance, in terms of profitability, thereby confirming previous studies (e.g., Anderson & Reeb, 2003; Andrés, 2008; Chrisman, Chua & Litz, 2004).

Results also show that FBs have a more committed and involved workforce and greater productivity. This is consistent with earlier research that also reports more positive accounts of employment practices in FBs (e.g., Bammens et al., 2015; Miller & Le Breton-Miller, 2006).

And, contrary to expectations, FBs invest fewer hours in employee training. This result concurs with Neckebrouck et al. (2018), who also found that employee earnings and productivity ratios were lower in FBs. Nevertheless, the result reported here should be interpreted with caution because of the greater commitment shown by FB employees to providing new innovation suggestions and their greater productivity ratios. These results suggest that human resources practices to motivate and instruct employees might be higher in FBs than in NFBs (Miller & Le Breton-Miller, 2006; Bammens et al., 2015), although they are not reflected in formal training programmes. These results concur with the study by Pittino et al. (2016), who observe that relational mechanisms originating from the family social capital may even act as substitutes of formal human resources practices.

The data also indicate that FBs are not only concerned with the involvement of internal stakeholders but also with society and the environment. FBs show greater ratios in R&D, a major adoption of quality certifications related to environmental issues, such as the ISO 14000 and the EMAS (Biscotti et al., 2018), and a stronger path in the development of cooperation agreements with external partners than NFBs (Miller & Le Breton-Miller, 2006).

Although some studies also confirm that FBs report higher investment ratios in R&D (e.g., Cassia et al., 2011; Kammerlander & Ganter, 2015; Zellweger, 2007), this finding differs with earlier research in the context of FBs that report a lower level of investment in R&D (e.g., Kotlar et al., 2014; Schmid et al., 2014; De Massis et al., 2013; Block, 2012).

FB acceptance of higher levels of R&D activities in comparison to NFBs should therefore be analyzed under specific circumstances, such as the presence of long-term FB goals and the transfer of control to the next generation (Chrisman & Patel, 2012). Moreover, consideration should be given to the fact that the tourism industry's high potential for growth may prompt FBs to focus more on R&D than NFBs, in order to secure their long-term viability and control over the company (Choi et al., 2015), and to differentiate themselves from their competitors and the homogenization of products characteristic of the tourism sector (Ding & Ma, 2018; Dredge & Jenkins, 2003).

The contribution of this work is important because it extends the SEW approach (Gómez-Mejía et al., 2007; Berrone et al., 2012) to identify family impact on the three spheres of sustainability performance: economic, social, and environmental. This study clearly identifies the performance in these three dimensions as independent and proposes clear, robust, objective measures to capture them. This research also attempts to distinguish between the impact of FBs on the social expectations and interests of both internal and external stakeholders.

This study also outlines implications for practice and for policymakers in the tourism sector, because it establishes that the SEW that characterizes the values, culture, strategies, and governing structures in FBs has positive effects for reaching an improved economic, social, and environmental performance, in comparison to NFBs. NFBs should therefore be challenged to involve and motivate employees to be productive and to develop the high-quality human practices associated with economic performance (Miller & Le Breton-Miller, 2006). NFBs should also construct more robust and differentiating positioning by investing in R&D, and in social and environmentally friendly activities, and in collaborating with external stakeholders.

FUTURE RESEARCH DIRECTIONS

Despite its merits, the generalizability of this study may be limited, as the sample was restricted to the Spanish tourism sector. Future research should include different sectors and regions, and explore how the specific characteristics of FBs affect sustainability positioning, especially in terms of ownership, governance structure, management, and succession, since existing results are highly inconsistent (Samara et al., 2018; Le Breton-Miler et al., 2016; Rees & Rodionova, 2015). Scant empirical studies on FBs in the tourism sector adds to this inconsistency in the literature (Memili et al., 2018).

ACKNOWLEDGMENT

This research has been funded by the Ministry of Science, Innovation, and Universities and the State Research Agency (AEI), and co-funded by the European Regional Development Fund (FEDER), project reference ECO2016-76796-P. Support was also provided by Universitat Jaume I, reference UJI-A2017-04.

REFERENCES

Aall, C. (2011). Energy use and leisure consumption in Norway: An analysis and reduction strategy. *Journal of Sustainable Tourism*, *19*(6), 729–745. doi:10.1080/09669582.2010.536241

Allouche, J., & Amann, B. (1997). Le retour de capitalisme familiale. *L'expansion. Management Review*, *85*, 92–99.

Altman, E. (1968). Financial ratios, discriminant analysis and the prediction of corporate bankruptcy. *The Journal of Finance*, *23*(4), 589–609. doi:10.1111/j.1540-6261.1968.tb00843.x

Ampenberger, M., Schmid, T., Achleitner, A., & Kasere, C. (2013). Capital structure decisions in family firms: Empirical evidence from a bank-based economy. *Review of Managerial Science*, *7*(3), 247–275. doi:10.100711846-011-0077-2

Anderson, R. C., & Reeb, D. M. (2003). Founding-family ownership, corporate diversification, and firm leverage. *The Journal of Law & Economics*, *46*(2), 653–684. doi:10.1086/377115

Andres, C. (2008). Large shareholders and firm performance. An empirical examination of founding-family ownership. *Journal of Corporate Finance*, *14*(4), 431–445. doi:10.1016/j.jcorpfin.2008.05.003

Arregle, J. L., Hitt, M. A., Sirmon, D. G., & Very, P. (2007). The development of organizational social capital: Attributes of family firms. *Journal of Management Studies*, *44*(1), 73–95. doi:10.1111/j.1467-6486.2007.00665.x

Bammens, Y., Notelaers, G., & Van Gils, A. (2015). Implications of family business employment for employees' innovative work involvement. *Family Business Review*, *28*(2), 123–144. doi:10.1177/0894486513520615

Bammens, Y., Voordeckers, W., & Van Gils, A. (2011). Boards of directors in family businesses: A literature review and research agenda. *International Journal of Management Reviews*, *13*(2), 134–152. doi:10.1111/j.1468-2370.2010.00289.x

Baron, R. A. (2008). The role of affect in the entrepreneurial process. *Academy of Management Review*, *33*(2), 328–340. doi:10.5465/amr.2008.31193166

Benito-Hernández, S., Platero-Jaime, M., & Esteban-Sánchez, P. (2016). The influence of cooperative relations of small businesses on environmental protection intensity. *Business Ethics (Oxford, England)*, *25*(4), 416–439. doi:10.1111/beer.12126

Bergamaschi, M., & Randerson, K. (2016). The futures of family businesses and the development of corporate social responsibility. *Futures*, *75*, 54–65. doi:10.1016/j.futures.2015.10.006

Berrone, P., Cruz, C., & Gomez-Mejia, L. R. (2012). Socioemotional wealth in family firms: Theoretical dimensions, assessment approaches, and agenda for future research. *Family Business Review*, *25*(3), 258–279. doi:10.1177/0894486511435355

Berrone, P., Cruz, C., Gomez-Mejia, L. R., & Larraza-Kintana, M. (2010). Socioemotional wealth and corporate responses to institutional pressures: Do family-controlled firms pollute less? *Administrative Science Quarterly*, *55*(1), 82–113. doi:10.2189/asqu.2010.55.1.82

Biscotti, A. M., D'Amico, E., & Monge, F. (2018). Do environmental management systems affect the knowledge management process? The impact on the learning evolution and the relevance of organisational context. *Journal of Knowledge Management*, *22*(3), 603–620. doi:10.1108/JKM-08-2017-0344

Bjuggren, C. M. (2015). Sensitivity to shocks and implicit employment protection in family firms. *Journal of Economic Behavior & Organization*, *119*, 18–31. doi:10.1016/j.jebo.2015.07.011

Blancas, F. J., Lozano-Oyola, M., González, M., & Caballero, R. (2016). Sustainable tourism composite indicators: A dynamic evaluation to manage changes in sustainability. *Journal of Sustainable Tourism*, *24*(10), 1403–1424. doi:10.1080/09669582.2015.1122014

Block, J. (2010). Family management, family ownership, and downsizing: Evidence from S&P 500 firms. *Family Business Review*, *23*(2), 109–130. doi:10.1177/089448651002300202

Block, J. H. (2012). R&D investments in family and founder firms: An agency perspective. *Journal of Business Venturing*, *27*(2), 248–265. doi:10.1016/j.jbusvent.2010.09.003

Brickson, S. L. (2005). Organizational identity orientation: Forging a link between organizational identity and organizations' relations with stakeholders. *Administrative Science Quarterly*, *50*(4), 576–609. doi:10.2189/asqu.50.4.576

Brickson, S. L. (2007). Organizational identity orientation: The genesis of the role of the firm and distinct forms of social value. *Academy of Management Review*, *32*(3), 864–888. doi:10.5465/amr.2007.25275679

Brown, B. J., Hanson, M. E., Liverman, D. M., & Merideth, R. W. Jr. (1987). Global sustainability: Toward definition. *Environmental Management*, *11*(6), 713–719. doi:10.1007/BF01867238

Campopiano, G., & De Massis, A. (2015). Corporate social responsibility reporting: A content analysis in family and non-family firms. *Journal of Business Ethics*, *129*(3), 511–534. doi:10.100710551-014-2174-z

Campopiano, G., De Massis, A., & Chirico, F. (2014). Firm philanthropy in small-and medium-sized family firms: The effects of family involvement in ownership and management. *Family Business Review*, *27*(3), 244–258. doi:10.1177/0894486514538450

Cassia, L., De Massis, A., & Pizzurno, E. (2011). An exploratory investigation on NPD in small family businesses from Northern Italy. *International Journal of Business. Management and Social Sciences*, *2*(2), 1–14.

Cennamo, C., Berrone, P., Cruz, C., & Gomez–Mejia, L. R. (2012). Socioemotional wealth and proactive stakeholder engagement: Why family–controlled firms care more about their stakeholders. *Entrepreneurship Theory and Practice*, *36*(6), 1153–1173. doi:10.1111/j.1540-6520.2012.00543.x

Choi, Y. R., Zahra, S. A., Yoshikawa, T., & Han, B. H. (2015). Family ownership and R&D investment: The role of growth opportunities and business group membership. *Journal of Business Research*, *68*(5), 1053–1061. doi:10.1016/j.jbusres.2014.10.007

Chrisman, J. J., Chua, J. H., De Massis, A., Frattini, F., & Wright, M. (2015). The ability and willingness paradox in family firm innovation. *Journal of Product Innovation Management*, *32*(3), 310–318. doi:10.1111/jpim.12207

Chrisman, J. J., Chua, J. H., & Litz, R. A. (2004). Comparing the agency costs of family and non-family firms: Conceptual issues and exploratory evidence. *Entrepreneurship Theory and Practice*, *28*(4), 335–354. doi:10.1111/j.1540-6520.2004.00049.x

Chrisman, J. J., Chua, J. H., Pearson, A. W., & Barnett, T. (2012). Family involvement, family influence, and family–centered non–economic goals in small firms. *Entrepreneurship Theory and Practice*, *36*(2), 267–293. doi:10.1111/j.1540-6520.2010.00407.x

Chrisman, J. J., & Patel, P. C. (2012). Variations in R&D investments of family and nonfamily firms: Behavioral agency and myopic loss aversion perspectives. *Academy of Management Journal*, *55*(4), 976–997. doi:10.5465/amj.2011.0211

Chua, J. H., Chrisman, J. J., & Steier, L. P. (2003). Extending the theoretical horizons of family business research. *Entrepreneurship Theory and Practice*, *27*(4), 331–338. doi:10.1111/1540-8520.00012

Collier, J., & Fuller, T. (2005). Corporations, ethics and global futures. *Futures*, *37*(2-3), 111–116. doi:10.1016/j.futures.2004.03.031

Corbetta, G., & Salvato, C. (2004). Self–Serving or Self–Actualizing? Models of Man and Agency Costs in Different Types of Family Firms: A Commentary on “Comparing the Agency Costs of Family and Non–family Firms: Conceptual Issues and Exploratory Evidence”. *Entrepreneurship Theory and Practice*, *28*(4), 355–362. doi:10.1111/j.1540-6520.2004.00050.x

Craig, J., & Dibrell, C. (2006). The natural environment, innovation, and firm performance: A comparative study. *Family Business Review*, *19*(4), 275–288. doi:10.1111/j.1741-6248.2006.00075.x

Daily, C. M., & Dollinger, M. J. (1992). An empirical examination of ownership structure in family and professionally managed firms. *Family Business Review*, *5*(2), 117–136. doi:10.1111/j.1741-6248.1992.00117.x

Davis, J., Schoorman, F., & Donaldson, L. (1997). Toward a stewardship theory of management. *Academy of Management Review*, *22*(1), 20–47. doi:10.5465/amr.1997.9707180258

De Massis, A., Frattini, F., & Lichtenthaler, U. (2013). Research on technological innovation in family firms: Present debates and future directions. *Family Business Review*, *26*(1), 10–31. doi:10.1177/0894486512466258

Deephouse, D. L., & Jaskiewicz, P. (2013). Do family firms have better reputations than non-family firms? An integration of socioemotional wealth and social identity theories. *Journal of Management Studies*, *50*(3), 337–360. doi:10.1111/joms.12015

Dehejia, R. H., & Wahba, S. (1999). Causal effects in nonexperimental studies: Reevaluating the evaluation of training programs. *Journal of the American Statistical Association*, *94*(448), 1053–1062. doi:10.1080/01621459.1999.10473858

Dehejia, R. H., & Wahba, S. (2002). Propensity score-matching methods for nonexperimental causal studies. *The Review of Economics and Statistics*, *84*(1), 151–161. doi:10.1162/003465302317331982

Déniz, M. D. L. C. D., & Suárez, M. K. C. (2005). Corporate social responsibility and family business in Spain. *Journal of Business Ethics*, *56*(1), 27–41. doi:10.100710551-004-3237-3

Dillman, D. A. (1978). *Mail and telephone surveys: The total design method* (Vol. 19). New York: Wiley.

Ding, F., & Ma, T. (2018). Dynamic Relationship Between Tourism and Homogeneity of Tourist Destinations. *IEEE Access: Practical Innovations, Open Solutions*, *6*, 51470–51476. doi:10.1109/ACCESS.2018.2841966

Doluca, H., Wagner, M., & Block, J. (2018). Sustainability and environmental behaviour in family firms: A longitudinal analysis of environment-related activities, innovation and performance. *Business Strategy and the Environment*, *27*(1), 152–172. doi:10.1002/bse.1998

Dredge, D., & Jenkins, J. (2003). Destination place identity and regional tourism policy. *Tourism Geographies*, *5*(4), 383–407. doi:10.1080/1461668032000129137

Dunn, B. (1999). The family factor: The impact of family relationship dynamics on business owning families during transitions. *Family Business Review*, *12*(1), 41–57. doi:10.1111/j.1741-6248.1999.00041.x

Dyer, W. G. Jr, & Whetten, D. A. (2006). Family firms and social responsibility: Preliminary evidence from the S & P 500. *Entrepreneurship Theory and Practice*, *30*(6), 785–802. doi:10.1111/j.1540-6520.2006.00151.x

Elkington, J. (2004). Enter the Triple Bottom Line. In A. Henriques & J. Richardson (Eds.), *The Triple Bottom Line: does it all add up?* London, UK: EarthScan.

Epstein, N. B., Bishop, D., Ryan, C., Miller, I., & Keitner, G. (1993). The McMaster model: View of healthy family functioning. In F. Walsh (Ed.), *Normal family processes* (pp. 138–160). New York: Guilford Press.

Fang, H., Memili, E., Van de Graaff Randolph, R., & Chrisman, J. J. (2016). Does size matter? The moderating effects of firm size on the employment of non-family managers in privately-held family SMEs. *Entrepreneurship Theory and Practice*, *40*(5), 1017–1039. doi:10.1111/etap.12156

Font, X., Garay, L., & Jones, S. (2016). Sustainability motivations and practices in small tourism enterprises in European protected areas. *Journal of Cleaner Production*, *137*, 1439–1448. doi:10.1016/j.jclepro.2014.01.071

Gallo, M. A., & Vilaseca, A. (1996). Finance in family business. *Family Business Review*, *9*(4), 387–401. doi:10.1111/j.1741-6248.1996.00387.x

Getz, D., & Carlsen, J. (2005). Family business in tourism: State of the art. *Annals of Tourism Research*, *32*(1), 237–258. doi:10.1016/j.annals.2004.07.006

Gómez-Mejía, L. R., Haynes, K. T., Núñez-Nickel, M., Jacobson, K. J., & Moyano-Fuentes, J. (2007). Socioemotional wealth and business risks in family-controlled firms: Evidence from Spanish olive oil mills. *Administrative Science Quarterly*, *52*(1), 106–137. doi:10.2189/asqu.52.1.106

Gomez-Mejia, L. R., Nunez-Nickel, M., & Gutierrez, I. (2001). The role of family ties in agency contracts. *Academy of Management Journal*, *44*(1), 81–95.

Hernández-Perlines, F., & Rung-Hoch, N. (2017). Sustainable entrepreneurial orientation in family firms. *Sustainability*, *9*(7), 1212. doi:10.3390u9071212

Jaskiewicz, P., Combs, J. G., Shanine, K. K., & Kacmar, K. M. (2017). Introducing the family: A review of family science with implications for management research. *The Academy of Management Annals, 11*(1), 309–341. doi:10.5465/annals.2014.0053

Juul, M. (2015). *The sharing economy and tourism: tourism accommodation*. Brussels: European Parliament Research Service Briefing.

Kachaner, N., Stalk, G., & Bloch, A. (2012). What you can learn from family business. *Harvard Business Review, 90*(11), 102–106.

Kallmuenzer, A., Strobl, A., & Peters, M. (2018). Tweaking the entrepreneurial orientation–performance relationship in family firms: The effect of control mechanisms and family-related goals. *Review of Managerial Science, 12*(4), 855–883. doi:10.100711846-017-0231-6

Kammerlander, N., & Ganter, M. (2015). An attention-based view of family firm adaptation to discontinuous technological change: Exploring the role of family CEOs' noneconomic goals. *Journal of Product Innovation Management, 32*(3), 361–383. doi:10.1111/jpim.12205

Kang, D. (2000). *Family ownership and performance in public corporations: A study of the U.S. fortune 500, 1982–1994*. Working Paper. Boston: Harvard Business School.

Kellermanns, F. W., Eddleston, K. A., Sarathy, R., & Murphy, F. (2012). Innovativeness in family firms: A family influence perspective. *Small Business Economics, 38*(1), 85–101. doi:10.100711187-010-9268-5

Khandker, S. (2010). *Handbook on Impact Evaluation. Quantitative Methods and Practices*. Washington, DC: World Bank.

Kim, J., Fairclough, S., & Dibrell, C. (2017). Attention, action, and greenwash in family-influenced firms? Evidence from polluting industries. *Organization & Environment, 30*(4), 304–323. doi:10.1177/1086026616673410

Kotlar, J., & De Massis, A. (2013). Goal setting in family firms: Goal diversity, social interactions, and collective commitment to family-centered goals. *Entrepreneurship Theory and Practice, 37*(6), 1263–1288. doi:10.1111/etap.12065

Kotlar, J., Fang, H., De Massis, A., & Frattini, F. (2014). Profitability goals, control goals, and the R & D investment decisions of family and nonfamily firms. *Journal of Product Innovation Management, 31*(6), 1128–1145. doi:10.1111/jpim.12165

Kruse, D. L., Freeman, R. B., & Blasi, J. R. (2010). Shared capitalism at work: Employee ownership, profit and gain sharing, and broad-based stock options. University of Chicago Press. Lamb, N. H., & Butler, F. C. (2018). The influence of family firms and institutional owners on corporate social responsibility performance. *Business & Society, 57*(7), 1374–1406.

Lamb, N. H., & Butler, F. C. (2018). The influence of family firms and institutional owners on corporate social responsibility performance. *Business & Society, 57*(7), 1374–1406. doi:10.1177/0007650316648443

Le Breton-Miller, I., & Miller, D. (2016). Family firms and practices of sustainability: A contingency view. *Journal of Family Business Strategy, 7*(1), 26–33. doi:10.1016/j.jfbs.2015.09.001

Le Breton-Miller, I., Miller, D., & Lester, R. H. (2011). Stewardship or agency? A social embeddedness reconciliation of conduct and performance in public family businesses. *Organization Science*, *22*(3), 704–721. doi:10.1287/orsc.1100.0541

López-Pérez, M., Melero-Polo, I., Vázquez-Carrasco, R., & Cambra-Fierro, J. (2018). Sustainability and Business Outcomes in the Context of SMEs: Comparing Family Firms vs. Non-Family Firms. *Sustainability*, *10*(11), 4080. doi:10.3390u10114080

Lubatkin, M. H., Ling, Y., & Schulze, W. S. (2007). An organizational justice-based view of self-control and agency costs in family firms. *Journal of Management Studies*, *44*(6), 955–971. doi:10.1111/j.1467-6486.2006.00673.x

Lumpkin, G. T., Brigham, K. H., & Moss, T. W. (2010). Long-term orientation: Implications for the entrepreneurial orientation and performance of family businesses. *Entrepreneurship and Regional Development*, *22*(3-4), 241–264. doi:10.1080/08985621003726218

Madison, K., Holt, D. T., Kellermanns, F. W., & Ranft, A. L. (2016). Viewing family firm behavior and governance through the lens of agency and stewardship theories. *Family Business Review*, *29*(1), 65–93. doi:10.1177/0894486515594292

Marques, P., Presas, P., & Simon, A. (2014). The heterogeneity of family firms in CSR engagement: The role of values. *Family Business Review*, *27*(3), 206–227. doi:10.1177/0894486514539004

Matten, D., & Crane, A. (2005). Corporate citizenship: Toward an extended theoretical conceptualization. *Academy of Management Review*, *30*(1), 166–179. doi:10.5465/amr.2005.15281448

Memili, E., Fang, H., Chrisman, J. J., & De Massis, A. (2015). The impact of small- and medium-sized family firms on economic growth. *Small Business Economics*, *45*(4), 771–785. doi:10.100711187-015-9670-0

Memili, E., Fang, H. C., Koç, B., Yildirim-Öktem, Ö., & Sonmez, S. (2018). Sustainability practices of family firms: The interplay between family ownership and long-term orientation. *Journal of Sustainable Tourism*, *26*(1), 9–28. doi:10.1080/09669582.2017.1308371

Micelotta, E. R., & Raynard, M. (2011). Concealing or revealing the family? Corporate brand identity strategies in family firms. *Family Business Review*, *24*(3), 197–216. doi:10.1177/0894486511407321

Miller, D., & Le Breton-Miller, I. (2005). *Managing for the long run: Lessons in competitive advantage from great family businesses*. Boston, MA: Harvard Business Press.

Miller, D., & Le Breton-Miller, I. (2006). Family governance and firm performance: Agency, stewardship, and capabilities. *Family Business Review*, *19*(1), 73–87. doi:10.1111/j.1741-6248.2006.00063.x

Miller, D., Le Breton-Miller, I., Lester, R. H., & Cannella, A. A. Jr. (2007). Are family firms really superior performers? *Journal of Corporate Finance*, *13*(5), 829–858. doi:10.1016/j.jcorpfin.2007.03.004

Miller, D., Le Breton-Miller, I., & Scholnick, B. (2008). Stewardship vs. stagnation: An empirical comparison of small family and non-family businesses. *Journal of Management Studies*, *45*(1), 51–78. doi:10.1017/S0021875807004379

Miller, D., Steier, L., & Le Breton-Miller, I. (2016). What Can Scholars of Entrepreneurship Learn From Sound Family Businesses? *Entrepreneurship Theory and Practice*, *40*(3), 445–455. doi:10.1111/etap.12231

Neckebrouck, J., Schulze, W., & Zellweger, T. (2018). Are family firms good employers? *Academy of Management Journal*, *61*(2), 553–585. doi:10.5465/amj.2016.0765

Nekhili, M., Nagati, H., Chtioui, T., & Rebolledo, C. (2017). Corporate social responsibility disclosure and market value: Family versus nonfamily firms. *Journal of Business Research*, *77*, 41–52. doi:10.1016/j.jbusres.2017.04.001

Orlitzky, M., Siegel, D. S., & Waldman, D. A. (2011). Strategic corporate social responsibility and environmental sustainability. *Business & Society*, *50*(1), 6–27. doi:10.1177/0007650310394323

Pace, L. A. (2016). How do tourism firms innovate for sustainable energy consumption? A capabilities perspective on the adoption of energy efficiency in tourism accommodation establishments. *Journal of Cleaner Production*, *111*, 409–420. doi:10.1016/j.jclepro.2015.01.095

Pieper, T. M., Klein, S. B., & Jaskiewicz, P. (2008). The impact of goal alignment on board existence and top management team composition: Evidence from family-influenced businesses. *Journal of Small Business Management*, *46*(3), 372–394. doi:10.1111/j.1540-627X.2008.00249.x

Pindado, J., Requejo, I., & de la Torre, C. (2011). Family control and investment-cash flow sensitivity: Empirical evidence from the Euro zone. *Journal of Corporate Finance*, *17*(5), 1389–1409. doi:10.1016/j.jcorpfin.2011.07.003

Pittino, D., Visintin, F., Lenger, T., & Sternad, D. (2016). Are high performance work practices really necessary in family SMEs? An analysis of the impact on employee retention. *Journal of Family Business Strategy*, *7*(2), 75–89. doi:10.1016/j.jfbs.2016.04.002

Porter, M. E., & Kramer, M. R. (2006). The link between competitive advantage and corporate social responsibility. *Harvard Business Review*, *84*(12), 78–92. PMID:17183795

Prud'homme, B., & Raymond, L. (2016). Implementation of sustainable development practices in the hospitality industry: A case study of five Canadian hotels. *International Journal of Contemporary Hospitality Management*, *28*(3), 609–639. doi:10.1108/IJCHM-12-2014-0629

Rees, W., & Rodionova, T. (2015). The influence of family ownership on corporate social responsibility: An international analysis of publicly listed companies. *Corporate Governance*, *23*(3), 184–202. doi:10.1111/corg.12086

Rindova, V. P., Williamson, I. O., Petkova, A. P., & Sever, J. M. (2005). Being good or being known: An empirical examination of the dimensions, antecedents, and consequences of organizational reputation. *Academy of Management Journal*, *48*(6), 1033–1049. doi:10.5465/amj.2005.19573108

Rosenbaum, P. R., & Rubin, D. B. (1983). The central role of the propensity score in observational studies for causal effects. *Biometrika*, *70*(1), 41–55. doi:10.1093/biomet/70.1.41

Sacristán-Navarro, M., Gómez-Ansón, S., & Cabeza-García, L. (2011). Family ownership and control, the presence of other large shareholders, and firm performance: Further evidence. *Family Business Review*, *24*(1), 71–93. doi:10.1177/0894486510396705

Samara, G., Jamali, D., Sierra, V., & Parada, M. J. (2018). Who are the best performers? The environmental social performance of family firms. *Journal of Family Business Strategy*, *9*(1), 33–43. doi:10.1016/j.jfbs.2017.11.004

Schmid, T. (2013). Control considerations, creditor monitoring, and the capital structure of family firms. *Journal of Banking & Finance*, *37*(2), 257–272. doi:10.1016/j.jbankfin.2012.08.026

Schmid, T., Achleitner, A. K., Ampenberger, M., & Kaserer, C. (2014). Family firms and R&D behavior–New evidence from a large-scale survey. *Research Policy*, *43*(1), 233–244. doi:10.1016/j.respol.2013.08.006

Schulze, W. S., Lubatkin, M. H., & Dino, R. N. (2003). Toward a theory of agency and altruism in family firms. *Journal of Business Venturing*, *18*(4), 473–490. doi:10.1016/S0883-9026(03)00054-5

Shanker, M. C., & Astrachan, J. H. (1996). Myths and realities: Family businesses' contribution to the US economy—A framework for assessing family business statistics. *Family Business Review*, *9*(2), 107–123. doi:10.1111/j.1741-6248.1996.00107.x

Sharma, P., & Sharma, S. (2011). Drivers of proactive environmental strategy in family firms. *Business Ethics Quarterly*, *21*(2), 309–334. doi:10.5840/beq201121218

Shepherd, D. A., Wiklund, J., & Haynie, J. M. (2009). Moving forward: Balancing the financial and emotional costs of business failure. *Journal of Business Venturing*, *24*(2), 134–148. doi:10.1016/j.jbusvent.2007.10.002

Sraer, D., & Thesmar, D. (2007). Performance and behavior of family firms: Evidence from the French stock market. *Journal of the European Economic Association*, *5*(4), 709–751. doi:10.1162/JEEA.2007.5.4.709

Wagner, D., Block, J. H., Miller, D., Schwens, C., & Xi, G. (2015). A meta-analysis of the financial performance of family firms: Another attempt. *Journal of Family Business Strategy*, *6*(1), 3–13. doi:10.1016/j.jfbs.2015.01.001

WCED, S. W. S. (1987). *World commission on environment and development*. Our common future.

Westhead, P., Cowling, M., & Howorth, C. (2001). The development of family companies: Management and ownership imperatives. *Family Business Review*, *14*(4), 369–385. doi:10.1111/j.1741-6248.2001.00369.x

Wood, D. J. (2010). Measuring corporate social performance: A review. *International Journal of Management Reviews*, *12*(1), 50–84. doi:10.1111/j.1468-2370.2009.00274.x

Zellweger, T. (2007). Time horizon, costs of equity capital, and generic investment strategies of firms. *Family Business Review*, *20*(1), 1–15. doi:10.1111/j.1741-6248.2007.00080.x

Zellweger, T. M., Kellermanns, F. W., Chrisman, J. J., & Chua, J. H. (2012). Family control and family firm valuation by family CEOs: The importance of intentions for transgenerational control. *Organization Science*, *23*(3), 851–868. doi:10.1287/orsc.1110.0665

ADDITIONAL READING

Adomako, S., Amankwah-Amoah, J., Danso, A., Konadu, R., & Owusu-Agyei, S. (2019). Environmental sustainability orientation and performance of family and nonfamily firms. *Business Strategy and the Environment*, *28*(6), 1250–1259. doi:10.1002/bse.2314

Carsrud, A. L., & Brännback, M. (2010). Fostering sustainability in family firms. *Sustainable economy: corporate, social and environmental responsibility*, 53-70.

Elkington, J. (2006). Governance for sustainability. *Corporate Governance*, *14*(6), 522–529. doi:10.1111/j.1467-8683.2006.00527.x

Hernández-Perlines, F., & Rung-Hoch, N. (2017). Sustainable entrepreneurial orientation in family firms. *Sustainability*, *9*(7), 1212. doi:10.3390u9071212

Le Breton-Miller, I., & Miller, D. (2016). Family firms and practices of sustainability: A contingency view. *Journal of Family Business Strategy*, *7*(1), 26–33. doi:10.1016/j.jfbs.2015.09.001

Neubauer, F., & Lank, A. G. (2016). *The family business: Its governance for sustainability*. Berlin: Springer.

Sharma, P., & Sharma, S. (2019). The Role of Family Firms in Corporate Sustainability. The Oxford Handbook of Management Ideas, 427.

Treviño, S. S. G., Flores, A. C., Durán, B. I. M., & Fraile, A. E. B. (2019). CSR Initiatives of Family Firms: An Analysis of Mexican Business Groups. In *Handbook of Research on Entrepreneurial Leadership and Competitive Strategy in Family Business*. Pennsylvania: IGI Global Publishing.

KEY TERMS AND DEFINITIONS

Binding Social Ties: The long-term orientation of FBs make them more willing to establish strong social bonds with broad sectors of the community, e.g., non-family employees, customers, suppliers, and the community at large.

Emotional Attachment: The role of emotions in an FB setting and how they permeate, influence, and shape decision-making processes.

Family Control and Influence: The control and influence over strategic decisions exerted by the family, which adopts the role of CEO or chairman of the board.

Family Firm: Typology of a company in which a family owning the capital exerts powers over the organization and its strategic direction through management or board positions.

Family Members' Identification With the Firm: The close identification of the family with the firm, which makes family members sensitive to the external image they project to stakeholders and explains why FBs exhibit higher levels of corporate responsibility and community citizenship.

Renewal of Family Bonds With the Firm Through Dynastic Succession: The family's willingness and desire for continuity in the business. Maintaining the business for future generations is commonly seen as a key goal for FBs.

Socioemotional Wealth: Socioemotional endowment of FBs which might drive the firm to make strategic choices that cannot be explained by applying economic logic or from a risk-averse financial perspective.

Section 6
Family Firm Performance

Chapter 13
Understanding Family Firm Profitability Heterogeneity:
Differences Within Family Managed Firms and the Interaction Effect of Innovative Effort

María J. Martínez-Romero
https://orcid.org/0000-0001-7891-1558
Universidad de Almería, Spain

Rubén Martínez-Alonso
https://orcid.org/0000-0001-7389-762X
Universidad de Almería, Spain

Alfonso A. Rojo-Ramírez
Universidad de Almería, Spain

Julio Diéguez-Soto
https://orcid.org/0000-0001-5116-5604
Universidad de Málaga, Spain

ABSTRACT

Understanding family firm heterogeneity has become a topic of critical importance among academics and practitioners in the family business research field. This chapter aims to provide new insights into this theme by examining the differences in profitability within the pool of family firms. Furthermore, this chapter introduces an exceptional strategic element, namely innovative effort, to analyse when and to what extent the deployed innovative effort influences the family involvement in management-firm profitability relationship. Using a panel dataset on 3,164 observations of Spanish private manufacturing firms over the 2000–2015 period, the findings reveal significant differences in the profitability of family firms depending on the degree of family involvement in the firm's management. The findings also show that innovative effort reinforces the positive effect that family involvement in management exerts on firm profitability.

DOI: 10.4018/978-1-7998-1655-3.ch013

INTRODUCTION

Firm profitability is essential to sustain the financial health of firms, regions and nations (Wolff & Pett, 2006). The study of profitability within family firms has been acknowledged as an issue of utmost importance (De Massis, Kotlar, Mazzola, Minola, & Sciascia, 2018; Kotlar, Fang, De Massis, & Frattini, 2014; Sciascia, Mazzola, & Kellermanns, 2014), insofar as family firms are ubiquitous and dominant forms of organizations in many countries of the world (La Porta, Lopez-De-Silanes, & Shleifer, 1999; Villalonga & Amit, 2006) and due to the critical nature of profitability to guarantee firm perpetuation and sustainability (Gottardo & Moisello, 2015). Nevertheless, there is little evidence in the existing literature on the study of profitability within the pool of family firms, despite the recognition of family firm heterogeneity and the acknowledgment of higher variability in profitability goals among family firms than between family and non-family firms (Chrisman & Patel, 2012; Chua, Chrisman, Steier, & Rau, 2012; Rau, Sabine, Schneider-Siebke, & Gunther, 2019).

Family firm heterogeneity can be expressed through goals (Chrisman, Chua, Pearson, & Barnett, 2012), governance structures (Carney, 2005), resources (Habbershon, Williams, & MacMillan, 2003), and founder values (García-Álvarez & López-Sintas, 2001). However, it has been argued that is the family involvement in the firm what really makes unique a family firm (Berrone, Cruz, & Gómez-Mejía, 2012; Chua, Chrisman, & Sharma, 1999), and more precisely, the family involvement in the firm management (Gallucci, Santulli, & Calabrò, 2015; Martínez-Alonso, Martínez-Romero, & Rojo-Ramírez, 2019). Specifically, a main source of family firm heterogeneity is in the degree to which family members occupy top management positions, as high or low levels of family involvement may determine the features of the management team (Diéguez-Soto & Martínez-Romero, 2019; Hambrick & Mason, 1984). Indeed, family involvement in management is generally recognized as a fundamental conditioning of firm profitability (Martínez-Romero, Martínez-Alonso, Casado-Belmonte, & Diéguez-Soto, 2019), since it enables family members to engage in decision-making processes and therefore, exert a significant influence on organizational outcomes (Hambrick & Mason, 1984). Therefore, more research is needed in analysing how family involvement in management, as a potential source of family firm heterogeneity, influences firm profitability within the pool of family firms.

Moreover, to further delve into family firm heterogeneity, this chapter introduces a moderating factor (Chrisman et al., 2012; Chua et al., 2012), which may help to unravel mixed findings from previous research on the family management-firm profitability relationship. In this respect, an important gap persists in the comprehension of how strategic decision making may moderate the relationship between family involvement in management and firm profitability within the pool of family firms. Thus, this study introduces innovative effort as an exceptional strategic element that might influence the impact of family involvement in management on firm profitability. Innovative effort is understood as the manner in which a business encourages investments in research and development (R&D) to get innovation outcomes. The authors' contention is that innovative effort might reinforce the distinctive influence that family involvement in management exerts on firm profitability.

Based on the aforementioned and using the resource-based view (RBV) as the theoretical approach, this chapter seeks to shed light on this theme addressing the following research questions. How does the level of family involvement in management influence the achievement of firm profitability in family firms? Does innovative effort moderate the expected impact of family involvement in management on firm profitability? To answer these questions, the authors performed an empirical analysis with different econometric models that cover the hypotheses, utilizing a panel data sample of 3,164 observations of

Spanish manufacturing firms over the 2000-2015 period. Data are obtained from the Spanish Survey on Business Strategies. The longitudinal nature of this data set allows analysing family firm profitability heterogeneity over time, in response of the variations in the level of family involvement in management.

The results of this chapter offer relevant contributions to the literature. First, in contrast to prior research, which has primarily focused on the differences in profitability between family and non-family firms, the authors assess such profitability outcomes within the pool of family firms. This is of great interest due to the phenomenon of family firm profitability heterogeneity is an under-researched topic. Specifically, to disclose heterogeneity among family firms, a continuous variable of family involvement in management counting the number of family members actively involved in firm management was used. Second, this study develops a more fine-grained comprehension of the innovation behaviour of family firms by introducing innovative effort as a specific strategic factor, which might influence the family involvement in management-firm profitability relationship. Even though previous literature has examined different elements that could affect the family firms' abilities to obtain profitability outcomes, to the best of the authors' knowledge, no research has analysed when and under what conditions the innovative effort influences such relationship among family firms. Third, a more comprehensive understanding of profitability in private firms through a longitudinal study of panel data was offered. In this vein, panel data studies analysing private firms are scarce in prior literature given the difficulties of access to reliable financial data of these firms (Carney, Van Essen, Gedajlovic, & Heugens, 2015; George, 2005).

This chapter is organized as follows: first, the relevant literature is outlined and the hypotheses are formulated. Second, the methodology is depicted, and then the empirical results are disclosed. Finally, the theoretical and practical implications of the obtained findings, the limitations and future research and conclusions are exposed.

THEORETICAL FRAMEWORK AND HYPOTHESES

Family Involvement in Management and Firm Profitability

Even though family managers pursue a broad range of goals, such as higher status or remuneration, they consider firm profitability as a priority goal (Kotlar et al., 2014). Firm profitability is an indicator of financial performance (Diéguez-Soto, López-Delgado, & Rojo-Ramírez, 2015), a primary driver of managers' compensation (Berle & Means, 1965) and also an essential factor in managers' career development (Mezias, Chen, & Murphy, 2002). Consequently, firm profitability ranks high on family firms' agenda (Chrisman & Patel, 2012; Kotlar et al., 2014), to the extent that the accomplishment of financial objectives is a prerequisite to the viability of the firm (Martínez-Romero, Rojo-Ramírez, & Casado-Belmonte, 2019) and a key variable for family managers keen on preserving their firm control (Gómez-Mejía, Makri, & Kintana, 2010).

Family managers' influence on firm profitability has been investigated under a variety of theories, such as, agency theory, stewardship theory, the socioemotional wealth approach and the resource-based view (RBV) (Chrisman, Kellermanns, Chan, & Liano, 2010; Martínez-Romero, Martínez-Alonso, & Casado-Belmonte, 2018; Sciascia et al., 2014). However, despite different theoretical approaches have been utilized to explain family firms' profitability, it is important to highlight that studies drawing on the RBV (Dyer, 2006; Habbershon & Williams, 1999) have prevailed in recent years (Diéguez-Soto, Garrido-Moreno, & Manzaneque, 2018).

Analysing family firms from the RBV perspective, enables capturing which resources and capabilities make family firms unique (Eddleston, Kellermanns, & Sarathy, 2008; Gallucci et al., 2015; Sirmon & Hitt, 2003). In this regard, there is a general consensus among family firm scholars establishing that what makes a family firm unique, is the involvement of the family in the firm (Habbershon & Williams, 1999), inasmuch as such family involvement is a "unique, inseparable, and synergistic resource", and thus, a "hard-to-duplicate capability" (Nordqvist, 2005, p. 287), representing a source of sustained competitive advantage. This family involvement is said to generate "familiness", i.e. a bundle of idiosyncratic arrays of family firms' resources and capabilities (Habbershon & Williams, 1999), which has been demonstrated to positively impact firm profitability (Chrisman, Chua, & Litz, 2003; Habbershon et al., 2003).

The family involvement within the family firm can be expressed through ownership and/or management (Diéguez-Soto & Martínez-Romero, 2019; Sciascia & Mazzola, 2008). Focusing the attention on family firms with family involvement in management, several studies highlighted the positive influence of family managers on firms' profitability (e.g. Gallucci et al., 2015; Sciascia et al., 2014; among others). For instance, Anderson and Reeb (2003) found that family managers evince a positive relationship to accounting profitability measurements, and justified their findings arguing that families understand their businesses and that family members conceive themselves as firms' stewards. Gómez-Mejía, Larraza-Kintana, and Makri (2003) also revealed a positive relationship between family managers and firm profitability, stating that due to their higher employment security, family managers are willing to trade such security for lower earnings, which in the end, increases firms' profitability. Lee (2006) argued that family managers command higher loyalty within their family firms, enhancing employee productivity, leading to better performance, and thus profitability. Finally, the recent study of Rojo-Ramírez and Martínez-Romero (2018) has also confirmed a positive impact of family managers on firms' profitability.

Based on the abovementioned studies, it can be argued that family managers contribute with several positive attributes to the firms' outcomes (Manzaneque, Ramírez, & Diéguez-Soto, 2017). In this respect, different arguments support such positive impact. First, family managers are characterised by high commitment to the business because they perceive firms' outcomes as an extension of their own well-being (Ward, 1987). Moreover, family managers usually develop friendly, sincere and close relationships with both internal and external stakeholders (Gómez-Mejía, Haynes, Núñez-Nickel, Jacobson, & Moyano-Fuentes, 2007). Specifically, family managers develop more personal relationships with employees and are usually more flexible regarding work practices, which occasion increased motivation among workers (Tagiuri & Davis, 1996). Because of these reasons and due to the altruistic behaviour of family managers towards their firms' employees, the latter tend to act in the best interest of the business (Huybrechts, Voordeckers, Lybaert, & Vandemaele, 2011; Voordeckers, Steijvers, & Peeters, 2010), and thus, it can be argued that family managers are able to bring out the best from their workers (Gallucci et al., 2015). Thereby, family managers are able to create a culture for trust, cooperation and shared codes, which in the end, improves the firm's ability to exchange and combine knowledge and to generate higher profitability (Collins & Smith, 2006).

Therefore, it seems that within the pool of family firms, family managers make the best of themselves to ensure their firm survival and their control over the firm, promote practices that evoke the best from their employees, and thereby, display higher performance and profitability (Gallucci et al., 2015; Huybrechts et al., 2011; Lee, 2006). In this regard, firm outcomes would be more family-influenced as family management increases (Martínez-Romero et al., 2019a). Thus, it can be stated that as family involvement in management increases, firms' profitablity will be higher. Stated formally:

Hypothesis 1: As family involvement in management increases, the obtained profitability by family firms will be higher.

The Moderating Role of Innovative Effort

In the former section, it has been hypothesized that, within the pool of family firms, a high involvement of family members in management is likely to improve firm profitability. At this point, it is argued that the abovementioned relationship might be moderated by the innovative effort deployed by family firms.

Innovation investments are critical to firms' organizational success and competitive advantage (Chan, Lakonishok, & Sougiannis, 2001; Muñoz-Bullón & Sanchez-Bueno, 2011), and R&D investments play a key role in the improvement of firms' productivity, economic growth and long-term performance (Block, 2012; Wakelin, 2001). According to OECD guidelines (2005, p. 92) R&D is the *creative work undertaken on a systematic basis in order to increase the stock of knowledge (including knowledge of man, culture and society) and the use of this knowledge to devise new applications.* Furthermore, R&D investment is a widely recognized indicator of the innovative effort of countries and businesses (e.g. Nieto, Santamaria, & Fernandez, 2015).

R&D is consistent with the survival instinct and long-term vision of family firms (Miller & Le-Breton-Miller, 2005; Sirmon, Arregle, Hitt, & Webb, 2008). In this regard, family managers are under less pressure to obtain higher short-term profits and often incur long-term expenditures (Munari, Oriani, & Sobrero, 2010; Sirmon & Hitt, 2003), making quintessentially farsighted investments (Diéguez-Soto, Manzaneque, González-García, & Galache-Laza, 2019), such as R&D investments, which can stimulate their firms' performance and competitiveness over their foreseeable long careers (Miller & Le Breton-Miller, 2006). The family managers' tendency to stay at their jobs for long periods gives them increased incentives to serve as good stewards of resources (Le Breton-Miller & Miller, 2006; Uhlaner, Wright, & Huse, 2007), and thus, their concern for the proper use and management of R&D resources will be greater. Hence, this higher commitment to R&D resources would make it possible to develop the resource orchestration and the dynamic capacities of family managers (Habbershon & Williams, 1999), which in turn, may enhance the relationship between family involvement in management and firm profitability (Diéguez-Soto, et al., 2019).

Previous research has revealed that R&D investment may increase the learning or absorptive capacity of firms as it generates new knowledge and improves the firm's ability to identify, assimilates and exploit existing information (Cohen & Levinthal, 1989, 1990). Moreover, scholars have found that family involvement in management actually boots a firm's economic motivation to learn from its environment and make the most of unique external opportunities (Zahra, 2012). In fact, family managed firms, because of its particular social capital (Arregle, Hitt, Sirmon, & Very, 2007; Sanchez-Famoso, Pittino, Chirico, Maseda, & Iturralde, 2019), are excel at cultivating, nurturing and developing long-standing relationships across generations with selected stakeholders (Berrone et al., 2012; Miller & Le-Breton-Miller, 2005), which allows the establishment of worthy technological networks. These networks are essential for a better assimilation of external technological knowledge, since they provide access to knowledge and knowledge-sharing, through the exchange of experiences and insights among network members (Martínez-Romero, Martínez-Alonso, Casado-Belmonte, & Rojo-Ramírez, 2019; Sirmon & Hitt, 2003). Stakeholders, who are widely aware of the innovative potential of family managed firms, as well as their stability in management, are eager to maintain and improve relationships with family firms

(Diéguez-Soto et al., 2019; Ward, 2004). Therefore, promoting innovative efforts would allow family managed firms to fully exploit their learning and absorptive capacities, and to have access to information, technological knowledge and resources that are not available internally (Martínez-Romero et al., 2019b; Weigelt, 2009), which can enhance their firm profitability.

Furthermore, as previously mentioned, the interplay between family and business systems (e.g. Kotlar & De Massis, 2013), bestows on family members certain idiosyncratic features, such as cement loyalties, unusual motivation and a unique family language that allow family members to communicate and share information in a more efficient and private manner (De Massis, Frattini, Pizzurno, & Cassia, 2015; Tagiuri & Davis, 1996; Vallejo-Martos & Puentes-Poyatos, 2014). In this respect, it can be argued that the innovative effort develop in family firms, as a result of high-quality communication flows among family members (Habbershon & Williams, 1999) and joint decision-making processes on a trust basis (Diéguez-Soto et al., 2018), will be aligned with the ultimate goal of improving firm profitability, which is considered a prerequisite for the viability of the firm (Chrisman & Patel, 2012; Kotlar et al., 2014; Martínez-Romero & Rojo-Ramírez, 2017). This innovative effort, which is based on decisions characterized by trustful and loyal relationships taken by family managers, may reinforce the commitment of all staff to achieve priority firms' goals (Kotlar et al., 2014; Lee, 2006), i.e. profitability goals.

Hence, it can be expected that, in family firms, deploying higher innovative efforts, while increasing the level of family involvement in management, will have a positive effect on firm profitability. Stated formally:

Hypothesis 2: The innovative effort deployed in family firms positively moderates the influence of family managers on firm profitability.

The research model and suggested hypotheses are illustrated in Figure 1.

Figure 1. Theoretical Model
Source: Own elaboration

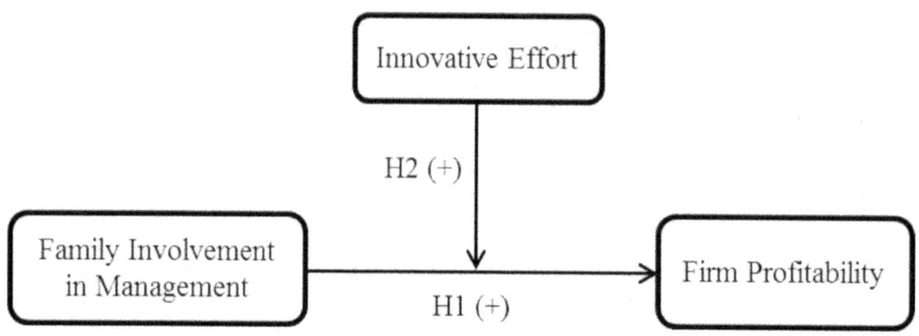

METHODOLOGY

Sample

To test the proposed hypotheses, the authors drew on a representative sample of Spanish private firms based on data from the Survey on Business Strategies (ESEE). The ESEE is an annual survey conducted by the State Partnership of Manufacturing Equity (SEPI) foundation on behalf of the Spanish Ministry of Industry and is composed by manufacturing firms. The sampling procedure of the ESEE guarantees the representativeness of the Spanish manufacturing industry by applying both exhaustive and random sampling criteria. Specifically, the data comprise the whole population of Spanish private manufacturing firms with 200 or more employees and include a stratified random sample of 5% of the firms' population with at least 10, but less than 200 employees. In this sense, this survey includes approximately 1,800 businesses per year, covering a wide range of information related to their management, their innovation strategies and their economic and financial outcomes, among other aspects. As the present study is interested in how innovative efforts influence the family involvement in management-firm profitability relationship, a focus on the manufacturing industry is considered appropriate to the extent that their products often suffer a high degree of obsolescence and consequently they are used to perform innovative efforts searching for competitive advantages (Kotlar, De Massis, Frattini, Bianchi, & Fang, 2013; Martínez-Alonso et al., 2019). Moreover, given that family firms tend to predominate in manufacturing industries (Diéguez-Soto & Martínez-Romero, 2019; IEF & Red de Cátedras de Empresa Familiar, 2015), the use of the ESEE database provides a unique context for analysing family firm profitability heterogeneity.

In this regard, the ESEE identifies family firms with a categorical variable, which indicates the identity between ownership and control depending on whether family members are involved in both the ownership and management of the firm. Therefore, to fulfil the research purpose, i.e. analysing family firm heterogeneity regarding profitability, a representative sample of family owned and managed firms was selected. This selection provides an unbalanced panel data of 3,164 (firm-year) observations, amounting to a total of 285 family managed firms for the 2000–2015 period. Table 1 presents a more detailed description of the sample firms.

Measures

Dependent Variable

In order to evaluate family firm profitability, the authors adopted gross margin, conceptualized as the difference between sales and the cost of goods sold scaled by sales (e.g. De Massis et al., 2018). Gross margin reflects the firms' financial health and represents the most appropriate indicator of profitability in this study as it allows measuring how efficiently family managers use their resources and abilities to generate organizational outcomes. In fact, the use of gross margin instead of other accounting indicators (e.g. return on assets or return on equity) provides certain advantages, since it only considers operating incomes and expenses. Accordingly, the gross margin does not contemplate taxes or interest generated by financial investments, which might undermine the reliability of performance estimates, providing a more reliable estimation of firm probability (De Massis et al., 2018; George, 2005).

Table 1. Sample description

	N	%
Sample composition by size[a]		
Large-size firms	420	13.27
Medium-size firms	413	13.05
Small-size firms	2,331	73.67
Total	3,164	100.00
Sample composition by sub-industry		
1. Meat industry	146	4.61
2. Foodstuffs and snuff	457	14.44
3. Drinks	31	0.98
4. Textiles and clothing	401	12.67
5. Leather and footwear	105	3.32
6. Timber industry	120	3.79
7. Paper Industry	142	4.49
8. Graphics	138	4.36
9. Chemical and pharmaceutical products	126	3.98
10. Rubber and plastic	265	8.38
11. Non-metallic mineral products	110	3.48
12. Ferrous and non-ferrous metals	44	1.39
13. Metal products	350	11.06
14. Agricultural and industrial machinery	185	5.85
15. Computer, electronic and optical products	39	1.23
16. Electrical machinery and material	86	2.72
17. Motor vehicles	91	2.88
18. Other transport equipment	51	1.61
19. Furniture industry	160	5.06
20. Other manufacturing	117	3.70
Total	3,164	100.00
[a]Small, medium, and large firms have been classified in compliance with European Commission criteria (2003/361/CE, 6th may).		

Source: Own elaboration

Independent Variable

Family involvement in management is conceived as the active participation of the controlling family in the firm management for all family owned firms (Kotlar et al., 2014). In this regard, for all those firms that are family owned the ESEE establishes the number of family members who occupy top managerial positions. Based on this definition, a continuous variable that includes the total number of family members who actively participate in top management teams is built to measure family involvement in management (Cruz, Gómez-Mejia, & Becerra, 2010; Kotlar et al., 2013).

Moderating Variable

To analyse the proposed moderating effect, a continuous variable that allows capturing the innovation effort developed by each firm was built. In this respect, the ratio of firms' R&D expenses over total sales was used as a proxy of innovative effort (e.g. Nieto et al., 2015). Furthermore, considering that R&D investment is a long-term process whose results are obtained in the following years after its execution (Liang, Li, Yang, Lin, & Zheng, 2013), a one-year lagged expression of innovative effort was used.

Control Variables

Several control variables were utilised to account for alternative explanations: firm size, leverage, supplier bargaining power, territorial subdivisions and sub-industries. The authors controlled for firm size, measured as the natural logarithm of total assets, because of larger firms have advantages in comparison to small and medium firms in terms of financial resources, internal knowledge or economies of scale, which might increase their firm profitability (Cohen & Klepper, 1996; Tsao & Lien, 2011). The authors also controlled for leverage, computed as debt to total assets ratio, due to firms with higher volume of financial resources are able to achieve both greater profitability and increased innovation levels (Martínez-Romero et al., 2019a; Revilla, Perez-Luno, & Nieto, 2016). Given that the concentration of suppliers can be perceived by family managers as a direct threat to their family control and thus, to their firms' profitability goals, supplier bargaining power was used as a control variable (Kotlar et al., 2014; Nieto et al., 2015), calculated as the percentage of purchases a firm makes from its three major suppliers. Furthermore, the authors control for territorial subdivisions or context conditions (Camagni & Capello, 2013; Manzaneque et al., 2017) through the inclusion of dummy variables representative of seven Spanish territorial subdivisions (NUTS1, Nomenclature des Unités Territoriales Statistiques), distinguishing 7 areas: 1. Northwest; 2. Northeastern; 3. Madrid; 4. Center; 5. East; 6. South; and, 7. Canarias. Finally, since strong support exists for the control of potential industry effects, twenty dummy variables denoting specific sub-industries were included in all models.

Analytical Method

This research aims to examine both the influence of family involvement in management on firm profitability and the interaction effect of innovative effort in the abovementioned relationship. With this aim, a panel data design was employed, which enables controlling for unobserved heterogeneity at the firm level. Moreover, panel data models offer higher resilience and explanatory power than cross-sectional designs. When using panel data it is common to distinguish between random effects and fixed effects, usually through the Hausman specification test (e.g. Tsao & Lien, 2011). Nevertheless, in this particular case, the invariant nature of key variables in the model, i.e., sub-industries and territorial specifications dummies, impedes the use of fixed effects models (Diéguez-Soto & López-Delgado, 2018; González, Guzmán, Pombo, & Trujillo, 2013). Therefore, to test the hypotheses, random effects models controlling for autocorrelation and heteroscedasticity were used. Specifically, the authors use lagged values of the dependent variable as regressors (Diéguez-Soto et al., 2019), which allows decreasing the potential serial correlation of errors and control for possible endogeneity problems (Cameron & Trivedi, 1998). Based on the abovementioned considerations, various models were estimated using the following equation:

Firm profitability=

$$\beta_0 + \beta_1 Family\ involvement\ in\ management_{t,i} + \beta_2 Innovative\ effort_{t-1,i}$$
$$+ \beta_3 Family\ involvement\ in\ management\ x\ Innovative\ effort_{t-1,i}$$
$$+ \beta_4 Firm\ profitability_{t-1} + \sum \beta_j x\ Controls + \varepsilon$$

RESULTS

Table 2 reports some descriptive statistics for continuous variables and frequencies for categorical variables. The mean value of firm profitability is 0.342, whereas the average value of family involvement in management is 1.635. The mean value of innovative effort is 0.007. With regard to other variables, for instance, the average firm size in the sample is 15.123 and the mean leverage is 0.517.

Table 3 presents the correlation and multicollinearity results of the examined variables. Since the highest correlation coefficient between independent variables is 0.215, and the variance inflation factors are well below the 2.5 threshold suggested in prior literature as the warning level above which multicollinearity problems could arise, there is sufficient evidence to rule out multicollinearity in the data (Belsley, Kuh, & Welsch, 1980; Hair, Anderson, Tatham, & Black, 1998).

Table 2. Descriptive statistics

Continuous Variables					
	Mean	**Median**	**25%**	**75%**	**Std. Dev.**
Firm profitability	0.342	0.336	0.234	0.446	0.170
Firm size	15.123	14.825	13.828	16.111	1.748
Leverage	0.517	0.522	0.328	0.701	0.235
Supplier bargaining power	44.942	40.000	28.000	60.000	21.770
Family involvement in management	1.635	1.000	1.000	2.000	0.786
Innovative effort	0.007	0.000	0.000	0.001	0.028
Categorical Variables					
Territorial subdivisions		**N**		**%**	
Northwest		343		10.84	
Northeastern		246		7.79	
Madrid		296		9.36	
Center		573		18.11	
East		1,252		39.56	
South		329		10.41	
Canarias		124		3.93	
Note: N = 3,164 observations.					

Source: Own elaboration

Table 3. Correlation matrix and multicollinearity analysis

	1	2	3	4	5	6
1. Firm profitability						
2. Firm size	-0.330***					
3. Leverage	-0.165***	-0.132***				
4. Supplier bargaining power	0.151***	-0.309***	0.038***			
5. Family involvement in management	0.016	0.215***	-0.020	0.066***		
6. Innovative effort	-0.059***	0.135***	0.016	-0.060***	-0.003	
Variance Inflation Factors		1.35	1.07	1.11	1.06	1.02
Note: N = 3,164 observations. ***Significant at 1%. Sub-industry and territorial subdivisions dummies are not added for space reasons, but results are available from the authors.						

Source: Own elaboration

Table 4 shows the random effects regression results. In accordance with the recommendations of Ruiz-Jiménez and Fuentes-Fuentes (2016), based on Cohen, Cohen, West, and Aiken (2003), the variables were incorporated into the models in four consecutive steps: first the control variables (Model 1), second the independent variable *Family involvement in management* (Model 2), then the main effect *Innovative effort* (Model 3), and finally the interaction effect *Family involvement in management x Innovative effort* (Model 4).

Model 1 shows a negative and statistically significant influence of firm size (β = -0.012; $p < 0.01$) and leverage (β = -0.028; $p < 0.05$) on firm profitability. Model 2 enables checking Hypothesis 1, confirming that family involvement in management positively influences firm profitability (β = 0.006; $p < 0.05$). These results are consistent with prior studies (e.g. Sciascia et al., 2014), which indicate that family managers make the most of their unique resources and abilities to improve their firms' profitability and thus, ensuring their survival for future generations. Then, Model 3 was run to analyse the direct influence of innovative effort on firm profitability. As shown in Model 3, innovative effort is negatively and significantly related to firm profitability (β = -0.187; p < 0.05). These results are also in line with previous literature (Cruz-Cázares, Bayona-Sáez, & García-Marco, 2013; Pantagakis, Terzakis, & Arvanitis, 2012), which revealed that R&D investments pose a substantial risk for the firms' profitability due to the non-immediate profits, the necessary investments in sunk costs and the high likelihood of failure (Chrisman & Patel, 2012; Martínez-Romero et al., 2019b). It can also be seen that when innovative effort is introduced, the effect of family involvement in management on firm profitability remains significant (β = 0.007; $p < 0.05$). However, the main goal is not analysing the direct effect of innovative effort on firm profitability; on the contrary, the main interest lies in Hypothesis 2, that is, in examining the moderating effect of innovative effort, and to this end, Model 4 introduces the interaction term *Family involvement in management x Innovative effort*. The results of Model 4 show that the abovementioned interaction effect is positive and statistically significant regarding firm profitability (β = 0.276; $p < 0.05$), suggesting that the positive effect that family involvement in management exerts on firm profitability is strengthened as innovative effort increase. That is, when increasing simultaneously family management and innovative effort, firm profitability is enhanced. It seems that as family involvement in management increases, family managers would develop more cautious and secure innovative efforts in an attempt to improve their firm profitability. Thus, these results strongly support hypothesis 2.

Moreover, to capture the total effect of family involvement in management on firm profitability when innovative efforts are undertaken, the authors present the sum of the coefficient of the individual variable and its interaction term, through the Wald test. The sum of the coefficients of family involvement in management and family involvement in management x Innovative effort ($\beta_1 + \beta_3$) is positive and significant ($\beta = 4.28$; $p < 0.05$), which confirms that innovative effort moderates the family involvement in management-firm profitability relationship.

Last, to provide a more accurate picture of the interaction effect of innovative effort in the family involvement in management-firm profitability relationship, Figure 2 depicts such interaction. In this sense, Figure 2 shows that when developing high innovative efforts, an augment in the number of family members actively participating in management positions is translated into a significant increase in firm

Table 4. Random effects regressions results

Dependent Variable: Firm Profitability				
	Model 1	**Model 2**	**Model 3**	**Model 4**
Independent Variable				
Family involvement in management (β_1)		0.006** (0.003)	0.007** (0.003)	0.006* (0.003)
Main Effect				
Innovative effort$_{t-1}$ (β_2)			-0.187** (0.098)	-0.599*** (0.227)
Interaction Effect				
Family involvement in management x Innovative effort$_{t-1}$ (β_3)				0.276** (0.137)
Lagged Dependent Variable				
Firm profitability$_{t-1}$ (β_4)	0.561*** (0.017)	0.558*** (0.017)	0.543*** (0.018)	0.540*** (0.018)
Controls				
Firm size$_{t-1}$ (β_5)	-0.012*** (0.002)	-0.013*** (0.002)	-0.012*** (0.002)	-0.013*** (0.002)
Leverage$_{t-1}$ (β_6)	-0.028** (0.011)	-0.029** (0.011)	-0.028** (0.011)	-0.028** (0.011)
Supplier bargaining power$_{t-1}$ (β_7)	0.001* (0.001)	0.001* (0.001)	0.002* (0.001)	0.002* (0.001)
Territorial subdivisions (β_8)	Included	Included	Included	Included
Industry effect (β_9)	Included	Included	Included	Included
Constant	0.354*** (0.032)	0.354*** (0.032)	0.379*** (0.036)	0.381*** (0.038)
Number of observations	3,164	3,164	3,164	3,164
Wald's X^2	1913.10***(21)	1914.84***(22)	2025.99***(31)	2014.15***(32)
Wald test: Total effects (β1+β3)				4.28**
R^2				
Within	0.0084	0.0082	0.0085	0.0091
Between	0.8324	0.8325	0.8153	0.8136
Overall	0.4996	0.5006	0.5071	0.5074
Note: Standard errors are in parentheses. ***Significant at 1%, **Significant at 5%, *Significant at 10%.				

Source: Own elaboration

Figure 2. Moderating effect of innovative effort on the relationship between family involvement in management and firm profitability
Source: Own elaboration based on the two-way interactions method of Dawson (2014)

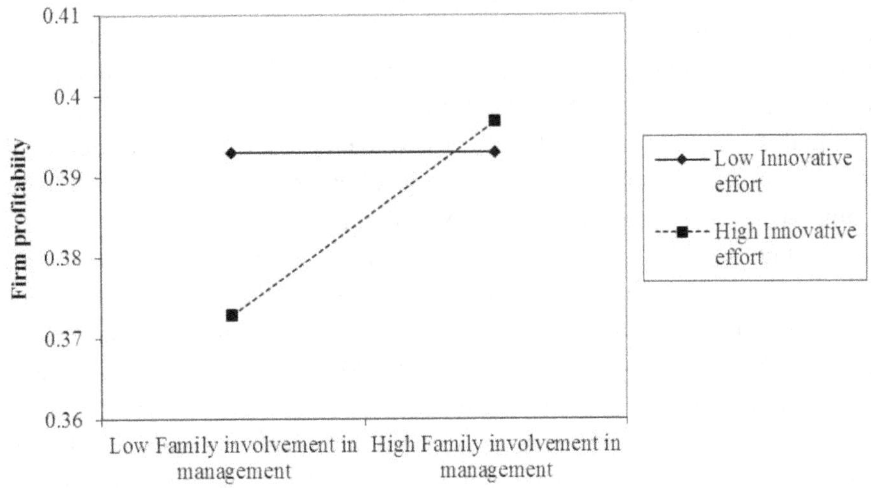

profitability. However, when the innovative effort is low, an increase in the number of family members in management results in a slight reduction of firm profitability. Thus, Figure 2 reinforces the obtained results in this study.

Robustness Test

As an additional robustness test to guarantee the consistency of the obtained results, the authors re-estimated models 1-4, but in this occasion, an alternative measurement of firm profitability was used. Therefore, in this case, firm profitability is computed as the return on assets ratio, conceptualised as the earnings before interest and tax to total assets. The obtained results are very similar to those obtained in the main analysis in Table 4 (robustness test results are available from authors), which provides further support for the hypotheses.

DISCUSSION

The findings reveal that, within the pool of family firms, an increase in the number of family members actively involved in the firm management, leads to higher profitability. Furthermore, the findings also show that an augment of family firms' innovative effort reinforces the positive effect that family involvement in management exerts on firm profitability.

Theoretical Implications

The results of this chapter offer significant contributions to both the family firm and the innovation research fields. First, this study is of great interest because while previous literature have devoted substantial attention on examining profitability differences among family and non-family firms (e.g. Allouche, Amann, Jaussaud, & Kurashina, 2008; Martínez, Stohr, & Quiroga, 2007), the authors go a step further by analysing profitability heterogeneity within the pool of family firms, a topic which has not received enough attention in the family firm research field (Chua et al., 2012). A major cause of family firm heterogeneity lies in the degree to which family members occupy upper echelon positions (Hambrick & Mason, 1984). Particularly, the high or low level of family participation may characterize the managerial team of the firm (Diéguez-Soto & Martínez-Romero, 2019; Klein, Astrachan, & Smyrnios, 2005). Thereby, in this study, the level of family involvement in management is identified as a potential source of heterogeneity that influences the achievement of organisational outcomes. In fact, this chapter expands the comprehension and the use of the RBV in family firms (Habbershon & Williams, 1999), by confirming that as family involvement in management increases, family managers will be more committed to the firm, will develop more personal relationships with employees and will make the best of themselves to improve firm profitability. Thus, the findings contribute to a better understanding of family firm heterogeneity (Chua et al., 2012; Pukall & Calabrò, 2014) and have important implications for the current debate on family firm profitability, to the extent that significant differences have been found in the profitability of these firms depending on the degree of family involvement in the firms' management.

Second, this manuscript offers a further in-depth theoretical analysis concerning the moderating role of innovative effort, highlighting the importance of the innovation behaviour of family firms. To the best of the authors' knowledge, this study is the first that empirically examines the moderating role of innovative effort on the relationship between family involvement in management and firm profitability within the pool of family firms. It has been argued that innovative effort reinforces the positive effect that family involvement in management exerts of firm profitability, because of, among other reasons, R&D investment horizons are aligned with the long-term vision of family firms (Diéguez-Soto et al., 2019; Muñoz-Bullón & Sanchez-Bueno, 2011). Moreover, innovative efforts are deployed with the final goal of improving firms' outcomes, not necessarily in the short term as these investments need time to succeed (Schmid, Achleitner, Ampenberger, & Kaserer, 2014), but in the middle and long-term, to ensure wealth creation across different family generations (Lumpkin & Brigham, 2011; Miller & Le Breton-Miller, 2014; Zellweger, Kellermanns, Chrisman, & Chua, 2012), and consequently, they are expected to improve the family management-profitability relationship. Likewise, the findings corroborate that, by increasing firms' learning and absorptive capacity (Cohen & Levinthal, 1989, 1990), innovative effort strengthens the relationship between family managers and firm profitability. Finally, the results seem to reveal that innovative strategic decisions in family firms, which are taken on the basis of trust, commitment and share vision (Diéguez-Soto et al., 2018; Diéguez-Soto & Martínez-Romero, 2019), will be deployed with the ultimate goal of guaranteeing the firm prosperity, reinforcing thus, family managers' ability to achieve higher profitability. Thus, the findings, in accordance with prior research acknowledging family firm heterogeneity (e.g. Schmid et al., 2014), confirm that R&D is crucial in reinforcing the distinctive characteristics of family managers, such as, for example, their tested ability to establish strong, prosperous technological collaboration networks, which in turn positively contributes to higher firm profitability. Thereby, this study stresses the relevance of considering family firm heterogeneity in terms of management when undertaking R&D investments.

Third, the present study contributes to the existing debate on performance, and namely on profitability, in private firms. It is widely known that current research on performance among private firms offers puzzling and conflicting results (Dyer, 2006; Rojo-Ramírez & Martínez-Romero, 2018). Empirical research on privately held family firms' performance is scant (Mazzi, 2011; Mazzola, Sciascia, &

Kellermanns, 2013), normally due to the absence of readily available financial data on these firms, which would also explain the reduced number of large sample longitudinal studies on this topic (Carney et al., 2015; George, 2005; Mazzi, 2011). Thereby, this chapter provides theoretical and empirical evidence on how strategic decisions, such as innovative effort, interact with family management, to generate financial consequences, i.e. higher profitability, in a context of private firms.

Finally, this chapter also contributes to the current literature on family firm performance inasmuch as it offers an alternative measure of firm profitability, i.e. gross margin, which has not been commonly utilized in past family firm research, but which is acquiring increased relevance in recent years (De Massis et al., 2018; Martínez-Romero, 2018; Martínez-Romero et al., 2019c). In this vein, up to now previous studies have opted for return on assets and/or return on equity ratios to measure firm profitability (Martínez et al., 2007; Mazzola et al., 2013; Rojo-Ramírez & Martínez-Romero, 2018; Sciascia et al., 2014). However, as previously mentioned, the use of gross margin as a profitability measure has several advantages such as, the unique consideration of operating incomes and expenses on the one hand; and, the non-consideration of taxes neither interest earned from financial investments, which may undermine the reliability of performance estimations (De Massis et al., 2018; George, 2005), on the other hand.

Practical Implications

This study also conveys insightful practical implications, particularly for those family firms that are keen on improving their profitability. A deeper understanding of the differences in firm profitability within the pool of family firms is crucial for family managers, family consultants and policy makers. Likewise, a better comprehension of the heterogeneity in the family firms' innovative behaviour is of extreme importance, inasmuch as these firms represent the backbone of the world economy (Family Firm Institute, 2018; La Porta et al., 1999; Villalonga & Amit, 2006).

Our results suggest that as the innovative effort of family firms increases, a greater family involvement in management implies higher profitability. Therefore, policy makers should stimulate R&D efforts in family firms via different initiatives, such as innovation subsidies or informative talks on the access and appropriate use of these resources. Furthermore, whereas the replacement of family managers by non-family managers is recognised as a key element to address innovation and to cope with declines in profitability (Detienne & Chirico, 2013; Diéguez-Soto, Duréndez, García-Pérez-de-Lema, & Ruiz-Palomo, 2016; Sciascia & Mazzola, 2008), this study demonstrates that a high family involvement in management combined with greater innovative efforts, is translated into higher profitability. According to Sciascia et al. (2014) and Stewart and Hitt (2011), this study emphasizes that the professionalization of a family firm does not necessarily involve recruiting non-family managers, as family firms with family members in management can also be professionally run. Thus, the family sphere should be aware that with appropriate training plans as well as with the development of close, strong and long-term technological networks, family managers can acquire the technical qualification, knowledge and skills required to face innovation with success and improve firm profitability. Nonetheless, family firms can also benefit from the inclusion of non-family members in their management teams (Martínez-Romero et al., 2019a), to the extent that it may help to align family and firm goals and to establish a culture of innovation that prevails in the long-term (Diéguez-Soto et al., 2016; Vandekerkhof, Steijvers, Hendriks, & Voordeckers, 2015).

Limitations and Future Research

While this chapter has found some new findings, the authors recognize some limitations that, in turn, open up new lines of research in the future. Although the total number of family members actively involved in the firm management is a direct and objective measure of family involvement in management (Kotlar et al., 2013; Manzaneque, Rojo-Ramírez, Diéguez-Soto, & Martínez-Romero, 2018), it suffers from a lack of consideration of certain components, such as managers' intentions, vision and goals, which could better elucidate family firm profitability heterogeneity. Future research should include these aspects in the analysis to better explain the variability of the dependent variable. Furthermore, although innovative effort was measured based on total R&D investments, recent studies (Bianchini, Pellegrino, & Tamagni, 2018; Diéguez-Soto et al., 2019; Diéguez-Soto & Martínez-Romero, 2019) have shown that different types of R&D strategies, i.e. intramural R&D investments vs. extramural R&D investments, might exert a different influence on innovation performance and thus, on firm profitability. Therefore, further research should consider the use of alternative R&D strategies to measure different types of innovative efforts, in order to see their possible consequences on firm profitability.

CONCLUSION

In conclusion, this chapter explores the heterogeneity of family firms by examining relationships of great relevance such as the effect of family involvement in management on firm profitability and the moderating role of innovative effort within the pool of family firms. In particular, the results show that an increase in the level of family involvement in management is positively associated with firm profitability, revealing differences in profitability gains among family firms depending on the degree of family implication in managerial positions. This manuscript also reveals that the deployment of greater innovative efforts is beneficial for family firm profitability, when interacting with high levels of family involvement in management. Therefore, although this study extends the theoretical contributions of prior literature (e.g. Nieto et al., 2015; Sciascia et al., 2014), more research is needed to better understand family firm heterogeneity regarding firm profitability and innovation.

ACKNOWLEDGMENT

Rubén Martínez-Alonso acknowledges the funding received by the Spanish Ministry of Science, Innovation and Universities in the form of a Research Grant to develop his PhD (FPU-17/01359), and thereby, this chapter.

REFERENCES

Allouche, J., Amann, B., Jaussaud, J., & Kurashina, T. (2008). The Impact of Family Control on the Performance and Financial Characteristics of Family Versus Nonfamily Businesses in Japan: A Matched-Pair Investigation. *Family Business Review*, *21*(4), 315–329. doi:10.1177/08944865080210040104

Anderson, R. C., & Reeb, D. M. (2003). Founding-family ownership and firm performance: Evidence from the S&P 500. *The Journal of Finance*, *58*(3), 1301–1329. doi:10.1111/1540-6261.00567

Arregle, J.-L., Hitt, M. A., Sirmon, D. G., & Very, P. (2007). The Development of Organizational Social Capital: Attributes of Family Firms*. *Journal of Management Studies*, *44*(1), 73–95. doi:10.1111/j.1467-6486.2007.00665.x

Belsley, D. A., Kuh, E., & Welsch, R. E. (1980). *Regression diagnostics: Identifying influential data and sources of collinearity*. New York: John Wiley & Sons. doi:10.1002/0471725153

Berle, A. A., & Means, G. C. (1965). *The modern corporation and private property*. New York: Macmillan.

Berrone, P., Cruz, C., & Gómez-Mejía, L. R. (2012). Socioemotional Wealth in Family Firms: Theoretical Dimensions, Assessment Approaches, and Agenda for Future Research. *Family Business Review*, *25*(3), 258–279. doi:10.1177/0894486511435355

Bianchini, S., Pellegrino, G., & Tamagni, F. (2018). Innovation complementarities and firm growth. *Industrial and Corporate Change*, *27*(4), 657–676. doi:10.1093/icc/dty008

Block, J. H. (2012). R&D investments in family and founder firms: An agency perspective. *Journal of Business Venturing*, *27*(2), 248–265. doi:10.1016/j.jbusvent.2010.09.003

Camagni, R., & Capello, R. (2013). Regional Innovation Patters and the EU Regional Policy Reform: Toward Smart Innovation Policies. *Growth and Change*, *44*(2), 355–389. doi:10.1111/grow.12012

Cameron, C., & Trivedi, P. (1998). *Regression Analysis of Count Data*. New York: Cambridge University Press. doi:10.1017/CBO9780511814365

Carney, M. (2005). Corporate Governance and Competitive Advantage in Family-Controlled Firms. *Entrepreneurship Theory and Practice*, *29*(3), 249–265. doi:10.1111/j.1540-6520.2005.00081.x

Carney, M., Van Essen, M., Gedajlovic, E. R., & Heugens, P. P. M. A. R. (2015). What do we know about private family firms? A meta-analytical review. *Entrepreneurship Theory and Practice*, *39*(3), 513–544. doi:10.1111/etap.12054

Chan, L. K. C., Lakonishok, J., & Sougiannis, T. (2001). The Stock Market Valuation of Research and Development Expenditures. *The Journal of Finance*, *56*(6), 2431–2456. doi:10.1111/0022-1082.00411

Chrisman, J. J., Chua, J. H., & Litz, R. A. (2003). A unified systems perspective of family firm performance: An extension and integration. *Journal of Business Venturing*, *18*(4), 467–472. doi:10.1016/S0883-9026(03)00055-7

Chrisman, J. J., Chua, J. H., Pearson, A. W., & Barnett, T. (2012). Family Involvement, Family Influence, and Family-Centered Non-Economic Goals in Small Firms. *Entrepreneurship Theory and Practice*, *36*(2), 267–293. doi:10.1111/j.1540-6520.2010.00407.x

Chrisman, J. J., Kellermanns, F. W., Chan, K. C., & Liano, K. (2010). Intellectual Foundations of Current Research in Family Business: An Identification and Review of 25 Influential Articles. *Family Business Review*, *23*(1), 9–26. doi:10.1177/0894486509357920

Chrisman, J. J., & Patel, P. C. (2012). Variations in R&D investments of family and nonfamily firms: Behavioral agency and myopic loss aversion perspectives. *Academy of Management Journal, 55*(4), 976–997. doi:10.5465/amj.2011.0211

Chua, J. H., Chrisman, J. J., & Sharma, P. (1999). Defining the family business by behavior. *Entrepreneurship Theory and Practice, 23*(4), 19–39. doi:10.1177/104225879902300402

Chua, J. H., Chrisman, J. J., Steier, L. P., & Rau, S. B. (2012). Sources of Heterogeneity in Family Firms: An Introduction. *Entrepreneurship Theory and Practice, 36*(6), 1103–1113. doi:10.1111/j.1540-6520.2012.00540.x

Cohen, J., Cohen, P., West, S. G., & Aiken, L. (2003). Applied Multiple Regression / Correlation Analysis for the Behavioral Sciences (3rd ed.). Mahwah, NJ: Lawrence Erlbaum Associates.

Cohen, W. M., & Klepper, S. (1996). A reprise of size and R & D. *Economic Journal (London), 106*(437), 925–951. doi:10.2307/2235365

Cohen, W. M., & Levinthal, D. A. (1989). Innovation and learning: The two faces of R&D. *Economic Journal (London), 99*(397), 569–596. doi:10.2307/2233763

Cohen, W. M., & Levinthal, D. A. (1990). Absorptive Capacity: A New Perspective on Learning and Innovation. *Administrative Science Quarterly, 35*(1), 128–152. doi:10.2307/2393553

Collins, C. J., & Smith, K. G. (2006). Knowledge exchange and combination: The role of human resource practices in the performance of high-technology firms. *Academy of Management Journal, 49*(3), 544–560. doi:10.5465/amj.2006.21794671

Cruz, C., Gómez-Mejia, L. R., & Becerra, M. (2010). Perceptions of benevolence and the design of agency contracts. *Academy of Management Journal, 53*(1), 69–89. doi:10.5465/amj.2010.48036975

Cruz-Cázares, C., Bayona-Sáez, C., & García-Marco, T. (2013). You can't manage right what you can't measure well: Technological innovation efficiency. *Research Policy, 42*(6–7), 1239–1250. doi:10.1016/j.respol.2013.03.012

Dawson, J. F. (2014). Moderation in management research: What, why, when and how. *Journal of Business and Psychology, 29*(1), 1–19. doi:10.100710869-013-9308-7

De Massis, A., Frattini, F., Pizzurno, E., & Cassia, L. (2015). Product innovation in family versus nonfamily firms: An exploratory analysis. *Journal of Small Business Management, 53*(1), 1–36. doi:10.1111/jsbm.12068

De Massis, A., Kotlar, J., Mazzola, P., Minola, T., & Sciascia, S. (2018). Conflicting Selves: Family Owners' Multiple Goals and Self-Control Agency Problems in Private Firms. *Entrepreneurship Theory and Practice, 42*(3), 362–389. doi:10.1111/etap.12257

Detienne, D. R., & Chirico, F. (2013). Exit strategies in family firms: How socioemotional wealth drives the threshold of performance. *Entrepreneurship Theory and Practice, 37*(6), 1297–1318. doi:10.1111/etap.12067

Diéguez-Soto, J., Duréndez, A., García-Pérez-de-Lema, D., & Ruiz-Palomo, D. (2016). Technological, management, and persistent innovation in small and medium family firms: The influence of professionalism. *Canadian Journal of Administrative Sciences*, *33*(4), 332–346. doi:10.1002/cjas.1404

Diéguez-Soto, J., Garrido-Moreno, A., & Manzaneque, M. (2018). Unravelling the link between process innovation inputs and outputs: The moderating role of family management. *Journal of Family Business Strategy*, *9*(2), 114–127. doi:10.1016/j.jfbs.2017.11.007

Diéguez-Soto, J., & López-Delgado, P. (2018). Does Family and Lone Founder Involvement Lead to Similar Indebtedness? *Journal of Small Business Management*. doi:10.1111/jsbm.12422

Diéguez-Soto, J., López-Delgado, P., & Rojo-Ramírez, A. A. (2015). Identifying and classifying family businesses. *Review of Managerial Science*, *9*(3), 603–634. doi:10.100711846-014-0128-6

Diéguez-Soto, J., Manzaneque, M., González-García, V., & Galache-Laza, T. (2019). A study of the moderating influence of R&D intensity on the family management-firm performance relationship: Evidence from Spanish private manufacturing firms. *BRQ Business Research Quarterly*, *22*(2), 105–118. doi:10.1016/j.brq.2018.08.007

Diéguez-Soto, J., & Martínez-Romero, M. J. (2019). Family Involvement in Management and Product Innovation: The Mediating Role of R&D Strategies. *Sustainability*, *11*(7), 2162. doi:10.3390u11072162

Dyer, W. G. (2006). Examining the "Family Effect" on Firm Performance. *Family Business Review*, *19*(4), 253–273. doi:10.1111/j.1741-6248.2006.00074.x

Eddleston, K. A., Kellermanns, F. W., & Sarathy, R. (2008). Resource Configuration in Family Firms: Linking Resources, Strategic Planning and Technological Opportunities to Performance. *Journal of Management Studies*, *45*(1), 26–50.

Family Firm Institute. (2018). *Global data points*. Available at: https://my.ffi.org/page/globaldatapoints

Gallucci, C., Santulli, R., & Calabrò, A. (2015). Does family involvement foster or hinder firm performance? The missing role of family-based branding strategies. *Journal of Family Business Strategy*, *6*(3), 155–165. doi:10.1016/j.jfbs.2015.07.003

García-Álvarez, E., & López-Sintas, J. (2001). A taxonomy of founders based on values: The root of family business heterogeneity. *Family Business Review*, *14*(3), 209–230. doi:10.1111/j.1741-6248.2001.00209.x

George, G. (2005). Slack resources and the performance of privately held firms. *Academy of Management Journal*, *48*(4), 661–676. doi:10.5465/amj.2005.17843944

Gómez-Mejía, L. R., Haynes, K. T., Núñez-Nickel, M., Jacobson, K. J. L., & Moyano-Fuentes, J. (2007). Socioemotional Wealth and Business Risks in Family-controlled Firms: Evidence from Spanish Olive Oil Mills. *Administrative Science Quarterly*, *52*(1), 106–137. doi:10.2189/asqu.52.1.106

Gómez-Mejía, L. R., Larraza-Kintana, M., & Makri, M. (2003). The determinants of executive compensation in family-controlled public corporations. *Academy of Management Journal*, *46*(2), 226–237.

Gómez-Mejía, L. R., Makri, M., & Kintana, M. L. (2010). Diversification Decisions in Family-Controlled Firms. *Journal of Management Studies*, *47*(2), 223–252. doi:10.1111/j.1467-6486.2009.00889.x

González, M., Guzmán, A., Pombo, C., & Trujillo, M. A. (2013). Family firms and debt: Risk aversion versus risk of losing control. *Journal of Business Research*, *66*(11), 2308–2320. doi:10.1016/j.jbusres.2012.03.014

Gottardo, P., & Moisello, A. M. (2015). The impact of socioemotional wealth on family firms' financial performance. *Problems and Perspectives in Management*, *13*(1), 67–77.

Habbershon, T. G., & Williams, M. (1999). A resource-based framework for assessing the strategic advantages of family firms. *Family Business Review*, *12*(1), 1–15. doi:10.1111/j.1741-6248.1999.00001.x

Habbershon, T. G., Williams, M., & MacMillan, I. C. (2003). A unified systems perspective of family firm performance. *Journal of Business Venturing*, *18*(4), 451–465. doi:10.1016/S0883-9026(03)00053-3

Hair, J. F., Anderson, R. E., Tatham, R. L., & Black, W. C. (1998). *Multivariate Data Analysis* (5th ed.). Upper Saddle River, NJ: Pearson.

Hambrick, D. C., & Mason, P. A. (1984). Upper echelons: The organization as a reflection of its top managers. *Academy of Management Review*, *9*(2), 193–206. doi:10.5465/amr.1984.4277628

Huybrechts, J., Voordeckers, W., Lybaert, N., & Vandemaele, S. (2011). The distinctiveness of family-firm intangibles: A review and suggestions for future research. *Journal of Management & Organization*, *17*(2), 268–287. doi:10.1017/S1833367200001656

IEF, & Red de Cátedras de Empresa Familiar. (2015). La Empresa Familiar en España (2015). Instituto de la Empresa Familiar. Barcelona, Spain.

Klein, S. B., Astrachan, J. H., & Smyrnios, K. X. (2005). The F-PEC Scale of Family Influence: Construction, Validation, and Further Implication for Theory. *Entrepreneurship Theory and Practice*, *29*(3), 321–339. doi:10.1111/j.1540-6520.2005.00086.x

Kotlar, J., & De Massis, A. (2013). Goal Setting in Family Firms: Goal Diversity, Social Interactions, and Collective Commitment to Family-Centered Goals. *Entrepreneurship Theory and Practice*, *37*(6), 1263–1288. doi:10.1111/etap.12065

Kotlar, J., De Massis, A., Frattini, F., Bianchi, M., & Fang, H. (2013). Technology acquisition in family and nonfamily firms: A longitudinal analysis of spanish manufacturing firms. *Journal of Product Innovation Management*, *30*(6), 1073–1088. doi:10.1111/jpim.12046

Kotlar, J., Fang, H., De Massis, A., & Frattini, F. (2014). Profitability Goals, Control Goals, and the R&D Investment Decisions of Family and Nonfamily Firms. *Journal of Product Innovation Management*, *31*(6), 1128–1145. doi:10.1111/jpim.12165

La Porta, R., Lopez-De-Silanes, F., & Shleifer, A. (1999). Corporate Ownership Around the World. *The Journal of Finance*, *54*(2), 471–517. doi:10.1111/0022-1082.00115

Laverty, K. J. (1996). Economic "short-termism": The debate, the unresolved issues, and the implications for management practice and research. *Academy of Management Review*, *21*(3), 825–860.

Le Breton-Miller, I., & Miller, D. (2006). Why Do Some Family Businesses Out-Compete? Governance, Long-Term Orientations, and Sustainable Capability. *Entrepreneurship Theory and Practice, 30*(6), 731–746. doi:10.1111/j.1540-6520.2006.00147.x

Lee, J. (2006). Family Firm Performance: Further Evidence. *Family Business Review, 19*(2), 103–114. doi:10.1111/j.1741-6248.2006.00060.x

Liang, Q., Li, X., Yang, X., Lin, D., & Zheng, D. (2013). How does family involvement affect innovation in China? *Asia Pacific Journal of Management, 30*(3), 677–695. doi:10.100710490-012-9320-x

Lumpkin, G. T., & Brigham, K. H. (2011). Long–Term Orientation and Intertemporal Choice in Family Firms. *Entrepreneurship Theory and Practice, 35*(6), 1149–1169. doi:10.1111/j.1540-6520.2011.00495.x

Manzaneque, M., Ramírez, Y., & Diéguez-Soto, J. (2017). Intellectual capital efficiency, technological innovation and family management. *Innovation: Management. Policy & Practice, 19*(2), 167–188. doi: 10.1080/14479338.2016.1272828

Manzaneque, M., Rojo-Ramírez, A. A., Diéguez-Soto, J., & Martínez-Romero, M. J. (2018). How negative aspiration performance gaps affect innovation efficiency. *Small Business Economics*. doi:10.100711187-018-0091-8

Martínez, J. I., Stohr, B. S., & Quiroga, B. F. (2007). Family ownership and firm performance: Evidence from public companies in Chile. *Family Business Review, 20*(2), 83–94. doi:10.1111/j.1741-6248.2007.00087.x

Martínez-Alonso, R., Martínez-Romero, M. J., & Rojo-Ramírez, A. A. (2019). The impact of technological innovation efficiency on firm growth: the moderating role of family involvement in management. *European Journal of Innovation Management*. doi:10.1108/EJIM-09-2018-0210

Martínez-Romero, M. J. (2018). *Financial performance and value creation in privately held family businesses: the influence of socioemotional wealth* (Doctoral thesis). Almería.

Martínez-Romero, M. J., Martínez-Alonso, R., & Casado-Belmonte, M. P. (2018). (Forthcoming). The influence of socioemotional wealth on firm financial performance: Evidence from small and medium privately held family businesses. *International Journal of Entrepreneurship and Small Business*.

Martínez-Romero, M. J., Martínez-Alonso, R., Casado-Belmonte, M. P., & Diéguez-Soto, J. (2019a). (Forthcoming) Family management and firm performance – The interaction effect of technological innovation efficiency. In Intrapreneurship and Sustainable Human Capital: Digital Transformation through Dynamic Competences. Springer.

Martínez-Romero, M. J., Martínez-Alonso, R., Casado-Belmonte, M. P., & Rojo-Ramírez, A. A. (2019b). The Moderating Effect of Family Management on R&D Productivity in Privately Held Firms. In N. M. Teixeira, T. G. Costa, & I. M. Lisboa (Eds.), *Handbook of Research on Entrepreneurship, Innovation, and Internationalization* (pp. 309–338). Hershey, PA: IGI Global. doi:10.4018/978-1-5225-8479-7.ch012

Martínez-Romero, M. J., & Rojo-Ramírez, A. A. (2017). Socioemotional wealth's implications in the calculus of the minimum rate of return required by family businesses' owners. *Review of Managerial Science, 11*(1), 95–118. doi:10.100711846-015-0181-9

Martínez-Romero, M. J., Rojo-Ramirez, A. A., & Casado-Belmonte, M. P. (2019c). Value creation in privately held family businesses: the moderating role of socioemotional wealth. *Canadian Journal of Administrative Sciences*. doi:10.1002/cjas.1540

Mazzi, C. (2011). Family business and financial performance: Current state of knowledge and future research challenges. *Journal of Family Business Strategy*, *2*(3), 166–181. doi:10.1016/j.jfbs.2011.07.001

Mazzola, P., Sciascia, S., & Kellermanns, F. W. (2013). Non-linear effects of family sources of power on performance. *Journal of Business Research*, *66*(4), 568–574. doi:10.1016/j.jbusres.2012.01.005

Mezias, S. J., Chen, Y. R., & Murphy, P. R. (2002). Aspiration-level adaptation in an American financial services organization: A field study. *Management Science*, *48*(10), 1285–1300. doi:10.1287/mnsc.48.10.1285.277

Miller, D., & Le-Breton-Miller, I. (2005). *Managing for the Long Run: Lessons in Competitive Advantage from Great Family Businesses*. Cambridge, MA: Harvard Business School Press.

Miller, D., & Le Breton-Miller, I. (2006). Family Governance and Firm Performance: Agency, Stewardship, and Capabilities. *Family Business Review*, *19*(1), 73–87. doi:10.1111/j.1741-6248.2006.00063.x

Miller, D., & Le Breton-Miller, I. (2014). Deconstructing Socioemotional Wealth. *Entrepreneurship Theory and Practice*, *38*(4), 713–720. doi:10.1111/etap.12111

Munari, F., Oriani, R., & Sobrero, M. (2010). The effects of owner identity and external governance systems on R&D investments: A study of Western European firms. *Research Policy*, *39*(8), 1093–1104. doi:10.1016/j.respol.2010.05.004

Muñoz-Bullón, F., & Sanchez-Bueno, M. J. (2011). The impact of family involvement on the R&D intensity of publicly traded firms. *Family Business Review*, *24*(1), 62–70. doi:10.1177/0894486510396870

Nieto, M. J., Santamaria, L., & Fernandez, Z. (2015). Understanding the Innovation Behavior of Family Firms. *Journal of Small Business Management*, *53*(2), 382–399. doi:10.1111/jsbm.12075

OECD. (2005). *Oslo Manual. Guidelines for collecting and interpreting innovation data*. OECD.

Pantagakis, E., Terzakis, D., & Arvanitis, S. (2012). *R&D Investments and Firm Performance: An Empirical Investigation of the High Technology Sector (Software and Hardware) in the E.U.* doi:10.2139srn.2178919

Pukall, T. J., & Calabrò, A. (2014). The Internationalization of Family Firms: A Critical Review and Integrative Model. *Family Business Review*, *27*(2), 103–125. doi:10.1177/0894486513491423

Rau, S. B., Schneider-Siebke, V., & Gunther, C. (2019). Family Firm Values Explaining Family Firm Heterogeneity. *Family Business Review*, *32*(2), 195–215.doi:10.1177/0894486519846670

Revilla, A. J., Perez-Luno, A., & Nieto, M. J. (2016). Does Family Involvement in Management Reduce the Risk of Business Failure? The Moderating Role of Entrepreneurial Orientation. *Family Business Review*, *29*(4), 365–379. doi:10.1177/0894486516671075

Rojo-Ramírez, A. A., & Martínez-Romero, M. J. (2018). Required and obtained equity returns in privately held businesses: The impact of family nature—evidence before and after the global economic crisis. *Review of Managerial Science*, *12*(3), 771–801. doi:10.100711846-017-0230-7

Ruiz-Jiménez, J. M., & Fuentes-Fuentes, M. del M. (2016). Management capabilities, innovation, and gender diversity in the top management team: An empirical analysis in technology-based SMEs. *BRQ Business Research Quarterly*, *19*(2), 107–121. doi:10.1016/j.brq.2015.08.003

Sanchez-Famoso, V., Pittino, D., Chirico, F., Maseda, A., & Iturralde, T. (2019). Social Capital and Innovation in Family Firms. The Moderating Roles of Family Control and Generational Involvement. *Scandinavian Journal of Management*. doi:10.1016/j.scaman.2019.02.002

Schmid, T., Achleitner, A.-K., Ampenberger, M., & Kaserer, C. (2014). Family firms and R&D behavior – New evidence from a large-scale survey. *Research Policy*, *43*(1), 233–244. doi:10.1016/j.respol.2013.08.006

Sciascia, S., & Mazzola, P. (2008). Family Involvement in Ownership and Management: Exploring Nonlinear Effects on Performance. *Family Business Review*, *21*(4), 331–345. doi:10.1177/08944865080210040105

Sciascia, S., Mazzola, P., & Kellermanns, F. W. (2014). Family management and profitability in private family-owned firms: Introducing generational stage and the socioemotional wealth perspective. *Journal of Family Business Strategy*, *5*(2), 131–137. doi:10.1016/j.jfbs.2014.03.001

Sirmon, D. G., Arregle, J.-L., Hitt, M., & Webb, J. W. (2008). The role of family influence in firms' strategic response to competitive threat of imitation. *Entrepreneurship Theory and Practice*, *32*(6), 979–998. doi:10.1111/j.1540-6520.2008.00267.x

Sirmon, D. G., & Hitt, M. A. (2003). Managing Resources: Linking Unique Resources, Management, and Wealth Creation in Family Firms. *Entrepreneurship Theory and Practice*, *27*(4), 339–358. doi:10.1111/1540-8520.t01-1-00013

Stewart, A., & Hitt, M. A. (2012). Why Can't a Family Business Be More Like a Nonfamily Business?: Modes of Professionalization in Family Firms. *Family Business Review*, *25*(1), 58–86. doi:10.1177/0894486511421665

Tagiuri, R., & Davis, J. (1996). Bivalent Attributes of the Family Firm. *Family Business Review*, *9*(2), 199–208. doi:10.1111/j.1741-6248.1996.00199.x

Tsao, S.-M., & Lien, W.-H. (2011). Family Management and Internationalization: The Impact on Firm Performance and Innovation. *Management International Review*, *53*(2), 189–213. doi:10.100711575-011-0125-9

Uhlaner, L., Wright, M., & Huse, M. (2007). Private Firms and Corporate Governance: An Integrated Economic and Management Perspective. *Small Business Economics*, *29*(3), 225–241. doi:10.100711187-006-9032-z

Vallejo-Martos, M. C., & Puentes-Poyatos, R. (2014). Family firms as incubators for ethical behavior: An exploratory study from the perspective of stewardship theory. *Journal of Management & Organization*, *20*(6), 784–807. doi:10.1017/jmo.2014.55

Vandekerkhof, P., Steijvers, T., Hendriks, W., & Voordeckers, W. (2015). The Effect of Organizational Characteristics on the Appointment of Nonfamily Managers in Private Family Firms: The Moderating Role of Socioemotional Wealth. *Family Business Review*, *28*(2), 104–122. doi:10.1177/0894486513514274

Villalonga, B., & Amit, R. (2006). How do family ownership, control and management affect firm value? *Journal of Financial Economics*, *80*(2), 385–417. doi:10.1016/j.jfineco.2004.12.005

Voordeckers, W., Steijvers, T., & Peeters, L. (2010). *The ownership-performance relationship: Agency issues in private family firms*. In Annual European Academy of Management (EURAM) Conference, Rome, Italy.

Wakelin, K. (2001). Productivity growth and R&D expenditure in UK manufacturing firms. *Research Policy*, *30*(7), 1079–1090. doi:10.1016/S0048-7333(00)00136-0

Ward, J. (2004). *Perpetuating the family business*. Marietta: Family Enterprise Publishers. doi:10.1057/9780230505995

Ward, J. L. (1987). *Keeping the family business healthy: how to plan for continuing growth, profitability, and family leadership*. San Francisco: Jossey-Brass.

Weigelt, C. (2009). The impact of outsourcing new technologies on integrative capabilities and performance. *Strategic Management Journal*, *30*(6), 595–616. doi:10.1002mj.760

Wolff, J. A., & Pett, T. L. (2006). Small-Firm Performance: Modeling the Role of Product and Process Improvements*. *Journal of Small Business Management*, *44*(2), 268–284. doi:10.1111/j.1540-627X.2006.00167.x

Zahra, S. A. (2012). Organizational learning and entrepreneurship in family firms: Exploring the moderating effect of ownership and cohesion. *Small Business Economics*, *38*(1), 51–65. doi:10.100711187-010-9266-7

Zellweger, T. M., Kellermanns, F. W., Chrisman, J. J., & Chua, J. H. (2012). Family Control and Family Firm Valuation by Family CEOs: The Importance of Intentions for Transgenerational Control. *Organization Science*, *23*(3), 851–868. doi:10.1287/orsc.1110.0665

ADDITIONAL READING

Chrisman, J. J., Chua, J. H., De Massis, A., Frattini, F., & Wright, M. (2015). The Ability and Willingness Paradox in Family Firm Innovation. *Journal of Product Innovation Management*, *32*(3), 310–318. doi:10.1111/jpim.12207

Daspit, J. J., Chrisman, J. J., Sharma, P., Pearson, A. W., & Mahto, R. V. (2018). Governance as a Source of Family Firm Heterogeneity. *Journal of Business Research*, *84*, 293–300. doi:10.1016/j.jbusres.2017.12.041

Li, Z., & Daspit, J. J. (2016). Understanding family firm innovation heterogeneity: A typology of family governance and socioemotional wealth intentions. *Journal of Family Business Management*, *6*(2), 103–121. doi:10.1108/JFBM-02-2015-0010

Martínez-Alonso, R., Martínez-Romero, M. J., & Rojo-Ramírez, A. (2018). Technological innovation and Socioemotional wealth in family firm research: Literature review and proposal of a conceptual framework. Management Research. *Journal of the Iberoamerican Academy of Management, 16*(3), 270–301. doi:10.1108/MRJIAM-01-2018-0803

Memili, E., & Dibrell, C. (2019). *The Palgrave Handbook of Heterogeneity among Family Firms* (E. Memili & C. Dibrell, Eds.). Palgrave Macmillan. doi:10.1007/978-3-319-77676-7

Zellweger, T. M. (2017). *Managing the Family Business: Theory and Practice*. Edward Elgar Publishing.

KEY TERMS AND DEFINITIONS

Absorptive Capacity: A firm's ability to acquire and use scientific, technological or other knowledge that exists outside the organization.

Family Firm Heterogeneity: Differences in the behaviours, goals, and values of family firms due to the high or low degree of family involvement in the firm.

Family Managed Firms: Family firms that are managed by the own family.

Family Managers: Family members of a family owned firm who are actively involved in the management team.

Firm Profitability: A firm's ability to generate profits from their activities.

Innovation Investments: Allocate money in the acquisition of a bundle of resources with the aim of generating innovation results.

Resource-Based View: Theory that facilitates the identification and exploitation of the resources that can lead a firm to achieve sustainable competitive advantages.

Social Capital: Intrinsic aspect of family firms that enables them to establish long-standing, fruitful, and quality relationships with potential stakeholders.

Chapter 14
Investigating Inner Dynamics in Family Firms: A Multilevel Analysis

Filippo Ferrari
https://orcid.org/0000-0002-7509-2320
Independent Researcher, Italy

ABSTRACT

This chapter shows that a multilevel model of analysis is a suitable approach in order to highlight hidden relationships among different structural units within organizations. In addition, current literature argued that the field of management could be enhanced by integrating the theory and empirical work of other related social science disciplines (e.g., psychology). In adopting analytical techniques from clinical, social, and I/O psychology, this chapter highlights the deepest (dysfunctional) organizational dynamics, thus demonstrating the effectiveness of a multidisciplinary approach to complex organizational phenomena. Finally, this chapter highlights implications and suggestions for scholars and consultants in the field of business analysis. In particular, the multiple nature of dysfunctional dynamics advocates for a wider diffusion of psychological diagnostic tools, integrating them into traditional economical and financial assessment.

INTRODUCTION

In order to investigate inner business dynamics and, more generally, understand the complexity of an organization, a multilevel analysis is advisable (McKenny et al., 2014). Managerial and family business literature (Hitt et al., 2007) traditionally uses a micro or macro analysis level, but that may not be sufficient for a full and deep understanding of the inner dynamics. The assumption at the base of the multilevel approach is that many outcomes are the result of a confluence of influences emanating from different levels of analysis (House, Rousseau & Thomas-Hunt, 1995; Rousseau, 1985).

DOI: 10.4018/978-1-7998-1655-3.ch014

All organizations, and family firms in particular, have *non-economic goals*: this is a well-established fact in managerial literature (e.g. Astrachan Jaskiewicz, 2008; Berrone et al., 2012; Chua, Chrisman, & Sharma, 1999; Zellweger & Astrachan, 2008). In pursuing these goals, organizations are particularly exposed to relationship conflicts (Davis & Harveston, 2001; Levinson, 1971; Zellweger & Astrachan, 2008) and/or rivalry (Grote, 2003), which can negatively affect firm performance (Eddleston & Kellermanns, 2007) or group dynamics and business processes (Pelled et al., 1999), thus generating non-financial costs (Astrachan & Jaskiewicz, 2008). These negative non-economic outcomes, usually unintended consequences of the positive ones, are often overlooked (Astrachan & Jaskiewicz, 2008) and, at least, are difficult to measure in spite of their potentially significant impact on firm performance and business value (Demetz & Lehn, 1985).

Following a multilevel analysis, the first purpose of this chapter is to analyse, discuss and largely further understand how organizations (family business especially) plays a role in generating unintended dysfunctional outcomes, at three different levels: the whole organization (i.e. the family firm), the group (i.e. the family), and the participants (the single family member).

Moreover, in order to proceed from 'how' to 'why', the second aim of the chapter is to offer an explanation for this dysfunctional phenomenon in terms of reciprocal interrelations between different organizational levels. This approach was chosen because other approaches (such as; organizational, managerial, and financial), focus more on success in terms of earnings, shareholder equity growth, and wealth retention, instead of human development and wellness.

With particular attention to methodological aspects, this study contributes to current literature in a twofold way.

By carrying out a multilevel analysis applied to family business field of research, this chapter demonstrates the feasibility of such an approach for obtaining a deeper understanding of organizational dynamics, thus responding to calls in organizational literature (Hitt et al., 2007). In addition, this research uses a qualitative approach, again reacting to a recent call (Fletcher et al, 2016) for a wider application of qualitative research in the family business field.

Furthermore, this chapter contributes more in general to organizational literature in two different ways.

First, by applying a multilevel analysis, this chapter highlights the deep dynamics which undermine family firm reliability and challenge its survival rate, thus offering a new, distinctive perspective on organizational (and family firms' in particular) inner processes. Moreover, by gathering data regarding Italian firms, this chapter contributes to international literature on organizational pathologies, literature so far almost exclusively focused on the Anglo-Saxon context.

THEORETICAL BACKGROUND

In pursuing non-economic advantages, family firms also sustain non-economic costs. Although scholars have suggested some criteria for considering both these aspects in business value appraisals, (e.g. Astrachan & Jaskiewicz, 2008), a complete and reliable evaluation of these non-economic costs is far from being accomplished. Occasionally a non-economic cost is an unintended consequence of a non-economic goal: literature following a Mertonian approach sustains (Griffin & O'Leary-Kelly's, 2004; Resick et al., 2009; Vaughan, 2009) that there could be a 'dark' dimension behind an apparently benign outcome. Due to the relevance of these kinds of goals for family firms, investigating positive non-economic outcomes that generate unintentionally harmful outcomes becomes a priority for scholars and researchers.

However, from a methodological point of view, the peculiar nature of family firms challenges scholars, and forces them to scratch beneath the surface of this organizational phenomena. For instance, Berrone and colleagues (2010) call for major attention to be paid to some family firm specific features such as; feelings, emotions, and relationships within the family controlling a firm. These features may vary from one firm to another and, within the firm, from one point in time to another (Hoy & Sharma, 2010), even with the same level of ownership. Moreover, a family firm is a very complex system: multilevel crossroads involving business and family goals, different generations and often different blood lines and siblings.

Consequently, studying family firms needs an adequate, multilevel approach (Hitt et al., 2007; McKenny et al., 2014), especially if the purpose is to investigate the 'dark side' of organizational phenomena. Socio-psychological literature suggests that each organization should be investigated on three different levels; (Cartwright & Zander, 1984; Spaltro & De Vito Piscitelli, 2001): organizational, group, and individual. Obviously, people in organizations are involved on all levels at the same time (*multiple belonging*).

Literature (Hitt et al., 2007) warns that it's fundamental, in order to avoid the 'fallacies of the wrong level' (Rousseau, 1985), to properly define the level of theory, measurement and data analysis. Thus, following these suggestions, this research investigates outcomes at an *organizational level* firstly. In a family firm, at this level, the analysis unit is the overlapping area between family and business. At this level, attempting to obtain an adequate balance between economic and non-economic goals plays a prominent role. For instance, recent literature has investigated the non-economic advantages that family member owners derive from corporate control (Berrone et al., 2010; Gomez-Mejia et al., 2007; Zellweger & A strachan, 2008).

However, literature suggests that there is also a *dark side* of trust and involvement that can lead to opportunism, complacency and blind faith, (Eddleston & Kidwell, 2012; Steier, 2001; Sundaramurthy, 2008), and can also negatively affect proactive stakeholder engagement (Kellermans et al., 2012). In spite of this empirical evidence, scholars have so far paid less attention to negative non-economic outcomes compared to positive ones (for a recent review, see Linstead et al., 2014). Thus, in order to fill this gap, this chapter focuses mainly on this organizational dark side, investigating in which conditions such pathologies arise from family relationships.

In adopting a multilevel approach, it's necessary to investigate this pathological situation at an organizational level of analysis primarily. Given these considerations, the first research question this chapter would suggest is:

RQ1: At an organizational level of analysis, which dynamics are at the base of negative non-economic outcomes in family firms?

Both organizational and social psychology suggest that, within an organization, a subset (such as a group or an organizational function) should represent a specific level of analysis, different from both the organisational and individual levels. Furthermore, following the small groups psychology approach (Cartwright & Zander, 1953, 1968), a family should be considered a small social group (Scabini, Iafrate, 2003; Uhlaner, 2006). In fact *group* is defined as a 'collection of two or more persons who interact with one another in such a way that each person influences and is influenced by the others' (Wagner & Hollenbeck, 1995, p. 310). By differentiating *team* and *group*, Uhlaner (2006) suggests that, within a family business, the family is a kind of stable group, different from the business family, which performs as a team. For the purpose of this chapter, the second level of analysis is the *family group*. At this level, the empirical evidence shows that a key factor in producing a positive outcome in family firms is the *kind of relationship* amongst *all* involved family members (Davis &

Harveston, 1998; Dunn, 1999; Lansberg & Astrachan, 1994; Morris et al., 1997). Family members' involvement could lead to positive outcomes such as *reciprocal altruism* (Eddleston, Kellermanns, & Sarathy, 2008; Lubatkin, Durand, & Ling, 2007), *family firm identity* (Zellweger, Kellermanns,

Eddleston, & Memili, 2012) and *stewardship* (Davis, Allen, & Hayes, 2010; Dibrell & Moeller, 2011; Eddleston & Kellermanns, 2007), but also to a *self-centred* and *strict family.* In fact, literature suggests, (for a review and an assessment of these dimensions, see Beavers & Hampson, 1995), that every situation experienced by a family group can be defined by assessing two different and variable family features: its *cohesiveness* (how self-oriented the family is) and its *flexibility* (how changeable and adaptable the relationships within the family are).

Each dimension/variable (both cohesiveness and flexibility) could be described in a curvilinear graph, where the extreme values are negative (dysfunctional). Due to the aforementioned familiar dimensions/ variables, and given the different values of both *cohesiveness* and *flexibility*, each combination could result in eight different kinds of family. Among these eight types, some positive non-economic goals (e.g. business transmission, second generation autonomy and wellness, and organizational trustful climate) are experienced. Families which are, at the same time, both connected *and* flexible/versatile show the highest likelihood of positive outcomes. Cohesiveness and flexibility are in some way correlated (Friedman, 1986; Gersick et al., 1997), and the former seems to play a prominent role in reducing variability around group/family norms (Schermerhorn et al., 2000). Given these considerations, the second research question this chapter would suggest is:

RQ2: At a family level of analysis, which dynamics affect family firm cohesiveness and flexibility?

Finally, when serious problems arise, the family business is treated, for all intents and purposes, as a patient (Kaye, 1996), and this patient - the family's continuity in their business - *must be saved.* However, what are (or could be) the psychological consequences for family members? For instance, past research suggests that in a family firm, high levels of emotional attachment and cohesiveness impede family employees from leaving (what Gomez-Mejia, Larraza-Kintana, & Makri, 2003 called the "family handcuff") and thereby preserve conflicting relationships: eventually, the family firm becomes a trap for the members themselves. Hence, at an *individual level* of analysis, it's possible to investigate these (and other) pathological outcomes involving a single family member.

At this level of analysis, Social Psychology of the Family literature underlines the fundamental role played by both *individuation/differentiation* and *legitimization* processes of the new generation in ensuring the overall success of transmission (Kaye, 1996; 1992; Scabini & Iafrate, 2003). Some anecdotal cases report, and a small amount of statistical evidence suggests, that the two variables are positively correlated (e.g., Swogger, 1991; Kaye, 1992; Lansberg & Astrachan, 1994). Several authors; (Barnes & Hershon, 1976; Kets de Vries, 1977, 1993; Lansberg, 1988; Peay & Dyer, 1989; Rubenson, Gupta, 1996), suggest that some sources of resistance to *legitimisation,* and *individuation/differentiation* of the second generation, could originate from characteristics of the founding entrepreneur (age, gender, attitude, and personality traits) and/or of the second generation. However, family business literature has so far paid scarce attention to these inner dynamics which involve both generations, thus offering little empirical evidence. Given these considerations, the third research question this chapter would suggest is:

RQ3: At an individual level of analysis, which dynamics affect the next generation's legitimisation and individuation/differentiation processes?

THE DATA COLLECTION

The author has worked for nearly 25 years as a consultant psychologist in family business. During these years, he has built up a database, gathering case studies characterized by pathologies, organizational dysfunctions and other hidden dimensions which lead family firms to the loss of what literature calls socio-emotional wealth or, more generally referred to as non-economic goals. To be included in the database, the firms must satisfy characteristic requirements:

- A single family must share at least 50% of the ownership;
- The strategic decisions must be managed by the family
- At least two generations belonging to the same family must be present in the firm
- At least one family member must experience his/her work situation negatively, from a psychological and/or relational point of view.

In that 5 year period, Author intervened in 36 family firms, which eventually formed the sample of this research. The sample is made up of firms belonging to several industrial sectors

Regarding the firm dimension/size, the sample was made up of SMEs, with a range of from 3 up to 174 employees As an I/O psychologist, since the beginnings of his professional career the Author have used a semi-structured grid in order to collect in-depth, detailed information about the clients during both individual and group interviews. On average each consultation process lasted approximately 8 months and Author usually met the participants around twice a month.

In psychological work, the process of analysis usually begins simultaneously with the process of data collection. This procedure is in line with both clinical and grounded theory procedures (Charmaz, 1995; Corbin & Strauss, 1990; McCollom, 1990;), which advocate data collection and analysis as interrelated processes. Meeting by meeting, month by month, nurturing my own firm's knowledge level, as each participant was interviewed these interviews in turn guided the next interview. The principle of constant comparison was also adhered to as each participant's experience, as told by them, was compared to that of the previous and following participants (see also Murphy & Lambrechts, 2015).

Following a multilevel and systemic approach well-established in clinical literature (McCollom, 1990; De Vito, 2001), the investigation focused on dysfunctional and even pathological behaviours; emerging data was coded and organized depending on the organizational level (family firm, family group, individual) affected by such dysfunctions.

During the data gathering, Author collected heterogeneous information regarding the nature, the strength, and the duration of each dysfunction. Hence, in order to systematize such data, dysfunctional dynamics were grouped according to which non-economic goal the firm was pursuing. Drawing on literature (Habbershom et al., 2003; Chrisman et al., 2003; Berrone et al., 2012), three clusters/groups have been defined, typically relating to family firms, and capturing the essence of the *familiness.* These three clusters represent non-economic and desired positive outcomes (Berrone et al., 2012): 1) the *Influence and control of family members over business*, that is family when members exert control over strategic decisions (Chua et al., 1999; Schulze, Lubatkin, & Dino, 2003b); 2) the *close identification of the family with the firm*, that is when the identity of a family firm's owner is inextricably linked to the organization (e.g., Berrone et al., 2010; Dyer & Whetten, 2006) and finally 3) the *intention to hand the business down to future generations,* that is the will/desire to preserve business continuity, (and) involving the next generation(e.g. Kets de Vries, 1993; Zellweger & Kellermanns, et al., 2011).

FINDINGS

Although managerial literature still often ignores the multilevel dynamics of organizations (Kozlowsi, Klein, 2000), a multilevel approach is a powerful instrument in order to develop a more complex understanding of a phenomenon. Thus, this qualitative research is more interested in deep interrelations within and among organizational levels, rather than merely producing a list of organizational dysfunctions and pathologies. Therefore, although this section presents the research findings, it also attempts to propose generalizations about a single organizational level, and at the same time begins to construct more higher-level theories starting from lower level data. This section is organized as follows;

In the first paragraph, the chapter presents and discusses the negative outcomes and undesired consequences emerging from each *single focal unit level* (Hitt et al., 2007): family firm, family group, family member. This paragraph answers research questions, providing evidence about organizational dysfunctions at each level.

Drawing on this first level evidence, the second paragraph presents a *three-level analysis*, in which each upper focal unit level affects the lower levels. In doing so, the chapter also presents a *throughout–level analysis,* suggesting some themes which recursively affect the family firm at all levels: organizational identity, emotional dynamics, and the founder's shadow.

Single Focal Units Level of Analysis

Following Hitt and colleagues (2007; see also Chan, 1998), this section presents a *composition* of the results, where simple, lower-level data (e.g. lack of managerialisation, nepotism, adverse selection) is associated with higher-level constructs (e.g. low level of organizational justice among non-family members). This paragraph provides a simple discussion of evidence, without inter-level influence. The following tables then present the key results, organizing the collected data as follows: the first column sets the cluster (that is the non-economic goal); the next column presents, level by level, the negative outcomes related to each non-economic goal; the third column proposes the potential undesired consequences. Due to the qualitative nature of this research, the limited dimension of the sample and its characteristics (non-randomized sample), it doesn't make sense to provide specific information about the quantitative diffusion of each negative outcome. Thus, this research provides simply a list of possible pathologies and related consequences. For convenience, and in order to clarify and simplify this complex analysis, discussion is provided level by level, immediately after the result presentation.

Influence and control of family members over business. This research (see table 1) seems to confirm that control and influence are integral parts of non-economic goals and are highly desired by family members (Zellweger & Kellermanns, et al., 2011). However, within the sample, this motivation is often associated with the discrimination of out-groups, and at the same time in-group favouritism. This finding is consistent with social-psychological literature (Tajfel, Turner, 1986) and previous research in the family business field (Ferrari, 2014; ; De Massis et al., 2012).

The *out-group discrimination* is associated with a high level of inter-group conflict versus non family members and, more frequently, with low level of organizational justice (OJ) as perceived by nonfamily members, according to current literature (Colquitt et al., 2001). Furthermore, literature supports the impact of the OJ dimensions (distributive, procedural, informational and relational) on organizational performance (Cropanzano et al., 2007), especially non-family member turnover rate (Colquitt et al., 2001; Ng et al., 2001).

Table 1. The influence and control of family members over business and related negative outcomes at a family firm level

Cluster (non-economic goal)	**RQ1 - Negative outcomes: family firm level**	**Undesired consequences for the business**
Influence and control of family members over business	• In-group favouritism and Outgroup's discrimination. • Lack of meritocracy in career and resource distribution. • Lack of managerialisation. • Imposed career on next generation. • Nepotism . • Adverse selection.	• Intergroup conflict vs. non family members. • Low level of organizational justice (both distributive and procedural). • High non-family member turn-over rate. • Skill shortage in managerial positions.

Table 2. The close identification of the family with the firm and related negative outcomes at a family firm level

Cluster (non-economic goal)	**RQ1 - Negative outcomes: family firm level**	**Undesired consequences for the business**
Close identification of the family with the firm;	• Family identity overwhelms firm identity. • Founder's total identification with the firm. • Mistrust of non-family members.	• Over-valuing of the current products, processes and managerial practices, Biases in strategic decision-making. • Postponed/Eluded succession. • Organizational failure. • Low level of organizational justice (both distributive and procedural). High non-family member turn-over rate.

Contrastingly, this data shows that *in-group favouritism* can explain dynamics such as nepotism (Salvato et al., 2012) and adverse selection (Schulze, Lubatkin, Dino, 2003; Chirsman, Chua, Litz, 2004), and more in general result in a lack of meritocracy, eventually resulting in severe skill shortage in managerial positions. This finding is consistent with literature: Italian firms have always showed a lack of *managerialisation* (Cagliano & Spina, 2000; Biasetti et al., 2009), and this research suggests that the situation is continuing unchanged. Furthermore, the Italian economy is characterized by small family-managed firms, with a lack of meritocracy in managerial selection and promotion (Bugamelli et al., 2012). Indeed, *Familism* and *Cronyism* appear to be the main causes of the delayed development of Italian organizations (Pellegrino & Zingales, 2014).

Close identification of the family with the firm. In the sample, family identity overwhelms firm identity (see table 2). This fact is often associated with an affective over-investment in family business, resulting in over-valuing of the current products, processes and managerial practices. The sample also shows biases in strategic decision-making, for example in launching new products or developing process innovation, pursuing the desire to preserve the current situation. Often, an innovation is perceived as a threat to the family firm past history. Literature highlights that the identity of a family firm's owner is inextricably tied to the organization: this causes the firm to be seen both by internal and external stakeholders as an extension of the family itself (Berrone et al., 2010; Dyer & Whetten, 2006). In particular, within the sample, there is almost always the founder's identification with the firm. This fact often leads to a lack of succession planning, that could easily result in an *eluded succession* (Piantoni, 1990) or even leads to organizational failure (Haveman, & Khaire, 2004). Finally, the close identification of the family with

Table 3. The intention to hand the business down to future generations and related negative outcomes at family firm level

Cluster (non-economic goal)	RQ1 - Negative outcomes: family firm level	Undesired consequences for the business
Intention to hand the business down to future generations	• Hazardous acquisitions and longterm investments in order to protect the next generation . • Refusal of mergers. • (Paradoxically) postponed/eluded succession.	• Waste of resources. • Chronically small firm dimension. • Demanded succession .

the firm could result in a sort of mistrust of nonfamily members, perceived as 'the others'. Once more, this fact could result in a low level of organizational justice (OJ) as perceived by non-family members, thus undermining their work engagement which in turn affects their Organizational Citizenship Behaviours - OCB and can even result in a high non-family member turn-over rate (Colquitt et al., 2001; Ng et al., 2001; Bowen et al., 2007).

Intention to hand the business down to future generations. Evidence shows (see table 3) that maintaining the business for future generations is commonly seen as a key goal for family firms (Berrone et al., 2012; Kets de Vries, 1993; Zellweger and Astrachan, 2008; Zellweger, Kellermanns, et al., 2011). In this research, this non-economic goal sometimes even results in hazardous behaviours in acquisitions and long-term investments in order to protect the next generation. Other times, the intention to protect next generation forces the founder into refusing a convenient, possible merger with a shareholder. In the former case the result is a waste resources, in the latter an under-sized firm. Not surprisingly, in a global economy, the Italian context is characterized by small firms, too small for the development of economies of scale, to fight bigger competitors or to invest in R&D. The result is low innovation rates, low capabilities in human resources and/or low improvement of human capital (Bugamelli et al., 2012).

Literature highlights that many family firms exhibit long-term planning horizons (Miller & Le Bret-onMiller, 2006b; Miller, Le Breton-Miller, & Scholnick, 2008; Sirmon & Hitt, 2003). However, these case studies show a different attitude to business transmission. Frequently, the intention to protect the business in order to transfer it to the to the next generation could paradoxically result in a postponed or eluded succession (Piantoni, 1990): the founder, year by year, waiting for the 'right moment', doesn't plan the transmission at all, thus by contrast eliciting a *demanded succession* in the successor.

The Influence and control of family members over business. Literature (Sorenson, 1999; Sorenson et al., 2009) suggests that family *cohesiveness* and firm integrity are prominent non-economic goals (see table 4).

Table 4. The intention to hand the business down to future generations and related negative outcomes at family level

Cluster (non-economic goal)	RQ2 - Negative outcomes: family level	Undesired consequences for the family
The influence and control of family members over business	• Strict family. • Self-centred family.	• Low level of member autonomy.

Table 5. The Close identification of the family with the firm and related negative outcomes at family level

Cluster (non-economic goal)	RQ2 - Negative outcomes: family level	Undesired consequences for the family
Close identification of the family with the firm	• Self-centred family	• Conflict avoidance/ intergenerational conflict. • Biases in strategic decision-making (e.g. next generation's educational path).

Social Psychology of the Family literature (Beavers & Hampson, 1995; Scabini, Iafrate, 2003) also suggests that family *flexibility* plays a strategic part both in facing daily events and sustaining the second generation in its development, fostering autonomy/independence and helping them to cope with unexpected events.

At family level of analysis, this research highlights that striving for control over non-family members is frequently associated with high level of cohesiveness and, at the same time, low level of flexibility. This association could be explained by social psychology of groups, which for a long time has shown the effect of a *perceived* out-group (Tajfel, Turner, 1986).

Close identification of the family with the firm. From a psychological point of view, an identity should ensure a return in terms of positive emotions, sense of belonging, and self-esteem. Social Identity Theory (Hogg et al., 1995; Stets & Burke, 2000) sustains that, although the effects are at an individual level, the roots of social identity are at a group/collective level. Emotional dynamics involving the family are strictly related to the correct definition of the firm's identity, due to the fact that the boundaries between family and corporation are rather blurred in family businesses (Berrone et al., 2010). Hence, this sample shows that the close identification of the family with the firm could easily lead to high level of cohesiveness, in order to preserve this positive emotional return (see table 5). Emotions permeate the organization, influencing the family business's decision-making process (Baron, 2008) and everyday activities (Ashforth & Humphrey, 1998). In this sample, the family frequently exerts strong pressure on next generation members in choosing their educational path, following the family's need for cohesiveness and identity rather than individual attitudes and aspiration level. Hence, intergenerational conflicts could arise due to frequently the next generation's frustration about a low satisfaction level regarding their educational path. Literature provides evidence of the fact that ignoring negative dynamics and conflict can often have a disastrous future impact on both family and business (Sorenson, 1999).

Furthermore, within the sample, the close identification of the family with the firm often results in a complex corporate structure (that is, the difficulty in separating family and business). For instance, the sample shows, especially regarding the small firms, an intermingling of personal and business finances, that could easily lead to a bias in firm value appraisal (Zellweger & Dehlen, 2012), and foster striving for non-economic goals, thus exacerbating the related dysfunctional dynamics.

The situation of 'firm complexity' is also considered from a socio-cognitive point of view by the Affect Infusion Model (Zellweger, Dehlen, 2012). This model offers useful insights in order to better understand why the family firm's complexity level could act as a moderator between affect dynamics and SEW (Berrone et al., 2010; Zellweger & Astrachan, 2008).

The intention to hand the business down to future generations. Transmitting the business is not only a key goal for a family firm: it's also frequently associated with high level of cohesiveness and low level of flexibility (see table 6). In this kind of family, the continuity of the business is a moral duty; in the founder's mind, the current situation is explicitly run in favour of the next generation ('One day, all this

Table 6. The intention to hand the business down to future generations and related negative outcomes at family level

Cluster (non-economic goal)	RQ2 - Negative outcomes: family level	Undesired consequences for the family
The intention to hand the business down to future generations	• Self-centred and strict family	• Blaming the next generation for failure in business transmission. • Next generation's low level or lack of gratefulness.

Table 7. The Influence and control of family members over business and related negative outcomes at individual level

Cluster (non-economic goal)	RQ3 - Negative outcomes: individual level	Undesired consequences for the family member
The Influence and control of family members over business	• Obstacles to the legitimisation of the next generation. • Pressure to join the family business.	• Low job satisfaction level. • High frustration level. • Conflict avoidance/ intergenerational conflict. • Family 'handcuff'.

will be yours...' 'I made all this for you'). At a family level, this situation can result in a twofold negative output. If the children aspire to a work outside the family firm, in a different sector, the founder's generation blames the next generation for refusing the business transmission. Conversely, if the next generation accept involvement in the family business, but with different attitudes and aspirations, it shows a low level of gratefulness. In both cases, the situation is characterized by permanent conflicts.

The influence and control of family members over business. Often during the consultation, family members belonging to the next generation referred to the fact that they felt 'trapped' within the family business (see table 7). This finding is consistent with previous research. For instance, scholars have suggested that family control and strong identification with the family firm can cause heirs to feel locked into and dependent upon the firm (Schulze, Lubatkin, Dino, & Buchholtz, 2001).

Other research has highlighted how heirs feel intense pressure to join the family business despite their reservations or personal preferences (Freudenberger, Freedheim, & Kurtz, 1989). Gomez-Mejia and colleagues (2003), called it the "family handcuff". This feeling of entrapment is often associated with a low job satisfaction level and high frustration levels. However, within the sample, the intention to quit the firm is very rare among the next generation. Clearly, the benefits of the situation are perceived as much more convenient/comfortable and acceptable than the negative aspects. Furthermore, the next generation usually avoids facing an explicit, intergenerational conflict. Thus, the 'family handcuff' is perpetuating.

Close identification of the family with the firm. Often this identification is especially prominent between the founder and the firm (see table 8). Following Zellweger et al. (2013), Organizational Identity Theory could provide an explanation for this abandoning of resistance and for such dynamics which undermine the next generation's legitimisation and differentiation. In particular, within the sample the so called 'founder's shadow' is widespread, which clearly has a negative impact on second generation development (Davis & Harveston, 1998; Ferrari, 2015;) and mostly undermines the next generation's differentiation (Ariely, Huber, & Wertenbroch, 2005; Dyer, 1986)

Table 8. The close identification of the family with the firm and related negative outcomes at individual level

Cluster (non-economic goal)	RQ3 - Negative outcomes: individual level	Undesired consequences for the family member
The close identification of the family with the firm	• Obstacles to the differentiation of the next generation. • Pressure to join the family business.	• Founder's shadow. • Boycott of individual's work aspirations.

Table 9. The intention to hand the business down to future generations and related negative outcomes at individual level

Cluster (non-economic goal)	RQ3 - Negative outcomes: individual level	Undesired consequences for the family member
The intention to hand the business down to future generations	• Obstacles to the legitimisation and differentiation of the next generation. • Pressure to join the family business.	• The 'Kid Brother' syndrome/ 'Fredo effect'. • Low innovation rate. • Boycott of individual's work aspirations. • Traditional rather than transitional career.

Moreover, prior research indicates that founders who maintain an influence after having largely removed themselves from operational responsibilities (Davis & Harveston, 1998) can negatively affect successors' job satisfaction and the overall success of the succession (Sharma, Chrisman, Pablo, & Chua, 2001; Sharma et al., 2003a; Sharma, Chrisman, & Chua, 2003b).

Additionally, the entrenchment of previous generations can be problematic because it inhibits the ability of successors to make necessary strategic adjustments (Sharma & Manikutty, 2005).

However, in other empirical studies the predecessor has been found to act as a mentor, allowing his/her tacit knowledge of the business and family-specific social capital to be passed on the next generation (Wasserman, 2003; Handler, 1994). Hence, it seems that the negative/positive outcomes of the 'founder shadow' could be due to the first generation's behaviour, rather than just to its presence (Mussolino & Calabrò 2014).

The intention to hand the business down to future generations. Within the sample, the senior generation seldom fosters the next generation's autonomy (see table 9). Moreover, if the family is also self-centred and strict, organizational identity can easily result in a boycott of the individual's identity development, (Haynes et al., 1999; Morck, Yeung, 2003; Villaneueva & Sapienza, 2009). This fact can easily undermine the business transmission process.

In particular, the sample shows that the association between the intention to transfer the business and a self-centred and strict firm often results in pressure to join the family firm but, mainly, in the next generation's career being traditional rather than transitional (Ferrari, 2016; Lazarova &Taylor, 2009). The next generation's career has a strong impact on both individual and organizational outcomes.

Literature (Chudzikowski, 2012; Kovalenko, Mortelmans, 2014; Verbruggen, 2012; Volmer, Spurk, 2011) is focused on the *individual* outcomes of the different kinds of careers: subjective success, skills development, commitment to the family business, person/organization fit. Literature also suggests that a *transitional* or *boundaryless career* (Arthur, 1994; Arthur & Rousseau, 1996) seems to improve the formation and deployment of social capital *and innovation rate* in organizations (Nahapiet & Ghoshal, 1998).

Furthermore, in some cases the sample shows a 'kid brother syndrome' (Kaye, 1992). This syndrome regards a child 'either as inadequate or as potentially able but unmotivated, lazy, incompetent, difficult to work with, unreliable, or irresponsible. Yet he not only receives financial support from the family, he does so through continued employment by the business despite their constant complaints about his poor performance (Kaye, 1992, 237)'.

The sample also sometimes shows a 'Fredo effect' (Kidwell et al., 2012; 2013), an on-the-surface quite similar (but substantially different) syndrome, emerging from peculiar behaviours of the first generation versus a younger member "who gets in the way of the business' success by engaging in dysfunctional behaviour or by not performing job duties effectively (Kidwell et al., 2012, 5).

Leibowitz (1986) observed that family businesses are most often formed by people trying to resolve a problem in their relationship with a particular relative, or to fix dysfunction in their whole family. Tragically, it often doesn't work, it only perpetuates the problem, and sometimes it even makes it much worse (Kaye, 1996).

Three-Level Relationship Analysis

A multilevel approach helps in clarifying dysfunctional processes, going beyond a simple focal unit level analysis.

The aim of this section is to present a *compilation analysis,* that is a three-level analysis where "measures collected from lower-level entities are combined in complex and non-linear ways" (Hitt et al., 2007), in order to highlight constructs and conceptual paths which are not reducible to the single parts (Kozlowski & Klein, 2000). This research has highlighted some non-linear ways which, starting from organizational level (e.g. the family identity overwhelming the firm), affect the family level (e.g. an excessive cohesiveness level), which in turn leads to pathological situations affecting family members at an individual level (e.g. the 'family handcuff').

In summary, in this research a throughout–level analysis (Hitt et al., 2007) identifies two themes which recursively affect the family firm at all levels: the *organizational identity* and the *infusion/emotional dynamics effect*. These themes could be considered for explaining variables in striving for non-economic goals, and related negative outcomes.

The First Identified Non-Linear Way: Organizational Identity

A multilevel analysis is useful for deeply understanding complex constructs, and non-the linear ways that can characterize organizational dynamics (see table 10). A first variable explaining organizational dysfunctions at all levels is *organizational identity*. In fact, due to its hybrid-identity nature (Albert & Whetten, 1985), family business faces several difficulties in operating, and a multilevel approach presents a good fit in analysing such dynamics (Whetten, Foreman, & Dyer, 2014).

According to social psychology research, family identity includes specific types of interpersonal relationships and internalized sets of behavioural expectations associated with these relationships (Shepherd & Haynie, 2009; Stryker, 1968).

Organizational identity encompasses the core values and beliefs of an organization that its members deem to be the most central, distinctive, and enduring (Kraatz & Block, 2008; Albert &Whetten, 1985). The continuity and coherence of organizational identity enables organizational members "to satisfy their inherent needs to be the same yesterday, today and tomorrow and to be unique actors or entities"

Table 10. Organizational identity, dysfunctional dynamics and consequences

Explaining variable	Non-economic goal	Family firm level	Family level	Family member level	Negative outcomes
• Organizational identity	• The close identification of the family with the firm	• The family identity overwhelms the firm.	• Cohesiveness level: selfcentred family	• Boycott of next generation's differentiation	• Failure in business transmission
		• In-group favouritism.	• Flexibility level: strict family	• 'Family handcuff'	• Low performance level • Frustration
	• The Influence and control of family members over business	• Nepotism -Adverse selection. • Out-group discrimination.	• Cohesiveness level: selfcentred family	• High frustration level	• Failure in business transmission
		• Imposed educational and organizational careers	• Flexibility level: strict family	• Traditional rather than transitional career	• -Low innovation rate. • Delegitimisation of the next generation.
		• Imposed educational career	• Imposed educational path	• 'Family handcuff'. • Low job satisfaction level.	• Failure in business transmission
	• The intention to hand the business down to future generations.	• (Paradoxically) postponed/ eluded succession	• Next generation's low autonomy level	• Boycott of next generation legitimisation. • Pressure to join the family business	• The 'founder's shadow'

(Whetten & Mackey, 2002, p. 396). This research shows that the strong identification of the family with the firm leads to the intention to hand the business down to future generations. However, this research also suggests that often the identification between the founder and the firm overtakes the family firm identity. As cited above (Zellweger et al., 2013), Organizational Identity Theory (OIT) could provide an explanation for dynamics such as founders abandoning resistance, paradoxically resulting in an eluded or postponed succession (Piantoni, 1990).

Furthermore, organizational identity fosters the desire for influence and control of family members over business, also provides an explanation for such dynamics which undermine the next generation's legitimisation and differentiation. For example, research has suggested that family control and strong identification with the family firm can cause the next generation to feel trapped into and dependent upon the firm (Schulze, Lubatkin, Dino, & Buchholtz, 2001). Other research has highlighted how the next generation feel intense pressure to join the family business despite their reservations or personal preferences (Freudenberger, Freedheim, & Kurtz, 1989).

Organizational identity could also result in discrimination of non-family members. When differences between groups are perceived, Social psychology (Tajfel, Turner, 1986) when applied to family firms (Ferrari, 2014; De Massis et al., 2012) shows that out-group discrimination and in-group favouritism arises, resulting in nepotism (Salvato et al., 2012) and adverse selection (Schulze, Lubatkin, & Dino, 2003; Chirsman, Chua, & Litz, 2004). Negative outcomes in terms of perceived Organizational Justice (Colquitt et al., 2001; Cropanzano et al., 2007) are frequently associated with such discrimination.

Organizational identity also affects the close identification of the family with the firm. In fact, the complexity of the corporate structure (that is, the difficulty in separating family and business) and the intermingling of personal and business finances could easily lead to a bias in firm value appraisal (Zellweger & Dehlen, 2012). It could also foster striving for non-economic goals, thus exacerbating the related dysfunctional dynamics. For instance, it could lead to boycotting the next generation's differentiation, thus undermining the firm reliability in business transmission process.

In summary, the concept of organizational identity offers a suitable instrument for family business scholars, in order to reach an in-depth understanding of the conflictual dynamics, and for differentiating among family firms. Furthermore, organizational identity offers useful insights for analysing and explaining the perhaps most compelling issues in family business (Whetten et al., 2014): goal setting, workplace relationships, hiring criteria and business transmission to name but a few . An ideal type of organizational identity model (Albert et al., 1998) posits that hybrid-identity organizations (HIO) presents the '3Is': the degree to which multiple identities are *incompatible, indispensable and inviolate* (see also Whetten et al., 2014 for a review). Differently from non-hybrid organizations, HIOs must mix/ put together/ or combine multiple 'organizing recipes' (Rao, 1994) to ensure legitimacy and reputation, and eventually permit the organization to survive (Kraatz & Block, 2008). This difficulty could help in explaining the current high family business failure rate (Davis & Harveston, 1998) or at least go so far as to explain enduring, intractable and substantial conflicts (Fiol et al., 2009; Pache & Santos, 2010; Pratt & Foreman, 2000) .

The Second Identified Non-Linear Way: Emotional Dynamics

A second variable explaining organizational dysfunctions at all levels is represented by emotional dynamics (see table 11). Emotions themselves could be considered an emotional return of the business (Astrachan & Jaskiewicz, 2008), both positive and negative Emotions permeate organizations (Hartel

Table 11. Emotional dynamics and consequences

<table>
<tr><th>Explaining variable</th><th>Non-economic goal</th><th>Family firm level</th><th>Family level</th><th>Family member level</th><th>Negative outcomes</th></tr>
<tr><td rowspan="5">• Emotional dynamics</td><td rowspan="3">• The intention to hand the business down to future generations</td><td>• Refusal of mergers.
• Biases in strategic decision-making.</td><td>• Strict family
• Self-centred family</td><td rowspan="2">• Low job satisfaction level.
• High frustration level.</td><td rowspan="2">• Failure in business transmission</td></tr>
<tr><td>• Conflict avoidance/ interg eneration-al conflict.</td><td>• Blaming the next generation for refused business transmission.</td></tr>
<tr><td>• Protecting the next generation: lack of meritocracy.</td><td>• Discrimination versus bestperformer child</td><td>• 'Kid brother syndrome'.
• 'Fredo effect.'</td><td>• Waste of resources</td></tr>
<tr><td>• The close identification of the family with the firm</td><td rowspan="2">• Pressure to join the family business.</td><td rowspan="2">• Strict family.
• Intergenerational conflict.</td><td rowspan="2">• Obstacles to the differentiation of the next generation</td><td rowspan="2">• Failure in business transmission.
• Conflict avoidance.</td></tr>
<tr><td>• The influence and control of family members over business</td></tr>
</table>

et al., 2011), for example influencing the family business's decision-making process (Baron, 2008) and everyday activities (Ashforth & Humphrey, 1998). Mood can also play an important part in biasing the appraisal processes, e.g. biasing the perceived value of the product and/or service delivered, or current managerial practices of the whole firm (Kellermans & Dehelen, 2012). Literature also provides evidence of the role that mood plays in the entrepreneur's decision making and evaluation (Foo, 2011). Emotional dynamics can affect the intention to hand the business down to future generations, protecting the trans-generational value and potential of the firm (Gomez-Mejia et al., 2007; Zellweger & Astrachan, 2008). As a possible consequence, over-valuing the firm can result in a refusal of mergers, even when the small size of the firm is to the detriment of future reliability. Moreover, these affective dynamics are the foundation of the intention to protect the next generation, especially if the successor is low skilled or shows low or even no aptitudes for the specific business. Sometimes, a next generation member could even show relational disorder, or personal problems sich as drug or alcohol abuse. In this case, the emotional involvement could lead to a 'kid brother syndrome' (Kaye, 1996) and/or to a 'Fredo effect' (Kidwell et al., 2013). Finally, literature highlights the positive and negative emotions' impact on intergenerational learning (Trevinyo-Rodriguez, 2010). Providing a non-economic return in term of self-esteem, emotional dynamics also foster the close identification of the family with the firm, leading to pressure on the next generation to join the family business. In fact, research has clearly highlighted how heirs feel intense pressure to join the family business despite their reservations or personal preferences (Freudenberger, Freedheim, & Kurtz, 1989). Conversely, the close identification with and the over-valuing of the family firm could also lead to blaming the next generation for refused business transmission.

The perception of environmental uncertainty fosters a persistent negative attitude, that in turn can easily result in strong need for control (Salovey, P., O'Leary, A., Stretton, M. S., Fishkin, S. A., & Drake, C. A. (1991), and helps to better explain the overwhelming of the non-economic goals on economic ones (Morck, et al., 1988; Cascino et al., 2010). Thus, emotional dynamics also affect the influence and control of family members over business, fostering an internal locus of control over a complex situation. Additionally, these dynamics often result in strong pressure on the next generation to join the family business.

In all these situations, an intergenerational conflict arises, and often striving for harmony and cohesiveness forces family members to ignore the conflict. Literature provides evidence of the fact that unfortunately ignoring negative dynamics and avoiding conflict can often have a disastrous future impact on both family and business (Sorenson, 1999).

In summary, this research suggests that emotional dynamics offer a suitable concept in order to explain several undesirable outcomes. Although a systematic reflection on the emotions in the family business literature is still at an early stage (see Brundin et al., 2014, for a review), the emotional labour and the display of the emotions (Hochschild, 1983) seem to follow specific rules within family firms, and deserve particular attention by scholars.

CONCLUSION

In conclusion, the strength of a multilevel approach is to provide the empirical evidence that striving for non-economic goals could be a myopic behaviour, over-valuing the business as a whole, and at the same time undermining the socio-emotional wealth of the next generation and eventually undermining the organizational reliability. The economic and managerial literature, unfortunately, often equates success with succession. For the purposes of this discussion, this chapter did not assume that succession by the next generation means the family business has succeeded. On the contrary, succession sometimes occurs as a result of developmental failure in a family, and conversely a thoroughly successful outcome for a family business can sometimes involve the decision to dispose of it.

According to the seminal research of Kaye (1991; 1992; 1996), this multiple case study suggests that "contrary to the course of normal life-cycle development, family-owned and/or family-managed enterprises are often used to *resist* the differentiation and development of children who join the business, and sometimes even of children who don't" (Kaye, 1996, p. 355).

MAIN CONTRIBUTIONS AND IMPLICATIONS

This chapter shows that a multilevel analysis is a suitable approach in order to highlight hidden relationships among different, structural units within organizations. In doing so, this chapter responds to previous calls in literature (Hitt and colleague, 2007) for a deeper understanding of complex organizational phenomena using a multilevel approach.

Furthermore, Hitt and colleagues (2007) called for more empirical studies to test the conceptual models that have already been developed. Thus, responding to their call, this chapter provides evidence supporting the idea that striving for non-economic goals could generate several negative outcomes for the family firm, in particular for the next generation. In doing so, this research represents an empirical study to test SEW (socio-emotional wealth). This approach (Gomez-Mejia et al., 2007; 2010; 2011; Berrone et al., 2012) suggests that "family firms are typically motivated by, and committed to, the preservation of their SEW, referring to non-financial aspects or "affective endowments" of family owners" Berrone et al., 2012, p. 259). The SEW construct has proven to be a good analytical lens for interpreting a wide variety of family firm phenomena. The SEW approach offers an explanation mainly for the *positive* non-economic outcomes, not for the negative ones. This study suggests that, in order to explain also the dark side of SEW, it's necessary go below the surface, investigating the multiple organizational levels involved in the pursuing of non-economic goals.

In addition, Agarwal & Hoetker (2007) argued that the field of management could be enhanced by integrating the theory and empirical work of other related social science disciplines (e.g., psychology). In adopting analytical techniques from clinical, social and I/O psychology, this chapter highlights the deepest (dysfunctional) organizational dynamics, thus demonstrating the effectiveness of a multidisciplinary approach to complex organizational phenomena.

An extended model of family enterprises (Chrisman et al., 2003; Habbershon et al., 2003) should consider not only resources and capabilities related to family involvement, but also features such as organizational identity and emotional dynamics peculiar to family firms. Thus, as this chapter suggests, if striving for non-economic goals almost always leads to undesired consequences, these unavoidable consequences should be considered in such extended models of family enterprise.

Finally, this research has some implications for scholars and consultants. In particular, the multiple nature of dysfunctional dynamics advocates for a wider diffusion of psychological diagnostic tools, integrating them into traditional economical and financial assessment. Both managerial and investigating practices should be grounded on a systemic and multilevel approach in order to better understand deep organizational dynamics, and their hidden relationships.

LIMITATIONS AND SUGGESTIONS FOR FUTURE RESEARCH

In addition to its results, this chapter does present some limitations.

Firstly, this multiple case study obviously doesn't permit a complete generalization of the findings. The position of the author, (an I/O psychologist) usually employeed by a firm when a perceived relational problem arises, could lead to an overestimation of the dysfunctional dynamics diffusion. Future research should investigate how widespread each single 'organizational pathology' actually is among SMEs, and if these pathologies are 'physiological' (that is unavoidable) rather than exceptional. Secondly, literature describes the 'long shadow' of the founder in shaping the overall image of the firm(). However, this research doesn't help to clarify if the 'dark side' of the firm is due to the noneconomic goals or to some of the founder's personal characteristics and/or personality traits. Hence, future research should investigate the relationship between organizational dysfunctional dynamics and founder's characteristics.

For example, analysing the different levels thoroughly, a promising stream of research could be how and why the entrepreneurial identity affects business transmission.

Thirdly, some undesired outcomes (for instance, boycotting second generation autonomy, legitimisation and differentiation) could be due to cultural factors rather to non-economic goals: that is, it's possible that Italian families show dysfunctional processes towards their children's education, which could also, in turn, lead to a scarce level of autonomy and differentiation.

Fourthly, there is growing evidence that family businesses are complex and diverse (Melin & Nordqvist, 2007; Westhead & Howorth, 2007) so a risk of this research could be to shift a prototype into a stereotype. Consequently, the aim of this chapter is not a generalization, but to offer a model of dysfunctional dynamics.

By adopting a multilevel analysis, this chapter also stimulates further research. For example, Hitt and colleagues sustain that "scholars' understanding of organizations could be enriched immensely by multilevel studies that investigate the forces of upward influence in addition to the top-down forces that shape complex phenomena (2007, 1394)". This chapter adopts a top-down approach, by investigating the influence the upper level (e.g. the family firm) exert to the lower (e.g. the family member). Future research should investigate how and if the individual level could affect the upper level. For instance, investigating how the next generation's personal skills and aptitude can affect the overall business strategy.

Finally, future research should investigate quantitatively the highlighted relations: for instance, the relationship between cohesiveness and innovation propensity, or between cohesiveness and the next generation's career; another interesting topic is the possible relationship between the discrimination of non-family members and perceived organizational justice.

REFERENCES

Agarwal, R., & Hoetker, G. (2007). A faustian bargain? The growth of management and its relationship with related disciplines. *Academy of Management Journal*, *50*(6), 1304–1322. doi:10.5465/amj.2007.28165901

Albert, S., & Whetten, D. (1985). Organizational identity. In L. L. Cummings & B. M. Staw (Eds.), *Research in organizational behavior* (Vol. 7, pp. 263–295). Greenwich, CT: JAI Press.

Ariely, D., Huber, J., & Wertenbroch, K. (2005). When do losses loom larger than gains? *JMR, Journal of Marketing Research*, *42*(2), 134–138. doi:10.1509/jmkr.42.2.134.62283

Arregle, J. L., Hitt, M. A., Sirmon, D. G., & Very, P. (2007). The development of organizational social capital: Attributes of family firms. *Journal of Management Studies*, *44*(1), 73–95. doi:10.1111/j.1467-6486.2007.00665.x

Astrachan, J. H., & Jaskiewicz, P. (2008). Emotional returns and emotional costs in privately held family businesses: Advancing traditional business valuation. *Family Business Review*, *21*(2), 139–149. doi:10.1111/j.1741-6248.2008.00115.x

Barach, J. A., & Gantisky, J. B. (1995). Successful succession in family business. *Family Business Review*, *8*(2), 131–155. doi:10.1111/j.1741-6248.1995.00131.x

Barnes, L. B., & Hershon, S. A. (1976). Transferring power in family business. *Harvard Business Review*, (July-August): 105–114.

Beavers, W. R., & Hampson, R. B. (1995). Misurare la competenza famigliare: il modello sistemico di Beavers, tr. it. In *Ciclo vitale e dinamiche familiari, a cura di F.* Milano: Walsh, Franco Angeli.

Berrone, P., Cruz, C., & Gomez-Mejia, L. R. (2012). Socioemotional wealth in family firms: Theoretical dimensions, assessment approaches, and agenda for future research. *Family Business Review*, *25*(3), 258–279. doi:10.1177/0894486511435355

Berrone, P., Cruz, C. C., Gomez-Mejia, L. R., & Larraza Kintana, M. (2010). Socioemotional wealth and corporate response to institutional pressures: Do family-controlled firms pollute less? *Administrative Science Quarterly*, *55*(1), 82–113. doi:10.2189/asqu.2010.55.1.82

Bryant, A., & Charmaz, K. (2007). *The Sage handbook of grounded theory*. London: Sage. doi:10.4135/9781848607941

Cartwright, D., & Zander, A. (Eds.). (1984). Group dynamics: Research and theory (2nd ed.). Evanston, IL: Row, Peterson, & Company.

Cascino, S., Pugliese, A., Mussolino, D., & Sansone, C. (2010). The influence of family ownership on the quality of accounting information. *Family Business Review*, *23*(3), 246–265. doi:10.1177/0894486510374302

Cater, J. J. III, & Justis, R. T. (2009). The development of successors from followers to leaders in small family firms: An exploratory study. *Family Business Review*, *22*(2), 109–124. doi:10.1177/0894486508327822

Chan, D. (1998). Functional relations among constructs in the same content domain at different levels of analysis: A typology of composition models. *The Journal of Applied Psychology*, *83*(2), 234–246. doi:10.1037/0021-9010.83.2.234

Charmaz, K. (1995). *Grounded Theory. A Practical Guide Through. Qualitative Analysis*. London: SAGE Publications.

Chenail, R. (2009). Qualitative research like politics can also be local: A review of interdisciplinary standards for systematic qualitative research. *The Weekly Qualitative Report*, *2*(11), 61–65.

Chrisman, J. J., Chua, J. H., & Litz, R. (2003). A unified systems perspective of family firm performance: An extension and integration. *Journal of Business Venturing*, *18*(4), 467–472. doi:10.1016/S0883-9026(03)00055-7

Chrisman, J. J., Chua, J. H., & Litz, R. (2004). Comparing the agency costs of family and nonfamily firms: Conceptual issues and exploratory evidence. *Entrepreneurship Theory and Practice*, *28*(4), 335–354. doi:10.1111/j.1540-6520.2004.00049.x

Chrisman, J. J., Sharma, P., & Taggar, S. (2007). Family influences on firms: An introduction. *Journal of Business Research*, *60*(10), 1005–1011. doi:10.1016/j.jbusres.2007.02.016

Chua, J. H., Chrisman, J. J., & Sharma, P. (1999). Defining the family business by behavior. *Entrepreneurship Theory and Practice*, *23*(4), 19–39. doi:10.1177/104225879902300402

Corbin, J., & Strauss, A. (2008). *Basics of qualitative research* (3rd ed.). Thousand Oaks, CA: Sage.

Daspit, J. J., Madison, K., Barnett, T., & Long, R. G. (2017). The emergence of bifurcation bias from unbalanced families: Examining HR practices in the family firm using Circumplex Theory. Human Resource Management Review.

Davis, J. H., Allen, M. R., & Hayes, H. D. (2010). Is blood thicker than water? A study of stewardship perceptions in family business. *Entrepreneurship Theory and Practice*, *34*(6), 1093–1116. doi:10.1111/j.1540-6520.2010.00415.x

Davis, P. S., & Harveston, P. D. (1998). The influence of family on the family business succession process: A multi-generational perspective. *Entrepreneurship Theory and Practice*, *22*(3), 31–53. doi:10.1177/104225879802200302

De Massis, A., Chua, J., & Chrisman, J. J. (2008). Factors Preventing Intra-Family Succession. *Family Business Review*, *21*(2), 183–199. doi:10.1111/j.1741-6248.2008.00118.x

Dibrell, C., & Moeller, M. (2011). The impact of a service-dominant focus strategy and stewardship culture on organizational innovativeness in family-owned businesses. *Journal of Family Business Strategy*, *2*(1), 43–51. doi:10.1016/j.jfbs.2011.01.004

Dukerich, J. M., Golden, B., & Shortell, S. M. (2002). Beauty is in the eye of the beholder: The impact of organizational identification, identity, and image on the cooperative behaviors of physicians. *Administrative Science Quarterly*, *47*(3), 507–533. doi:10.2307/3094849

Dunn, B. (1999). The family factor: The impact of family relationship dynamics on business-owning families during transitions. *Family Business Review*, *12*(1), 41–60. doi:10.1111/j.1741-6248.1999.00041.x

Dutton J.E., & Dukerich J.M. (1991). Keeping An Eye on the Mirror: Image and Identity In Organizational Adaptation. *Academy Of Management Journal, 34*, 517-554.

Dyck, B., Mauws, M., Starke, F. A., & Mischke, G. A. (2002). Passing the baton: The importance of sequence, timing, technique and communication in executive succession. *Journal of Business Venturing*, *17*(2), 143–162. doi:10.1016/S0883-9026(00)00056-2

Eddleston, K. A., & Morgan, R. M. (2014). Trust, commitment and relationships in family business: Challenging conventional wisdom. *Journal of Family Business Strategy*, *5*(3), 213–216. doi:10.1016/j.jfbs.2014.08.003

Eddleston, K. A., & Kellermanns, F. W. (2007). Destructive and productive family relationships: A stewardship theory erspective. *Journal of Business Venturing*, *22*(4), 545–565. doi:10.1016/j.jbusvent.2006.06.004

Eddleston, K. A., & Kidwell, R. E. (2012). Parent–child relationships: Planting the seeds of deviant behavior in the family firm. *Entrepreneurship Theory and Practice*, *36*(2), 369–386. doi:10.1111/j.1540-6520.2010.00403.x

Eddleston, K. A., Kellermanns, F. W., & Sarathy, R. (2008). Resource configuration in family firms: Linking resources, strategic planning and technological opportunities to performance. *Journal of Management Studies*, *45*(1), 26–50.

Eddleston, K. A., Kellermanns, F. W., & Zellweger, T. M. (2012). Exploring the entrepre-neurial behavior of family firms: Does the stewardship perspective explain differ-ences? *Entrepreneurship Theory and Practice*, *36*(2), 347–367. doi:10.1111/j.1540-6520.2010.00402.x

Fendt, J., & Sachs, W. (2008). Grounded theory method in management research. Users' perspectives. *Organizational Research Methods*, *11*(3), 430–455. doi:10.1177/1094428106297812

Fiol, C. M., Pratt, G. M., & O'Connor, E. J. (2009). Managing Intractable Identity Conflicts. *Academy of Management Review*, *34*(1), 32–55. doi:10.5465/amr.2009.35713276

Fletcher, D., De Massis, A., & Nordqvist, M. (2016). Qualitative research practices and family business scholarship: A review and future research agenda. *Journal of Family Business Strategy*, *7*(1), 8–25. doi:10.1016/j.jfbs.2015.08.001

Foo, M.-D. (2011). Emotions and entrepreneurial opportunity evaluation. *Entrepreneurship Theory and Practice*, *35*(2), 375–393. doi:10.1111/j.1540-6520.2009.00357.x

Frank, H., Lueger, M., Nose´, L., & Suchy, D. (2010). The concept of "Familiness": Literature review and systems theory-based reflections. *Journal of Family Business Strategy*, *1*(3), 119–130. doi:10.1016/j.jfbs.2010.08.001

Freudenberger, H. J., Freedheim, D. K., & Kurtz, T. S. (1989). Treatment of individuals in family business. *Psychotherapy (Chicago, Ill.)*, *26*(1), 47–53. doi:10.1037/h0085404

Gomez-Mejia, L. R., Larraza-Kintana, M., & Makri, M. (2003). The determinants of executive compensation in family-controlled public corporations. *Academy of Management Journal*, *46*, 226237.

Gomez-Mejia, L. R., Makri, M., & Larraza-Kintana, M. (2010). Diversification decisions in familycontrolled firms. *Journal of Management Studies*, *47*(2), 223–252. doi:10.1111/j.1467-6486.2009.00889.x

Gómez-Mejía, L. R., Cruz, C., Berrone, P., & De Castro, J. (2011). The Bind that Ties: Socioemotional Wealth Preservation in Family Firms. *The Academy of Management Annals*, *5*(1), 653–707. doi:10.1080/19416520.2011.593320

Gomez-Mejia, L. R., Haynes, K. T., Nunez-Nickel, M., Jacobson, K. J. L., & Moyano-Fuentes, J. (2007). Socioemotional wealth and business risks in family-controlled firms: Evidence from Spanish olive oil mills. *Administrative Science Quarterly*, *52*(1), 106–137. doi:10.2189/asqu.52.1.106

Habbershon, T. G., Williams, M., & MacMillan, I. C. (2003). 'A unified systems perspective of family firm performance'. *Journal of Business Venturing*, *18*(4), 451–465. doi:10.1016/S0883-9026(03)00053-3

Haynes, G. W., Walker, R., Rowe, B. R., & Hong, G. S. (1999). The intermingling of business and family finances in family-owned businesses. *Family Business Review*, *12*(3), 225–239. doi:10.1111/j.1741-6248.1999.00225.x

Haveman, H. A., & Khaire, M. V. (2004). Survival beyond succession? The contingent impact of founder succession on organizational failure. *Journal of Business Venturing*, *19*(3), 437–463. doi:10.1016/S0883-9026(03)00039-9

Hitt, M. A., Beamish, P. W., Jackson, S. E., & Mathieu, J. E. (2007). Building theoretical and empirical bridges across levels: Multilevel research in management. *Academy of Management Journal*, *50*(6), 1385–1399. doi:10.5465/amj.2007.28166219

House, R., Rousseau, D. M., & Thomas-Hunt, M. (1995). The meso paradigm: A framework for the integration of micro and macro organizational behavior. In L. L. Cummings & B. M. Staw (Eds.), *Research in organizational behavior* (Vol. 17, pp. 71–114). Greenwich, CT: JAI Press.

Irava, W. J., & Moores, K. (2010). Clarifying the strategic advantage of familiness: Unbundling its dimensions and highlighting its paradoxes. *Journal of Family Business Strategy*, *1*(3), 131–144. doi:10.1016/j.jfbs.2010.08.002

Kaye, K. (1991). Penetrating the Cycle of Sustained Conflict. *Family Business Review*, *4*(1), 21-44.

Kaye, K. (1992). The Kid Brother. *Family Business Review*, *5*(3), 237–256. doi:10.1111/j.1741-6248.1992.00237.x

Kaye, K. (1996). When the Family Business Is a Sickness. *Family Business Review*, *9*(4), 347–368. doi:10.1111/j.1741-6248.1996.00347.x

Kellermanns, F.W., Eddleston, K. A., & Zellweger, T. M. (2012). Extending the Socioemotional Wealth Perspective: A Look at the Dark Side. *Entrepreneurship Theory and Practice*, *36*, 1175–1182.

Kets de Vries, M. F. (1977). The entrepreneurial personality: A person at the crossroads. *Journal of Management Studies*, *14*(1), 34–57. doi:10.1111/j.1467-6486.1977.tb00616.x

Kets de Vries, M. F. (1993). The dynamics of family controlled firms: The good and the bad news. *Organizational Dynamics*, *21*(3), 59–71. doi:10.1016/0090-2616(93)90071-8

Kidwell, R. E., Eddleston, K. A., Cater, J. J. III, & Kellermanns, F. W. (2013). How one bad family member can undermine a family firm: Preventing the Fredo effect. *Business Horizons*, *56*(1), 5–12. doi:10.1016/j.bushor.2012.08.004

Kidwell, R. E., Kellermanns, F. W., & Eddleston, K. A. (2012). Harmony, justice, confusion, and conflict in the family firm: Implications for ethical climate and the "Fredo effect." *Journal of Business Ethics*, *106*(4), 503–517. doi:10.100710551-011-1014-7

Kozlowski, S. W. J., & Klein, K. J. (2000). A Multilevel Approach to Theory and Research in Organizations Contextual, Temporal, and Emergent Processes. In Multilevel Theory, Research, and Methods in Organizations Foundations, Extensions, and New Directions. Jossey-Bass.

Kraatz, M., & Block, E. (2008). Organizational implications of institutional pluralism. In Handbook of organizational institutionalism (pp. 243-275). London: Sage Publication. doi:10.4135/9781849200387.n10

Lambrecht, J. (2005). Multigenerational transition in family businesses: A new explanatory model. *Family Business Review*, *28*(4), 267–282. doi:10.1111/j.1741-6248.2005.00048.x

Lambrecht, J., & Lievens, J. (2008). Pruning the family tree: An unexplored path to family business continuity and family harmony. *Family Business Review*, *21*(4), 295–313. doi:10.1177/089448650802 10040103

Lansberg, I., & Astrachan, J. H. (1994). Influence of family relationships on succession planning and training: The importance of mediating factors. *Family Business Review*, *7*(1), 39–59. doi:10.1111/j.1741-6248.1994.00039.x

Lansberg, I. (1988). The succession conspiracy. In C. E. Aronoff, J. H. Astrachan, & J. L. Ward (Eds.), *Family business sourcebook II* (pp. 70–86). Marietta, GA: Business Owner Resources.

Le Breton-Miller, I., Miller, D., & Steier, L. P. (2004). Toward an integrative model of effective FOB succession. *Entrepreneurship Theory and Practice*, *28*(4), 305–328. doi:10.1111/j.1540-6520.2004.00047.x

Leibowitz, B. (1986). Resolving conflict in the family owned business. *Consultation*, *5*(3), 191–205.

Linstead, S., Marechal, G., & Griffin, R. W. (2014). Theorizing and researching the dark side of organization. *Organization Studies*, *35*(2), 165–188. doi:10.1177/0170840613515402

Lubatkin, M. H., Durand, R., & Ling, Y. (2007). The missing lens in family firm governance theory: A self-other typology of parental altruism. *Journal of Business Research*, *60*(10), 1022–1029. doi:10.1016/j.jbusres.2006.12.019

McCollom, M. E. (1990). Problems and Prospects in Clinical Research on Family Firms. *Family Business Review*, *3*(3), 245–262. doi:10.1111/j.1741-6248.1990.00245.x

McKenny, A. F., Payne, G. T., Zachary, M. A., & Short, J. C. (2014). In L. Melin, M. Nordqvist, & P. Sharma (Eds.), *The SAGE Handbook of Family Business* (pp. 594–608). Thousand Oaks, CA: SAGE Publications. doi:10.4135/9781446247556.n30

Melin, L., & Nordqvist, M. (2007). The reflexive dynamics of institutionalization: The case of the family business. *Strategic Organization*, *5*(3), 321–333. doi:10.1177/1476127007079959

Miller, D., Steier, L., & Le Breton-Miller, I. (2003). Lost in time: Intergenerational succession, change, and failure in family business. *Journal of Business Venturing*, *18*(4), 513–531. doi:10.1016/S0883-9026(03)00058-2

Morck, R., Shleifer, A., & Vishny, R. W. (1988). Management ownership and market valuation: An empirical nalysis. *Journal of Financial Economics*, *20*, 293–315. doi:10.1016/0304-405X(88)90048-7Morck, R., & Yeung, B. (2003). Agency problems in large family business groups. *Entrepreneurship Theory and Practice*, *27*(4), 367–382. doi:10.1111/1540-8520.t01-1-00015

Murphy, L., & Lambrechts, F. (2015). Investigating the actual career decisions of the next generation: The impact of family business involvement. *Journal of Family Business Strategy*, *6*(1), 33–44. doi:10.1016/j.jfbs.2014.10.003

Murray, B. (2003). The succession transition process: A longitudinal perspective. *Family Business Review*, *16*(1), 17–33. doi:10.1111/j.1741-6248.2003.00017.x

Nordqvist, M., Hall, A., & Melin, L. (2009). Qualitative research on family businesses: The relevance and usefulness of the interpretive approach. *Journal of Management & Organization*, *15*(3), 294–308. doi:10.1017/S1833367200002637

Olson, D. H. (2000). Circumplex model of marital and family systems. *Journal of Family Therapy*, *22*(2), 144–167. doi:10.1111/1467-6427.00144 PMID:6840263

Pache, A.-C., & Santos, F. M. (2010). *Inside the Hybrid Organization: An* Organizational Level View of Responses to Conflicting Institutional Demands. Research Center ESSEC Working Paper 1101. Available at SSRN: https://ssrn.com/abstract=2328257

Pearson, A. W., Carr, J. C., & Shaw, J. C. (2008). Toward a theory of familiness: A social capital perspective. *Entrepreneurship Theory and Practice*, *32*(6), 949–969. doi:10.1111/j.1540-6520.2008.00265.x

Peay, R. T., & Dyer, G. (1989). Power orientations of entrepreneurs and succession planning. *Journal of Small Business Management*, *27*(1), 47–52.

Pratt, M. G., & Foreman, P. O. (2000). Classifying managerial responses to multiple organizational identities. *Academy of Management Review*, *25*(1), 18–42. doi:10.5465/amr.2000.2791601

Rousseau, D. M. (1985). Issues of level in organizational research: Multi-level and cross-level perspectives. In L. L. Cummings & B. M. Staw (Eds.), *Research in organizational behavior* (Vol. 7, pp. 1–37). Greenwich, CT: JAI Press.

Rubenson, G. C., & Gupta, A. K. (1996). The initial succession: A contingency model of founder tenure. *Entrepreneurship Theory and Practice*, *21*(2), 21–32. doi:10.1177/104225879602100202

Salovey, P., O'Leary, A., Stretton, M. S., Fishkin, S. A., & Drake, C. A. (1991). Influence of mood on judgments about health and illness. In J. P. Forgas (Ed.), *Emotion and social judgments* (p. 241262). Elmsford, NY: Pergamon Press.

Santiago, A. L. (2000). Succession experiences in Philippine family businesses. *Family Business Review*, *13*(1), 15–35. doi:10.1111/j.1741-6248.2000.00015.x

Scabini, E. (1995). *Psicologia sociale della famiglia*. Torino: Bollati Boringhieri.

Scabini, E., & Iafrate, R. (2003). Psicologia dei legami familiari. Roma: Carocci.

Schulze, W. S., Lubatkin, M. H., & Dino, R. N. (2003). Toward a theory of agency and altruism in family firms. Journal of Business Venturing, 18(4), 473–490. doi:10.1016/S0883-9026(03)00054-5 doi:10.1016/S0883-9026(03)00054-5

Schulze, W. S., Lubatkin, M. H., Dino, R. N., & Buchholtz, A. K. (2001). Agency relationships in family firms: Theory and evidence. *Organization Science*, *12*(2), 99–116. doi:10.1287/orsc.12.2.99.10114

Shepherd, D., & Haynie, J. M. (2009). Family business, identità conflict, and an expedited entrepreneurial process: A process of resolving identity conflict. *Entrepreneurship Theory and Practice*, *33*(6), 1245–1264. doi:10.1111/j.1540-6520.2009.00344.x

Sirmon, D. G., & Hitt, M. A. (2003). Managing resource: Linking unique resource, management and wealth creation in family firms. *Entrepreneurship Theory and Practice*, *27*(4), 339–358. doi:10.1111/1540-8520.t01-1-00013

Sorenson, R. (1999). Conflict management strategies used by successful family businesses. *Family Business Review*, *12*(4), 325–340. doi:10.1111/j.1741-6248.1999.00325.x

Sorenson, R. L., Goodpaster, K. E., Hedberg, P. R., & Yu, A. (2009). The family point of view, family social capital, and firm performance: An exploratory test. *Family Business Review*, *22*(3), 239–253. doi:10.1177/0894486509332456

Spaltro, E., & de Vito Piscicelli, P. (1990). *Psicologia per le organizzazioni*. Roma: Carocci.

Steier, L. (2001). Family firms, plural forms of governance, and the evolving role of trust. *Family Business Review*, *14*(4), 353–367. doi:10.1111/j.1741-6248.2001.00353.x

Steier, L., & Miller, D. (2010). Pre- and post-succession governance philosophies in entrepreneurial family firms. *Journal of Family Business Strategy*, *1*(3), 145–154. doi:10.1016/j.jfbs.2010.07.001

Stewart, A., & Hitt, M. A. (2012). Why Can't a Family Business Be More Like a Nonfamily Business? Modes of Professionalization in Family Firms. *Family Business Review*, *25*(1), 58–86. doi:10.1177/0894486511421665

Strauss, A., & Corbin, J. (1998). *Basics of qualitative research: grounded theory procedures and techniques* (2nd ed.). Newbury Park, CA: Sage.

Stryker, S. (1968). Identity salience and role performance. *Journal of Marriage and the Family*, *4*(4), 558–564. doi:10.2307/349494

Sundaramurthy, C. (2008). Sustaining trust within family businesses. *Family Business Review*, *21*(1), 89–102. doi:10.1111/j.1741-6248.2007.00110.x

Swogger, G. (1991). Assessing the successor generation in family businesses. *Family Business Review*, *4*(4), 397–411. doi:10.1111/j.1741-6248.1991.00397.x

Tajfel, H., & Turner, J. C. (1986). The social identity theory of intergroup behaviour. In S. Worchel & W. G. Austin (Eds.), *Psychology of intergroup relations* (pp. 7–24). Chicago: Nelson-Hall Publishers.

Tsang, E. W. K. (2002). Learning from overseas venturing experience: The case of Chinese family business. *Journal of Business Venturing*, *17*(1), 21–40. doi:10.1016/S0883-9026(00)00052-5

Uhlaner, L. M. (2006). Business family as a team: Underlying force for sustained competitive advantage. In P. Z. Poutziouris, K. X. Smyrnios, & S. B. Klein (Eds.), *Handbook of research on family business* (pp. 125–144). Cheltenham, UK: Edward Elgar. doi:10.4337/9781847204394.00016

Villanueva, J., & Sapienza, H. J. (2009). Goal tolerance, outside investors, and family firm governance. *Entrepreneurship Theory and Practice, 33*(6), 1193–1199. doi:10.1111/j.1540-6520.2009.00340.x

Westhead, P., & Howorth, C. (2007). "Types" of private family firms: An exploratory conceptual and empirical analysis. *Entrepreneurship and Regional Development, 19*(5), 405–431. doi:10.1080/08985620701552405

Whetten, D., & Mackey, A. (2002). A social actor conception of organizational identity and its implications for the study of organizational reputation. *Business & Society, 41*(4), 393–415. doi:10.1177/0007650302238775

Whetten, D. A., Foreman, P., & Dyer, W. G. (2014). Organizational Identity and Family Business. In The SAGE Handbook of Family Business. Thousand Oaks, CA: SAGE Publications Ltd. doi:10.4135/9781446247556.n24

Yin, R. K. (2003). *Case study research: Design and methods* (3rd ed.). Thousand Oaks, CA: Sage.

Zahra, S. A., Hayton, J. C., & Salvato, C. (2004). Entrepreneurship in family vs. non-family firms: A resource-based analysis of the effect of organizational culture. *Entrepreneurship Theory and Practice, 28*(4), 363–381. doi:10.1111/j.1540-6520.2004.00051.x

Zahra, S. A., Hayton, J. C., Neubaum, D. O., Dibrell, C., & Craig, J. (2008). Culture of family commitment and strategic flexibility: The moderating effect of stewardship. *Entrepreneurship Theory and Practice, 32*(6), 1035–1054. doi:10.1111/j.1540-6520.2008.00271.x

Zellweger, T. M., & Dehlen, T. (2012). Value Is in the Eye of the Owner: Affect Infusion and Socioemotional Wealth Among Family Firm Owners. *Family Business Review, 25*(3), 280–297. doi:10.1177/0894486511416648

Zellweger, T. M., Nason, R. S., Nordqvist, M., & Brush, V. (2013). Why Do Family Firms Strive for Nonfinancial Goals? An Organizational Identity Perspective. *Entrepreneurship Theory and Practice, 37*(2), 229–248. doi:10.1111/j.1540-6520.2011.00466.x

Zellweger, T. M., & Astrachan, J. H. (2008). On the emotional value of owning a firm. *Family Business Review, 21*(4), 347–363. doi:10.1177/08944865080210040106

Zellweger, T. M., Eddleston, K. A., & Kellermanns, F. W. (2010). Exploring the concept of familiness: Introducing family firm identity. *Journal of Family Business Strategy, 1*(1), 54–63. doi:10.1016/j.jfbs.2009.12.003

Zellweger, T. M., Kellermanns, F. W., Chrisman, J. J., & Chua, J. H. (2011). Family control and family firm valuations by family CEOs: The importance of intentions for transgenerational control. *Organization Science, 23*(3), 851–868. doi:10.1287/orsc.1110.0665

Zellweger, T. M., Kellermanns, F. W., Eddleston, K. A., & Memili, E. (2012). Building a family firm image: How family firms capitalize on their family ties. *Journal of Family Business Strategy, 3*(4), 239–250. doi:10.1016/j.jfbs.2012.10.001

ADDITIONAL READING

Kets de Vries, M. F. R., Carlock, R. S., & Florent-Treacy, E. (2007). *Family Business on the Couch: A Psychological Perspective*. London: Wiley.

Kets de Vries, M. F. R., & Miller, D. (1984). *The Neurotic Organization: Diagnosing and Changing Counterproductive Styles of Management*. San Francisco, CA: Jossey-Bas.

Kumra, S., Simpson, R., & Burke, R. J. (2014). *The Oxford Handbook of Gender in Organizations*. Oxford: Oxford University Press. doi:10.1093/oxfordhb/9780199658213.001.0001

Melin, L., Nordqvist, M., & Sharma, P. (2014). *The SAGE Handbook of Family Business*. London: SAGE. Publications Inc. doi:10.4135/9781446247556

Nordqvist, M., Melin, L., Waldkirch, M., & Kumeto, G. (Eds.). (2015). *Theoretical perspectives on family businesses*. Cheltenham: Edward Elgar Publishing. doi:10.4337/9781783479665

Poutziouris, P. Z., Smyrnios, K. X., & Klein, S. B. (2006). *Handbook of research on family business*. Cheltenham; Northampton (MA): Edward Elgar Pub. doi:10.4337/9781847204394

Zellweger, T. (2017). *Managing the Family Business: Theory and Practice*. Cheltenham, UK: Edward Elgar.

KEY TERMS AND DEFINITIONS

Dysfunctional Behaviour: The term dysfunctional is defined as "abnormal or impaired functioning" on the part of an individual person, between people in any sort of relationship, or amongst members of a family. Poor functioning refers to both behaviour and relationships that aren't working and have one or more negative, unhealthy aspects to them, such as poor communication or frequent conflict. This is a term used often by mental health professionals for interactions between people and is often used to describe any relationship in which there are significant problems or struggles.

Multilevel Analysis: The fundamental premise of this paradigm comes from the theory of organizational systems and resides in the fact that organizations are complex and dynamic systems with multiple levels. Thus, in any organizational system we find multiple levels such as industry, organization, group, individual, etc.; with lower levels nested and integrated within the upper ones.

Socio-Emotional Wealth: Is conceptualized in broad terms to capture the stock of affect-related value that a family derives from its controlling position in a particular firm.

Section 7
Anlysing the Family Firm From the Family Side

Chapter 15
A Configurational Approach to Analyze Family Governance and Family Firm Outcome Preferences

Antonio Carlos Cuenca
University of Valencia, Spain

Tomás F. González-Cruz
https://orcid.org/0000-0001-7479-7268
University of Valencia, Spain

ABSTRACT

This chapter follows the new research current that looks for heterogeneity between family businesses and its consequences. Through a cluster analysis, the chapter presents a taxonomy of four groups with different family government profiles, depending on the scope—number of issues considered—and the level of formalization. Alike, the research describes the different relative importance that each group attaches a to financial and non-financial performance measures, as well as to the dimensions of business and family success. The chapter analyzes a sample of 147 SME family businesses that belong to the tourism industry. All of them are closely held family businesses that range between the first and third generation. Results show how family businesses with wide and formalized family government systems place a special emphasis on those success measures related to stakeholder satisfaction, family satisfaction, and wealth preservation. They present a stronger continuity intention.

INTRODUCTION

Along the last two decades Family-Business Academy focus his effort in developing a sound theoretical rationale, sometimes borrowed from mainstream general management literature –Agency Theory, Resource Based View, etc.–, sometimes as an own theoretical development that contributes to the general

DOI: 10.4018/978-1-7998-1655-3.ch015

management Academy –Socio-Emotional Wealth–. In general terms, this theoretical background is useful in order to increase knowledge about family-firm distinctive mindset, resources, processes, practices and performance assessment, in comparison to non-family-firms.

Meanwhile, some papers began to analyze family-business as a heterogeneous phenomenon, looking to gain better understanding about how different family-business bear different mindsets, deploy resources following a distinctive logic; enact different financial, management and organizational practices; and look for a different mix of firm outcomes.

Two main research strategies allow facing this challenge. First, departing from a sound rationale based on accepted theories, the development of typologies of family-firms that share common characteristics that differentiate each type from other family-business(Dyer, 2006; Li & Daspit, 2016, Nordqvist, Sharma, & Chirico, 2014; Scholes & Wilson, 2014; Sharma, 2002). The Second one, consist on exploring family-business features looking for taxonomies. This research strategy is inductive and empirically driven, and results in classifications that are valuable to develop new theory and advance in understanding family-business as a rich and diverse phenomenon. This chapter is going to follow this second research strategy.

Papers presenting family-business taxonomies are recent and to some extent scarce, in fact Neubaum, et al., (2019) report 16 papers that count 1,639 citations, being the most cited contribution Tagiuri & Davis (1992). However, the majority of papers date form the last ten years.

With regard, the main issues that past research considers for building family-business taxonomies, research aligns into two main categories:

On the *firm side*, research considers criteria like:

- Firm features, like size and ownership concentration (Miller et al., 2013) –;
- Firm practices, like management professionalization–
- firm orientations and capabilities, strategic (Basco & Rodriguez, 2009; Dekker et al., 2013), Internationalization (Swoboda & Olejnik, 2013) or innovation (Erdogan et al., 2019)–;
- Family-firm resource endowment, Social capital (Sanchez-Ruiz et al., 2019)–;
- Family-business goals/outcome profiles (Basco, 2017; Tagiuri & Davis, 1992).

On the family side:

- family involvement and degree of family orientation (Birley et al., 1999; Basco & Rodriguez, 2011; Uhlaner, 2005);
- family size and complexity (Westhead & Howorth, 2007);
- communication patterns between the family and the firm, as well as inside and across the family group (Dalpiaz et al., 2014; Distelberg & Blow, 2011; Leiß & Zehrer, 2018; Zody et al., 2006);
- founder and family values (García-Álvarez & López-Sintas, 2001; Rau, Schneider-Siebke & Günther, 2019).

Like the rest of specialized literature in family-business, papers that explore the family side through taxonomies, focus on individual relations –mainly incumbent-successor and communication patterns–, family complexity as a liability, and the family as a resource provider: social capital, familiness, etc. However, papers addressing family governance and its consequences in terms of: resource endowment, firm capabilities or firm orientations remain scant in family-business literature, and to author's best knowledge, there is no family-business taxonomy based on the scope and formalization of the family government system. Analyzing family-business from this perspective is a necessary step to better understanding the context that frames family views and intentions, where family relationships are enacted and family resources developed, protected and enhanced.

In order to close this gap, this chapter explores and sample of 147 Spanish family-business that belong to the tourism industry. Beyond industry, the sample presents a set of similarities, like firm size, age and family generation, alike, all of them are closely held family-business that also represent a significant share of family wealth. The research goal is looking for a family-firm taxonomy that responds to the family intention of self-government in terms of scope and formalization. Alike this paper describes how each group presents a different orientation in terms of relative importance given to different family-firm outcomes.

From now on, the chapter structures as follows: First paragraph succinctly presents background about family government. Family regulatory framework, that refers to the set of uses, traditions, mores and norms that regulate the family group, which can be tacit-informal or explicit-formal rules; these norms could be formal or informal. Likewise, family government structure refers to devices that serve to communicate, deliberate and update criteria, and above all to develop and strengthen family cohesion and harmony. The background paragraph closes with a brief description of family-firm outcome model. This multidimensional concept is a good reflection of the owner family intention, and represent the set of financial and non-financial outcomes that the dominant coalition bears in mind when assessing family-firm success. Then, the chapter describes the method and the sample. Next, the paper presents and characterizes the groups that make up the taxonomy in terms of its family-government development –number of issues considered and level of formalization– and the usefulness that they attribute to the family council. The research cast an eye to the family-firm outcome profile of each cluster –depending on the relative importance they attach to each outcome–. Last, but not least, the paper looks for differences regarding how groups envision family-firm continuity. The chapter closes with a set of conclusions and recommendations.

FAMILY GOVERMENT

The analysis of the family-business from the owner-family side is one of the aspects of the research object that has received less attention from Academy (Jaskiewicz & Dyer, 2017). Especially how the kin group manages their relationship between them, and with the firm, and the consequences of such self-regulation in terms of family government.

Literature is neat in reporting that family growth and evolution usually goes with a reduction in familial-shared meanings and purposes, and more divergences between factional interest and intentions that damage financial and non-financial performance. To counterbalance this negative impact, mainstream research proposes a set of practices that come from the Corporate Governance field, and are oriented toward preventing and managing conflict of interests.

However, the number of papers that analyze the issue from the family side is scant. To our best knowledge, research that explores how family government systems: rules –as a family constitution– and family-government devices –as family council– impact on the family-business performance is anecdotal –an exception is the paper of Arteaga & Menendez-Requejo (2017)–.

Family governance has to do with managing relationship, resources and emotions of an affinity group. Contrary to mainstream research in family-business, family governance requires a clear differentiation from the government and management of the firm that the family holds. Given that, the main goal of this chapter is providing a taxonomy of family-business based on the family decision about the level of development of their family governance structure, authors devote this paragraph to briefly describing rules and devices that enable family government. This chapter distinguishes two complementary but different family-family government parts: family regulatory framework and family governance devices.

Family Regulatory framework

The elaboration, enactment and deployment of rules regulating ownership, power and work are well-known recipes to manage the owner-family in relation to the family-business. These regulatory frameworks provide protection against owner-owner agency cost (Arteaga & Menendez-Requejo, 2017), develops and protects familiness (Minichilli & Corbetta, 2010; Suess, 2014), regulates ownership transmission without draining financial resources nor reducing family control (Neubauer & Lank, 2016), frames owner-family logic, and provides institutional legitimacy to the family and to the business (Raymond et al., 2015).

These rules usually refer to three main dimensions:

- **Human Resource Polices Concerning Family Members** (Kidwell et al., 2018)
- **Management:** Presence of family members in managerial positions and CEO succession (Chittoor & Das, 2007)
- **Ownership Transference:** Valuation and transmission of share (Villalonga et al., 2015).

These regulatory frameworks generally enhance corporate governance and rules regarding the incorporation of family members, limiting managerial opportunism and promoting firm professionalization, which in turn will improve performance. On the family side, a proper regulatory framework increases feelings of procedural justice between family members, (Van den Berghe & Carchon, 2003). Alike, owner-family agreements, formalized in different rules, prevent block-holder conflicts. However not all family issues and challenges can be managed through a set of rules. Norms cannot be stone-written, and some issues need the development of a family governance structure that updates, develops and interprets the application of the regulatory framework.

Family Governance Structure

Family governance also refers to different structural devices addressed to manage family wealth and harmony. Literature identifies two main kind of family government devices: *Family office*, that is a structure addressed to professionalize wealth management and optimize profitability, while reducing financial risk and tax burden (Rivo-López et al., 2017; Naldi et al., 2015). Family office separates the family from its wealth reducing the risk of irresponsible altruistic tendencies and wasteful financial behaviors (Miller et al, 2017). Depending on family circumstances double agency cost are well below of cost associated to behaviors derived from incompetence, irresponsibility or directly from a situation of conflict between family factions (Zellweger & Kammerlander, 2015).

A second family governance structure is the *family council*, that enables and channels regular meetings between family members (Suess, 2014; Gersick et al., 1997), which main function is "to achieve, maintain, and increase family members' unity both among themselves and with their family-business" (Gallo and Kenyon-Rouvinez, 2005: 53). Family council purpose has to do with cultivating trust and a shared vision between family members (Gnan and Montemerlo, 2010), to enhance their emotional commitment and identification with the family and the firm (Börjnberg & Nicholson, 2012). Alike, family council improves family communication (Labaki, 2011; Suess, 2014), and it is an orderly and structured transmission vehicle of the needs and expectations of the family with respect to the firm (Nordqvist & Melin, 2010).

Family council should be a clearly differentiated family government device, which finality is to preserve and enhance family harmony and unity of purpose. Family council emphasizes on family values, education and communications, and focuses on family relationships. Threfore, the main outcome of a family council has to do with family unity and harmony (Poza, 2013).

From this view, family council is the formal forum where family members interact in order to enhance communication and increase transparency. Family council is the context where the family builds an explicit set of common values (Tapies & Fernandez-Moya, 2012) and policies (Sundaramurthy, 2008), that guide intra-family interactions and family-firm relationships. As a result, trust, commitment, harmony, common intention and unity of purpose, are the basement of a functional family that contributes to the firm (Chittoor & Das, 2007; Gnan & Montemerlo, 2010; Sundaramurthy, 2008; Vilaseca, 2002). Alike, other authors underline the role of family council as transmission channel of family history, values, mind-set, identity and intention toward de firm (Craig et al, 2008; Nordqvist & Melin, 2010; Tapies & Fernandez-Moya, 2012).

With regard to the impact of family-governance devices on family-business performance, results are not conclusive, while De Massis et al (2015) reports a negative but not statically significant relationship between family council and gross profit margin in general terms, Suess (2017) states that this kind of family governance devices have a positive influence on the attainment of financial performance.

With regard to non-financial performance, family office and especially family council, minimize the potential family conflicts (Arteaga and Menéndez-Requejo, 2017; Cruz, Larraza-Kintana, Garcés-Galdeano, & Berrone, 2014; Vardaman & Gondo, 2014). Alike, family council promotes family cohesion, which in turn also minimizes the negative effects of family problems on family-firm reputation (Arteaga and Menéndez-Requejo, 2017; Vardaman & Gondo, 2014). It also enhances stewardship behavior by promoting cohesion, values and open communication between family members (Gallo & Kenyon-Rouvinez, 2005; Suess, 2014).

Family-government structural devices contribute to create an adequate organizational environment (Chirico et al., 2011; Sirmon et al., 2008), where the family-firm can benefit from the interaction and ties between family members, that is necessary to leverage the diverse and rich endowment of knowledge, relationships and competences that a complex family produces (Brenes et al., 2011; Umans et al., 2018).

Finally yet importantly, family regulatory framework and family-government structure should be considered as part of a system, given the complementary function between them, where family-government devices are the proper forum to interpret, develop and update the rules that regulate the relationship between family and business (Alderson, 2015).

Family-Firm Outcome Profile

The business outcome model describes the set of criteria, and its polarity and hierarchy –relative weight– that each firm has to measure success and gauge performance. Of course, this outcome model reflects mind-sets, intentions, mission and vision of the dominant coalition. Performance conceptualization is a topic that is receiving attention, and is the research goal of papers in top journals (Holt, Pearson, Carr & Barnett, 2017), doctoral dissertations (Williams, 2015), and open calls for new research it top general management journals special issues.

For the case of family-business, given the sustained relationship between the family and the firm, *Firm Outcome Model* should be a multidimensional and fine-grained reflection of family values, aspirations, goals and priorities (Miller & Le Breton-Miller, 2014).

There is some agreement about the main six categories that make up the conceptualization of performance measurement. Outcomes reported by published family-business literature fit in a 2X3 grid of five dimensions (Holt, Pearson, Carr & Barnett, 2017):

- **Outcome dimensions:**
  - Financial
  - Non-financial – external
  - Non-financial – Internal
- **Sphere dimensions:**
  - Firm
  - Family

Given that Academy reports empirical findings suggesting that, there are wide variations in the behaviors of family-firms (Chrisman & Patel, 2012), the way for properly measuring family-firm performance should first consider the relative importance that each owner-family puts on different dimensions and categories of performance (Williams, 2015). Following this recommendation, this chapter is going to explore and describe in which way different groups of family-firms –considering its level of family government development– place importance on different firm outputs.

METHODOLOGY

Sample and Data Collection

We use a database from a primary study on Spanish tourism industry, the economic activity considered in the definition of Tourism set by the Instituto de Estudios Turísticos. This definition follows the recommendations of international institutions such as the World Tourism Organization (UNWTO) and the United Nation Statistic Commission. The sample comes from the entire population of Spanish tourism companies presented in the 2009 Central Companies Directory (DIRCE) compiled by the National Institute of Statistics. According to this census, there was a total population of approximately 140,900 tourism businesses. The initial sample of 8,148 companies was selected using a stratified random sampling procedure with proportional allocation to ensure the representativeness of the sample in terms of activity (considering four groups), size (taking the number of employees as a measure of the size of the

Table 1. Sample distribution by activity

Activity	Frequency	Valid Percentage	Accumulated Percentage
Hospitality	71	48,3	48,2
Restaurants & Cafeterias	35	23,8	72,1
Travel Ag	14	9,5	81,6
Passenger Transport	5	3,4	85
Sport & Wellness	4	2,7	87,7
Other	18	12,3	100,0
Total	147	100,0	

company) and location. The result of the fieldwork, after various data cleansing processes, was a sample of 1,019 companies with a confidence level of 95% and an error interval of ± 3.1%. This final sample represents a response rate of 25.6%.

For data collection, we use a questionnaire, conducted through personal interviews with the firms' CEO or general manager in 2015. In order to correct potential problems regarding questionnaires as a data collection method, the project team follow a set of recommended procedures; based on the Dillman's Total Design Method (1978) for questionnaire-based research. The data collection process lasted from December 2009 to March 2010. We got a total sample of 165 non-family-business and 378 family-business.

Given the extended length of the questionnaire –is part of a wider research project– we work only with family-firms that give complete and reliable answers. Alike, given the small number of large firms and the research goals, authors remove large and micro firms, so the final sample was made of 147 SME family-firms. Figure 1 presents the sample distribution by activity.

With regard to other sample features, 80% of the firms are founded in the early 80`s, so they are in the transition between the first and second generation with a few in third and later generations. In fact, the generation in charge is: 46,3% first generation; 39,5% second generation; and 14,2% third or later generation. Of course, all of them are non-listed and closely held family-business, where the family holds over 70% of the share in all cases.

Measures

Independent Variables

Given that the research goal is describing a taxonomy of family-firms, depending on the degree of development of their family government system, the chapter considers the presence or not of an array of different agreements, policies, rules and government devices. Alike the questionnaire ask for the degree of formalization, that is, if there are informal/ verbal agreement or, on the contrary, it they are formal/ written. Specifically the survey asks for:

- Family council,
- Family constitution,
- Wealth management policies,
- Requirements to work in the firm –for family members–,

- Human Resource Policies concerning family members,
- Succession in management,
- Power distribution between family branches,
- Share transmission,
- Ownership transmission to next generations,

Alike, given that family council is the most specific family government device, and given that it is one of the most unknown and misunderstood tools to preserve family capabilities, the questionnaire asks –using a Likert scale from 1 to 7– for the usefulness of the family council in relation to:

- *'Allows the exchange of opinions'*,
- *'Enables harmony and prevents conflict'*,
- *'Promotes family commitment toward the firm'*,
- *'Channel to inform family members about the company's performance'*,
- *'Developing a plan for family members' education, training and development'*,
- *'Planning leisure activities to encourage family life and interaction'*,
- *'Discuss and review the family constitution content'*,
- *'Discuss the policies that regulate family members' access to work or management positions'*,
- *'Discuss and develop financial policies to preserve and enhance family wealth'*,
- *'Promote firm growth and competitiveness'*.

Independent Variables

Following Williams (2015), this chapter considers the relative importance that the family-firm puts on different outcomes as a necessary previous step to measure performance. In line with Holt et al. (2017), this research considers financial and non-financial outcomes, for both, the firm and the family. The questionnaire asses the outcome relevance asking through a 1 to 7 likert scale *'What do you think is the importance given by your company to the following aspects as a measure of success?'*

- **Financial outcomes:**
  - EBIT growth,
  - Net profit,
  - Next generations' wealth,
- **Non-financial external outcomes:**
  - Customer satisfaction
  - Competitiveness improvement,
  - Job creation
- **Non-financial internal outcomes:**
  - Employees satisfaction
  - Ownership satisfaction

CLUSTER IDENTIFICATON AND DESCRIPTION

Cluster Analysis

In order to find an appropriate number of family-firm groups characterized by its family-government system, the research uses cluster analysis as an approach to sort firms into similar sets of homogeneous groups and develop a taxonomy (Hair, et al, 1998). Because the limited size of the sample, authors consider that hierarchical cluster analysis is more suitable (Hair et al., 1998), alike and following Lehman (1979) the number of clusters should be 3 to 5. To ensure stability of the results, we iterated by generating three, four, and five clusters. Results indicate that four clusters represented the best solution with the strongest values. Table 2 shows the sample distribution among clusters and the number of cases in each group.

With regard to some general features that are useful to describe each cluster, table 3 presents firm age, generation in charge, number of shareholders, and percentage of share owned by the main shareholder and the five first family owners, as well as the proportion of family wealth compromised in the firm. Data shows that *cluster 1* groups the oldest family-firms, that present more family and ownership complexity and, in relative terms, the less closely held firm. On the other side, *cluster 2* groups the youngest family-firms with and average family and ownership complexity, alike is the group where the firm represents the lowest percentage of family wealth.

Cluster Description

The family-government system is different between cluster 2 the less developed, and cluster 3, the most developed one in terms of scope and formalization, while clusters 1 and 4 present a similar level of development but with a different profile.

Cluster 1- government of family involvement. Presents a family government profile that places relative importance on those aspects related to family involvement in the business: criteria to get access to work in the firm, distribution of power between family members and human resource policies concerning family members. The percentage of formalization is low.

Cluster 2-ungoverned family. Presents the less developed system of family government, a little 20% of the firms in this group report some verbal agreement, and formalization is nearly non-existent. This cluster groups the youngest family-business and those firms that represent less portion of family wealth.

Cluster 3-governed family-firm. This is the group that presents the most developed family-government system, that stands out for its wide scope –all items considered present at least a high degree of verbal agreement–, alike is the group that presents the highest percentage of formalization, especially in those

Table 2. Sample distribution by cluster

		Frequency	Percentage	Valid Percentage	Accumulated Percentage
Cluster	1	32	21,8	21,8	21,8
	2	41	27,9	27,9	49,7
	3	20	13,6	13,6	63,3
	4	54	36,7	36,7	100,0
	Total	147	100,0	100,0	

Table 3. Cluster features by firm age, generation in charge, number of shareholders, ownership distribution and wealth family in firm

		Cluster				
		1	2	3	4	Total
	Age	46	32	39	36	37
Generation	1,00	34,4%	56,1%	55,0%	42,6%	46,3%
	2,00	43,7%	36,6%	40,0%	38,9%	39,5%
	3,00	9,7%	7,3%	5,0%	18,5%	11,6%
	4,00	12,5%				2,7%
Total		**100,0%**	**100,0%**	**100,0%**	**100,0%**	**100,0%**
Family Shareholder	1		10,0%	10,0%	7,4%	6,9%
	2-5	90,6%	82,5%	90,0%	85,2%	86,2%
	6-20	9,4%	7,5%		7,4%	6,9%
Total		**100,0%**	**100,0%**	**100,0%**	**100,0%**	**100,0%**
Share distrib	Main	64,4%	85,5%	88,2%	70,5%	75,7%
	5 main	84,9%	96,7%	100%	98,1%	95,1%
Fam Wealth.		63%	50%	68%	75%	65%

Figure 1. Family government profile - Cluster 1: government of family involvement.

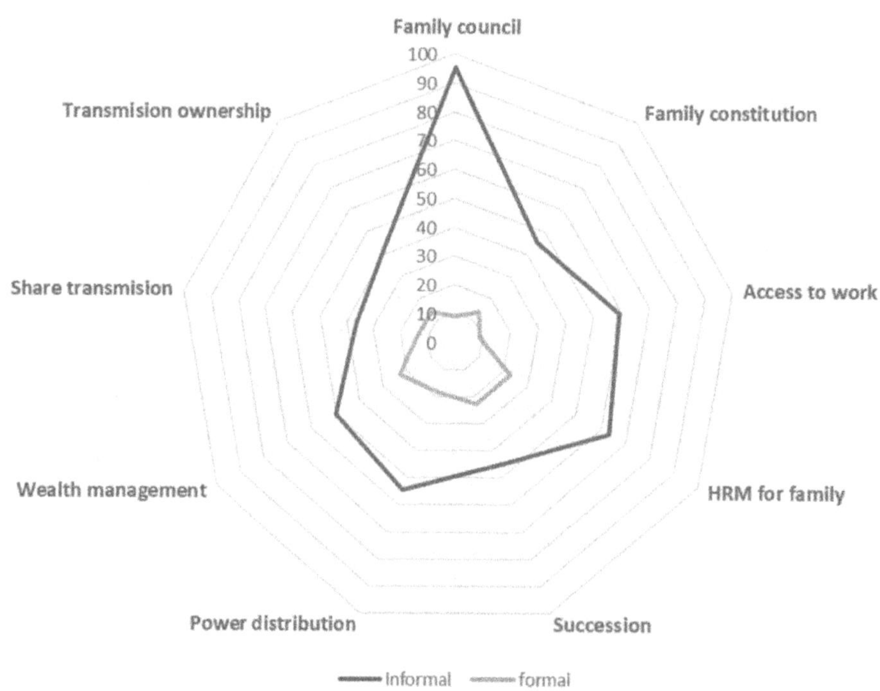

Figure 2. Family government profile - Cluster 2: ungoverned family

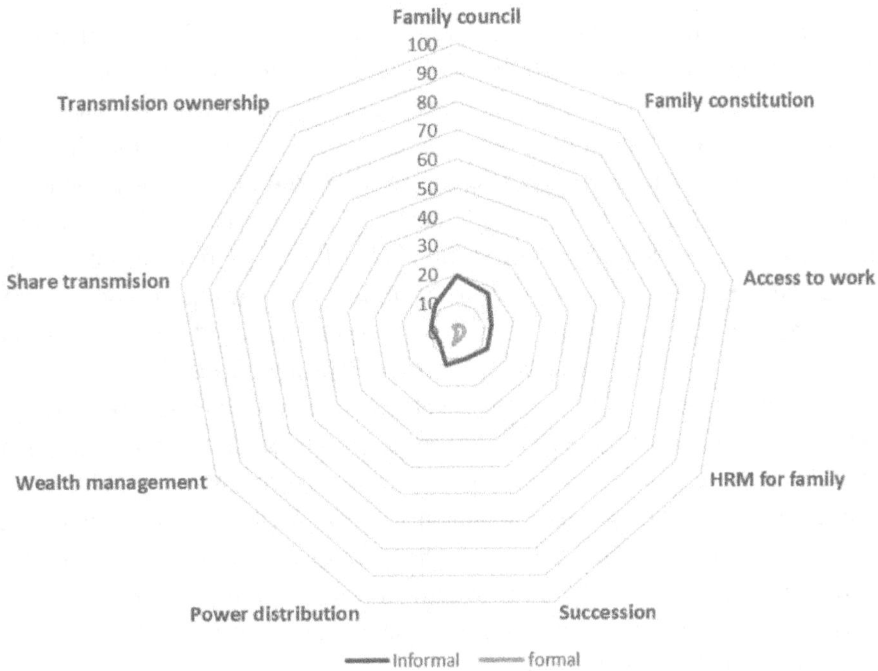

Figure 3. Family government profile - Cluster 3: governed family

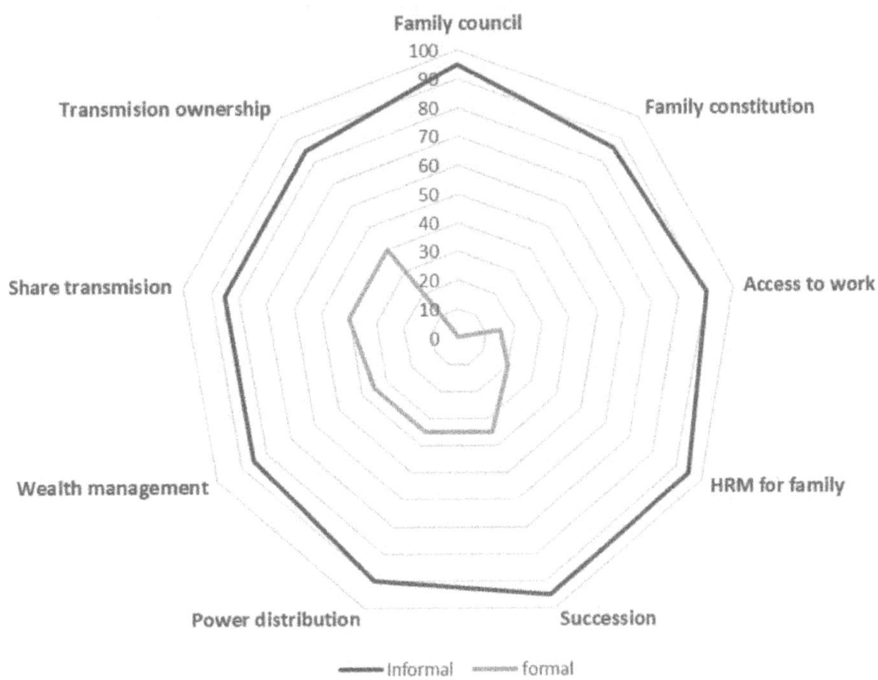

issues related to family involvement in the firm, succession in management, ownership transmission and wealth management.

Cluster 4-government of family ownership. Like cluster 1, presents and intermediate level of development, and a low percentage of formalization. In this group family government places emphasis on stock transmission, succession, and HRM policies concerning family members. Therefore, the governance system focus on ownership and benefit distribution in terms of financial and non-financial returns.

Clusters where also made considering the usefulness attributed to the family council. Family-firms in *Cluster 3 –governed family-firm,* report a high degree of usefulness for all issues considered in the questionnaire. Receive an especially high appreciation issues that refer to family constitution enactment and actualization, and the cohesion and development of the family group through leisure and training activities. On the opposite side, firms in *cluster 2 –ungoverned family,* do not perceive family council as a useful tool for any of the issues asked in the questionnaire as figure 5 shows.

In line with the stages of family government development, family-business belonging to *Cluster 1–government of family involvement,* and *cluster 4 –government of family ownership,* report similar levels of usefulness to family council as a device to govern the array of family issues considered in this research.

In accordance to the post hoc analysis, two statements receive similar usefulness assessment in clusters 1, 3 and 4: *'family council as a useful device to promote family commitment'*, and *'family council as a channel to inform family members'*. Alike, the statement: *'family council as a valuable device to plan family education and development'* receives similar assessment in cluster 1 and 3, and in both cases is higher than for firms that belong to cluster 4.

Figure 4. Family government profile - Cluster 4: government of family benefits

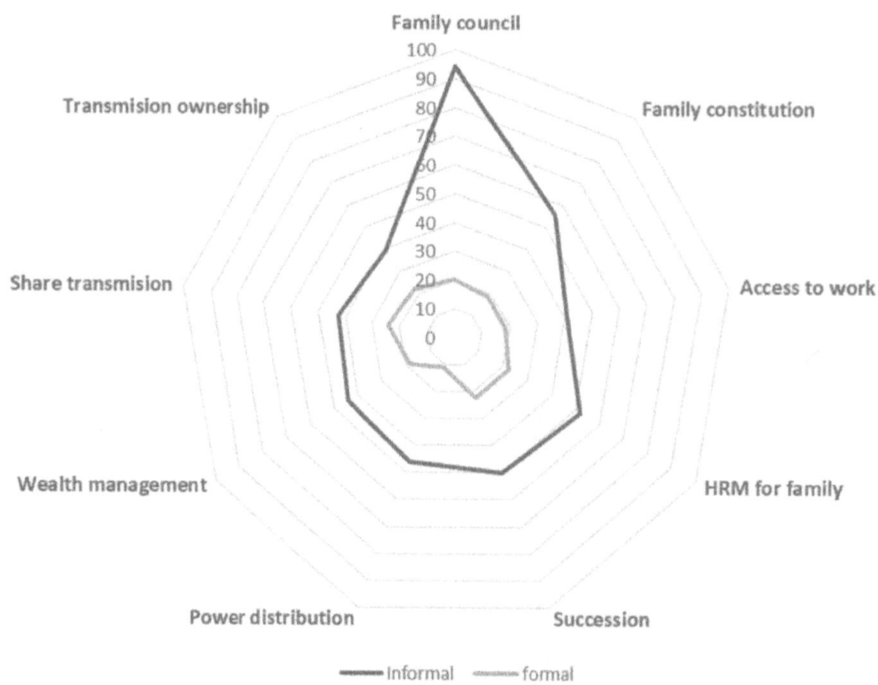

Figure 5. Family council usefulness

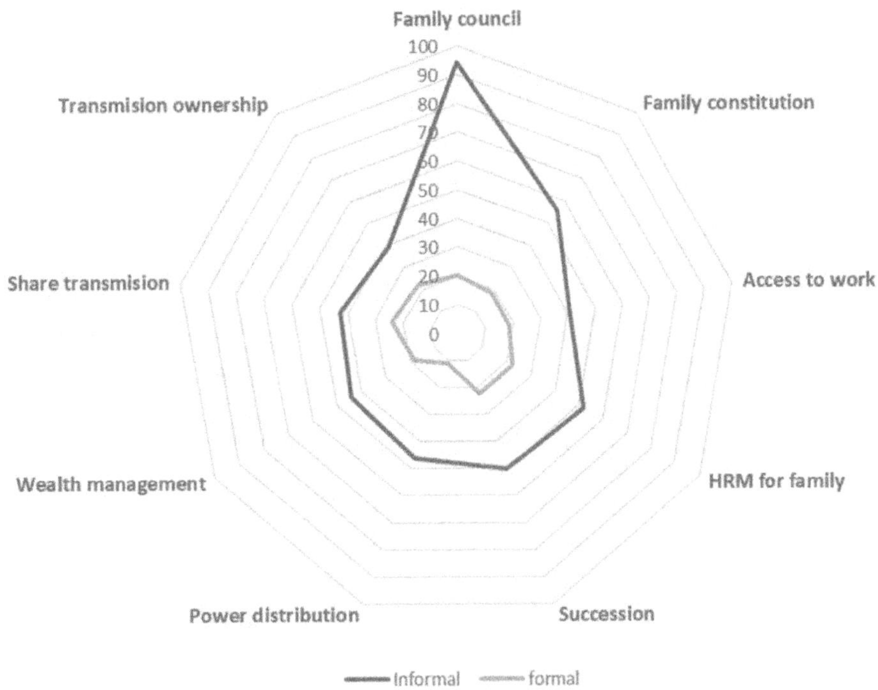

Family-Firm Outcome Profile

The main research goal of this chapter is developing a SME-family-business taxonomy depending on the scope and formalization degree of its family governance system. After cluster identification and description, the paper shows the outcome profile for each group. Following Williams (2015) researchers consider the relative importance that the family-business places on different outcomes.

As figure 6 shows, family-firms that belong to *cluster 1 –government of family involvement,* place the highest relevance to all outcomes. Family-business that fit in *cluster 2 –ungoverned family,* present a very-low non-financial outcome profile, in terms of importance attributed by the firm to this kind of outcomes, and in comparison with business financial outcomes.

With regard to family-business that belong to *cluster 3 –governed family,* they attribute great relevance to non-financial outcomes, for both family and business spheres, alike attach a relative low importance to family financial outcomes. Finally yet importantly, firms in *cluster 4 –governed ownership,* place a comparatively high emphasis on business financial and operational outcomes in comparison to business non-financial outcomes (employee satisfaction; job creation).

Least but not least, this research considers how family-government profiles are related to the vision that family-firms have about their own future. Table 4 shows that firms in *cluster 3 –governed family–* have a coherent vision of the future: incumbents want that the firm remains in family hands, are confident about future generations' competences, and do not consider the family as a liability for firm's growth and development. For the case of *Cluster 4 –government of family ownership*, both incumbents and successors mostly want family-firm continuity, however, 35% do not trust in next generations' competences

Figure 6. Family-firm outcome profile

and 25% consider the family as a liability for firm's growth. More striking is the case of family-firms in *cluster 2 –ungoverned family*, while present the lowest incumbents' willingness for family continuity, as well as the lowest confidence in next generations' competences, is the group that reports the lowest percentage of responses considering the family as a liability for firm's growth. Data suggests that a developed system of family government lead to positive realism, while partial family governance or an ungoverned family leads to naïve optimism and incoherent statements

Table 4. Considerations about family-firm future

	Cluster				
	1	**2**	**3**	**4**	**Post hoc comparison**
Incumbents want family continuity	72,7%	68,3%	85%	90,7%	**4,3>1,2**
Successors want family continuity	59,1%	56,1%	50%	77,8%	**4>1,2,3**
Competent family in next generation?	63,6%	56,1%	80%	64,8%	**3>4,1,2**
Family as a liability for firm growth	35,8%	14,6%	15%	25,7%	**1,4>3,2**

CONCLUSION

This chapter contributes to the emerging vein of research that explores the family-firm as a complex and heterogeneous phenomenon. The paper presents an exploratory and data-driven survey that looks for a taxonomy that distinguishes family-business depending on the level of family government development in terms of scope –number of different issues considered–, degree of formalization and usefulness attributed to the family council –the most clearly and differentiated family government structural device–.

Family government is an under-researched issue in specialized literature. Usually, Family-Business Academy relies in Corporate Governance knowledge to propose ways to face and manage firm and owner-family complexity. This predominant vein of research proposes devices and government practices addressed to prevent, and manage conflict of interest, but that ignore the essentials of family dynamics: a set of harmonic and long-term relationships focused on human fulfillment for every one belonging to the kin group. In fact, academic research devoted to analyze family government and its impact on family-firm performance is scant, and results remain contradictory and inconclusive, and, to researchers' best knowledge, there is no family-business taxonomy based on how families develop their family government system.

With the intention to close this gap, this study explores a sample of 147 SME Family Business that belong to the Spanish tourism industry. In order to bound other sources of heterogeneity, the sample is limited to non-listed and closely held family-business, which are transitioning between first-second and second-third generation.

The research looks for family-firm groups with homogenous family-governance. The elements considered to create clusters are three: the regulatory framework, which includes the norms, uses and mores that the family group grants to themselves to rule their relations of coexistence; Family government structural devices, that support proper communication and decision-making patterns about issues concerning the family group; and the perception of usefulness of this devices. As a secondary research goal, the survey explores the firm's outcome model profile for each group, as well as their view about family-firm continuity.

Through a cluster analysis, the chapter describes four family-business groups: *The ungoverned family –Cluster 2*, are family firms with an underdeveloped system of family government, the number of issues considered is limited, and formalization is nearly non-existent. This group attributes near cero usefulness to family council. With regard to the outcome model, they give low relevance to non-financial outcomes, especially in comparison to business financial outcomes. Alike, these family-firms belong to the group with less intention and confidence on family continuity.

Government of family involvement –Cluster 1, this group places relative importance on those aspects related to family involvement in the business, that is, issues like: criteria to get access to work in the firm, distribution of power between family branches and human resource policies concerning family members. In this group, the percentage of formalization is low and attribute an intermediate level of usefulness to the family council. This cluster places the highest importance to all family-firm outcomes considered in the survey. Alike they present a low confidence in family firm continuity and consider the family as a liability to family growth.

Government of family ownership –Cluster 4. In this group, like cluster 1, the number of issues considered in the family government system is limited, and presents a low percentage of formalization. The family government system places emphasis on stock transmission, succession, and HRM policies concerning family members. Therefore, the governance system focus on ownership and benefit distribution in terms of financial and non-financial returns. With regard to family council usefulness, this group reports similar assessment to cluster 1. With respect to the family-firm outcome model, this group reports lower relevance to all outcomes in comparison with cluster 1. Likewise, these family-firms attribute importance to business financial and operational outcomes, in comparison to business non-financial outcomes (employee satisfaction; job creation). As a distinctive feature, this is the group where both incumbents and successors report the high percentage of willingness to continue the family-business, and, with cluster 1, alike, is the group that provides higher rates to the family as a liability to growth.

Governed family-firm –Cluster 3 presents the most developed family-government system that stands out for its wide scope and formalization, especially in those issues related to family involvement in the firm, succession in management, ownership transmission and wealth management. This group reports a high degree of usefulness of family council, especially as a device for family constitution enactment and actualization, and as a means to increase cohesion and development of the family. These family-firms attribute great relevance to non-financial outcomes, for both family and business spheres, alike attach relative importance to family financial outcomes. Cluster 3 contains the family-business that most confident in future generations' competence to continue the firm.

To summarize, this research offers several contributions. First, it extends the emergent vein of research that analyzes family-firm heterogeneity. Second, it contributes to the scant literature that analyzes the family government system and its influence on family-firm outcomes. Third, it considers the relative relevance that the dominant coalition gives to different organizational outcomes, as a previous and relevant step to measure performance. Fourth, it shows that the willingness to continue is not necessarily dependent on family governance and, in consequence reflects a will that not always is accompanied of coherent family-firm behaviors. On the contrary, family-firms with more developed family government systems present a coherent behavior: incumbents want continuity, are confident on next generation's competences and don´t consider the family as liability for the future growth of the firm. These results suggest that family government leads to an informed awareness of the capabilities and liabilities of the familial group, in clear contrast to the optimistic voluntarism of the rest of the clusters.

This research is not without limitations. First, due to the sample, that considers family firms from one country and one industry. Second, while the homogeneity of the sample is an advantage to increase the relevance of the main variables considered to draw the clusters that made the taxonomy, it is a serious drawback for results generalization. Third, cluster analysis requires some test, like a second round in a split sample or in a second sample. In this case, the limited size of the sample made it impossible. Fourth, the survey report information from a single informant.

In order to overcome these limitations, future research should consider different samples from other countries and different industries. Alike, the regulatory framework needs to consider a wide scope of questions related to pure family issues. Additional research ought to explore data with alternative techniques like Latent Profile Analysis. Finally yet importantly, longitudinal survey would show the real impact of family governance in family firm future performance.

ACKNOWLEDGMENT

This research was supported by the Spanish Ministry of Science, Innovation and Universities, co-financed with FEDER funds [grant number ECO2016-26796-P].

REFERENCES

Alderson, K. (2015). Conflict management and resolution in family-owned businesses: A practitioner focused review. *Journal of Family Business Management*, *5*(2), 140–156. doi:10.1108/JFBM-08-2015-0030

Arteaga, R., & Menéndez-Requejo, S. (2017). Family constitution and business performance: Moderating factors. *Family Business Review*, *30*(4), 320–338. doi:10.1177/0894486517732438

Basco, R. (2017). "Where do you want to take your family firm?" A theoretical and empirical exploratory study of family business goals. *BRQ Business Research Quarterly*, *20*(1), 28–44. doi:10.1016/j.brq.2016.07.001

Basco, R., & Pérez Rodríguez, M. J. (2009). Studying the family enterprise holistically: Evidence for integrated family and business systems. *Family Business Review*, *22*(1), 82–95. doi:10.1177/0894486508327824

Basco, R., & Rodríguez, M. J. P. (2011). Ideal types of family business management: Horizontal fit between family and business decisions and the relationship with family business performance. *Journal of Family Business Strategy*, *2*(3), 151–165. doi:10.1016/j.jfbs.2011.07.004

Birley, S., Ng, D., & Godfrey, A. (1999). The family and the business. *Long Range Planning*, *32*(6), 598–608. doi:10.1016/S0024-6301(99)00076-X

Björnberg, Å., & Nicholson, N. (2012). Emotional ownership: The next generation's relationship with the family firm. *Family Business Review*, *25*(4), 374–390. doi:10.1177/0894486511432471

Brenes, E. R., Madrigal, K., & Requena, B. (2011). Corporate governance and family business performance. *Journal of Business Research*, *64*(3), 280–285. doi:10.1016/j.jbusres.2009.11.013

Chirico, F., Sirmon, D. G., Sciascia, S., & Mazzola, P. (2011). Resource orchestration in family firms: Investigating how entrepreneurial orientation, generational involvement, and participative strategy affect performance. *Strategic Entrepreneurship Journal*, *5*(4), 307–326. doi:10.1002ej.121

Chittoor, R., & Das, R. (2007). Professionalization of management and succession performance—A vital linkage. *Family Business Review*, *20*(1), 65–79. doi:10.1111/j.1741-6248.2007.00084.x

Chrisman, J. J., & Patel, P. C. (2012). Variations in R&D investments of family and nonfamily firms: Behavioral agency and myopic loss aversion perspectives. *Academy of Management Journal*, *55*(4), 976–997. doi:10.5465/amj.2011.0211

Craig, J. B., Dibrell, C., & Davis, P. S. (2008). Leveraging family-based brand identity to enhance firm competitiveness and performance in family businesses. *Journal of Small Business Management*, *46*(3), 351–371. doi:10.1111/j.1540-627X.2008.00248.x

Cruz, C., Larraza–Kintana, M., Garcés–Galdeano, L., & Berrone, P. (2014). Are family firms really more socially responsible? *Entrepreneurship Theory and Practice*, *38*(6), 1295–1316.

Dalpiaz, E., Tracey, P., & Phillips, N. (2014). Succession narratives in family business: The case of Alessi. *Entrepreneurship Theory and Practice*, *38*(6), 1375–1394.

De Massis, A., Kotlar, J., Campopiano, G., & Cassia, L. (2015). The Impact of Family Involvement on SME s′ Performance: Theory and Evidence. *Journal of Small Business Management*, *53*(4), 924–948. doi:10.1111/jsbm.12093

Dekker, J. C., Lybaert, N., Steijvers, T., Depaire, B., & Mercken, R. (2013). Family firm types based on the professionalization construct: Exploratory research. *Family Business Review*, *26*(1), 81–99. doi:10.1177/0894486512445614

Dillman, D. A. (1978). *Mail and telephone surveys: The total design method* (Vol. 19). New York: Wiley.

Distelberg, B. J., & Blow, A. (2011). Variations in family system boundaries. *Family Business Review*, *24*(1), 28–46. doi:10.1177/0894486510393502

Dyer Gibb Jr, W. (2006). Examining the "family effect" on firm performance. *Family Business Review*, *19*(4), 253–273. doi:10.1111/j.1741-6248.2006.00074.x

Erdogan, I., Rondi, E., & De Massis, A. (2019). Managing the tradition and innovation paradox in family firms: A family imprinting perspective. *Entrepreneurship Theory and Practice*.

Gallo, M. A., & Kenyon-Rouvinez, D. (2005). The importance of family and business governance. In *Family Business* (pp. 45–57). London: Palgrave Macmillan. doi:10.1057/9780230287730_4

García-Álvarez, E., & López-Sintas, J. (2001). A taxonomy of founders based on values: The root of family business heterogeneity. *Family Business Review*, *14*(3), 209–230. doi:10.1111/j.1741-6248.2001.00209.x

Gersick, K. E., Gersick, K. E., Davis, J. A., Hampton, M. M., & Lansberg, I. (1997). *Generation to generation: Life cycles of the family business*. Harvard Business Press.

Gnan, L., Montemerlo, D., & Sharma, P. (2005). Ownership and governance structures: towards a typology of Italian family firms. *The Family business network: annual world conference*.

Hair, J. F., Anderson, R. E., Tatham, R. L., & Black, W. C. (1998). *Multivariate data analysis*. Englewood Cliffs, NJ: Prentice Hall.

Holt, D. T., Pearson, A. W., Carr, J. C., & Barnett, T. (2017). Family firm (s) outcomes model: Structuring financial and nonfinancial outcomes across the family and firm. *Family Business Review*, *30*(2), 182–202. doi:10.1177/0894486516680930

Jaskiewicz, P., & Dyer, W. G. (2017). Addressing the elephant in the room: Disentangling family heterogeneity to advance family business research. *Family Business Review*, *30*(2), 111–118. doi:10.1177/0894486517700469

Kidwell, R. E., Eddleston, K. A., & Kellermanns, F. W. (2018). Learning bad habits across generations: How negative imprints affect human resource management in the family firm. *Human Resource Management Review*, *28*(1), 5–17. doi:10.1016/j.hrmr.2017.05.002

Lehman, D. R. (1979). *Market research and analysis*. Homewood, IL: Irwin.

Leiß, G., & Zehrer, A. (2018). Intergenerational communication in family firm succession. *Journal of Family Business Management*, *8*(1), 75–90. doi:10.1108/JFBM-09-2017-0025

Li, Z., & Daspit, J. J. (2016). Understanding family firm innovation heterogeneity: A typology of family governance and socioemotional wealth intentions. *Journal of Family Business Management*, *6*(2), 103–121. doi:10.1108/JFBM-02-2015-0010

Miller, D., & Le Breton–Miller, I. (2014). Deconstructing socioemotional wealth. *Entrepreneurship Theory and Practice*, *38*(7), 713–720. doi:10.1111/etap.12111

Miller, D., Le Breton-Miller, I., Amore, M. D., Minichilli, A., & Corbetta, G. (2017). Institutional logics, family firm governance and performance. *Journal of Business Venturing*, *32*(6), 674–693. doi:10.1016/j.jbusvent.2017.08.001

Miller, D., Minichilli, A., & Corbetta, G. (2013). Is family leadership always beneficial? *Strategic Management Journal*, *34*(5), 553–571. doi:10.1002mj.2024

Minichilli, A., Corbetta, G., & MacMillan, I. C. (2010). Top management teams in family-controlled companies:'familiness','faultlines', and their impact on financial performance. *Journal of Management Studies*, *47*(2), 205–222. doi:10.1111/j.1467-6486.2009.00888.x

Naldi, L., Chirico, F., Kellermanns, F. W., & Campopiano, G. (2015). All in the family? An exploratory study of family member advisors and firm performance. *Family Business Review*, *28*(3), 227–242. doi:10.1177/0894486515581951

Neubauer, F., & Lank, A. G. (2016). *The family business: Its governance for sustainability*. Springer.

Neubaum, D. O., Kammerlander, N., & Brigham, K. H. (2019). Capturing Family Firm Heterogeneity: How Taxonomies and Typologies Can Help the Field Move Forward. *Family Business Review*, *32*(2), 106–130.

Nordqvist, M., & Melin, L. (2010). The promise of the strategy as practice perspective for family business strategy research. *Journal of Family Business Strategy*, *1*(1), 15–25. doi:10.1016/j.jfbs.2009.12.001

Nordqvist, M., Sharma, P., & Chirico, F. (2014). Family firm heterogeneity and governance: A configuration approach. *Journal of Small Business Management*, *52*(2), 192–209. doi:10.1111/jsbm.12096

Poza, E. J. (2013). *Family business*. Cengage Learning.

Rau, S. B., Schneider-Siebke, V., & Günther, C. (2019). Family firm values explaining family firm heterogeneity. *Family Business Review*, *32*(2), 195–215.

Raymond, L., Marchand, M., St-Pierre, J., Cadieux, L., & Labelle, F. (2013). Dimensions of small business performance from the owner-manager's perspective: A re-conceptualization and empirical validation. *Entrepreneurship and Regional Development*, *25*(5-6), 468–499. doi:10.1080/08985626.2013.782344

Rivo-Lopez, E., Villanueva-Villar, M., Vaquero-García, A., & Lago-Peñas, S. (2017). Family offices. What, why and what for. *Organizational Dynamics*, *46*(4), 262–270. doi:10.1016/j.orgdyn.2017.03.002

Sanchez-Ruiz, P., Daspit, J. J., Holt, D. T., & Rutherford, M. W. (2019). Family Social Capital in the Family Firm: A Taxonomic Classification, Relationships With Outcomes, and Directions for Advancement. *Family Business Review*, *32*(2), 131–153.

Scholes, L., & Wilson, N. (2014). The importance of family firm trusts in family firm governance. *Entrepreneurship Theory and Practice*, *38*(6), 1285–1293.

Sharma, P. (2002, August). *Stakeholder mapping technique: Toward the development of a family firm typology*. Paper presented at the Academy of Management conference, Denver, CO.

Sirmon, D. G., Arregle, J. L., Hitt, M. A., & Webb, J. W. (2008). The role of family influence in firms' strategic responses to threat of imitation. *Entrepreneurship Theory and Practice*, *32*(6), 979–998. doi:10.1111/j.1540-6520.2008.00267.x

Suess, J. (2014). Family governance–Literature review and the development of a conceptual model. *Journal of Family Business Strategy*, *5*(2), 138–155. doi:10.1016/j.jfbs.2014.02.001

Suess, J. (2017). Understanding the transgenerational orientation of family businesses: The role of family governance and business family identity. *Journal of Business Economics*, *87*(6), 749–777. doi:10.100711573-016-0835-3

Sundaramurthy, C. (2008). Sustaining trust within family businesses. *Family Business Review*, *21*(1), 89–102. doi:10.1111/j.1741-6248.2007.00110.x

Swoboda, B., & Olejnik, E. (2013). A taxonomy of small-and medium-sized international family firms. *Journal of International Entrepreneurship*, *11*(2), 130–157. doi:10.100710843-012-0101-x

Tagiuri, R., & Davis, J. A. (1992). On the goals of successful family companies. *Family Business Review*, *5*(1), 43–62. doi:10.1111/j.1741-6248.1992.00043.x

Tàpies, J., & Fernández Moya, M. (2012). Values and longevity in family business: Evidence from a cross-cultural analysis. *Journal of Family Business Management*, *2*(2), 130–146. doi:10.1108/20436231211261871

Uhlaner, L., Matser, I., Berent, M., & Flören, R. (2015). Linking Bonding and Bridging Ownership Social Capital in Private Firms: Moderating Effects of Ownership–Management Overlap and Family Firm Identity. *Family Business Review*, *28*(3), 1–18. doi:10.1177/0894486515568974

Umans, I., Lybaert, N., Steijvers, T., & Voordeckers, W. (2018). Succession planning in family firms: Family governance practices, board of directors, and emotions. *Small Business Economics*, 1–19.

Van den Berghe, L. A., & Carchon, S. (2003). Agency relations within the family business system: An exploratory approach. *Corporate Governance*, *11*(3), 171–179. doi:10.1111/1467-8683.00316

Vardaman, J. M., & Gondo, M. B. (2014). Socioemotional wealth conflict in family firms. *Entrepreneurship Theory and Practice*, *38*(6), 1317–1322.

Vilaseca, A. (2002). The shareholder role in the family business: Conflict of interests and objectives between nonemployed shareholders and top management team. *Family Business Review*, *15*(4), 299–320. doi:10.1111/j.1741-6248.2002.00299.x

Villalonga, B., Amit, R., Trujillo, M. A., & Guzmán, A. (2015). Governance of family firms. *Annual Review of Financial Economics*, *7*(1), 635–654. doi:10.1146/annurev-financial-110613-034357

Westhead, P., & Howorth, C. (2007). 'Types' of private family firms: An exploratory conceptual and empirical analysis. *Entrepreneurship and Regional Development*, *19*(5), 405–431.

Williams, R. I., Jr. (2015). *Measuring family business performance: a holistic, idiosyncratic approach* (Doctoral Dissertation). Kennesaw State University. Doctor of Business Administration Dissertations. Paper 13.

Zellweger, T., & Kammerlander, N. (2015). Article Commentary: Family, Wealth, and Governance: An Agency Account. *Entrepreneurship Theory and Practice*, *39*(6), 1281–1303. doi:10.1111/etap.12182

Zody, Z., Sprenkle, D., MacDermid, S., & Schrank, H. (2006). Boundaries and the functioning of family and business systems. *Journal of Family and Economic Issues*, *27*(2), 185–206. doi:10.100710834-006-9017-8

KEY TERMS AND DEFINITIONS

Closely Held Family Business: A family firm whose stock is held by a small number of people pertaining to the same kin group.

Family Business: A business governed and/or managed by a dominant coalition that are members of the same family or a small number of families, in a manner that is potentially sustainable across generations of the family or families.

Family Constitution: It is an agreement that sets out the rights, values, responsibilities and rules applying to stakeholders in the family business, and provides plans and structures to deal with situations that arise in the course of the family business's operation.

Family Council: A structural device that supports meetings of the familial group. The entire family, or a representative group of their members, sets plans, creates policies and strength family communications and bonds.

Family Firm Outcome Model: Firm outcomes can be determined by assessing a set of appropriate financial, operational, and external outcomes. A FFO is a reflection of the dominant coalition—mainly the owner family—intention and vision.

Family Government System: Describes the process of joint decision-making that a family chooses to adopt based on their unique needs and characteristics. As a system, it can manage family members' competing and interrelated interests, defining roles and boundaries, and supporting the family's collective vision.

Taxonomy: Categorization that uses inductive and empirically driven methods to identify similarities and assign corresponding cases into groups. These sets of similar groups are built into larger groups, allowing for comparison between and among groups across dimensions.

Compilation of References

Aall, C. (2011). Energy use and leisure consumption in Norway: An analysis and reduction strategy. *Journal of Sustainable Tourism, 19*(6), 729–745. doi:10.1080/09669582.2010.536241

Abdellatif, M., Amann, B., & Jaussaud, J. (2010). Family versus nonfamily business: A comparison of international strategies. *Journal of Family Business Strategies, 1*(2), 108–116. doi:10.1016/j.jfbs.2010.04.004

Acosta-Prado, J. C., Longo-Somoza, M., & Lozano, M. B. (2017). Does family ownership affect innovation activity? A focus on the biotechnological industry. *Innovar (Universidad Nacional de Colombia), 27*(65), 11–23. doi:10.15446/innovar.v27n65.64886

Acquaah, M. (2003). Corporate management, industry competition and the sustainability of firm abnormal profitability. *The Journal of Management and Governance, 7*(1), 57–85. doi:10.1023/A:1022489324208

Acquaah, M., & Agyapong, A. (2015). The relationship between competitive strategy and firm performance in micro and small businesses in Ghana: The moderating role of managerial and marketing capabilities. *Africa Journal of Management, 1*(2), 172–193. doi:10.1080/23322373.2015.1025684

Addae-Boateng, S., Xiao, W., & Brew, Y. (2014). Governance Issues in Family Businesses. International *Journal of Economics. Commerce and Management, 2*(12), 1–28.

Agarwal, R., & Hoetker, G. (2007). A faustian bargain? The growth of management and its relationship with related disciplines. *Academy of Management Journal, 50*(6), 1304–1322. doi:10.5465/amj.2007.28165901

Agrawal, A., & Mandelker, G. (1990). Large shareholders and the monitoring of managers: The case of antitakeover charter amendments. *Journal of Financial and Quantitative Analysis, 25*(2), 143–161. doi:10.2307/2330821

Ahsan, M. (2017). The right people at the right time—The place does not matter. *Academy of Management Review, 42*(1), 145–148. doi:10.5465/amr.2015.0276

Ajzen, I. (1985). From intentions to actions: A theory of planned behavior. In J. Kuhl & J. Beckmann (Eds.), *Action Control* (pp. 11–39). Berlin: Springer. doi:10.1007/978-3-642-69746-3_2

Alayo, M., Maseda, A., Iturralde, T., & Arzubiaga, U. (2019). Internationalization and entrepreneurial orientation of family SMEs: The influence of the family character. *International Business Review, 28*(1), 48–59. doi:10.1016/j.ibusrev.2018.06.003

Albert, S., & Whetten, D. (1985). Organizational identity. In L. L. Cummings & B. M. Staw (Eds.), *Research in organizational behavior* (Vol. 7, pp. 263–295). Greenwich, CT: JAI Press.

Alchian, A. A. (1991). Rent. In J. Eatwell, M. Milgate, & P. Newman (Eds.), *The world of economics* (pp. 591–597). Nueva York, NY: W.W. Norton. doi:10.1007/978-1-349-21315-3_79

Alcorn, P. B. (1982). *Success and survival in the family-owned business.* Nueva York, NY: McGraw-Hill.

Alderson, K. (2015). Conflict management and resolution in family-owned businesses: A practitioner focused review. *Journal of Family Business Management, 5*(2), 140–156. doi:10.1108/JFBM-08-2015-0030

Aldrich, H. E., & Cliff, J. E. (2003). The Pervasive Effects of Family on Entrepreneurship: Toward a Family Embeddedness Perspective. *Journal of Business Venturing, 18*(5), 573–596. doi:10.1016/S0883-9026(03)00011-9

Allison, T. H., McKenny, A. F., & Short, J. C. (2014). Integrating time into family business research: Using random coefficient modelling to examine temporal influences on family firm ambidexterity. *Family Business Review, 27*(1), 20–34. doi:10.1177/0894486513494782

Allouche, J., & Amann, B. (1997). Le retour de capitalisme familiale. *L'expansion. Management Review, 85*, 92–99.

Allouche, J., Amann, B., Jaussaud, J., & Kurashina, T. (2008). The Impact of Family Control on the Performance and Financial Characteristics of Family Versus Nonfamily Businesses in Japan: A Matched-Pair Investigation. *Family Business Review, 21*(4), 315–329. doi:10.1177/08944865080210040104

Almodóvar, P. (2012). The International performance of standardizing and customizing Spanish firms. The M curve relationships. *Multinational Business Review, 20*(4), 306–330. doi:10.1108/15253831211286246

Almodóvar, P., & Rugman, A. M. (2014). The M Curve and the Performance of Spanish International New Ventures. *British Journal of Management, 2*, S6–S23. doi:10.1111/1467-8551.12022

Altman, E. I. (1968). Financial ratios, discriminant analysis and the prediction of corporate bankruptcy. *The Journal of Finance, 23*(4), 589–609. doi:10.1111/j.1540-6261.1968.tb00843.x

Altman, E. I., & Sabato, G. (2007). Modelling credit risk for SMEs: Evidence from the US market. *Abacus, 43*(3), 332–357. doi:10.1111/j.1467-6281.2007.00234.x

Álvarez, S., & González, V. (2005). Performance of Spanish firms going public: Windows of opportunity and the informative effect. *Applied Financial Economics, 15*(18), 1283–1297. doi:10.1080/09603100500391479

Amabile, T., Conti, R., Coon, H., Lazenby, J., & Herron, M. (1996). Assessing the work environment for creativity. *Academy of Management Journal, 39*, 1154–1184.

Amann, B., & Jaussaud, J. (2012). Family and non-family business resilience in an economic downturn. *Asia Pacific Business Review, 18*(2), 203–223. doi:10.1080/13602381.2010.537057

Amat, J.M. (1998). *La continuidad de la empresa familiar.* Barcelona, España: Ediciones Gestión 2000.

American Psychological Association. (2018). Retrieved from https://www.apa.org

Amit, R., & Belcourt, M. (1999). Human resources management processes: A value-creating source of competitive advantage. *European Journal of Management, 71*(2), 174–181. doi:10.1016/S0263-2373(98)00076-0

Amit, R., & Schoemaker, P. (1993). Strategic assets and organizational rent. *Strategic Management Journal, 14*(1), 33–46. doi:10.1002mj.4250140105

Ampenberger, M., Bennedsen, M., & Zhu, H. (2012). The capital structure of family firms. In D. Cumming (Ed.), *Oxford Handbook of Entrepreneurial Finance* (pp. 167–191). Oxford, UK: Oxford University Press.

Ampenberger, M., Schmid, T., Achleitner, A., & Kasere, C. (2013). Capital structure decisions in family firms: Empirical evidence from a bank-based economy. *Review of Managerial Science, 7*(3), 247–275. doi:10.100711846-011-0077-2

Andersen, A. (1997). Research findings: Amercian family business survey 1997. Arthur Andersen.

Anderson, C. R., & Paine, F. T. (1975). Managerial perceptions and strategic behavior. *Academy of Management Journal*, *18*(4), 811–823.

Anderson, R. C., Mansi, S. A., & Reeb, D. M. (2003). Founding family ownership and the agency cost of debt. *Journal of Financial Economics*, *68*(2), 263–285. doi:10.1016/S0304-405X(03)00067-9

Anderson, R. C., & Reeb, D. M. (2003). Founding-family ownership, corporate diversification, and firm leverage. *The Journal of Law & Economics*, *46*(2), 653–684. doi:10.1086/377115

Anderson, R., & Reeb, D. (2003). Founding-family ownership and firm performance: Evidence from the S&P 500. *The Journal of Finance*, *58*(3), 1301–1328. doi:10.1111/1540-6261.00567

Andersson, S., Gabrielsson, J., & Wictor, I. (2004). International Activities in Small Firms: Examining Factors Influencing the Internationalisation and Export Growth of Small Firms. *Canadian Journal of Administrative Sciences*, *21*(1), 22–34. doi:10.1111/j.1936-4490.2004.tb00320.x

Andersson, T., Carlsen, J., & Getz, D. (2002). Family business goals in the tourism and hospitality sector: Case studies and cross-case analysis from Australia, Canada, and Sweden. *Family Business Review*, *15*(2), 89–106. doi:10.1111/j.1741-6248.2002.00089.x

Andres, C. (2008). Large shareholders and firm performance – An empirical examination of founding-family ownership. *Journal of Corporate Finance*, *14*(4), 431–445. doi:10.1016/j.jcorpfin.2008.05.003

Andrews, K. R. (1987). *The concept of corporate strategy* (3rd ed.). Homewood, IL: Richard D. Irwin.

Aragón, A., Barba, M. I., & Sanz, R. (2003). Efectos de la formación de directivos en las PYMES españolas. Estudios Financieros. *Revista de Trabajo y Seguridad Social*, *243*, 103–134.

Arellano, M., & Bond, S. (1991). Some tests of specification for panel data: Monte Carlo evidence and an application to employment equations. *The Review of Economic Studies*, *58*(2), 277–297. doi:10.2307/2297968

Arend, R. J., & Bromiley, P. (2009). Assessing the dynamic capabilities view: Spare change, everyone? *Strategic Organization*, *7*(1), 75–90. doi:10.1177/1476127008100132

Ariely, D., Huber, J., & Wertenbroch, K. (2005). When do losses loom larger than gains? *JMR, Journal of Marketing Research*, *42*(2), 134–138. doi:10.1509/jmkr.42.2.134.62283

Armstrong, J. S., & Overton, T. S. (1977). Estimating non response bias in mail surveys. *JMR, Journal of Marketing Research*, *16*(3), 396–402. doi:10.1177/002224377701400320

Aronoff, C. E., & Ward, J. L. (1995). Family-owned business. A thing of the past or a model of the future? *Family Business Review*, *8*(2), 121–130. doi:10.1111/j.1741-6248.1995.00121.x

Aronoff, C., & Ward, J. (2016). *Family Business Governance*. London: Springer.

Arregle, J. L., Batjargal, B., Hitt, M. A., Webb, J. W., Miller, T., & Tsui, A. S. (2015). Family ties in entrepreneurs' social networks and venture growth. *Entrepreneurship Theory and Practice*, *39*(2), 313–344. doi:10.1111/etap.12044

Arregle, J. L., Hitt, M. A., Sirmon, D. G., & Very, P. (2007). The development of organizational social capital: Attributes of family firms. *Journal of Management Studies*, *44*(1), 73–95. doi:10.1111/j.1467-6486.2007.00665.x

Arregle, J.-L., Naldi, L., Nordqvist, M., & Hitt, M. A. (2012). Internationalization of family-controlled firms: A study of the effects of external involvement in governance. *Entrepreneurship Theory and Practice*, *36*(6), 1115–1143. doi:10.1111/j.1540-6520.2012.00541.x

Arteaga, R., & Menéndez-Requejo, S. (2017). Family constitution and business performance: Moderating factors. *Family Business Review*, *30*(4), 320–338. doi:10.1177/0894486517732438

Arzubiaga, U., Kotlar, J., De Massis, A., Maseda, A., & Iturralde, T. (2018). Entrepreneurial orientation and innovation in family SMEs: Unveiling the (actual) impact of the Board of Directors. *Journal of Business Venturing*, *33*(4), 455–469. doi:10.1016/j.jbusvent.2018.03.002

Astrachan, J. H. (2010). Strategy in family business: Toward a multidimensional research agenda. *Journal of Family Business Strategy*, *1*(1), 6–14. doi:10.1016/j.jfbs.2010.02.001

Astrachan, J. H., & Jaskiewicz, P. (2008). Emotional returns and emotional costs in privately held family businesses: Advancing traditional business valuation. *Family Business Review*, *21*(2), 139–149. doi:10.1111/j.1741-6248.2008.00115.x

Astrachan, J. H., Klein, S. B., & Smyrnios, K. X. (2002). The F-PEC scale of family influence: A proposal for solving the family business definition problem. *Family Business Review*, *15*(1), 45–58. doi:10.1111/j.1741-6248.2002.00045.x

Astrachan, J. H., Zahra, S. A., & Sharma, P. (2003). *Family-sponsored ventures*. Kansas City, MO: Kauffman Fondation.

Ateljevic, I., & Doorne, S. (2000). Staying within the fence: Lifestyle entrepreneurship in tourism. *Journal of Sustainable Tourism*, *8*(5), 378–392. doi:10.1080/09669580008667374

Ateljevic, J. (2007). Small tourism firms and management practices in New Zeland: The Centre Stage Macro Region. *Tourism Management*, *28*(1), 307–316. doi:10.1016/j.tourman.2006.07.004

Athreye, S. S. (2005). The Indian software industry and its evolving service capability. *Industrial and Corporate Change*, *14*(3), 393–418. doi:10.1093/icc/dth056

Atinc, G., Kroll, M., & Walters, B. (2017). Detrimental effects of post-IPO corporate governance changes: The case of young entrepreneurial firms. *Management Decision*, *55*(2), 234–247. doi:10.1108/MD-02-2016-0084

Audretsch, D. B., Hülsbeck, M., & Lehmann, E. E. (2013). Families as active monitors of firm performance. *Journal of Family Business Strategy*, *4*(2), 118–130. doi:10.1016/j.jfbs.2013.02.002

Axinn, C. N., Savitt, R., Sinkula, J. M., & Thatch, S. V. (1995). Export Intention, Beliefs, and Behaviors in Smaller Industrial Firms. *Journal of Business Research*, *32*(1), 49–55. doi:10.1016/0148-2963(94)00009-4

Ayala, J. C., & Navarrete, E. (2004). Efectos, tamaño y sector sobre la rentabilidad, endeudamiento y coste de la deuda de las empresas familiares riojanas. *Cuadernos de Gestión*, *4*(1), 35–53.

Backes-Gellner, U. (2001). *Das insdustrielle Familienunternehmen – Kontinuität im Wandel*. Bonn: Institut für Mittelstandforschung.

Bamiatzi, V., Bozos, K., Cavusgil, S. T., & Hult, G. T. M. (2016). Revisiting the firm, industry and country effects on profitability under recessionary and expansion periods: A multi-level analysis. *Strategic Management Journal*, *22*(1), 1–26.

Bamiatzi, V., & Hall, G. (2009). Firm versus sector effects on profitability and growth: The importance of size and interaction. *International Journal of the Economics of Business*, *16*(2), 205–220. doi:10.1080/13571510902917517

Bammens, Y., Notelaers, G., & Gils, A. (2015). Implications of family business employment for employees' innovative work involvement. *Family Business Review*, *28*(2), 123–144. doi:10.1177/0894486513520615

Bammens, Y., Voordeckers, W., & Van Gils, A. (2011). Boards of directors in family businesses: A literature review and research agenda. *International Journal of Management Reviews*, *13*(2), 134–152. doi:10.1111/j.1468-2370.2010.00289.x

Banalieva, E. R., & Eddleston, K. A. (2011). Home-region focus and performance of family firms: The role of family vs. non-family leaders. *Journal of International Business Studies*, *42*(8), 1060–1072. doi:10.1057/jibs.2011.28

Bannò, M., & Sgobbi, F. (2016). Family business characteristics and the approach to HRM in overseas ventures. *Journal of Small Business Management*, *54*(2), 640–658. doi:10.1111/jsbm.12162

Barach, J. A., Ganitsky, J. B., Carson, J. A., & Doochin, B. A. (1988). Entry of the next generation: Strategic challenge for family business. *Journal of Small Business Management*, *26*, 49–56.

Barach, J. A., & Gantisky, J. B. (1995). Successful succession in family business. *Family Business Review*, *8*(2), 131–155. doi:10.1111/j.1741-6248.1995.00131.x

Barber, B. M., & Lyon, J. D. (1996). Detecting abnormal operating performance: The empirical power of specification of test-statistics. *Journal of Financial Economics*, *41*(3), 359–399. doi:10.1016/0304-405X(96)84701-5

Barnes, L. B., & Hershon, S. A. (1976). Transferring power in family business. *Harvard Business Review*, (July-August): 105–114.

Barnes, L. B., & Hershon, S. A. (1976). Trasfering power in the family business. *Harvard Business Review*, 105–114.

Barney, J. B., Clark, C., & Alvarez, S. (2002). *Where does entrepreneurship come from: Network models of opportunity and resource acquisition with application to the family firm*, Second Annual Conference on Theories of the Family Enterprise, Philadelphia, PA.

Barney, J. B. (1986). Organizational culture: Can it be a source of sustained competitive advantage? *Academy of Management Review*, *11*(3), 656–665. doi:10.5465/amr.1986.4306261

Barney, J. B. (1986). Strategic factor markets: Expectations, luck and business strategy. *Management Science*, *32*(10), 1231–1241. doi:10.1287/mnsc.32.10.1231

Barney, J. B. (1991). Firms resources and sustained competitive advantage. *Journal of Management*, *17*(1), 191–210. doi:10.1177/014920639101700108

Barney, J. B. (1997). *Gaining and sustaining competitive advantage*. Aldershot, UK: Addison-Wesley Publishing.

Barney, J. B., & Tyler, B. (1990). The attributes of top management teams and sustained competitive advantage. In M. Lawless & L. Gómez-Mejía (Eds.), *Managing the high technology firms* (pp. 33–48). Nueva York, NY: JAI Press.

Barney, J. B., Wright, M., & Ketchen, D. J. Jr. (2001). The resource-based view of the firm: Ten years after 1991. *Journal of Management*, *27*(6), 625–641. doi:10.1177/014920630102700601

Barney, J. B., & Wright, P. M. (1998). On becoming a strategic partner: The role of human resources in gaining competitive advantage. *Human Resource Management*, *37*(1), 31–47. doi:10.1002/(SICI)1099-050X(199821)37:1<31::AID-HRM4>3.0.CO;2-W

Baron, J. N., Hannan, M. T., & Burton, M. D. (2001). Labor pains: Change in organizational models and employee turnover in young, high-tech firms. *American Journal of Sociology*, *106*(4), 960–1012. doi:10.1086/320296

Baron, R. A. (2008). The role of affect in the entrepreneurial process. *Academy of Management Review*, *33*(2), 328–340. doi:10.5465/amr.2008.31193166

Barontini, R., & Caprio, L. (2006). The effect of family control on firm value and performance: Evidence from continental Europe. *European Financial Management*, *12*(5), 689–723. doi:10.1111/j.1468-036X.2006.00273.x

Barroso, A., Sanguino, R., & Bañegil, T. M. (2012). Diferentes criterios del concepto de empresa familiar. Una aportación desde Extremadura, España. *Ide@as. CONCYTEG, 7*(83), 611–622.

Barroso, C., Villegas, M. M., & Pérez-Calero, L. (2011). Board influence on a firm's internationalization. *Corporate Governance, 19*(4), 351–367. doi:10.1111/j.1467-8683.2011.00859.x

Barry, B. (1975). The development of organization structure in the family firm. *Journal of General Management, otoño*, 42-60.

Barua, A., Konana, P., Whinston, A. B., & Yin, F. (2004). An empirical investigation of net-enabled business value. *Management Information Systems Quarterly, 28*(4), 585–620. doi:10.2307/25148656

Basco, J. T. (2006). La investigación en la empresa familiar: Un debate sobre la existencia de un campo independiente". *Investigaciones Europeas, 12*(1), 33–54.

Basco, R. (2006). La investigación en la empresa familiar: Un debate sobre la existencia de un campo independiente. *Investigaciones Europeas, 12*(1), 33–54.

Basco, R. (2014). Exploring the influence of the family upon firm performance: Does strategic behaviour matter? *International Small Business Journal, 32*(8), 967–995. doi:10.1177/0266242613484946

Basco, R. (2017). "Where do you want to take your family firm?" A theoretical and empirical exploratory study of family business goals. *BRQ Business Research Quarterly, 20*(1), 28–44. doi:10.1016/j.brq.2016.07.001

Basco, R., Calabro, A., & Campopiano, G. (2018). Transgenerational entrepreneurship around the World: Implications for family business research and practice. *Journal of Family Business Strategy, 31*(3), 1–16.

Basco, R., & Perez Rodríguez, M. J. (2009). Studying the family enterprise holistically evidence for integrated family and business systems. *Family Business Review, 22*(1), 82–95. doi:10.1177/0894486508327824

Basco, R., & Rodríguez, M. J. P. (2011). Ideal types of family business management: Horizontal fit between family and business decisions and the relationship with family business performance. *Journal of Family Business Strategy, 2*(3), 151–165. doi:10.1016/j.jfbs.2011.07.004

Basile, R. (2001). Export behaviour if Italian manufacturing firms over the nineties: The role of innovation. *Research Policy, 30*(8), 1185–1201. doi:10.1016/S0048-7333(00)00141-4

Basly, S. (2007). The internationalization of family SME. An organizational learning and knowledge development perspective. *Baltic Journal of Management, 2*(2), 154–180. doi:10.1108/17465260710750973

Baum, C. F., Schaffer, M. E., & Stillman, S. (2007). Enhanced routines for instrumental variables/generalized method of moments estimation and testing. *The Stata Journal, 7*(4), 465–506. doi:10.1177/1536867X0800700402

Bayo, A., & Merino, J. (2002). Las prácticas de recursos humanos de alto compromiso: Un estudio de los factores que influyen sobre su adopción en la industria española. *Cuadernos de Economía y Dirección de la Empresa, 12*, 227–246.

Baysinger, B. D., Kosnik, R. D., & Turk, T. A. (1991). Effects of board and ownership structure on corporate R&D strategy. *Academy of Management Journal, 34*, 205–214.

Beavers, W. R., & Hampson, R. B. (1995). Misurare la competenza famigliare: il modello sistemico di Beavers, tr. it. In *Ciclo vitale e dinamiche familiari, a cura di F.* Milano: Walsh, Franco Angeli.

Bebchuk, L. A., & Stole, L. A. (1993). Do short-term objectives lead to under- or overinvestment in long-term projects? *The Journal of Finance, 48*(2), 719–729. doi:10.1111/j.1540-6261.1993.tb04735.x

Becattini, G. (1979). Del settore industriale al distretto industriale. Alcune considerazioni sull l'unita di indagine dell'economia industriale. *Rivista di Economia e Politica Industriale*, *1*, 7–21.

Becker, B., & Gerhart, B. (1996). The impact of human resource management on organizational performance: Progress and prospects. *Academy of Management Journal*, *39*(4), 779–801.

Becker, G. (1981). *A treatise on the family*. Cambridge, MA: Harvard University Press.

Beckhard, R., & Dyer, W. G. Jr. (1983). SMR forum: Managing change in the family firm – Issues and strategies. *Sloan Management Review*, *24*, 59–65.

Beck, L., Janssens, W., Debruyne, M., & Lommelen, T. (2011). A study of the relationships between generation, market orientation, and innovation in family firms. *Family Business Review*, *24*(3), 252–272. doi:10.1177/0894486511409210

Belsley, D. A., Kuh, E., & Welsch, R. E. (1980). *Regression diagnostics: Identifying influential data and sources of collinearity*. New York: John Wiley & Sons. doi:10.1002/0471725153

Benavides, C. A., Guzmán, V. F., & Quintana, C. (2011). Evolución de la literatura sobre empresa familiar como disciplina científica. *Cuadernos de Economía de la Empresa*, *14*(2), 78–90.

Benavides-Velasco, C. A., Quintana-García, C., & Guzmán-Parra, V. F. (2013). Trends in family business research. *Small Business Economics*, *40*(1), 41–57. doi:10.100711187-011-9362-3

Benito, G. R. G., & Welch, L. S. (1994). Foreign market servicing: Beyond choice of entry mode. *Journal of International Marketing*, *2*(2), 7–28. doi:10.1177/1069031X9400200202

Benito-Hernández, S., Platero-Jaime, M., & Esteban-Sánchez, P. (2016). The influence of cooperative relations of small businesses on environmental protection intensity. *Business Ethics (Oxford, England)*, *25*(4), 416–439. doi:10.1111/beer.12126

Bennedsen, M., & Foss, N. (2015). Family assets and liabilities in the innovation process. *California Management Review*, *58*(1), 65–81. doi:10.1525/cmr.2015.58.1.65

Bennedsen, M., Nielsen, K. M., Pérez-González, F., & Wolfenzon, D. (2007). Inside the family firm: The role of families in succession decisions and performance. *The Quarterly Journal of Economics*, *122*(2), 647–691. doi:10.1162/qjec.122.2.647

Berchicci, L. (2013). Towards an open R&D system: Internal R&D investment, external knowledge acquisition and innovative performance. *Research Policy*, *42*(1), 117–127. doi:10.1016/j.respol.2012.04.017

Bergamaschi, M., & Randerson, K. (2016). The futures of family businesses and the development of corporate social responsibility. *Futures*, *75*, 54–65. doi:10.1016/j.futures.2015.10.006

Berggren, B., Olofsson, C., & Silver, L. (2000). Control Aversion and The Search for External Financing in Swedish SMEs. *Small Business Economics*, *15*(3), 233–242. doi:10.1023/A:1008153428618

Berle, A. & Means, G. (1932). *The modern corporation and private property*. Nueva York: McMillan.

Berle, A., & Means, G. (1932). *The modern corporation and private property*. New York, NY: MacMillan.

Berrone, P., Cruz, C., & Gomez-Mejia, L. R. (2012). Socioemotional wealth in family firms: Theoretical dimensions, assessment approaches, and agenda for future research. *Family Business Review*, *25*(3), 258–279. doi:10.1177/0894486511435355

Berrone, P., Cruz, C., Gomez-Mejia, L. R., & Larraza-Kintana, M. (2010). Socioemotional wealth and corporate responses to institutional pressures: Do family-controlled firms pollute less? *Administrative Science Quarterly*, *55*(1), 82–113. doi:10.2189/asqu.2010.55.1.82

Bertrand, M., & Schoar, A. (2006). The role of family in family firms. *The Journal of Economic Perspectives*, *20*(2), 73–96. doi:10.1257/jep.20.2.73

Bhattacharya, S., & Ritter, J. R. (1983). Innovation and communication: Signalling with partial disclosure. *The Review of Economic Studies*, *50*(2), 331–346. doi:10.2307/2297419

Bhattacharya, U., & Ravikumar, B. (2001). Capital markets and the evolution of family business. *The Journal of Business*, *74*(2), 187–220. doi:10.1086/209670

Bianchini, S., Pellegrino, G., & Tamagni, F. (2018). Innovation complementarities and firm growth. *Industrial and Corporate Change*, *27*(4), 657–676. doi:10.1093/icc/dty008

Bigliardi, B., & Ivo Dormio, A. (2009). Successful generational change in family business. *Measuring Business Excellence*, *13*(2), 44–50. doi:10.1108/13683040910961207

Birley, S., Ng, D., & Godfrey, A. (1999). The family and the business. *Long Range Planning*, *32*(6), 598–608. doi:10.1016/S0024-6301(99)00076-X

Biscotti, A. M., D'Amico, E., & Monge, F. (2018). Do environmental management systems affect the knowledge management process? The impact on the learning evolution and the relevance of organisational context. *Journal of Knowledge Management*, *22*(3), 603–620. doi:10.1108/JKM-08-2017-0344

Björnberg, Å., & Nicholson, N. (2012). Emotional ownership: The next generation's relationship with the family firm. *Family Business Review*, *25*(4), 374–390. doi:10.1177/0894486511432471

Bjuggren, C. M. (2015). Sensitivity to shocks and implicit employment protection in family firms. *Journal of Economic Behavior & Organization*, *119*, 18–31. doi:10.1016/j.jebo.2015.07.011

Bjuggren, P. O., Duggal, R., & Giang, D. T. (2012). Ownership dispersion and capital structures in family firms: A study of closed medium-sized enterprises. *Journal of Small Business and Entrepreneurship*, *25*(2), 185–200. doi:10.1080/08276331.2012.10593568

Bjuggren, P. O., & Palmberg, J. (2010). The impact of vote differentiation on investment performance in listed family firms. *Family Business Review*, *23*(4), 327–340. doi:10.1177/0894486510379001

Blancas, F. J., Lozano-Oyola, M., González, M., & Caballero, R. (2016). Sustainable tourism composite indicators: A dynamic evaluation to manage changes in sustainability. *Journal of Sustainable Tourism*, *24*(10), 1403–1424. doi:10.1080/09669582.2015.1122014

Block, J. (2010). Family management, family ownership, and downsizing: Evidence from S&P 500 firms. *Family Business Review*, *23*(2), 109–130. doi:10.1177/089448651002300202

Block, J. H. (2012). R&D investments in family and founder firms: An agency per-spective. *Journal of Business Venturing*, *27*(2), 248–265. doi:10.1016/j.jbusvent.2010.09.003

Block, J., Miller, D., Jaskiewicz, P., & Spiegel, F. (2013). Economic and technological importance of innovations in large family and founder firms: An analysis of patent data. *Family Business Review*, *26*(2), 180–199. doi:10.1177/0894486513477454

Bloom, N., & Van Reenen, J. (2007). Measuring and explaining management practices across firms and countries. *The Quarterly Journal of Economics*, *122*(4), 1351–1408. doi:10.1162/qjec.2007.122.4.1351

Blyler, M., & Coff, R. W. (2003). Dynamic capabilities, social capital, and rent appropriation: Ties that split pies. *Strategic Management Journal*, *24*(7), 677–686. doi:10.1002mj.327

Boeker, W. (1997). Strategic change: The influence of managerial characteristics and organizational growth. *Academy of Management Journal*, *40*(1), 152–170.

Bonaccorsi, A. (1992). On the relationship between firm size and export intensity. *Journal of International Business Studies*, *23*(4), 605–635. doi:10.1057/palgrave.jibs.8490280

Boubakri, N., & Ghouma, H. (2010). Control/ownership structure, creditor rights protection, and the cost of debt financing: International evidence. *Journal of Banking & Finance*, *34*(10), 2481–2499. doi:10.1016/j.jbankfin.2010.04.006

Boxall, P., & Steeneveld, M. (1999). Human resource strategy and competitive advantage: A longitudinal study of engineering consultancies. *Journal of Management Studies*, *36*(4), 443–463. doi:10.1111/1467-6486.00144

Boyd, B. K., Dess, G. G., & Rasheed, A. M. (1993). Divergence between archival and perceptual measures of the environment: Causes and consequences. *Academy of Management Review*, *18*(2), 204–226. doi:10.5465/amr.1993.3997514

Bradburd, R. M., & Ross, D. R. (1989). Can small firms find and defend strategic niches? A test of the Porter Hypotheses. *The Review of Economics and Statistics*, *71*(2), 258–262. doi:10.2307/1926971

Bradley, M., Jarrell, G., & Kim, E. (1984). On the Existence of an Optimal Capital Structure: Theory and Evidence. *The Journal of Finance*, *39*(3), 857–878. doi:10.1111/j.1540-6261.1984.tb03680.x

Braun, M., & Sharma, A. (2007). Should the CEO also be chair of the board?: An empirical examination of family-controlled public firms. *Family Business Review*, *20*(2), 111–126. doi:10.1111/j.1741-6248.2007.00090.x

Brav, O. (2009). Access to capital, capital structure, and the funding of the firm. *The Journal of Finance*, *64*(1), 263–308. doi:10.1111/j.1540-6261.2008.01434.x

Brenes, E. R., Madrigal, K., & Requena, B. (2011). Corporate governance and family business performance. *Journal of Business Research*, *64*(3), 280–285. doi:10.1016/j.jbusres.2009.11.013

Brennan, M. J., & Schwartz, E. S. (1978). Corporate income taxes, valuation and the problem of optimal capital structure. *The Journal of Business*, *51*(1), 103–114. doi:10.1086/295987

Brickson, S. L. (2005). Organizational identity orientation: Forging a link between organizational identity and organizations' relations with stakeholders. *Administrative Science Quarterly*, *50*(4), 576–609. doi:10.2189/asqu.50.4.576

Brickson, S. L. (2007). Organizational identity orientation: The genesis of the role of the firm and distinct forms of social value. *Academy of Management Review*, *32*(3), 864–888. doi:10.5465/amr.2007.25275679

Brinkerink, J., & Bammens, Y. (2018). Family influence and R&D spending in Dutch manufacturing SMEs: The role of identity and socioemotional decision considerations. *Journal of Product Innovation Management*, *35*(4), 588–608. doi:10.1111/jpim.12428

Brown, B. (1987). Recent tourism research in South East Dorset. In Tourism and development: Overviews and Case Studies of the UK and the South West Region (pp. 57-66). Department of Geography, University of Exeter.

Brown, B. J., Hanson, M. E., Liverman, D. M., & Merideth, R. W. Jr. (1987). Global sustainability: Toward definition. *Environmental Management*, *11*(6), 713–719. doi:10.1007/BF01867238

Brunninge, O., Nordqvist, M., & Wiklund, J. (2007). Corporate Governance and Strategic Change in SMEs: The Effects of Ownership, Board Composition and Top Management Teams. *Small Business Economics*, *29*(3), 295–308. doi:10.100711187-006-9021-2

Brusco, S. (1982). The Emilian Model: Productive decentralisation and social integration. *Cambridge Journal of Economics*, *6*, 167–184.

Brush, C. (1992). *Factors motivating small firms to internationalize: The effect of firm age* (Doctoral dissertation). Boston University.

Brush, T. H., & Artz, K. W. (1999). Toward a contingent resource-based theory: The impact of information asymmetry on the value of capabilities in veterinary medicine. *Strategic Management Journal*, *20*(3), 223–250. doi:10.1002/(SICI)1097-0266(199903)20:3<223::AID-SMJ14>3.0.CO;2-M

Bryant, A., & Charmaz, K. (2007). *The Sage handbook of grounded theory*. London: Sage. doi:10.4135/9781848607941

Bubolz, M. (2001). Family as source, user and builder of social capital. *Journal of Socio-Economics*, *30*(2), 129–131. doi:10.1016/S1053-5357(00)00091-3

Buchanan, J. M. (1975). The Samaritan's dilemma. In E. S. Phelps (Ed.), *Altruism, morality and economic theory* (pp. 71–75). New York, NY: Russell Sage Foundation.

Buckley, P. J. (1989). Foreign investment by small-and-medium-sized enterprises: The theoretical background. *Small Business Economics*, *1*(2), 89–100. doi:10.1007/BF00398627

Burack, E. H., & Calero, C. M. (1981). Seven perils of family business. *Nation's Business*, *69*(1), 62–64.

Bushee, B. (1998). The influence of institutional investors on myopic R&D investment behavior. *The Accounting Review*, *73*(3), 305–333.

Buyl, T., Boone, C., & Wade, J. B. (2019). CEO narcissism, risk-taking, and resilience: An empirical analysis in US commercial banks. *Journal of Management*, *45*(4), 1372–1400. doi:10.1177/0149206317699521

Cabrera, K., De Saá, P., & Garcia, D. (2001). The succession process from a resource -and knowledge- based view of the family firm. *Family Business Review*, *14*(1), 37–46. doi:10.1111/j.1741-6248.2001.00037.x

Cabrera, K., & García, J. M. (2000). Planteamiento multinivel para el estudio del proceso de sucesión en la empresa familiar. *Cuadernos de Economía y Dirección de la Empresa*, *6*, 187–212.

Cacciolatti, L., & Lee, S. H. (2016). Revisiting the relationship between marketing capabilities and firm performance: The moderating role of market orientation, marketing strategy and organisational power. *Journal of Business Research*, *69*(12), 5597–5610. doi:10.1016/j.jbusres.2016.03.067

Cai, J., & Wei, K. C. (1997). The investment and operating performance of Japanese initial public offerings. *Pacific-Basin Finance Journal*, *5*(4), 289–417. doi:10.1016/S0927-538X(97)00021-8

Calabrò, A., Minichilli, A., Amore, M. D., & Brogi, M. (2018). The courage to choose! Primogeniture and leadership succession in family firms. *Strategic Management Journal*, *39*(7), 2014–2035. doi:10.1002mj.2760

Calabro, A., Torchia, M., Pukall, T., & Mussolino, D. (2013). The influence of ownership structure and board strategic involvement on international sales: The moderating effect of family involvement. *International Business Review*, *22*(3), 509–523. doi:10.1016/j.ibusrev.2012.07.002

Calabrò, A., Vecchiarini, V., Gast, J., Campopiano, G., De Massis, A., & Kraus, S. (2019). Innovation in Family Firms: A Systematic Literature Review and Guidance for Future Research. *International Journal of Management Reviews*, *21*(3), 317–355. doi:10.1111/ijmr.12192

Calder, G. H. (1961). The peculiar problems of a family business. *Business Horizons*, *4*(3), 93–102. doi:10.1016/0007-6813(61)90029-5

Calvo, A. R., & López, V. A. (2003). Modelo RBV y rendimiento empresarial: Análisis discriminante en PYMEs gallegas. *Boletín de Estudios Económicos*, *59*(180), 503–521.

Camagni, R., & Capello, R. (2013). Regional Innovation Patters and the EU Regional Policy Reform: Toward Smart Innovation Policies. *Growth and Change*, *44*(2), 355–389. doi:10.1111/grow.12012

Cameron, C., & Trivedi, P. (1998). *Regression Analysis of Count Data*. New York: Cambridge University Press. doi:10.1017/CBO9780511814365

Camisón, C. (2002). Las competencias distintivas basadas en activos intangibles. In Nuevas claves para la dirección estratégica. Barcelona, España: Editorial Ariel.

Camisón, C., & Monfort, V. M. (2012). La empresa turística familiar en España: importancia, perfil y competitividad. Madrid: Ministerio de Industria, Energía y Turismo (Estudios del IET).

Camisón, C. (1996). Dinámica de la competitividad de la PYME industrial española en la década 1984-94: Análisis del efecto país, efecto industria y efecto empresa. *Economía Industrial*, *310*, 121–140.

Camisón, C. (1997). *La competitividad de la PYME industrial española: estrategia y competencias distintivas*. Madrid, España: Civitas.

Camisón, C. (2001). *La competitividad de la empresa industrial de la Comunidad Valenciana: análisis del efecto del atractivo del entorno, los distritos industriales y las estrategias empresariales*. Valencia, España: Tirant lo Blanch.

Camisón, C. (2002). *Las competencias distintivas basadas en activos intangibles. In Nuevas claves para la dirección estratégica* (pp. 117–151). Barcelona: Editorial Ariel.

Camisón, C. (2004). Shared, competitive and comparative advantages: A competence-based view of industrial-district competitiveness. *Environment & Planning A*, *36*(12), 2227–2256. doi:10.1068/a3759

Camisón, C. (2005). On how to measure managerial and organizational capabilities. *Management Research*, *3*(1), 27–48.

Camisón, C. (2005). On how to measure managerial and organizational capabilities: Multi-Item models for measuring distinctive competences. *Management Research*, *3*(1), 27–48.

Camisón, C., & Boronat, M. (2004). Factores determinantes del desempeño organizativo: Efecto industria, incertidumbre y competencias distintivas. *Investigaciones Europeas de Dirección y Economía de la Empresa*, *10*(3), 127–143.

Camisón, C., & Cruz, S. (2008). La medición del desempeño organizativo desde una perspectiva estratégica: Creación de un instrumento de medida. *Revista Europea de Dirección y Economía de la Empresa*, *17*(1), 79–102.

Camisón, C., & Forés, B. (2010). Knowledge absorptive capacity: New insights for its conceptualization and measurement. *Journal of Business Research*, *63*(7), 707–715. doi:10.1016/j.jbusres.2009.04.022

Camisón, C., & Forés, B. (2015). Is tourism firm competitiveness driven by different internal or external specific factors?: New empirical evidence from Spain. *Tourism Management*, *48*(1), 477–499. doi:10.1016/j.tourman.2015.01.001

Camisón, C., Forés, B., & Puig-Denia, A. (2016). Return on capital in Spanish tourism businesses: A comparative analysis of family vs non-family businesses. *European Journal of Management and Business Economics*, *25*(3), 91–110. doi:10.1016/j.redeen.2016.04.002

Camisón, C., & Monfort, V. (2011). *La empresa turística familiar en España: importancia, perfil y competitividad*. Madrid, España: Ministerio de Industria, Turismo y Comercio.

Campopiano, G., & De Massis, A. (2015). Corporate social responsibility reporting: A content analysis in family and non-family firms. *Journal of Business Ethics*, *129*(3), 511–534. doi:10.100710551-014-2174-z

Campopiano, G., De Massis, A., & Chirico, F. (2014). Firm philanthropy in small-and medium-sized family firms: The effects of family involvement in ownership and management. *Family Business Review*, *27*(3), 244–258. doi:10.1177/0894486514538450

Canals, J. (1991). *Competitividad internacional y estrategia de la empresa*. Barcelona, España: Ariel.

Canals, J. (1995). Firm, industry and country specific advantages in international competition. In H. Thomas, D. O'Neal, & J. Kelly (Eds.), *Strategic Renaissance and Business Transformation* (pp. 107–134). Nueva York, NY: John Wiley & Sons.

Cannella, A. A. Jr, Jones, C. D., & Withers, M. C. (2015). Family- versus lone-founder-controlled public corporations: Social identity theory and boards of directors. *Academy of Management Journal*, *58*(2), 436–459. doi:10.5465/amj.2012.0045

Cao, Q., Gedajlovic, E., & Zhang, H. (2009). Unpacking organizational ambidexterity: Dimensions, contingencies, and synergistic effects. *Organization Science*, *20*(4), 781–796. doi:10.1287/orsc.1090.0426

Capasso, A. (2004). Stakeholder theory and corporate governance: The role of intangible assets. *Working Paper Series, Social Sciencesearch Network SSRN*. Retrieved from http://papers.ssm.com/sol3/papers.cfm?abstract_id:610661

Carmeli, A. (2001). High -and low- performance firms: Do they have different profiles of perceived core intangible resources and business environment? *Technovation*, *21*(10), 661–671. doi:10.1016/S0166-4972(01)00050-5

Carmeli, A., & Tishler, A. (2006). The relative importance of the top management team's managerial skills. *International Journal of Manpower*, *27*(1), 9–36. doi:10.1108/01437720610652817

Carney, M. (2005). Corporate governance and competitive advantage in family-controlled firms. *Entrepreneurship Theory and Practice*, *29*(May), 249–265. doi:10.1111/j.1540-6520.2005.00081.x

Carney, M., & Nason, R. S. (2018). Family business and the 1%. *Business & Society*, *57*(6), 1191–1215. doi:10.1177/0007650316661165

Carney, M., Van Essen, M., Gedajlovic, E. R., & Heugens, P. (2015). What do we know about private family firms? A Meta-Analytical Review. *Entrepreneurship Theory and Practice*, *39*(3), 513–544. doi:10.1111/etap.12054

Carsrud, A. (1994). Meanderings of a resurrected psychologist, or lessons learned in creating a family business program. *Entrepreneurship Theory and Practice*, *19*(1), 39–48. doi:10.1177/104225879401900103

Cartwright, D., & Zander, A. (Eds.). (1984). Group dynamics: Research and theory (2nd ed.). Evanston, IL: Row, Peterson, & Company.

Cascino, S., Pugliese, A., Mussolino, D., & Sansone, C. (2010). The influence of family ownership on the quality of accounting information. *Family Business Review*, *23*(3), 246–265. doi:10.1177/0894486510374302

Casillas, J. C., Moreno-Menéndez, A. M., Barbero, J. L., & Clinton, E. (2019). Retrenchment strategies and family involvement: The role of survival. *Family Business Review*, *32*(1), 58–75.

Casillas, J., Moreno, A., & Barbero, J. (2010). A configurational approach of the relationship between entrepreneurial orientation and growth of family firms. *Family Business Review*, *23*(1), 27–44. doi:10.1177/0894486509345159

Cassia, L., De Massis, A., & Pizzurno, E. (2011). An exploratory investigation on NPD in small family businesses from Northern Italy. *International Journal of Business. Management and Social Sciences*, *2*(2), 1–14.

Castanias, R. P., & Helfat, C. E. (1991). Managerial Resources and Rents. *Journal of Management*, *17*(1), 155–171. doi:10.1177/014920639101700110

Castanias, R. P., & Helfat, C. E. (2001). The managerial rents model: Theory and empirical analysis. *Journal of Management, 27*(6), 661–678. doi:10.1177/014920630102700604

Castrogiovanni, G. J. (1991). Environmental munificence; a theoretical assessment. *Academy of Management Review, 16*(3), 542–565.

Cater, J. J. III, & Justis, R. T. (2009). The development of successors from followers to leaders in small family firms: An exploratory study. *Family Business Review, 22*(2), 109–124. doi:10.1177/0894486508327822

Cauffman, L. (1996). El desafío de la empresa familiar: Sus relaciones. In M. A. Gallo (Ed.), *La empresa familiar 5* (pp. 99–113). Barcelona, España: IESE, Publicaciones de la Cátedra de Empresa Familiar.

Caves, R. E., & Porter, M. E. (1977). From Entry Barriers to Mobility Barriers: Conjectural Decisions and Contrived Deterrence to New Competition. *The Quarterly Journal of Economics, 91*(2), 241–261. doi:10.2307/1885416

Cavusgil, S., & Knight, G. (2015). The born global firm: An entrepreneurial and capabilities perspective on early and rapid internationalization. *Journal of International Business Studies, 46*(1), 3–16. doi:10.1057/jibs.2014.62

Cennamo, C., Berrone, P., Cruz, C., & Gomez–Mejia, L. R. (2012). Socioemotional wealth and proactive stakeholder engagement: Why family–controlled firms care more about their stakeholders. *Entrepreneurship Theory and Practice, 36*(6), 1153–1173. doi:10.1111/j.1540-6520.2012.00543.x

Cerrato, D., & Piva, M. (2012). The internationalization of small and medium-sized enterprises: The effect of family management, human capital and foreign ownership. *The Journal of Management and Governance, 16*(4), 617–644. doi:10.100710997-010-9166-x

Céspedes, J., González, M., & Molina, C. (2009). Ownership and capital structure in Latin America. *Journal of Business Research, 63*(3), 248–254. doi:10.1016/j.jbusres.2009.03.010

Chahine, S., & Goergen, M. (2013). The effects of management-board ties on IPO performance. *Journal of Corporate Finance, 21*, 153–179. doi:10.1016/j.jcorpfin.2013.02.001

Chakravarthy, B., McEvily, S., Doz, Y., & Devaki, R. (2003). Knowledge management and competitive advantage. In M. Easterby-Smith & M. A. Lyles (Eds.), *Handbook of Organizational Learning and Knowledge Management* (pp. 305–323). New York: Blackwell Publishing.

Chakravarty, A., & Grewal, R. (2011). The stock market in the driver's seat! Implications for R&D and marketing. *Management Science, 57*(9), 1594–1609. doi:10.1287/mnsc.1110.1317

Chan, D. (1998). Functional relations among constructs in the same content domain at different levels of analysis: A typology of composition models. *The Journal of Applied Psychology, 83*(2), 234–246. doi:10.1037/0021-9010.83.2.234

Chandler, A. D. (1990). *Scale and Scope: The dynamics of industrial capitalism*. Cambridge, MA: Harvard University Press.

Chandler, A. D. (1990). *Scale and Scope: The Dynamics of Industrial Capitalism*. Cambridge: Harvard University Press.

Chandra, Y., Styles, C., & Wilkinson, I. (2009). The recognition of first time international entrepreneurial opportunities: Evidence from firms in knowledge-based industries. *International Marketing Review, 26*(1), 30–61. doi:10.1108/02651330910933195

Chang, S., Wu, W., & Wong, Y. (2010). Family control and stock market reactions to innovation announcements. *British Journal of Management, 21*(1), 152–170. doi:10.1111/j.1467-8551.2008.00618.x

Chan, L. K. C., Lakonishok, J., & Sougiannis, T. (2001). The Stock Market Valuation of Research and Development Expenditures. *The Journal of Finance, 56*(6), 2431–2456. doi:10.1111/0022-1082.00411

Charmaz, K. (1995). *Grounded Theory. A Practical Guide Through. Qualitative Analysis*. London: SAGE Publications.

Chenail, R. (2009). Qualitative research like politics can also be local: A review of interdisciplinary standards for systematic qualitative research. *The Weekly Qualitative Report*, *2*(11), 61–65.

Chen, H. (2011). Internationalization in Taiwanese family firms. *Global Journal of Business Research*, *5*(4), 15–23.

Chen, H. L., & Hsu, W. T. (2009). Family ownership, board independence, and R&D investment. *Family Business Review*, *22*(4), 347–362. doi:10.1177/0894486509341062

Chen, R., & Martin, J. M. (2001). Foreign expansion of small firms: The impact of domestic alternatives and prior foreign business involvement. *Journal of Business Venturing*, *16*(6), 557–574. doi:10.1016/S0883-9026(99)00058-0

Cheung, Y. L., Rau, P. R., & Stouraitis, A. (2006). Tunneling, propping and expropriation: Evidence from connected party transactions in Hong Kong. *Journal of Financial Economics*, *82*(2), 343–386. doi:10.1016/j.jfineco.2004.08.012

Chi, J. (2005). Understanding the Endogeneity between Firm Value and Shareholder Rights. *Financial Management*, *34*(4), 65–76. doi:10.1111/j.1755-053X.2005.tb00118.x

Child, J. (1972). Organization structure, environment and performance: The role of strategic choice. *Sociology*, *6*(January), 1–22. doi:10.1177/003803857200600101

Chin, C. L., Chen, Y. J., Kleinman, G., & Lee, P. (2009). Corporate ownership struc-ture and innovation: Evidence from Taiwan's electronics industry. Journal ofAccounting. *Auditing & Finance*, *24*(1), 145–175. doi:10.1177/0148558X0902400108

Chirico, F., & Nordqvist, M. (2010). Dynamic capabilities and trans-generational value creation in family firms: The role of organizational culture. *International Small Business Journal*, *28*(5), 487–504. doi:10.1177/0266242610370402

Chirico, F., & Salvato, C. (2008). Knowledge integration and dynamic organizational adaptation in family firms. *Family Business Review*, *21*(2), 169–181. doi:10.1111/j.1741-6248.2008.00117.x

Chirico, F., Sirmon, D. G., Sciascia, S., & Mazzola, P. (2011). Resource orchestration in family firms: Investigating how entrepreneurial orientation, generational involvement, and participative strategy affect performance. *Strategic Entrepreneurship Journal*, *5*(4), 307–326. doi:10.1002ej.121

Chittoor, R., & Das, R. (2007). Professionalization of management and succession performance—A vital linkage. *Family Business Review*, *20*(1), 65–79. doi:10.1111/j.1741-6248.2007.00084.x

Chmielewski, D. A., & Paladino, A. (2007). Driving a resource orientation: Reviewing the role of resource and capability characteristics. *Management Decision*, *45*(3), 462–483. doi:10.1108/00251740710745089

Choi, Y. R., Zahra, S. A., Yoshikawa, T., & Han, B. H. (2015). Family ownership and R&D investment: The role of growth opportunities and business group membership. *Journal of Business Research*, *68*(5), 1053–1061. doi:10.1016/j.jbusres.2014.10.007

Chrisman, J. J., Chua, J. H., & Sharma, P. (2003). Current trends and future directions in family business management studies: Toward a theory of the family firm. *Colerman White Paper Series*. Available at www.usabe.org/knowledge/whitepapers/index.asp

Chrisman, J. J., Chua, J. H., & Sharma, P. (2003). *Current trends and future directions in family business management studies: Toward a theory of the family firm*. Colerman White Paper Series. Disponible en www.usabe.org/knowledge/whitepapers/index.asp

Chrisman, J. J., Chua, J. H., De Massis, A., Frattini, F., & Wright, M. (2015). The ability and willingness paradox in family firm innovation. *Journal of Product Innovation Management*, *32*(3), 310–318. doi:10.1111/jpim.12207

Chrisman, J. J., Chua, J. H., & Litz, R. A. (2003). A unified systems perspective of family firm performance: An extension and integration. *Journal of Business Venturing*, *18*(4), 467–472. doi:10.1016/S0883-9026(03)00055-7

Chrisman, J. J., Chua, J. H., & Litz, R. A. (2004). Comparing the agency costs of family and non-family firms: Conceptual issues and exploratory evidence. *Entrepreneurship Theory and Practice*, *28*(4), 335–354. doi:10.1111/j.1540-6520.2004.00049.x

Chrisman, J. J., Chua, J. H., Pearson, A. W., & Barnett, T. (2012). Family involvement, family influence, and family-centered non-economic goals in small firms. *Entrepreneurship Theory and Practice*, *36*(2), 267–293. doi:10.1111/j.1540-6520.2010.00407.x

Chrisman, J. J., Chua, J. H., & Sharma, P. (2005). Trends and directions in the development of a strategic management theory of the family firm. *Entrepreneurship Theory and Practice*, *29*(5), 555–576. doi:10.1111/j.1540-6520.2005.00098.x

Chrisman, J. J., Kellermanns, F. W., Chan, K. C., & Liano, K. (2010). Intellectual foundations of current research in family business: An identification and review of 25 influential articles. *Family Business Review*, *23*(1), 9–26. doi:10.1177/0894486509357920

Chrisman, J. J., & Patel, P. C. (2012). Variations in R&D investments of family and non-family firms: Behavioral agency and myopic loss aversion perspectives. *Academy of Management Journal*, *55*(4), 976–997. doi:10.5465/amj.2011.0211

Chrisman, J. J., Sharma, P., & Taggar, S. (2007). Family influences on firms: An introduction. *Journal of Business Research*, *60*(10), 1005–1011. doi:10.1016/j.jbusres.2007.02.016

Chrisman, J. J., Steier, L. P., & Chua, J. H. (2008). Toward a theoretical basis for understanding the dynamics of strategic performance in family firms. *Entrepreneurship Theory and Practice*, *32*(6), 935–947. doi:10.1111/j.1540-6520.2008.00264.x

Chua, J. H., Chrisman, J. J., De Massis, A., & Wang, H. (2018). Reflections on family firm goals and the assessment of performance. *Journal of Family Business Strategy*, *9*(2), 107–113. doi:10.1016/j.jfbs.2018.02.001

Chua, J. H., Chrisman, J. J., & Sharma, P. (1999). Defining the family business by behavior. *Entrepreneurship Theory and Practice*, *23*(Summer), 19–39. doi:10.1177/104225879902300402

Chua, J. H., Chrisman, J. J., & Sharma, P. (2003). Succession and nonsuccession concerns of family firms and agency relationship with nonfamily managers. *Family Business Review*, *16*(2), 89–107. doi:10.1111/j.1741-6248.2003.00089.x

Chua, J. H., Chrisman, J. J., & Steier, L. P. (2003b). Extending the theoretical horizons of family business research. *Entrepreneurship Theory and Practice*, *27*(4), 331–338. doi:10.1111/1540-8520.00012

Chua, J. H., Chrisman, J. J., Steier, L. P., & Rau, S. B. (2012). Sources of Heterogeneity in Family Firms: An Introduction. *Entrepreneurship Theory and Practice*, *36*(6), 1103–1113. doi:10.1111/j.1540-6520.2012.00540.x

Chua, J., Chrisman, J. J., Kellermanns, F., & Wu, Z. (2011). Family Involvement and New Venture Debt Financing. *Journal of Business Venturing*, *26*(4), 472–488. doi:10.1016/j.jbusvent.2009.11.002

Churchill, G. Jr. (1979). A paradigm for developing better measures of marketing constructs. *JMR, Journal of Marketing Research*, *16*(1), 64–73. doi:10.1177/002224377901600110

Cirillo, A., Ossorio, M. & Pennacchio, L. (in press). Family ownership and R&D investment: the moderating role of banks and private equity. *Management Decision*, *57*(7), 1675-1694.

Claessens, S., Djankov, S., Fan, J. P., & Lang, L. H. (2002). Disentangling the incentive and entrenchment effects of large shareholdings. *The Journal of Finance*, *57*(6), 2741–2771. doi:10.1111/1540-6261.00511

Classen, N., Van Gils, A., Bammens, Y., & Carree, M. (2012). Accessing resources from innovation partners: The search breadth of family SMEs. *Journal of Small Business Management*, *50*(2), 191–215. doi:10.1111/j.1540-627X.2012.00350.x

Claver, E., Rienda, L., Pertusa, E.M. (2004). Un marco teórico para la continuidad de la empresa familiar desde un punto de vista estratégico. *Esic Market, Mayo-Agosto*, 229-257.

Claver, E., Rienda, L., & Quer, D. (2007). The internationalisation process in family firms: Choice of market entry strategies. *Journal of General Management*, *33*(1), 1–14. doi:10.1177/030630700703300101

Claver, E., Rienda, L., & Quer, D. (2009). Family firms´ international commitment: The influence of family-related factors. *Family Business Review*, *22*(2), 25–135. doi:10.1177/0894486508330054

Clemente, J. A., & Soborg, F. (2018). Costs of debt, tax benefits and a new measure of non-debt tax shields: Examining debt conservatism in Spanish listed firms. *Spanish Accounting Review*, *21*(2), 162–175.

Cohen, J., Cohen, P., West, S. G., & Aiken, L. (2003). Applied Multiple Regression / Correlation Analysis for the Behavioral Sciences (3rd ed.). Mahwah, NJ: Lawrence Erlbaum Associates.

Cohen, A., & Sharma, P. (2016). *Entrepreneurs in every generation: How successful family businesses develop their next leaders*. Oakland, CA: Berrett-Koehler Publishers.

Cohen, W. M., & Klepper, S. (1996). A reprise of size and R & D. *Economic Journal (London)*, *106*(437), 925–951. doi:10.2307/2235365

Cohen, W. M., & Klepper, S. (1996). Firm size and the nature of innovation within industries: The case of product and process R&D. *The Review of Economics and Statistics*, *78*(2), 232–243. doi:10.2307/2109925

Cohen, W. M., & Levinthal, D. A. (1989). Innovation and learning: The two faces of R&D. *Economic Journal (London)*, *99*(397), 569–596. doi:10.2307/2233763

Cohen, W. M., & Levinthal, D. A. (1990). Absorptive Capacity: A New Perspective on Learning and Innovation. *Administrative Science Quarterly*, *35*(1), 128–152. doi:10.2307/2393553

Coleman, S., & Carski, M. (1999). Sources of capital for small family-owned businesses: Evidence from the National Survey of Small Business Finances. *Family Business Review*, *12*(1), 73–86. doi:10.1111/j.1741-6248.1999.00073.x

Cole, R. A. (2013). What Do We Know about the Capital Structure of Privately Held US Firms? Evidence from the Surveys of Small Business Finance. *Financial Management*, *42*(4), 777–813. doi:10.1111/fima.12015

Collier, J., & Fuller, T. (2005). Corporations, ethics and global futures. *Futures*, *37*(2-3), 111–116. doi:10.1016/j.futures.2004.03.031

Collins, C. J., & Smith, K. G. (2006). Knowledge exchange and combination: The role of human resource practices in the performance of high-technology firms. *Academy of Management Journal*, *49*(3), 544–560. doi:10.5465/amj.2006.21794671

Collis, D. J. (1991). A resource-based analysis of global competition: The case of bearings industry. *Strategic Management Journal*, *12*(S1), 49–68. doi:10.1002mj.4250120906

Collis, D. J. (1994). Research note: How valuable are organizational capabilities? *Strategic Management Journal*, *15*(S1), 143–152. doi:10.1002mj.4250150910

Combs, J. G., & Ketchen, D. J. Jr. (1999). Explaining interfirm cooperation and performance: Toward a reconciliation of predictions. *Strategic Management Journal*, *20*(9), 867–888. doi:10.1002/(SICI)1097-0266(199909)20:9<867::AID-SMJ55>3.0.CO;2-6

Conant, J. S., Mokwa, M. P., & Varadarajan, P. R. (1990). Strategic types, distinctive marketing competencies and organizational performance: A Multiple Measures-Based Study. *Strategic Management Journal, 11*(5), 365–383. doi:10.1002mj.4250110504

Cool, K., & Schendel, D. (1987). Strategic group formation and performance: The case of U.S. pharmaceutical industry, 1963-1982. *Management Science, 33*(9), 1102–1124. doi:10.1287/mnsc.33.9.1102

Cool, K., & Schendel, D. (1988). Performance differences among strategic group members. *Strategic Management Journal, 9*(3), 207–223. doi:10.1002mj.4250090302

Cooper, M. J., Upton, N., & Seaman, S. (2005). Customer relationship management: A comparative analysis of family and nonfamily business practices. *Journal of Small Business Management, 43*(3), 242–256. doi:10.1111/j.1540-627X.2005.00136.x

Corbetta, G., Salvato, C. (2004). Self-serving or self-actualizing? Models of man and agency costs in different types of family firms: A commentary on 'comparing the agency costs of family and non-family firms: Conceptual issues and exploratory evidence. *Entrepreneurship Theory and Practice, summer*, 7-25.

Corbetta, G., & Salvato, C. (2004). Self-serving or self-actualizing? Models of man and agency costs in different types of family firms: A commentary on "comparing the agency costs of family and non-family firms: Conceptual issues and exploratory evidence.". *Entrepreneurship Theory and Practice, 28*(4), 355–362. doi:10.1111/j.1540-6520.2004.00050.x

Corbin, J., & Strauss, A. (2008). *Basics of qualitative research* (3rd ed.). Thousand Oaks, CA: Sage.

Covin, J. G., & Slevin, D. P. (2002). The entrepreneurial imperatives of strategic leadership. In M. A. Hitt (Ed.), *Strategic Entrepreneurship: Creating a New Mindset* (pp. 309–327). Oxford, UK: Blackwell Publishing.

Covin, J. G., Slevin, D. P., & Schultz, R. L. (1994). Implementing strategic missions: Effective strategic, structural and tactical choices. *Journal of Management Studies, 31*(4), 481–506. doi:10.1111/j.1467-6486.1994.tb00627.x

Craig, J. B. L., & Moores, K. (2006). A 10 year longitudinal investigation of strategy, systems, and environment on innovation in family firms. *Family Business Review, 19*(1), 1–10. doi:10.1111/j.1741-6248.2006.00056.x

Craig, J. B., Dibrell, C., & Davis, P. S. (2008). Leveraging family-based brand identity to enhance firm competitiveness and performance in family businesses. *Journal of Small Business Management, 46*(3), 351–371. doi:10.1111/j.1540-627X.2008.00248.x

Craig, J. B., & Moores, K. (2017). *Leading a Family Business: Best Practices for Long-term Stewardship*. ABC-CLIO.

Craig, J., & Dibrell, C. (2006). The natural environment, innovation, and firm performance: A comparative study. *Family Business Review, 19*(4), 275–288. doi:10.1111/j.1741-6248.2006.00075.x

Crespí, R., & Martín-Oliver, A. (2015). Do family firms have better access to external finance during crises? *Corporate Governance, 23*(3), 249–265. doi:10.1111/corg.12100

Croci, E., Doukas, J., & Gonenc, H. (2011). Family Control and Financing Decisions. *European Financial Management, 17*(5), 860–897. doi:10.1111/j.1468-036X.2011.00631.x

Cromie, S., Stevenson, B., & Montieth, D. (1995). The management of family firms: An empirical investigation. *International Small Business Journal, 13*(4), 11–34. doi:10.1177/0266242695134001

Cronbach, L. J. (1951). Coefficient alpha and the internal structure of tests. *Psychometrika, 16*(3), 297–334. doi:10.1007/BF02310555

Cruz, C., Gómez-Mejia, L. R., & Becerra, M. (2010). Perceptions of benevolence and the design of agency contracts. *Academy of Management Journal, 53*(1), 69–89. doi:10.5465/amj.2010.48036975

Cruz, C., Larraza–Kintana, M., Garcés–Galdeano, L., & Berrone, P. (2014). Are family firms really more socially responsible? *Entrepreneurship Theory and Practice, 38*(6), 1295–1316.

Cruz, C., & Nordqvist, M. (2012). Entrepreneurial Orientation in Family Firms: A Generational Perspective. *Small Business Economics, 38*(1), 33–49. doi:10.100711187-010-9265-8

Cruz-Cázares, C., Bayona-Sáez, C., & García-Marco, T. (2013). You can't manage right what you can't measure well: Technological innovation efficiency. *Research Policy, 42*(6–7), 1239–1250. doi:10.1016/j.respol.2013.03.012

Cuadrado Roura, J. R., & López Morales, J.M. (2015). *El turismo, motor del crecimiento y de la recuperación de la economía española.* Documentos de trabajo. IAES- Instituto Universitario de Análisis Económico y Social, Universidad de Alcalá, No. 04/15.

Cubbin, J. S., & Leech, D. (1983). The effeft of shareholding dispersion on the degree of control in British companies: Theory and measurement. *Economic Journal (London), 93*(37), 351–369. doi:10.2307/2232797

Cucculelli, M., & Bettinelli, C. (2016). Corporate governance in family firms, learning and reaction to recession: Evidence from Italy. *Futures, 75*, 92–103. doi:10.1016/j.futures.2015.10.011

Cucculelli, M., & Micucci, G. (2008). Family succession and firm performance: Evidence from Italian family firms. *Journal of Corporate Finance, 14*(1), 17–31. doi:10.1016/j.jcorpfin.2007.11.001

Cuervo, A. (1993). El papel de la empresa en la competitividad. *Papeles de Economía Española, 56*, 363-378.

Daellenbach, U. S., McCarthy, A. M., & Schoenecker, T. S. (1999). Commitment to innovation: The impact of top management characteristics. *Strategic Management Journal, 29*, 199–209.

Daily, C. M., & Dollinger, M. J. (1992). An empirical examination of ownership structure in family and professionally managed firms. *Family Business Review, 5*(2), 117–136. doi:10.1111/j.1741-6248.1992.00117.x

Daily, C. M., & Dollinger, M. J. (1993). Alternative methodologies for identifying family- versus nonfamily- managed business. *Journal of Small Business Management, 31*(2), 79–90.

Dalpiaz, E., Tracey, P., & Phillips, N. (2014). Succession narratives in family business: The case of Alessi. *Entrepreneurship Theory and Practice, 38*(6), 1375–1394.

Daspit, J. J., Madison, K., Barnett, T., & Long, R. G. (2017). The emergence of bifurcation bias from unbalanced families: Examining HR practices in the family firm using Circumplex Theory. Human Resource Management Review.

Daspit, J. J., Holt, D. T., Chrisman, J. J., & Long, R. G. (2016). Examining family firm succession from a social Exchange perspective: A multiphase, multistakeholder review. *Family Business Review, 29*(1), 44–64. doi:10.1177/0894486515599688

Davis, J. H., Allen, M. R., & Hayes, H. D. (2010). Is blood thicker than water? A study of stewardship perceptions in family business. *Entrepreneurship Theory and Practice, 34*(6), 1093–1116. doi:10.1111/j.1540-6520.2010.00415.x

Davis, J. H., Schoorman, F. D., & Donaldson, L. (1997). Toward a stewardship theory of management. *Academy of Management Review, 22*(1), 20–47. doi:10.5465/amr.1997.9707180258

Davis, J. H., Schoorman, R., Mayer, R., & Tan, H. (2000). The trusted general manager and business unit performance. *Strategic Management Journal, 21*(5), 563–576. doi:10.1002/(SICI)1097-0266(200005)21:5<563::AID-SMJ99>3.0.CO;2-0

Davis, P. (1983). Realizing the potential of the family business. *Organizational Dynamics*, *12*(1), 47–56. doi:10.1016/0090-2616(83)90026-8

Davis, P. S., & Harveston, P. D. (1998). The influence of family on the family business succession process: A multi-generational perspective. *Entrepreneurship Theory and Practice*, *22*(3), 31–53. doi:10.1177/104225879802200302

Davis, P. S., & Harveston, P. D. (2000). Internationalization and organizational grow: The impact of internet usage and technology involvement among entrepreneur-led family businesses. *Family Business Review*, *18*(2), 107–120. doi:10.1111/j.1741-6248.2000.00107.x

Davis, P., & Harveston, P. D. (2001). The Phenomenon of Substantive Conflict in the Family Firm: A Cross-Generational Study. *Journal of Small Business Management*, *39*(1), 14–30. doi:10.1111/0447-2778.00003

Dawson, J. F. (2014). Moderation in management research: What, why, when and how. *Journal of Business and Psychology*, *29*(1), 1–19. doi:10.100710869-013-9308-7

Day, G. S. (1994). The capabilities of market-driven organizations. *Journal of Marketing*, *58*(4), 37–52. doi:10.1177/002224299405800404

De Angelo, H., & Masulis, R. W. (1980). Optimal capital structure under corporate and personal taxation. *Journal of Financial Economics*, *8*(1), 3–29. doi:10.1016/0304-405X(80)90019-7

De Massis, A., Audretsch, D., Uhlaner, L., & Kammerlander, N. (2018). Innovation with limited resources: Management lessons from the German Mittelstand. *Journal of Product Innovation Management*, *35*(1), 125–146. doi:10.1111/jpim.12373

De Massis, A., Chirico, F., Kotlar, J., & Naldi, L. (2014). The temporal evolution of proactiveness in family firms: The horizontal S-curve hypothesis. *Family Business Review*, *27*(1), 35–50. doi:10.1177/0894486513506114

De Massis, A., Chua, J., & Chrisman, J. J. (2008). Factors Preventing Intra-Family Succession. *Family Business Review*, *21*(2), 183–199. doi:10.1111/j.1741-6248.2008.00118.x

De Massis, A., Di Minin, A., & Frattini, F. (2015). Family-driven innovation: Resolving the paradox in family firms. *California Management Review*, *58*(1), 5–19. doi:10.1525/cmr.2015.58.1.5

De Massis, A., Frattini, F., & Lichtenthaler, U. (2012b). Research on Technological Innovation in Family Firms: Present Debates and Future Directions. *Family Business Review*, *20*(10), 1–22.

De Massis, A., Frattini, F., & Lichtenthaler, U. (2013). Research on technological innovation in family firms: Present debates and future directions. *Family Business Review*, *26*(1), 10–31. doi:10.1177/0894486512466258

De Massis, A., Frattini, F., Majocchi, A., & Piscitello, L. (2018). Family firms in the global economy: Toward a deeper understanding of internationalization determinants, processes, and outcomes. *Global Strategy Journal*, *8*(1), 3–21. doi:10.1002/gsj.1199

De Massis, A., Frattini, F., Pizzurno, E., & Cassia, L. (2015). Product innovation in family versus nonfamily firms: An exploratory analysis. *Journal of Small Business Management*, *53*(1), 1–36. doi:10.1111/jsbm.12068

De Massis, A., & Kotlar, J. (2015). Learning resources for family business education: A review and directions for future developments. *Academy of Management Learning & Education*, *14*(3), 415–422. doi:10.5465/amle.2014.0246

De Massis, A., Kotlar, J., Campopiano, G., & Cassia, L. (2013). Dispersion of family ownership and the performance of small-to-medium size private family firms. *Journal of Family Business Strategy*, *4*(3), 166–175. doi:10.1016/j.jfbs.2013.05.001

De Massis, A., Kotlar, J., Campopiano, G., & Cassia, L. (2015). The Impact of Family Involvement on SME s′ Performance: Theory and Evidence. *Journal of Small Business Management*, *53*(4), 924–948. doi:10.1111/jsbm.12093

De Massis, A., Kotlar, J., & Cassia, L. (2012c). How do entrepreneurs of family firms perceive their competitive advantages and disadvantages compared to non-family companies? Empirical evidence from the transportation industry. *International Journal of Entrepreneurship and Small Business*, *51*(1).

De Massis, A., Kotlar, J., Chua, J. H., & Chrisman, J. J. (2014). Ability and willingness as sufficiency conditions for family-oriented particularistic behavior: Implications for theory and empirical studies. *Journal of Small Business Management*, *52*(2), 344–364. doi:10.1111/jsbm.12102

De Massis, A., Kotlar, J., Mazzola, P., Minola, T., & Sciascia, S. (2018). Conflicting Selves: Family Owners' Multiple Goals and Self-Control Agency Problems in Private Firms. *Entrepreneurship Theory and Practice*, *42*(3), 362–389. doi:10.1111/etap.12257

De Massis, A., Sharma, P. A., Chua, J. H., & Chrisman, J. J. (2012a). *Family business studies: An annotated bibliography*. Northhampton, MA: Edward Elgar. doi:10.4337/9781781002988

Deardorff, A. (1984). Testing Trade Theories and Predicitng Trade Flows´. In R. Jones & P. Kenen (Eds.), *Handbook of International Economics I*. Amsterdam: Elsevier Science Publishers. doi:10.1016/S1573-4404(84)01013-3

Decker, C., & Günther, C. (2017). The impact of family ownership on innovation: Evidence from the German machine tool industry. *Small Business Economics*, *48*(1), 199–212. doi:10.100711187-016-9775-0

Deephouse, D. L. (1999). To be different, or to be the same? It's a question (a theory) of strategic balance. *Strategic Management Journal*, *20*(2), 147–166. doi:10.1002/(SICI)1097-0266(199902)20:2<147::AID-SMJ11>3.0.CO;2-Q

Deephouse, D. L., & Jaskiewicz, P. (2013). Do family firms have better reputations than non-family firms? An integration of socioemotional wealth and social identity theories. *Journal of Management Studies*, *50*(3), 337–360. doi:10.1111/joms.12015

Dehejia, R. H., & Wahba, S. (1999). Causal effects in nonexperimental studies: Reevaluating the evaluation of training programs. *Journal of the American Statistical Association*, *94*(448), 1053–1062. doi:10.1080/01621459.1999.10473858

Dehejia, R. H., & Wahba, S. (2002). Propensity score-matching methods for nonexperimental causal studies. *The Review of Economics and Statistics*, *84*(1), 151–161. doi:10.1162/003465302317331982

Dekker, J. C., Lybaert, N., Steijvers, T., Depaire, B., & Mercken, R. (2013). Family firm types based on the professionalization construct: Exploratory research. *Family Business Review*, *26*(1), 81–99. doi:10.1177/0894486512445614

Dekker, J., Lybaert, N., Steijvers, T., & Depaire, B. (2015). The effect of family business professionalization as a multidimensional construct on firm performance. *Journal of Small Business Management*, *53*(2), 516–538. doi:10.1111/jsbm.12082

Delgado-Gómez, J. M., Ramírez-Alesón, M., & Espitia-Escuer, M. A. (2004). Intangible Resource as a key factor in the internationalisation of Spanish firms. *Journal of Economic Behavior & Organization*, *53*(4), 477–494. doi:10.1016/j.jebo.2002.11.001

Demsetz, H., & Lehn, K. (1985). The structure of corporate ownership: Causes and consequences. *Journal of Political Economy*, *93*(6), 1155–1177. doi:10.1086/261354

Demsetz, H., & Villalonga, B. (2001). Ownership structure and corporate performance. *Journal of Corporate Finance*, *7*(3), 209–233. doi:10.1016/S0929-1199(01)00020-7

Denison, D., Lief, C., & Ward, J. (2004). Culture in family-owned enterprises: Recognizing and leveraging unique strengths. *Family Business Review*, *17*(1), 61–70. doi:10.1111/j.1741-6248.2004.00004.x

Déniz, M. D. L. C. D., & Suárez, M. K. C. (2005). Corporate social responsibility and family business in Spain. *Journal of Business Ethics*, *56*(1), 27–41. doi:10.100710551-004-3237-3

DesJardine, M., Bansal, P., & Yang, Y. (2019). Bouncing Back: Building resilience through social and environmental practices in the context of the 2008 global financial crisis. *Journal of Management*, *45*(4), 1434–1460. doi:10.1177/0149206317708854

Dess, G. G., & Lumpkin, G. T. (2005). The role of entrepreneurial orientation in stimulating effective corporate entrepreneurship. *The Academy of Management Perspectives*, *19*(1), 147–156. doi:10.5465/ame.2005.15841975

Dess, G. G., & Robinson, R. B. Jr. (1984). Measuring organizational performance in the absence of objective measures: The case of the privately-held firm and conglomerate business unit. *Strategic Management Journal*, *5*(3), 265–273. doi:10.1002mj.4250050306

Detienne, D. R., & Chirico, F. (2013). Exit strategies in family firms: How socioemotional wealth drives the threshold of performance. *Entrepreneurship Theory and Practice*, *37*(6), 1297–1318. doi:10.1111/etap.12067

Devins, D. (2008). Encouraging skills acquisitions and SMEs. In R. Barret & S. Mayson (Eds.), International Handbook of Entrepreneurship and HRM, (pp. 420–433). Cheltenham, UK: Elgar.

Dharwadkar, R., Gerard, G., & Brandes, P. (2000). Privatization in emerging economies: An agency theory perspective. *Academy of Management Review*, *25*(3), 650–669. doi:10.5465/amr.2000.3363533

Dibrell, C., & Moeller, M. (2011). The impact of a service-dominant focus strategy and stewardship culture on organizational innovativeness in family-owned businesses. *Journal of Family Business Strategy*, *2*(1), 43–51. doi:10.1016/j.jfbs.2011.01.004

Diéguez-Soto, J., & López-Delgado, P. (2018). Does Family and Lone Founder Involvement Lead to Similar Indebtedness? *Journal of Small Business Management*. doi:10.1111/jsbm.12422

Diéguez-Soto, J., Duréndez, A., García-Pérez-de-Lema, D., & Ruiz-Palomo, D. (2016). Technological, management, and persistent innovation in small and medium family firms: The influence of professionalism. *Canadian Journal of Administrative Sciences*, *33*(4), 332–346. doi:10.1002/cjas.1404

Diéguez-Soto, J., Garrido-Moreno, A., & Manzaneque, M. (2018). Unravelling the link between process innovation inputs and outputs: The moderating role of family management. *Journal of Family Business Strategy*, *9*(2), 114–127. doi:10.1016/j.jfbs.2017.11.007

Diéguez-Soto, J., López-Delgado, P., & Rojo-Ramírez, A. A. (2015). Identifying and classifying family businesses. *Review of Managerial Science*, *9*(3), 603–634. doi:10.100711846-014-0128-6

Diéguez-Soto, J., Manzaneque, M., González-García, V., & Galache-Laza, T. (2019). A study of the moderating influence of R&D intensity on the family management-firm performance relationship: Evidence from Spanish private manufacturing firms. *BRQ Business Research Quarterly*, *22*(2), 105–118. doi:10.1016/j.brq.2018.08.007

Diéguez-Soto, J., & Martínez-Romero, M. J. (2019). Family Involvement in Management and Product Innovation: The Mediating Role of R&D Strategies. *Sustainability*, *11*(7), 2162. doi:10.3390u11072162

Dierickx, I., & Cool, K. (1989). Asset stock accumulation and sustainability of competitive advantage. *Management Science*, *35*(12), 1504–1513. doi:10.1287/mnsc.35.12.1504

Díez Vial, I., & Fernández-Olmos, M. (2013). Internal resources, local externalities and export performance: An application in the Iberian ham cluster in Spain. *Journal of Management & Organization, 19*(4), 478–497. doi:10.1017/jmo.2013.32

Dillman, D.A. (1978). *Mail and telephone surveys: The Total Design Method.* John Wiley & Sons.

Dillman, D. A. (1978). *Mail and telephone surveys: The total design method* (Vol. 19). New York: Wiley.

Dillman, D. A. (1978). *Mail and Telephone Surveys: The Total Design Method.* New York: John Wiley & Sons.

Ding, F., & Ma, T. (2018). Dynamic Relationship Between Tourism and Homogeneity of Tourist Destinations. *IEEE Access: Practical Innovations, Open Solutions, 6,* 51470–51476. doi:10.1109/ACCESS.2018.2841966

Distelberg, B. J., & Blow, A. (2011). Variations in family system boundaries. *Family Business Review, 24*(1), 28–46. doi:10.1177/0894486510393502

Distelberg, B., & Sorenson, R. L. (2009). Updating Systems Concepts in Family Businesses. *Family Business Review, 22*(1), 65–81. doi:10.1177/0894486508329115

Doluca, H., Wagner, M., & Block, J. (2018). Sustainability and environmental behaviour in family firms: A longitudinal analysis of environment-related activities, innovation and performance. *Business Strategy and the Environment, 27*(1), 152–172. doi:10.1002/bse.1998

Dolz, C., Iborra, M., & Safón, V. (2015). Empresa familiar, equipos directivos, diversidad y ambidiestría en las Pymes. *Revista de Administração de Empresas, 55*(6), 673–687. doi:10.1590/S0034-759020150606

Dolz, C., Iborra, M., & Safón, V. (2019). Improving the likelihood of SME survival during financial and economic crises: The importance of TMTs and family ownership for ambidexterity. *BRQ Business Research Quarterly, 22*(2), 119–136. doi:10.1016/j.brq.2018.09.004

Donaldson, L., & Davis, J. H. (1991). Stewardship theory or agency theory: CEO governance and shareholder returns. *Australian Journal of Management, 16*(1), 49–64. doi:10.1177/031289629101600103

Donckels, R., & Frölich, E. (1991). Are family businesses really different? European experiences from Stratos. *Family Business Review, 4*(2), 149–160. doi:10.1111/j.1741-6248.1991.00149.x

Donckels, R., & Lambrecht, T. (1999). Are family business really different? What we know from Western European business research that could be applied to the re-emergence of family-based. Enterprises in East Central Europe. *Family Business Review, 12*(2), 171–191. doi:10.1111/j.1741-6248.1999.00171.x

Donnelley, R. (1964). The family business. *Harvard Business Review, 42*(4), 93–105.

Donnelly, R. G. (1964). The Family Business. *Harvard Business Review, 42*(4), 93–105.

Dosi, G., Freeman, C., Nelson, R. R., Silverberg, G., & Soete, L. (Eds.). (1988). Technical change and economic theory. Pinter Publishers.

Dosi, G. (1982). Technological paradigms and technological trajectories. A suggested interpretation of the determinants and directions of technical change. *Research Policy, 11*(3), 147–162. doi:10.1016/0048-7333(82)90016-6

Dosi, G. (1988a). Sources, procedures, and microeconomic effects of innovation. *Journal of Economic Literature, 26,* 1120–1171.

Dosi, G. (1988b). The nature of the innovative process. In G. Gosi, C. Freeman, R. Nelson, G. Silverberg, & L. Soete (Eds.), *Technical Change and Economic Theory.* London: Pinter.

Dosi, G., & Marengo, L. (1993). Some elements of an evolutionary theory of organisational competences. In R. W. England (Ed.), *Evolutionary Concepts in Contemporary Economics*. Ann Arbor, MI: University of Michigan Press.

Dosi, G., Nelson, R., & Winter, S. (2000). Introduction: the nature and dynamics of organizational capabilities. In G. Dosi, R. Nelson, & S. G. Winter (Eds.), *Nature and Dynamics of Organizational Capabilities* (pp. 1–21). New York: Oxford University Press.

Dosi, G., Teece, D. J., & Winter, S. (1992). Towards a theory of corporate coherence: Preliminary remarks. In G. Dosi, R. Giannetti, & P. A. Toninelli (Eds.), *Technology and Enterprise in a Historical Perspective* (pp. 185–211). Oxford, UK: Clarendon Press.

Dredge, D., & Jenkins, J. (2003). Destination place identity and regional tourism policy. *Tourism Geographies*, *5*(4), 383–407. doi:10.1080/1461668032000129137

Drnevich, P. L., & Kriauciunas, A. P. (2011). Clarifying the conditions and limits of the contributions of ordinary and dynamic capabilities to relative firm performance. *Strategic Management Journal*, *32*(3), 254–279. doi:10.1002mj.882

Duchek, S. (2019). Organizational resilience: a capability-based conceptualization. *Business Research, 1-32, https://doi.org/10.1007/s40685-019-0085-7.*

Duh, M. (2015). Succession process: A chance for rebirth or failure of a family business. *International Journal of Business and Management*, *10*(3), 45–52. doi:10.5539/ijbm.v10n3p45

Dukerich, J. M., Golden, B., & Shortell, S. M. (2002). Beauty is in the eye of the beholder: The impact of organizational identification, identity, and image on the cooperative behaviors of physicians. *Administrative Science Quarterly*, *47*(3), 507–533. doi:10.2307/3094849

Dul, J. (2016). Identifying single necessary conditions with NCA and fsQCA. *Journal of Business Research*, *69*(4), 1516–1523. doi:10.1016/j.jbusres.2015.10.134

Duncan, R. B. (1976). The ambidextrous organization: Designing dual structures for innovation. *The Management of Organization, 1*(1), 167-188.

Duncan, R. (1973). Multiple decision making structures in adapting to the environmental uncertainty: The impact of organizational effectiveness. *Human Relations*, *26*(3), 273–291. doi:10.1177/001872677302600301

Dunn, B. (1995). Success themes in Scottish family enterprises: Philosophies and practices through the generations. *Family Business Review*, *8*(1), 17–28. doi:10.1111/j.1741-6248.1995.00017.x

Dunn, B. (1999). The family factor: The impact of family relationship dynamics on business owning families during transitions. *Family Business Review*, *12*(1), 41–57. doi:10.1111/j.1741-6248.1999.00041.x

Durán Herrera, J. J. (2008). La Geografía de la Empresa Multinacional Española. *Boletín de Estudios Económicos. 63, 193*, 15–44.

Duran, J., & Úbeda, F. (2003). A Dynamic Analysis of the Inward and Outward Direct Investment of the Newly Developed Countries. *29th Annual Conference of the European International Business Academy.*

Duréndez, A., García, D., & Madrid, A. (2007). *Culture management control systems and performance in SME family firms. VII International Family Enterprise Research Academy Conference*, June, Germany.

Duréndez, A., García-Pérez-de-Lema, D., & Mariño, T. (2015). The behaviour of family firms in relation to the Alternative Stock Market (MAB): Empirical evidence. *Spanish Journal of Finance and Accounting*, *44*(2), 208–237.

Dutta, S., Narasimhan, O., & Rajiv, S. (1999). Success in high-technology markets: Is marketing capability critical. *Marketing Science*, *18*(4), 547–568. doi:10.1287/mksc.18.4.547

Dutton J.E., & Dukerich J.M. (1991). Keeping An Eye on the Mirror: Image and Identity In Organizational Adaptation. *Academy Of Management Journal, 34*, 517-554.

Dyck, B., Mauws, M., Starke, F. A., & Mischke, G. A. (2002). Passing the baton: The importance of sequence, timing, technique and communication in executive succession. *Journal of Business Venturing*, *17*(2), 143–162. doi:10.1016/S0883-9026(00)00056-2

Dyer Jr, W. G., & Panicheva Mortensen, S. (2005). Entrepreneurship and family business in a hostile environment: The case of Lithuania. *Family Business Review*, *18*(3), 247–258. doi:10.1111/j.1741-6248.2005.00045.x

Dyer, W. G. (2006). Examining the family effect on firm performance. *Family Business Review*, *19*(4), 253–273. doi:10.1111/j.1741-6248.2006.00074.x

Dyer, W. G. (2018). Are family firms really better? Reexamining "examining the 'family effect'on firm performance". *Family Business Review*, *31*(2), 240–248. doi:10.1177/0894486518776516

Dyer, W. G. Jr. (1994). Potential contributions of organizational behaviour to the study of family-owned businesses. *Family Business Review*, *7*(2), 109–131. doi:10.1111/j.1741-6248.1994.00109.x

Dyer, W. G. Jr, & Handler, W. (1994). Entrepreneurship and family business: Exploring the connections. *Entrepreneurship Theory and Practice*, *19*(Fall), 71–83. doi:10.1177/104225879401900105

Dyer, W. G. Jr, & Whetten, D. A. (2006). Family firms and social responsibility: Preliminary evidence from the S & P 500. *Entrepreneurship Theory and Practice*, *30*(6), 785–802. doi:10.1111/j.1540-6520.2006.00151.x

Easterby-Smith, M., Lyles, M. A., & Peteraf, M. A. (2009). Dynamic capabilities: Current debates and future directions. *British Journal of Management*, *20*, S1–S8. doi:10.1111/j.1467-8551.2008.00609.x

Eaton, C., Yuan, L., & Wu, Z. (2002). *Reciprocal altruism and the theory of the family firm.* Paper presented at the Second Annual Conference on Theories of the Family Enterprise, Philadelphia, PA.

Eckrich, C. J., & Loughead, T. A. (1996). Effects of family business membership and psychological separation on the career development of late adolescents. *Family Business Review*, *9*(4), 369–386. doi:10.1111/j.1741-6248.1996.00369.x

Eddleston, K. A., & Kellermanns, F. W. (2007). Destructive and productive family relationships: A stewardship theory perspective. *Journal of Business Venturing*, *22*(4), 545–565. doi:10.1016/j.jbusvent.2006.06.004

Eddleston, K. A., Kellermanns, F. W., & Sarathy, R. (2008). Resource Configuration in Family Firms: Linking Resources, Strategic Planning and Technological Opportunities to Performance. *Journal of Management Studies*, *45*(1), 26–50.

Eddleston, K. A., Kellermanns, F. W., & Sarathy, R. (2008). Resource configuration in family firms: Linking resources, strategic planning and technological opportunities to performance. *Journal of Management Studies*, *45*, 26–50.

Eddleston, K. A., Kellermanns, F. W., & Zellweger, T. M. (2012). Exploring the entrepre-neurial behavior of family firms: Does the stewardship perspective explain differ-ences? *Entrepreneurship Theory and Practice*, *36*(2), 347–367. doi:10.1111/j.1540-6520.2010.00402.x

Eddleston, K. A., & Kidwell, R. E. (2012). Parent-child relationships: Planting the seeds of deviant behavior in the family firm. *Entrepreneurship Theory and Practice*, *36*(2), 369–386. doi:10.1111/j.1540-6520.2010.00403.x

Eddleston, K. A., & Morgan, R. M. (2014). Trust, commitment and relationships in family business: Challenging conventional wisdom. *Journal of Family Business Strategy*, *5*(3), 213–216. doi:10.1016/j.jfbs.2014.08.003

Edelman. (2006). *La imagen de la empresa familiar en España*. Madrid: Instituto de Empresa Familiar.

Efron, B. (1982). *The jackknife, bootstrap, and other resampling plans. Society for industrial and Applied Mathematics monograph 38*. CBMS-NSF. doi:10.1137/1.9781611970319

Eisenberger, R., Armeli, S., Rexwinkel, B., Lynch, P., & Rhoades, L. (2001). Reciprocation of perceived organizational support. *The Journal of Applied Psychology*, *86*(1), 42–51. doi:10.1037/0021-9010.86.1.42 PMID:11302232

Eisenhardt, K. M., & Brown, S. L. (1998). Competing on the edge: Strategy as structured chaos. *Long Range Planning*, *31*(5), 786–789. doi:10.1016/S0024-6301(98)00092-2

Eisenhardt, K. M., & Martin, J. A. (2000). Dynamic Ccpabilities: What are they? *Strategic Management Journal*, *21*(10-11), 1105–1121. doi:10.1002/1097-0266(200010/11)21:10/11<1105::AID-SMJ133>3.0.CO;2-E

Eldridge, S., Balubaif, M., & Barber, K. D. (2006). Using a knowledge management approach to support quality costing. *International Journal of Quality & Reliability Management*, *23*(1), 81–101. doi:10.1108/02656710610637569

Elkington, J. (2004). Enter the Triple Bottom Line. In A. Henriques & J. Richardson (Eds.), *The Triple Bottom Line: does it all add up?* London, UK: EarthScan.

Ellington, E. P., Jones, R. T., & Deane, R. (1996). TQM adoption practices in the family-owned business. *Family Business Review*, *9*(1), 5–14. doi:10.1111/j.1741-6248.1996.00005.x

Ellul, A. (2009). *Control Motivations and Capital Structure Decision*. Working Paper, Indiana University.

Epstein, N. B., Bishop, D., Ryan, C., Miller, I., & Keitner, G. (1993). The McMaster model: View of healthy family functioning. In F. Walsh (Ed.), *Normal family processes* (pp. 138–160). New York: Guilford Press.

Erdogan, I., Rondi, E., & De Massis, A. (2019). Managing the tradition and innovation paradox in family firms: A family imprinting perspective. *Entrepreneurship Theory and Practice*.

Ernst, H. (2002). Success factors of new product development: A review of the empirical literature. *International Journal of Management Reviews*, *4*(1), 1–40. doi:10.1111/1468-2370.00075

Escribá-Esteve, A., Sánchez-Peinado, L., & Sánchez-Peinado, E. (2009). The influence of top management teams in the strategic orientation and performance of small and medium-sized enterprises. *British Journal of Management*, *20*(4), 581–597. doi:10.1111/j.1467-8551.2008.00606.x

Eshel, I., Samuelson, L., & Shaked, A. (1998). Altruists, egoists, and hooligans in a local interaction model. *The American Economic Review*, *88*(1), 157–179.

Esparza, J. L., García, D., & Duréndez, A. (2009). Gestión estratégica y competitiva de las empresas familiares turísticas mexicanas: Un estudio empírico. *Revista EAN*, *66*(Mayo-Agosto), 5–30.

European Central Bank. (2013). *Survey on the Access to Finance of Enterprises in the euro area – October 2012 to March 2013*. Author.

European Central Bank. (2018). *Survey on the Access to Finance of Enterprises in the euro area – October 2018 to March 2019*. Author.

European Commission. (2017). *2017 EU Industrial R&D Investment Scoreboard*. Luxembourg: European Commission.

Faems, D., Van Looy, B., & Debackere, K. (2005). Interorganizational collaboration and innovation: Toward a portfolio approach. *Journal of Product Innovation Management*, *22*(3), 238–250. doi:10.1111/j.0737-6782.2005.00120.x

Fahed-sreih, J., & Djoundourian, S. (2006). Determinants of longevity and success in Lebanese family businesses: An exploratory study. *Family Business Review*, *19*(3), 225–234. doi:10.1111/j.1741-6248.2006.00071.x

Fama, E. F., & French, K. R. (2002). Testing trade-off and pecking order predictions about dividends and debt. *Review of Financial Studies*, *15*(1), 1–33. doi:10.1093/rfs/15.1.1

Fama, E. F., & Jensen, M. C. (1985). Organizational forms and investment decisions. *Journal of Financial Economics*, *14*(1), 101–119. doi:10.1016/0304-405X(85)90045-5

Fama, E., & Jensen, M. (1983). Separation of ownership and control. *The Journal of Law & Economics*, *26*(2), 301–325. doi:10.1086/467037

Fama, E., & Jensen, M. (1983b). Agency problems and residual claims. *The Journal of Law & Economics*, *26*(2), 327–349. doi:10.1086/467038

Family Firm Institute. (2018). *Global data points*. Available at: https://my.ffi.org/page/globaldatapoints

Fang, H., Memili, E., Van de Graaff Randolph, R., & Chrisman, J. J. (2016). Does size matter? The moderating effects of firm size on the employment of non-family managers in privately-held family SMEs. *Entrepreneurship Theory and Practice*, *40*(5), 1017–1039. doi:10.1111/etap.12156

Farinas, J. C., & Jaumandreu, J. (1999). *La empresa industrial en la década de los noventa*. Madrid: Fundación Argentaria/ Visor Dis.

Farinós, J. E., García, C. J., & Ibáñez, A. M. (2007). Operating and stock market performance of state-owned enterprise privatizations: The Spanish experience. *International Review of Financial Analysis*, *16*(4), 367–389. doi:10.1016/j.irfa.2007.01.001

Felin, T., Foss, N. J., Heimeriks, K. H., & Madsen, T. L. (2012). Microfoundations of routines and capabilities: Individuals, processes, and structure. *Journal of Management Studies*, *49*(8), 1351–1374. doi:10.1111/j.1467-6486.2012.01052.x

Fendt, J., & Sachs, W. (2008). Grounded theory method in management research. Users' perspectives. *Organizational Research Methods*, *11*(3), 430–455. doi:10.1177/1094428106297812

Fernández-Mesa, A., Iborra, M., & Safón, V. (2013). CEO-TMT interaction: Do tenure and age affect ambidexterity dynamism? *European Journal of International Management*, *7*(1), 31–55. doi:10.1504/EJIM.2013.052098

Fernández-Olmos, M. (2011). The determinants of internationalization: Evidence from the wine industry. *Applied Economic Perspectives and Policy*, *33*(3), 384–401. doi:10.1093/aepp/ppr017

Fernandez, Z., & Nieto, M. J. (2005). Internationalization strategy of small and medium-sized family businesses: Some influential factors. *Family Business Review*, *18*(1), 77–89. doi:10.1111/j.1741-6248.2005.00031.x

Fernández, Z., & Nieto, M. J. (2005). La estrategia de internacionalización de la pequeña empresa familiar. *Cuadernos de Economía y Dirección de la Empresa*, *22*, 107–126.

Fernández, Z., & Nieto, M. J. (2006). Impact of ownership on the international involvement of SMEs. *Journal of International Business Studies*, *37*(3), 340–351. doi:10.1057/palgrave.jibs.8400196

Ferreira, J. V. (2016). *The Performance of Family Firms after Going Public*. Working paper available at SSRN: https://ssrn.com/abstract=2906411

Ferreira, J. V. (2008). Determinants of performance of closely-held (family) firms after going public: The role of the ownership structure, economy, changes in top management, partial sale, equity concentration after the IPO and shareholders in management. *Corporate Ownership & Control*, *5*(2), 55–67. doi:10.22495/cocv5i2p5

Fiegener, M. K. (2005). Determinants of board participation in the strategic decisions of small corporations. *Entrepreneurship Theory and Practice*, *29*(5), 627–650. doi:10.1111/j.1540-6520.2005.00101.x

Fiegener, M. K., Brown, B. M., Prince, R. A., & File, K. M. (1996). Passing on strategic vision. *Journal of Small Business Management*, *34*(3), 15–26.

Fiegener, M., Brown, B., Prince, R., & File, K. (1994). A comparison of successor development in family and non-family businesses. *Family Business Review*, *7*(4), 313–329. doi:10.1111/j.1741-6248.1994.00313.x

Filser, M., De Massis, A., Gast, J., Kraus, S., & Niemand, T. (2018). Tracing the roots of innovativeness in family SMEs: The effect of family functionality and socioemotional-wealth. *Journal of Product Innovation Management*, *35*(4), 609–628. doi:10.1111/jpim.12433

Finkelstein, D., & Hambrick, D. C. (1990). Top management team tenure and organizational outcomes: The moderating role of managerial discretion. *Administrative Science Quarterly*, *35*(3), 484–503. doi:10.2307/2393314

Fiol, C. M. (1991). Managing culture as a competitive resource: An identity-based view of sustainable competitive advantage. *Journal of Management*, *17*(1), 191–211. doi:10.1177/014920639101700112

Fiol, C. M., Pratt, G. M., & O'Connor, E. J. (2009). Managing Intractable Identity Conflicts. *Academy of Management Review*, *34*(1), 32–55. doi:10.5465/amr.2009.35713276

Fiss, P. C. (2007). A set-theoretic approach to organizational configurations. *Academy of Management Review*, *32*(4), 1180–1198. doi:10.5465/amr.2007.26586092

Fiss, P. C. (2011). Building better causal theories: A fuzzy set approach to typologies in organization research. *Academy of Management Journal*, *54*(2), 393–420. doi:10.5465/amj.2011.60263120

Fletcher, D., De Massis, A., & Nordqvist, M. (2016). Qualitative research practices and family business scholarship: A review and future research agenda. *Journal of Family Business Strategy*, *7*(1), 8–25. doi:10.1016/j.jfbs.2015.08.001

Fondas, N., & Wiersema, M. (1997). Changing of the guard: The influence of CEO socialization on strategic change. *Journal of Management Studies*, *34*(4), 561–584. doi:10.1111/1467-6486.00063

Font, X., Garay, L., & Jones, S. (2016). Sustainability motivations and practices in small tourism enterprises in European protected areas. *Journal of Cleaner Production*, *137*, 1439–1448. doi:10.1016/j.jclepro.2014.01.071

Foo, M.-D. (2011). Emotions and entrepreneurial opportunity evaluation. *Entrepreneurship Theory and Practice*, *35*(2), 375–393. doi:10.1111/j.1540-6520.2009.00357.x

Forbes, D. P., & Milliken, F. J. (1999). Cognition and corporate governance: Understanding boards of directors as strategic decision-making groups. *Academy of Management Review*, *24*(3), 489–505. doi:10.5465/amr.1999.2202133

Ford, C. M., & Gioia, D. A. (1995). *Creative action in organizations: Ivory tower visions and real world voices*. Newbury Park, MA: Sage Publications.

Frambach, R. T., Fiss, P. C., & Ingenbleek, P. T. (2016). How important is customer orientation for firm performance? A fuzzy set analysis of orientations, strategies and environments. *Journal of Business Research*, *69*(4), 1428–1436. doi:10.1016/j.jbusres.2015.10.120

Frank, H., Lueger, M., Nose´, L., & Suchy, D. (2010). The concept of "Familiness": Literature review and systems theory-based reflections. *Journal of Family Business Strategy*, *1*(3), 119–130. doi:10.1016/j.jfbs.2010.08.001

Franks, J., Mayer, C., Volpin, P., & Wagner, H. F. (2012). The life cycle of family ownership: International evidence. *Review of Financial Studies*, *25*(6), 1675–1712. doi:10.1093/rfs/hhr135

Freeman, C. (1976). *Economics of industrial innovation*. London, UK: Pinter.

Freudenberger, H. J., Freedheim, D. K., & Kurtz, T. S. (1989). Treatment of individuals in family business. *Psychotherapy (Chicago, Ill.)*, *26*(1), 47–53. doi:10.1037/h0085404

Friedman, M., & Friedman, S. (1994). How to run a family business. Cincinnati, OH: Better way Books.

Friedman, E., Johnson, S., & Mitton, T. (2003). Propping and tunneling. *Journal of Comparative Economics*, *31*(4), 732–750. doi:10.1016/j.jce.2003.08.004

Froot, K. A., Perold, A. F., & Stein, J. C. (1992). Shareholder trading practices and corporate investment horizons. *Journal of Applied Corporate Finance*, *5*(2), 42–58. doi:10.1111/j.1745-6622.1992.tb00489.x

Fuchs, P. H., Mifflin, K. E., Miller, D., & Whitney, J. O. (2000). Strategic integration: Competing in the age of capabilities. *California Management Review*, *42*(3), 118–147. doi:10.2307/41166045

Fukuyama, F. (1995). *Trust: The Social Virtues and the Creation of Prosperity*. New York: Free Press.

Gagne, M., & Deci, E. (2005). Self-determination theory and work motivation. *Journal of Organizational Behavior*, *26*(4), 331–362. doi:10.1002/job.322

Gajewski, P., & Tchorek, G. (2017). What drives export performance of firms in Eastern and Western Poland? *European Planning Studies*, *25*(12), 2250–2271. doi:10.1080/09654313.2017.1355890

Galende, J. (2006). Analysis of technological innovation from business economics and management. *Technovation*, *26*(3), 300–311. doi:10.1016/j.technovation.2005.04.006

Galende, J., & Suárez, I. (1998). Los factores determinantes de las inversiones empresariales en I+D. *Economía Industrial*, *319*, 63–76.

Gallego, I. (2012). *La empresa familiar, su concepto y delimitación jurídica*. Universidad de Córdoba, España: Cuadernos de Reflexión de la Cátedra PRASA de Empresa Familiar, Cuaderno nº 14.

Gallo, M.A. (2002). Unidad y confianza en la empresa familiar. *Revista IESE, junio*, 28-35.

Gallo, M. A. (1995). *Empresa familiar: Textos y casos*. Barcelona, España: Praxis.

Gallo, M. A., & Amat, J. A. (2003). *Los secretos de las empresas familiares centenarias*. Barcelona: Deusto.

Gallo, M. A., & Kenyon-Rouvinez, D. (2005). The importance of family and business governance. In *Family Business* (pp. 45–57). London: Palgrave Macmillan. doi:10.1057/9780230287730_4

Gallo, M. A., & Melé, D. (1998). *Ética en la empresa familiar*. Barcelona, España: Praxis.

Gallo, M. A., & Pont, C. G. (1996). Important factors in family business internationalization. *Family Business Review*, *9*(1), 45–59. doi:10.1111/j.1741-6248.1996.00045.x

Gallo, M. A., & Sveen, J. (1991). Internationalizing the family business: Facilitating and restraining factors. *Family Business Review*, *4*(2), 181–190. doi:10.1111/j.1741-6248.1991.00181.x

Gallo, M. A., Tàpies, J., & Cappuyns, K. (2004). Comparison of family and nonfamily business: Financial logic and personal preferences. *Family Business Review*, *17*(4), 303–318. doi:10.1111/j.1741-6248.2004.00020.x

Gallo, M. A., & Vilaseca, A. (1996). Finance in family business. *Family Business Review*, *9*(4), 387–401. doi:10.1111/j.1741-6248.1996.00387.x

Gallo, M. A., & Vilaseca, A. (1998). A financial perspective on structure, conduct, and performance in the family firms: An empirical study. *Family Business Review*, *11*, 35–47.

Gallucci, C., Santulli, R., & Calabrò, A. (2015). Does family involvement foster or hinder firm performance? The missing role of family-based branding strategies. *Journal of Family Business Strategy*, *6*(3), 155–165. doi:10.1016/j.jfbs.2015.07.003

Galve, C. (2002). Propiedad y gobierno: La empresa familiar, *Ekonomiaz, 50*(2), 158-181.

Galve, C., & Salas, V. (1993). Propiedad y resultados de la gran empresa española. *Investigacion Economica*, *17*(2), 207–238.

Galve, C., & Salas, V. (2003). *La empresa familiar en España. Fundamentos económicos y resultados*. Bilbao, España: Fundación BBVA.

Galve, C., & Salas, V. (2011). ¿Determina la propiedad familiar diferencias en las relaciones entre preferencias, comportamiento y resultados en las empresas españolas cotizadas? *Revista de Economía Aplicada*, *19*(57), 5–34.

Garces-Galdeano, L., Larazza-Kintana, M., Garcia-Olaverri, C., & Makri, M. (2016). Entrepreneurial orientation in family firms: The moderating role of technological intensity and performance. *The International Entrepreneurship and Management Journal*, *12*(1), 27–45. doi:10.100711365-014-0335-2

García-Álvarez, E., & López-Sintas, J. (2001). A taxonomy of founders based on values: The root of family business heterogeneity. *Family Business Review*, *14*(3), 209–230. doi:10.1111/j.1741-6248.2001.00209.x

García-Álvarez, E., López-Sintas, J., & Saldaña Gonzalvo, P. (2002). Socialization patterns of successors in first-to second-generation family businesses. *Family Business Review*, *15*(3), 189–203.

García-Castro, R. G., & Sharma, P. (2011). Family involvement-firm performance link: Winning configurations revealed by set-theoretic methods. *Universia Business Review*, (32): 54–69.

Gedajlovic, E. R. (1993). Ownership, strategy and performance: Is the dichotomy sufficient? *Organization Studies*, *14*(5), 731–752. doi:10.1177/017084069301400507

Gedajlovic, E. R., & Shapiro, D. M. (1998). Management and ownership effects: Evidence from five countries. *Strategic Management Journal*, *19*(6), 533–553. doi:10.1002/(SICI)1097-0266(199806)19:6<533::AID-SMJ957>3.0.CO;2-#

Gedajlovic, E., Cao, Q., & Zhang, H. (2012). Corporate shareholdings and organizational ambidexterity in high-tech SMEs: Evidence form a transitional economy. *Journal of Business Venturing*, *27*(6), 652–665. doi:10.1016/j.jbusvent.2011.06.001

Gedajlovic, E., Lubatkin, M. H., & Schulze, W. S. (2004). Crossing the threshold from founder management to professional management: A governance perspective. *Journal of Management Studies*, *41*(5), 899–912. doi:10.1111/j.1467-6486.2004.00459.x

George, G. (2005). Slack resources and the performance of privately held firms. *Academy of Management Journal*, *48*(4), 661–676. doi:10.5465/amj.2005.17843944

Geroski, P., Machin, S., & Van Reenen, J. (1993). The profitability of innovating firms. *The Rand Journal of Economics*, *24*(2), 198–211. doi:10.2307/2555757

Gersick, K. E., Davis, J. A., Hampton, M. M., & Lansberg, I. (1997). *Generation to generation: Life cycles of the family business*. Boston, MA: Harvard Business School Press.

Gersick, K. E., Davis, J. A., Hampton, M., & Lansberg, I. (1997). *Generation to generation - Life cycles of the family business*. Harvard Business School Press.

Gersick, K. E., Davis, J. A., Hampton, M., & Lansberg, I. (1997). *Generation to generation—Life cycles of the family business*. Boston: Harvard Business School Press.

Getz, D., & Carlsen, J. (2000). Characteristics and goals of family and owner-operated business in the rural tourism and hospitality sectors. *Tourism Management, 21*(6), 547–560. doi:10.1016/S0261-5177(00)00004-2

Getz, D., & Carlsen, J. (2005). Family business in tourism. State of the art. *Annals of Tourism Research, 32*(1), 237–258. doi:10.1016/j.annals.2004.07.006

Gibson, C. B., & Birkinshaw, J. (2004). The antecedents, consequences, and mediating role of organizational ambidexterity. *Academy of Management Journal, 47*(2), 209–226.

Gilbert, N. (1989). Can a family business survive merger mania and divorce? *Management Review, 78*(1), 38–42.

Gilding, M., Gregory, S., & Cosson, B. (2015). Motives and outcomes in family business succession planning. *Entrepreneurship Theory and Practice, 39*(2), 299–312. doi:10.1111/etap.12040

Gimeno, A., Baulenas, G., & Coma-Cros, J. (2010). Family business models. In *Family business models* (pp. 57–77). London: Palgrave Macmillan. doi:10.1057/9780230282148_4

Gimeno, J., Folta, T., Cooper, A. C., & Woo, C. Y. (1997). Survival of the fittest? Entrepreneurial human capital. *Administrative Science Quarterly, 42*(4), 750–784. doi:10.2307/2393656

Ginebra, J. (1997). *Las empresas familiares. Su dirección y su continuidad.* México: Panorama.

Gittell, J. H., Cameron, K., Lim, S., & Rivas, V. (2006). Relationships, layoffs, and organizational resilience: Airline industry responses to September 11. *The Journal of Applied Behavioral Science, 42*(3), 300–329. doi:10.1177/0021886306286466

Gnan, L., Montemerlo, D., & Sharma, P. (2005). Ownership and governance structures: towards a typology of Italian family firms. *The Family business network: annual world conference.*

Goel, S., & Jones, R. J. III. (2016). Entrepreneurial exploration and exploitation in family business: A systematic review and future directions. *Family Business Review, 29*(1), 94–120. doi:10.1177/0894486515625541

Goffee, R., & Scase, R. (1985). Proprietorial control in family firms: Some functions of quasi-organic management systems. *Journal of Management Studies, 22*(1), 54–68. doi:10.1111/j.1467-6486.1985.tb00242.x

Goh, S., & Richards, G. (1997). Benchmarking the learning capability of organizations. *European Management Journal, 15*(5), 575–583. doi:10.1016/S0263-2373(97)00036-4

Gómez-Mejia, L. (1988). The Role of Human Resources Strategy in Export Performance: A Longitudinal Study. *Strategic Management Journal, 9*(5), 493–505. doi:10.1002mj.4250090508

Gomez-Mejía, L. R., Campbell, J. T., Martin, G., Hoskisson, R. E., Makri, M., & Sirmon, D. G. (2014). Socioemotional wealth as a mixed gamble: Revisiting family firm R&D investments with the behavioural agency model. *Entrepreneurship Theory and Practice, 38*(6), 1351–1374.

Gómez-Mejía, L. R., Cruz, C., Berrone, P., & De Castro, J. (2011). The bind that ties: Socioemotional wealth preservation in family firms. *The Academy of Management Annals, 5*(1), 653–707. doi:10.1080/19416520.2011.593320

Gómez-Mejía, L. R., Haynes, K. T., Núñez-Nickel, M., Jacobson, K. J., & Moyano-Fuentes, J. (2007). Socioemotional wealth and business risks in family-controlled firms: Evidence from Spanish olive oil mills. *Administrative Science Quarterly, 52*(1), 106–137. doi:10.2189/asqu.52.1.106

Gómez-Mejía, L. R., Larraza-Kintana, M., & Makri, M. (2003). The determinants of executive compensation in family-controlled public corporations. *Academy of Management Journal*, *46*(2), 226–237.

Gómez-Mejía, L. R., Larrazar-Kintana, M., & Makri, M. (2003). The determinants of executive compensation in family- controlled public corporations. *Academy of Management Journal*, *46*(2), 226–237.

Gómez-Mejia, L. R., Makri, M., & Larraza-Kintana, M. (2010). Diversification decisions in family-controlled firms. *Journal of Management Studies*, *47*(2), 223–252. doi:10.1111/j.1467-6486.2009.00889.x

Gomez-Mejia, L. R., Nuñez-Nickel, M., & Gutierrez, I. (2001). The role of family ties in agency contracts. *Academy of Management Journal*, *44*, 81–95.

González-Cruz, T. F., & Cruz-Ros, S. (2016). When does family involvement produce superior performance in SME family business? *Journal of Business Research*, *69*(4), 1452–1457. doi:10.1016/j.jbusres.2015.10.124

González, E., & Ventura, J. (2002). How much do strategic groups matter? *Review of Industrial Organization*, *21*(1), 55–71. doi:10.1023/A:1016001219134

González, M., Guzmán, A., Pombo, C., & Trujillo, M. A. (2013). Family firms and debt: Risk aversion versus risk of losing control. *Journal of Business Research*, *66*(11), 2308–2320. doi:10.1016/j.jbusres.2012.03.014

Gottardo, P., & Moisello, A. M. (2015). The impact of socioemotional wealth on family firms' financial performance. *Problems and Perspectives in Management*, *13*(1), 67–77.

Gottardo, P., & Moisello, A. M. (2017). Family Firms, Risk-taking and Financial Distress. *Problems and Perspectives in Management*, *15*(2), 168–177. doi:10.21511/ppm.15(2-1).2017.01

Grant, R.M. (1996). Toward a knowledge-based theory of the firm. *Strategic Management Journal, 17*(winter special issue), 109–122.

Grant, R. M. (1991). *Contemporary Strategy Analysis: Concepts, Techniques, Applications*. Cambridge: Blackwell Publishers.

Grant, R. M. (1991a). The resource-based theory of competitive advantages: Implications for strategy formulation. *California Management Review*, *33*(3), 114–135. doi:10.2307/41166664

Grant, R. M., Jammine, A. P., & Thomas, H. (1988). Diversity, diversification, and profitability among British manufacturing companies, 1972–1984. *Academy of Management Journal*, *31*(4), 771–801.

Graves, C., & Shan, Y. G. (2014). An Empirical Analysis of the Effect of Internationalization on the Performance of Unlisted Family and Nonfamily Firms in Australia. *Family Business Review*, *27*(2), 142–160. doi:10.1177/0894486513491588

Graves, C., & Thomas, J. (2006). Internationalization of Australian family business: A managerial capabilities perspective. *Family Business Review*, *19*(3), 207–224. doi:10.1111/j.1741-6248.2006.00066.x

Graves, C., & Thomas, J. (2008). Determinants of the Internationalization Pathways of Family Firms: An Examination of Family Influence. *Family Business Review*, *21*(2), 151–167. doi:10.1111/j.1741-6248.2008.00119.x

Grewal, R., & Tansuhaj, P. (2001). Building organizational capabilities for managing economic crises: The role of market orientation and strategic flexibility. *Journal of Marketing*, *65*(2), 67–80. doi:10.1509/jmkg.65.2.67.18259

Griffin, A., & Hauser, J. R. (1996). Integrating R&D and marketing: A review and analysis of the literature. *Journal of Product Innovation Management*, *13*(3), 191–215. doi:10.1111/1540-5885.1330191

Gruber-Muecke, T., & Hofer, K. M. (2015). Market orientation, entrepreneurial orientation and performance in emerging markets. *International Journal of Emerging Markets*, *10*(3), 560–571. doi:10.1108/IJoEM-05-2013-0076

Gudmundson, D., Tower, C. B., & Hartman, E. A. (2003). Innovation in small businesses: Culture and ownership structure do matter. *Journal of Developmental Entrepreneurship*, *8*, 1–17.

Gupta, A. K., Smith, K. G., & Shalley, C. E. (2006). The interplay between exploration and exploitation. *Academy of Management Journal*, *49*(4), 693–706. doi:10.5465/amj.2006.22083026

Habbershon, T. G. (2006). Commentary: A framework for managing the familiness and agency advantages in family firms. *Entrepreneurship Theory and Practice*, *30*(6), 879–886. doi:10.1111/j.1540-6520.2006.00158.x

Habbershon, T., & Williams, M. (1999). A resource-based framework for assessing the strategic advantage of family firms. *Family Business Review*, *12*(1), 27–39. doi:10.1111/j.1741-6248.1999.00001.x

Habbershon, T., & Williams, M. (2000). A model for understanding the competitiveness of family-controlled companies. In P. Poutziouris (Ed.), *Tradition or entrepreneurship in the New Economy* (pp. 94–115). Manchester, UK: Manchester Business School.

Habbershon, T., Williams, M., & MacMillan, L. C. (2003). A unified systems perspective of family firm performance. *Journal of Business Venturing*, *18*(4), 451–465. doi:10.1016/S0883-9026(03)00053-3

Hagedoorn, J. (1993). Understanding the rationale of strategic technology partnering: Interorganizational modes of cooperation and sectoral differences. *Strategic Management Journal*, *14*(3), 371–385. doi:10.1002mj.4250140505

Hair, J. F., Anderson, R. E., Tatham, R. L., & Black, W. C. (1998). *Multivariate Data Analysis* (5th ed.). Upper Saddle River, NJ: Pearson.

Hair, J. F., Anderson, R. E., Tatham, R. L., & Black, W. C. (1998). *Multivariate data analysis*. Englewood Cliffs, NJ: Prentice Hall.

Hair, J. F., Anderson, R. E., Tatham, R. L., & Black, W. C. (1998). *Multivariate data analysis*. Prentice Hall.

Hall, A., Melin, L., & Nordqvist, M. (2001). Entrepreneurship as radical change in family business: Exploring the role of cultural patterns. *Family Business Review*, *14*(3), 193–208. doi:10.1111/j.1741-6248.2001.00193.x

Hall, R. H. (1992). The strategic analysis of intangible resources. *Strategic Management Journal*, *13*(2), 135–144. doi:10.1002mj.4250130205

Hall, R. H. (1993). A framework linking intangible resources and capabilities to sustainable competitive advantage. *Strategic Management Journal*, *14*(8), 607–618. doi:10.1002mj.4250140804

Hambrick, D. C. (Ed.). (1988). The executive effect: concepts and methods for studying top managers. JAI Press.

Hambrick, D. C. (1983). Some tests of the effectiveness and functional attributes of Miles and Snow's strategic types. *Academy of Management Journal*, *26*, 5–25. PMID:10299037

Hambrick, D. C. (1988). *The executive effect: concepts and methods for studying top managers*. Greenwich, CT: JAI Press.

Hambrick, D. C., Cho, T. S., & Chen, M. J. (1996). The influence of top management team heterogeneity on firms competitive moves. *Administrative Science Quarterly*, *41*(4), 659–684. doi:10.2307/2393871

Hambrick, D. C., & Finkelstein, S. (1987). Managerial discretion: A bridge between polar views of organizational outcomes. In L. L. Cummings & B. Staw (Eds.), *Research in Organizational Behavior* (Vol. 9, pp. 369–406). Greenwich, CT: JAI Press.

Hambrick, D. C., & Mason, P. (1984). Upper echelons: The organization as a reflection of its top managers. *Academy of Management Review*, *9*(2), 193–206. doi:10.5465/amr.1984.4277628

Hamel, G. (2007). *The future of management*. Boston, MA: Harvard Business School Press.

Hamel, G., & Prahalad, C. K. (1994). *Competing for the future*. Cambridge, MA: Harvard Business School Press.

Hamel, G., & Välikangas, L. (2003). The Quest for Resilience 2003. *Harvard Business Review*, (Sept), 52–62. PMID:12964393

Handler, W. C. (1989). Methodological issues and considerations in studying family businesses. *Family Business Review*, *2*(3), 257–276. doi:10.1111/j.1741-6248.1989.00257.x

Hansen, G., & Wernerfelt, B. (1989). Determinants of firm performance: The relative importance of economic and organizational factors. *Strategic Management Journal*, *10*(5), 399–411. doi:10.1002mj.4250100502

Hansmann, H. (1988). Ownership of the firm. *Journal of Law Economics and Organization*, *4*(2), 267–304.

Hansmann, H. (1996). *The ownership of enterprise*. Cambridge, MA: Belknap Press of the Harvard University Press.

Harries, T., McEwen, L., & Wragg, A. (2018). Why it takes an 'ontological shock' to prompt increases in small firm resilience: Sense making, emotions and flood risk. *International Small Business Journal*, *36*(6), 712–733. doi:10.1177/0266242618765231

Harris, R., Martinez, J., & Ward, J. (1994). Is strategy different for the family-owned business? *Family Business Review*, *VII*(2), 159–173. doi:10.1111/j.1741-6248.1994.00159.x

Hart, O., Shleifer, A., & Vishny, R. W. (1997). The Proper Scope of Government: Theory and an Application to Prisons. *The Quarterly Journal of Economics*, *112*(4), 1127–1161. doi:10.1162/003355300555448

Harvey, M., & Evans, R. (1994). Family business and multiple levels of conflict. *Family Business Review*, *7*(4), 331–347. doi:10.1111/j.1741-6248.1994.00331.x

Harvey, S. (1999). Owner as a manager, extended horizons and the family firm. *International Journal of the Economics of Business*, *6*(1), 41–55. doi:10.1080/13571519984304

Haugen, R. A., & Senbet, I. W. (1986). Corporate finance and taxes: A review. *Financial Management*, *15*(3), 5–21. doi:10.2307/3664840

Haveman, H. A., & Khaire, M. V. (2004). Survival beyond succession? The contingent impact of founder succession on organizational failure. *Journal of Business Venturing*, *19*(3), 437–463. doi:10.1016/S0883-9026(03)00039-9

Hawawini, G., Subramanian, V., & Verdin, P. (2003). Is performance driven by industry or firm-specific factors?: A new look at the evidence. *Strategic Management Journal*, *24*(1), 1–16. doi:10.1002mj.278

Hayes, J. L. (1981). All in the family. *Management Review*, *70*(7), 4–7. PMID:10310146

Haynes, G. W., Walker, R., Rowe, B. R., & Hong, G. S. (1999). The intermingling of business and family finances in family-owned businesses. *Family Business Review*, *12*(3), 225–239. doi:10.1111/j.1741-6248.1999.00225.x

Hayward, S. (1992). *Managing the family business in the UK: A Stoy Hayward survey in conjunction with the London Business School*. London: Stoy Hayward.

Heavy, C., & Simsek, Z. (2010). A dynamic capabilities model of organizational ambidexterity. *10th European Academy of Management Annual Conference*.

Heck, R. K. Z., & Walker, R. (1993). Family-owned home-business: Their employees and unpaid helpers. *Family Business Review*, *6*(4), 397–415. doi:10.1111/j.1741-6248.1993.00397.x

Helfat, C. E. (1997). Know-how and asset complementarity and dynamic capability accumulation: The case of R&D. *Strategic Management Journal*, *18*(5), 339–360. doi:10.1002/(SICI)1097-0266(199705)18:5<339::AID-SMJ883>3.0.CO;2-7

Helfat, C. E., Finkelstein, S., Mitchell, W., Peteraf, M., Singh, H., Teece, D., & Winter, S. G. (2007). *Dynamic Capabilities: Understanding Strategic Change in Organizations*. Malden, MA: Wiley-Blackwell.

Helfat, C. E., & Peteraf, M. (2003). The dynamic resource-based view: Capability lifecycles. *Strategic Management Journal*, *24*(10), 997–1010. doi:10.1002mj.332

Henderson, J., & Cool, K. (2003). Learning to time capacity expansions: An empirical analysis of the worldwide petrochemical industry, 1975–1995. *Strategic Management Journal*, *24*(5), 393–413. doi:10.1002mj.309

Henderson, R., & Cockburn, I. (1994). Measuring competence? Exploring firm effects in pharmaceutical research. *Strategic Management Journal*, *15*(S1), 63–84. doi:10.1002mj.4250150906

Hennart, J. F., Majocchi, A., & Forlani, E. (2019). The myth of the stay-at-home family firm: How family-managed SMEs can overcome internationalization limitations. *Journal of International Business Studies*, *50*(5), 758–782. doi:10.105741267-017-0091-y

Herhausen, D. (2015). Unfolding the ambidextrous effects of proactive and responsive market orientation. *Journal of Business Research*, *69*(7), 2585–2593. doi:10.1016/j.jbusres.2015.10.139

Hernandez-Espallardo, M., & Arcas-Lario, N. (2003). The effects of authoritative mechanisms of coordination on market orientation in asymmetrical channel partnerships. *International Journal of Research in Marketing*, *20*(2), 133–152. doi:10.1016/S0167-8116(03)00015-6

Hernández-Linares, R., Sarkar, S., & López-Fernádez, M. C. (2017). How has the family firm literature addressed the heterogeneity through classification systems? An integrated analysis. *European Journal of family. Business (Atlanta, Ga.)*, *7*, 1–13.

Hernández-Perlines, F., & Rung-Hoch, N. (2017). Sustainable entrepreneurial orientation in family firms. *Sustainability*, *9*(7), 1212. doi:10.3390u9071212

Heyman, D., Deloof, M., & Ooghe, H. (2008). The financial structure of private held Belgian firms. *Small Business Economics*, *30*(3), 301–313. doi:10.100711187-006-9031-0

He, Z. L., & Wong, P. K. (2004). Exploration vs. exploitation: An empirical test of the ambidexterity hypothesis. *Organization Science*, *15*(4), 481–494. doi:10.1287/orsc.1040.0078

Hiebl, M. R. (2015). Family involvement and organizational ambidexterity in later-generation family businesses: A framework for further investigation. *Management Decision*, *53*(5), 1061–1082. doi:10.1108/MD-04-2014-0191

Hill, C. W. L., Hwang, P., & Kim, C. (1990). An eclectic theory of the choice of international entry mode. *Strategic Management Journal*, *11*(2), 117–128. doi:10.1002mj.4250110204

Hillman, A. J., & Dalziel, T. (2003). Boards of directors and firm performance: Integrating agency and resource dependence perspectives. *Academy of Management Review*, *28*(3), 383–396. doi:10.5465/amr.2003.10196729

Hitt, M. A., Beamish, P. W., Jackson, S. E., & Mathieu, J. E. (2007). Building theoretical and empirical bridges across levels: Multilevel research in management. *Academy of Management Journal*, *50*(6), 1385–1399. doi:10.5465/amj.2007.28166219

Hitt, M. A., Hoskisson, R. E., & Kim, H. (1997). International diversification: Effects on innovation and firm performance in product-diversified firms. *Academy of Management Journal*, *40*, 767–798.

Hitt, M. A., & Ireland, R. D. (1985). Corporate distinctive competence, strategy, industry, and performance. *Strategic Management Journal*, *6*(3), 273–293. doi:10.1002mj.4250060307

Hitt, M. A., Ireland, R. D., & Hoskisson, R. E. (2001). *Strategic Management: Competitiveness and Globalization*. Cincinnati, OH: Southwestern College Publishing Company.

Hitt, M. A., Tihanyi, L., Miller, T., & Connelly, B. (2006). International diversification: Antecedents, outcomes, and moderators. *Journal of Management*, *32*(6), 831–867. doi:10.1177/0149206306293575

Hoffman, J., Hoelscher, M., & Sorenson, R. (2006). Achieving sustained competitive advantage: A family capital theory. *Family Business Review*, *19*(2), 135–145. doi:10.1111/j.1741-6248.2006.00065.x

Ho, K. L. P., Nguyen, C. N., Adhikari, R., Miles, M. P., & Bonney, L. (2018). Exploring market orientation, innovation, and financial performance in agricultural value chains in emerging economies. *Journal of Innovation & Knowledge*, *3*(3), 154–163. doi:10.1016/j.jik.2017.03.008

Holland, J. (2001). Financial institutions, intangibles and corporate governance. *Accounting, Auditing & Accountability Journal*, *14*(4), 497–529. doi:10.1108/EUM0000000005871

Holmström, B., & Tirole, J. (1998). Private and public supply of liquidity. *Journal of Political Economy*, *106*(1), 1–40. doi:10.1086/250001

Holt, D. T., Pearson, A. W., Carr, J. C., & Barnett, T. (2017). Family firm(s) outcomes model: Structuring financial and nonfinancial outcomes across the family and firm. *Family Business Review*, *30*(2), 182–202. doi:10.1177/0894486516680930

Hooley, G. J., Broderick, A., & Möller, K. (1998). Competitive positioning and the resource-based view of the firm. *Journal of Strategic Marketing*, *6*(2), 97–115. doi:10.1080/09652549800000003

Hooley, G. J., Greenley, G. E., Cadogan, J. W., & Fahy, J. (2005). The performance impact of marketing resources. *Journal of Business Research*, *58*(1), 18–27. doi:10.1016/S0148-2963(03)00109-7

Hoopes, D. G., & Madsen, T. L. (2008). A capability-based view of competitive heterogeneity. *Industrial and Corporate Change*, *17*(3), 393–426. doi:10.1093/icc/dtn008

Hoopes, D. G., & Miller, D. (2006). Owner preferences, competitive heterogeneity and strategic capabilities. *Family Business Review*, *19*(2), 89–101. doi:10.1111/j.1741-6248.2006.00064.x

Horton, T. (1986). Managing in a Family Way. *Management Review*, *75*(2), 3.

Horton, T. P. (1986). Managing in a family way. *Management Review*, *75*(2), 3.

House, R., Rousseau, D. M., & Thomas-Hunt, M. (1995). The meso paradigm: A framework for the integration of micro and macro organizational behavior. In L. L. Cummings & B. M. Staw (Eds.), *Research in organizational behavior* (Vol. 17, pp. 71–114). Greenwich, CT: JAI Press.

Hsu, L. C., & Wang, C. H. (2012). Clarifying the effect of intellectual capital on performance: The mediating role of dynamic capability. *British Journal of Management*, *23*(2), 179–205. doi:10.1111/j.1467-8551.2010.00718.x

Hughes, M., Filser, M., Harms, R., Kraus, S., Chang, M. L., & Cheng, C. F. (2018). Family firm configurations for high performance: The role of entrepreneurship and ambidexterity. *British Journal of Management*, *29*(4), 595–612. doi:10.1111/1467-8551.12263

Hunt, S. D. (2000). *A general theory of competition*. Thousand Oaks, CA: Sage Publications.

Hunt, S. D., & Morgan, R. M. (1995). The comparative advantage theory of competition. *Journal of Marketing*, *59*(2), 1–15. doi:10.1177/002224299505900201

Hutchinson, R. (1995). The capital structure and investment decisions of the small owner-managed firm: Some exploratory issues. *Small Business Economics*, *7*(3), 231–239. doi:10.1007/BF01135368

Huybrechts, J., Voordeckers, W., Lybaert, N., & Vandemaele, S. (2011). The distinctiveness of family-firm intangibles: A review and suggestions for future research. *Journal of Management & Organization*, *17*(2), 268–287. doi:10.1017/S1833367200001656

Ibrahim, A. B., & Ellis, W. (1994). *Family business management. Concepts and practice*. Dubuque, IA: Kendall/Hunt Publishing Company.

Ibrahim, A. B., Soufani, K., & Lam, J. (2001). A study of succession in a family firm. *Family Business Review*, *14*(3), 245–258. doi:10.1111/j.1741-6248.2001.00245.x

IEF, & Red de Cátedras de Empresa Familiar. (2015). La Empresa Familiar en España (2015). Instituto de la Empresa Familiar. Barcelona, Spain.

Ifera. (2003). Family business dominate. *Family Business Review*, *16*(4), 235-9.

Instituto de Empresa Familiar. (2015). *La empresa Familiar en España*. Barcelona: Author.

Irava, W. J., & Moores, K. (2010). Clarifying the strategic advantage of familiness: Unbundling its dimensions and highlighting its paradoxes. *Journal of Family Business Strategy*, *1*(3), 131–144. doi:10.1016/j.jfbs.2010.08.002

Isaksen, S., & Tidd, J. (2006). *Meeting the innovation challenge: Leadership for transformation and growth*. Hoboken, NJ: John Wiley & Sons.

Itami, H., & Roehl, T. W. (1987). *Mobilizing Invisible Assets*. Cambridge, MA: Harvard University Press.

Jain, B. A., & Kini, O. (1994). The post-issue operating performance of IPO firms. *The Journal of Finance*, *49*(5), 1699–1726. doi:10.1111/j.1540-6261.1994.tb04778.x

James, H. (2009). *Family capitalism: Wendels, Haniels, Falcks, and the continental European model*. Harvard University Press. doi:10.2307/j.ctvjz811m

James, H. Jr. (1999). What can the family contribute to business? Examining contractual relationships. *Family Business Review*, *12*(1), 61–71. doi:10.1111/j.1741-6248.1999.00061.x

Jaskiewicz, P., Combs, J. G., Shanine, K. K., & Kacmar, K. M. (2016). Introducing the family: A review of family science with implications for management research. *The Academy of Management Annals*, *11*(1), 309–341. doi:10.5465/annals.2014.0053

Jaskiewicz, P., & Dyer, W. G. (2017). Addressing the elephant in the room: Disentangling family heterogeneity to advance family business research. *Family Business Review*, *30*(2), 111–118. doi:10.1177/0894486517700469

Jaworski, B. J., & Kohli, A. K. (1996). Market orientation: Review, refinement, and roadmap. *Journal of Market-Focused Management*, *1*(2), 119–135. doi:10.1007/BF00128686

Jell, F., Block, J., Henkel, J., Spiegel, F., & Zischka, H. (2015). Cross-functional patent management in family firms. *Journal of Business Economics*, *85*(2), 181–203. doi:10.100711573-014-0732-6

Jennings, R., & Lumpkin, G. T. (1989). Functioning Modeling Corporate Entrepreneurship: An Empirical Integrative Analysis. *Journal of Management*, *15*(3), 485–502. doi:10.1177/014920638901500310

Jensen, M. C. (1986). Agency costs of free cash flow, corporate finance and takeovers. *The American Economic Review*, *76*(2), 323–329.

Jensen, M. C., & Meckling, W. H. (1976). Theory of the firm: Managerial behavior, agency costs, and ownership structure. *Journal of Financial Economics*, *3*(4), 305–360. doi:10.1016/0304-405X(76)90026-X

Jensen, M. C., & Meckling, W. H. (1994). The nature of man. *Journal of Applied Corporate Finance*, *7*(2), 4–19. doi:10.1111/j.1745-6622.1994.tb00401.x

Jha, S., & Bhattacharyya, S. S. (2017). Deveoplemt of model integrating determinants of job performance and competitor orientation. *International Journal of Indian Culture and Business Management*, *15*(3), 326–349. doi:10.1504/IJICBM.2017.087313

Jogaratnam, G. (2017). How organizational culture influences market orientation and business performance in the restaurant industry. *Journal of Hospitality and Tourism Management*, *31*, 211–219. doi:10.1016/j.jhtm.2017.03.002

Johannisson, B., & Huse, M. (2000). Recruiting outside board members in the small family business: An ideological challenge. *Entrepreneurship and Regional Development*, *12*(4), 353–378. doi:10.1080/08985620050177958

Johanson, J., & Mattsson, L. G. (1993). Internationalization in industrial systems – a network approach, strategies in global competition´. In P. J. Buckley & P. N. Ghauri (Eds.), *The Internationalization of the Firm: A Reader* (pp. 303–322). London: Academic Press.

Johanson, J., & Vahlne, J. E. (1977). The internationalization process of the firm: A model of knowledge development and increasing market commitment. *Journal of International Business Studies*, *8*(1), 23–32. doi:10.1057/palgrave.jibs.8490676

Jorinsen, A., Laveren, E., Martens, R., & Reheul, A. (2001). *Planning and control practices in family firms versus non-family firms: empirical evidence from SMEs in the wholesale sector*. Antwerp, Belgium: Faculty of Applied Economics.

Josefy, M. A., Harrison, J. S., Sirmon, D. G., & Carnes, C. (2017). Living and dying: Synthesizing the literature on firm survival and failure across stages of development. *The Academy of Management Annals*, *11*(2), 770–799. doi:10.5465/annals.2015.0148

Judge, W. (2012). Owner type as emerging area of governance research. *Corporate Governance*, *20*(3), 231–232. doi:10.1111/j.1467-8683.2012.00908.x

Juul, M. (2015). *The sharing economy and tourism: tourism accommodation*. Brussels: European Parliament Research Service Briefing.

Kabbach de Castro, L. R., Aguilera, R. V., & Crespí-Cladera, R. (2017). Family firms and compliance: Reconciling the conflicting predictions within the socioemotional wealth perspective. *Family Business Review*, *30*(2), 137–159. doi:10.1177/0894486516685239

Kachaner, N., Stalk, G., & Bloch, A. (2012). What you can learn from family business. *Harvard Business Review*, *90*(11), 102–106.

Kahn, K. B. (1996). Interdepartmental integration: A definition with implications for product development performance. *Journal of Product Innovation Management*, *13*(2), 137–151. doi:10.1111/1540-5885.1320137

Kajolo, S., & Lindblom, A. (2015). Market orientation, entrepreneurial orientation and business performance among small retailers. *International Journal of Retail & Distribution Management*, *43*(7), 580–596. doi:10.1108/IJRDM-04-2014-0044

Kaleka, A. (2002). Resources and capabilities driving competitive advantage in export markets: Guidelines for industrial exporters. *Industrial Marketing Management*, *31*(3), 273–283. doi:10.1016/S0019-8501(00)00148-6

Kallmuenzer, A., Strobl, A., & Peters, M. (2018). Tweaking the entrepreneurial orientation–performance relationship in family firms: The effect of control mechanisms and family-related goals. *Review of Managerial Science*, *12*(4), 855–883. doi:10.100711846-017-0231-6

Kammerlander, N., & Ganter, M. (2015). An attention-based view of family firm adaptation to discontinuous technological change: Exploring the role of family CEOs' noneconomic goals. *Journal of Product Innovation Management*, *32*(3), 361–383. doi:10.1111/jpim.12205

Kamoche, K. (1996). Strategic human resource management within a resource-capability view of the firm. *Journal of Management Studies*, *33*(2), 213–233. doi:10.1111/j.1467-6486.1996.tb00158.x

Kampouri, K., Plakoyiannaki, E., & Leppäaho, T. (2017). Family business internationalisation and networks: Emerging pathways. *Journal of Business and Industrial Marketing*, *32*(3), 357–370. doi:10.1108/JBIM-04-2015-0066

Kang, D. (1998). *The impact of ownership type on performance in public corporations: a study of the US textile industry 1983-1992*. Available at SSRN 10592.

Kang, D. (2000). *Family ownership and performance in public corporations: A study of the U.S. fortune 500, 1982–1994*. Working Paper. Boston: Harvard Business School.

Karagozoglu, N., & Brown, W. B. (1988). Adaptive responses by conservative and entrepreneurial firms. *Journal of Product Innovation Management*, *5*(4), 269–281. doi:10.1111/1540-5885.540269

Kartika, R. (2012). *Family ownership and post-IPO performance: evidence in Malaysia* (Unpublished doctoral dissertation). Universiti Utara, Malaysia.

Katz, R. L. (1974). Skills of and effective administrator. *Harvard Business Review*, *52*(September-October), 90–102.

Kaye, K. (1991). Penetrating the Cycle of Sustained Conflict. *Family Business Review*, *4*(1), 21-44.

Kaye, K. (1992). The Kid Brother. *Family Business Review*, *5*(3), 237–256. doi:10.1111/j.1741-6248.1992.00237.x

Kaye, K. (1996). When the Family Business Is a Sickness. *Family Business Review*, *9*(4), 347–368. doi:10.1111/j.1741-6248.1996.00347.x

Keasey, K., Martinez, B., & Pindado, J. (2015). Young family firms: Financing decisions and the willingness to dilute control. *Journal of Corporate Finance*, *34*, 47–63. doi:10.1016/j.jcorpfin.2015.07.014

Kellerman, F. W., Eddleston, K. A., Barnett, T., & Pearson, A. (2008). An exploratory study of family member characteristics and involvement effects on entrepreneurial behavior in the family firm. *Family Business Review*, *21*(1), 1–14. doi:10.1111/j.1741-6248.2007.00107.x

Kellermanns, F.W., Eddleston, K. A., & Zellweger, T. M. (2012). Extending the Socioemotional Wealth Perspective: A Look at the Dark Side. *Entrepreneurship Theory and Practice, 36*, 1175–1182.

Kellermanns, F. W. (2005). Family firm resource management: Comments and extensions. *Entrepreneurship Theory and Practice*, *29*(3), 313–319. doi:10.1111/j.1540-6520.2005.00085.x

Kellermanns, F. W., & Eddleston, K. A. (2006). Corporate entrepreneurship in family firms: A family perspective. *Entrepreneurship Theory and Practice*, *30*(6), 809–830. doi:10.1111/j.1540-6520.2006.00153.x

Kellermanns, F. W., Eddleston, K. A., Sarathy, R., & Murphy, F. (2012). Innovativeness in family firms: A family influence perspective. *Small Business Economics*, *38*(1), 85–101. doi:10.100711187-010-9268-5

Kepner, E. (1983). The family and the firm: A coevolutionary perspective. *Organizational Dynamics*, *12*(1), 57–70. doi:10.1016/0090-2616(83)90027-X

Ketchen, D. J., Hult, G. T. M., & Slater, S. F. (2007). Toward greater understanding of market orientation and the resource-based view. *Strategic Management Journal*, *28*(9), 961–964. doi:10.1002mj.620

Ketchen, D. J. Jr, Thomas, J. B., & Snow, C. C. (1993). Organizational configurations and performance: A comparison of theoretical approaches. *Academy of Management Journal*, *36*(6), 1278–1313.

Kets de Vries, M. F. (1977). The entrepreneurial personality: A person at the crossroads. *Journal of Management Studies*, *14*(1), 34–57. doi:10.1111/j.1467-6486.1977.tb00616.x

Kets de Vries, M. F. R. (1993). The dynamics of family controlled firms: The good and the bad news. *Organizational Dynamics*, *21*(3), 59–71. doi:10.1016/0090-2616(93)90071-8

Kets de Vries, M. F. R. (1993b). Lo bueno y lo malo de las empresas de titularidad familiar. *Harvard Business Review*, *4*, 32–44.

Kets de Vries, M. F. R. (1996). *Family business: Human dilemmas in the family firm*. London, UK: Thomson Business Press.

Khandker, S. (2010). *Handbook on Impact Evaluation. Quantitative Methods and Practices*. Washington, DC: World Bank.

Khanna, T., & Rivkin, J. W. (2001). Estimating the performance effects of business groups in emerging markets. *Strategic Management Journal*, *22*(1), 45–74. doi:10.1002/1097-0266(200101)22:1<45::AID-SMJ147>3.0.CO;2-F

Khurshed, A., Paleari, S., & Vismara, S. (2005). *The Operating Performance of Initial Public Offerings: The UK Experience*. Università di Bergamo Working Paper. Available at SSRN: https://ssrn.com/abstract=439240 or doi:10.2139srn.439240

Kidwell, R. E., Eddleston, K. A., Cater, J. J. III, & Kellermanns, F. W. (2013). How one bad family member can undermine a family firm: Preventing the Fredo effect. *Business Horizons*, *56*(1), 5–12. doi:10.1016/j.bushor.2012.08.004

Kidwell, R. E., Eddleston, K. A., & Kellermanns, F. W. (2018). Learning bad habits across generations: How negative imprints affect human resource management in the family firm. *Human Resource Management Review*, *28*(1), 5–17. doi:10.1016/j.hrmr.2017.05.002

Kidwell, R. E., Kellermanns, F. W., & Eddleston, K. A. (2012). Harmony, justice, confusion, and conflict in the family firm: Implications for ethical climate and the "Fredo effect." *Journal of Business Ethics*, *106*(4), 503–517. doi:10.100710551-011-1014-7

Kim, J., Fairclough, S., & Dibrell, C. (2017). Attention, action, and greenwash in family-influenced firms? Evidence from polluting industries. *Organization & Environment*, *30*(4), 304–323. doi:10.1177/1086026616673410

Kim, K. A., Kitsabunnarat, P., & Nofsinger, J. R. (2004). Ownership and operating performance in an emerging market: Evidence from Thai IPO firms. *Journal of Corporate Finance*, *10*(3), 355–381. doi:10.1016/S0929-1199(02)00019-6

Kim, W. C., Hwang, P., & Burgers, W. P. (1989). Global Diversification Strategy and Corporate Profit Performance. *Strategic Management Journal*, *10*(1), 45–57. doi:10.1002mj.4250100105

Kim, Y., & Gao, F. Y. (2013). Does family involvement increase business performance?: Family-longevity goals´ moderating role in Chinese family firms. *Journal of Business Research*, *66*(2), 265–274. doi:10.1016/j.jbusres.2012.08.018

Kim, Y., & Gray, S. J. (2008). The impact of entry mode choice on foreign affiliate performance: The case of foreign MNEs in South Korea. *Management International Review*, *48*(2), 165–188. doi:10.100711575-008-0010-3

King, M., & Santor, E. (2008). Family values: Ownership structure, performance and capital structure of Canadian firms. *Journal of Banking & Finance*, *32*(11), 2423–2432. doi:10.1016/j.jbankfin.2008.02.002

Kirchhoff, B. A., & Kirchhoff, J. J. (1987). Family contributions to productivity and profitability in small business. *Journal of Small Business Management*, *25*(4), 25–31.

Klein, B., Crawford, R. A., & Alchian, A. A. (1978). Vertical integration, appropriable rents, and the competitive contracting process. *The Journal of Law & Economics*, *21*(2), 297–326. doi:10.1086/466922

Klein, B., & Leffler, K. (1981). The role of market forces in assuring contractual performance. *Journal of Political Economy*, *89*(agosto), 615–641. doi:10.1086/260996

Klein, P., Shapiro, D., & Young, J. (2005). Corporate governance, family ownership and firm value: The Canadian evidence. *Corporate Governance*, *13*(6), 769–784. doi:10.1111/j.1467-8683.2005.00469.x

Klein, S. B., Astrachan, J. H., & Smyrnios, K. X. (2005). The F-PEC scale of family influence: Construction, validation, and further implication for theory. *Entrepreneurship Theory and Practice*, *29*(3), 321–339. doi:10.1111/j.1540-6520.2005.00086.x

Kogut, B., & Zander, U. (1992). Knowledge of the firm, combinative capabilities, and the replication of technology. *Organization Science*, *3*(3), 383–397. doi:10.1287/orsc.3.3.383

Kogut, B., & Zander, U. (1996). What firms do? Coordination, learning, and learning. *Organization Science*, *7*(5), 502–518. doi:10.1287/orsc.7.5.502

König, A., Kammerlander, N., & Enders, A. (2013). The family innovator's dilemma: How family influence affects the adoption of discontinuous technologies by incumbent firms. *Academy of Management Review*, *38*(3), 418–441. doi:10.5465/amr.2011.0162

Konopaski, M., Jack, S., & Hamilton, E. (2016). How family business members learn about continuity. *Academy of Management Learning & Education*, *14*(3), 347–364. doi:10.5465/amle.2014.0244

Kontinen, T., & Ojala, A. (2010). The internationalization of family businesses: A review of extant research. *Journal of Family Business Strategy*, *1*(2), 97–107. doi:10.1016/j.jfbs.2010.04.001

Koopman, M., & Sebel, K. (2009). *The internationalization of family firms: Facilitating and Constraining Features.* Jönköping: Jönköping University.

Koropp, C., Kellermanns, F., Grichnik, D., & Stanley, L. (2014). Financial Decision Making in Family Firms. *Family Business Review*, *27*(4), 307–327. doi:10.1177/0894486514522483

Kor, Y. Y. (2003). Experience-based Top management team competence and sustained growth. *Organization Science*, *14*(6), 707–719. doi:10.1287/orsc.14.6.707.24867

Kosmidou, V., & Ahuja, M. K. (2019). A configurational approach to family firm innovation. *Family Business Review*, *32*(2), 154–173.

Kotabe, M., & Kothari, T. (2016). Emerging market multinational companies' evolutionary paths to building a competitive advantage from emerging markets to developed countries. *Journal of World Business*, *51*(5), 729–743. doi:10.1016/j.jwb.2016.07.010

Kotlar, J., & De Massis, A. (2013). Goal setting in family firms: Goal diversity, social interactions, and collective commitment to family-centered goals. *Entrepreneurship Theory and Practice*, *37*(6), 1263–1288. doi:10.1111/etap.12065

Kotlar, J., De Massis, A., Frattini, F., Bianchi, M., & Fang, H. (2013). Technology acquisition in family and nonfamily firms: A longitudinal analysis of spanish manufacturing firms. *Journal of Product Innovation Management*, *30*(6), 1073–1088. doi:10.1111/jpim.12046

Kotlar, J., Fang, H., De Massis, A., & Frattini, F. (2014). Profitability goals, control goals, and the R & D investment decisions of family and nonfamily firms. *Journal of Product Innovation Management*, *31*(6), 1128–1145. doi:10.1111/jpim.12165

Kozlowski, S. W. J., & Klein, K. J. (2000). A Multilevel Approach to Theory and Research in Organizations Contextual, Temporal, and Emergent Processes. In Multilevel Theory, Research, and Methods in Organizations Foundations, Extensions, and New Directions. Jossey-Bass.

Kraatz, M., & Block, E. (2008). Organizational implications of institutional pluralism. In Handbook of organizational institutionalism (pp. 243-275). London: Sage Publication. doi:10.4135/9781849200387.n10

Kraus, A., & Litzenberger, R. (1973). A State-Preference Model of Optimal Financial Leverage. *The Journal of Finance*, *28*(4), 911–922. doi:10.1111/j.1540-6261.1973.tb01415.x

Kruse, D. L., Freeman, R. B., & Blasi, J. R. (2010). Shared capitalism at work: Employee ownership, profit and gain sharing, and broad-based stock options. University of Chicago Press. Lamb, N. H., & Butler, F. C. (2018). The influence of family firms and institutional owners on corporate social responsibility performance. *Business & Society*, *57*(7), 1374–1406.

Ku, E. C., Wu, W. C., & Chen, Y. J. (2016). The relationships among supply chain partnerships, customer orientation, and operational performance: The effect of flexibility. *Information Systems and e-Business Management*, *14*(2), 415–441. doi:10.100710257-015-0289-0

La Porta, R., Lopez-De-Silanes, F., & Shleifer, A. (1999). Corporate ownership around the world. *The Journal of Finance*, *54*(2), 471–514. doi:10.1111/0022-1082.00115

Lachenmaier, S., & Wößmann, L. (2006). Does Innovation Cause Export? Evidence from Exogenous Innovation Impulses and Obstacles Using German Micro Data. Oxford Economic Press.

Lado, A. A., Boyd, N. G., & Wright, P. (1992). A competency-based model of sustainable competitive advantage: Toward a conceptual integration. *Journal of Management*, *18*(1), 77–91. doi:10.1177/014920639201800106

Lado, A. A., & Wilson, M. C. (1994). Human resource systems and sustained competitive advantage: A competency-based perspective. *Academy of Management Review*, *19*(4), 699–727. doi:10.5465/amr.1994.9412190216

Lai, F., Li, D., Qiang, Q., & Zhao, X. (2008). The information technology capability of third party logistics providers: A resource-based view and empirical test from China. *The Journal of Supply Chain Management*, *9*(1), 21–36.

Lai, J. H., Chen, L. Y., & Chen, I. J. (2014). The value of outside director experience to firm strategies: Evidence from joint ventures. *Journal of Management & Organization*, *20*(3), 387–409. doi:10.1017/jmo.2014.18

Lamb, N. H., & Butler, F. C. (2018). The influence of family firms and institutional owners on corporate social responsibility performance. *Business & Society*, *57*(7), 1374–1406. doi:10.1177/0007650316648443

Lambrecht, J. (2005). Multigenerational transition in family businesses: A new explanatory model. *Family Business Review*, *28*(4), 267–282. doi:10.1111/j.1741-6248.2005.00048.x

Lambrecht, J., & Lievens, J. (2008). Pruning the family tree: An unexplored path to family business continuity and family harmony. *Family Business Review*, *21*(4), 295–313. doi:10.1177/08944865080210040103

Lampel, J., & Shamsie, J. (2003). Capabilities in motion: New organizational forms and the reshaping of the Hollywood movie industry. *Journal of Management Studies*, *40*(8), 2189–2210. doi:10.1046/j.1467-6486.2003.00417.x

Landes, D. S. (1951). French business and businessman in social and cultural analysis. In E. Mead (Ed.), *Modern France* (pp. 334–353). Princeton, NJ: Princeton University Press.

Landeta, J., Barrutia, J., Araujo, A., & Hoyos, J. (2007). *Claves del comportamiento de la empresa respecto a la formación continua de sus directivos*. Thomson Cívitas, Navarra.

Lansberg, I. (1988). The succession conspiracy. In C. E. Aronoff, J. H. Astrachan, & J. L. Ward (Eds.), *Family business sourcebook II* (pp. 70–86). Marietta, GA: Business Owner Resources.

Lansberg, I. S. (1983). Managing human resources in family firms: The problem of institutional overlap. *Organizational Dynamics*, *12*(1), 39–46. doi:10.1016/0090-2616(83)90025-6

Lansberg, I., & Astrachan, J. H. (1994). Influence of family relationships on succession planning and training: The importance of mediating factors. *Family Business Review*, *7*(1), 39–59. doi:10.1111/j.1741-6248.1994.00039.x

Lansberg, I., & Gersick, K. (2015). Educating family business owners: The fundamental intervention. *Academy of Management Learning & Education*, *14*(3), 400–413. doi:10.5465/amle.2014.0254

Lansberg, L., Perrow, E., & Rogolsky, S. (1988). Family business as an emerging field. *Family Business Review*, *4*(2), 1–8. doi:10.1111/j.1741-6248.1988.00001.x

Larrinaga, C., & Vallejo, R. (2013). El turismo en el desarrollo español contemporáneo. *TST: Transportes. Servicios y Telecomunicaciones*, *24*, 12–29.

Laverty, K. J. (1996). Economic "short-termism": The debate, the unresolved issues, and the implications for management practice and research. *Academy of Management Review*, *21*(3), 825–860.

Lawson, B., & Samson, D. (2001). Developing innovation capability in organisations: A dynamic capabilities approach. *International Journal of Innovation Management*, *5*(3), 377–400. doi:10.1142/S1363919601000427

Lazonick, W. (1991). *Business organization and the myth of the market economy*. Nueva York, NY: Cambridge University Press.

Le Breton–Miller, I., & Miller, D. (2006). Why do some family businesses out–compete? Governance, long–term orientations, and sustainable capability. *Entrepreneurship Theory and Practice*, *30*(6), 731–746. doi:10.1111/j.1540-6520.2006.00147.x

Le Breton-Miller, I., & Miller, D. (2008). To grow or to harvest? Governance, strategy and performance in family and lone founder firms. *Journal of Strategy and Management*, *1*(1), 41–56. doi:10.1108/17554250810909419

Le Breton-Miller, I., & Miller, D. (2009). Agency vs. stewardship in public family firms: A social embeddedness reconciliation. *Entrepreneurship Theory and Practice*, *33*(6), 1169–1191. doi:10.1111/j.1540-6520.2009.00339.x

Le Breton-Miller, I., & Miller, D. (2011). Commentary: Family firms and the advantage of multitemporality. *Entrepreneurship Theory and Practice*, *35*(6), 1171–1177. doi:10.1111/j.1540-6520.2011.00496.x

Le Breton-Miller, I., & Miller, D. (2013). Socioemotional wealth across the family firm life cycle: A commentary on "Family Business Survival and the Role of Boards". *Entrepreneurship Theory and Practice*, *37*(6), 1391–1397. doi:10.1111/etap.12072

Le Breton–Miller, I., & Miller, D. (2015). Article Commentary: The Arts and Family Business: Linking Family Business Resources and Performance to Industry Characteristics. *Entrepreneurship Theory and Practice*, *39*(6), 1349–1370. doi:10.1111/etap.12177

Le Breton-Miller, I., & Miller, D. (2015). Learning stewardship in family firms: For family, by family, across the life cycle. *Academy of Management Learning & Education*, *14*(3), 386–399. doi:10.5465/amle.2014.0131

Le Breton-Miller, I., & Miller, D. (2016). Family firms and practices of sustainability: A contingency view. *Journal of Family Business Strategy*, *7*(1), 26–33. doi:10.1016/j.jfbs.2015.09.001

Le Breton-Miller, I., Miller, D., & Lester, R. H. (2011). Stewardship or agency? A social embeddedness reconciliation of conduct and performance in public family businesses. *Organization Science*, *22*(3), 704–721. doi:10.1287/orsc.1100.0541

Le Breton-Miller, I., Miller, D., & Steier, L. P. (2004). Toward an integrative model of effective FOB succession. *Entrepreneurship Theory and Practice*, *28*(4), 305–328. doi:10.1111/j.1540-6520.2004.00047.x

Leach, P. (1993). *La empresa familiar*. Barcelona, España: Granica.

Leal-Rodrìguez, A. L., Peris-Ortiz,M. & Leal-Mill´an, A.G. (2017). Fostering entrepreneurship by linking organizational unlearning and innovation: the moderating role of family business. *Management International/International Management/Gestion Internacional*, *21*, 86-94.

Leech, D., & Leahy, J. (1991). Ownership structure, control type classifications and the performance of large British companies. *The Economical Journal*, *101*, 1418–1437.

Lee, J. (2006). Family Firm Performance: Further Evidence. *Family Business Review*, *19*(2), 103–114. doi:10.1111/j.1741-6248.2006.00060.x

Lee, P. M., & O'Neill, H. M. (2003). Ownership structures and R&D investments of U.S. and Japanese firms: Agency and stewardship perspectives. *Academy of Management Journal*, *46*(2), 212–225.

Lehman, D. R. (1979). *Market research and analysis*. Homewood, IL: Irwin.

Leiblein, M. J., & Madsen, T. L. (2009). Unbundling competitive heterogeneity: Incentive structures and capability influences on technological innovation. *Strategic Management Journal*, *30*(7), 711–735. doi:10.1002mj.746

Leibowitz, B. (1986). Resolving conflict in the family owned business. *Consultation*, *5*(3), 191–205.

Leiß, G., & Zehrer, A. (2018). Intergenerational communication in family firm succession. *Journal of Family Business Management*, *8*(1), 75–90. doi:10.1108/JFBM-09-2017-0025

Lemmon, M., & Lins, K. (2003). Ownership Structure, Corporate Governance, and Firm Value: Evidence from the East Asian Financial Crisis. *The Journal of Finance*, *58*(4), 1445–1468. doi:10.1111/1540-6261.00573

Leonard-Barton, D. (1992). Core capabilities and core rigidities: A paradox in managing new product development. *Strategic Management Journal*, *13*(special issue summer), 111-126.

Leonidou, L. C. (2004). An analysis of the barriers hindering small business export development. *Journal of Small Business Management*, *42*(3), 279–302. doi:10.1111/j.1540-627X.2004.00112.x

Lerner, M., & Almor, T. (2002). Relationships among strategic capabilities and the performance of women-owned small ventures. *Journal of Small Business Management*, *40*(2), 109–125. doi:10.1111/1540-627X.00044

Levin, S. G., & Levin, S. L. (1982). Ownership and control of large industrial firms. Some new evidence. *Review of Business and Economic Research*, *18*(1), 37–49.

Levinson, H. (1971). Conflicts that plague family business. *Harvard Business Review*, *49*(2), 90–98.

Levinson, R. E. (1987). Problems in managing a family-owned business. In C. E. Aronoff & J. L. Ward (Eds.), *Family business sourcebook* (pp. 169–174). Detroit, MI: Omnigraphics.

Levinthal, D. A., & March, J. G. (1993). The myopia of learning. *Strategic Management Journal*, *14*(S2), 95–112. doi:10.1002mj.4250141009

Levring, R., & Moskowitz, M. (1993). The ten best companies to work for in *America. Business and Society Review*, *85*(1), 26–38.

Liang, Q., Li, X., Yang, X., Lin, D., & Zheng, D. (2013). How does family involvement affect innovation in China? *Asia Pacific Journal of Management*, *30*(3), 677–695. doi:10.100710490-012-9320-x

Liang, X., Wang, L., & Cui, Z. (2014). Chinese Private Firms and Internationalization: Effects of Family Involvement in Management and Family Ownership. *Family Business Review*, *1*, 259–274.

Lichtenthaler, U., & Muethel, M. (2012). Retracted: The impact of family involvement on dynamic innovation capabilities: Evidence from German manufacturing firms. *Entrepreneurship Theory and Practice*, *36*(6), 1235–1253. doi:10.1111/j.1540-6520.2012.00548.x

Li, J., & Hambrick, D. C. (2005). Factional groups: A new vantage on demographic faultlines, conflict, and disintegration in work teams. *Academy of Management Journal*, *48*(5), 794–813. doi:10.5465/amj.2005.18803923

Lindbeck, A., & Weibull, J. W. (1988). Altruism and time consistency: The economics of fait accompli. *Journal of Political Economy*, *96*(6), 1165–1182. doi:10.1086/261582

Ling, Y., & Kellermanns, F. W. (2010). The effects of family firm specific sources of TMT diversity: The moderating role of information exchange frequency. *Journal of Management Studies*, *47*(2), 322–344. doi:10.1111/j.1467-6486.2009.00893.x

Linnenluecke, M. K. (2017). Resilience in business and management research: A review of influential publications and a research agenda. *International Journal of Management Reviews*, *19*(1), 4–30. doi:10.1111/ijmr.12076

Linstead, S., Marechal, G., & Griffin, R. W. (2014). Theorizing and researching the dark side of organization. *Organization Studies*, *35*(2), 165–188. doi:10.1177/0170840613515402

Litz, R. A. (1995). The family business: Toward definitional clarity. *Family Business Review*, *8*(2), 71–81. doi:10.1111/j.1741-6248.1995.00071.x

Liu, Y., Chen, Y.-J., & Wang, L. C. (2017). Family business, innovation and organizational slack in Taiwan. *Asia Pacific Journal of Management*, *34*(1), 193–213. doi:10.100710490-016-9496-6

Li, Z., & Daspit, J. J. (2016). Understanding family firm innovation heterogeneity: A typology of family governance and socioemotional wealth intentions. *Journal of Family Business Management*, *6*(2), 103–121. doi:10.1108/JFBM-02-2015-0010

Lonial, S. C., & Carter, R. E. (2015). The impact of organizational orientations on medium and small firm performance: A resource-based perspective. *Journal of Small Business Management*, *53*(1), 94–113. doi:10.1111/jsbm.12054

López-Gracia, J., & Sánchez-Andújar, S. (2007). Financial Structure of the Family Business: Evidence From a Group of Small Spanish Firms. *Family Business Review*, *20*(4), 269–287. doi:10.1111/j.1741-6248.2007.00094.x

López-Gracia, J., & Sogorb-Mira, F. (2008). Testing trade-off and pecking order theories financing SMEs. *Small Business Economics*, *31*(2), 117–136. doi:10.100711187-007-9088-4

López-Pérez, M., Melero-Polo, I., Vázquez-Carrasco, R., & Cambra-Fierro, J. (2018). Sustainability and Business Outcomes in the Context of SMEs: Comparing Family Firms vs. Non-Family Firms. *Sustainability*, *10*(11), 4080. doi:10.3390u10114080

Loughran, T., & Ritter, J. R. (1997). The operating performance of firms conducting seasoned equity offerings. *The Journal of Finance*, *52*(5), 1823–1850. doi:10.1111/j.1540-6261.1997.tb02743.x

Love, L. G., Priem, R. L., & Lumpkin, G. T. (2002). Explicitly articulated strategy and firm performance under alternative levels of centralization. *Journal of Management*, *28*(5), 611–627. doi:10.1177/014920630202800503

Lubatkin, M. H., Durand, R., & Ling, Y. (2007). The missing lens in family firm governance theory: A self-other typology of parental altruism. *Journal of Business Research*, *60*(10), 1022–1029. doi:10.1016/j.jbusres.2006.12.019

Lubatkin, M. H., Ling, Y., & Schulze, W. S. (2007). An organizational justice-based view of self-control and agency costs in family firms. *Journal of Management Studies*, *44*(6), 955–971. doi:10.1111/j.1467-6486.2006.00673.x

Lubatkin, M. H., Simsek, Z., Ling, Y., & Veiga, J. F. (2006). Ambidexterity and performance in small-to medium-sized firms: The pivotal role of top management team behavioral integration. *Journal of Management*, *32*(5), 646–672. doi:10.1177/0149206306290712

Lubatkin, M., Schulze, W., Ling, Y., & Dino, R. (2005). The effects of parental altruism on the governance of family-managed firms. *Journal of Organizational Behavior*, *26*(3), 313–330. doi:10.1002/job.307

Luhmann, N. (1996). *Introducción a la teoría de sistemas*. Universidad Iberoamericana.

Lu, J. W., & Beamish, P. W. (2006). SME internationalization and performance: Growth vs. profitability. *Journal of International Entrepreneurship*, *4*(1), 27–48. doi:10.100710843-006-8000-7

Lumpkin, G. T., & Brigham, K. H. (2011). Long-term orientation and intertemporal choice in family firms. *Entrepreneurship Theory and Practice*, *35*(6), 1149–1169. doi:10.1111/j.1540-6520.2011.00495.x

Lumpkin, G. T., Brigham, K. H., & Moss, T. W. (2010). Long-term orientation: Implications for the entrepreneurial orientation and performance of family businesses. *Entrepreneurship and Regional Development*, *22*(3-4), 241–264. doi:10.1080/08985621003726218

Ly, M., & Simerly, R. L. (1998). The moderating effect of environmental dynamism on the ownership and performance relationship. *Strategic Management Journal*, *19*(2), 169–179. doi:10.1002/(SICI)1097-0266(199802)19:2<169::AID-SMJ939>3.0.CO;2-2

Lyman, A. R. (1991). Customer Service: Does Family Ownership Make a Difference? *Family Business Review*, *4*(3), 303–324. doi:10.1111/j.1741-6248.1991.00303.x

Madhok, A. (1997). Cost, value, and foreign market entry mode: The transaction and the firm. *Strategic Management Journal*, *18*(1), 39–61. doi:10.1002/(SICI)1097-0266(199701)18:1<39::AID-SMJ841>3.0.CO;2-J

Madison, K., Holt, D. T., Kellermanns, F. W., & Ranft, A. L. (2016). Viewing family firm behavior and governance through the lens of agency and stewardship theories. *Family Business Review*, *29*(1), 65–93. doi:10.1177/0894486515594292

Mahoney, J. T. (1995). The management of resources and the resource of management. *Journal of Business Research*, *33*(2), 91–101. doi:10.1016/0148-2963(94)00060-R

Mahoney, J. T., & Pandian, J. R. (1992). The resource-based view within the conversation of strategic management. *Strategic Management Journal*, *13*(5), 363–380. doi:10.1002mj.4250130505

Maijoor, S., & Witteloostuijn, A. V. (1996). An empirical test of the resource-based theory: Strategic regulation in the Dutch audit industry. *Strategic Management Journal, 17*(7), 549–569. doi:10.1002/(SICI)1097-0266(199607)17:7<549::AID-SMJ827>3.0.CO;2-R

Majumdar, S. K. (1999). Sluggish giants, sticky cultures, and dynamic capability transformation. *Journal of Business Venturing, 15*(1), 59–78. doi:10.1016/S0883-9026(98)00010-X

Makadok, R. (1999). Interfirm differences in scale economies and the evolution of market shares. *Strategic Management Journal, 20*(10), 935–952. doi:10.1002/(SICI)1097-0266(199910)20:10<935::AID-SMJ56>3.0.CO;2-G

Makadok, R. (2001). Toward a synthesis of the resource-based and dynamic-capability views of rent creation. *Strategic Management Journal, 22*(5), 387–401. doi:10.1002mj.158

Makadok, R. (2010). The interaction effect of rivalry restraint and competitive advantage on profit: Why the whole is less than the sum of the parts. *Management Science, 56*(2), 356–372. doi:10.1287/mnsc.1090.1102

Manzaneque, M., Rojo-Ramírez, A. A., Diéguez-Soto, J., & Martínez-Romero, M. J. (2018). How negative aspiration performance gaps affect innovation efficiency. *Small Business Economics.* doi:10.100711187-018-0091-8

Manzaneque, M., Ramírez, Y., & Diéguez-Soto, J. (2017). Intellectual capital efficiency, technological innovation and family management. *Innovation: Management. Policy & Practice, 19*(2), 167–188. doi:10.1080/14479338.2016.1272828

March, J. G. (1991). Exploration and exploitation in organizational learning. *Organization Science, 2*(1), 71–87. doi:10.1287/orsc.2.1.71

Margaritis, D., & Psillaki, M. (2010). Capital structure, equity ownership and firm performance. *Journal of Banking & Finance, 34*(3), 621–632. doi:10.1016/j.jbankfin.2009.08.023

Mariussen, A., Wheelock, J., & Baines, S. (1997). The family business Tradition in Britain and Norway. *International Studies of Management & Organization, 27*(3), 64–85. doi:10.1080/00208825.1997.11656713

Markides, C.C., Williamson, P.J. (1994). Related diversification, core competences and corporate performance. *Strategic Management Journal 15*(special issue, summer), 149-165.

Marques, P., Presas, P., & Simon, A. (2014). The heterogeneity of family firms in CSR engagement: The role of values. *Family Business Review, 27*(3), 206–227. doi:10.1177/0894486514539004

Martínez-Alonso, R., Martínez-Romero, M. J., & Rojo-Ramírez, A. A. (2019). The impact of technological innovation efficiency on firm growth: the moderating role of family involvement in management. *European Journal of Innovation Management.* doi:10.1108/EJIM-09-2018-0210

Martínez, J. I., Stohr, B. S., & Quiroga, B. F. (2007). Family ownership and firm performance: Evidence from public companies in Chile. *Family Business Review, 20*(2), 83–94. doi:10.1111/j.1741-6248.2007.00087.x

Martínez, R., Charterina, J., & Araujo, A. (2010). Un modelo causal de competitividad empresarial planteado desde la VBR: Capacidades directivas, de innovación, marketing y calidad. *Investigaciones Europeas de Dirección y Economía de la Empresa, 16*(2), 1135–2523.

Martínez-Romero, M. J. (2018). *Financial performance and value creation in privately held family businesses: the influence of socioemotional wealth* (Doctoral thesis). Almería.

Martínez-Romero, M. J., Martínez-Alonso, R., Casado-Belmonte, M. P., & Diéguez-Soto, J. (2019a). (Forthcoming) Family management and firm performance – The interaction effect of technological innovation efficiency. In Intrapreneurship and Sustainable Human Capital: Digital Transformation through Dynamic Competences. Springer.

Martínez-Romero, M. J., Rojo-Ramirez, A. A., & Casado-Belmonte, M. P. (2019c). Value creation in privately held family businesses: the moderating role of socioemotional wealth. *Canadian Journal of Administrative Sciences*. doi:10.1002/cjas.1540

Martínez-Romero, M. J., Martínez-Alonso, R., & Casado-Belmonte, M. P. (2018). (Forthcoming). The influence of socioemotional wealth on firm financial performance: Evidence from small and medium privately held family businesses. *International Journal of Entrepreneurship and Small Business*.

Martínez-Romero, M. J., Martínez-Alonso, R., Casado-Belmonte, M. P., & Rojo-Ramírez, A. A. (2019b). The Moderating Effect of Family Management on R&D Productivity in Privately Held Firms. In N. M. Teixeira, T. G. Costa, & I. M. Lisboa (Eds.), *Handbook of Research on Entrepreneurship, Innovation, and Internationalization* (pp. 309–338). Hershey, PA: IGI Global. doi:10.4018/978-1-5225-8479-7.ch012

Martínez-Romero, M. J., & Rojo-Ramírez, A. A. (2017). Socioemotional wealth's implications in the calculus of the minimum rate of return required by family businesses' owners. *Review of Managerial Science*, *11*(1), 95–118. doi:10.100711846-015-0181-9

Martin, S. L., & Javalgi, R. R. G. (2016). Entrepreneurial orientation, marketing capabilities and performance: The moderating role of competitive intensity on Latin American International new ventures. *Journal of Business Research*, *69*(6), 2040–2051. doi:10.1016/j.jbusres.2015.10.149

Mascarenhas, B., Baveja, A., & Jamil, M. (1998). Dynamics of Core Competencies in Leading Multinational Companies. *California Management Review*, *40*(4), 117–132. doi:10.2307/41165967

Matlay, H. (2002). Training and HRD strategies in family and non-family owned small businesses: A comparative approach. *Education + Training*, *44*(8/9), 357–369. doi:10.1108/00400910210449196

Matten, D., & Crane, A. (2005). Corporate citizenship: Toward an extended theoretical conceptualization. *Academy of Management Review*, *30*(1), 166–179. doi:10.5465/amr.2005.15281448

Matzler, K., Veider, V., Hautz, J., & Stadler, C. (2015). The impact of family ownership, management, and governance on innovation. *Journal of Product Innovation Management*, *32*(3), 319–333. doi:10.1111/jpim.12202

Mauri, A. J., & Michaels, M. P. (1998). Firm and industry effects within strategic management: An empirical examination. *Strategic Management Journal*, *19*(3), 211–219. doi:10.1002/(SICI)1097-0266(199803)19:3<211::AID-SMJ947>3.0.CO;2-T

Maury, B. (2006). Family ownership and firm performance: Empirical evidence from Western European corporations. *Journal of Corporate Finance*, *12*(2), 321–341. doi:10.1016/j.jcorpfin.2005.02.002

Mazzelli, A., De Massis, A., Petruzzelli, A. M., Del Giudice, M., & Khan, Z. (in press). Behind ambidextrous search: The microfoundations of search in family and non-family firms. *Long Range Planning*.

Mazzi, C. (2011). Family business and financial performance: Current state of knowledge and future research challenges. *Journal of Family Business Strategy*, *2*(3), 166–181. doi:10.1016/j.jfbs.2011.07.001

Mazzola, P., & Marchisio, G. (2002). The role of going public in family businesses' long-lasting growth: A study of Italian IPOs. *Family Business Review*, *15*(2), 133–148. doi:10.1111/j.1741-6248.2002.00133.x

Mazzola, P., Sciascia, S., & Kellermanns, F. W. (2013). Non-linear effects of family sources of power on performance. *Journal of Business Research*, *66*(4), 568–574. doi:10.1016/j.jbusres.2012.01.005

McCann, J. E. III, Leon-Guerrero, A., & Haley, J. D. (2001). Strategic goals and practices of innovative family businesses. *Journal of Small Business Management*, *39*(1), 50–59. doi:10.1111/0447-2778.00005

McCollom, M. E. (1990). Problems and Prospects in Clinical Research on Family Firms. *Family Business Review*, *3*(3), 245–262. doi:10.1111/j.1741-6248.1990.00245.x

McConaughy, D. L. (2000). Family CEOs vs. nonfamily CEOs in the family-controlled firm: An examination of the level and sensitivity of pay to performance. *Family Business Review*, *13*(2), 121–131. doi:10.1111/j.1741-6248.2000.00121.x

McConaughy, D. L., Matthews, C. H., & Fialko, A. S. (2001). Founding family controlled firms: Performance, risk, and value. *Journal of Small Business Management*, *39*(1), 31–50. doi:10.1111/0447-2778.00004

McConaughy, D. L., Walker, M., Henderson, G. V. Jr, & Mishra, C. S. (1998). Founding family controlled firms: Efficiency and value. *Review of Financial Economics*, *7*(1), 1–19. doi:10.1016/S1058-3300(99)80142-6

McConnell, J. J., & Servaes, H. (1990). Additional evidence on equity ownership and Corporate value. *Journal of Financial Economics*, *27*(2), 595–612. doi:10.1016/0304-405X(90)90069-C

McGahan, A., & Porter, M. (1998): *What do we know about variance in accounting profitability?* Working paper. Harvard Business School.

McGahan, A., Porter, M. (1997): How much does industry matter, really? *Strategic Management Journal, 18*(special summer issue), 15-30.

McGahan, A. (1999). The performance of U.S. corporations: 1981-1994. *The Journal of Industrial Economics*, *47*(4), 373–398. doi:10.1111/1467-6451.00105

McGahan, A., & Porter, M. (1999). The persistence of shock to profitability. *The Review of Economics and Statistics*, *81*(1), 143–153. doi:10.1162/003465399767923890

McGuinness, G., Hogan, T., & Powell, R. (2018). European trade credit use and SME survival. *Journal of Corporate Finance*, *49*, 81–103. doi:10.1016/j.jcorpfin.2017.12.005

McKelvie, A., & Davidsson, P. (2009). From Resource Base to Dynamic Capabilities: An Investigation of New Firms. *British Journal of Management*, *20*, 63–80. doi:10.1111/j.1467-8551.2008.00613.x

McKenny, A. F., Payne, G. T., Zachary, M. A., & Short, J. C. (2014). In L. Melin, M. Nordqvist, & P. Sharma (Eds.), *The SAGE Handbook of Family Business* (pp. 594–608). Thousand Oaks, CA: SAGE Publications. doi:10.4135/9781446247556.n30

McKiernan, M. H., & Morris, C. (1994). Strategic planning and financial performance in UK SMEs: Does formality matter? *British Journal of Management*, *5*(special issue), 31–41. doi:10.1111/j.1467-8551.1994.tb00128.x

McNamara, G., Deephouse, D. L., & Luce, R. A. (2003). Competitive positioning within and across a strategic group structure: The performance of core, secondary, and solitary firms. *Strategic Management Journal*, *24*(2), 161–181. doi:10.1002mj.289

Mehra, A. (1996). Resource and market based determinants of performance in the US banking industry. *Strategic Management Journal*, *17*(4), 307–322. doi:10.1002/(SICI)1097-0266(199604)17:4<307::AID-SMJ820>3.0.CO;2-2

Melin, L., & Nordqvist, M. (2007). The reflexive dynamics of institutionalization: The case of the family business. *Strategic Organization*, *5*(3), 321–333. doi:10.1177/1476127007079959

Memili, E., Chrisman, J. J., & Chua, J. H. (2011). Transaction Costs and Outsourcing Decisions in Small- and Medium-Sized Family Firms. *Family Business Review*, *24*(1), 47–61. doi:10.1177/0894486510396706

Memili, E., Fang, H. C., Koç, B., Yildirim-Öktem, Ö., & Sonmez, S. (2018). Sustainability practices of family firms: The interplay between family ownership and long-term orientation. *Journal of Sustainable Tourism*, *26*(1), 9–28. doi:10.1080/09669582.2017.1308371

Memili, E., Fang, H., Chrisman, J. J., & De Massis, A. (2015). The impact of small-and medium sized family firms on economic growth. *Small Business Economics*, *45*(4), 771–785. doi:10.100711187-015-9670-0

Menéndez-Requejo, S. (2005). Growth and internationalization of family businesses. *International Journal of Globalisation and Small Business*, *1*(2), 122–133. doi:10.1504/IJGSB.2005.008009

Menéndez-Requejo, S. (2006). Ownership structure and firm performance: evidence from Spanish family firms. In P. Z. Poutziouris, K. X. Smyrnios, & S. B. Klein (Eds.), *Handbook of Research on Family Business* (pp. 575–593). Edward Elgar Publishing Limited.

Merchant, P., Kumar, A., & Malik, D. (2018). Factors Influencing Family Business Continuity in Indian Small and Medium Enterprises (SMEs). *Journal of Family and Economic Issues*, *39*(2), 177–190. doi:10.100710834-017-9562-3

Merino, F., Monreal-Pérez, J., & Sánchez-Marín, G. (2015). Family SMEs´ internationalization: Disentangling the Influence of Familiness on Spanish Firms´ Export Activity. *Journal of Small Business Management*, *53*(4), 1164–1184. doi:10.1111/jsbm.12111

Merino, F., & Salas, V. (2002). Causes and consequences of exports´ channel integration. *Spanish Economic Review*, *4*(4), 239–259. doi:10.1007101080200056

Meyer, A. D. (1982). Adapting to environmental jolts. *Administrative Science Quarterly*, *27*(4), 515–537. doi:10.2307/2392528 PMID:10257768

Mezias, S. J., Chen, Y. R., & Murphy, P. R. (2002). Aspiration-level adaptation in an American financial services organization: A field study. *Management Science*, *48*(10), 1285–1300. doi:10.1287/mnsc.48.10.1285.277

Micelotta, E. R., & Raynard, M. (2011). Concealing or revealing the family? Corporate brand identity strategies in family firms. *Family Business Review*, *24*(3), 197–216. doi:10.1177/0894486511407321

Michaelas, N., Chittenden, F., & Poutziouris, P. (1999). Financial policy and capital structure choice in U.K. SMEs: Empirical evidence from company panel data. *Small Business Economics*, *12*(2), 113–130. doi:10.1023/A:1008010724051

Michiels, A., & Molly, V. (2017). Financial decisions in family businesses: A review and suggestions for developing the field. *Family Business Review*, *30*(4), 369–399. doi:10.1177/0894486517736958

Mikkelson, W. H., Partch, M. M., & Shah, K. (1997). Ownership and operating performance of companies that go public. *Journal of Financial Economics*, *44*(3), 281–307. doi:10.1016/S0304-405X(97)00006-8

Miles, R. E., & Snow, C. C. (1978). *Organisational Strategy, Structure and Process*. New York: McGraw-Hill.

Miles, R. E., & Snow, C. C. (1978). *Organizational strategy, structure, and process*. McGraw-Hill.

Milfelner, B., Gabrijan, V., & Snoj, B. (2008). Can marketing resources contribute to company performance? *Organizacija*, *14*(1), 3–13.

Miller, D., & Le Breton-Miller, I. (2005). Management insights from great and struggling family business. *Long Range Planning*, *38*(6), 517–530. doi:10.1016/j.lrp.2005.09.001

Miller, D., & Le Breton-Miller, I. (2005). *Managing for the long run: Lessons in competitive advantage from great family businesses*. Harvard Business Press.

Miller, D., & Le Breton-Miller, I. (2006). Family governance and firm performance: Agency, stewardship, and capabilities. *Family Business Review*, *19*(1), 73–87. doi:10.1111/j.1741-6248.2006.00063.x

Miller, D., & Le Breton-Miller, I. (2006). Family Governance and Firm Performance: Agency, Stewardship, and Capabilities. *Family Business Review*, 19.

Miller, D., & Le Breton-Miller, I. (2006). Priorities, practices and strategies in successful and failing family businesses: An elaboration and test of the configuration perspective. *Strategic Organization*, *4*(4), 379–407. doi:10.1177/1476127006069575

Miller, D., & Le Breton-Miller, I. (2014). Deconstructing Socioemotional Wealth. *Entrepreneurship Theory and Practice*, *38*(4), 713–720. doi:10.1111/etap.12111

Miller, D., Le Breton-Miller, I., Amore, M. D., Minichilli, A., & Corbetta, G. (2017). Institutional logics, family firm governance and performance. *Journal of Business Venturing*, *32*(6), 674–693. doi:10.1016/j.jbusvent.2017.08.001

Miller, D., Le Breton-Miller, I., & Lester, R. H. (2010). Family ownership and acquisition behavior in publicly-traded companies. *Strategic Management Journal*, *31*(2), 201–223.

Miller, D., Le Breton-Miller, I., Lester, R. H., & Cannella, A. A. Jr. (2007). Are family firms really superior performers? *Journal of Corporate Finance*, *13*(5), 829–858. doi:10.1016/j.jcorpfin.2007.03.004

Miller, D., Le Breton-Miller, I., & Scholnick, B. (2008). Stewards vs. stagnation: An empirical comparison of small family and non-family businesses. *Journal of Management Studies*, *45*(1), 51–78. doi:10.1017/S0021875807004379

Miller, D., & Le-Breton-Miller, I. (2005). *Managing for the Long Run: Lessons in Competitive Advantage from Great Family Businesses*. Cambridge, MA: Harvard Business School Press.

Miller, D., Minichilli, A., & Corbetta, G. (2012). Is family leadership always beneficial? *Strategic Management Journal*, *34*(5), 553–571. doi:10.1002mj.2024

Miller, D., & Shamsie, J. (1996). The resource-based view of the firm in two environments: The Hollywood film studios from 1936 to 1965. *Academy of Management Journal*, *39*(3), 519–543.

Miller, D., Steier, L., & Le Breton-Miller, I. (2003). Lost in time: Intergenerational succession, change, and failure in family business. *Journal of Business Venturing*, *18*(4), 513–531. doi:10.1016/S0883-9026(03)00058-2

Miller, D., Steier, L., & Le Breton-Miller, I. (2016). What Can Scholars of Entrepreneurship Learn From Sound Family Businesses? *Entrepreneurship Theory and Practice*, *40*(3), 445–455. doi:10.1111/etap.12231

Miller, E. J., & Rice, A. K. (1988). The family business in contemporary society. *Family Business Review*, *1*(2), 193–210. doi:10.1111/j.1741-6248.1988.00193.x

Miller, N. J., McLeod, H., & Oh, K. Y. (2001). Managing family business in small communities. *Journal of Small Business Management*, *39*(1), 73–87. doi:10.1111/0447-2778.00007

Milliken, F., & Martins, L. L. (1996). Searching for common threads: Understanding the multiple effects of diversity in organizational groups. *Academy of Management Review*, *21*(2), 402–433. doi:10.5465/amr.1996.9605060217

Minichilli, A., Corbetta, G., & MacMillan, I. C. (2010). Top management teams in family-controlled companies: Familiness, fualtlines and their impact of financial performance. *Journal of Management Studies*, *47*(2), 205–222. doi:10.1111/j.1467-6486.2009.00888.x

Minola, T., Brumana, M., Campopiano, G., Garrett, R. P., & Cassia, L. (2016). Corporate venturing in family business: A developmental approach of the enterprising family. *Strategic Entrepreneurship Journal*, *10*(4), 395–412. doi:10.1002ej.1236

Modigliani, F., & Miller, M. (1963). Corporate income taxes and the cost of capital: A correction. *The American Economic Review*, *53*(3), 433–443.

Moen, O. (1999). The relationship between firm size, competitive advantage and export performance revisited. *International Small Business Journal*, *18*(1), 53–72. doi:10.1177/0266242699181003

Mokhber, M., Gi Gi, T., Abdul Rasid, S. Z., Vakilbashi, A., Mohd Zamil, N., & Woon Seng, Y. (2017). Succession planning and family business performance in SMEs. *Journal of Management Development*, *36*(3), 330–347. doi:10.1108/JMD-12-2015-0171

Molina, C. A. (2005). Are firms underleveraged? An examination of the effect of leverage on default probabilities. *The Journal of Finance*, *60*(3), 1427–1459. doi:10.1111/j.1540-6261.2005.00766.x

Molly, V., Laveren, E., & Deloof, M. (2010). Family business succession and its impact on financial structure and performance. *Family Business Review*, *23*(2), 131–147. doi:10.1177/089448651002300203

Monferrer, D., Blesa, A., & Ripolles, M. (2015). Born global through knowledge-based dynamic capabilities and network market orientation. *BRQ Business Research Quarterly*, *18*(1), 18–36. doi:10.1016/j.brq.2014.04.001

Morck, R., & Yeung, B. (2004b), Special issues relating to corporate governance and family control. *World Bank Policy Research Working Paper 3406.*

Morck, R., Shleifer, A., & Vishny, R. (1988). Management ownership and market valuation: An empirical analysis. *Journal of Financial Economics*, *20*, 293–316. doi:10.1016/0304-405X(88)90048-7

Morck, R., Stangeland, D. A., & Yeung, B. (2000). Inherited wealth, corporate control, and economic growth: The Canadian disease. In R. Morck (Ed.), *Concentrated Corporate Ownership* (pp. 319–369). Chicago: University of Chicago Press. doi:10.7208/chicago/9780226536828.001.0001

Morck, R., Wolfenzon, D., & Yeung, B. (2005). Corporate governance, economic entrenchment, and growth. *Journal of Economic Literature*, *43*(3), 655–720. doi:10.1257/002205105774431252

Morgan, N. A., & Rego, L. L. (2009). Brand Portfolio Strategy and Firm Performance. *Journal of Marketing*, *73*(1), 59–74. doi:10.1509/jmkg.73.1.59

Morris, M. H. (1998). *Entrepreneurial intensity*. Westport, CT: Quorum Books.

Morris, M. H. (1998). *Entrepreneurial Intensity*. Westport, CT: Quorum.

Morris, M. H., Williams, R. O., Allen, J. A., & Avila, R. A. (1997). Correlates of success in family business transitions. *Journal of Business Venturing*, *12*(5), 358–401. doi:10.1016/S0883-9026(97)00010-4

Moss, T. W., Payne, G. T., & Moore, C. B. (2014). Strategic consistency of exploration and exploitation in family businesses. *Family Business Review*, *27*(1), 51–71. doi:10.1177/0894486513504434

Mudambi, R., & Nicosia, C. (1998). Ownership structure and firm performance: Evidence from the UK financial services industry. *Applied Financial Economics*, *8*(2), 175–180. doi:10.1080/096031098333159

Munari, F., Oriani, R., & Sobrero, M. (2010). The effects of owner identity and external governance systems on R&D investments: A study of Western European firms. *Research Policy*, *39*(8), 1093–1104. doi:10.1016/j.respol.2010.05.004

Muñoz-Bullón, F., & Sánchez-Bueno, M. J. (2011). The impact of family involvement on the R&D intensity of publicly traded firms. *Family Business Review*, *24*(1), 62–70. doi:10.1177/0894486510396870

Murphy, L., & Lambrechts, F. (2015). Investigating the actual career decisions of the next generation: The impact of family business involvement. *Journal of Family Business Strategy*, *6*(1), 33–44. doi:10.1016/j.jfbs.2014.10.003

Murray, B. (2003). The succession transition process: A longitudinal perspective. *Family Business Review*, *16*(1), 17–33. doi:10.1111/j.1741-6248.2003.00017.x

Muskataillo, M., Autio, E., & Zahra, S. A. (2002). Relational and contractual governance in family firms: Effects on strategic decision making. *Family Business Review*, *15*(3), 205–222. doi:10.1111/j.1741-6248.2002.00205.x

Mustakallio, M., & Autio, E. (2001). *Optimal governance in family firms*. Paper presented at the Babson Entrepreneurship Conference.

Myers, S. C. (1977). Determinants of corporate borrowing. *Journal of Financial Economics*, *5*(2), 147–175. doi:10.1016/0304-405X(77)90015-0

Myers, S. C. (1984). The capital structure puzzle. *The Journal of Finance*, *39*(3), 574–592. doi:10.1111/j.1540-6261.1984.tb03646.x

Myers, S. C. (2001). Capital structure. *The Journal of Economic Perspectives*, *15*(2), 81–102. doi:10.1257/jep.15.2.81

Myers, S. C., & Majluf, N. (1984). Corporate financing and investment decisions when firms have information that investors do not have. *Journal of Financial Economics*, *13*(2), 187–221. doi:10.1016/0304-405X(84)90023-0

Nagy, S. (2013). The internationalisation of the Spanish SME sector. *Society and Economy*, *35*(1), 71–86. doi:10.1556/SocEc.2012.0005

Naldi, L., Chirico, F., Kellermanns, F. W., & Campopiano, G. (2015). All in the family? An exploratory study of family member advisors and firm performance. *Family Business Review*, *28*(3), 227–242. doi:10.1177/0894486515581951

Naldi, L., Nordqvist, M., Sjöberg, K., & Wiklund, J. (2007). Entrepreneurial orientation, risk taking and performance in family firms. *Family Business Review*, *23*(1), 33–47. doi:10.1111/j.1741-6248.2007.00082.x

Navis, C., & Ozbek, O. V. (2016). The right people in the wrong places: The paradox of entrepreneurial entry and successful opportunity realization. *Academy of Management Review*, *41*(1), 109–129. doi:10.5465/amr.2013.0175

Navis, C., & Ozbek, O. V. (2017). Why context matters: Overconfidence, narcissism, and the role of objective uncertainty in entrepreneurship. *Academy of Management Review*, *42*(1), 148–153. doi:10.5465/amr.2016.0208

Neckebrouck, J., Schulze, W., & Zellweger, T. (2018). Are family firms good employers? *Academy of Management Journal*, *61*(2), 553–585. doi:10.5465/amj.2016.0765

Nekhili, M., Nagati, H., Chtioui, T., & Rebolledo, C. (2017). Corporate social responsibility disclosure and market value: Family versus nonfamily firms. *Journal of Business Research*, *77*, 41–52. doi:10.1016/j.jbusres.2017.04.001

Nelson, R.R. (1991). Why do firms differ and how does industry matter?, *Strategic Management Journal, 12*(special issue winter), 61-74.

Nelson, R.R. (1991): Why do firms differ and how does industry matter? *Strategic Management Journal, 12* (special issue winter), 61-74.

Nelson, R. R. (1995). Recent evolutionary theorizing about economic change. *Journal of Economic Literature*, *33*(March), 48–90.

Nelson, R. R., & Winter, S. (1982). *An evolutionary theory of economic change*. Cambridge, MA: Harvard University Press.

Neubauer, F., & Lank, A. G. (1998). *The family business: it's governance for sustainability*. New York: Routledge. doi:10.1007/978-1-349-14465-5

Neubauer, F., & Lank, A. G. (2003). *La empresa familiar: cómo dirigirla para que perdure*. Bilbao, España: Deusto.

Neubauer, F., & Lank, A. G. (2016). *The Family Business: Its governance for sustainability*. London: Springer.

Neubauer, F., & Lank, A. G. (2016). *The family business: Its governance for sustainability*. Springer.

Neubaum, D. O., Dibrell, C., & Craig, J. B. (2012). Balancing natural environmental con-cerns of internal and external stakeholders in family and non-family businesses. *Journal of Family Business Strategy*, *3*(1), 28–37. doi:10.1016/j.jfbs.2012.01.003

Neubaum, D. O., Kammerlander, N., & Brigham, K. H. (2019). Capturing family firm heterogeneity: How taxonomies and typologies can help the field move forward. *Family Business Review*, *32*(2), 106–130.

Neubaum, D. O., Kammerlander, N., & Brigham, K. H. (2019). Capturing Family Firm Heterogeneity: How Taxonomies and Typologies Can Help the Field Move Forward. *Family Business Review*, *32*(2), 106–130.

Newbert, S. L. (2007). Empirical research on the resource-based view of the firm: An assessment and suggestions for future research. *Strategic Management Journal*, *28*(2), 121–146. doi:10.1002mj.573

Nickel, S., Nicolitsas, D., & Dryden, N. (1997). What makes firms perform well? *European Economic Review*, *41*(3-5), 783–796. doi:10.1016/S0014-2921(97)00037-8

Nielsen, S. (2010). Top management team diversity: A review of theories and methodologies. *International Journal of Management Reviews*, *12*(3), 301–316.

Nieto, M. J., Fernández, Z., Casasola, M. J., & Usero, B. (2009). Impacto de la implicación familiar y de otros accionistas de referencia en la creación de valor, *Revista de Estudios Empresariales. Segunda Época*, *2*, 5–20.

Nieto, M. J., Santamaria, L., & Fernandez, Z. (2015). Understanding the innovation behaviour of family firms. *Journal of Small Business Management*, *53*(2), 382–399. doi:10.1111/jsbm.12075

Nohria, N., & Gulati, R. (1996). Is Slack Good or Bad for Innovation? *Academy of Management Journal*, *39*(5), 1245–1264. doi:10.5465/256998

Nonaka, I., & Takeuchi, H. (1998). A Theory of the Firm's Knowledge-Creation Dynamics., In A. Chandler, P. Hagström & Ö. Sölvell (Eds.), The Dynamic Firm, The Role of Technology, Strategy, Organization, and Regions. Oxford University Press.

Nonaka, I., & Konno, N. (1998). The concept of Ba: Building a foundation for knowledge creation. *California Management Review*, *40*(3), 40–54. doi:10.2307/41165942

Nordqvist, M., Habbershon, T. G., & Melin, L. (2009). Transgenerational entrepreneurship: Exploring entrepreneurial orientation in family firms. In H. Landström, D. Smallbone, H. Crijns, & E. Laveren (Eds.), *Entrepreneurship, sustainable growth, and performance: Frontiers in European entrepreneurship research* (pp. 93–116). Londres, UK: Edward Elgar.

Nordqvist, M., Hall, A., & Melin, L. (2009). Qualitative research on family businesses: The relevance and usefulness of the interpretive approach. *Journal of Management & Organization*, *15*(3), 294–308. doi:10.1017/S1833367200002637

Nordqvist, M., & Melin, L. (2002). The dynamics of family firms: An institutional perspective on corporate governance and strategic change. In D. Fletcher (Ed.), *Understanding the small family business*. Londres: Routledge.

Nordqvist, M., & Melin, L. (2010). The promise of the strategy as practice perspective for family business strategy research. *Journal of Family Business Strategy*, *1*(1), 15–25. doi:10.1016/j.jfbs.2009.12.001

Nordqvist, M., Sharma, P., & Chirico, F. (2014). Family firm heterogeneity and governance: A configuration approach. *Journal of Small Business Management*, *52*(2), 192–209. doi:10.1111/jsbm.12096

Nunnally, J. C. (1978). *Psychometric theory*. New York: McGraw-Hill.

O'Reilly, C. A. III, & Tushman, M. L. (2008). Ambidexterity as a dynamic capability: Resolving the innovator's dilemma. *Research in Organizational Behavior*, *28*, 185–206. doi:10.1016/j.riob.2008.06.002

O'Reilly, C. A. III, & Tushman, M. L. (2011). Organizational ambidexterity in action: How managers explore and exploit. *California Management Review*, *53*(4), 5–22. doi:10.1525/cmr.2011.53.4.5

O'Reilly, C. A. III, & Tushman, M. L. (2013). Organizational ambidexterity: Past, present, and future. *The Academy of Management Perspectives*, *27*(4), 324–338. doi:10.5465/amp.2013.0025

OECD. (2005). *Oslo Manual. Guidelines for collecting and interpreting innovation data*. OECD.

Okoroafo, S. (1999). Internationalization of family businesses: Evidence from Northwest Ohio, USA. *Family Business Review*, *21*, 147–158.

Olivares-Mesa, A., & Cabrera-Suárez, K. (2006). Factors affecting the timing of the export development process: Does the family influence on the business make a difference? *International Journal of Globalisation and Small Business*, *1*(4), 326–339. doi:10.1504/IJGSB.2006.012183

Olson, D. H. (2000). Circumplex model of marital and family systems. *Journal of Family Therapy*, *22*(2), 144–167. doi:10.1111/1467-6427.00144 PMID:6840263

Olson, P. D., Zuiker, V. S., Danes, S. M., Stafford, K., Heck, R. K. Z., & Duncan, K. A. (2003). The impact of the family and the business on family business sustainability. *Journal of Business Venturing*, *18*(5), 639–666. doi:10.1016/S0883-9026(03)00014-4

Orlitzky, M., Siegel, D. S., & Waldman, D. A. (2011). Strategic corporate social responsibility and environmental sustainability. *Business & Society*, *50*(1), 6–27. doi:10.1177/0007650310394323

Ortín, P. (1998). El proceso de acumulación de capacidades directivas: Evidencia empírica a partir de una muestra de directivos españoles. *CEDE*, *2*, 253–274.

Osbaldeston, M., & Barham, K. (1992). Using management development for competitive advantage. *Long Range Planning*, *25*(6), 18–24. doi:10.1016/0024-6301(92)90165-X

Osterman, P. (1994). Supervision, discretion and work organization. *The American Economic Review*, *84*(2), 380–384.

Oswald, S. L., & Janera, J. S. (1991). The influence of ownership on performance: An empirical study. *Strategic Management Journal*, *12*(4), 321–326. doi:10.1002mj.4250120407

Oudah, M., Jabeen, F., & Dixon, C. (2018). Determinants linked to family business sustainability in UAE: An AHP approach. *Sustainability*, *10*(1), 1–23. doi:10.3390u10010246 PMID:30607262

Ozkaya, H. E., Droge, C., Hult, G. T. M., Calantone, R., & Ozkaya, E. (2015). Market orientation, knowledge competence, and innovation. *International Journal of Research in Marketing*, *32*(3), 309–318. doi:10.1016/j.ijresmar.2014.10.004

Pace, L. A. (2016). How do tourism firms innovate for sustainable energy consumption? A capabilities perspective on the adoption of energy efficiency in tourism accommodation establishments. *Journal of Cleaner Production*, *111*, 409–420. doi:10.1016/j.jclepro.2015.01.095

Pache, A.-C., & Santos, F. M. (2010). *Inside the Hybrid Organization: An* Organizational Level View of Responses to Conflicting Institutional Demands. Research Center ESSEC Working Paper 1101. Available at SSRN: https://ssrn.com/abstract=2328257

Pagano, M., Panetta, F., & Zingales, L. (1998). Why do companies go public? An empirical analysis. *The Journal of Finance*, *53*(1), 27–64. doi:10.1111/0022-1082.25448

Pal, R., Torstensson, H., & Mattila, H. (2014). Antecedents of organizational resilience in economic crises—An empirical study of Swedish textile and clothing SMEs. *International Journal of Production Economics*, *147*, 410–428. doi:10.1016/j.ijpe.2013.02.031

Pangarkar, N. (2008). Internationalization and performance of small- and medium sized enterprises. *Journal of World Business*, *43*(4), 475–485. doi:10.1016/j.jwb.2007.11.009

Pantagakis, E., Terzakis, D., & Arvanitis, S. (2012). *R&D Investments and Firm Performance: An Empirical Investigation of the High Technology Sector (Software and Hardware) in the E.U.* doi:10.2139srn.2178919

Papadakis, V. M., & Barwise, P. (2002). How Much Do CEOs and Top Managers Matter in Strategic Decision- Making? *British Journal of Management*, *13*(1), 83–95. doi:10.1111/1467-8551.00224

Parker, H., & Ameen, K. (2018). The role of resilience capabilities in shaping how firms respond to disruptions. *Journal of Business Research*, *88*, 535–541. doi:10.1016/j.jbusres.2017.12.022

Patel, P. C., & Fiet, J. O. (2011). Knowledge combination and the potential advantages of family firms in searching for opportunities. *Entrepreneurship Theory and Practice*, *35*(6), 1179–1197. doi:10.1111/j.1540-6520.2011.00497.x

Patel, V. K., Pieper, T. M., & Hair, J. F. Jr. (2012). The global family business: Challenges and drivers for cross-border growth. *Business Horizons*, *55*(3), 231–239. doi:10.1016/j.bushor.2012.01.002

Pattanayak, D., Koilakuntla, M., & Punyatoya, P. (2017). Investigating the influence of TQM, service quality and market orientation on customer satisfaction and loyality in the Indian banking sector. *International Journal of Quality & Reliability Management*, *34*(3), 362–377. doi:10.1108/IJQRM-04-2015-0057

Pavitt, K. (1991). Key characteristics of the large innovating firm. *British Journal of Management*, *2*(1), 41–50. doi:10.1111/j.1467-8551.1991.tb00014.x

Pearson, A. W., Carr, J. C., & Shaw, J. C. (2008). Toward a theory of familiness: A social capital perspective. *Entrepreneurship Theory and Practice*, *32*(6), 949–969. doi:10.1111/j.1540-6520.2008.00265.x

Peay, R. T., & Dyer, G. (1989). Power orientations of entrepreneurs and succession planning. *Journal of Small Business Management*, *27*(1), 47–52.

Pedreño, A., & Ramón, A. (2009). El turismo: Globalización, competitividad y sostenibilidad. *Colección Mediterráneo Económico*, *16*, 227–256.

Pelham, A. M. (2015). Strategy, Market Orientation, or Environment: Relative Influence on Small Manufacturing Firms. In *Proceedings of the 1998 Academy of Marketing Science (AMS) Annual Conference*. Cham: Springer. 10.1007/978-3-319-13084-2_107

Pena, A. I. P., Jamilena, D. M. F., & Molina, M. A. R. (2017). The effects of perceived value on loyalty: The moderating effect of market orientation adoption. *Service Business*, *11*(1), 93–116. doi:10.100711628-016-0303-8

Peng, M. W. (2001). The resource-based view and international business. *Journal of Management*, *27*(6), 803–829. doi:10.1177/014920630102700611

Peng, M. W., & York, A. S. (2001). Behind intermediary performance in export trade: Transactions, agents, and resources. *Journal of International Business Studies*, *32*(2), 327–346. doi:10.1057/palgrave.jibs.8490955

Penrose, E. (1959). *The Theory of the growth of the firm*. New York: John Wiley & Sons.

Penrose, E. (1959). *The Theory of the Growth of the Firm*. New York: John Wiley & Sons.

Pereira, T., & Sousa, M. (2017). Is there still a Berlin Wall in the post-issue operating performance of European IPOs? *International Journal of Finance & Economics*, *22*(2), 139–158. doi:10.1002/ijfe.1573

Pérez-Cabañero, C., González-Cruz, T., & Cruz-Ros, S. (2012). Do family SME managers value marketing capabilities' contribution to firm performance? *Marketing Intelligence & Planning*, *30*(2), 116–142. doi:10.1108/02634501211211948

Pérez-González, F. (2006). Inherited control and firm performance. *The American Economic Review*, *96*(5), 1559–1588. doi:10.1257/aer.96.5.1559

Perez-Luno, A., Saparito, P., & Gopalakrishnan, S. (2016). Small and Medium-Sized Enterprise's Entrepreneurial versus Market Orientation and the Creation of Tacit Knowledge. *Journal of Small Business Management*, *54*(1), 262–278. doi:10.1111/jsbm.12144

Pérez, M. J., Basco, R., García-Tenorio, J., Giménez, J., & Sánchez, I. (2007). *Fundamentos en la dirección de la empresa familiar. Emprendedor, empresa y familia*. Madrid, España: Thomson.

Pervin, A. (1997). A conversation with Henry Mintzberg. *Family Business Review*, *10*(2), 1985–198. doi:10.1111/j.1741-6248.1997.00185.x

Peteraf, M. A. (1993). The cornerstone of competitive advantage: A resource-based view. *Strategic Management Journal*, *14*(3), 179–191. doi:10.1002mj.4250140303

Peters, M., & Buhalis, D. (2004). Family hotel business: Strategic planning and the need for education and training. *Education + Training*, *46*(8/9), 406–415. doi:10.1108/00400910410569524

Pettit, R. R., & Singer, R. F. (1985). Small business finance: A research agenda. *Financial Management*, *14*(3), 47–60. doi:10.2307/3665059

Pfeffer, J., & Salancik, G. R. (2003). *The External Control of Organizations: A Resource Dependence Perspective*. Stanford, CA: Stanford University Press.

Piccoli, G., & Ives, B. (2005). IT-dependent strategic initiatives and sustained competitive advantage: A review and synthesis of the literature. *Management Information Systems Quarterly*, *29*(4), 747–776. doi:10.2307/25148708

Pickett, L. (1998). Competencies and managerial effectiveness: Putting competencies to work. *Public Personnel Management*, *27*(1), 103–115. doi:10.1177/009102609802700110

Pieper, T. M., Klein, S. B., & Jaskiewicz, P. (2008). The impact of goal alignment on board existence and top management team composition: Evidence from family-influenced businesses. *Journal of Small Business Management*, *46*(3), 372–394. doi:10.1111/j.1540-627X.2008.00249.x

Pindado, J., & Requejo, I. (2015). Family business performance from a governance perspective: A review of empirical research. *International Journal of Management Reviews*, *17*(3), 279–331. doi:10.1111/ijmr.12040

Pindado, J., Requejo, I., & de la Torre, C. (2011). Family control and investment-cash flow sensitivity: Empirical evidence from the Euro zone. *Journal of Corporate Finance*, *17*(5), 1389–1409. doi:10.1016/j.jcorpfin.2011.07.003

Pindado, J., Requejo, I., & la Torre, C. (2015). Does family control shape corporate capital structure? An empirical analysis of eurozone firms. *Journal of Business Finance & Accounting*, *42*(7-8), 965–1006. doi:10.1111/jbfa.12124

Pisano, G.P. (1994). Knowledge, integration, and the locus of learning: An empirical analysis of process development. *Strategic Management Journal, 15*(winter special issue), 85-100.

Pisano, G. P. (2000). In search of dynamic capabilities: the origins of R&D competence in biopharmaceuticals. In G. Dosi, R. R. Nelson, & S. G. Winter (Eds.), *The Nature and Dynamics of Organizational Capabilities*. Oxford, UK: Oxford University Press.

Pittino, D., & Visintin, F. (2009). Innovation and strategic types of family SMEs – a test and extension of Miles and Snow's configurational model. *Journal of Enterprising Culture*, *17*(03), 257–295. doi:10.1142/S0218495809000382

Pittino, D., Visintin, F., Lenger, T., & Sternad, D. (2016). Are high performance work practices really necessary in family SMEs? An analysis of the impact on employee retention. *Journal of Family Business Strategy*, *7*(2), 75–89. doi:10.1016/j.jfbs.2016.04.002

Plá Barber, J. (1999). Filiales de Entrada en los Mercados Internacionales: Factores Determinantes. *Revista de Economía Aplicada*, *20*, 29–51.

Pollak, R. (1985). A transaction cost approach to families and households. *Journal of Economic Literature*, *23*, 581–608.

Porter, M.E. (1991). Towards a dynamic theory of strategy. *Strategic Management Journal, 12*(special issue winter), 95-117.

Porter, M. E. (1979). The Structure within Industries and Companies Performance. *The Review of Economics and Statistics*, *61*(2), 214–227. doi:10.2307/1924589

Porter, M. E. (1980). *Competitive strategy. Techniques for analyzing industries and competitors*. Nueva York, NY: The Fress Press.

Porter, M. E. (1985). *Competitive advantage. Creating and sustaining superior performance*. Nueva York, NY: The Fress Press.

Porter, M. E. (1985). *Competitive Advantage: creating and sustaining superior performance*. New York: Free Press.

Porter, M. E. (1985). *Competitive Advantages*. New York: Free Press.

Porter, M. E. (1990a). *The competitive advantage of nations*. Nueva York, NY: The Fress Press. doi:10.1007/978-1-349-11336-1

Porter, M. E. (1990b). The competitive advantage of nations. *Harvard Business Review*, *68*(2), 73–93.

Porter, M. E., & Kramer, M. R. (2006). The link between competitive advantage and corporate social responsibility. *Harvard Business Review*, *84*(12), 78–92. PMID:17183795

Poutziouris, P. Z. (2001). The views of family companies on venture capital: Empirical evidence from the UK small to medium-size enterprising economy. *Family Business Review*, *14*(3), 277–291. doi:10.1111/j.1741-6248.2001.00277.x

Poza, E. (1995). *A la sombra del roble: La empresa privada familiar y su continuidad*. Editorial Universitaria para la Empresa Familiar.

Poza, E. J. (2013). *Family business.* Cengage Learning.

Poza, E. J., & Daugherty, M. S. (2014). *Family Business.* Cengage Learning.

Prajogo, D. (2016). The Role of Human Capital and Market Orientation as Determinants of Service Innovation. *International Academy of Management and Business Conference.*

Pratono, A. H., & Mahmood, R. (2015). Mediating effect of marketing capability and reward philosophy in the relationship between entrepreneurial orientation and firm performance. *Journal of Global Entrepreneurship Research, 5*(1), 5–15. doi:10.118640497-015-0023-x

Pratt, M. G., & Foreman, P. O. (2000). Classifying managerial responses to multiple organizational identities. *Academy of Management Review, 25*(1), 18–42. doi:10.5465/amr.2000.2791601

Prud'homme, B., & Raymond, L. (2016). Implementation of sustainable development practices in the hospitality industry: A case study of five Canadian hotels. *International Journal of Contemporary Hospitality Management, 28*(3), 609–639. doi:10.1108/IJCHM-12-2014-0629

Pukall, T. J., & Calabrò, A. (2014). The Internationalization of family firms: A critical review and integrative model. *Family Business Review, 27*(2), 323–332. doi:10.1177/0894486513491423

Qureshi, S., Chen, C., & Wang, M. (2017). A multi-dimensional professionalisation construct for UK family businesses–building internal capabilities and improving business performance. In *ICSB World Conference Proceedings* (pp. 1-10). International Council for Small Business (ICSB).

Ragin, C. C., & Fiss, P. C. (2008). Net effects analysis versus configurational analysis: An empirical demonstration. *Redesigning social inquiry: Fuzzy sets and beyond, 240*, 190-212.

Ragin, C. (2000). *Fuzzy-set social science.* Chicago: University of Chicago Press.

Ragin, C. C. (2008). *Redesigning social inquiry: Fuzzy sets and beyond.* Chicago, IL: University of Chicago Press. doi:10.7208/chicago/9780226702797.001.0001

Ragin, C. C., & Sean, D. (2016). *Fuzzy-set/qualitative comparative analysis 3.0.* Irvine, CA: University of California.

Raisch, S., & Birkinshaw, J. (2008). Organizational ambidexterity: Antecedents, outcomes, and moderators. *Journal of Management, 34*(3), 375–409. doi:10.1177/0149206308316058

Raisch, S., Birkinshaw, J., Probst, G., & Tushman, M. L. (2009). Organizational ambidexterity: Balancing exploitation and exploration for sustained performance. *Organization Science, 20*(4), 685–695. doi:10.1287/orsc.1090.0428

Rakthin, S., Calantone, R. J., & Wang, J. F. (2016). Managing market intelligence: The comparative role of absorptive capacity and market orientation. *Journal of Business Research, 69*(12), 5569–5577. doi:10.1016/j.jbusres.2016.03.064

Ramón-Llorens, M. C., García-Meca, E., & Duréndez, A. (2017). Influence of CEO characteristics in family firms internationalization. *International Business Review, 26*(4), 786–799. doi:10.1016/j.ibusrev.2017.01.007

Rauch, A., Frese, M., & Utsch, A. (2005). Effects of human capital and long-term human resources development and utilization on employment growth of small-scale businesses: A causal analysis. *Entrepreneurship Theory and Practice, 29*(6), 681–698.

Rau, S. B., Schneider-Siebke, V., & Gunther, C. (2019). Family Firm Values Explaining Family Firm Heterogeneity. *Family Business Review, 32*(2), 195–215.doi:10.1177/0894486519846670

Rau, S. B., Schneider-Siebke, V., & Günther, C. (2019). Family firm values explaining family firm heterogeneity. *Family Business Review*, *32*(2), 195–215.

Raymond, L., Marchand, M., St-Pierre, J., Cadieux, L., & Labelle, F. (2013). Dimensions of small business performance from the owner-manager's perspective: A re-conceptualization and empirical validation. *Entrepreneurship and Regional Development*, *25*(5-6), 468–499. doi:10.1080/08985626.2013.782344

Reddrop, A., & Mapunda, G. (2015). Family businesses: Seekers of advice. *Journal of Family Business Management*, *5*(1), 90–115. doi:10.1108/JFBM-08-2014-0018

Reed, R., Lemak, D. J., & Montgomery, J. C. (1996). Beyond process: TQM content and firm performance. *Academy of Management Review*, *12*(1), 173–202. doi:10.5465/amr.1996.9602161569

Rees, W., & Rodionova, T. (2015). The influence of family ownership on corporate social responsibility: An international analysis of publicly listed companies. *Corporate Governance*, *23*(3), 184–202. doi:10.1111/corg.12086

Reuber, A. R., & Fischer, E. (1997). The influence of the management team's international experience on the internationalization behaviors of SMEs. *Journal of International Business Studies*, *28*(4), 807–825. doi:10.1057/palgrave.jibs.8490120

Revilla, A. J., Perez-Luno, A., & Nieto, M. J. (2016). Does Family Involvement in Management Reduce the Risk of Business Failure? The Moderating Role of Entrepreneurial Orientation. *Family Business Review*, *29*(4), 365–379. doi:10.1177/0894486516671075

Rhoades, L., & Eisenberger, R. (2002). Perceived organizational support: A review of the literature. *The Journal of Applied Psychology*, *87*(4), 698–714. doi:10.1037/0021-9010.87.4.698 PMID:12184574

Rialp, A. (1999). Los Enfoques Micro-organizativos de la Internacionalización de la Empresa: Una Revisión y Síntesis de la Literatura. *ICE: Revista de Economía*, *781*, 117–128.

Rindova, V. P., & Kotha, S. (2001). Continuous morphing: Competing through dynamic capabilities, form, and function. *Academy of Management Journal*, *44*, 1263–1280.

Rindova, V. P., Williamson, I. O., Petkova, A. P., & Sever, J. M. (2005). Being good or being known: An empirical examination of the dimensions, antecedents, and consequences of organizational reputation. *Academy of Management Journal*, *48*(6), 1033–1049. doi:10.5465/amj.2005.19573108

Rivo-Lopez, E., Villanueva-Villar, M., Vaquero-García, A., & Lago-Peñas, S. (2017). Family offices. What, why and what for. *Organizational Dynamics*, *46*(4), 262–270. doi:10.1016/j.orgdyn.2017.03.002

Robins, J., & Wiersema, M. F. (1995). A resource-based approach to the multibusiness firm: Empirical analysis of portfolio interrelationships and corporate financial performance. *Strategic Management Journal*, *16*(4), 277–299. doi:10.1002mj.4250160403

Roca Junyet, M. (2005). La empresa familiar en el ordenamiento jurídico interno y comunitario, en la obra El patrimonio familiar, profesional y empresarial. Sus protocolos, coordinado por M. Garrido Melero y J.M. Fugardo Estivill, tomo IV, Ordenamiento jurídico y empresa familiar (p.30). El protocolo familiar, coordinado por V.M. Garrido de Palma, Consejo General del Notariado. Barcelona, España: Bosch.

Rodríguez-Sánchez, A., Guinot, J., Chiva, R., & López-Cabrales, Á. (2019). How to emerge stronger: Antecedents and consequences of organizational resilience. *Journal of Management & Organization*, 1–18. doi:10.1017/jmo.2019.5

Rogoff, E. G., Lee, M., & Suh, D. (2004). Who done it? Attributions by entrepreneurs and experts of the factors that cause and impede small business success. *Journal of Small Business Management*, *42*(4), 374–376. doi:10.1111/j.1540-627X.2004.00117.x

Roida, H. Y., & Sunarjanto, N. A. (2012). Family ownership type and the international involvement of SMEs: Empirical study of agency theory in East Java Indonesia. *The China Business Review*, *11*, 224–232.

Rojas, A. (2019). *Conditions for innovation in family firms. A configurational approach.* XXIX Conference ACEDE, Globalization under complexity and uncertainty environments.

Rojo, A., Diéguez, J., & López, P. (2011). Importancia del concepto de Empresa Familiar en investigación: Utilización de la base de datos SABI para su clasificación. *Revista de Empresa Familiar*, *1*(1), 53–67.

Rojo-Ramírez, A. A., & Martínez-Romero, M. J. (2018). Required and obtained equity returns in privately held businesses: The impact of family nature—evidence before and after the global economic crisis. *Review of Managerial Science*, *12*(3), 771–801. doi:10.100711846-017-0230-7

Romano, C., Tanewski, G., & Smyrnios, K. (2001). Capital structure decision making. *Journal of Business Venturing*, *16*(3), 285–310. doi:10.1016/S0883-9026(99)00053-1

Rondi, E., De Massis, A. & Kotlar, J. (2018). Unlocking innovation potential: a typology of family business innovation postures and the critical role of the family system. *Journal of Family Business Strategy*. DOI: doi:10.1016/j.jfbs.2017.12.001

Roquebert, J., Phillips, R., & Westfall, P. (1996). Market vs management: What drives profitability? *Strategic Management Journal*, *17*(8), 653–664. doi:10.1002/(SICI)1097-0266(199610)17:8<653::AID-SMJ840>3.0.CO;2-O

Rosenbaum, P. R., & Rubin, D. B. (1983). The central role of the propensity score in observational studies for causal effects. *Biometrika*, *70*(1), 41–55. doi:10.1093/biomet/70.1.41

Rosenblatt, P. C., deMik, L., Anderson, R. M., & Johnson, P. A. (1985). *The family in business: Understanding and dealing with the challenges entrepreneurial families face*. San Francisco: Jossey Bass.

Rothwell, R. (1977). The characteristics of successful innovators and technically progressive firms. *R & D Management*, *7*(3), 191–206. doi:10.1111/j.1467-9310.1977.tb01334.x

Rousseau, D. M. (1985). Issues of level in organizational research: Multi-level and cross-level perspectives. In L. L. Cummings & B. M. Staw (Eds.), *Research in organizational behavior* (Vol. 7, pp. 1–37). Greenwich, CT: JAI Press.

Rubenson, G. C., & Gupta, A. K. (1996). The initial succession: A contingency model of founder tenure. *Entrepreneurship Theory and Practice*, *21*(2), 21–32. doi:10.1177/104225879602100202

Rubenstein, C. (1990). Power and priorities. *Family Business Magazine*, *2*(2), 37.

Rubio, A., & Aragón, A. (2002). Factores explicativos del éxito competitivo. Un estudio empírico en la PYME. *Cuadernos de Gestión*, *2*(1), 49–63.

Rubio, A., & Aragón, A. (2006). Competitividad y recursos estratégicos en las PYMEs. *Revista de Empresa*, *17*, 32–47.

Rubio, A., & Aragón, A. (2008). Recursos estratégicos en las PYMEs. *Revista Europea de Dirección y Economía de la Empresa*, *17*(1), 103–126.

Ruiz-Jiménez, J. M., & Fuentes-Fuentes, M. del M. (2016). Management capabilities, innovation, and gender diversity in the top management team: An empirical analysis in technology-based SMEs. *BRQ Business Research Quarterly*, *19*(2), 107–121. doi:10.1016/j.brq.2015.08.003

Rumelt, R. P. (1984). Toward a strategic theory of the firm. In E. Lamb (Ed.), *Competitive Strategic Management* (pp. 556–570). Englewood Cliffs, NJ: Prentice-Hall.

Rumelt, R. P. (1991). How much does industry matter? *Strategic Management Journal, 12*(3), 167–185. doi:10.1002mj.4250120302

Rumelt, R. P., Schendel, D., & Teece, D. (1991). Strategic management and economics. *Strategic Management Journal, 12*(S2), 5–29. doi:10.1002mj.4250121003

Russo, M., & Fouts, P. (1997). A resource-based perspective on corporate environmental performance and profitability. *Academy of Management Journal, 40*(3), 534–559.

Sacristán, M., Rico, G. & Lafuente, C. (2011). Spanish SMEs and Family Firms export behavior: are there differences in their incremental approach? *Revista de Empresa Familiar, 1*(1), 7-21.

Sacristán, M., & Gómez, S. (2006). Family ownership, corporate governance and firm value: evidence from the Spanish market. In P. Z. Poutziouris, K. X. Smyrnios, & S. B. Klein (Eds.), *Handbook of Research on Family Business* (pp. 593–613). Edward Elgar Publishing Limited.

Sacristán-Navarro, M., Gómez-Ansón, S., & Cabeza-García, L. (2011). Family ownership and control, the presence of other large shareholders, and firm performance: Further evidence. *Family Business Review, 24*(1), 71–93. doi:10.1177/0894486510396705

Salas, V. (1992a). La empresa: un análisis económico frente a Europa. In *Albi, E. (coord.): Europa y la competitividad de la economía española* (pp. 233–250). Barcelona, España: Ariel.

Salas, V. (1992b). *Aspectos microorganizativos de la competitividad, Documento de Trabajo nº 9205*. Madrid, España: Fundación Empresa Pública.

Salas, V. (1993a). Factores de competitividad empresarial: Consideraciones generales. *Papeles de Economía Española, 56*, 379–396.

Salas, V. (1993b). El papel de los mecanismos de asignación de capital en la competitividad a largo plazo de la economía española. In J. Velarde (Ed.), *Empresas y empresarios españoles en la encrucijada de los noventa. VII Jornadas de Alicante sobre Economía Española* (pp. 109–132). Madrid, España: Civitas.

Salomon, R., & Shaver, M. (2005). Export and domestic sales: Their interrelationship and determinants. *Strategic Management Journal, 26*(9), 855–871. doi:10.1002mj.481

Salovey, P., O'Leary, A., Stretton, M. S., Fishkin, S. A., & Drake, C. A. (1991). Influence of mood on judgments about health and illness. In J. P. Forgas (Ed.), *Emotion and social judgments* (p. 241262). Elmsford, NY: Pergamon Press.

Salvato, C. (2004). Predictors of entrepreneurship in family firms. *Journal of Private Equity, 7*(3), 68–76. doi:10.3905/jpe.2004.412339

Salvato, C., Chirico, F., Melin, L., & Seidl, D. (2019). Coupling family business research with organization studies: Interpretations, issues and insights. *Organization Studies, 40*(6), 775–791. doi:10.1177/0170840619841402

Salvato, C., & Melin, L. (2008). Creating value across generations in family-controlled businesses: The role of family social capital. *Family Business Review, 21*(3), 259–276. doi:10.1177/08944865080210030107

Samara, G., Jamali, D., Sierra, V., & Parada, M. J. (2018). Who are the best performers? The environmental social performance of family firms. *Journal of Family Business Strategy, 9*(1), 33–43. doi:10.1016/j.jfbs.2017.11.004

Sánchez.Ruiz, P., Daspit, J. J., Holt, D. T., & Rutherford, M. W. (2019). Family social capital in the family firm: A taxonomic classification, relationships with outcomes, and directions for advancement. *Family Business Review, 32*(2), 131–153.

Sanchez-Famoso, V., Pittino, D., Chirico, F., Maseda, A., & Iturralde, T. (2019). Social Capital and Innovation in Family Firms. The Moderating Roles of Family Control and Generational Involvement. *Scandinavian Journal of Management*. doi:10.1016/j.scaman.2019.02.002

Sanchez-Famoso, V., Maseda, A., & Iturralde, T. (2017). Family involvement in top management team: Impact on relationships between internal social capital and innovation. *Journal of Management & Organization*, *23*(1), 136–162. doi:10.1017/jmo.2016.2

Sanchez-Ruiz, P., Daspit, J. J., Holt, D. T., & Rutherford, M. W. (2019). Family Social Capital in the Family Firm: A Taxonomic Classification, Relationships With Outcomes, and Directions for Advancement. *Family Business Review*, *32*(2), 131–153.

Santiago, A. L. (2000). Succession experiences in Philippine family businesses. *Family Business Review*, *13*(1), 15–35. doi:10.1111/j.1741-6248.2000.00015.x

Sarbah, A., & Xiao, W. (2015). Good corporate governance structures: A must for family businesses. *Open Journal of Business and Management*, *3*(1), 40–57. doi:10.4236/ojbm.2015.31005

Sardeshmukh, S. R., & Corbett, A. C. (2011). The duality of internal and external development of successors: Opportunity recognition in family firms. *Family Business Review*, *24*(2), 111–125. doi:10.1177/0894486510391783

Sarkees, M., Hulland, J., & Chatterjee, R. (2014). Investments in exploitation and exploration capabilities: Balance versus focus. *Journal of Marketing Theory and Practice*, *22*(1), 7–24. doi:10.2753/MTP1069-6679220101

Scabini, E., & Iafrate, R. (2003). Psicologia dei legami familiari. Roma: Carocci.

Scabini, E. (1995). *Psicologia sociale della famiglia*. Torino: Bollati Boringhieri.

Schenkel, A., & Teigland, R. (2016). Why doesn't downsizing deliver? A multi-level model integrating downsizing, social capital, dynamic capabilities, and firm performance. *International Journal of Human Resource Management*.

Schmalensee, R. (1985). Do markets differ much? *The American Economic Review*, *75*, 341–351.

Schmid, T. (2013). Control considerations, creditor monitoring, and the capital structure of family firms. *Journal of Banking & Finance*, *37*(2), 257–272. doi:10.1016/j.jbankfin.2012.08.026

Schmid, T., Achleitner, A. K., Ampenberger, M., & Kaserer, C. (2014). Family firms and R&D behavior–New evidence from a large-scale survey. *Research Policy*, *43*(1), 233–244. doi:10.1016/j.respol.2013.08.006

Schmitt, A., & Raisch, S. (2013). Corporate turnarounds: The duality of retrenchment and recovery. *Journal of Management Studies*, *50*(7), 1216–1244.

Schneider, M. R., & Eggert, A. (2014). Embracing complex causality with the QCA method: An invitation. *Journal of Business Market Management*, *7*(1), 312–328.

Schneider, M. R., Schulze-Bentrop, C., & Paunescu, M. (2010). Mapping the institutional capital of high-tech firms: A fuzzy-set analysis of capitalist variety and export performance. *Journal of International Business Studies*, *41*(2), 246–266. doi:10.1057/jibs.2009.36

Scholes, L., & Wilson, N. (2014). The importance of family firm trusts in family firm governance. *Entrepreneurship Theory and Practice*, *38*(6), 1285–1293.

Schulze, W. S., & Gedajlovic, E. R. (2010). Whither family business? *Journal of Management Studies*, *47*(2), 191–204. doi:10.1111/j.1467-6486.2009.00887.x

Schulze, W. S., Lubatkin, M. H., & Dino, R. N. (2003). Exploring the agency consequences of ownership dispersion among the directors of private family firms. *Academy of Management Journal, 46*(2), 179–194.

Schulze, W. S., Lubatkin, M. H., & Dino, R. N. (2003). Toward a theory of agency and altruism in family firms. *Journal of Business Venturing, 18*(4), 473–490. doi:10.1016/S0883-9026(03)00054-5

Schulze, W. S., Lubatkin, M. H., Dino, R. N., & Buchholtz, A. K. (2001). Agency relationships in family firms: Theory and evidence. *Organization Science, 12*(2), 99–116. doi:10.1287/orsc.12.2.99.10114

Schulze, W. S., Lubatkin, M. H., Dino, R. N., & Buchholtz, A. K. (2002). Altruism, agency and the competitiveness of family firms. *Managerial and Decision Economics, 23*(4-5), 247–259. doi:10.1002/mde.1064

Sciascia, S., & Mazzola, P. (2008). Family involvement in ownership and management: Exploring nonlinear effects on performance. *Family Business Review, 21*(4), 331–345. doi:10.1177/08944865080210040105

Sciascia, S., Mazzola, P., & Chirico, F. (2013). Generational involvement in the top management team of family firms: Exploring nonlinear effects on entrepreneurial orientation. *Entrepreneurship Theory and Practice, 37*(1), 69–85. doi:10.1111/j.1540-6520.2012.00528.x

Sciascia, S., Mazzola, P., & Kellermanns, F. W. (2014). Family management and profitability in private family-owned firms: Introducing generational stage and the socioemotional wealth perspective. *Journal of Family Business Strategy, 5*(2), 131–137. doi:10.1016/j.jfbs.2014.03.001

Seaman, C. (2015). Creating space for the business family: Networks, social capital & family businesses in rural development. *Journal of Family Business Management, 5*(2), 182–191. doi:10.1108/JFBM-08-2015-0032

Setia-Atmaja, L., Tanewski, G. A., & Skully, M. (2009). The role of dividends, debt and board structure in the governance of family controlled firms. *Journal of Business Finance & Accounting, 36*(7-8), 863–898. doi:10.1111/j.1468-5957.2009.02151.x

Shanker, M. C., & Astrachan, J. H. (1996). Myths and realities: Family businesses´ contribution to the US economy. A framework for assessing family business statistics. *Family Business Review, 9*(2), 107–123. doi:10.1111/j.1741-6248.1996.00107.x

Sharma, P. (2002, August). *Stakeholder mapping technique: Toward the development of a family firm typology*. Paper presented at the Academy of Management conference, Denver, CO.

Sharma, P. (2008). Commentary: Familiness: Capital stocks and flows between family and business. *Entrepreneurship Theory and Practice, 32*(6), 971–977. doi:10.1111/j.1540-6520.2008.00266.x

Sharma, P., Chrisman, J. J., & Chua, J. H. (1996). *A review and annotated bibliography of family business studies*. Boston: Kluwer. doi:10.1007/978-1-4419-8768-6

Sharma, P., Chrisman, J. J., & Chua, J. H. (1997). Strategic management of the family business: Past research and future challenges. *Family Business Review, 10*(1), 1–36. doi:10.1111/j.1741-6248.1997.00001.x

Sharma, P., Christman, J., Pablo, A., & Chua, J. H. (2001). Determinants of initial satisfaction with the succession process in family firms: A conceptual model. *Entrepreneurship Theory and Practice, 25*(3), 17–36. doi:10.1177/104225870102500302

Sharma, P., & Irving, P. G. (2005). Four bases of family business successor commitment: Antecedents and consequences. *Entrepreneurship Theory and Practice, 29*(1), 13–33. doi:10.1111/j.1540-6520.2005.00067.x

Sharma, P., & Manikutty, S. (2005). Strategic divestments in family firms: Role of family structure and community culture. *Entrepreneurship Theory and Practice, 29*(3), 293–311. doi:10.1111/j.1540-6520.2005.00084.x

Sharma, P., & Sharma, S. (2011). Drivers of proactive environmental strategy in family firms. *Business Ethics Quarterly*, *21*(2), 309–334. doi:10.5840/beq201121218

Shepherd, D. A., Wiklund, J., & Haynie, J. M. (2009). Moving forward: Balancing the financial and emotional costs of business failure. *Journal of Business Venturing*, *24*(2), 134–148. doi:10.1016/j.jbusvent.2007.10.002

Shepherd, D., & Haynie, J. M. (2009). Family business, identità conflict, and an expedited entrepreneurial process: A process of resolving identity conflict. *Entrepreneurship Theory and Practice*, *33*(6), 1245–1264. doi:10.1111/j.1540-6520.2009.00344.x

Shleifer, A., & Vishny, R. W. (1986). Large shareholders and corporate control. *Journal of Political Economy*, *94*(3, Part 1), 461–488. doi:10.1086/261385

Shleifer, A., & Vishny, R. W. (1997). A survey of corporate governance. *The Journal of Finance*, *52*(2), 737–783. doi:10.1111/j.1540-6261.1997.tb04820.x

Short, H. (1994). Ownership, control, financial structure and the performance of the firm. *Journal of Economic Surveys*, *8*(3), 203–249. doi:10.1111/j.1467-6419.1994.tb00102.x

Siebels, J. F., & zu Knyphausen-Aufseß, D. (2012). A review of theory in family business research: The implications for corporate governance. *International Journal of Management Reviews*, *14*(3), 280–304. doi:10.1111/j.1468-2370.2011.00317.x

Siggelkow, N. (2002). Evolution toward fit. *Administrative Science Quarterly*, *47*(1), 125–159. doi:10.2307/3094893

Simon, H. A. (1993). Altruism and economics. *The American Economic Review*, *83*(2), 156–161.

Simsek, Z. (2009). Organizational ambidexterity: Towards a multilevel understanding. *Journal of Management Studies*, *46*(4), 597–624. doi:10.1111/j.1467-6486.2009.00828.x

Simsek, Z., Heavey, C., Veiga, J. F., & Souder, D. (2009). A typology for aligning organizational ambidexterity's conceptualizations, antecedents, and outcomes. *Journal of Management Studies*, *46*(5), 864–894. doi:10.1111/j.1467-6486.2009.00841.x

Sirmon, D. G., Arregle, J.-L., Hitt, M., & Webb, J. W. (2008). The role of family influence in firms' strategic response to competitive threat of imitation. *Entrepreneurship Theory and Practice*, *32*(6), 979–998. doi:10.1111/j.1540-6520.2008.00267.x

Sirmon, D. G., & Hitt, M. A. (2003). Managing resources: Linking unique resources, management, and wealth creation in family firms. *Entrepreneurship Theory and Practice*, *27*(4), 339–358. doi:10.1111/1540-8520.t01-1-00013

Slatten, T., Lien, G., & Svensson, G. (2018). The value of cultivating norms for market orientation in Professional service firms. *International Journal of Quality and Service Sciences*, *10*(3), 316–330. doi:10.1108/IJQSS-09-2017-0086

Smith, A. (1796). An inquiry into the nature and causes of the wealth of nations (2nd ed.). Philadelphia: Thomas Dobson.

Snow, C. C., & Hrebiniak, L. G. (1980). Strategy, distinctive competence and organizational performance. *Administrative Science Quarterly*, *25*(2), 317–336. doi:10.2307/2392457

Sogorb, F. (2005). How SME uniqueness affects capital structure: Evidence from a 1994-1998 Spanish data panel. *Small Business Economics*, *25*(5), 447–457. doi:10.100711187-004-6486-8

Somech, A., & Drach-Zahavy, A. (2013). Translating team creativity to innovation implementation: The role of team composition and climate for innovation. *Journal of Management*, *39*(3), 684–708. doi:10.1177/0149206310394187

Sorenson, R. (1999). Conflict management strategies used by successful family businesses. *Family Business Review*, *12*(4), 325–340. doi:10.1111/j.1741-6248.1999.00325.x

Sorenson, R. L., Goodpaster, K. E., Hedberg, P. R., & Yu, A. (2009). The family point of view, family social capital, and firm performance: An exploratory test. *Family Business Review*, *22*(3), 239–253. doi:10.1177/0894486509332456

Spaltro, E., & de Vito Piscicelli, P. (1990). *Psicologia per le organizzazioni*. Roma: Carocci.

Sraer, D., & Thesmar, D. (2007). Performance and behaviour of family firms: Evidence from the French stock market. *Journal of the European Economic Association*, *5*(4), 709–751. doi:10.1162/JEEA.2007.5.4.709

Srivastava, R. K., Shervani, T. A., & Fahey, L. (1998). Market-based assets and shareholder value: A framework for analysis. *Journal of Marketing*, *62*(1), 2–18. doi:10.1177/002224299806200102

Srivastava, R. K., Shervani, T. A., & Fahey, L. (1999). Marketing business process, and shareholder value: An organizationally embedded view of marketing activities and the discipline of marketing. *Journal of Marketing*, *63*(special issue), 168–179. doi:10.1177/00222429990634s116

Stanley, L. J., Hernández-Linares, R., López-Fernández, M. C., & Kellermanns, F. W. (2019). A typology of family firms: An investigation of entrepreneurial orientation and performance. *Family Business Review*, *32*(2), 174–194.

Stanley, L. J., Hernández-Linares, R., López-Fernández, M. C., & Kellermanns, F. W. (2019). A Typology of Family Firms: An Investigation of Entrepreneurial Orientation and Performance. *Family Business Review*.

Stanley, L., Kellermanns, F. W., & Zellweger, T. M. (2017). Latent profile analysis: Understanding family firm profiles. *Family Business Review*, *30*(1), 84–102. doi:10.1177/0894486516677426

Stark, O. (1995). *Altruism and beyond: An economic analysis of transfers and exchanges within families and groups*. New York: Cambridge University Press. doi:10.1017/CBO9780511493607

Stavrou, E. T. (1999). Succession in family business: Exploring the effects of demographic factor on offspring intentions to join and take over the business. *Journal of Small Business Management*, *37*(3), 43–61.

Steier, L. (2001). Family firms, plural forms of governance, and the evolving role of trust. *Family Business Review*, *14*(4), 353–367. doi:10.1111/j.1741-6248.2001.00353.x

Steier, L. (2003). Variants of agency contracts in family-financed ventures as a continuum of familial altruistic and market rationalities. *Journal of Business Venturing*, *18*(5), 597–618. doi:10.1016/S0883-9026(03)00012-0

Steier, L., & Miller, D. (2010). Pre- and post-succession governance philosophies in entrepreneurial family firms. *Journal of Family Business Strategy*, *1*(3), 145–154. doi:10.1016/j.jfbs.2010.07.001

Steiger, T., Duller, C., & Hiebl, M. R. W. (2015). No consensus in sight: An analysis of ten years of family business definitions in empirical research studies. *Journal of Enterprising Culture*, *23*(01), 36. doi:10.1142/S0218495815500028

Stein, J. (1988). Takeover threats and managerial myopia. *Journal of Political Economy*, *96*(1), 61–80. doi:10.1086/261524

Stein, J. C. (1989). Efficient capital markets, inefficient firms: A model of myopic corporate behavior. *The Quarterly Journal of Economics*, *104*(4), 655–669. doi:10.2307/2937861

Stenholm, P., Pukkinen, T., & Heinonen, J. (2016). Firm growth in family businesses-The role of entrepreneurial orientation and the entrepreneurial activity. *Journal of Small Business Management*, *54*(2), 687–713. doi:10.1111/jsbm.12166

Sterlacchini, A. (1999). Do innovative activities matter to small firms in non R&D intensive industries? An application to export performance. *Research Policy*, *28*(8), 819–832. doi:10.1016/S0048-7333(99)00023-2

Stewart, A., & Hitt, M. A. (2012). Why can't a family business be more like a nonfamily business? Modes of professionalization in family firms. *Family Business Review*, *25*(1), 58–86. doi:10.1177/0894486511421665

Stinnett, N., & De Frain, J. (1985). *Secrets of strong families*. Nueva York, NY: Berkeley Books.

Strauss, A., & Corbin, J. (1998). *Basics of qualitative research: grounded theory procedures and techniques* (2nd ed.). Newbury Park, CA: Sage.

Stryker, S. (1968). Identity salience and role performance. *Journal of Marriage and the Family*, *4*(4), 558–564. doi:10.2307/349494

Stubner, S., Blarr, W. H., Brands, C., & Wulf, T. (2012). Organizational ambidexterity and family firm performance. *Journal of Small Business and Entrepreneurship*, *25*(2), 217–229. doi:10.1080/08276331.2012.10593570

Stulz, R. M. (1990). Managerial discretion and optimal financing policies. *Journal of Financial Economics*, *26*(1), 3–27. doi:10.1016/0304-405X(90)90011-N

Suess, J. (2014). Family governance–Literature review and the development of a conceptual model. *Journal of Family Business Strategy*, *5*(2), 138–155. doi:10.1016/j.jfbs.2014.02.001

Suess, J. (2017). Understanding the transgenerational orientation of family businesses: The role of family governance and business family identity. *Journal of Business Economics*, *87*(6), 749–777. doi:10.100711573-016-0835-3

Sundaramurthy, C. (2008). Sustaining trust within family businesses. *Family Business Review*, *21*(1), 89–102. doi:10.1111/j.1741-6248.2007.00110.x

Sutcliffe, K. M., & Vogus, T. J. (2003). Organization for resilience. In K. Cameron, J. E. Dutton, & R. E. Quinn (Eds.), Positive Organizational Scholarship (pp. 94–110). San Francisco: Academic Press.

Swinth, R., & Vinton, K. (1993). Do Family-Owned Businesses have a Strategic Advantage in International Joint Ventures? *Family Business Review*, *4*(1), 19–30. doi:10.1111/j.1741-6248.1993.00019.x

Swoboda, B., & Olejnik, E. (2013). A taxonomy of small-and medium-sized international family firms. *Journal of International Entrepreneurship*, *11*(2), 130–157. doi:10.100710843-012-0101-x

Swogger, G. (1991). Assessing the successor generation in family businesses. *Family Business Review*, *4*(4), 397–411. doi:10.1111/j.1741-6248.1991.00397.x

Tagiuri, R., & Davis, J. A. (1992). Bivalent attributes of the family firm. Family Business Review, 9(2), 199-208.

Tagiuri, R., & Davis, J. (1996). Bivalent attributes of the family firm. *Family Business Review*, *9*(2), 199–208. doi:10.1111/j.1741-6248.1996.00199.x

Tagiuri, R., & Davis, J. A. (1992). On the Goals of Successful Family Companies. *Family Business Review*, *5*(1), 263–281. doi:10.1111/j.1741-6248.1992.00043.x

Tajeddini, K., Altinay, L., & Ratten, V. (2017). Service innovativeness and the structuring of organizations: The moderating roles of learning orientation and inter-functional coordination. *International Journal of Hospitality Management*, *65*, 100–114. doi:10.1016/j.ijhm.2017.06.010

Tajfel, H., & Turner, J. C. (1986). The social identity theory of intergroup behaviour. In S. Worchel & W. G. Austin (Eds.), *Psychology of intergroup relations* (pp. 7–24). Chicago: Nelson-Hall Publishers.

Tallon, P. P. (2008). Inside the adaptive enterprise: An information technology capabilities perspective on business process agility. *Information Technology Management*, *9*(1), 21–36. doi:10.100710799-007-0024-8

Tanewski, G. A., Prajogo, D., & Sohal, A. (2003, January). Strategic orientation and innovation performance between family and non-family firms. In *ICSB 2003: 48th World Conference Proceedings* (pp. 1-22). International Council for Small Business.

Tàpies, J., & Fernández Moya, M. (2012). Values and longevity in family business: Evidence from a cross-cultural analysis. *Journal of Family Business Management*, *2*(2), 130–146. doi:10.1108/20436231211261871

Taylor, A., & Greve, H. R. (2006). Superman or the fantastic four? Knowledge combination and experience in innovative teams. *Academy of Management Journal*, *49*(4), 723–740. doi:10.5465/amj.2006.22083029

Teece, D. J., & Pisano, G. (1998). The dynamic capabilities of the firm: An introduction. In Technology, organization, and competitiveness. Perspectives on industrial and corporate change (pp. 193-212). Oxford, UK: Oxford University Press.

Teece, D. J., Pisano, G. P., & Shuen, A. (1990). *Firm capabilities, resources, and the concept of strategy*. Working Paper, Berkeley, University of California.

Teece, D. J. (1986). Profiting from technological innovation: Implications for integration, collaboration, licensing and public policy. *Research Policy*, *15*(6), 285–305. doi:10.1016/0048-7333(86)90027-2

Teece, D. J. (2006). Reflections on "profiting from innovation". *Research Policy*, *35*(8), 1131–1146. doi:10.1016/j.respol.2006.09.009

Teece, D. J. (2007). Explicating dynamic capabilities: The nature and microfoundations of (sustainable) enterprise performance. *Strategic Management Journal*, *28*(13), 1319–1350. doi:10.1002mj.640

Teece, D. J. (2014). A dynamic capabilities-based entrepreneurial theory of the multinational enterprise. *Journal of International Business Studies*, *45*(1), 8–37. doi:10.1057/jibs.2013.54

Teece, D. J., & Pisano, G. (1998). The dynamic capabilities of the firm: An introduction. In G. Dosi, D. J. Teece, & J. Chytry (Eds.), *Technology, organization, and competitiveness. Perspectives on industrial and corporate change* (pp. 193–212). Oxford, UK: Oxford University Press. doi:10.1093/0198290969.003.0006

Teece, D. J., Pisano, G., & Shuen, A. (1997). Dynamic capabilities and strategic management. *Strategic Management Journal*, *18*(7), 509–533. doi:10.1002/(SICI)1097-0266(199708)18:7<509::AID-SMJ882>3.0.CO;2-Z

Teece, D. J., Rumelt, R., Dosi, G., & Winter, S. (1994). Understanding corporate coherence. Theory and evidence. *Journal of Economic Behavior & Organization*, *23*(1), 1–30. doi:10.1016/0167-2681(94)90094-9

Thomas, J. B., Clark, S. M., & Gioia, D. A. (1993). Strategic sensemaking and organizational performance: Linkages among scanning, interpretation, action and outcomes. *Academy of Management Journal*, *36*(2), 239–270.

Thomsen, S., & Pedersen, T. (2000). Ownership structure and economic performance in the largest European Companies. *Strategic Management Journal*, *21*(6), 689–705. doi:10.1002/(SICI)1097-0266(200006)21:6<689::AID-SMJ115>3.0.CO;2-Y

Tidd, J., & Bessant, J. R. (2009). *Managing innovation: Integrating technological, market and organizational change*. New York, NY: John Wiley.

Tognazzo, A., Gubitta, P., & Favaron, S. D. (2016). Does slack always affect resilience? A study of quasi-medium-sized Italian firms. *Entrepreneurship and Regional Development*, *28*(9-10), 768–790. doi:10.1080/08985626.2016.1250820

Tokarczyk, J., Hansen, E., Green, M., & Down, J. (2007). A resource-based view and market orientation theory examination of the role of "familiness" in family business success. *Family Business Review*, *20*(1), 17–31. doi:10.1111/j.1741-6248.2007.00081.x

Tosi, H. L., & Gómez-Mejía, L. R. (1989). The decoupling of CEO pay and performance: An agency theory perspective. *Administrative Science Quarterly*, *34*(2), 169–189. doi:10.2307/2989894

Tsai, W. H., Hung, J. H., Kuo, Y. C., & Kuo, L. (2006). CEO tenure in Taiwanese family and nonfamily firms: An agency theory perspective. *Family Business Review*, *19*(1), 11–28. doi:10.1111/j.1741-6248.2006.00057.x

Tsang, E. W. K. (1999). Internationalization as a learning process: Singapore MNCs in China. *The Academy of Management Executive*, *13*(1), 91–101. doi:10.5465/ame.1999.1567359

Tsang, E. W. K. (2002). Learning from overseas venturing experience: The case of Chinese family business. *Journal of Business Venturing*, *17*(1), 21–40. doi:10.1016/S0883-9026(00)00052-5

Tsao, S., & Lien, W. (2013). Family management and internationalization: The impact on firm performance and innovation. *Management International Review*, *53*(2), 189–213. doi:10.100711575-011-0125-9

Tushman, M. L., & O'Reilly, C. A. III. (1996). Ambidextrous organizations: Managing evolutionary and revolutionary change. *California Management Review*, *38*(4), 8–29. doi:10.2307/41165852

Uhlaner, L. M. (2006). Business family as a team: Underlying force for sustained competitive advantage. In P. Z. Poutziouris, K. X. Smyrnios, & S. B. Klein (Eds.), *Handbook of research on family business* (pp. 125–144). Cheltenham, UK: Edward Elgar. doi:10.4337/9781847204394.00016

Uhlaner, L., Matser, I., Berent, M., & Flören, R. (2015). Linking Bonding and Bridging Ownership Social Capital in Private Firms: Moderating Effects of Ownership–Management Overlap and Family Firm Identity. *Family Business Review*, *28*(3), 1–18. doi:10.1177/0894486515568974

Uhlaner, L., Wright, M., & Huse, M. (2007). Private Firms and Corporate Governance: An Integrated Economic and Management Perspective. *Small Business Economics*, *29*(3), 225–241. doi:10.100711187-006-9032-z

Ulrich, D., & Smallwood, N. (2004). Capitalizing on capabilities. *Harvard Business Review*, *82*(6), 119–127. PMID:15202293

Umans, I., Lybaert, N., Steijvers, T., & Voordeckers, W. (2018). Succession planning in family firms: Family governance practices, board of directors, and emotions. *Small Business Economics*, 1–19.

Urbinati, A., Franzo, S., DeMassis, A., & Frattini, F. (2017). Innovation in family firms: a review of prior studies and a framework for future research. In A. Brem & E. Viardot (Eds.), *Revolution of Innovation Management*. London, UK: Palgrave Macmillan. doi:10.1057/978-1-349-95123-9_8

Vago, M. (2004). Integrating change management: Challenges for family business clients and consultants. *Family Business Review*, *17*(1), 71–80. doi:10.1111/j.1741-6248.2004.00005.x

Vallejo-Martos, M. C., & Puentes-Poyatos, R. (2014). Family firms as incubators for ethical behavior: An exploratory study from the perspective of stewardship theory. *Journal of Management & Organization*, *20*(6), 784–807. doi:10.1017/jmo.2014.55

Van Caneghem, T., & Van Campenhout, G. (2012). Quantity and quality of information and SME financial structure. *Small Business Economics*, *39*(2), 341–358. doi:10.100711187-010-9306-3

Van den Berghe, L. A., & Carchon, S. (2003). Agency relations within the family business system: An exploratory approach. *Corporate Governance*, *11*(3), 171–179. doi:10.1111/1467-8683.00316

van der Vegt, G. S., Essens, P., Walshtröm, M., & George, G. (2015). Managing Risk and Resilience. *Academy of Management Journal*, *59*(4), 971–980. doi:10.5465/amj.2015.4004

Van Essen, M., Carney, M., Gedajlovic, E., & Heugens, P. (2015). How does family control influence firm strategy and performance: A meta-analysis of US publicly listed firms. *Corporate Governance*, *23*(1), 3–24. doi:10.1111/corg.12080

van Essen, M., Strike, V. M., Carney, M., & Sapp, S. (2015). The resilient family firm: Stakeholder outcomes and institutional effects. *Corporate Governance*, *23*(3), 167–183. doi:10.1111/corg.12087

Van Gils, A., Voordeckers, W., & van den Heuvel, J. (2004). Environmental uncertainty and strategic behavior in Belgian family firms. *European Management Journal*, *22*(5), 588–595. doi:10.1016/j.emj.2004.09.015

Vandekerkhof, P., Steijvers, T., Hendriks, W., & Voordeckers, W. (2015). The Effect of Organizational Characteristics on the Appointment of Nonfamily Managers in Private Family Firms: The Moderating Role of Socioemotional Wealth. *Family Business Review*, *28*(2), 104–122. doi:10.1177/0894486513514274

Vardaman, J. M., & Gondo, M. B. (2014). Socioemotional wealth conflict in family firms. *Entrepreneurship Theory and Practice*, *38*(6), 1317–1322.

Veider, V., & Matzler, K. (2016). The ability and willingness of family-controlled firms to arrive at organizational ambidexterity. *Journal of Family Business Strategy*, *7*(2), 105–116. doi:10.1016/j.jfbs.2015.10.001

Venkatraman, N. (1990). Performance implications of strategic coalignment: A methodological perspective. *Journal of Management Studies*, *27*(1), 19–41. doi:10.1111/j.1467-6486.1990.tb00751.x

Venkatraman, N., & Ramanujam, V. (1987). Measurement of business economic performance: An examination of method convergence. *Journal of Management*, *13*(1), 109–122. doi:10.1177/014920638701300109

Vera, F., & Marchena, M. (1996). *El modelo turístico español. In Introducción a la economía del turismo en España* (pp. 327–364). Madrid: Civitas.

Vilaseca, A. (2002). The shareholder role in the family business: Conflict of interests and objectives between nonemployed shareholders and top management team. *Family Business Review*, *15*(4), 299–320. doi:10.1111/j.1741-6248.2002.00299.x

Villalonga, B., & Amit, R. (2006). How do family ownership, control and management affect firm value? *Journal of Financial Economics*, *80*(2), 385–417. doi:10.1016/j.jfineco.2004.12.005

Villalonga, B., Amit, R., Trujillo, M. A., & Guzmán, A. (2015). Governance of family firms. *Annual Review of Financial Economics*, *7*(1), 635–654. doi:10.1146/annurev-financial-110613-034357

Villanueva, J., & Sapienza, H. J. (2009). Goal tolerance, outside investors, and family firm governance. *Entrepreneurship Theory and Practice*, *33*(6), 1193–1199. doi:10.1111/j.1540-6520.2009.00340.x

Vives, X. (Ed.). (2000). Corporate governance: Theoretical and empirical perspectives. Nueva York, NY: Cambridge University Press.

Von Hippel, E. (1988). *Sources of Innovation*. Oxford, UK: Oxford University Press.

Voordeckers, W., Steijvers, T., & Peeters, L. (2010). *The ownership-performance relationship: Agency issues in private family firms*. In Annual European Academy of Management (EURAM) Conference, Rome, Italy.

Voordeckers, W., Le Breton-Miller, I., & Miller, D. (2014). In search of the best of both worlds: Crafting a finance paper for the Family Business Review. *Family Business Review*, *27*(4), 281–286. doi:10.1177/0894486514552175

Voordeckers, W., Van Gils, A., & Van den Heuvel, J. (2007). Board composition in small and medium-sized family firms. *Journal of Small Business Management*, *45*(1), 137–156. doi:10.1111/j.1540-627X.2007.00204.x

Vorhies, D. W., Harker, M., & Rao, C. P. (1999). The capabilities and performance advantages of market-driven firms. *European Journal of Marketing, 33*(11-12), 1171–1202. doi:10.1108/03090569910292339

Wagner, D., Block, J. H., Miller, D., Schwens, C., & Xi, G. (2015). A meta-analysis of the financial performance of family firms: Another attempt. *Journal of Family Business Strategy, 6*(1), 3–13. doi:10.1016/j.jfbs.2015.01.001

Wakelin, K. (2001). Productivity growth and R&D expenditure in UK manufacturing firms. *Research Policy, 30*(7), 1079–1090. doi:10.1016/S0048-7333(00)00136-0

Wallace, J. C., Little, L. M., Hill, A. D., & Ridge, J. W. (2010). CEO regulatory foci, environmental dynamism, and small firm performance. *Journal of Small Business Management, 48*(4), 580–604. doi:10.1111/j.1540-627X.2010.00309.x

Wall, T. D., Michie, J., Patterson, M., Wood, S. J., Sheehan, M., Clegg, C. W., & West, M. (2004). On the validity of subjective measures of company performance. *Personnel Psychology, 57*(1), 95–118. doi:10.1111/j.1744-6570.2004.tb02485.x

Wang, C. (2005). Ownership and operating performance of Chinese IPOs. *Journal of Banking & Finance, 29*(7), 1835–1856. doi:10.1016/j.jbankfin.2004.07.003

Wang, C. K., & Ang, B. L. (2004). Determinants of venture performance in Singapore. *Journal of Small Business Management, 42*(4), 347–363. doi:10.1111/j.1540-627X.2004.00116.x

Wang, C. L., & Ahmed, P. K. (2007). Dynamic capabilities: A review and research agenda. *International Journal of Management Reviews, 9*(1), 31–51. doi:10.1111/j.1468-2370.2007.00201.x

Wang, G., & Miao, C. F. (2015). Effects of sales force market orientation on creativity, innovation implementation and sales performance. *Journal of Business Research, 68*(11), 2374–2382. doi:10.1016/j.jbusres.2015.03.041

Wang, Q., Zhao, X., & Voss, C. (2016). Customer orientation and innovation: A comparative study of manufacturing and service firms. *International Journal of Production Economics, 171*, 221–230. doi:10.1016/j.ijpe.2015.08.029

Wanhill, S. (1997). Peripheral area tourism: A European perspective. *Progress in Tourism and Hospitality Research, 3*(1), 47–70. doi:10.1002/(SICI)1099-1603(199703)3:1<47::AID-PTH38>3.0.CO;2-F

Wanhill, S. (2000). Small and medium tourism enterprises. *Annals of Tourism Research, 27*(1), 132–147. doi:10.1016/S0160-7383(99)00072-9

Ward, J.L. (1986). How many will survive in 2046? *Family Enterprise, 9.*

Ward, J. (2016). *Keeping the family business healthy: How to plan for continuing growth, profitability and family leadership*. London: Springer.

Ward, J. (2016). *Perpetuating the family business: 50 lessons learned from long lasting, successful families in business.* London: Springer.

Ward, J. L. (1987). *Keeping the Family Business Healthy: How to plan for continuing growth, profitability, and family leadership.* San Francisco, CA: Jossey-Bass.

Ward, J. L. (1987). *Keeping the family business healthy: How to plan for continuing growth, profitability, and family leadership.* San Francisco: Jossey-Bass.

Ward, J. L. (1987). *Keeping the family business healthy: how to plan for continuing growth, profitability, and family leadership.* San Francisco: Jossey-Brass.

Ward, J. L. (1988). The special role of strategic planning for family business. *Family Business Review*, *1*(2), 105–117. doi:10.1111/j.1741-6248.1988.00105.x

Ward, J. L. (1997). Growing the family business: Special challenges and best practices. *Family Business Review*, *10*(4), 323–337. doi:10.1111/j.1741-6248.1997.00323.x

Ward, J. L. (2004). *Perpetuating the Family Business: 50 Lessons Learned from Long Lasting, Successful Families in Business*. Marietta, GA: Family Enterprise Publishers. doi:10.1057/9780230505995

Wayne, S., Shore, L., & Liden, R. (1997). Perceived organizational support and leader-member exchange: A social exchange perspective. *Academy of Management Journal*, *40*, 82–111.

WCED, S. W. S. (1987). *World commission on environment and development*. Our common future.

Webb, J. W., Ketchen, D. J. Jr, & Ireland, R. D. (2010). Strategic entrepreneurship within family-controlled firms: Opportunities and challenges. *Journal of Family Business Strategy*, *1*(2), 67–77. doi:10.1016/j.jfbs.2010.04.002

Weber, J., Lavelle, L., Lowry, T., Zellner, W., & Barrett, A. (2003). Family Inc. *Business Week*, *3857*, 100-110.

Webster, F. E. Jr. (1992). The changing role of marketing in the corporation. *Journal of Marketing*, *56*(4), 1–17. doi:10.1177/002224299205600402

Wehrens, R., Putter, H., & Buydens, L. M. (2000). The bootstrap: A tutorial. *Chemometrics and Intelligent Laboratory Systems*, *50*(1), 35–53. doi:10.1016/S0169-7439(00)00102-7

Weigelt, C. (2009). The impact of outsourcing new technologies on integrative capabilities and performance. *Strategic Management Journal*, *30*(6), 595–616. doi:10.1002mj.760

Welch, L. (1992). The use of alliances by small firms in achieving internationalization. *Scandinavian International Business Review*, *1*(2), 21–37. doi:10.1016/0962-9262(92)90019-3

Welsh, J. H. M. (1993). The impact of family ownership and involvement on the process of management succession. *Family Business Review*, *6*(1), 31–45. doi:10.1111/j.1741-6248.1993.00031.x

Wernerfelt, B. (1984). A resource-based view of the firm. *Strategic Management Journal*, *5*(2), 171–180. doi:10.1002mj.4250050207

Werts, C. E., Linn, R. L., & Jöreskog, K. G. (1974). Interclass reliability estimates: Testing structural assumptions. *Educational and Psychological Measurement*, *34*(1), 25–33. doi:10.1177/001316447403400104

Westhead, P. (1997). Ambitions, 'external' environment and strategic factor differences between family and non-family companies. *Entrepreneurship and Regional Development*, *9*(2), 127–157. doi:10.1080/08985629700000007

Westhead, P., & Cowling, M. (1997). Performance contrasts between family and non-family unquoted companies in the UK. *International Journal of Entrepreneurial Behaviour & Research*, *3*(1), 30–52. doi:10.1108/13552559710170892

Westhead, P., Cowling, M., & Howorth, C. (2001). The development of family companies: Management and ownership imperatives. *Family Business Review*, *14*(4), 369–385. doi:10.1111/j.1741-6248.2001.00369.x

Westhead, P., Cowling, M., & Storey, D. J. (1997). *The management and performance of unquoted family companies in the United Kingdom. Centre for Small and medium Sized Enterprises*. Warwick Business School.

Westhead, P., & Howorth, C. (2006). Ownership and Management Issues Associated with Family Firm Performance and Company Objectives. *Family Business Review*, *19*(4), 301–316. doi:10.1111/j.1741-6248.2006.00077.x

Westhead, P., & Howorth, C. (2007). 'Types' of private family firms: An exploratory conceptual and empirical analysis. *Entrepreneurship and Regional Development, 19*(5), 405–431. doi:10.1080/08985620701552405

Westhead, P., Wright, M., & Ucbasaran, D. (2004). Internationalization of private firms: Environmental turbulence and organizational strategies and resources. *Entrepreneurship and Regional Development, 16*(6), 501–522. doi:10.1080/0898562042000231929

Westley, F., Mintzberg, H. (1989). Visionary leadership and strategic management. *Strategic Management Journal, 10*(summer special issue), 17-32.

Whetten, D. A., Foreman, P., & Dyer, W. G. (2014). Organizational Identity and Family Business. In The SAGE Handbook of Family Business. Thousand Oaks, CA: SAGE Publications Ltd. doi:10.4135/9781446247556.n24

Whetten, D., & Mackey, A. (2002). Asocial actor conception of organizational identity and its implications for the study of organizational reputation. *Business & Society, 41*(4), 393–415. doi:10.1177/0007650302238775

Whipp, R., Rosenfeld, R., & Pettigrew, A. (1989). Culture and competitiveness: Evidence from two mature UK industries. *Journal of Management Studies, 26*(6), 561–585. doi:10.1111/j.1467-6486.1989.tb00745.x

Whiteside, M. F., Aronoff, C. E., & Ward, J. L. (1993). *How families work together.* Marietta, GA: Business Owner Resources.

Wiersema, M., & Bantel, K. (1992). Top management team demography and corporate strategic change. *Academy of Management Journal, 35*(1), 91–121.

Williams, R. I., Jr. (2015). *Measuring family business performance: a holistic, idiosyncratic approach* (Doctoral Dissertation). Kennesaw State University. Doctor of Business Administration Dissertations. Paper 13.

Williamson, O. E. (1985). *The Economic Institutions of Capitalism. Firms, Markets, Relational Contracting.* Nueva York, NY: The Free Press.

Williamson, O. E. (1988). Corporate finance and corporate governance. *The Journal of Finance, 43*(3), 567–591. doi:10.1111/j.1540-6261.1988.tb04592.x

Williamson, O. E. (1991). Strategizing, economizing, and economic organization. *Strategic Management Journal, 12*(S2), 75–94. doi:10.1002mj.4250121007

Williams, T. A., Gruber, D. A., Sutcliffe, K. M., Shepherd, D. A., & Zhao, E. Y. (2017). Organizational response to adversity: Fusing crisis management and resilience research streams. *The Academy of Management Annals, 11*(2), 733–769. doi:10.5465/annals.2015.0134

Wilson, N., Wright, M., & Scholes, L. (2013). Family Business Survival and the Role of Boards. *Entrepreneurship Theory and Practice, 37*(Nov), 1369–1389. doi:10.1111/etap.12071

Winter, S. G. (1995). Four Rs of profitability: Rents, resources, routines and replication. In C. A. Montgomery (Ed.), *Resource-based and evolutionary theories of the Firm: Toward a Synthesis* (pp. 147–178). Boston: Kluwer Academic Publishers. doi:10.1007/978-1-4615-2201-0_7

Winter, S. G. (2003). Understanding dynamic capabilities. *Strategic Management Journal, 24*(10), 991–995. doi:10.1002mj.318

Wiseman, R., & Gomez-Mejia, L. (1998). A Behavioral Agency Model of Managerial Risk Taking. *Academy of Management Review, 23*(1), 133–153. doi:10.5465/amr.1998.192967

Wolff, J. A., & Pett, T. L. (2006). Small-Firm Performance: Modeling the Role of Product and Process Improvements*. *Journal of Small Business Management*, *44*(2), 268–284. doi:10.1111/j.1540-627X.2006.00167.x

Wood, D. J. (2010). Measuring corporate social performance: A review. *International Journal of Management Reviews*, *12*(1), 50–84. doi:10.1111/j.1468-2370.2009.00274.x

Wright, P. M., McMahan, G. C., & McWilliams, A. (1994). Human resources and sustained competitive advantage: A resource-based perspective. *International Journal of Human Resource Management*, *5*(2), 301–326. doi:10.1080/09585199400000020

Wright, P., Kroll, M., Load, A., & Van, B. (2002). The structure of ownership and corporate acquisition strategies. *Strategic Management Journal*, *23*(1), 41–53. doi:10.1002mj.208

Xi, J. M., Kraus, S., Filser, M., & Kellermanns, F. W. (2015). Mapping the field of family business research: Pats trends and future directions. *The International Entrepreneurship and Management Journal*, *11*(1), 113–132. doi:10.100711365-013-0286-z

Yen, J. F., Lin, C. Y., Chen, Y. S., & Huang, Y. C. (2015). Founding family firms and bank loan contracts. *Journal of Financial Services Research*, *48*(1), 53–82. doi:10.100710693-014-0199-1

Yeoth, P. L., & Roth, K. (1999). An empirical analysis of sustained advantage in the U.S. pharmaceutical industry: Impact of firm resources and capabilities. *Strategic Management Journal*, *20*(7), 637–653. doi:10.1002/(SICI)1097-0266(199907)20:7<637::AID-SMJ42>3.0.CO;2-Z

Yeung, H. W. (2000). Limits to the growth of family owned business? The case of Chinese transnational corporations from Hong Kong. *Family Business Review*, *13*(1), 55–70. doi:10.1111/j.1741-6248.2000.00055.x

Yin, R. K. (2003). *Case study research: Design and methods* (3rd ed.). Thousand Oaks, CA: Sage.

Yu, A., Lumpkin, G. T., Sorenson, R. L., & Brigham, K. H. (2012). The landscape of family business outcomes: A summary and numerical taxonomy of dependent variables. *Family Business Review*, *25*(1), 33–57. doi:10.1177/0894486511430329

Zahra, S. A. (2003). `International expansion of US manufacturing family businesses: The effect of ownership and involvement´. *Journal of Business Venturing*, *18*(4), 495–512. doi:10.1016/S0883-9026(03)00057-0

Zahra, S. A. (2005). Entrepreneurial risk taking in family firms. *Family Business Review*, *18*(1), 23–40. doi:10.1111/j.1741-6248.2005.00028.x

Zahra, S. A. (2012). Organizational Learning and Entrepreneurship in Family Firms: Exploring the Moderating Effect of Ownership and Cohesion. *Small Business Economics*, *38*(1), 51–65. doi:10.100711187-010-9266-7

Zahra, S. A., Hayton, J. C., Neubaum, D. O., Dibrell, C., & Craig, J. (2008). Culture of family commitment and strategic flexibility: The moderating effect of stewardship. *Entrepreneurship Theory and Practice*, *32*(6), 1035–1054. doi:10.1111/j.1540-6520.2008.00271.x

Zahra, S. A., Hayton, J. C., & Salvato, C. (2004). Entrepreneurship in family vs. non-family firms: A resource based analysis of the effect of organizational culture. *Entrepreneurship Theory and Practice*, *28*(Summer), 363–381. doi:10.1111/j.1540-6520.2004.00051.x

Zahra, S. A., Matherne, B. P., & Carleton, J. M. (2003). `Technological resource leveraging and the internationalization of new ventures´. *Journal of International Entrepreneurship*, *1*(2), 163–186. doi:10.1023/A:1023852201406

Zahra, S. A., Neubaum, D. O., & Huse, M. (2000). Entrepreneurship in medium-size companies: Exploring the effects of ownership and governance systems. *Journal of Management*, *26*(5), 947–976. doi:10.1177/014920630002600509

Zahra, S. A., Sapienza, H. J., & Davidsson, P. (2006). Entrepreneurship and dynamic capabilities. A review, model and research agenda. *Journal of Management Studies*, *43*(4), 917–955. doi:10.1111/j.1467-6486.2006.00616.x

Zahra, S., Rawhouser, H., Bhawe, N., Neubaum, D., & Hayton, J. (2008). Globalization of Social Entrepreneurship. *Strategic Entrepreneurship Journal*, *2*(2), 117–131. doi:10.1002ej.43

Zellweger, T. (2007). Time horizon, costs of equity capital, and generic investment strategies of firms. *Family Business Review*, *20*(1), 1–15. doi:10.1111/j.1741-6248.2007.00080.x

Zellweger, T. (2017). *Managing the family business: Theory and Practice*. Cheltenham, UK: Edward Elgar Publishing.

Zellweger, T. M., & Astrachan, J. H. (2008). On the emotional value of owning a firm. *Family Business Review*, *21*(4), 347–363. doi:10.1177/08944865080210040106

Zellweger, T. M., & Dehlen, T. (2012). Value Is in the Eye of the Owner: Affect Infusion and Socioemotional Wealth Among Family Firm Owners. *Family Business Review*, *25*(3), 280–297. doi:10.1177/0894486511416648

Zellweger, T. M., Eddleston, K. A., & Kellermanns, F. W. (2010). Exploring the concept of familiness: Introducing family firm identity. *Journal of Family Business Strategy*, *1*(1), 54–63. doi:10.1016/j.jfbs.2009.12.003

Zellweger, T. M., Kellermanns, F. W., Chrisman, J. J., & Chua, J. H. (2012). Family control and family firm valuation by family CEOs: The importance of intentions for transgenerational control. *Organization Science*, *23*(3), 851–868. doi:10.1287/orsc.1110.0665

Zellweger, T. M., Kellermanns, F. W., Eddleston, K. A., & Memili, E. (2012). Building a family firm image: How family firms capitalize on their family ties. *Journal of Family Business Strategy*, *3*(4), 239–250. doi:10.1016/j.jfbs.2012.10.001

Zellweger, T. M., Nason, R. S., Nordqvist, M., & Brush, V. (2013). Why Do Family Firms Strive for Nonfinancial Goals? An Organizational Identity Perspective. *Entrepreneurship Theory and Practice*, *37*(2), 229–248. doi:10.1111/j.1540-6520.2011.00466.x

Zellweger, T., & Kammerlander, N. (2015). Article Commentary: Family, Wealth, and Governance: An Agency Account. *Entrepreneurship Theory and Practice*, *39*(6), 1281–1303. doi:10.1111/etap.12182

Zellweger, T., Nason, R., & Nordqvist, M. (2012). From longevity of firms to transgenerational entrepreneurship of families: Introducing family entrepreneurial orientation. *Family Business Review*, *25*(2), 136–155. doi:10.1177/0894486511423531

Zellweger, T., & Sieger, P. (2012). Entrepreneurial orientation in long-lived family firms. *Small Business Economics*, *38*(1), 67–84. doi:10.100711187-010-9267-6

Zhang, L., Kara, A., Spillan, J. E., & Mintu-Wimsatt, A. (2015). Exploring market orientation among Chinese small and medium-sized enterprises. *Chinese Management Studies*, *11*(4), 617–636. doi:10.1108/CMS-08-2016-0158

Zhou, K. Z., Li, J. J., Zhou, N., & Su, C. (2008). Market orientation, job satisfaction, product quality and firm performance: Evidence from China. *Strategic Management Journal*, *29*(5), 985–1000. doi:10.1002mj.700

Zhu, K., & Kraemer, K. L. (2002). E-commerce metrics for net-enhanced organizations: Assessing the value of e-commerce to firm performance in the manufacturing sector. *Information Systems Research, 13*(3), 275–295. doi:10.1287/isre.13.3.275.82

Zody, Z., Sprenkle, D., MacDermid, S., & Schrank, H. (2006). Boundaries and the functioning of family and business systems. *Journal of Family and Economic Issues, 27*(2), 185–206. doi:10.100710834-006-9017-8

Zollo, M., & Winter, S. (2002). Deliberate learning and the evolution of dynamic capabilities. *Organization Science, 13*(3), 339–351. doi:10.1287/orsc.13.3.339.2780

Zona, F., Minichilli, A., & Zattoni, A. (2011). Boards of Directors and Firm Innovation: An Empirical Analysis on Large Italian Companies. In The Value Creating Board. Corporate Governance and Organizational Behaviour. Routledge, Taylor & Francis Group.

Zou, S., Fang, E., & Zhao, S. (2003). The effect of export marketing capabilities on export performance: An investigation of Chinese exporters. *Journal of International Marketing, 11*(4), 32–55. doi:10.1509/jimk.11.4.32.20145

Zucker, L. G. (1987). Normal change or risky business: Institutional effects of the hazard of change in hospital organizations, 1959-79. *Journal of Management Studies, 24*(6), 671–701. doi:10.1111/j.1467-6486.1987.tb00468.x

About the Contributors

Cesar Camison has a PhD in Economics and Business Sciences. Principal Professor in Business Administration at Director of Family Business Chair at University of Valencia. Principal Researcher of Research Group on Strategy, Competitiveness and Knowledge and Innovation Management (GRECO). Visiting Professor in London School of Economics and Political Science, Surrey, Universitá Commerciale Luigi Bocconi de Milán, Viena University, Université de Montpellier I, Texas A&M University). His fields of expertise are the sources of international competitive advantages based on intangible assets and dynamic capabilities, firm as a knowledge and learning organization, strategic alliances and competitive dynamic inside inter-organizational networks and industrial districts; specially, he has worked on these topics in tourism and small and medium-sized firms. He has published works as articles in closely 100 journals as British Journal of Management, Scandinavian Journal of Management, Journal of Small Business Management, Journal of Business Research, Environment and Planning A, Organization Studies, and Tourism Management.

Tomás F. González Cruz was born in Zaragoza (Spain) in 1969. Associated Professor in Business Administration at the University of Valencia, Spain. Bachelor's degree in Business Administration from Valencia University. Doctorate in Business Administration at Valencia University.

* * *

Özgür Atılgan is an assistant professor in the Business Department at Istanbul Kültür University where he has been a faculty member since 2011. Özgür completed his Ph.D. at Istanbul University in the Management and Organization Department. His research interests lie in the area of corporate governance, family businesses in emerging economies, entrepreneurship, career success.

Montserrat Boronat-Navarro is an assistant professor in Strategic Management at Jaume I University in Castellón (Spain). She received her PhD in November 2007 with Cum Laude qualification. She has published her research in international book chapters and in journals as Environment & Planning C, Current Issues in Tourism, Organization Studies or Management Decision. She has presented her research in several international conferences organized by different associations such as European Group for Organization Studies and European Academy of Management. Her research interests include dynamic capabilities, innovation, knowledge development, family firms, and corporate social responsibility.

Sergio Camisón-Haba is an Associate Professor in Strategic Management at the University of Valencia and the Universidad Internacional de la Rioja (UNIR), as well as a part-time researcher at the Chair of Enterprise and Humanism of the University of Valencia. Sergio studies interactions between information asymmetries, capital structure, information and technologies and the development of competitive capabilities in organizations.

José Antonio Clemente is a full time profesor at UNIR (Universidad Internacional de La Rioja). Visiting scholar at Vives University (Belgium). PhD in Finance, CIIA, CEVE. Forensic Economist. Research fields focus on capital structure in corporate finance and family firm. In parallel to teaching and research activity, he develops his professional activity in the field of accounting and financial consulting (debt restructuring, feasibility plans, business reorganization, …) and Forensic-REFor-CGCEE Economist (judicial expert, pre-bankruptcy situations, …). During 1995-2010 he was Chief Accountant, CFO, CEO and Financial Advisor in SMEs from various sectors (industrial, distribution, social health, restoration). Member of Board of Directors' and Senior Management Committee.

Julio Diéguez-Soto is an Associate Professor of Finance and Accounting at the University of Málaga (Spain). He is the Director of the Finance and Accounting Department and the Academic Director of Firm Feasibility Chair. His main research interests include Performance, Capital Structure, Innovation, Professionalization and MCS in Family Firms. He has published his latest research findings in International journals such as Small Business Economics, Journal of Small Business Management, Family Business Review, Journal of Family Business Strategy, Business Research Quarterly, Review of Managerial Science, Canadian Journal of Administrative Sciences, Innovation: Organization and Management, Journal of Scientific and Industrial Research, and Review of Business Management, among others.

Jose Farinos is Professor at the Department of Corporate Finance of the University of Valencia (Spain). He has taught in the area of Corporate Finance both undergraduate and postgraduate, as well as specialization diplomas and master degrees. His areas of interest in research are IPOs and firm acquisitions, topics on which he has supervised several doctoral theses and has published numerous articles in both national and international journals. He collaborates as an evaluator of prestigious national and international scientist journals.

Marta Fernández-Olmos obtained his PhD in 2008 (Extraordinary Award for doctoral thesis from University of Zaragoza, Spain) and is currently Assistant Professor of Business Organization at the University of Zaragoza. Research interests are innovation, family firms, and internationalization of SMEs. The author belongs to the Compete Research Group of the University of Zaragoza. She has published in Technovation, Journal of Technology Transfer, Applied Economic Perspectives and Policy, Food Policy and British Food Journal, among others.

Filippo Ferrari holds a Bachelor degree in Work and Organizational Psychology and a Masters degree in Adult Training and Education. He currently serves as a Lecturer at Bologna University, School of Economics, Management and Statistics, where he teaches Organizational Behaviour and Design and Human Resources Management. His fields of interests are International Human Resources Management, Organizational Reliability, Change Management, Adult Training.

Beatriz Forés-Julián is a Lecturer of the Business Administration and Marketing Department of the Universitat Jaume I of Castellón. She holds a PhD in Business Management (2009) with Cum Laude and Extraordinary Prize from the Universitat Jaume I. Her fields of expertise are strategic management, specially the sources of dynamic capabilities, firm as a knowledge and learning organization, family business, and districts. Her work has been published in Tourism Management, Journal of Business Research, International Journal of Tourism Research, Management Decision,Current Issues in Tourism, Scandinavian Journal of Management, International Journal of Technology Management and Revista Española de Financiación y Contabilidad among others.

Melanie Grueso-Gala is a PhD student at University of Valencia (UV). She has worked for the Chair of Enterprise and Humanism (UV) and now is a researcher and lecturer in business at University of Valencia.

María Iborra is an Associate Professor at University of Valencia.

Rubén Martínez-Alonso is a junior researcher at the University of Almería, Spain. He collaborates with the Santander Family Business Chair at this University. His research interests include family firm research focusing on technological innovation and emotional considerations. He has published his latest research findings in international journals such as European Journal of Innovation Management, International Journal of Entrepreneurship and Small Business and, Management Research: Journal of the Iberoamerican Academy of Management.

Fuencisla Martínez-Lobato is a lecturer with 26 years of experience at the Faculty of Economics, University of Valencia (Spain).

María J. Martínez-Romero is an assistant professor of Accounting and Finance in the Economics and Business Department at the University of Almería, Spain. She collaborates with the Santander Family Business Chair at this University. Her primary research interests include family firm research focusing on emotional, innovative, finance and corporate governance aspects. She has published her latest research findings in international journals such as Small Business Economics, Review of Managerial Science, European Journal of Innovation Management, International Journal of Entrepreneurship and Small Business, Management Research: Journal of the Iberoamerican Academy of Management.

Mario Ossorio is Assistant professor of Management at Università degli Studi della Campania Luigi Vanvitelli. He earned his MSc in Economics and Finance from University of Naples "Federico II" and his PhD in Entrepreneurship and Innovation from University of Naples II. His primary research interests include innovation, family businesses and corporate governance. He has published his latest research findings in international journal such as Management Decision and Career Development International.

Alba Puig-Denia is lecturer at Universitat Jaume I in Castellón. She has a degree in Business Management and a PhD (Cum Laude) in Business Administration from the Universitat Jaume I. In 2014, she got the PhD extraordinary award in the field of Economics and Business Sciences from this university. She participated as an exchange tutor of the Tourism Degree and she is currently the exchange coordinator of the Business Management Degree at this university. Her teaching lines are related to business organization and management and business information systems. Her main research interests are family business, quality management and innovation. She has participated in national and international conferences and publications. Among her contributions, she has published in journals such as International Journal of Production Research, International Journal of Tourism Research, Spanish Journal of Finance and Accounting, or European Journal of Management and Business Economics. Moreover, she has received some awards in several conferences. She has also collaborated on different projects and research contracts at state, regional and the university level and in various research projects of educational nature at Universitat Jaume I.

Norat Roig-Tierno is professor at the ESIC Business & Marketing School. His research is focused on innovation, regional development and the application of qualitative methodologies. He has presented numerous papers at international conferences. He has published articles and books in international journals including Applied Geography, Journal of Human Development and Capabilities, Social and Policy Administration, Journal of Business Research, among others. He is or has been on the editorial board of several journals.

Alfonso A. Rojo-Ramírez is a professor of accounting and finance in the Department of Economics and Business at Almeria University, Spain. He is also manage The Family Business Chair at this university since 2009. He headed the Department of Business Management and is a member of the Valuation Committee of the Spanish Association of Accounting and Business Administration. He has published his latest research findings in international journals such as Small Business Economics, Family Business Review, Review of Managerial Science, European Journal of Innovation Management, and Management Research: Journal of the Iberoamerican Academy of Management.

Vicente Safón is an Associate Professor at University of Valencia.

Index

T

U

www.ingramcontent.com/pod-product-compliance
Lightning Source LLC
LaVergne TN
LVHW060354300926
849162LV00006B/1260